Rational Reasoning with Finite Conditional Knowledge Bases

Christian Eichhorn

Rational Reasoning with Finite Conditional Knowledge Bases

Theoretical and Implementational Aspects

J.B. METZLER

Christian Eichhorn
Iserlohn, Germany

Zugleich Dissertation an der Fakultät Informatik, TU Dortmund, Dortmund (DE) 2018
unter dem Titel "Qualitative Rational Reasoning with Finite Conditional Knowledge
Bases – Theoretical and Implementational Aspects"

This work was supported by Grant KI1413/5-1 of Deutsche Forschungsgemeinschaft
(DFG) to Gabriele Kern-Isberner as part of the priority program "New Frameworks of
Rationality" (SPP 1516).

ISBN 978-3-476-04823-3   ISBN 978-3-476-04824-0   (eBook)
https://doi.org/10.1007/978-3-476-04824-0

Library of Congress Control Number: 2018965124

This J.B. Metzler imprint is published by the registered company Springer-Verlag GmbH, DE part
of Springer Nature
The registered company address is: Heidelberger Platz 3, 14197 Berlin, Germany

Acknowledgements

There a many people to whom I am very grateful for their support during the past years. First of all I want to thank Gabriele Kern-Isberner for being my supervisor both scientifically as with respect to my career. If she did not had believed that I could acquire the necessary formal skills to work in knowledge representation and reasoning, this thesis would never have been. Apart from that she supported my research, pulled me back when ideas went astray, guided me round various obstacles of scientific research, and supported me whenever I was in need for support. I thank Marco Ragni for being my second reviewer, for being an excellent host in a wonderful city and a marvellous discussion partner. Furthermore I thank Günter Rudolph and Peter Padawitz for agreeing to be part of my disseration committee. I also thank Lars Hildebrand, who accepted being my mentor, for his insights, be it scientifically or with respect to other issues during my dissertation period.

Many thanks go to my colleagues Daan Apeldoorn, Tanja Bock, Diana Howey, Steffen Schieweck, Andre Thevapalan, and Marco Wilhelm of the Information Engineering group as well as the whole Chair 1 of Computer Science at TU Dortmund for their discussions, ideas, and joint publications. I thank Christoph Beierele, Steven Kutsch, and Kai Sauerwald of the Lehrgebiet Wissensbasierte Systeme from the University of Hagen for interesting discussions, joint publications, and enjoyable travels.

I thank my wife, Claudia Eichhorn, for having endured the busy and stressful time of me having to finish this dissertation, for raising me up when this project pushed me down, and generally being there.

I am grateful that I had the possibility to conduct my research in the community of the priority program "New Frameworks of Rationality" and I thank all friends and colleagues for the great time we had. Finally, I thank all co-authors of joint articles, cited or not cited in this thesis, for working with me on all these fascinating and interesting things.

This work was supported by Grant KI1413/5-1 of Deutsche Forschungsgemeinschaft (DFG) to Gabriele Kern-Isberner as part of the priority program "New Frameworks of Rationality" (SPP 1516).

Contents

List of Figures

List of Tables

List of Algorithms

List of Symbols

The following list contains the symbols and functions used in this work. Please note that the listing here contains the usual usage of the symbols, it may happen that this usage is overwritten, locally, for the reason of making proofs or longer texts easier legible (for instance using Latin Majuscules in ascending order for different variables).

Propositional Logic

$\wedge$ .... conjunction, logical *and*
$\vee$ .... disjunction, logical *or*
$\underline{\vee}$ .... exclusive disjunction, logical exclusive or, xor
$\neg, \overline{\cdot}$ .... negation, logical *not*
$\Rightarrow$ .... material implication
$\Leftrightarrow$ .... logical equivalence, *if and only if*
$\equiv$ .... semantical equivalence
$\top$ .... Tautology, $\top \equiv \phi \vee \overline{\psi}$
$\bot$ .... Contradiction, $\top \equiv \phi \wedge \overline{\psi}$
true .... logical truth
false .... logical falseness
undefined .... third evaluation outcome of conditionals

Set Operations

$\times$ .... Cartesian product
$\in$ .... is element of
$\cup$ .... union
$\cap$ .... intersection
$\subseteq$ .... subset or equal
$\subsetneq$ .... strict subset
$\setminus$ .... difference
$|\cdot|$ .... cardinality of a set
$\varnothing$ .... empty set

Relations of Entailment, Inference, and Satisfaction

$\vDash$ .... classical satisfaction / entailment
.... also acceptance of conditionals / knowledge bases in epistemic states

Greek Majuscules

Greek Minuscules

(γ'') . . . . Suppression Task with "If the library is closed. . ." as modifier

δ . . . . a conditional $\delta \in (\mathfrak{L}|\mathfrak{L})$

. . . . also used as $\delta \in [0,1]$ of ε, δ-inference

ε . . . . a small value, usually $\varepsilon \in [0,1]$ of ε, δ-inference

ζ . . . . Inference rule, like Monotony, Cautious Monotony, etc.

$\vec{\eta}$ . . . . solution to $CSP(\Delta)$

ι . . . . inference $\iota = \phi \mathrel{\vert\!\approx} \psi$

κ . . . . ranking function, $\kappa : \Omega \to \mathbb{N}_0^\infty$

κ_Γ . . . . global ranking function of an OCF-network, $\kappa_\Gamma : \Omega \to \mathbb{N}_0^\infty$

κ_V . . . . local ranking table at vertex V of an OCF-network

κ_Δ^Z . . . . ranking function generated by System Z of Δ, $\kappa_\Delta^Z : \Omega \to \mathbb{N}_0$

κ_Γ^Z . . . . global System Z OCF of an OCF-network, $\kappa_\Gamma : \Omega \to \mathbb{N}_0^\infty$

$\kappa_\mathcal{H}^Z$ . . . . System Z OCF of local knowledge base $\Delta_\mathcal{H}$

κ_Z^* . . . . temporary plausibility function in System Z^+

κ_Δ^c . . . . ranking function of a c-representation of Δ, $\kappa_\Delta^c : \Omega \to \mathbb{N}_0^\infty$

$\kappa_{\vec{\eta}}$ . . . . ranking function of a c-representation composed from vector $\vec{\eta}$

κ_i^- . . . . integer impact of a conditional for c-representations

$\lambda(\cdot)$ local OCF from the local OCF tables in an OCF-network, $\lambda : \Omega \to \mathbb{N}_0$

μ . . . . default in Reiter Default Logic

ξ . . . . propositional formula, $\xi \in \mathfrak{L}$

ϱ . . . . inference pattern as formalisation of psychological studies

σ_Δ . . . . conditional structure of a world

$\sigma_{\Delta,i}$ . . . . individual conditional evaluation of a world

τ_Δ^c . . . . generic c-representation

ϕ . . . . propositional formula, $\phi \in \mathfrak{L}$, often antecedent of a conditional

χ . . . . propositional formula, $\chi \in \mathfrak{L}$

ψ . . . . propositional formula, $\psi \in \mathfrak{L}$, often consequent of a conditional

ω . . . . possible world $\omega \in \Omega$

Latin Majuscules

P . . . . a probability function

$\overline{P}$ . . . . the improbability function to P, $\overline{P}(\omega) = 1 - P(\omega)$

V . . . . a variable of the alphabet or vertex in a graph, $V \in \Sigma$

W . . . . a variable of the alphabet or vertex in a graph, $W \in \Sigma$

Latin Minuscules

f .... often used as firmness of a conditional $f \in \mathbb{N}_0^\infty$
i .... often used as running variable with locally defined range
j .... often used as running variable with locally defined range
n .... usually number of conditionals in a knowledge base, $n \in \mathbb{N}_0$
m .... usually number of variables in an alphabet, $m \in \mathbb{N}_0$
v .... positive outcome of a variable $V \in \Sigma$
$\overline{v}$ .... negative outcome of a variable $V \in \Sigma$
$\dot{v}$ .... fixed but undetermined outcome of $V \in \Sigma$, $\dot{v} \in \{v, \overline{v}\}$
x .... often used as probability of a conditional, $x \in [0, 1]$

Bold Latin Majuscules

A .... set of variables $\mathbf{A} \subseteq \Sigma$
B .... set of variables $\mathbf{B} \subseteq \Sigma$
C .... set of variables $\mathbf{C} \subseteq \Sigma$
D .... set of variables $\mathbf{D} \subseteq \Sigma$
I .... set of inferences $\{\iota_1, \ldots\}$
O .... set of variables $\mathbf{P} \subseteq \Sigma$
P .... set of variables $\mathbf{O} \subseteq \Sigma$
V .... set of variables $\mathbf{V} \subseteq \Sigma$

Bold Latin Minuscules

$\mathbf{a}_i^+$ .... indicator of the verification of a conditional i
$\mathbf{a}_i^-$ .... indicator of the falsification of a conditional i
$\mathbf{a}$ .... outcome of / complete conjunction over a variable set $\mathbf{A}$
$\mathbf{b}$ .... outcome of / complete conjunction over a variable set $\mathbf{B}$
$\mathbf{c}$ .... outcome of / complete conjunction over a variable set $\mathbf{C}$
$\mathbf{d}$ .... outcome of / complete conjunction over a variable set $\mathbf{D}$
$\mathbf{o}$ .... outcome of / complete conjunction over a variable set $\mathbf{O}$
$\mathbf{p}$ .... outcome of a variable set $\mathbf{P}$
$\mathbf{p}_V$ .... outcome of the variables $pa(V)$
$\mathbf{p}_W$ .... outcome of the variables $pa(W)$
$\mathbf{v}$ .... outcome of / complete conjunction over a set of variables $\mathcal{V} \subseteq \Sigma$

Gothic Majuscules

$\mathfrak{E}$ ....hyperedges in a hypertree
$\mathfrak{K}$ ....set of all *CP*-compatible OCF to a CP-network
$\mathfrak{L}$ ....propositional language from an alphabet Σ and junctors $\wedge$, $\vee$, $\neg$
$(\mathfrak{L}|\mathfrak{L})$ .... language of conditionals
$(\mathfrak{L}|\mathfrak{L})\mathbb{N}_0^\infty$ .... language of conditionals with integer weights
$(\mathfrak{L}|\mathfrak{L})[0,1]$ .... language of conditionals with real weights
$\mathfrak{M} = (\cdot, \cdot, \cdot)$ ....preferential model
$\mathfrak{M}^\Delta$ ....preferential model $(\Omega, \vDash, \prec_\Delta^\sigma)$ obtained from conditional structures
$\mathfrak{P}(\cdot)$ .... power set of the associated set
$\mathfrak{R}$...Reiter Default Theory
$\mathfrak{S}$ ....set of propositional constraints / strict knowledge base $\mathfrak{S} \subseteq \mathfrak{L}$
$\mathfrak{X}$ ....totally $\leq$ (with $<$ as usual) ordered set of elements
$\mathfrak{Z}$ ....temporary set of conditionals in System Z$^+$

Blackboard Majuscules

$\mathbb{C}$ ....hyperedge in a hypergraph, also clique in a undirected graph, $\mathbb{C} \subseteq \Sigma$
$\mathbb{N}$.............................set of natural numbers (positive integers)
$\mathbb{N}_0$...................set of natural numbers and 0 (non-negative integers)
$\mathbb{N}_0^\infty$ .... set of natural numbers with 0 and ∞
$\mathbb{R}$..residues in a hypertree, $\mathbb{R} \subseteq \Sigma$
$\mathbb{S}$ .... separator in a hypertree, $\mathbb{S} \subseteq \Sigma$

Calligraphic Majuscules

$\mathcal{A}$ .... set of formulas $\mathcal{A} \subseteq \mathfrak{L}$
$\mathcal{C}$ .... set of inference rules ζ
$\mathcal{D}$.............................set of defaults in a Reiter Default Theory
$\mathcal{E}$ ....set of edges in a graph
$\mathcal{F}$ .... strict knowledge in a Reiter Default Theory
$\mathcal{F}(\Delta)$....set of verification / falsification indicators of a knowledge base Δ
$\mathcal{G}$...undirected graph, $\mathcal{G} = (\Sigma, \mathcal{E})$
$\mathcal{G}_\Delta$...undirected graph constructed from a knowledge base Δ, $\mathcal{G}_\Delta = (\Sigma, \mathcal{E})$
$\mathcal{I}$ .... set of all inference patterns
$\mathcal{L}$ .... Set of literals of a propositional language
$\mathcal{M}$ .... general set of states of a preferential model
$\mathcal{O}$ ....Landau symbol, asymptotically bounded above

$\mathcal{P}_{\Delta}^{<\varepsilon}$ . . . . set of probability functions that ε-accepts Δ

$\mathcal{R}$ . . . . qualitative knowledge base with strict knowledge, $\mathcal{R} \subseteq \{\mathfrak{L}, (\mathfrak{L}|\mathfrak{L})\}$

$\mathcal{R}_V$ . . . . local knowledge base at vertex V in an OCF-network

$\mathcal{R}_{\mathcal{H}}$ . . . . local knowledge base at hyperedge $\mathcal{H}$ in an OCF-LEG network

$\mathcal{R}^{\mathbb{N}_0^{\infty}}$ . . . . semi-quantitative knowledge base with strict knowledge,

. . . . $\mathcal{R} \subseteq \{\mathfrak{L}, (\mathfrak{L}|\mathfrak{L}), \mathbb{N}_0^{\infty}\}$

$\mathcal{R}^{[0,1]}$ . . . . quantitative KB with strict knowledge, $\mathcal{R} \subseteq \{\mathfrak{L}, (\mathfrak{L}|\mathfrak{L}), [0,1]\}$

$\mathcal{S}_\Delta$ . . . elements of the free abelian group induced by conditional structures

$\mathcal{T}$ . . . . transformation system for conditional knowledge bases

$\mathcal{T}^\Delta$ . . . . outcome of transformation of Δ with $\mathcal{T}$

$\mathcal{T}(\Delta)$ . . . . outcome of transformation of Δ with $\mathcal{T}$

$\mathcal{T}_2$ . . . . transformation system for conditional knowledge bases

Further Symbols

$<$ . . . . strictly smaller as

$\leq$ . . . . not larger as

$>$ . . . . strictly larger as

$\geq$ . . . . not smaller as

$<_\kappa$ . . . . κ-preferred, $\omega <_\kappa \omega'$ iff $\kappa(\omega) < \kappa\omega(\omega')$

$\prec$ . . . . general preference or preferential relation (strict)

$\preccurlyeq$ . . . . general preference or preferential relation (not strict)

$\prec_\Psi$ . . . . preferred in epistemic state Ψ

$\prec_{\mathbf{p}}$ . . . . (local) conditional preference table in a CP-network

$\prec_{CP}$ . . . . global preference relation of a CP-network

$\prec_{CP}^*$ . . . . preference relation of a CP-network

$\prec_c^\circ$ . . . . strict preference of c-representations under measure $\circ$

$\preccurlyeq_c^\circ$ . . . . preference of c-representations under measure $\circ$

$\prec_\Delta^\sigma$ . . . . structural preference (induced by conditional structures)

$\asymp$ . . . . equally preferred as

$\equiv$ . . . . *true* if a variable appears in a formula $\equiv \subseteq \Sigma \times \mathfrak{L}$

$\circ$ . . . . generic symbol for index out of locally defined set

$\bullet$ . . . . generic symbol for index out of locally defined set

$\models$ . . . . general satisfaction relation of a preferential model

$(\cdot|\cdot)$ . . . . qualitative conditional of language $(\mathfrak{L}|\mathfrak{L})$

$(\!|\cdot|\!|\cdot)$ . . . . weak conditional of language $(\!|\mathfrak{L}|\mathfrak{L}\!|)$

$(\cdot|\cdot)[\cdot]$ . . . . semi-quantitative conditional of language $(\mathfrak{L}|\mathfrak{L}) \times \mathbb{N}$

$(\cdot|\cdot)[\cdot]$ . . . . quantitative conditional of language $(\mathfrak{L}|\mathfrak{L}) \times [0,1]$

Abstract

Knowledge representation and reasoning is a discipline of artificial intelligence dealing with formally representing knowledge the agent already has, and approaches to inferring new information about facts and dependencies based on said knowledge. The formal framework for the latter are nonmonotonic logics, that is, logics in which a valid inference can be invalidated by additional information, thus having room for representing rules with exceptions.

Conditionals are vital building blocks of nonmonotonic logics: As formal statements, they establish relationships between their premise and their conclusion. As trivalent logical entities, they provide room for dealing with situations where their premise is falsified, that is, where the conditional is to be evaluated outside its designated context. As formalisation, they capture defeasible statements "If ϕ then usually ψ" into formal language and thus extend the classical logical representation of strict knowledge with a representation of defeasible knowledge. Knowledge bases containing conditionals capture the knowledge of an intelligent agent and serve as base for its reasoning and inference.

The contribution of this thesis to the field is trifold: On the conceptual side, it recalls established approaches to representing knowledge, inductively generating epistemic states, and realising reasoning upon the latter. We examine techniques that inductively generate purely qualitative and semi-quantitative epistemic states, that is, orderings on the possible worlds, from knowledge bases. These epistemic states instantiate the generic approach of preferential models to define nonmonotonic inference relations, and these relations realise the information formalised in the knowledge base and license for the inference of additional knowledge. In addition to the established techniques, it discusses recent development of such approaches. These relations are examined, compared and rated using formal properties of nonmonotonic inference relations.

On the implementational side, it recalls network approaches to representing semi-quantitative epistemic states: Bayesian Networks and LEG networks are well-established graph methods that distribute a global knowledge base and probability function over a set of connected, directed local components. We recall how to transfer these techniques to the semi-quantitative area of ordinal conditional functions and also that the so defined networks endorse the strong properties regarding both independence and combina-

tion of local information. We discuss how these networks reduce spatial
complexity of this representation, and also if and how they impact the time
complexity of the inductive approaches positively.

On the applicational side, we research if and how different approaches to
nonmonotonic inference can be applied to modelling human inference using
the results of a renowned psychological experiment as baseline: Starting
from the established logic programming approach to the so-called Suppression Task, we recall that careful implementation of implicit connections
between variables is necessary to correctly model human inference. With
the technique of inference patterns, we recall an algorithmic method of
making these implicit connections explicit. Their holistic view of the complete results of the experiment makes it possible to apply preferential inference and thus gives us a notion of nonmonotonic rationality. Employing
c-representations on these results yields a method of reverse-engineering a
hypothesis for the background knowledge used by the participants: A conditional knowledge that, used with an inductive approach to nonmonotonic
inference, yields the same results as the majority of the human participants
in the experiment.

Overall, this thesis uses conditionals as building blocks of inductive inference methods. It examines, studies and rates these methods with respect to
their inferential strength, and finally brings these methods to a full circle by
using them to yield sets of conditionals as hypotheses for the background
knowledge of human reasoners.

1 Introduction

This section gives an overview over the topic of this thesis in its scientific context, motivates the work, phrases major research questions, and gives an outline over the structure of the thesis.

1.1 Context and Motivation

This thesis is located in the area of knowledge representation and reasoning, that is, the area of artificial intelligence that deals with formally representing knowledge of an intelligent agent, and using this knowledge to infer new or additional knowledge. The knowledge is represented in the compact form of conditionals, formalisations of defeasible rules of the form "If ϕ then (usually) ψ"; logics over conditionals extend classical logic with their trivalent evaluation to *true*, *false*, and *undefined*. Sets of conditionals, so-called knowledge bases, serve as compact representation of the background knowledge the reasoning is to be based upon. The reasoning itself is performed as formal inference based on epistemic states in the sense of [Hal05]. These epistemic states are represented as preferential models [Mak94] and yield inferences in the way of the Ramsey test for nonmonotonic logic [Ram29], that is, accepting a conditional if and only if its premise licenses for the inference of its conclusion. As preferential relation we use, among others, structural preference, probabilities, and mainly ordinal conditional functions (OCF, [Spo88, Spo12]). Inductive methods which bring forth such preferential relations inductively upon conditional knowledge bases bridge the gap between the compact knowledge bases and the complete epistemic states. We recall formal properties to evaluate and compare the inferences presented, and examine to which extend the presented approaches to inference are capable to mimic and model human inference captured by psychological experiments. The latter reveals hidden assumptions of the participants in the tested tasks. In this way, we connect the way humans reason with formal inference towards an artificial intelligence that can work alongside human beings.

But why address this problem at the first place? A motivation is that it seems that as long as human beings possess and use tools, the wish for having these tools to do their work without the need for wielding them by themselves is present in stories passed on [McC04]. However, with the stories of autonomous tools or machines a warning about these automatons

© Springer-Verlag GmbH Germany, part of Springer Nature 2018
C. Eichhorn, *Rational Reasoning with Finite Conditional Knowledge Bases*, https://doi.org/10.1007/978-3-476-04824-0_1

being rather dangerous if not cared for or not instructed properly is told[1]. Nowadays, automated helpers[2] which are able to command other household appliances, play music, place online orders, and serve as relay in communication enter the homes of many. These helpers are voice controlled so the human users need to express their orders verbally to these non-human agents. In human communication, a great deal of information is kept implicit, so the appliances may misunderstand their human employer, bearing the risks foretold in the mentioned stories. The risk of misunderstandings would be reduced if these appliances were capable of understanding their owners in the way humans understand each other. Here, to "understand" means not only with respect to the used language, words, and commands, but with respect to the actual message (and its maybe hidden meaning) which was send by the human[3]. This can be achieved by making the noted machines capable of following the ways of reasoning in the way humans do.

But how to realise this reasoning, how to test whether it correctly models the (generic) commonsensical human reasoner, and how to compare different formal approaches to this reasoning? One way of doing so is using formal properties of inference which originate in 5th century BC ancient Greek syllogistic reasoning with the works of Aristotle, and are still object of current research, be it in their original form (see, for instance, [SPG14]) or as derived properties (as introduced, for instance, by [Ada65, KLM90, LM92, Boc01, Haw07]). In the philosophical tradition, such rules and properties are used in a normative way, that is, inference rules are used to describe correct inferences, and the performance of systems as well as human reasoners are evaluated with them. For instance the trivalent evaluation of conditional sentences which does not coincide with the interpretation of such as material implication has been described as *defective truth table* [Was68]. Apart from this normative approach to human reasoning we have the psychological tradition of a descriptive approach towards human reasoning, which does not evaluate whether a given choice or decision is right or wrong, but describes which decision or choice

---

[1]   Confer the stories of the *Golem of Prague* (oratory, 16th century), Johann Wolfgang von Goethe: *The Sorcerer's Apprentice* (1797), Sir Terence David John Pratchett: *Thief of Time* (2001) as just three historical and recent examples from many.

[2]   For instance Amazon Echo, Google Home, or Apple's HomePod.

[3]   However, even humans struggle with this problem, the necessity of communication coaches and the popularity of the "four sides model" of von Thun (Friedemann Schulz von Thun: *Miteinander reden: Störungen und Klärungen. Psychologie der zwischenmenschlichen Kommunikation.* (1981)) among them is not by chance.

was made by human reasoners for questions which are similar in form, but different with respect to the situation, environment or emotional context (see, for instance, [GCK16]). In this environment of the venerable disciplines of philosophy and psychology, computer science with its birth in the early twentieth century is, in terms of relative age, not even a teenager. Nonetheless the increasing experience with and computational power of the automated calculation machines lead to an ongoing shift from the simple processing of numbers to sophisticated information processing.

As noted, knowledge representation and reasoning is the discipline of artificial intelligence in computer science dealing with formally representing knowledge which is already acquainted, and approached to inferring new information about facts and dependencies on the basis of this. It can be located in the intersection of the philosophy of reasoning, the psychology of reasoning, and computer scientific information processing. However, other than the human and social sciences, it explicitly focusses "on the knowledge, not on the knower" [BL04, Page xvii], that is, on how any intelligent agent could exploit the represented knowledge to display intelligent or rational behaviour. If we intersect this area with simulating the inferences human reasoners draw in "natural" situations, we find the pocket where this thesis is located; it deals with the following:

- Approaches to *reasoning* as it deals with methods that, given represented knowledge, infer new knowledge thereof.

- *Qualitative* reasoning insofar as it focuses on methods that, in contrast to, for instance, probabilistic methods, do not necessarily use numbers or numeric grades for inferences, or use numbers in a qualitative way to base their results on the direct comparison of possible worlds.

- *Rational* reasoning in that it assesses these methods with respect to measures of rationality, be it formal properties or in direct comparison with the human reasoner.

In this thesis, inference is realised on top of epistemic states in the sense of [Hal05]. These epistemic states are represented as preorders on a set of possible worlds, and inference is realised via preferential models [Mak94]. The methods applied and researched in this thesis are *inductive* insofar as they are applied to *finite conditional knowledge bases*, that is, sets of conditionals, and fill in the information given in these sets to bring forth complete epistemic states thereupon.

This course of action again is "commonsensical", as most of human knowledge seems to be represented as rules "If ϕ then (usually) ψ", for instance "If the traffic lights are red, you usually have to stop", "If a glass hits the ground, it breaks", or the standard example of nonmonotonic reasoning: "If something is a bird, it usually can fly". Technically, these rules are evaluated as trivalent logical entities, in that they can be verified (the traffic lights are red and you stop; something is a bird and can fly), falsified (the traffic lights are red and you do not stop; something is a bird and cannot fly) or not applicable (the traffic lights are green; something is not a bird). This trivalent formal evaluation following [Fin74] is shown to be part of human reasoning by [Was68]. Such rules also may have exceptions and are nonmonotonic insofar as additional information may override the generic information encoded in the rule (right of way for vehicles with switched on emergency lights; penguins or kiwis), which was also found to be present in human reasoning [Byr89].

Finally, this thesis deals with *theoretical* or conceptual aspects in that it recalls, summarises and defines formal methods and properties which can be used to realise reasoning based on sets of such rules, and with *implementational aspects* as it recalls and analyses algorithms to apply these methods.

This thesis, the presented methods, models, and formalisations are intended to sit on the fence between normative and descriptive application of its findings: Viewing the results from the viewpoint of the knowledge engineer, the methods and especially the quality criteria are to be used as normative tools insofar as they rate the inferential power as well as correctness of inference relations and formal methods with respect to the method used for comparison. Viewing the results from the viewpoint of a researcher from cognition or psychology, these models and formalisations are meant to be descriptive in that they describe and mimic human inference processes. This means turning around the role of the human participants who are traditionally judged to be irrational, or to reason incorrectly with respect to formal models, towards the human participants being the normative model for automated reasoning. This is done under the impression that a system that mimics the inferences of its human user is easier to understand, to interact, and to work with – frankly the difference of having the Golem[4] or

---

[4]   See Footnote 1

Frankenstein's Monster[5] as co-worker in comparison to working alongside with the Bicentennial Man[6] or Lieutenant Commander Data[7].

1.2 Research Questions

The general research questions that underlie this thesis can be paraphrased as follows:

> *Quantitative, that is, probabilistic approaches to reasoning are very successful but sometimes hard to understand and communicate. Which qualitative or semi-quantitative methods can be used that are able to compete with these approaches with respect to inferential power?*

To answer these general question, Section 3 concentrates on two approaches to representing epistemic states as a relation between possible worlds: The purely qualitative *conditional structures* [KI01, KI02] and the semi-quantitative *ordinal conditional functions* (OCF, [Spo88, Spo12]). The formalisms both order the worlds in a transitive way; this ordering is used to instantiate the preferential relation of preferential models [Mak94], whereas we keep the models (as the set of possible worlds) and the satisfaction relation (as satisfaction relation from classical logic) constant. We recall the fundamentals of inference relations based on preferential models, which form the basics of most of the inferences examined in this thesis, from the literature (see, for instance, [GP96, KI01, Spo12]). On top of these the contribution to the basics of conditional structures is done by recalling an alternative formulation of condition of structural preference [KIE12, KIE14]. Additionally this thesis extends the basics of ranking theory by proving that the axiomatic characterisation of (conditional) independence of probabilistic models [Pea88, Theorem 1] is invalid for ranking models, as one of the axioms is violated by OCF.

> *How can we evaluate and compare these inference relations with respect to their formal properties?*

---

[5] Mary Shelley: *Frankenstein; or, The Modern Prometheus* (1818)
[6] 1999 Canadian-American science fiction comedy-drama based on Isaac Asimov: *The Bicentennial Man* (1976)
[7] Star Trek franchise, television series *Star Trek: The Next Generation*, (1987 – 1993)

To formally examine, rate and compare the inferential strength of (non-monotonic) inference relations independently from concrete settings, formal properties are needed. A canon of such properties is joined as axioms of five nested systems known by the name of System O, O^+, C, P, and R [Ada65, Ada75, Gab85, KLM90, LM92, Mak94, Boc01, Haw07]. These systems define calculi of syntactical inferences which serve as reference point for semantical inference relations and are recalled in Section 4.1. In this thesis we consolidate these systems, their properties and syntactical inferences with a uniform notation and running example, while at the same time use a suitable semantical inference to illustrate the inferences licensed by the axioms. We contribute to the clarity of the systems by illustrating how the properties derivable are related. However the properties of these calculi are not sufficient to distinguish between some inference relations, as the differentiation in five system is too coarsely meshed and there is no stronger system than System R. Therefore we select additional properties found in the literature (for instance [Boc01, FL96]) to provide additional, finer woven layers which are able to differentiate between the inference relations presented. This thesis extends these properties by defining additional ones (as, for instance, the property *Integrity* which ensures that non-contradictory formulas do not license for contradictions), as well as reveal relations between the different properties presented (for instance that Weak Contraposition is indeed a consequence of Contraposition).

These formal properties are used to formally distinguish the inference relations presented in this thesis using well-known results from the literature [Pea90, BCD$^+$93, Haw07, EKI15a], the results of joint articles and this thesis' author's own contributions to the field [KIE12, BEKI16, BEKIK18], and hitherto unpublished novel contributions to the answer of this question. For instance we will see that inference with conditional structures satisfies System P, violates all presented properties outside System P, and licenses for meaningful inferences even upon inconsistent knowledge bases. For System Z, in comparison, it is well known that it satisfies System R, suffers from the Drowning Problem, and does not yield any inference for inconsistent knowledge bases.

Inference relations can be constructed inductively upon conditional knowledge bases. One approach to this is the technique of c-representations, which provide a schema for OCF and thereof induced inference. How can we evaluate the inference with these relations with respect to formal properties regarding one, several, or all c-representations of a given knowledge base?

Inference with single c-representations was defined on top of ranking inference in [KI01, KI04], the technique of which is recalled in Section 3.3.3.3. The technique of generating c-representations on top of a conditional knowledge base is transferred to the domain of constraint satisfaction problems, which leads to inference relations on all c-representations of a knowledge base with varying degrees of scepticism [BEKI16, BEKIK16]. We recall formal properties of these inferences, which prove that sceptical c-inference licenses for more inferences than System P but less that System R [BEKIK18]. This thesis sheds light upon this gap by proving additional properties for both sceptical and weakly sceptical c-inference. The examination of the inference with sets of c-representations is completed by recalling notions of preference on c-representations and the inferences that are realised by taking not all, but only the maximally preferred c-representations into account [BEKIK16, BEKIK18]. Here the main contribution of the author of this thesis is to be found in finding formal properties for these relations and this thesis extends the cited literature with respect to these properties.

Approaches to nonmonotonic reasoning that generate an epistemic state inductively upon a conditional knowledge base depend strongly on the form of the knowledge base. How can we define equivalence for knowledge bases and with this transfer knowledge bases to a normal form thereof?

Knowledge formalised in conditional knowledge bases can be represented by different conditionals. Like in propositional logic, semantical equivalent information can be expressed by different syntactic constructs. When using inductive methods as the ones illuminated in this thesis, these different formulations can involuntarily lead to different inferences. We recall the results of the articles [BEKI17a, BEKI17b] which propose two different notions of equivalence for conditional knowledge bases, as well as confluent terminating and minimising transformation systems that lead to normalised knowledge bases.

Network approaches to formalising conditional independence like Bayesian Networks are successful in organising and expediting different representations and inferences. How and to what extent can we use these techniques in the area of semi-quantitative ranking inference?

The majority of inference relations of this thesis are based on ordinal conditional functions. We recall network approaches to OCF and compare them to major network approaches to other formalisms. These deliberations can be divided in three major parts:

OCF-networks in comparison to Bayesian networks: It is safe to say that Bayesian Networks have been the disruptive innovation which made the application, implementation, and general employment of probabilistic methods possible [Pea88]: These networks render the efficient storing of exponentially large probability tables as well as algorithms on learning and changing probabilities feasible. This is achieved by separating the global probability function into small and manageable tables which still can be combined efficiently. This technique has already been used for ordinal conditional functions [GP96, BT10]; we recall findings in [KIE13a, KIE13b, EKI15b] that prove the underlying properties and show that these techniques can be used in a static context, but not inductively. We recall algorithms to inductively generate such networks based on conditional knowledge bases [KIE13a, KIE13b, EKI15b]. This thesis extends these findings by thoroughly analysing these algorithms and by providing a property for the inductive generation of such networks to directly obtain the resulting OCF-tables out of a conditional knowledge base to speed up the generation process. It has been shown that this process is not always successful [EKI15b] but may lead to networks which do not model the knowledge used to set them up; this thesis contributes to the solution of this problem by providing a method of locally testing for global consistency, which does not overcome the problem but allows the user to notice this in the step of setting up the network, so the procedure can be cancelled without the need to wait for the construction of the whole network before the failure becomes apparent. This thesis also presents a method of safely inducing an OCF-network from a knowledge base that profits from the efficient storing and local computation of OCF-networks, but lacks the efficiency in setting-up this formalism.

OCF-networks in comparison to CP-networks: In addition to representing probabilistic independencies, directed acyclic networks also are used to represented preferences, especially conditional preferences which are constant under the assumption that all other variables are fixed. These are the so-called *ceteris paribus* (or CP-) networks. OCF-networks have been compared to CP-networks [BBD$^+$04] as Bachelor Thesis [Fey12] under supervision of the author of this thesis and Gabriele Kern-Isberner. The findings of [Fey12] have been extended, streamlined, and concreted in the article [EFKI16] which in this thesis are embedded further into the context of knowledge representation and reasoning.

Definition of OCF-LEG networks and comparison to LEG networks: Inference with c-representations and reasoning with maximum entropy are related in that the system of inequalities used to set-up c-representations are closely connected to the equations from the MaxEnt approach (see [KI01, KI04]). The article [EKI14] defines OCF-LEG networks and an algorithm to inductively generate this application of hypergraphs for OCF following LEG networks, which are hypergraphs with local probability functions associated to the hyperedges, in probabilistics [LB82, Mey98]. In this thesis, we recall these findings and further analyse the algorithms necessary to generate an OCF-LEG network from a conditional knowledge base, especially with respect to complexity and correctness. This thesis extends the prior work in this area by investigating whether and under which circumstances the consistency condition for OCF-LEG networks can be guaranteed to be met. We also extend the literature in showing that the global OCF of an OCF-LEG network cannot be the System Z OCF of the original knowledge base, but may be a c-representation thereof. A discussion of the differences, advantages and disadvantages of OCF-LEG networks compared to OCF-networks complement these contributions.

> *We already motivated that it is desirable to enable an artificial intelligence to reason in a human way. But can the methods of knowledge representation and reasoning actually model or mimic human reasoning?*

To compare the results of formal approaches to nonmonotonic reasoning to human reasoning, studies about human reasoning have to be conducted. In principle, this can be done in two different ways: One way is to apply formal approaches to inference tasks, and use these tasks and their formal results as normative view in studies with human participants. The other is to use studies on human reasoning already conducted and apply formal approaches to knowledge representation and reasoning on the tasks of these studies to model the human reasoners. Recalling and extending on the articles [REKI16, REB$^+$17, ERKI18] this thesis takes the latter path.

In the tradition of [SvL08, HR09] we take on formalising the Suppression Task [Byr89], an experiment on human reasoning on conditional statements, in different formal logics. A plain modelling [REKI16] of the tasks fails to show the effect found in the empirical study, but we recall that carefully including additional background knowledge about the conditional statements into the modelling under systematic variation [REB$^+$17] leads to formalisations that properly draw (and avoid to draw) the same inferences as the majority of human test persons in [Byr89]. This method makes the additional information the participants use to the statements given by the examiner explicit. This systematic variation of additional is complemented with a systematic variation of the strength of the modelling [REB$^+$17] used in [REKI16].

These modellings reveal that formal approaches to nonmonotonic reasoning can mimic human reasoning. However, to achieve this a careful and meticulous analysis of the task and the involved dependencies between the variables and their meaning in the context of human experience is necessary. For formal techniques to be used in automated systems, a thorough analysis like this is not always possible or desired. Prior results (see, for instance, [PK05, KR14]) indicate that human reasoning can be covered by a set of formal properties which are also satisfied by preferential reasoning in the sense of [Mak88, Mak94]. This preferential reasoning in combination with the capturing of the combined qualitative results of inference studies in style of [Byr89] lead to the definition of inference patterns [ERKI18] which serve as formalisation of the results conducted. These inference patterns also reveal the epistemic state of the participants and, based on this, the beliefs and possible background knowledge in the form of a generic representation detached from the actual variables and cover story of the experiment.

1.3 Own contributions to joint articles

Some findings in this dissertation are already published in joint articles with involvement of the author of this thesis. These findings as well are their formal proofs included in this thesis are referred to the articles which the originate from. References to these findings as well as proofs are directed at the propositions of the articles, where applicable, in all conscience. The introduction of each chapter (or section in the case of network approaches) enumerates the articles serving as base for this chapter; the interim summaries concluding the chapters (sections) not only summarise the chapter-/section, but also point out my own contributions to these articles, as well as how and to what extent the chapter (and thus this dissertation) extends the articles.

1.4 Overview

The topics of this thesis can be arranged in following loop depicted in Figure 1.1: Inductive methods as the ones presented in Chapters 3 and 5 are applied to conditional knowledge bases (Chapter 2) which are representations of the (background) knowledge of intelligent agents. These knowledge bases can be normalised for an even more compact and clear presentation (Chapter 6). Inductive methods fill in the compact information of the knowledge base to a complete epistemic state. Instantiating preferential models with these states we obtain inference relations. In this way each of the inductive methods directly realises a semantical nonmonotonic inference (Chapter 3) which are assessed by and compared to syntactical inferences based on axioms and additional properties (Chapter 4). To close the loop, results of experiments regarding human inference are used to reveal the background knowledge and implicit assumptions under which the inferences of the participants can be deemed rational (Chapter 8). All these methods leading to and making use of epistemic states can be optimised with respect to time and space complexity by using network approaches rather than exponentially large tables (Chapter 7).

Presented in a more linear fashion, this thesis is organised in four major parts as follows: In the first part we introduce the topic and main research questions of the thesis as well as indicate how the contributions of the thesis answer these questions in Chapter 1. After this we recall the necessary preliminaries (Chapter 2) including but not limited to classical (bivalent) propositional logic, conditionals as trivalent logical entities, knowledge bases, and the general concept of inference relations. Consecutively in Chapter 3 we recall the basic techniques which form the foundation of the methods of this thesis. These techniques include, but are not limited to, conditional structures and ordinal conditional functions, inductive methods to generate inference relations as well as formal properties thereof. On top of the graphs

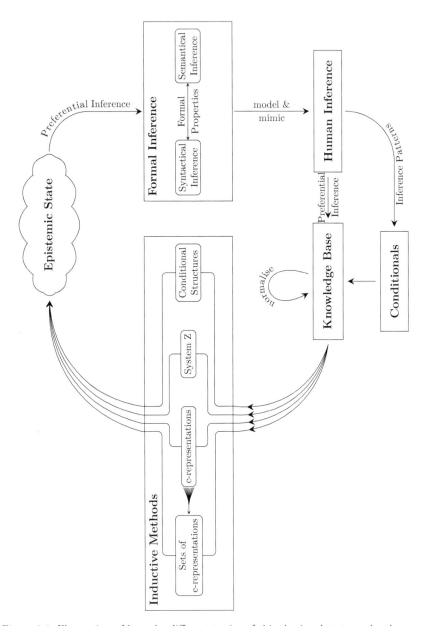

Figure 1.1: Illustration of how the different topics of this thesis relate to each other

recalled in the previous chapter we use the basics of probabilistic reasoning to recall Bayesian Networks, LEG networks, and finally, using preference relations instead of probabilities, CP-networks.

The second part focusses on conceptual properties of inference relations: Chapter 4 recalls major properties and axiom systems for nonmonotonic reasoning. In addition to just reporting these properties, this section also shows how the properties are related. In this section we apply these properties to the inductive methods of the previous chapter to show how the resulting inferences are related to each other. Chapter 5 extends the already presented technique of reasoning with (single) c-representations to reasoning with sets of c-representations and shows the formal properties of these relations. All inductive methods use conditional knowledge bases as input. Chapter 6 recalls and summarises two articles on how conditional knowledge bases can be normalised in order to make these approaches to inductive reasoning more efficient.

The third part of this thesis purports network approaches to organising ordinal conditional functions: Chapter 7 recalls OCF-networks as semi-quantitative counterpart to Bayesian networks, and OCF-LEG networks as semi-quantitative counterparts to LEG networks. The factorising / stratification properties of these network types have been the breakthrough for the implementation and employment of probabilities, and this research in general are to help ordinal conditional functions to achieve the same. Finally, this chapter shows that OCF-networks can simulate the preference networks known as CP-networks.

The fourth part focusses on connections to and applications in psychology and cognition. Chapter 8 recalls that methods of formal inference can indeed model and mimic human inference provided that the knowledge engineer employing the methods carefully and thoroughly implements the background knowledge of the human reasoners the system is to model. This is completed by recalling the technique of inference patterns which is capable of revealing the background knowledge applied by the participants of an inference study and assessing the inherent rationality of the answers given by the participants.

The thesis concludes in Chapter 9, which is followed by an appendix containing, among others, the formal proofs for the technical results in this thesis.

2 Preliminaries

This chapter recalls the formal background which provides the formal base this thesis is built upon. We start by introducing the running example, a variant of the iconic example from nonmonotonic reasoning speaking about birds and penguins with respect to their ability to fly. This example is then used to illustrate the stepwise recallection of the necessary preliminaries in propositional logic and classical entailment (Section 2.1), conditionals and knowledge bases (Section 2.2), and nonmonotonic inference (Section 2.3). These definitions culminate in Δ-inference as first implementable nonmonotonic inference relation in this dissertation, which licenses for inferences based on the context of the background knowledge of the agent. This background knowledge is represented as a qualitative conditional knowledge base.

Example 2.1 (Introduction of the Running Example). The running example in this dissertation is an elaboration of the exemplary nonmonotonicity example about penguins, birds, and flying. So we work with the defeasible knowledge that *birds usually fly, birds usually have wings, penguins usually are birds, penguins usually do not fly, chickens usually are birds, chicken-birds usually do not fly,* and *being chicken or penguin is mutually exclusive.* Figure 2.1 illustrates this scenario.

In this example, both penguins and chickens are exceptional birds in that they are birds that lack the ability to fly, which is a specific property of birds. This is a scenario in which some properties (namely "ability to fly") of a superclass ("bird") are not inherited by all subclasses ("penguin", "chicken"), while others (namely "having wings") are inherited (or the inheritance is blocked for the property "ability to fly", and not blocked for the property "having wings"). Such scenarios are called *subclass-superclass problem* (confer, for instance, [Pea90, ST12, BKI14]) and are one of the main motivations for researching nonmonotonic reasoning in the first place, because for these problems classical, monotone logic leads to inconsistencies.

2.1 Propositional Logic and Satisfaction

For this dissertation, we use propositional logic based on a set of propositional variables, the *alphabet*, $\Sigma = \{V_1, ..., V_n\}$. A *literal* is the positive (v_i) or negative $(\overline{v}_i)$ form of a variable $V_i \in \Sigma$; we denote by $\dot{v}_i$ an un-

© Springer-Verlag GmbH Germany, part of Springer Nature 2018
C. Eichhorn, *Rational Reasoning with Finite Conditional Knowledge Bases*, https://doi.org/10.1007/978-3-476-04824-0_2

Figure 2.1: Graphical introduction of the running example: Penguins and chickens contemplating about their subclass-superclass problem, as they both are winged birds that cannot fly (drawing of Katharina Dieckmann, 2012)

determined but fixed outcome of V_i. With the connectives $\wedge$ (*conjunction*, logical "and") and $\neg$ (*negation*, logical "not"), the propositional language $\mathfrak{L}$ is recursively defined as follows (please confer [BKI14] as reference for this section if no other reference is given):

- Every literal is an atomic formula of $\mathfrak{L}$.

- If ϕ is a formula in $\mathfrak{L}$, then $\neg\phi$ is a formula in $\mathfrak{L}$.

- If ϕ and ψ are formulas in $\mathfrak{L}$, then $\phi \wedge \psi$ is a formula in $\mathfrak{L}$.

For a formula $\phi \in \mathfrak{L}$ we write $V \Subset \phi$ if and only if v or $\overline{v}$ appears in ϕ and define the the set of all variables of a formula as $Vars(\phi) = \{V \mid V \Subset \phi\}$. For shorter formulas we abbreviate $\neg\phi$ with $\overline{\phi}$, and omit the connective $\wedge$, indicating conjunction by juxtaposition, that is, we abbreviate $\phi \wedge \psi$ by $\phi\psi$. We use the usual logical connectives as abbreviations of the following

Table 2.1: Evaluation of the propositional connectives

$[\![\phi]\!]_\omega$	$[\![\psi]\!]_\omega$	implies	$[\![\phi \wedge \psi]\!]_\omega$	$[\![\phi \vee \psi]\!]_\omega$	$[\![\phi \Rightarrow \psi]\!]_\omega$	$[\![\phi \Leftrightarrow \psi]\!]_\omega$	$[\![\phi \triangledown \psi]\!]_\omega$
true	*true*		*true*	*true*	*true*	*true*	*false*
true	*false*		*false*	*true*	*false*	*false*	*true*
false	*true*		*false*	*true*	*true*	*false*	*true*
false	*false*		*false*	*false*	*true*	*true*	*false*

formulas:

$\phi \vee \psi$	abbreviates	$\neg(\overline{\phi}\,\overline{\psi})$	*(disjunction)*
$\phi \Rightarrow \psi$	abbreviates	$\overline{\phi} \vee \psi$	*(material implication)*
$\phi \Leftrightarrow \psi$	abbreviates	$(\phi \Rightarrow \psi) \wedge (\psi \Rightarrow \phi)$	*(biconditional, if and only if)*
$\phi \triangledown \psi$	abbreviates	$\phi\overline{\psi} \vee \overline{\phi}\psi$	*(exclusive or)*

Interpretations, or *(possible) worlds*, are represented by complete conjunctions over Σ; Ω is the set of all possible worlds over Σ. The established evaluation function $[\![\cdot]\!] . : \mathcal{L} \times \Omega \to \{true, false\}$ evaluates a formula ϕ under a possible world ω with respect to the recursive construction of the language, that is:

- If ϕ is a literal, then $[\![\phi]\!]_\omega = true$ if and only if ϕ is an element of the conjunction ω, and *false*, otherwise.

- For a negation we have $[\![\neg\phi]\!]_\omega = true$ if and only if $[\![\phi]\!]_\omega = false$, and *false*, otherwise.

- For a conjunction we have $[\![\phi\psi]\!]_\omega = true$ if $[\![\phi]\!]_\omega = true$ and $[\![\psi]\!]_\omega = true$, as well, and *false*, otherwise.

Table 2.1 gives the evaluation of the connectives above with respect to the evaluation of formulas ϕ and ψ.

The set of *models of a formula* $\phi \in \mathcal{L}$ is the set of possible worlds which evaluate ϕ to *true*, formally $Mod(\phi) = \{\omega | [\![\phi]\!]_\omega = true\}$. For a set $\mathbf{V} \subseteq \Sigma$, $\mathbf{v}$ denotes a complete conjunction $\bigwedge_{\dot{v} \in \mathbf{V}} \dot{v}$, also called an *outcome* of $\mathbf{V}$. We define by $\Omega(\mathbf{V}) = \Omega_\mathbf{V}$ the set of *local possible worlds* over the variables $\mathbf{V}$, that is, the set of all complete conjunctions $\mathbf{v}$ over the variables $\mathbf{V}$.

A possible world *satisfies* a formula ϕ if and only if ω is a model of ϕ, formally $\omega \vDash \phi$ if and only if $\omega \in Mod(\phi)$. A formula ϕ is *satisfiable* if and only if it has models, that is, $Mod(\phi) \neq \varnothing$. We overload the satisfaction operator to represent *entailment* (also referred to as *classical entailment*) as a relation between formulas such that a formula ϕ entails a formula ψ if and only if every model of ϕ is also a model of ψ, formally $\phi \vDash \psi$ if and only if $Mod(\phi) \subseteq Mod(\psi)$. The set of all formulas ψ that are entailable from a formula ψ, called the (classical) *consequences* of ϕ, is $Cn(\phi) = \{\psi | \phi \vDash \psi\}$. A set of formulas $\mathcal{A} \subseteq \mathfrak{L}$ is called *deductively closed* if it contains all is consequences, that is, if $\mathcal{A} = Cn(\mathcal{A})$. A formula ϕ is *semantically equivalent* to a formula ψ, written $\phi \equiv \psi$ if and only if $\phi \vDash \psi$ and $\psi \vDash \phi$. The symbols $\top$ for *tautology* with the semantics $\top \equiv \phi \vee \overline{\phi}$ and $\bot$ for *contradiction* with the semantics $\bot \equiv \phi\overline{\phi}$ are to be symbols of $\mathfrak{L}$. We recall major properties of the entailment relation (see [Tar30]).

MONOTONY (M). Set up on the subset-relation on sets of models, classical entailment is *monotone*, that is, for arbitrary formulas $\phi, \psi, \chi \in \mathfrak{L}$ it holds that if χ can be entailed from ϕ, then χ can be entailed from $\phi\psi$, as well, formally

$$\phi \vDash \chi \qquad \text{implies} \qquad \phi\psi \vDash \chi \qquad \text{for all } \psi \in \mathfrak{L}. \qquad \text{(M)}$$

TRANSITIVITY (T). Classical entailments can be chained:

$$\phi \vDash \psi \qquad \text{and} \qquad \psi \vDash \chi \qquad \text{imply} \qquad \phi \vDash \chi \qquad \text{(T)}$$

DEDUCTION THEOREM (DThm). For classical entailment, every syntactical implication is a semantical one, and vice versa, formally

$$\top \vDash (\phi \Rightarrow \psi) \qquad \text{if and only if} \qquad \phi \vDash \psi. \qquad \text{(DThm)}$$

CONTRAPOSITION (CPS). With the deduction theorem we obtain directly that Contraposition holds for classical entailment:

$$\phi \vDash \psi \qquad \text{implies} \qquad \overline{\psi} \vDash \overline{\phi} \qquad \text{(CPS)}$$

EXPLOSION (EFQ). The definition of $\vDash$ via subsets of models accounts for the principle of Explosion or "ex falso sequitur quodlibet", that is, any formula ψ can be inferred from a contradiction, which is written as

$$\bot \vDash \psi \qquad \text{for all } \psi \in \mathfrak{L}. \qquad \text{(EFQ)}$$

Example 2.2 (Propositional Preliminaries). We formalise the penguin example introduced as Example 2.1 to illustrate these preliminaries of propositional logic Let $\Sigma = \{P, C, B, F, W\}$ be a propositional alphabet with the boolean variables penguin (P), chicken (C), bird (B), flying (F) and wings (W), each with positive (for instance, p for "being a penguin") and negative (for instance, $\overline{p}$ for "not being a penguin") outcome. The set of possible worlds for this example is the set

$$\Omega = \left\{ \begin{array}{l} p\,c\,b\,f\,w,\ p\,c\,b\,f\,\overline{w},\ p\,c\,b\,\overline{f}\,w,\ p\,c\,b\,\overline{f}\,\overline{w},\ p\,c\,\overline{b}\,f\,w,\ p\,c\,\overline{b}\,f\,\overline{w},\ p\,c\,\overline{b}\,f\,w, \\ p\,c\,\overline{b}\,\overline{f}\,\overline{w},\ p\,\overline{c}\,b\,f\,w,\ p\,\overline{c}\,b\,f\,\overline{w},\ p\,\overline{c}\,b\,\overline{f}\,w,\ p\,\overline{c}\,b\,\overline{f}\,\overline{w},\ p\,\overline{c}\,\overline{b}\,f\,w,\ p\,\overline{c}\,\overline{b}\,f\,\overline{w}, \\ p\,\overline{c}\,\overline{b}\,\overline{f}\,w,\ p\,\overline{c}\,\overline{b}\,\overline{f}\,\overline{w},\ \overline{p}\,c\,b\,f\,w,\ \overline{p}\,c\,b\,f\,\overline{w},\ \overline{p}\,c\,b\,\overline{f}\,w,\ \overline{p}\,c\,b\,\overline{f}\,\overline{w},\ \overline{p}\,c\,\overline{b}\,f\,w, \\ \overline{p}\,c\,\overline{b}\,f\,\overline{w},\ \overline{p}\,c\,\overline{b}\,\overline{f}\,w,\ \overline{p}\,c\,\overline{b}\,\overline{f}\,\overline{w},\ \overline{p}\,\overline{c}\,b\,f\,w,\ \overline{p}\,\overline{c}\,b\,f\,\overline{w},\ \overline{p}\,\overline{c}\,b\,\overline{f}\,w,\ \overline{p}\,\overline{c}\,b\,\overline{f}\,\overline{w}, \\ \overline{p}\,\overline{c}\,\overline{b}\,f\,w,\ \overline{p}\,\overline{c}\,\overline{b}\,f\,\overline{w},\ \overline{p}\,\overline{c}\,\overline{b}\,\overline{f}\,w,\ \overline{p}\,\overline{c}\,\overline{b}\,\overline{f}\,\overline{w} \end{array} \right\}$$

which contains fairly usual entities like flying birds with wings which are neither chickens nor penguins ($\overline{p}\,\overline{c}\,b\,f\,w$) and also quite surprising fellows like the chicken-penguin that is a wingless non-bird that flies ($p\,c\,\overline{b}\,f\,\overline{w}$). The set models of pc, that is, the worlds with chicken-penguins is

$$Mod(pc) = \left\{ \begin{array}{llll} p\,c\,b\,f\,w, & p\,c\,b\,f\,\overline{w}, & p\,c\,b\,\overline{f}\,w, & p\,c\,b\,\overline{f}\,\overline{w}, \\ p\,c\,\overline{b}\,f\,w, & p\,c\,\overline{b}\,f\,\overline{w}, & p\,c\,\overline{b}\,\overline{f}\,w, & p\,c\,\overline{b}\,\overline{f}\,\overline{w} \end{array} \right\}$$

which gives us that the set of worlds that satisfy that chickens and penguins are, as stated in Example 2.1, mutually exclusive is the set $Mod(\neg(pc)) = \Omega \setminus Mod(pc)$. Being a penguin-bird entails being a bird, that is $pb \vDash b$ as $Mod(pb) \subseteq Mod(pb) \cup Mod(p\overline{b}) = Mod(b)$.

2.2 Conditionals and Knowledge Bases

With the binary operator $|$ we obtain the set $(\mathfrak{L}|\mathfrak{L})$ of *conditionals*. A conditional $(\psi|\phi)$ formalises the conditional assertion "if ϕ then usually/-typically/normally ψ". This is also called a *defeasible rule* because even if the connection between the premise ϕ and the conclusion ψ exists "usually", there may be exceptions to this. Other than the propositional evaluation of the material implication $\phi \Rightarrow \psi$ used to formalise strict rules of the form "if ϕ then (always) ψ", the evaluation of a conditional is trivalent (see [Fin74, KI01]): If the formalised rule holds in ω, that is, if premise and conclusion are *true* in ω, the conditional is verified. If the formalised rule is violated in ω, that is, if the premise is *true* and conclusion is *false* in ω,

Table 2.2: Comparison of the evaluation of the material implication, the biconditional, and the conditional

$[\![\phi]\!]_\omega$	$[\![\psi]\!]_\omega$	implies	$[\![\phi \Rightarrow \psi]\!]_\omega$	$[\![\phi \Leftrightarrow \psi]\!]_\omega$	$[\![(\psi|\phi)]\!]_\omega$
true	*true*		*true*	*true*	*true*
true	*false*		*false*	*false*	*false*
false	*true*		*true*	*false*	*undefined*
false	*false*		*true*	*true*	*undefined*

the conditional is falsified. If the premise is *false* in ω, the formalised rule and thus the conditional is not applicable in ω. We overload the evaluation function $[\![\cdot]\!]$. to evaluate conditionals in such a way, that is, [Fin74]

$$[\![(\psi|\phi)]\!]_\omega = \begin{cases} true & \text{iff} \quad \omega \vDash \phi\psi & \text{(verification)} \\ false & \text{iff} \quad \omega \vDash \phi\overline{\psi} & \text{(falsification)} \\ undefined & \text{iff} \quad \omega \vDash \overline{\phi} & \text{(non-applicability)}. \end{cases} \qquad (2.1)$$

This trivalent evaluation has also been discovered to be used by human reasoners when reasoning about a rule [Was68]. Up to this time, the material conditional was considered as the normative correct formalisation of conditional statements. As the trivalent evaluation of conditionals differs from the evaluation of the material conditional, this evaluation scheme was named *defective truth table*. Because the evaluation function was defined by [Fin74] on formal conditionals, there is a recent name-shift to calling this evaluation scheme a *deFinetti truth table* [BOP13]. Table 2.2 compares the different evaluations of the material implication, the biconditional, and the conditional. Note that the evaluation of all of these formal constructs is identical if the premise is satisfied and differs only in the cases where the premise does not hold.

Let $\delta = (\psi|\phi)$ be a conditional, then $(\overline{\psi}|\phi)$ is the *(strict) negation of* δ, also written as $\neg\delta$ or $\overline{\delta}$, and $(\phi|\psi)$ the *inverse of the conditional*. If $\phi \vDash \psi$ the conditional cannot be falsified and is called *self-fulfilling* (confer [BEKIK16, ERKI18]).

The trivalent evaluation function (2.1) is a relation between conditionals and worlds. With the notion of *tolerance* we recall a relation between conditionals and sets of conditional

Definition 2.3 (Tolerance [Pea90]). Let Δ be be a finite set of conditionals $\Delta = \{(\psi_1|\phi_1), \ldots, (\psi_n|\phi_n)\} \subseteq (\mathfrak{L} \mid \mathfrak{L})$ and let $\delta = (\psi|\phi)$ be a conditional. Δ *tolerates* δ if and only if there is a world $\omega \in \Omega$ that verifies δ and does not falsify any conditional in Δ, that is, if there is a world ω with the property

$$\omega \models \phi\psi \bigwedge_{i=1}^{n} (\phi_i \Rightarrow \psi_i). \tag{2.2}$$

Example 2.4 (Formalising Conditionals from the Running Example). We continue the formalisation of Example 2.1 by representing the defeasible rules given in the example text as conditionals as follows:

$\delta_1 : (f|b)$ "Birds usually fly."
$\delta_2 : (w|b)$ "Birds usually have wings."
$\delta_3 : (b|p)$ "Penguins usually are birds."
$\delta_4 : (\overline{f}|p)$ "Penguins usually do not fly."
$\delta_5 : (b|c)$ "Chickens usually are birds."
$\delta_6 : (\overline{f}|cb)$ "Chicken-birds usually do not fly."

Here, for example, the flying bird with wings which is neither a chicken nor a penguin from Example 2.2 ($\overline{p}\,\overline{c}bfw$) verifies δ_1 and δ_2, falsifies no conditional, whilst in this world the conditionals δ_3, δ_4, δ_5, and δ_6 are not applicable. The chicken-penguin that is a wingless non-bird that flies ($pc\overline{b}f\overline{w}$) also mentioned in Example 2.2, verifies not a single conditional, falsifies the conditionals δ_3, δ_4, and δ_5, whilst δ_1, δ_2, and δ_6 are not applicable. Table 2.3 shows the evaluation of the conditionals in the worlds of this example. The set $\Delta = \{\delta_1, \delta_2, \delta_3, \delta_4, \delta_5, \delta_6\}$ tolerates δ_1, as the formula $\left((b \wedge f) \wedge (b \Rightarrow w) \wedge (p \Rightarrow b) \wedge (p \Rightarrow \overline{f}) \wedge (c \Rightarrow b) \wedge (cb \Rightarrow \overline{f})\right)$ is satisfied, for instance, by the world $\overline{p}\,\overline{c}\,bf\,w$; Δ does not tolerate δ_3 as

$$\left((b \Rightarrow f) \wedge (b \Rightarrow w) \wedge (p \wedge b) \wedge (p \Rightarrow \overline{f}) \wedge (c \Rightarrow b) \wedge (cb \Rightarrow \overline{f})\right) \equiv \bot.$$

Sometimes approaches to (or being based on) conditionals need a simpler, more restricted form of these formalisation of rules, because using the whole propositional language in premise and conclusion is not possible or too complex. In this case we may restrict ourselves to single-elementary conditionals which we recall as follows.

Definition 2.5 (Single-Elementary Conditionals [KI01, KIE13a]). A *single-elementary conditional* $(\psi|\phi)$ is a conditional where the conclusion ψ is a literal and the premise ϕ is a conjunction of literals.

Table 2.3: Illustration of the evaluation behaviour the conditionals and worlds given in Example 2.4

ω	$[\![(f|b)]\!]_\omega$	$[\![(w|b)]\!]_\omega$	$[\![(b|p)]\!]_\omega$	$[\![(\overline{f}|p)]\!]_\omega$	$[\![(b|c)]\!]_\omega$	$[\![(\overline{f}|cb)]\!]_\omega$
$p\,c\,b\,f\,w$	true	true	true	false	true	false
$p\,c\,b\,f\,\overline{w}$	true	false	true	false	true	false
$p\,c\,b\,\overline{f}\,w$	false	true	true	true	true	true
$p\,c\,b\,\overline{f}\,\overline{w}$	false	false	true	true	true	true
$p\,c\,\overline{b}\,f\,w$	undefined	undefined	false	false	false	undefined
$p\,c\,\overline{b}\,f\,\overline{w}$	undefined	undefined	false	false	false	undefined
$p\,c\,\overline{b}\,\overline{f}\,w$	undefined	undefined	false	true	false	undefined
$p\,c\,\overline{b}\,\overline{f}\,\overline{w}$	undefined	undefined	false	true	false	undefined
$p\,\overline{c}\,b\,f\,w$	true	true	true	false	undefined	undefined
$p\,\overline{c}\,b\,f\,\overline{w}$	true	false	true	false	undefined	undefined
$p\,\overline{c}\,b\,\overline{f}\,w$	false	true	true	true	undefined	undefined
$p\,\overline{c}\,b\,\overline{f}\,\overline{w}$	false	false	true	true	undefined	undefined
$p\,\overline{c}\,\overline{b}\,f\,w$	undefined	undefined	false	false	undefined	undefined
$p\,\overline{c}\,\overline{b}\,f\,\overline{w}$	undefined	undefined	false	false	undefined	undefined
$p\,\overline{c}\,\overline{b}\,\overline{f}\,w$	undefined	undefined	false	true	undefined	undefined
$p\,\overline{c}\,\overline{b}\,\overline{f}\,\overline{w}$	undefined	undefined	false	true	undefined	undefined
$\overline{p}\,c\,b\,f\,w$	true	true	undefined	undefined	true	false
$\overline{p}\,c\,b\,f\,\overline{w}$	true	false	undefined	undefined	true	false
$\overline{p}\,c\,b\,\overline{f}\,w$	false	true	undefined	undefined	true	true
$\overline{p}\,c\,b\,\overline{f}\,\overline{w}$	false	false	undefined	undefined	true	true
$\overline{p}\,c\,\overline{b}\,f\,w$	undefined	undefined	undefined	undefined	false	undefined
$\overline{p}\,c\,\overline{b}\,f\,\overline{w}$	undefined	undefined	undefined	undefined	false	undefined
$\overline{p}\,c\,\overline{b}\,\overline{f}\,w$	undefined	undefined	undefined	undefined	false	undefined
$\overline{p}\,c\,\overline{b}\,\overline{f}\,\overline{w}$	undefined	undefined	undefined	undefined	false	undefined
$\overline{p}\,\overline{c}\,b\,f\,w$	true	true	undefined	undefined	undefined	undefined
$\overline{p}\,\overline{c}\,b\,f\,\overline{w}$	true	false	undefined	undefined	undefined	undefined
$\overline{p}\,\overline{c}\,b\,\overline{f}\,w$	false	true	undefined	undefined	undefined	undefined
$\overline{p}\,\overline{c}\,b\,\overline{f}\,\overline{w}$	false	false	undefined	undefined	undefined	undefined
$\overline{p}\,\overline{c}\,\overline{b}\,f\,w$	undefined	undefined	undefined	undefined	undefined	undefined
$\overline{p}\,\overline{c}\,\overline{b}\,f\,\overline{w}$	undefined	undefined	undefined	undefined	undefined	undefined
$\overline{p}\,\overline{c}\,\overline{b}\,\overline{f}\,w$	undefined	undefined	undefined	undefined	undefined	undefined
$\overline{p}\,\overline{c}\,\overline{b}\,\overline{f}\,\overline{w}$	undefined	undefined	undefined	undefined	undefined	undefined

In this thesis, single-elementary conditionals are, for instance, used to formalise causal relationships between (multiple) causes ϕ and their effect ψ.

The evaluation function $[\![(\cdot|\cdot)]\!]_\omega$ (see (2.1)) is not sufficient to give appropriate semantics to conditionals. Hence, conditionals have to be considered within richer structures such as epistemic states in the sense of [Hal05]. Such epistemic states usually order worlds and by this, formulas, with respect to a notion of plausibility, possibility, probability, or necessity. For most of these methods, which are the subject of Chapter 3, a conditional is *accepted* if and only if its verification (or "confirmation", when we talk about conditionals as formalisation of rules) is (strictly) preferred (more plausible, possible, probable, . . . , as defined by the respective semantics) than its falsification (or "refutation"). So, to forestall the formal semantics in Chapter 3, a conditional $(\psi|\phi)$ is *accepted* in an epistemic state Ψ, written $\Psi \models (\psi|\phi)$ overloading the relation $\models$, if the rule "If ϕ then usually ψ" is confirmed in Ψ with respect to the semantics characterising Ψ.

This dissertation deals mainly with qualitative conditionals. For quantitative or semi-quantitative purposes, the language of conditionals can be extended to the sets $(\mathfrak{L}|\mathfrak{L})[0,1]$ or $(\mathfrak{L}|\mathfrak{L})\mathbb{N}_0^\infty$; Chapter 3 will also give formal details on the semantics characterising an appropriate epistemic state.

In addition to the conditional in the sense of [Fin74] we also use *weak* or *might conditionals* [ERKI18] in the sense of [Lew73]: A weak conditional $(\![\psi|\phi]\!)$ has the same evaluation as the strong conditional $(\psi|\phi)$, that is, $[\![(\![\psi|\phi]\!)]\!]_\omega = [\![(\psi|\phi)]\!]_\omega$ for all $\omega \in \Omega$ but encodes the conditional assertion "If ϕ, then ψ is possible", "If ϕ then it might be that ψ", or "If ϕ it is not the case that $\overline{\psi}$". The language of all weak conditionals is denoted as $(\![\mathfrak{L}|\mathfrak{L}]\!)$. A weak conditional is accepted in an epistemic state Ψ if and only if its negation is not accepted in the epistemic state with respect to the semantics characterising Ψ.

In the most general sense with respect to this dissertation, a *knowledge base* is a finite set of formalised knowledge of some kind. We here distinguish between the following types:

A *strict knowledge base* is a finite set of propositional formulas $\mathfrak{S} \subseteq \mathfrak{L}$. The knowledge formalised in a strict knowledge base describes strict facts and classical nexuses that are always true and do not have exceptions. This means, worlds that falsify any of the formulas in $\mathfrak{S}$ are not possible given this knowledge, that is, are *impossible* worlds, and are excluded from the set of possible worlds. So for any knowledge based system, the set of possible worlds with respect to $\mathfrak{S}$ is defined as $\Omega^{\mathfrak{S}} = \{\omega | \omega \in \Omega \text{ and } \omega \models \bigwedge_{\phi \in \mathfrak{S}} \phi\}$. For clarity of formal propositions, we exclude the superscript where there is no danger of confusion and keep in mind that given a non-empty set of strict knowledge, the set of possible worlds consists only of the worlds actually possible with respect to this knowledge. A strict knowledge base is *consistent* if and only if the conjunction of the formulas in the knowledge base is satisfiable, that is, if there is a possible world ω that satisfies all formulas in $\mathfrak{S}$, which is the case if and only if $\bigwedge_{\phi \in \mathfrak{S}} \phi \not\equiv \bot$.

Example 2.6 (Illustrating the Effect of Strict Knowledge). In the penguin-example, we know that being a penguin or a chicken is mutually exclusive, thus we define $\mathfrak{S}_{\text{Bird}} = \{\neg(pc)\}$. This restricts the worlds Ω from Example 2.2 to $\Omega^{\mathfrak{S}_{\text{Bird}}} = \Omega_{\text{Bird}}$ as follows:

$$\Omega_{\text{Bird}} = \left\{ \begin{array}{l} p\,\overline{c}\,b\,f\,w \,,\, p\,\overline{c}\,b\,f\,\overline{w} \,,\, p\,\overline{c}\,b\,\overline{f}\,w \,,\, p\,\overline{c}\,b\,\overline{f}\,\overline{w} \,,\, p\,\overline{c}\,\overline{b}\,f\,w \,,\, p\,\overline{c}\,\overline{b}\,f\,\overline{w}, \\ p\,\overline{c}\,\overline{b}\,\overline{f}\,w \,,\, p\,\overline{c}\,\overline{b}\,\overline{f}\,\overline{w} \,,\, \overline{p}\,c\,b\,f\,w \,,\, \overline{p}\,c\,b\,f\,\overline{w} \,,\, \overline{p}\,c\,b\,\overline{f}\,w \,,\, \overline{p}\,c\,b\,\overline{f}\,\overline{w}, \\ \overline{p}\,c\,\overline{b}\,f\,w \,,\, \overline{p}\,c\,\overline{b}\,f\,\overline{w} \,,\, \overline{p}\,c\,\overline{b}\,\overline{f}\,w \,,\, \overline{p}\,c\,\overline{b}\,\overline{f}\,\overline{w} \,,\, \overline{p}\,\overline{c}\,b\,f\,w \,,\, \overline{p}\,\overline{c}\,b\,f\,\overline{w}, \\ \overline{p}\,\overline{c}\,b\,\overline{f}\,w \,,\, \overline{p}\,\overline{c}\,b\,\overline{f}\,\overline{w} \,,\, \overline{p}\,\overline{c}\,\overline{b}\,f\,w \,,\, \overline{p}\,\overline{c}\,\overline{b}\,f\,\overline{w} \,,\, \overline{p}\,\overline{c}\,\overline{b}\,\overline{f}\,w \,,\, \overline{p}\,\overline{c}\,\overline{b}\,\overline{f}\,\overline{w} \end{array} \right\}$$

Set up from the formalisation of defeasible rules, a *conditional knowledge base* formalises the knowledge of an agent or knowledge based system about rules that are not always, but usually true. So, a *qualitative conditional knowledge base* $\Delta = \{(\psi_1|\phi_1), \ldots, (\psi_n|\phi_n)\} \subseteq (\mathfrak{L} \mid \mathfrak{L})$ is a finite set of conditionals. This holds for the most, if not all, knowledge of human reasoners. The folk saying goes "the exception proves the rule" because there is very few, if any, strict knowledge in the "real world"[1]. Being set up from (defeasible, exception-permitting) conditionals rather than strict rules, conditional knowledge bases do not render worlds impossible in the way strict knowledge bases do. In contrast to that, they are often used to induce a notion of probability, plausibility or possibility on the possible worlds based on the conditionals verified or falsified, in that providing a base for inductively setting up an epistemic state Ψ.

---

[1] Actually we made it a tradition to ask the students at the beginnings of the lectures "Darstellung, Verarbeitung und Erwerb von Wissen" and "Commonsense Reasoning" to come up with rules without exceptions; so far, no rule was presented where we could not find an exception to.

Example 2.7 (Illustrating Conditional Knowledge Bases). We join the qualitative conditionals obtained by formalising the defeasible rules of the running example in Example 2.4 to the conditional knowledge base of the running example as

$$\Delta_{\text{Bird}} = \{\delta_1 : (f|b), \delta_2 : (w|b), \delta_3 : (b|p), \delta_4 : (\overline{f}|p), \delta_5 : (b|c), \delta_6 : (\overline{f}|cb)\}.$$

A *(semi-) quantitative conditional knowledge base* is a finite set of conditionals $\Delta^{\mathbb{N}_0^\infty} = \{(\psi_1|\phi_1)[f_1], \ldots, (\psi_n|\phi_n)[f_n]\} \subseteq (\mathcal{L} \mid \mathcal{L})\mathbb{N}$ if integer weights are used, or $\Delta^{[0,1]} = \{(\psi_1|\phi_1)[x_1], \ldots, (\psi_n|\phi_n)[x_n]\} \subseteq (\mathcal{L} \mid \mathcal{L})[0,1]$ if rational weights are used.

A conditional knowledge base is *consistent* if and only if there is an epistemic state Ψ that accepts all conditionals in the knowledge base. We further overload the relation $\vDash$ and write $\Psi \vDash \Delta$ if and only if $\Psi \vDash (\psi_i|\phi_i)$, $\Psi \vDash (\psi_i|\phi_i)[f_i]$, or $\Psi \vDash (\psi_i|\phi_i)[x_i]$ for all $1 \leq i \leq n$, respectively, with respect to the the the formalisation of Ψ.

Additionally to the model-theoretic definition of consistency for a qualitative conditional knowledge base Δ, the relation of tolerance between conditionals and sets of conditionals makes an algorithmic testing of consistency possible: A conditional knowledge base Δ is consistent if and only if in every non-empty subset $\Delta' \subseteq \Delta$ there is a conditional δ that is tolerated by Δ' [Ada75]. This is the case if and only if there is an ordered partition $(\Delta_0, \ldots \Delta_k)$ of Δ with $\Delta = \bigcup_{i=1}^k \Delta_i$ and $\Delta_i \cap \Delta_j = \varnothing$ for all $1 \leq i, j \leq k$, $i \neq j$ such that every conditional in Δ_i is tolerated by the set $\bigcup_{j=i}^k \Delta_j$ [Pea90, Ada75]. Algorithm 2.1, illustrated in Figure 2.2, is an algorithm to test a qualitative conditional knowledge base for consistency by generating a unique, inclusion-maximal partitioning of Δ that satisfies the consistency condition of [Ada75]. The algorithm traverses through the knowledge base and in each iteration either stops or removes at least one conditional from the knowledge base. The algorithm stops if the knowledge base is empty. In each iteration, the algorithm inspects all remaining conditionals in the knowledge base for tolerance, hence the tolerance test has to be invoked $\mathcal{O}(|\Delta|^2)$ times. The tolerance test itself is a test on satisfiability and can be worst-case estimated to be in $\mathcal{O}(2^{|\Sigma|})$, thus the overall consistency test algorithm has the non-polynomial time complexity $\mathcal{O}(|\Delta|^2 \cdot 2^{|\Sigma|})$ (see [Pea90] for a formal proof).

Example 2.8 (Illustrating Algorithm 2.1). We illustrate Algorithm 2.1 with an excerpt of the running example. Let $\Delta = \{\delta_1 : (f|b), \delta_3 : (b|p), \delta_4 :$

Listing 2.1: Algorithm to test for consistency of Δ (cf. [Pea90])

```
INPUT   : Qualitative conditional knowledge base
          Δ = {(ψ₁|φ₁),...,(ψₙ|φₙ)} ⊆ (𝔏 | 𝔏)
OUTPUT  : Ordered partition (Δ₀,Δ₁,...,Δᵢ) if Δ is consistent,
          NULL otherwise

BEGIN
  INT i:=0;
  WHILE(Δ ≠ ∅) DO
    Δᵢ:=∅
    FOR-EACH((ψ|φ) in Δ) DO
      IF(Δ tolerates (ψ|φ))      // Tolerance test
      THEN
          Δᵢ:=Δᵢ ∪ {(ψ|φ)}
      ENDIF
    END
    IF(Δᵢ ≠ ∅)
    THEN
        Δ:=Δ \ Δᵢ
        i:=i+1
    ELSE
      RETURN NULL                // Δ is inconsistent
    ENDIF
  END
  RETURN (Δ₀,Δ₁,...,Δᵢ)          // Δ is consistent
END
```

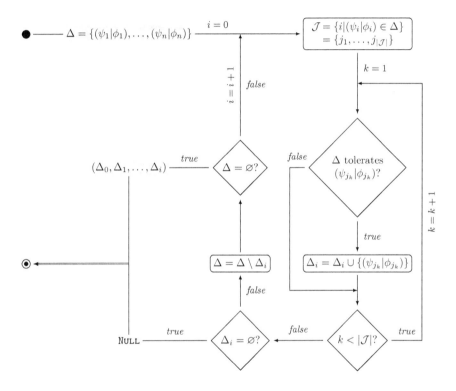

Figure 2.2: Flowchart of Algorithm 2.1 [Pea90] to test the consistency of a qualitative conditional knowledge base Δ

$(\overline{f}|p)\}$ be the knowledge base to examine, and we reduce the alphabet to the needed variables, such that $\Sigma = \{P, B, F\}$ with a respective set of worlds. In the first iteration, the algorithm tests whether Δ tolerates δ_1, δ_2 and δ_3. Here, δ_1 is tolerated because the proposition $b \wedge f \wedge (p \Rightarrow \overline{f}) \wedge (p \Rightarrow b)$ is satisfiable, the world $\overline{p}bf$ is a model for this formula. The conditional δ_4 is not tolerated because the proposition $(b \Rightarrow f) \wedge p \wedge b \wedge (p \Rightarrow \overline{f})$ resolves to $\bot$, and δ_4 is not tolerated because the proposition $(b \Rightarrow f) \wedge (p \Rightarrow b) \wedge (p \wedge \overline{f})$ also resolves to $\bot$, rendering both propositions inconsistent and hence not satisfiable. Therefore, $\Delta_0 = \{\delta_1\}$. For the second iteration, this set is removed from Δ, such that the knowledge base $\Delta \setminus \{\delta_1\} = \{\delta_3, \delta_4\}$ is inspected. We obtain that both propositions $p \wedge \overline{f} \wedge (p \Rightarrow b)$ and $(p \Rightarrow \overline{f}) \wedge p \wedge b$ are satisfiable, for instance with the world pbf, thus $\Delta_1 = \{\delta_3, \delta_4\}$. For the third iteration, the algorithm also removes Δ_1 from Δ; the algorithm stops because the knowledge base $\Delta \setminus (\Delta_0 \cup \Delta_1)$ is empty, and returns the partitioning $(\Delta_0 = \{\delta_1\}, \Delta_1 = \{\delta_3, \delta_4\})$.

To avoid confusion between the different types of knowledge bases and for clear reference to each part, we follow the approach of [Gil93] and split (semi-) quantitative knowledge bases into the qualitative and the numeric part, such that we use the tuple $\Delta^{[0,1]} = (\{(\psi_1|\phi_1), ..., (\psi_n|\phi_n)\}, \{x_1, ..., x_n\})$ if and only if $\Delta^{[0,1]} = \{(\psi_1|\phi_1)[x_1], ..., (\psi_n|\phi_n)[x_n]\} \subseteq (\mathcal{L} \mid \mathcal{L})[0, 1]$ and likewise the tuple $\Delta^{\mathbb{N}_0^\infty} = (\{(\psi_1|\phi_1), ..., (\psi_n|\phi_n)\}, \{f_1, ..., f_n\})$ for a knowledge base with integer weights $\Delta^{\mathbb{N}_0^\infty} = \{(\psi_1|\phi_1)[f_1], ..., (\psi_n|\phi_n)[f_n]\} \subseteq (\mathcal{L} \mid \mathcal{L})\mathbb{N}$. For knowledge bases which consist of strict and defeasible knowledge we write a pair $\mathcal{R} \subseteq (\mathcal{L}, (\mathcal{L}|\mathcal{L}))$ if the knowledge is qualitative, or triplet $\mathcal{R}^{[0,1]} \subseteq (\mathcal{L}, (\mathcal{L}|\mathcal{L}), [0, 1])$ $(\mathcal{R}^{\mathbb{N}_0^\infty} \subseteq (\mathcal{L}, (\mathcal{L}|\mathcal{L}), \mathbb{N}_0^\infty))$ if the knowledge is quantitative, for referring to the the different parts, if necessary. If it is clear from the context which representation is meant, a knowledge base of either type is simply referred to as knowledge base. A knowledge base $\mathcal{R}$ is consistent if and only if $\mathfrak{S}$ is consistent and $\Delta = \{(\psi|\phi)|(\psi|\phi)[x] \in \mathcal{R}\}$ is consistent with respect to the possible worlds $\Omega^{\mathfrak{S}}$.

Example 2.9 (Illustrating Knowledge Base $\mathcal{R}$ and Consistency Thereof). Joining the knowledge of the running example formalised in Examples 2.6 and 2.7 we obtain the overall knowledge base

$$\mathcal{R}_{\text{Bird}} = \left(\{\neg(pc)\}, \left\{ \begin{array}{lll} \delta_1 : (f|b), & \delta_2 : (w|b), & \delta_3 : (b|p), \\ \delta_4 : (\overline{f}|p), & \delta_5 : (b|c), & \delta_6 : (\overline{f}|cb) \end{array} \right\} \right)$$

as complete formalisation of the background knowledge provided in Example 2.1. This knowledge base is consistent: For the strict part, Example 2.6 enumerates the set of possible worlds that satisfy $\{\neg(pc)\}$. Using Table 2.3 we see that there is a world that verifies δ_1 and falsifies no other world, namely $\overline{p}\,\overline{c}\,b\,f\,w$, this world also verifies δ_2. So both conditionals are tolerated by Δ_{Bird}; the conditionals δ_3 to δ_6 are not tolerated by Δ. But $\Delta_{\text{Bird}} \setminus \{\delta_1, \delta_2\}$ tolerates these conditionals: $p\,\overline{c}\,b\,\overline{f}\,w$ verifies δ_3 and δ_4 and does not falsify any conditional in this knowledge base, and $\overline{p}\,c\,b\,\overline{f}\,w$ verifies δ_5 and δ_6 and does not falsify any conditional in this knowledge base. Therefore, Δ_{Bird} is consistent and thus $\mathcal{R}_{\text{Bird}}$ is consistent, as well.

2.3 Inference Relations

An *inference relation* $\mathrel{|\!\approx}\ \subseteq \mathfrak{L} \times \mathfrak{L}$ is a generalisation of the entailment relation $\vDash$ in such a way that inference relations share the domain of this relation and encode a similar relationship between formulas: As already defined in Section 2.1, a formula $\psi \in \mathfrak{L}$ is entailed from a formula $\phi \in \mathfrak{L}$ if it follows logically from ϕ, that is, by means of classical logic, formally, $\phi \vDash \psi$. A formula ψ is *inferred* from a formula ϕ if it follows from ϕ given the semantics tied to the respective inference relation $\mathrel{|\!\approx}$. In this section we recall inference relations as a general and generic concept [Mak94, BKI14]; the approaches presented in the following chapters (especially in Chapter 3) will instantiate this generic concept to obtain concrete inference relations based on these approaches and semantics.

Even if the entailment is a particular inference relation instantiated according to Section 2.1, in the context of this dissertation inference relations $\mathrel{|\!\approx}$ are usually meant to be *nonmonotonic*, that is, if not otherwise stated we assume in inference relation $\mathrel{|\!\approx}$ not to satisfy (M) (and neither (T), (DThm), nor (CPS)). Other than logical entailment, nonmonotonic inference licenses for inferences with exceptions, that is, it is possible for an inference relation $\mathrel{|\!\approx}$ to license for the entailment of χ from ϕ but not from $\phi\psi$, thus violating (M).

Example 2.10 (Illustrating Nonmonotonicity). In Example 2.1 we have the rules "Birds usually can fly" and "Penguins usually cannot fly". So for birds it is reasonable to infer that they can fly, $b \mathrel{|\!\approx} f$, whereas for penguin-birds this inference should not be drawn, $pb \mathrel{|\!\not\approx} f$, in contrast to (M).

As this example indicates, nonmonotonic inference and conditionals are closely connected, such that for most of the approaches to nonmonotonic inference which use / set up an epistemic state Ψ we can infer ψ from ϕ in $(\phi \hspace{0.2em}\vdash\mkern-9mu\sim_\Psi \psi)$ if and only if Ψ accepts the conditional $(\psi|\phi)$ ($\Psi \models (\psi|\phi)$). This connection is also called the *Ramsey Test for nonmonotonic logic* [Ram29].

We finish this general introduction to inference relations by recalling a first nonmonotonic inference relation based on conditional knowledge bases.

Definition 2.11 (Δ-inference $\hspace{0.2em}\vdash\mkern-9mu\sim_\Delta$ [GP91a, DP96]). A formula ψ can be inferred from a formula ϕ using Δ-inference over a conditional knowledge base $\Delta = \{(\psi_1|\phi_1), \dots, (\psi_n|\phi_n)\} \subseteq (\mathfrak{L} \mid \mathfrak{L})$, written $\phi \hspace{0.2em}\vdash\mkern-9mu\sim_\Delta \psi$, if and only if the extension of Δ with the conditional $(\overline{\psi}|\phi)$ is inconsistent.

We illustrate Δ-inference with the running example.

Example 2.12 (Illustration of Δ-Inference). Let Δ_{Bird} be the knowledge base specified in Example 2.7. From these knowledge base we obtain that winged penguins cannot fly, that is, $pw \hspace{0.2em}\vdash\mkern-9mu\sim_\Delta \overline{f}$: In the subset $\{(\overline{f}|p), (f|pw)\} \subseteq (\Delta \cup \{(f|pw)\})$, both propositions $p\overline{f} \wedge (pw \Rightarrow f)$ and $(p \Rightarrow \overline{f}) \wedge pfw$ are inconsistent. Hence there is a non-empty subset of $\Delta \cup \{(f|pw)\}$ which contains conditionals that are not tolerated by the subset, and thus the so extended knowledge base is inconsistent, which gives us $pw \hspace{0.2em}\vdash\mkern-9mu\sim_\Delta \overline{f}$ according to Definition 2.11.

Δ-inference is a nonmonotonic inference:

Observation 2.13 (Δ-Inference Violates (M)). There are knowledge bases such that $\hspace{0.2em}\vdash\mkern-9mu\sim_\Delta$ violates (M).

This can be observed from the following counterexample to the opposite:

Example 2.14 (Example for Δ-Inference Violating (M)). Let Δ_{Bird} be the knowledge base specified in Example 2.7. With this example we directly obtain that Δ-inference violates (M): $\Delta \cup \{(\overline{f}|b)\}$ is inconsistent, because the conditionals $(f|b)$ and $(\overline{f}|b)$ directly contradict each other, but $\Delta \cup \{(\overline{f}|pb)\}$ is consistent: If we apply Algorithm 2.1 to $\Delta \cup \{(\overline{f}|pb)\}$ we obtain the tolerance partitioning

$$\left(\{(f|b),(w|b)\}, \{(b|p),(\overline{f}|p),(b|c),(\overline{f}|cb),(\overline{f}|pb)\} \right).$$

Therefore we have $b\!\mid\!\approx_\Delta f$ but $pb\!\mid\!\not\approx_\Delta f$ in contrast to (M).

With the consistency test algorithm (Algorithm 2.1), this inference is implementable with non-polynomial time-complexity: the complexity analysis of Algorithm 2.1 (see Section 2.2) yields that Δ-inferences can be calculated with a time complexity of $\mathcal{O}(|\Delta|^2 \cdot 2^{|\Sigma|})$.

DIRECT INFERENCE (DI) [Luk05]. An inference relation set up upon a conditional knowledge base Δ satisfies *Direct Inference* if and only if it infers the knowledge used to set it up, that is, if we have $\phi\!\mid\!\approx\psi$ for every $(\psi|\phi) \in \Delta$. Another way of stating this is that an inference relation satisfies (DI) if and only if it *recovers* all knowledge in the underlying knowledge base.

Proposition 2.15 ([Luk05]). Δ-inference satisfies (DI).

We noted that the monotone entailment endorses the principle of explosion. This property follows from the definition of $\models$ via set-inclusion on the models of formulas, hence it is not to be expected that this property holds for nonmonotonic inference, in general.

But Δ-inference is defined utilising inconsistency not on the level of formulas, but on the level of conditionals. We define the following properties to capture inference properties on this level.

META-EXPLOSION (MExp) An inference relation $\mid\!\approx^*_\Delta$ based on a set of conditionals $\Delta = \{(\psi_1|\phi_1),\dots,(\psi_n|\phi_n)\} \subseteq (\mathfrak{L} \mid \mathfrak{L})$ satisfies the property of *Meta-Explosion* if and only if it licenses for arbitrary inferences given the knowledge base is inconsistent, that is, an inconsistent knowledge base yields $\phi\!\mid\!\approx\psi$ for all formulas $\phi, \psi \in \mathfrak{L}$.

SEMI-MONOTONY (SM) [ST12] An inference relation $\mid\!\approx^*_\Delta$ based on a set of conditionals $\Delta = \{(\psi_1|\phi_1),\dots,(\psi_n|\phi_n)\} \subseteq (\mathfrak{L} \mid \mathfrak{L})$ satisfies the property of *Meta-Monotony* if and only if we can add arbitrary conditionals to Δ without rendering the inferences invalid, formally

$$\phi\!\mid\!\approx^*_\Delta\psi \qquad \text{implies} \qquad \phi\!\mid\!\approx^*_{\Delta'}\psi \qquad \text{for any } \Delta' \supseteq \Delta \qquad \text{(SM)}$$

Δ-inference satisfies both of these properties, which we formalise as follows.

Proposition 2.16. Δ-inference satisfies (MExp).

Proposition 2.17 ([ST12]). Δ-inference satisfies (SM).

2.4 Graphs and Hypergraphs

Graphs and Hypergraphs are graphical illustrations of relations between elements of a given set. In this section we briefly recall the notation of these constructs; see [Par94, HHM08] for a more thorough introduction in the field of graph and hypergraph theory.

Let $\mathbf{V}$ be a set of elements called *vertices*, a set of *edges* $\mathcal{E}$ is a set of pairs of vertices; the tuple $\mathcal{G} = (\mathbf{V}, \mathcal{E})$ is called a *graph*. If these pairs are sets, that is, $\mathcal{E} \subseteq \{V, V' | V, V' \in \mathbf{V}\}$ the graph is called *undirected*, if these pairs are tuples, that is, $\mathcal{E} \subseteq \mathbf{V} \times \mathbf{V}$, the graph is called *directed*. Note that we use $\mathcal{E}$ as set of edges for both directed and undirected graphs. In this we avoid unnecessary clutter of formal symbols and make it clear from the context whether the graph is meant to be directed or undirected.

We say that there is an edge between V and V' if and only if $(V, V') \in \mathcal{E}$ or $\{V, V'\} \in \mathcal{E}$. There is a *path* from V to V', written $V \rightsquigarrow V'$ if and only if either there is an edge between V and V' or there is a vertex V'' such that there is an edge between V and V'' and a path from V'' to V'. A graph contains *cycles* if and only if there are edges $V \in \mathbf{V}$ with the property that there are paths $V \rightsquigarrow V$; the graph is called *acyclic*, otherwise.

In a directed graph we call the vertex V in an edge $(V, V') \in \mathcal{E}$ the *parent* of V' and V' the *child* of V. The set of parents of a vertex is $pa(V') = \{V | (V, V') \in \mathcal{E})$ and the set of children of a vertex is the set $ch(V) = \{V' | (V, V') \in \mathcal{E}\}$. The vertex V in a path $V \rightsquigarrow V'$ is called the *source* of the path, and V' is called the *target*, *sink*, or *well* of the path. The set of *descendants* of a vertex V is the set $desc(V) = \{V' | V \rightsquigarrow V'\}$, and the set of *ancestors* of V' is the set $anc(V') = \{V | V \rightsquigarrow V'\}$. Finally, the set of vertices that are neither descendants nor parents of V, and also not V itself, that is, $nd(V) = \mathbf{V} \setminus \{\{V\} \cup desc(V) \cup pa(V)\}$ is called the *non-descendants* of V

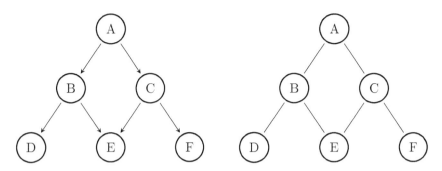

Figure 2.3: Illustration of directed (left) and undirected (right) graphs over a set of vertices $\mathbf{V} = \{A, B, C, D, E, F\}$ with edges given in Example 2.18

Example 2.18 (Directed and Undirected Graphs). Let the set of vertices $\mathbf{V}$ be $\mathbf{V} = \{A, B, C, D, E, F\}$. We define the directed graph

$$\mathcal{G} = (\mathbf{V}, \{(A, B), (A, C), (B, D), (B, E), (C, E), (C, F)\}),$$

and the undirected graph

$$\mathcal{G}' = (\mathbf{V}, \{\{A, B\}, \{A, C\}, \{B, D\}, \{B, E\}, \{C, E\}, \{C, F\}\});$$

both are illustrated in Figure 2.3. In both graphs we find the paths $A \rightsquigarrow D$ and $A \rightsquigarrow F$, but only in $\mathcal{G}'$ there is a path $D \rightsquigarrow F$. $\mathcal{G}$ is acyclic, but $\mathcal{G}'$ contains, among others, the cycle $A \rightsquigarrow B \rightsquigarrow E \rightsquigarrow C \rightsquigarrow A$. In $\mathcal{G}$, A is the parent of B and C which are both children of A, and A is the source, and E the sink of the path $A \rightsquigarrow E$.

A *subgraph* $\mathcal{G}^* = (\mathbf{V}^*, \mathcal{E}^*)$ of a graph $\mathcal{G} = (\mathbf{V}, \mathcal{E})$ is a tuple where $\mathbf{V}^* \subseteq \mathbf{V}$ and $\mathcal{E}^* = \{(V, V') | \{V, V'\} \in \mathbf{V}^* \text{ and } (V, V') \in \mathcal{E}\} \subseteq \mathcal{E}$ (likewise for undirected graphs). We overload the subset relation and write $\mathcal{G}^* \subseteq \mathcal{G}$ to indicate that $\mathcal{G}^*$ is a subgraph of $\mathcal{G}$. In an undirected graph $\mathcal{G}$, two vertices V, V' are *connected* if there is a path $V \rightsquigarrow V'$. The graph $\mathcal{G}$ is connected if and only if there is a path $V \rightsquigarrow V'$ for every pair $\{V, V'\} \subseteq \mathbf{V}$ and *disconnected* otherwise. A *connection component* is a (with respect to inclusion) maximal subgraph $\mathcal{G}^* \subseteq \mathcal{G}$ where each pair of vertices $\{V, V'\} \in \mathbf{V}^*$ is connected. A directed graph $\mathcal{G} = (\mathbf{V}, \mathcal{E})$ is *weakly connected* if its *undirected counterpart* $\mathcal{G}' = (\mathbf{V}, \{\{V, V'\} | (V, V') \in \mathcal{E}\})$ is connected. The graph $\mathcal{G}$ is *strongly connected* if $V \rightsquigarrow V'$ for every pair $\{V, V'\} \subseteq \mathbf{V}$. A

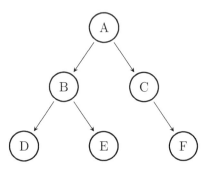

Figure 2.4: Illustration of a tree over the set of vertices $\mathbf{V} = \{A, B, C, D, E, F\}$ with edges given in Example 2.19

directed acyclic graph (DAG) is a graph $\mathcal{G}$ where the edges are directed and which contains no cycles. A *tree* is a weakly connected DAG with the additional constraint that each node has no more than one parent; the vertex V with $pa(V) = \varnothing$ is called the *root* of the tree and the vertices V' with $ch(V') = \varnothing$ are called the *leaves* of the tree.

Example 2.19 (Trees). None of the graphs from Example 2.18 are trees: One is no DAG, and in the other the vertex E has more than one parent. Figure 2.4 gives an example for a tree over the set of vertices $\mathbf{V} = \{A, B, C, D, E, F\}$. Here A is the root, and D, E, and F are the leaves of the tree.

A *Hypergraph* $\mathcal{H} = (\mathbf{V}, \mathfrak{E} \subseteq \mathfrak{P}(\mathfrak{P}(\mathbf{V})))$ is a generalisation of graphs in such a way that its hyperedges $\mathbf{V}_i$ connect not pairs, but subsets $\mathbf{V}_i$ of the vertices $\mathbf{V}$. Let the set $\mathfrak{E} \subseteq \mathfrak{P}(\mathfrak{P}(\mathbf{V})) = \{\mathbf{V}_1, \dots, \mathbf{V}_k\}$ of hyperedges to be enumerated with an index set $\mathcal{I} = \{1, \dots, k\}$. For $1 < i \leq k$ we call $\mathbb{S}_i = \{V | V \in \mathbf{V} \cap (\bigcup_{j=1}^{i-1} \mathbf{V}_j)$ the *separator* of $\mathbf{V}_i$ and define $\mathbb{S}_1 = \varnothing$. Furthermore we call $\mathbb{R}_i = \mathbf{V}_i \setminus \mathbb{S}_i$ the *residues* of $\mathbf{V}_i$. A hypergraph is a *hypertree* if and only if there is an enumeration of the hyperedges such that for each $\mathbf{V}_i$ its separators are a subset of a hyperedge with a lower index, that is, for each $1 \leq i \leq k$ there is a $1 \leq j < i$ such that $\mathbb{S}_i \subseteq \mathbf{V}_j$. This is called the *running intersection property* (RIP). We illustrate hypergraphs with the following example.

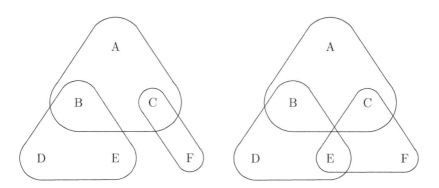

Figure 2.5: Illustration of a hypertree (left) and a hypergraph that is no hypertree (right) over the same alphabet as used in Example 2.20.

Example 2.20 (Hypergraphs and Hypertrees). Figure 2.5 gives two examples for hypergraphs. The left is $\mathcal{H} = (\mathbf{V} = \{A, B, C, D, E, F\}, \{\mathbf{V}_1, \mathbf{V}_2, \mathbf{V}_3\})$ with the hyperedges $\mathbf{V}_1 = \{A, B, C\}$, $\mathbf{V}_2 = \{B, D, E\}$, and $\mathbf{V}_3 = \{C, F\}$ and the right is $\mathcal{H}^* = (\mathbf{V}, \{\mathbf{V}_1^* = \mathbf{V}_1, \mathbf{V}_2^* = \mathbf{V}_1, \mathbf{V}_3^* = \{C, E, F\}\})$ with the following separators and residues:

$$\mathbb{S}_1 = \varnothing \qquad\qquad \mathbb{R}_1 = \mathbf{V}_1 = \{A, B, C\}$$
$$\mathbb{S}_2 = \{B\} \qquad\qquad \mathbb{R}_2 = \{D, E\}$$
$$\mathbb{S}_3 = \{C\} \qquad\qquad \mathbb{R}_2 = \{F\}$$
$$\mathbb{S}_1^* = \varnothing \qquad\qquad \mathbb{R}_1^* = \mathbf{V}_1^* = \{A, B, C\}$$
$$\mathbb{S}_2^* = \{B\} \qquad\qquad \mathbb{R}_2^* = \{D, E\}$$
$$\mathbb{S}_3^* = \{C, E\} \qquad\qquad \mathbb{R}_3^* = \{F\}$$

In these examples, $\mathcal{H}$ is a hypertree as $\mathcal{S}_2 \subseteq \mathbf{V}_1$ and $\mathcal{S}_3 \subseteq \mathcal{S}_1$, but $\mathcal{H}^*$ is not because $\mathcal{S}_3 = \{C, E\} \nsubseteq \mathbf{V}_1$ and also $\mathcal{S}_3 = \{C, E\} \nsubseteq \mathbf{V}_2$.

In the context of this thesis we usually use graphs over the set of variables, thus directly substituting $\mathbf{V}$ with Σ and, in case of hypergraphs, writing Σ_i for hyperedges instead of $\mathbf{V}_i$.

2.5 Interim Summary

This chapter lays the formal groundwork of this thesis by recalling the necessary preliminaries and basic definitions in propositional logic, conditionals, and knowledge bases needed to understand the rest of the dissertation. It recalls a generic framework of inference and with it a first inference relation based on conditional knowledge bases, only, and recalled a selection of basic properties of inference relations, including, but not limited to, Monotony, Transitivity and Explosion. It also recalls nonmonotonic inference relations, inference relation that violate Monotony, and some basic properties of nonmonotonic inference relations, for instance Direct Inference and Semi-Monotony. In addition to these established properties, this chapter extends the literature by formally stating the property of Meta-Explosion which is closely connected to Semi-Monotony in the way Explosion is closely connected to Monotony. Finally this introduction of basic concepts finishes by recalling directed and undirected graphs and their generalisation, which are hypergraphs.

3 Basic Techniques

In this section, we recall basic techniques which, on top of the formal preliminaries of the previous one, provide the formal and scientific groundwork for the dissertation. We start by recalling preferential models and preferential entailment as underlying formalism of the qualitative and semi-quantitative inferences used in Section 3.1. Based on this, we recall the approach of conditional structures (Section 3.2) as purely qualitative approach for reasoning on the base of a knowledge base with the qualitative information provided in the knowledge base, only. This is followed by the semi-quantitative ordinal conditional functions (Section 3.3); we close this section by briefly recalling probabilistic reasoning in Section 3.4.

3.1 Preferential Models and Preferential Inference

When defining nonmonotonic logics or nonmonotonic inference relations, one wants to abandon the strict bodice of classical logic, rendering conditional assertions or rules possible hold "usually" or "typically", but may have exceptions. One approach of formalising this idea of *typicality* are preferential models and the herefrom arising preferential inference. Here, the preferential relation orders the states of the preferential model. On top of this ordering, preferential inference licenses for the inference of a formula ψ from a formula ϕ if the states that verify the conditional assertion "if ϕ then usually ψ" are typical states (that is, if the preferential relation prefers these states to states that falsify the conditional assertion).

Preferential models [Mak94] are a generic approach to model inferences from arbitrary satisfaction relations, connecting any models with formulas, and preferential relations between the models themselves. Hence we start following [Mak94] by recalling the approach in the most generic way, which we then instantiate to meet the satisfaction relation used in this dissertation, leaving room to instantiate the preferential relation with respect to the approach used.

Definition 3.1 (Preferential Model [Mak94]). Let $\mathcal{M}$ be a set of states, let $\models$ be a satisfaction relation $\models\ \subseteq \mathcal{M} \times \mathfrak{L}$, and let $\prec$ be a preferential relation $\prec\ \subseteq \mathcal{M} \times \mathcal{M}$. The triple $\mathfrak{M} = (\mathcal{M}, \models, \prec)$ is called *preferential model*.

© Springer-Verlag GmbH Germany, part of Springer Nature 2018
C. Eichhorn, *Rational Reasoning with Finite Conditional Knowledge Bases*, https://doi.org/10.1007/978-3-476-04824-0_3

Based on this definition, we recall preferential inference[1] such that ψ is inferred from ϕ if and only for every model of the violation of the conditional $(\phi|\psi)$ there is a $\prec$-preferred model of its verification. With $m, m' \in \mathcal{M}$ this is written formally as

$$\phi \mathrel{\mathop{\sim}\limits_{\mathfrak{M}}} \psi \quad \text{iff} \quad \forall\, m' \models \phi \overline{\psi} \quad \exists\, m \models \phi \psi \quad \text{such that} \quad m \prec m'. \quad (3.1)$$

For this dissertation, we fix the set of models to be the set of possible worlds Ω, the satisfaction relation to be the classical satisfaction $\models$.

Definition 3.2 (Classical Preferential Model [Mak94]). Let $\mathfrak{M} = (\mathcal{M}, \models, \prec)$ be a preferential model, let $\phi, \psi \in \mathfrak{L}$ be formulas. $\mathfrak{M}$ is called *classical preferential model* (or simply *classical* for short), if and only if for all $m \in \mathcal{M}$ it is

$$m \models \overline{\phi} \qquad \text{if and only if} \qquad m \not\models \phi$$
$$m \models \phi \vee \psi \qquad \text{if and only if} \qquad m \models \phi \quad \text{or} \quad m \models \psi$$

Lemma 3.3 (confer [Mak94]). If the satisfaction relation of a preferential model $(\mathcal{M}, \models, \prec)$ is identical to the classical satisfaction relation $\models$, the preferential model is classical.

For simplicity, in the following we will refer to a relation $\prec$ as strict variant of a total relation $\preccurlyeq$ and set up as usual, that is, $\omega \prec \omega'$ if and only if $\omega \preccurlyeq \omega'$ and $\omega' \not\preccurlyeq \omega$ as a strict and total relation. For total relations $\preccurlyeq$ we define the relation $\asymp \subseteq \Omega \times \Omega$ such that $\omega \asymp \omega'$ if and only if $\omega \preccurlyeq \omega'$ and $\omega' \preccurlyeq \omega$.

Definition 3.4 (Stoppered Preferential Model [Mak94]). A preferential model set up according to Definition 3.1, that is, $(\mathcal{M}, \models, \prec)$ is called *stoppered* if and only if for every set of formulas $\mathcal{A}$ there is a (not necessarily unique) minimal state in the set $\mathcal{M}_{\mathcal{A}} = \{m \in \mathcal{M} | m \models \phi \; \forall\, \phi \in \mathcal{A}\}$ of states that satisfy $\mathcal{A}$ such that for each $m \in \mathcal{M}_{\mathcal{A}}$ there is a state $n \in \mathcal{M}_{\mathcal{A}}$ such that $n \preccurlyeq m$.

So a preferential model is stoppered if the preferential relation does not contain infinite descending chains and for each set of states there is a set of $\prec$-minimal states.

---

[1]   This inference relation is called "preferential entailment" in the literature. For clarity of presentation, in this dissertation the term "entailment" is used only to describe the relation $\models \subseteq \mathfrak{L} \times \mathfrak{L}$ as defined in Section 2.1, while referring to relations of non-monotonic inference as "inference".

Lemma 3.5 ([Mak94]). Let $\mathcal{M}$ be a finite set of states and let $\prec$ be a strict and transitive relation $\prec\ \subseteq\ \mathcal{M}\times\mathcal{M}$. Then the preferential model $(\mathcal{M}, \models, \prec)$ is stoppered.

This lemma ensures that for the preferential models we consider in this dissertation we only have to show that $\prec$ is transitive (and strict) to obtain that the preferential model is stoppered.

A preferential model that is both classical and stoppered is referred to as *classical stoppered preferential model*. As the inference relation of different classical stoppered preferential models differ in the definition of the preferential relation, only, we use $\mathrel{\vert\!\approx_{\prec}}$ as inference relation of a classical stoppered preferential model according to (3.1), with the relation $\prec$ to be instantiated by the respective approach.

Definition 3.6 ((Classical Stoppered) Preferential Inference [Mak94]). Let $\phi, \psi \in \mathfrak{L}$ be formulas. ϕ *preferentially entails* ψ based on the preferential model $\mathfrak{M} = (\Omega, \models, \prec)$, written $\phi\mathrel{\vert\!\approx_{\prec}}\psi$, if and only if for every model of $\phi\overline{\psi}$ there is a $\prec$-preferred model of $\phi\psi$, formally

$$\phi\mathrel{\vert\!\approx_{\prec}}\psi \quad \text{if and only if} \quad \forall\,\omega' \models \phi\overline{\psi} \;\; \exists\,\omega \models \phi\psi \quad \text{such that} \quad \omega \prec \omega'. \quad (3.2)$$

Let $C_{\prec} : \mathfrak{L} \to \mathfrak{P}(\mathfrak{L})$ with $C_{\prec}(\phi) = \{\psi \mid \phi\mathrel{\vert\!\approx_{\prec}}\psi\}$ be the *preferential inference operation*, in parallel to the definition of the classical consequences of a formula in Section 2.1, be the preferential inference operation.

We illustrate preferential models and preferential inference using a subset of the running example.

Example 3.7. Let $\Sigma = \{P, B, F\}$ be the alphabet covering issues of penguins, birds, and ability to fly, as introduced in Example 2.1, with a respective set of worlds Ω_{PBF}. We define the preferential relation to be

$$\prec_{PBF} = \left\{ \begin{array}{llll} (\overline{p}\,b\,f, p\,b\,\overline{f}), & (\overline{p}\,b\,f, p\,b\,f), & (\overline{p}\,b\,f, p\,\overline{b}\,\overline{f}), & (\overline{p}\,b\,f, \overline{p}\,b\,\overline{f}), \\ (\overline{p}\,\overline{b}\,f, p\,b\,\overline{f}), & (\overline{p}\,\overline{b}\,f, p\,b\,f), & (\overline{p}\,\overline{b}\,f, p\,\overline{b}\,\overline{f}), & (\overline{p}\,\overline{b}\,f, \overline{p}\,b\,\overline{f}), \\ (\overline{p}\,\overline{b}\,\overline{f}, p\,b\,\overline{f}), & (\overline{p}\,\overline{b}\,\overline{f}, p\,b\,f), & (\overline{p}\,\overline{b}\,\overline{f}, p\,\overline{b}\,\overline{f}), & (\overline{p}\,\overline{b}\,\overline{f}, \overline{p}\,b\,\overline{f}), \\ (p\,b\,f, p\,\overline{b}\,f), & (p\,\overline{b}\,\overline{f}, p\,\overline{b}\,f), & (\overline{p}\,b\,f, p\,\overline{b}\,f), & (\overline{p}\,\overline{b}\,f, p\,\overline{b}\,f), \\ (\overline{p}\,\overline{b}\,\overline{f}, p\,\overline{b}\,f) & & & \end{array} \right\}$$

illustrated in Figure 3.1. Here we have, for instance $\top\mathrel{\vert\!\approx_{\prec_{PBF}}}\overline{p}$ because to every $\omega' \models p$ a world $\omega \in \{\overline{p}bf, \overline{p}\,\overline{b}f, \overline{p}\,\overline{b}\,\overline{f}\}$ is preferred (and is a model of $\overline{p}$),

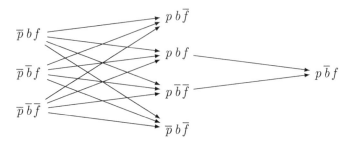

Figure 3.1: Preferential relation for Example 3.7: $\omega \to \omega'$ indicates $\omega \prec \omega'$, we left out edges that arise through transitivity for clarity of presentation

and also "birds that are no penguins usually fly", that is $b\overline{p} \mathrel{|\!\approx}_{\prec_{PBF}} f$, because $\overline{p}bf \prec_{PBF} \overline{p}b\overline{f}$.

With preferential models and the respective inference, the definition of an inference relation boils down to definition a relation $\prec$ on the possible worlds. In the following section we recall a first approach to obtain this relation inductively from a conditional knowledge base.

3.2 Conditional Structures

Having recalled conditionals and their individual evaluation in possible worlds following the semantics of [Fin74] in Section 2.2, this section is dedicated to bring this formalism of defeasible rules to practical use for a first concrete nonmonotonic inference relation. This relation will be based on the background knowledge of an agent formalised as conditional knowledge base. The preference relation on the set of possible worlds is obtained on the structure of the qualitative information of the conditionals, only. We use in this preference relation to instantiate the general definition of preferential models (see Section 3.1) to obtain a nonmonotonic inference relation. We start recalling a function that expresses the evaluation of a conditional with an abstract symbol.

Definition 3.8 (Individual Conditional Evaluation Indicators $\mathbf{a}_i^+, \mathbf{a}_i^-$ [KI01]). Let $\Delta = \{(\psi_1|\phi_1), \ldots, (\psi_n|\phi_n)\} \subseteq (\mathfrak{L} \mid \mathfrak{L})$ be a conditional knowledge base and let $\mathcal{F}(\Delta) = \{\mathbf{a}_1^+, \mathbf{a}_1^-, \ldots, \mathbf{a}_n^+, \mathbf{a}_n^-\}$ be a set of abstract symbols. The function $\sigma_{\Delta,i} : \Omega \to \mathcal{F}(\Delta)$ assigns to each world $\omega \in \Omega$ a symbol out of

$\{\mathbf{a}_i^+, \mathbf{a}_i^-, 1\}$ dependent on the evaluation of the conditional $(\psi_i|\phi_i) \in \Delta$ in ω, such that

$$
\sigma_{\Delta,i}(\omega) = \begin{cases} \mathbf{a}_i^+ & \text{iff} \quad [\![(\psi_i|\phi_i)]\!]_\omega = \text{true} & \text{iff} \quad \omega \vDash \phi_i \psi_i \\ \mathbf{a}_i^- & \text{iff} \quad [\![(\psi_i|\phi_i)]\!]_\omega = \text{false} & \text{iff} \quad \omega \vDash \phi_i \overline{\psi}_i \\ 1 & \text{iff} \quad [\![(\psi_i|\phi_i)]\!]_\omega = \text{undefined} & \text{iff} \quad \omega \vDash \overline{\phi}_i. \end{cases} \tag{3.3}
$$

In this way the set $\mathcal{F}(\Delta)$ is a set of indicators for the verification or falsification of each individual conditional in Δ. We use this set as generator of an algebraic structure that can be used to formalise the evaluation of all conditionals in the knowledge base:

Definition 3.9 $((\mathcal{S}_\Delta, \cdot)$ [KI01, Chapter 3.5]). Let $\mathcal{F}(\Delta)$ be a set of abstract symbols, $\mathcal{F}(\Delta) = \{\mathbf{a}_1^+, \mathbf{a}_1^-, \ldots, \mathbf{a}_n^+, \mathbf{a}_n^-\}$, indicating verification or falsification of conditionals in a knowledge base $\Delta = \{(\psi_1|\phi_1), \ldots, (\psi_n|\phi_n)\}$. Let $\cdot$ be a binary operation on $\mathcal{F}(\Delta)$ that is invertible, associative, and commutative and has 1 as neutral element[2]. With this operation and $\mathcal{F}(\Delta)$ as set of generators, we obtain the free abelian group $(\mathcal{S}_\Delta, \cdot)$.

With $|\Delta| = n$ and integer exponents $r_{i,1}, r_{i,2} \in \mathbb{Z}$, $1 \le i \le n$, the group $(\mathcal{S}_\Delta, \cdot)$ consists of elements $(\mathbf{a}_1^+)^{r_{1,1}}(\mathbf{a}_1^-)^{r_{1,2}} \cdots (\mathbf{a}_n^+)^{r_{n,1}}(\mathbf{a}_1^-)^{r_{n,2}}$, combining multiple occurrences of an impact as it is usual for multiplication, that is, for instance $\mathbf{a}_1^+ \mathbf{a}_1^+ = (\mathbf{a}_1^+)^2$. Following the usual definition of groups, a negative exponent indicates the inverse of an element such that $(\mathbf{a}_1^+)^1 \cdot (\mathbf{a}_1^+)^{-1} = (\mathbf{a}_1^+)^0 = 1$. As $(\mathcal{S}_\Delta, \cdot)$ is a free abelian group there are only trivial cancellations of this sort. With this group, we obtain the combined evaluation of all conditionals in a knowledge base as conditional structures.

Definition 3.10 (Conditional Structure [KI01]). Let Δ be a knowledge base, $\Delta = \{(\psi_1|\phi_1), \ldots, (\psi_n|\phi_n)\} \subseteq (\mathfrak{L} \mid \mathfrak{L})$, with the free abelian group $(\mathcal{S}_\Delta, \cdot)$ according to Definition 3.9. The *conditional structure* $\sigma_\Delta : \Omega \to (\mathcal{S}_\Delta, \cdot)$ of a world ω is

$$
\sigma_\Delta(\omega) = \prod_{i=1}^n \sigma_{\Delta,i}(\omega) = \prod_{\omega \vDash \phi_i \psi_i} \mathbf{a}_i^+ \cdot \prod_{\omega \vDash \phi_i \overline{\psi}_i} \mathbf{a}_i^-. \tag{3.4}
$$

---

[2]   that is, $\cdot$ behaves like the multiplication operation on numbers, but is used on $\mathcal{F}(\Delta)$ instead.

The conditional structure of a world combines all verification and falsification indicators of the evaluation of all conditionals in the knowledge base for each individual world $\omega \in \Omega$. Note that when used in this way, the exponents of the generators can be only 1 or 0 as each conditional applies its impact not more than once and (3.4) does not introduce negative exponents[3]. For practical purposes we sometimes are interested in the verified or falsified conditionals rather than the full conditional structure, therefore we define the following sets:

Definition 3.11 (Verifying / Falsifying Sets of Conditionals (*ver/fal*)). For a knowledge base $\Delta = \{(\psi_1|\phi_1), \ldots, (\psi_n|\phi_n)\} \subseteq (\mathfrak{L} \mid \mathfrak{L})$ with $\sigma_{\Delta,i}$ as defined as in Definition 3.8, we define the set of conditionals verified (falsified) by a world $\omega \in \Omega$ to be

$$ver_\Delta(\omega) := \{(\psi_i|\phi_i) | [\![(\psi_i|\phi_i)]\!]_\omega = true\} = \{(\psi_i|\phi_i)|\sigma_{\Delta,i} = \mathbf{a}_i^+\} \qquad (3.5)$$

$$fal_\Delta(\omega) := \{(\psi_i|\phi_i) | [\![(\psi_i|\phi_i)]\!]_\omega = false\} = \{(\psi_i|\phi_i)|\sigma_{\Delta,i} = \mathbf{a}_i^-\}. \qquad (3.6)$$

We now have functions to indicate for each world the verification and falsification of each conditional in the knowledge base. This information is be used to obtain a preference relation to worlds as follows.

Definition 3.12 (Structural Preference $\prec_\sigma^\Delta$ [KI01]). Let $\sigma_{\Delta,i}$ and σ_Δ be functions set up upon a conditional knowledge base $\Delta = \{(\psi_1|\phi_1), \ldots, (\psi_n|\phi_n)\}$ according to to Definitions 3.8 and 3.10. A world ω is *structurally preferred* to a world ω', written $\omega \prec_\Delta^\sigma \omega'$ if and only if for each $1 \leq i \leq n$ we have $\sigma_{\Delta,i}(\omega) = \mathbf{a}_i^-$ implies $\sigma_{\Delta,i}(\omega') = \mathbf{a}_i^-$ and there is at least one $1 \leq i \leq n$ such that $\sigma_{\Delta,i}(\omega) \in \{\mathbf{a}_i^+, 1\}$ and $\sigma_{\Delta,i}(\omega') = \mathbf{a}_i^-$.

This definition recalls a preference between worlds with respect to falsification that can be formulated alternatively such that ω is preferred to ω' if and only if ω' falsifies, ceteris paribus, strictly more worlds that ω, or, formally

$$\omega \prec_\Delta^\sigma \omega' \qquad \text{if and only if} \qquad fal(\omega) \subsetneq fal(\omega'); \qquad (3.7)$$

---

[3]   Using conditional structures for inference from a single conditional knowledge base does not extend these structures to the full capabilities of their algebraic structure. See, for instance, [KI01] for application of this to conditional indifference, or [KTFF09] for an application of this method to qualitative data mining.

this alternative definition was pointed out in [KIE12]. Note that $\prec_\Delta^\sigma$ is a partial ordering on Ω. From its alternative formulation with the strict subset relation we directly obtain:

Corollary 3.13 (confer [KIE12]). The preference relation $\prec_\Delta^\sigma$ is strict and transitive.

Using $\prec_\Delta^\sigma$ as preference relation in a preferential model gives us *structural inference* as instantiation of inference with preferential models (see Definition 3.6).

Definition 3.14 (Structural Inference [KI02, KIE12]). Let $\prec_\Delta^\sigma$ be a preference relation defined by the conditional structure of a knowledge base Δ. Let $\mathfrak{M}_\sigma^\Delta = (\Omega, \vDash, \prec_\Delta^\sigma)$ be a preferential model as instantiation of Definition 3.1. Following Definition 3.6, on this model from ϕ we *structurally infer* ψ, written $\phi \hspace{0.5mm}\vdash\hspace{-3mm}\approx_\Delta^\sigma \psi$, if and only if for each world that falsifies the conditional $(\psi|\phi)$ there is a $\prec_\Delta^\sigma$-preferred world that verifies it, formally

$$\phi \hspace{0.5mm}\vdash\hspace{-3mm}\approx_\Delta^\sigma \psi \quad \text{iff} \quad \forall\, \omega' \vDash \phi\overline{\psi} \quad \exists\, \omega \vDash \phi\psi \quad \text{s.t.} \quad \omega \prec_\Delta^\sigma \omega'. \quad (3.8)$$

These definition of conditional structures, preference and inference are illustrated in the following example.

Example 3.15. We use an excerpt of the ornithological knowledge base defined in Example 2.8 to illustrate conditional structures and the preference induced by these structures: Let $\Sigma_{pbf} = \{P, B, F\}$ with the respective set of possible worlds

$$\Omega(\Sigma_{pbf}) = \{p\,b\,f, p\,b\,\overline{f}, p\,\overline{b}\,f, p\,\overline{b}\,\overline{f}, \overline{p}\,b\,f, \overline{p}\,b\,\overline{f}, \overline{p}\,\overline{b}\,f, \overline{p}\,\overline{b}\,\overline{f}\}$$

and let $\Delta_{pbf} = \{\delta_1 \ : \ (b|f), \delta_3 \ : \ (b|p), \delta_4 \ : \ (\overline{f}|p)\}$ be the knowledge base formalising our knowledge about penguins, birds, and flying. Here, for instance, the world pbf verifies the conditionals δ_1 and δ_3, but falsifies δ_4, hence $\sigma_{\Delta_{pbf}}(pbf) = \mathbf{a}_1^+\mathbf{a}_3^+\mathbf{a}_4^-$. The world $p\overline{b}f$ falsifies δ_3 and δ_4, whereas δ_1 is not applicable to $p\overline{b}f$, hence the conditional structure of this world is $\sigma_{\Delta_{pbf}}(p\overline{b}f) = 1\mathbf{a}_3^-\mathbf{a}_4^- = \mathbf{a}_3^-\mathbf{a}_4^-$. We have $fal_{\Delta_{pbf}}(pbf) = \{\delta_4\} \subsetneqq \{\delta_3, \delta_4\} = fal_{\Delta_{pbf}}(p\overline{b}f)$ and thus $pbf \prec_\sigma^{\Delta_{pbf}} p\overline{b}f$, which gives us that flying penguins are usually birds, $pf \hspace{0.5mm}\vdash\hspace{-3mm}\approx_{\Delta_{pbf}}^\sigma b$ according to Definition 3.14. But it is $pbf \not\prec_\sigma^{\Delta_{pbf}} pb\overline{f}$ since $fal_{\Delta_{pbf}}(pbf) = \{\mathbf{a}_4^-\} \not\subseteq \{\mathbf{a}_1^-\} = fal_{\Delta_{pbf}}(pb\overline{f})$ (and vice versa), so pbf

Table 3.1: Conditional structures in Example 3.15

ω	$p\,b\,f$	$p\,b\,\overline{f}$	$p\,\overline{b}\,f$	$p\,\overline{b}\,\overline{f}$	$\overline{p}\,b\,f$	$\overline{p}\,b\,\overline{f}$	$\overline{p}\,\overline{b}\,f$	$\overline{p}\,\overline{b}\,\overline{f}$
$\sigma_{\Delta_{pbf}}$	$a_1^+ a_3^+ a_4^-$	$a_1^- a_3^+ a_4^+$	$a_3^- a_4^-$	$a_3^- a_4^+$	a_1^+	a_1^-	1	1

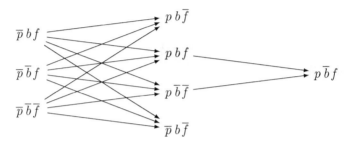

Figure 3.2: Conditional preference in Example 3.15; a path $\omega \rightsquigarrow \omega'$ indicates $\omega \prec_\sigma^{\Delta_{pbf}} \omega'$. We highlighted the worlds pbf and $p\overline{b}f$ which are responsible for the inference $pf \vDash_{\Delta_{pbf}}^\sigma b$.

and $p\overline{b}\overline{f}$ are incomparable with respect to $\prec_\sigma^{\Delta_{pbf}}$. Table 3.1 gives all conditional structures for this example, and Figure 3.2 depicts the relation $\prec_\sigma^{\Delta_{pbf}}$ such that $\omega \prec_\sigma^{\Delta_{pbf}} \omega'$ if and only if there is a path $\omega \rightsquigarrow \omega'$. We highlighted the worlds responsible for the inference $pf \vDash_{\Delta_{pbf}}^\sigma b$. Having illustrated the relation $\prec_\sigma^{\Delta_{pbf}}$ it is also easily seen that from the knowledge base Δ_{pbf} we obtain the inference that usually objects are no penguins, $\top \vDash_{\Delta_{pbf}}^\sigma \overline{p}$, because for every model of p there is structurally preferred model of $\overline{p}$.

In the next section, we leave the domain of purely qualitative representation and move on to a semi-quantitative representation, that is, an approach to representing an epistemic state using numbers, but in a qualitative way.

3.3 Ordinal Conditional Functions (OCF)

Ordinal conditional functions (OCF, also called *ranking functions* [Spo88, Spo12]) are used to express the insecure knowledge of an agent by means of its epistemic state in the sense of [Hal05]. This formalism assigns a semi-positive integer to each possible world, indicating its implausibility.

3.3.1 Definition and Properties

OCF express the implausibility of the possible worlds, that is, the higher the rank of a possible world in a given OCF, the less plausible it is. OCF use integer values for this notion, resulting in countable infinite ranks, in distinction to the uncountable many values bestowed by the better known approach of probability (see also Section 3.4).

Definition 3.16 (Ordinal Conditional Function (OCF, [Spo88, Spo12]). An *Ordinal conditional function* (OCF) or *ranking function* κ is a function $\kappa : \Omega \to \mathbb{N}_0^\infty$ that assigns to each world $\omega \in \Omega$ an implausibility rank $\kappa(\omega)$. An OCF has to be *normalised*, that is, there have to be worlds with a rank of 0 and thus are maximally plausible, which is formally expressed in that the inverse of 0 cannot be empty, $\kappa^{-1}(0) \neq \varnothing$.

Being a function indicating implausibility or disbelief, the *belief set*, that is, the set of formulas believed by the agent with an OCF as epistemic state, is the set of formulas for which the worlds that are maximally believed (or minimally disbelieved) are models, formally

$$\mathrm{Bel}(\kappa_\Delta^c) = \mathit{Th}(\{\omega | \kappa_\Delta^c(\omega) = 0\}). \tag{3.9}$$

An OCF κ is extended to a function that expresses the rank of formulas $\phi \in \mathcal{L}$ and conditionals $(\psi|\phi) \in (\mathcal{L}|\mathcal{L})$. The rank of a formula ϕ is the rank of the least implausible world that satisfies ϕ, we overload κ to this extent. Note that since for totally ordered sets (like the codomain of κ), the minimum and the infimum coincide, this means that for a inconsistent proposition $\kappa(\bot) = \infty$ because ∞ is the greatest lower bound as there are no elements in $Mod(\bot)$ which constrain the bound. This further gives us that the rank of a disjunction is the rank of the minimal model of either element of the disjunction, and the rank of a conjunction is at least the rank of either element of the conjunction. The rank of a conditional is the rank of the verification of the conditional, that is, the rank of the conjunction of premise and conclusion of the conditional, normalised by the rank of the premise of the conditional. We summarise the formalities of these as follows (confer [Spo88, Spo12]).

$$\kappa(\phi) = \min\left\{\kappa(\omega)|\omega \vDash \phi\right\} \tag{3.10}$$

$$\kappa(\phi \vee \psi) = \min\left\{\kappa(\phi), \kappa(\psi)\right\} \tag{3.11}$$

$$\kappa(\phi\psi) \geq \min\left\{\kappa(\phi), \kappa(\psi)\right\} \tag{3.12}$$

$$\kappa(\psi|\phi) = \kappa(\phi\psi) - \kappa(\phi) \tag{3.13}$$

Note that the rank of a conditional (3.13) is nonnegative. As κ is a function with a domain Ω, to store an OCF we need exponential space, to be more exact, the space complexity is $\mathcal{O}(\Omega) = \mathcal{O}(2^{|\Sigma|})$.

For OCF, the notions of total rank and total conditional rank can be formulated in parallel to the respective definitions of total probability and total conditional probability (see, for instance, [BKI14] or Proposition 3.41 in Section 3.4, confer also "Jeffrey Conditionalization" or "Probability Kinematics" (e.g., [Spo12, BKI14])):

Lemma 3.17 (Law of Total (Conditional) Rank [EKI15b, Lem. 2] (cf. [Spo12])). For ranking functions κ, for all $\phi, \psi\chi \in \mathfrak{L}$ we have

$$\kappa(\phi) = \min\{\kappa(\phi|\psi) + \kappa(\psi), \kappa(\phi|\overline{\psi}) + \kappa(\overline{\psi})\} \tag{3.14}$$

called *total rank* and

$$\kappa(\phi|\chi) = \min\{\kappa(\phi|\psi\chi) + \kappa(\phi|\chi), \kappa(\phi|\overline{\psi}\chi) + \kappa(\overline{\psi}|\chi)\}. \tag{3.15}$$

called *total conditional rank*.

Independence between (sets of) variables can be captured as follows:

Definition 3.18 (κ-Independence [Spo12]). Let $\mathbf{A}, \mathbf{B} \subseteq \Sigma$ be sets of variables. $\mathbf{A}$ is *κ-independent from $\mathbf{B}$ given $\mathbf{C}$*, written $\mathbf{A} \perp\!\!\!\perp_\kappa \mathbf{B}$, if and only if for all complete conjunctions $\mathbf{a}$ of $\mathbf{A}$ and $\mathbf{b}$ of $\mathbf{B}$ the rank of the conjunction $\mathbf{ab}$ is identical to the sum of the ranks of $\mathbf{a}$ and $\mathbf{b}$, that is,

$$\mathbf{A} \perp\!\!\!\perp_\kappa \mathbf{B} \qquad \text{if and only if} \qquad \kappa(\mathbf{ab}) = \kappa(\mathbf{a}) + \kappa(\mathbf{b}). \tag{3.16}$$

Other than being independent, two formulas can also be independent given a third formula, this is called conditional κ-independence.

Definition 3.19 (Conditional κ-Independence [Spo12]). Let $\mathbf{A}, \mathbf{B}, \mathbf{C} \subseteq \Sigma$ be sets of variables. $\mathbf{A}$ is *conditionally κ-independent* from $\mathbf{B}$ (also called independent from $\mathbf{B}$ in the context $\mathbf{C}$), written

$$\mathbf{A} \perp\!\!\!\perp_\kappa \mathbf{B} \mid \mathbf{C}, \qquad \text{if and only if} \qquad \kappa(\mathbf{ab}|\mathbf{c}) = \kappa(\mathbf{a}|\mathbf{c}) + \kappa(\mathbf{b}|\mathbf{c}). \qquad (3.17)$$

for all complete conjunctions $\mathbf{a}$, $\mathbf{b}$, and $\mathbf{c}$, of $\mathbf{A}$, $\mathbf{B}$, and $\mathbf{C}$, respectively.

If $\mathbf{A}$ is independent from $\mathbf{B}$ in the context $\mathbf{C}$, then conditioning $\mathbf{A}$ on $\mathbf{B}$ has no effect on the plausibility of $\mathbf{A}$, which is shown in the following lemma.

Lemma 3.20 ([EKI15b, Lemma 1]). Let $\mathbf{A}, \mathbf{B}, \mathbf{C} \subseteq \Sigma$ be sets of Variables. $\mathbf{A}$ is conditionally κ-independent from $\mathbf{B}$ given $\mathbf{C}$ if and only if

$$\kappa(\mathbf{a}|\mathbf{bc}) = \kappa(\mathbf{a}|\mathbf{c}). \qquad (3.18)$$

for all complete conjunctions $\mathbf{a}$, $\mathbf{b}$ and $\mathbf{c}$ of $\mathbf{A}$, $\mathbf{B}$ and $\mathbf{C}$, respectively.

Example 3.21 (Car Start Example). We illustrate OCF with the car start example of [GP96]: Let the alphabet of this example be $\Sigma = \{H, B, F, S\}$ where H indicates whether the headlights of a car have been left switched on (h) overnight or have been switched off ($\overline{h}$), B indicates whether the battery of the car is charged (b) or nor ($\overline{b}$), F indicates whether the fuel tank of the car is filled (f) or empty ($\overline{f}$) and, finally, S indicates whether the car will start (s) or not ($\overline{s}$). The set of possible worlds is the set

$$\Omega = \left\{ \begin{array}{c} hbfs,\ hbf\overline{s},\ hb\overline{f}s,\ hb\overline{f}\overline{s},\ h\overline{b}fs,\ h\overline{b}f\overline{s},\ h\overline{b}\overline{f}s,\ h\overline{b}\overline{f}\overline{s}, \\ \overline{h}bfs,\ \overline{h}bf\overline{s},\ \overline{h}b\overline{f}s,\ \overline{h}b\overline{f}\overline{s},\ \overline{h}\overline{b}fs,\ \overline{h}\overline{b}f\overline{s},\ \overline{h}\overline{b}\overline{f}s,\ \overline{h}\overline{b}\overline{f}\overline{s} \end{array} \right\},$$

containing intuitively plausible worlds like the one where the headlights have been switched off, the battery is charged, the fuel tank filled and the car starts ($\overline{h}bfs$), as well as intuitively implausible worlds like the one where the headlights have been switched off, the battery and the fuel tank are empty, and the car starts ($\overline{h}\,\overline{b}\,\overline{f}s$). Overall we would suppose that it is plausible that the car starts, and that from an empty fuel tank we can infer that the car would not start. Also, we would assume that the state of the headlights is independent from the filling level of the fuel tank. Table 3.2 shows an OCF for this example. We illustrate the properties of OCF with this concrete

Table 3.2: Ranking function for the car start example (Example 3.21)

	$hbfs$	$hbf\bar{s}$	$hb\bar{f}s$	$hb\bar{f}\bar{s}$	$h\bar{b}fs$	$h\bar{b}f\bar{s}$	$h\bar{b}\bar{f}s$	$h\bar{b}\bar{f}\bar{s}$
$\kappa(\omega)$	19	22	42	29	26	15	52	25

	$\bar{h}bfs$	$\bar{h}bf\bar{s}$	$\bar{h}b\bar{f}s$	$\bar{h}b\bar{f}\bar{s}$	$\bar{h}\bar{b}fs$	$\bar{h}\bar{b}f\bar{s}$	$\bar{h}\bar{b}\bar{f}s$	$\bar{h}\bar{b}\bar{f}\bar{s}$
$\kappa(\omega)$	0	3	23	10	19	8	45	18

function as follows:

$$\kappa(\bar{h}bfs) = 0$$
$$\kappa(\bar{h}\,\bar{b}\bar{f}s) = 45$$
$$\kappa(s) = \min \left\{ \begin{array}{llll} \kappa(hbfs), & \kappa(hb\bar{f}s), & \kappa(h\bar{f}s), & \kappa(h\bar{b}\bar{f}s), \\ \kappa(\bar{h}bfs), & \kappa(\bar{h}b\bar{f}s), & \kappa(\bar{h}\bar{f}s), & \kappa(\bar{h}\,\bar{b}\bar{f}s) \end{array} \right\}$$
$$= \min\{19, 42, 26, 52, 0, 23, 19, 45\} = 0$$
$$\kappa(\bar{f}\bar{s}) = 10 < 23 = \kappa(\bar{f}s) \qquad \text{hence} \qquad \bar{f} \not\approx_\kappa \bar{s}$$
$$\kappa(hf) = 15 = 15 + 0 = \kappa(h) + \kappa(f)$$
$$\kappa(\bar{h}f) = 0 + 0 = \kappa(\bar{h}) + \kappa(f)$$
$$\kappa(h\bar{f}) = 25 = 15 + 10 = \kappa(h) + \kappa(\bar{f})$$
$$\kappa(\bar{h}\bar{f}) = 10 = 0 + 10 = \kappa(\bar{h}) + \kappa(\bar{f}) \qquad \text{hence} \qquad H \perp\!\!\!\perp_\kappa F.$$

Independence and conditional independence has been researched thoroughly for probability functions [Pea88]. This research finally resulted in an axiomatisation of conditional independence [Pea88, Theorem 1]. We show which of these axioms are valid for OCF as follows.

Independence is a symmetric concept, that is, if, in the context of **C**, **B** has no impact on **A**, then also **A** has no impact in **B** (see Figure 3.3a). This property is called symmetry [Pea88] and for OCF is formalised as

Proposition 3.22 (Symmetry [Pea88] of Conditional κ-Independence). If, for sets of variables $\mathbf{A}, \mathbf{B}, \mathbf{C} \subseteq \Sigma$, **A** is conditionally independent from **B** given **C**, then **B** is conditionally independent from **A** given **C**, formally

$$\mathbf{A} \perp\!\!\!\perp_\kappa \mathbf{B} \mid \mathbf{C} \qquad \text{if and only if} \qquad \mathbf{B} \perp\!\!\!\perp_\kappa \mathbf{A} \mid \mathbf{C}. \qquad (3.19)$$

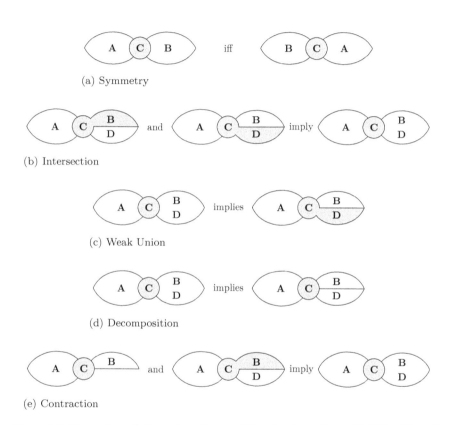

Figure 3.3: Illustration of the axioms for conditional independence [Pea88]. The left white set (usually **A**) is independent to the white right set(s) given the grey sets. Note that κ-independence satisfies the axioms (a), (b), (d), and (e), but violates (c)

If both **B** and **D** are irrelevant for **A** in context of the mutually other joined with **C**, then the joined set **B** ∪ **D** is irrelevant for **A** in the context of **C**; this property is called *intersection* [Pea88] and for OCF is formalised as follows.

Proposition 3.23 (Intersection [Pea88] for Conditional κ-Independence). If, for sets of variables $\mathbf{A}, \mathbf{B}, \mathbf{C} \subseteq \Sigma$, both $\mathbf{A} \perp\!\!\!\perp_\kappa \mathbf{B} \mid (\mathbf{C} \cup \mathbf{D})$ and $\mathbf{A} \perp\!\!\!\perp_\kappa \mathbf{D} \mid (\mathbf{B} \cup \mathbf{C})$, then also $\mathbf{A} \perp\!\!\!\perp_\kappa (\mathbf{B} \cup \mathbf{D}) \mid \mathbf{C}$.

The property *weak union* requires that the context of conditional independence can be safely extended by irrelevant information [Pea88]: Given sets of variables **A**, **B**, **C**, and $\mathbf{D} \subseteq \Sigma$, a conditional independence satisfies weak union if and only if $\mathbf{A} \perp\!\!\!\perp (\mathbf{B} \cup \mathbf{D}) \mid \mathbf{C}$ implies $\mathbf{A} \perp\!\!\!\perp \mathbf{B} \mid (\mathbf{C} \cup \mathbf{D})$. This is violated by OCF, which we observe as follows.

Observation 3.24 (Conditional κ-Independence Violates Weak Union [Pea88]). There are OCF over sets of variables $\mathbf{A}, \mathbf{B}, \mathbf{C} \subseteq \Sigma$ such that $\mathbf{A} \perp\!\!\!\perp_\kappa (\mathbf{B} \cup \mathbf{D}) \mid \mathbf{C}$ but $\mathbf{A} \not\perp\!\!\!\perp_\kappa \mathbf{B} \mid (\mathbf{C} \cup \mathbf{D})$.

The following example is such an OCF.

Example 3.25. Let κ be an OCF as given in Table 3.3. In this ranking function we have $\{A\} \perp\!\!\!\perp_\kappa (\{B\} \cup \{D\}) \mid \{C\}$. Here we find the ranks

$$\kappa(a\,\overline{b}\,\overline{c}\,d) = 2$$
$$\kappa(\overline{b}\,\overline{c}\,d) = \min\{a\,\overline{b}\,\overline{c}\,d, \overline{a}\,\overline{b}\,\overline{c}\,d\} = \min\{2, 1\} = 1$$
$$\kappa(a\,\overline{c}) = \min\{a\,b\,\overline{c}\,d, a\,\overline{b}\,\overline{c}\,d, a\,b\,\overline{c}\,\overline{d}, a\,\overline{b}\,\overline{c}\,\overline{d}\} = \min\{1, 2, 1, 1\} = 1$$
$$\kappa(\overline{c}) = \min\left\{\begin{array}{l} a\,b\,\overline{c}\,d, \; a\,b\,\overline{c}\,\overline{d}, \; a\,\overline{b}\,\overline{c}\,d, \; a\,\overline{b}\,\overline{c}\,\overline{d} \\ \overline{a}\,b\,\overline{c}\,d, \; \overline{a}\,b\,\overline{c}\,\overline{d}, \; \overline{a}\,\overline{b}\,\overline{c}\,d, \; \overline{a}\,\overline{b}\,\overline{c}\,\overline{d} \end{array}\right\} = \min\left\{\begin{array}{l} 1, 1, 2, 1 \\ 1, 0, 1, 16 \end{array}\right\} = 0$$
$$\kappa(a\,\overline{c}\,d) = \min\{a\,b\,\overline{c}\,d, a\,\overline{b}\,\overline{c}\,d\} = \min\{1, 2\} = 1$$
$$\kappa(\overline{c}\,\overline{d}) = \min\{a\,b\,\overline{c}\,d, a\,\overline{b}\,\overline{c}\,d, \overline{a}\,b\,\overline{c}\,d, \overline{a}\,\overline{b}\,\overline{c}\,d\} = \min\{1, 2, 1, 1\} = 1$$

and, for instance,

$$\kappa(a\,|\,\overline{b}\,\overline{c}\,d) = \kappa(a\,\overline{b}\,\overline{c}\,d) - \kappa(\overline{b}\,\overline{c}\,d) = 2 - 1$$
$$= 1 = 1 - 0 = \kappa(a|\overline{c}) = \kappa(a\,\overline{c}) - \kappa(\overline{c})$$

Table 3.3: OCF of Example 3.25 that violates weak union for conditional independence

ω	$abcd$	$abc\overline{d}$	$ab\overline{c}d$	$ab\overline{c}\overline{d}$	$a\overline{b}cd$	$a\overline{b}c\overline{d}$	$a\overline{b}\overline{c}d$	$a\overline{b}\overline{c}\overline{d}$
$\kappa(\omega)$	1	1	1	1	1	1	2	1

ω	$\overline{a}bcd$	$\overline{a}bc\overline{d}$	$\overline{a}b\overline{c}d$	$\overline{a}b\overline{c}\overline{d}$	$\overline{a}\overline{b}cd$	$\overline{a}\overline{b}c\overline{d}$	$\overline{a}\overline{b}\overline{c}d$	$\overline{a}\overline{b}\overline{c}\overline{d}$
$\kappa(\omega)$	1	1	1	0	1	1	1	16

as one configuration (of 16) to ensure the conditional indepence of A from B and D in the context of C. However, we also find

$$\kappa(a|\,\overline{b}\,\overline{c}\,d) = \kappa(a\,\overline{b}\,\overline{c}\,d) - \kappa(\overline{b}\,\overline{c}\,d) = 2 - 1 = 1$$
$$\neq 0 = 1 - 1 = \kappa(a\,\overline{c}\,d) - \kappa(\overline{c}\,d) = \kappa(a|\overline{c}\,d)$$

and thus $\{A\}\,\cancel{\perp\!\!\!\perp}_\kappa\,\{B\} \mid (\{C\} \cup \{D\})$ violating weak union.

Conditional independence satisfies decomposition [Pea88] if given a joined set of variables $(\mathbf{C} \cup \mathbf{D})$ is irrelevant for the set $\mathbf{A}$ in the context of $\mathbf{C}$, then the individual information are, in the same context, also irrelevant for $\mathbf{A}$ (see Figure 3.3d).

Proposition 3.26 (Decomposition [Pea88] for Conditional κ-Independence). Let $\mathbf{A}, \mathbf{B}, \mathbf{C} \subseteq \Sigma$ be sets of variables. $\mathbf{A} \perp\!\!\!\perp_\kappa (\mathbf{B} \cup \mathbf{D}) \mid \mathbf{C}$ implies both $\mathbf{A} \perp\!\!\!\perp_\kappa \mathbf{B} \mid \mathbf{C}$ and $\mathbf{A} \perp\!\!\!\perp_\kappa \mathbf{D} \mid \mathbf{C}$.

We finally examine the property named contraction [Pea88], illustrated in Figure 3.3e.

Proposition 3.27 (Contraction [Pea88] for Conditional κ-Independence). For sets of variables $\mathbf{A}, \mathbf{B}, \mathbf{C} \subseteq \Sigma$, $\mathbf{A} \perp\!\!\!\perp_\kappa \mathbf{B} \mid \mathbf{C}$ and $\mathbf{A} \perp\!\!\!\perp_\kappa \mathbf{D} \mid (\mathbf{C} \cup \mathbf{B})$ imply $\mathbf{A} \perp\!\!\!\perp_\kappa (\mathbf{B} \cup \mathbf{D}) \mid \mathbf{C}$.

Additionally to the stated properties if OCF, these function provide a semantic for conditionals such that an agent with an epistemic state κ believes (in a) conditional $(\psi|\phi) \in (\mathfrak{L}|\mathfrak{L})$ if and only if its verification is believed to be more plausible as its refutation. Following the literature (for instance [KI01]) we overload the symbol for the satisfaction relation on this behalf and write $\kappa \vDash (\psi|\phi)$ to indicate that $(\psi|\phi)$ is believed in κ, in this case we synonymously say that κ *accepts* $(\psi|\phi)$ or κ is *a model of* $(\psi|\phi)$, formally

$$\kappa \models (\psi|\phi) \qquad \text{if and only if} \qquad \kappa(\phi\psi) < \kappa(\phi\overline{\psi}). \qquad (3.20)$$

Likewise an OCF κ accepts a weak conditional $(\!|\psi|\phi|\!)$ if and only if κ does not accept its negation [ERKI18], that is,

$$\kappa \models (\!|\psi|\phi|\!) \qquad \text{iff} \qquad \kappa \not\models (\overline{\psi}|\phi) \qquad \text{iff} \qquad \kappa(\phi\psi) \leq \kappa(\phi\overline{\psi}). \qquad (3.21)$$

A ranking function κ is *admissible with respect to a conditional knowledge base* $\Delta = \{(\psi_1|\phi_1), \ldots, (\psi_n|\phi_n)\} \subseteq (\mathfrak{L} \mid \mathfrak{L})$ [KI01] if and only if κ accepts all conditionals in the knowledge base according to (3.20), formally

$$\kappa \models \Delta \qquad \text{if and only if} \qquad \kappa \models (\psi_i|\phi_i) \qquad \text{for all} \qquad 1 \leq i \leq n. \qquad (3.22)$$

So far, the acceptance relation (3.20) between an OCF and a conditional is only qualitative. We now extend this relation for an OCF also accept conditionals weighted with a *firmness* [Spo12] $f \in \mathbb{N}$, which expresses a degree of disbelief in the refutation of the conditional: An OCF κ accepts a conditional $(\psi|\phi)[f]$ with $(\psi|\phi) \in (\mathfrak{L}|\mathfrak{L})$ and $f \in \mathbb{N}$ if and only if the verification of the conditional increased with the firmness of the conditional is as least as plausible as the rank of the refutation of the conditional [Spo12], formally

$$\kappa \models (\psi|\phi)[f] \qquad \text{if and only if} \qquad \kappa(\phi\psi) + f \leq \kappa(\phi\overline{\psi}); \qquad (3.23)$$

likewise, an OCF κ is admissible with respect to a knowledge base composed from firmness-weighted conditionals if and only if κ accepts all conditionals in this knowledge base with respect to (3.23).

A conditional is accepted qualitatively if it is accepted with any strictly positive firmness, with gives us the following relation between qualitative and semi-quantitative acceptance of a conditional:

Lemma 3.28 ([EKI15b]). *If a conditional* $(\psi|\phi)[f]$ *with* $\phi, \psi \in \mathfrak{L}$ *and* $f \in \mathbb{N}$ *is accepted semi-quantitatively for any* $f \in \mathbb{N}$ *then it is also accepted qualitatively. The reverse does not hold in general.*

Finally, we restrict the acceptance relation between OCF and conditionals such that an OCF *strictly* accepts a conditional if and only if the verification of the conditional lifted by its firmness is exactly as plausible as the refutation of the conditional, formally

$$\kappa \vDash^s (\psi|\phi)[f] \qquad \text{if and only if} \qquad \kappa(\phi\psi) + f = \kappa(\phi\overline{\psi}), \qquad (3.24)$$

with the same extension to strictly admissibility of an OCF with respect to a firmness weighted knowledge base. It is clear that each OCF that strictly accepts a conditional (or is strict admissible with respect to a firmness weighted knowledge base) also accepts the conditional (is admissible with respect to the knowledge base).

In the acceptance of conditionals we find a different between strict facts $\phi \in \mathcal{L}$ and conditional facts $(\psi|\top) \in (\mathcal{L}|\mathcal{L})$ in a knowledge base $\mathcal{R} = (\mathfrak{S}, \Delta)$: For a strict fact $\phi \in \mathfrak{S}$, there is no $\omega \in \Omega$ such that $\omega \vDash \overline{\phi}$ and hence $\kappa(\overline{\phi}) = \infty$ (as already discussed for the rank of the contradiction above). For a conditional fact $(\psi|\top) \in \Delta$, for every $\omega \in \Omega$ with $\omega \vDash \overline{\psi}$ for κ to be admissible to Δ it is required that $\kappa(\psi) < \kappa(\overline{\psi})$ but not necessarily $\kappa(\overline{\psi}) = \infty$.

3.3.2 Inference with Ordinal Conditional Functions

An OCF κ induces a preference relation $\leq_\kappa$ on Ω such that for two worlds we have $\omega \leq_\kappa \omega'$ if and only if $\kappa(\omega) \leq \kappa(\omega')$. The strict variant of $\leq_\kappa$ is defined as usual, that is, $\omega <_\kappa \omega'$ if and only if $\omega \leq_\kappa \omega'$ and $\omega' \not\leq_\kappa \omega$. By definition of $\leq_\kappa$ this maps to the $<$-relation between natural numbers, and thus we obtain $\omega <_\kappa \omega'$ if and only if $\kappa(\omega) < \kappa(\omega')$.

Using $<_\kappa$ as preference relation of a preferential model that, apart from this, uses the set of possible worlds Ω as set of models and the classical satisfaction relation $\vDash$ as satisfaction relation, we obtain the preferential model $(\Omega, \vDash, <_\kappa)$.

By Definition 3.6 of preferential entailment from this model we obtain the inference relation $\succnapprox_\kappa \subseteq \mathcal{L} \times \mathcal{L}$ such that for formulas $\phi, \psi \in \mathcal{L}$ we have

$$\phi \succnapprox_\kappa \psi \qquad \text{iff} \qquad \forall \omega' \vDash \phi\overline{\psi} \quad \exists \omega \vDash \phi\psi \quad \text{s.t.} \quad \omega <_\kappa \omega'. \qquad (3.25)$$

Proposition 3.29 (κ-Inference [Spo88, Spo12]). Let κ be an OCF. A formula $\phi \in \mathcal{L}$ that is not-contradictory, $\phi \not\equiv \bot$, κ-*infers* a formula ψ if and only if κ accepts the conditional $(\psi|\phi)$, formally

$$\phi \succnapprox_\kappa \psi \qquad \text{iff} \qquad \kappa(\phi\psi) < \kappa(\phi\overline{\psi}) \qquad \text{iff} \qquad \kappa \vDash (\psi|\phi) \qquad (3.26)$$

This close connection between the acceptance of a conditional in an epistemic state κ and the inference of ψ from ϕ basically states that an agent accepts the conditional rule "if ϕ then normally ψ" if and only if it believes ψ given that it already believes ϕ. Even more, this also opens the door to counterfactual reasoning, because even if the agent does not believe ϕ, it accepts that ϕ licenses for the inference of ψ and hence believes that it would believe ψ if it came to believe in ϕ.

3.3.3 Inductive Approaches to Generating OCF

In the previous sections we discussed the formal properties of ordinal conditional functions and the preferential entailment induced by this ordering of the possible worlds. The question how we obtain such a ranking function is still open; we will catch up on this in this section.

3.3.3.1 System Z

System Z [Pea90] is an approach to inductively generating an OCF to a conditional knowledge base and uses the partitions determined in the consistency test algorithm (Algorithm 2.1, [Pea90]) to assign a plausibility rank to each world. The basic idea in this assignment is that the higher the partition number of a conditional, the fewer other conditionals tolerate the conditional, which means that is describes a (proportionally to its partition number far fetched) exception to the (with respect to this more) general rule on a layer with a smaller partition number.

Definition 3.30 (System Z OCF κ_Δ^Z [Pea90]). Let Δ be a conditional knowlegde base, $\Delta = \{(\psi_1|\phi_1), \ldots, (\psi_n|\phi_n)\}$, with a partitioning $(\Delta_j)_{j=0}^m$ determined by Algorithm 2.1. Let $Z : (\mathfrak{L}|\mathfrak{L}) \to \mathbb{N}_0^\infty$ to be a function that assigns to each $(\psi_i|\phi_i) \in \Delta$ an integer value such that $Z(\psi_i|\phi_i) = j$ if and only if $(\psi_i|\phi_i) \in \Delta_j$. The respective OCF κ_Δ^Z is the function

$$\kappa_\Delta^Z(\omega) = \begin{cases} 0 \text{ if and only if } \omega \text{ does not falsify any conditional in } \Delta \\ \max_{\omega \models \phi_i \overline{\psi_i}} \{Z(\phi_i|\phi_i)\} + 1 \text{ otherwise.} \end{cases}$$

$$(3.27)$$

Intuitively this system proceeds on the assumption that only exceptions violate exceptional rules and thus a world is implausible if it is an exception with respect to this definition. It has been shown 3.30 that Definition 3.30

defines the unique Pareto-minimal OCF that is admissible with respect to Δ^4. We illustrate System Z with the following example:

Example 3.31. We extend Example 2.8 and use the subset $\Delta = \{\delta_1 : (b|f), \delta_3 : (b|p), \delta_4 : (\overline{f}|p)\}$ of the knowledge in Example 2.1 respectively 2.4 with the aligned alphabet $\Sigma = \{P, B, F\}$ to illustrate System Z. The consistency test algorithm partitions this knowledge base into the partitions $\Delta_0 = \{\delta_1\}$ and $\Delta_1 = \{\delta_3, \delta_4\}$. So rules about birds in general are put into partitions with smaller numbers than the rules about the exceptional birds, that is, penguins. So the example confirms the the intuition about the algorithm about the exceptionality of conditionals in the partitions. Table 3.4 (upper row) shows which conditionals are falsified by the worlds, which then leads to the OCF κ_Δ^Z also given in Table 3.4 (bottom row). We ensure ourselves that κ_Δ^Z is admissible with respect to Δ and observe

$$\kappa_\Delta^Z(bf) = \min\{\kappa_\Delta^Z(pbf), \kappa_\Delta^Z(\overline{p}bf)\} = \min\{2, 0\} = 0$$
$$\kappa_\Delta^Z(b\overline{f}) = \min\{\kappa_\Delta^Z(pb\overline{f}), \kappa_\Delta^Z(\overline{p}b\overline{f})\} = \min\{1, 1\} = 1$$
$$\kappa_\Delta^Z(pb) = \min\{\kappa_\Delta^Z(pbf), \kappa_\Delta^Z(pb\overline{f})\} = \min\{2, 1\} = 1$$
$$\kappa_\Delta^Z(p\overline{b}) = \min\{\kappa_\Delta^Z(p\overline{b}f), \kappa_\Delta^Z(p\overline{b}\overline{f})\} = \min\{2, 2\} = 2$$
$$\kappa_\Delta^Z(pf) = \min\{\kappa_\Delta^Z(pbf), \kappa_\Delta^Z(p\overline{b}f)\} = \min\{2, 2\} = 2$$
$$\kappa_\Delta^Z(p\overline{f}) = \min\{\kappa_\Delta^Z(pb\overline{f}), \kappa_\Delta^Z(p\overline{b}\overline{f})\} = \min\{1, 2\} = 1$$

and therefore, as proposed,

$$\kappa_\Delta^Z(bf) = 0 < 1 = \kappa_\Delta^Z(b\overline{f}) \qquad \text{and thus} \qquad \kappa_\Delta^Z \models (f|b)$$
$$\kappa_\Delta^Z(pb) = 1 < 2 = \kappa_\Delta^Z(p\overline{b}) \qquad \text{and thus} \qquad \kappa_\Delta^Z \models (b|p)$$
$$\kappa_\Delta^Z(p\overline{f}) = 1 < 2 = \kappa_\Delta^Z(pf) \qquad \text{and thus} \qquad \kappa_\Delta^Z \models (\overline{f}|p).$$

3.3.3.2 System Z^+

System Z inductively generates an OCF for a purely qualitative knowledge base and does hot have means of handling firmness annotated conditionals.

---

[4] Note that if Algorithm 2.1 would start the numbering of the partitions with 1, this could more conveniently be defined as $\kappa_\Delta^Z(\omega) = \max\{Z(\phi_i|\phi_i)|\omega \models \phi_i\overline{\psi_i}\}$ without the case differentiation and the increment in the second case. Here the algorithm and the definition have been kept as defined originally because this definition is the widely known and used.

Table 3.4: Falsification behaviour of the worlds and conditionals in Example 3.31 (upper row) and resulting OCF κ_Δ^Z (bottom row) by means of System Z

ω	$p\,b\,f$	$p\,b\,\overline{f}$	$p\,\overline{b}\,f$	$p\,\overline{b}\,\overline{f}$	$\overline{p}\,b\,f$	$\overline{p}\,b\,\overline{f}$	$\overline{p}\,\overline{b}\,f$	$\overline{p}\,\overline{b}\,\overline{f}$
falsifies	δ_4	δ_1	δ_3, δ_4	δ_3	—	δ_1	—	—
$\kappa_\Delta^Z(\omega)$	2	1	2	2	0	1	0	0

This is where System Z^+ [GP91b] comes into play. This approach generalises the notion of tolerance to semi-quantitative knowledge bases in such a way that a knowledge base $\Delta^{N_0^\infty} = \{(\psi_1|\phi_1)[f_1], \ldots, (\psi_n|\phi_n)[f_n]\} \subseteq (\mathfrak{L} \mid \mathfrak{L})N$ tolerates a conditional $(\xi|\chi)[f]$ if and only if the qualitative conterpart of $\Delta^{N_0^\infty}$, that is, the knowledge base $\Delta = \{(\psi_i|\phi_i)|(\psi_i|\phi_i)[f_i] \in \Delta^{N_0^\infty}\}$ tolerates the conditional $(\xi|\chi)$. The first step of the System Z^+ algorithm is identical to the System Z approach, that is, from $\Delta^{N_0^\infty}$ we select a subset $\mathfrak{Z}$ with the property that $\mathfrak{Z}$ tolerates all conditionals in $\Delta^{N_0^\infty}$. To each of the conditionals in $\mathfrak{Z}$ we assign a Z-value identical to their firmness, that is $Z((\psi_i|\phi_i)[f_i]) := f_i$ for all $(\psi_i|\phi_i)[f_i] \in \mathfrak{Z}$. Then we iteratively add conditionals from the remainder knowledge base to $\mathfrak{Z}$ until $\mathfrak{Z} = \Delta^{N_0^\infty}$ and assign Z-values to these conditionals according to Algorithm 3.1.

When all conditional in $\Delta^{N_0^\infty}$ are added to $\mathfrak{Z}$ we obtain the ranking function κ_Δ^Z as for System Z, that is

$$\kappa_\Delta^Z(\omega) = \begin{cases} 0 \text{ if and only if } \omega \text{ does not falsify any conditional in } \Delta^{N_0^\infty} \\ \max_{\omega \models \phi_i \overline{\psi_i}} \{Z(\psi_i|\phi_i)\} \text{ otherwise.} \end{cases}$$

(3.28)

Note that for totally ordered sets, the maximum and the supremum coincide, thus it would suffice to define $\kappa_\Delta^Z(\omega) = \max\{Z(\psi_i|\phi_i)|\omega \models \phi_i\overline{\psi_i}\}$ as $\max\{\varnothing\} = 0$. Further note that here the $+1$ increment is added in step (2) of the iteration and thus is not added in (3.28), as it is the case for the qualitative variant of System Z (see (3.27)).

Formal background and the proof of correctness of System Z^+ can be found in [GP91b], we here just give some intuitions to the steps of the iteration.

Listing 3.1: Algorithm for System Z^+ (confer [GP91b])

```
INPUT   : Semi-Quantitative conditional knowledge base
          Δ^{N_0^∞} = {(ψ_1|φ_1)[f_1],...,(ψ_n|φ_n)[f_n]} ⊆ (𝔏 | 𝔏)ℕ
OUTPUT  : Function Z : (𝔏|𝔏) → ℕ_0 for all (ψ_i|φ_i) ∈ Δ if Δ is
          consistent, NULL otherwise

BEGIN
    ℑ := {(ψ_i|φ_i)[f_i]|(ψ_i|φ_i)[f_i] ∈ Δ^{N_0^∞}} s.t. ℑ tolerates Δ^{N_0^∞}.
    IF(ℑ = ∅)          // that is, if Δ^{N_0^∞} is inconsistent (1)
      RETURN NULL
    END IF
    Z(ψ_i|φ_i)[f_i]:=f_i for all (ψ_i|φ_i)[f_i] ∈ ℑ
    WHILE(ℑ ≠ Δ^{N_0^∞}) DO
       Ω(ℑ):={ω|ω falsifies only conditionals (ψ_i|φ_i)[f_i] ∈ Δ^{N_0^∞} \ ℑ}
       FOR-EACH(ω ∈ Ω(ℑ))
         κ_Z^*(ω):=     max      {Z((ψ_i|φ_i)[f_i])|ω ⊨ φ_i\overline{ψ_i}}+1 // (2)
                   (ψ_i|φ_i)[f_i]∈ℑ
       END FOR-EACH
       \widehat{ω}:= min  {κ_Z^*(ω)}
               ω∈Ω(ℑ)
       FOR EACH((ψ_i|φ_i)[f_i] ∈ Δ^{N_0^∞} \ ℑ)
         IF([[(ψ_i|φ_i)]]_{\widehat{ω}} = true) //(3)
            ℑ:=ℑ ∪ {(ψ_i|φ_i)[f_i]
            Z(ψ_i|φ_i)[f_i]:=f_i + κ_Z^*(\widehat{ω})
         END IF
       END FOR-EACH
    END WHILE
    RETURN Z
END
```

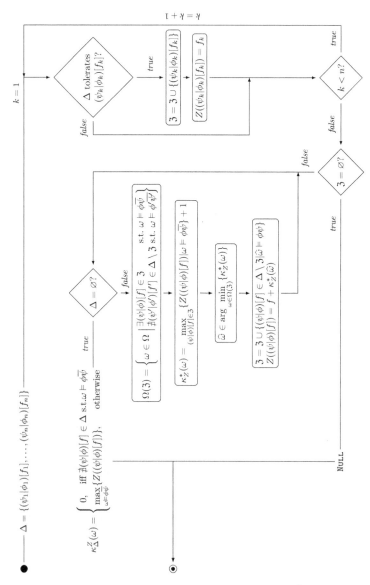

Figure 3.4: Flowchart of Algorithm 3.1 for setting up the System Z^+-OCF for a firmness-annotated knowledge base

Table 3.5: System Z^+-ranking for the knowledge base in Example 3.32

ω	pbf	$pb\overline{f}$	$p\overline{b}f$	$p\overline{b}\overline{f}$	$\overline{p}bf$	$\overline{p}b\overline{f}$	$\overline{p}\overline{b}f$	$\overline{p}\overline{b}\overline{f}$
$\kappa_\Delta^Z(\omega)$	4	1	12	12	0	1	0	0

(1) Initially, $\mathfrak{Z}$ contains conditionals that tolerate the whole knowledge base, thus every conditional in the remainder knowledge base does not tolerate the conditionals in $\mathfrak{Z}$ and thus must be verified by a world that falsifies conditionals in $\mathfrak{Z}$. The existence of these sets and world is guaranteed if Δ is consistent, and System Z^+ generates no OCF if Δ is inconsistent.

(2) Here the $+1$ increment, which in the System Z approach is applied in the final step, is applied in each iteration and ensures that the Z-value of the conditionals is "large enough" to ensure that the resulting OCF is admissible with respect to $\Delta^{\mathbb{N}_0^\infty}$.

(3) By construction, the worlds $\Omega(\mathfrak{Z})$ must verify at least one conditional outside $\mathfrak{Z}$.

We illustrate this approach with an Example.

Example 3.32 ([KIE13b]). To illustrate System Z^+ we use a semi-quantitative variant of the knowledge base used in Example 2.8, the knowledge base $\Delta^{\mathbb{N}_0^\infty} = \{(f|b)[1], (b|p)[10], (\overline{f}|p)[2]\}$. In the preliminary steps we set $\mathfrak{Z}_0 = \{(f|b)[1]\}$ and set $Z((f|b)[1]) = 1$. In the iteration obtain the world $\Omega(\mathfrak{Z}_0) = \{pb\overline{f}\}$ which is assigned with a value $\kappa_Z^*(pb\overline{f}) = 2$. We select the only world possible and observe that $pb\overline{f} \vDash pb$ as well as $pb\overline{f} \vDash p\overline{f}$, thus both conditionals are added to $\mathfrak{Z}$ and are assigned with a Z-value $Z((b|p)[10]) = 12$ and $Z((\overline{f}|p)[2]) = 4$. The resulting OCF is shown in Table 3.5.

3.3.3.3 c-Representations

As we have seen, System Z pools conditionals together to generate an OCF from a knowledge base, contemplating the most exceptional conditional falsified in this step. In contrast to this, the approach of c-representations considers each conditional individually. In this, each conditional in knowledge base exerts an impact on the OCF. These impacts are set to generate OCF which are admissible with respect to this knowledge base.

Definition 3.33 (c-Representation [KI01, KI04]). Let Δ be a conditional knowledge base, $\Delta = \{(\psi_1|\phi_1), \ldots, (\psi_n|\phi_n)\} \subseteq (\mathfrak{L} \mid \mathfrak{L})$. Let $\vec{\eta} = \left(\kappa_i^-\right)_{i=1}^{|\Delta|}$ be a vector of integer *impacts*, $\kappa_i^- \in \mathbb{N}_0$ for each $1 \leq i \leq n$, and that each impact κ_i^- is associated with the conditional $(\psi_i|\phi_i) \in \Delta$. A *c-representation* κ_Δ^c of Δ is a ranking function

$$\kappa_\Delta^c(\omega) = \sum_{\substack{\omega \models \phi_i \overline{\psi}_i \\ i=1}}^{n} \kappa_i^- \tag{3.29}$$

such that the rank of each world ω is composed from the impacts of conditionals falsified by ω, and where the values of the impacts are instantiated such that $\kappa_\Delta^c \models \Delta$ which can be achieved if and only if the impacts are chosen such that

$$\kappa_i^- > \min_{\omega \models \phi_i \psi_i} \left\{ \sum_{\substack{\omega \models \phi_i \overline{\psi}_i \\ i \neq j}} \kappa_i^- \right\} - \min_{\omega \models \phi_i \overline{\psi}_i} \left\{ \sum_{\substack{\omega \models \phi_i \overline{\psi}_i \\ i \neq j}} \kappa_i^- \right\} \tag{3.30}$$

for all $1 \leq i \leq n$.

We illustrate the approach of c-representations with an excerpt of the running example.

Example 3.34. We use the subset $\Delta = \{\delta_1 : (b|f), \delta_3 : (b|p), \delta_4 : (\overline{f}|p)\}$ of the knowledge in Example 2.1 respectively 2.4 with the aligned alphabet $\Sigma = \{P, B, F\}$ to illustrate c-representations. Table 3.6 (upper rows) shows the verification/falsification behaviour of the worlds in this example with respect to the conditionals and the schema (middle row) that follows from this with respect to (3.29). We substitute this information into the system of inequalities (3.30) which gives us

$$\kappa_1^- > \min\{\kappa_4^-, 0\} - \min\{0, 0\}$$
$$\kappa_3^- > \min\{\kappa_1^-, \kappa_4^-\} - \min\{\kappa_4^-, 0\}$$
$$\kappa_4^- > \min\{\kappa_1^-, \kappa_3^-\} - \min\{\kappa_3^-, 0\}$$

and therefore

$$\kappa_1^- > 0$$
$$\kappa_3^- > \min\{\kappa_1^-, \kappa_4^-\} \tag{3.31}$$
$$\kappa_4^- > \min\{\kappa_1^-, \kappa_3^-\}. \tag{3.32}$$

So κ_1^- can be set independently from the other two impacts. For the other ones we do the following case analysis: If $\kappa_4^- \leq \kappa_1^-$, then by (3.31) we had $\kappa_3^- > \kappa_4^-$. However, then we had both $\kappa_1^- \geq \kappa_4^-$ and $\kappa_4^- > \kappa_3^-$ which would render (3.32) inconsistent. Therefore we have $\kappa_4^- > \kappa_1^-$. With this, line (3.31) implies $\kappa_3^- > \kappa_1^-$ and (3.32) then coincides with this assumption. So we obtain

$$\kappa_1^- > 0$$
$$\kappa_3^- > \kappa_1^-$$
$$\kappa_4^- > \kappa_1^-.$$

For a minimal solution to this system, we set $\kappa_1^- = 1$, and $\kappa_2^- = \kappa_3^- = 2$ and thus obtain the vector $(1, 2, 2)$ which leads to an OCF κ_Δ^c as given in Table 3.6 (bottom row). We ensure ourselves that $\kappa_\Delta^c \models \Delta$ and from the table obtain

$$\kappa_\Delta^c \models (b|f) \quad \text{as } \kappa(bf) = \min\{2,0\} = 0 < 1 = \min\{1,1\} = \kappa(b\overline{f}) \tag{3.33}$$
$$\kappa_\Delta^c \models (b|p) \quad \text{as } \kappa(pb) = \min\{1,2\} = 1 < 1 = \min\{2,4\} = \kappa(p\overline{b}) \tag{3.34}$$
$$\kappa_\Delta^c \models (\overline{f}|p) \quad \text{as } \kappa(p\overline{f}) = \min\{1,2\} = 1 < 1 = \min\{2,4\} = \kappa(pf). \tag{3.35}$$

Lemma 3.35 ([KI01]). Let $\Delta = \{(\psi_1|\phi_1), \ldots, (\psi_n|\phi_n)\} \subseteq (\mathcal{L} \mid \mathcal{L})$ be a conditional knowledge base. Every c-representation of Δ is an OCF.

Every c-representation set up according to Definition 3.33 is admissible with respect to the underlying knowledge base, which we show with the following proposition.

Proposition 3.36 (Correctness of c-Representations [KI01]). Let κ_Δ^c be a c-representation of a knowledge base $\Delta = \{(\psi_1|\phi_1), \ldots, (\psi_n|\phi_n)\} \subseteq (\mathcal{L} \mid \mathcal{L})$. Then $\kappa_\Delta^c \models \Delta$ as proposed in Definition 3.33

Table 3.6: Verification / falsification behaviour of the worlds and conditionals in Example 3.34 (upper rows), the schema of c-representations for this knowledge base according to (3.29) (middle row) and one concrete c-representation as instantiation of the schema with the solution $(1, 2, 2)$ to the system of inequalities (3.30) (bottom row).

ω	pbf	$pb\overline{f}$	$p\overline{b}f$	$p\overline{b}\,\overline{f}$	$\overline{p}bf$	$\overline{p}b\overline{f}$	$\overline{p}\,\overline{b}f$	$\overline{p}\,\overline{b}\,\overline{f}$
verifies	δ_1,δ_3	δ_3,δ_4	—	δ_4	δ_1	—	—	—
falsifies	δ_4	δ_1	δ_3,δ_4	δ_3	—	δ_1	—	—
schema (3.29)	κ_4^-	κ_1^-	$\kappa_3^- + \kappa_4^-$	κ_3^-	0	κ_1^-	0	0
$\kappa_\Delta^c(\omega)$	2	1	4	2	0	1	0	0

At the same time, there are OCF admissible with respect to a knowledge base which are no c-representations, so this approach is correct, but not complete with respect to Δ-admissible OCF.

Observation 3.37 (Not-Completeness of c-Representations). There are OCF κ with the property $\kappa \vDash \Delta$ for a knowledge base $\Delta = \{(\psi_1|\phi_1), \ldots, (\psi_n|\phi_n)\}$ that are no c-representations of Δ.

Example 3.38. Example 3.31 contains such an OCF: Here for the System Z OCF we find $\kappa_\Delta^Z(pbf) = 2 = \kappa_\Delta^Z(p\overline{b}f)$. For c-representations, the schema (3.29) specifies $\kappa_\Delta^c(pbf) = \kappa_4^-$ and $\kappa_\Delta^c(p\overline{b}f) = \kappa_3^- + \kappa_4^-$. As we have seen in Example 3.34, κ_3^- and κ_4^- are strictly positive, thus for every c-representation we have $\kappa_\Delta^c(pbf) < \kappa_\Delta^c(p\overline{b}f)$ and therefore the is no c-representation identical to κ_Δ^Z.

We finally recall that there are c-representations for every consistent knowledge base:

Lemma 3.39 ([KI01]). Let $\Delta = \{(\psi_1|\phi_1), \ldots, (\psi_n|\phi_n)\} \subseteq (\mathfrak{L} \mid \mathfrak{L})$ be a conditional knowledge base. There are c-representations for Δ if and only if Δ is consistent if and only if the system of inequalities (3.30) is solvable.

This provides us with an additional way of testing a conditional knowledge base for consistency: If we set up the system of inequalities (3.30) for a knowledge base Δ and find a solution, then we know the knowledge base to be consistent. If, on the other hand, we prove that no solution is possible, the knowledge base is inconsistent. Using c-representations in this way was pointed out in [BEKI16].

The inference relation of c-representations according to the inference relation of OCF in general (3.26) is

$$\phi \approx_{\kappa_\Delta^c} \psi \qquad \text{if and only if} \qquad \kappa_\Delta^c(\phi\psi) < \kappa_\Delta^c(\phi\overline{\psi}). \qquad (3.36)$$

Thus for every c-representation κ_Δ^c of Δ we obtain an inference operation

$$C_{\kappa_\Delta^c}(\phi) = \{\psi | \phi \approx_{\kappa_\Delta^c} \psi\}. \qquad (3.37)$$

Note that c-representations provide a schema for a subset of all Δ-admissible OCF. Chapter 5 further examines the set of all c-representations and how to define inferences relations to sets of c-representations.

Following [ERKI18] we extend Definition 3.33 to also cover conditional knowledge bases which contain weak conditionals.

Proposition 3.40. Let $\Delta = \{\delta_1, \ldots, \delta_n\} \subseteq (\mathcal{L}|\mathcal{L}) \cup (\!(\mathcal{L}|\mathcal{L})\!)$ be a conditional knowledge base. A ranking function κ_Δ^c is a c-representation of Δ if and only if it is composed from the impacts according to (3.29) and $\kappa_\Delta^c \vDash \Delta$, which is the case if and only if the impacts κ_i^- are chosen according to (3.30) if, for all $1 \leq i \leq n$, δ_i is a strong conditional $\delta_i \in (\mathcal{L}|\mathcal{L})$ and

$$\kappa_i^- \geq \min_{\omega \vDash \phi_i \psi_i} \left\{ \sum_{\substack{\omega \vDash \phi_i \overline{\psi}_i \\ i \neq j}} \kappa_i^- \right\} - \min_{\omega \vDash \phi_i \overline{\psi}_i} \left\{ \sum_{\substack{\omega \vDash \phi_i \overline{\psi}_i \\ i \neq j}} \kappa_i^- \right\} \qquad (3.38)$$

if δ_i is a weak conditional $\delta_i \in (\!(\mathcal{L}|\mathcal{L})\!)$.

Finally, the technique of c-representations can be used to inductively generate epistemic states κ_Δ^c for knowledge bases where each conditional is annotated with a firmness of belief that is, a semi-qualitative knowledge base $\Delta^{\mathbb{N}_0^\infty} = \{(\psi_1|\phi_1)[f_1], \ldots, (\psi_n|\phi_n)[f_n]\} \subseteq (\mathcal{L} | \mathcal{L})\mathbb{N}$, as well. This was demonstrated in [KI01] as well as [EKI15b, Definition 4] and involves applying (3.23) to (3.30) to obtain the system of inequalities

$$\kappa_i^- \geq f_i + \min_{\omega \vDash \phi_i \psi_i} \left\{ \sum_{\substack{\omega \vDash \phi_i \overline{\psi}_i \\ i \neq j}} \kappa_i^- \right\} - \min_{\omega \vDash \phi_i \overline{\psi}_i} \left\{ \sum_{\substack{\omega \vDash \phi_i \overline{\psi}_i \\ i \neq j}} \kappa_i^- \right\}. \qquad (3.39)$$

this finishes the overview of OCF as one of the major basic techniques of this thesis.

3.4 Probabilistic Reasoning

A probability function [Fin74, BKI14] is a non-negative real-valued finitely additive function $P : \Omega \to [0, 1]$ that assigns each world $\omega \in \Omega$ a probability $0 \leq P(\omega) \leq 1$ with the normalisation property that $\sum_{\omega \in \Omega} P(\omega) = 1$ and, for every $\widehat{\Omega} \subseteq \Omega$,

$$P(\widehat{\Omega}) := \sum_{\omega \in \widehat{\Omega}} P(\omega). \tag{3.40}$$

This *finite additivity property* lifts P from the domain of possible worlds Ω with sets of models to the domain of formulas $\phi \in \mathfrak{L}$ in such a way that

$$P(\phi) = P(Mod(\phi)) = \sum_{\omega \in Mod(\phi)} P(\omega). \tag{3.41}$$

From these axioms, we directly obtain that the probability of the contradiction is $P(\bot) = P(\varnothing) = 0$ and the probability of the tautology is $P(\top) = P(\Omega) = 1$. Also, the probability of the negation of a formula equals the *improbability* $\overline{P}$ [ST12] of the formula, formally

$$P(\overline{\phi}) = 1 - P(\phi) =: \overline{P}(\phi). \tag{3.42}$$

For for $P(\phi) > 0$, the conditional probability $P(\psi|\phi)$ is [Fin74]

$$P(\psi|\phi)[x] = \frac{P(\phi\psi)}{P(\phi)}. \tag{3.43}$$

and undefined for $P(\phi) = 0$.

Proposition 3.41 (Law of Total (Conditional) Probability [BKI14]). Let Σ be a finite propositional alphabet with a set of possible worlds Ω, let $\phi, \psi, \chi \in \mathfrak{L}$ be formulas and let P be a probability function over Ω. Then we have

$$P(\phi) = P(\phi|\psi) \cdot P(\psi) + P(\phi|\overline{\psi}) \cdot P(\overline{\psi}) \tag{3.44}$$

$$P(\chi|\phi) = P(\chi|\phi\psi) \cdot P(\psi|\phi) + P(\chi|\phi\overline{\psi}) \cdot P(\overline{\psi}|\phi) \tag{3.45}$$

A probability function to *accepts* a weighted conditional $(\psi|\phi)[x]$, written

$$P \vDash (\psi|\phi)[x] \qquad \text{if and only if} \qquad P(\psi|\phi) = x = \frac{P(\phi\psi)}{P(\phi)}, \qquad (3.46)$$

that is, the probability function accepts the conditional if the probability of the conditional coincides with its the conditional probability. It is common (see, for instance, [Thi09]) to relax this definition to overcome the singularity and to make the handling of conditionals $(\psi|\phi)$ under probability functions with $P(\phi) = 0$ possible: We follow [Thi09] in such a way that a probability function *zero-accepts* a conditional if and only if

$$P \vDash^0 (\psi|\phi)[x] \qquad \text{if and only if} \qquad x \cdot P(\phi) = P(\phi\psi). \qquad (3.47)$$

The two different acceptance relations coincide for cases where $P(\phi) > 0$, and differ completely where $P(\phi) = 0$, which we formalise in the following lemma.

Lemma 3.42. Let P be a probability function, let $\phi, \psi, \chi \in \mathfrak{L}$ be formulas with $P(\phi) > 0$ and $P(\chi) = 0$, and let $x \in [0,1]$. Then $P \vDash (\psi|\phi)[x]$ if and only if $P \vDash^0 (\psi|\phi)[x]$, and also $P \nvDash (\psi|\chi)[x]$ and $P \vDash^0 (\psi|\chi)[x]$ for any $x \in [0,1]$.

For this dissertation, we concentrate on two inference relations set up upon probability functions: The relation called *threshold inference* [HM07] follows the Lockean thesis [Fol92] which in its original phrasing reads as follows:

> *"It is epistemically rational for us to believe a proposition just in case it is epistemically rational for us to have a sufficiently high degree of confidence in it."*[5]

With this line of argumentation a conditional is to be accepted if its probability is "large enough" given a fixed threshold. The sceptical relation called ε, δ-*inference* [Pea88], accepts a conditional if it is "probable enough" in all probability functions that accept the knowledge base with a floating improbability-threshold.

---

[5]   Quoted from [Fol92, Page 111], inspiration attributed to John Locke: *An Essay Concerning Human Understanding*, P. H. Nidditch (Editor); Oxford: Clarendon Press, 1975.

Definition 3.43 (Threshold Acceptance [HM07]). A probability function P *accepts a conditional* $(\psi|\phi) \in (\mathfrak{L}|\mathfrak{L})$ *under threshold* $x \in (0,1]$, written $P \models^{\geq x} (\psi|\phi)$ if and only if the probability of the conditional is at least x, that is, $P(\psi|\phi) \geq x$. The probability function P accepts a knowledge base $\Delta^{[0,1]} = \{(\psi_1|\phi_1)[x_1], \ldots, (\psi_n|\phi_n)[x_n]\} \subseteq (\mathfrak{L} \mid \mathfrak{L})[0,1]$ if and only if P accepts all conditionals in the knowledge base, formally,

$$P \models \Delta^{[0,1]} \quad \text{if and only if} \quad P \models (\psi_i|\phi_i) \quad \text{for all } 1 \leq i \leq n. \quad (3.48)$$

This acceptance relation defines an inference relation under Ramsey Test for nonmonotonic logic (see [Ram29], Section 2.3) such that a formula is inferred from another if the respective conditional is accepted.

Definition 3.44 (Threshold Inference [HM07]). Let P be a probability function. A formula ψ is *probabilistically inferred under threshold* x from a formula ϕ if and only if the conditional $(\psi|\phi)$ is accepted by P under threshold x, formally,

$$\phi \mathrel{\mkern-1mu\vert\mkern-4mu\sim}^{P,\geq x} \psi \quad \text{iff} \quad P \models^{\geq x} (\psi|\phi) \quad \text{iff} \quad P(\psi|\phi) \geq x. \quad (3.49)$$

Example 3.45. We illustrate threshold inference with the probability function given in Table 3.7. This function accepts all conditional of the excerpt of the running example in Example 2.8 with a threshold of 0.5, as we have (rounded half away from zero)

$$P(f|b) \approx 0.55$$
$$P(b|p) \approx 0.87$$
$$P(\overline{f}|p) \approx 0.62$$

and thus, according to Definition 3.44,

$$b \mathrel{\mkern-1mu\vert\mkern-4mu\sim}^{P,\geq 0.5} f$$
$$p \mathrel{\mkern-1mu\vert\mkern-4mu\sim}^{P,\geq 0.5} b$$
$$p \mathrel{\mkern-1mu\vert\mkern-4mu\sim}^{P,\geq 0.5} \overline{f}.$$

Another well-established probabilistic inference relation is the ε, δ-semantics of [Pea88]. This inference relation is tied closely to probabilistic knowledge bases $\Delta^{[0,1]} = \{(\psi_1|\phi_1)[x_1], \ldots, (\psi_n|\phi_n)[x_n]\} \subseteq (\mathfrak{L} \mid \mathfrak{L})[0,1]$ and ε-acceptance.

Table 3.7: Probability function for Example 3.45 to illustrate threshold inference

ω	$p\,b\,f$	$p\,b\,\overline{f}$	$p\,\overline{b}\,f$	$p\,\overline{b}\,\overline{f}$	$\overline{p}\,b\,f$	$\overline{p}\,b\,\overline{f}$	$\overline{p}\,\overline{b}\,f$	$\overline{p}\,\overline{b}\,\overline{f}$
$P(\omega)$	0.22	0.37	0.04	0.05	0.25	0.02	0.01	0.04

Definition 3.46 (ε-Acceptance [Pea88]). Let $(\psi|\phi)$ be a conditional. A probability function P ε-*accepts* $(\psi|\phi)$ if and only if the improbability of the conditional is less than ε

$$P \models^{<\varepsilon} (\psi|\phi) \quad \left\{ \begin{array}{l} \text{if and only if} \quad \overline{P}(\psi|\phi) < \varepsilon \\ \text{if and only if} \quad P(\psi|\phi) \geq 1 - \varepsilon \end{array} \right\} \quad \text{and} \quad P(\phi) > 0 \tag{3.50}$$

Based on this acceptance relation, we the set of probability functions that ε-accept all conditionals in a knowledge base $\Delta = \{(\psi_1|\phi_1), \ldots, (\psi_n|\phi_n)\}$ is

$$\mathcal{P}_\Delta^{<\varepsilon} = \left\{ P | P \models^{<\varepsilon} (\psi|\phi), (\phi|\psi) \in \Delta \right\}. \tag{3.51}$$

We now nest ε-acceptance (with a value δ in the role of the ε from Definition 3.46) into this definition to obtain ε, δ-inference as follows:

Definition 3.47 (ε, δ-Inference [Pea88]). A formula ψ can be ε, δ entailed from a formula ϕ in the context of a qualitative conditional knowledge base $\Delta = \{(\psi_1|\phi_1), \ldots, (\psi_n|\phi_n)\}$ (written $\phi \approx_\Delta^{\varepsilon,\delta} \psi$), if and only if for every $\delta > 0$ there is an $\varepsilon > 0$ such that for each $P \in \mathcal{P}_\Delta^{\leq \varepsilon}$ the conditional $(\psi|\phi)$ is δ-accepted by P, formally

$$\phi \approx_\Delta^{P, <\varepsilon, \delta} \psi \qquad \begin{array}{l} \text{if and only if} \quad \forall\, \delta > 0 \qquad \exists\, \varepsilon > 0 \\ \text{such that} \quad \forall\, P \in \mathcal{P}_\Delta^{\leq \varepsilon} \quad P \models^{<\delta} (\psi|\phi) \end{array} \tag{3.52}$$

Note that both inference relations are set up upon qualitative knowledge bases, that is, knowledge bases containing strictly qualitative conditionals without any probabilistic weights. Approaches to nonmonotonic reasoning that operate upon probabilistic quantitative knowledge bases like, for instance, the MaxEnt approach [Par94, Par98, KI01, KI04, BKI14] which infers using the unique probability function that accept all conditionals in a probability annotated knowledge base $\Delta^{[0,1]}$ and has minimal (Shannon-) entropy are no matters of this dissertation. We refer the reader interested in these inference relations and their properties to the aforementioned literature.

3.5 Bayesian Networks and LEG Networks

Bayesian networks [Pea88, Par94, BKI14] are a graphical tool that represents a probability distribution over a set of variables and the independences between the variables. It is safe to claim that these networks are the disruptive innovation that is responsible for the breakthrough of applied probability methods in many areas.

We use the following example from the literature where conditionals represent causal connections to illustrate networks in general and Bayesian networks in particular.

Example 3.48 (Car Start Example [GP96, BT10]). Let S indicate whether a car starts (s) or not ($\bar{s}$), H indicate whether the headlights of the car have been left switches on overnight (h) or not ($\bar{h}$), B indicate whether the battery of the car is sufficiently charged (b) or not ($\bar{b}$), and F indicate whether the fuel tank of the car is sufficiently filled (f) or not ($\bar{f}$). In this example we use the following background knowledge formalised as single-elementary conditionals:

$(s|b)$ If the battery is sufficiently charged, the car usually starts.

$(\bar{s}|\bar{b})$ If the battery is not charged sufficiently, the car usually does not start.

$(s|f)$ If the fuel tank is sufficiently filled, the car usually starts.

$(\bar{s}|\bar{f})$ If the fuel tank is not filled sufficiently, the car usually does not start.

$(\bar{s}|b\bar{f})$ If the battery is sufficiently charged and the fuel tank is not filled sufficiently, the car usually does not start.

$(\bar{s}|\bar{b}f)$ If the battery is not charged sufficiently and the fuel tank is sufficiently filled, the car usually does not start.

$(\bar{h}|\top)$ Usually the headlights have not been switched on overnight.

$(f|\top)$ Usually the fuel tank is sufficiently filled.

$(\bar{b}|h)$ If the headlights have been left switched on overnight, the battery usually is not filled sufficiently.

$(b|\bar{h})$ If the headlights have not been left switched on overnight, the battery usually is sufficiently filled.

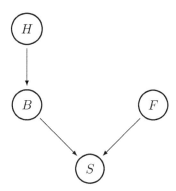

Figure 3.5: Network component for the car start example in Example 3.48

These conditional statements are joined to the knowledge base

$$\Delta = \left\{ \begin{array}{ccccc} (s|b), & (\overline{s}|\overline{b}), & (s|f), & (\overline{s}|\overline{f}), & (\overline{s}|b\overline{f}), \\ (\overline{s}|\overline{b}f), & (\overline{h}|\top), & (f|\top), & (\overline{b}|h), & (b|\overline{h}) \end{array} \right\}.$$

The network given in Figure 3.5 serves as examples for this knowledge base.

In a Bayesian Network, each vertex $V \in \Sigma$ of an acyclic directed graph $\Gamma = (\Sigma, \mathcal{E})$ is annotated with a conditional probability table $P(V|pa(V))$. The joint probability distribution is factorised by the graph such that

$$P(\Sigma) = \prod_{V \in \Sigma} P(V|pa(V)). \tag{3.53}$$

In a these networks, the local directed Markov Property holds, that is, every vertex is independent from its non-descendants in the context of its parents,

$$\{V\} \perp\!\!\!\perp_P nd(V) \mid pa(V), \tag{3.54}$$

whilst each edge in $\mathcal{E}$ reveals a direct dependence between the incident vertices.

Example 3.49. We annotate the network of the car start example with probabilities as given in Figure 3.6 to illustrate Bayesian networks. Table 3.8 shows how the local conditional probability tables are combined to a global probability distribution over Σ.

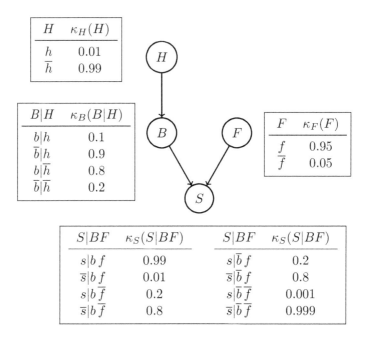

H	$\kappa_H(H)$
h	0.01
$\overline{h}$	0.99

$B\mid H$	$\kappa_B(B\mid H)$
$b\mid h$	0.1
$\overline{b}\mid h$	0.9
$b\mid\overline{h}$	0.8
$\overline{b}\mid\overline{h}$	0.2

F	$\kappa_F(F)$
f	0.95
$\overline{f}$	0.05

$S\mid BF$	$\kappa_S(S\mid BF)$	$S\mid BF$	$\kappa_S(S\mid BF)$
$s\mid b\,f$	0.99	$s\mid\overline{b}\,f$	0.2
$\overline{s}\mid b\,f$	0.01	$\overline{s}\mid\overline{b}\,f$	0.8
$s\mid b\,\overline{f}$	0.2	$s\mid\overline{b}\,\overline{f}$	0.001
$\overline{s}\mid b\,\overline{f}$	0.8	$\overline{s}\mid\overline{b}\,\overline{f}$	0.999

Figure 3.6: Bayesian network of the car start example in Example 3.49

Table 3.8: Illustration of (3.53) in Example 3.49

ω	$h\,b\,f\,s$	$h\,b\,f\,\overline{s}$	$h\,b\,\overline{f}\,s$	$h\,b\,\overline{f}\,\overline{s}$	$h\,\overline{b}\,f\,s$	$h\,\overline{b}\,f\,\overline{s}$	$h\,\overline{b}\,\overline{f}\,s$	$h\,\overline{b}\,\overline{f}\,\overline{s}$
$P(H)$	0.01	0.01	0.01	0.01	0.01	0.01	0.01	0.01
$P(B\mid H)$	0.1	0.1	0.1	0.1	0.9	0.9	0.9	0.9
$P(F)$	0.95	0.95	0.05	0.05	0.95	0.95	0.05	0.05
$P(S\mid BF)$	0.99	0.01	0.2	0.8	0.2	0.8	0.001	0.999
$P(HBFS)$	0.0009405	0.0000095	0.00001	0.00004	0.00171	0.00684	0.00000045	0.00044955

ω	$\overline{h}\,b\,f\,s$	$\overline{h}\,b\,f\,\overline{s}$	$\overline{h}\,b\,\overline{f}\,s$	$\overline{h}\,b\,\overline{f}\,\overline{s}$	$\overline{h}\,\overline{b}\,f\,s$	$\overline{h}\,\overline{b}\,f\,\overline{s}$	$\overline{h}\,\overline{b}\,\overline{f}\,s$	$\overline{h}\,\overline{b}\,\overline{f}\,\overline{s}$
$P(H)$	0.99	0.99	0.99	0.99	0.99	0.99	0.99	0.99
$P(B\mid H)$	0.8	0.8	0.8	0.8	0.2	0.2	0.2	0.2
$P(F)$	0.95	0.95	0.05	0.05	0.95	0.95	0.05	0.05
$P(S\mid BF)$	0.99	0.01	0.2	0.8	0.2	0.8	0.001	0.999
$P(HBFS)$	0.744876	0.007524	0.00792	0.03168	0.03762	0.15048	0.0000099	0.0098901

Another established class of graphs for probabilities are LEG networks [LB82]. Like Bayesian networks, LEG networks arrange the probabilities in a directed, stratified fashion, but unlike these, they are build upon hypergraphs instead of graphs.

Definition 3.50 (LEG Network). Let $\mathcal{H} = (\Sigma, \mathcal{E} \subseteq \mathfrak{P}(\Sigma))$ be a hypertree. The tuple $(\Sigma_i, P(\Sigma_i))$ where $\Sigma_i \in \mathcal{E}$ is a hyperedge in $\mathcal{H}$ and $P(\Sigma_i)$ is a probability distribution over the variables in Σ_i is called a *local event group* (LEG, [LB82]). The system $\langle(\Sigma_i, P_i(\Sigma_i))\rangle_{\Sigma_i \in \mathcal{E}}$ is called a *LEG network*.

We use the usual notation of residues and separators recalled for hypertrees in Section 2.4. Like Bayesian networks, LEG networks factorise the global probability distribution $P(\Sigma)$ such that

$$P(\Sigma) = \prod_{\substack{\Sigma_i \in \mathcal{E} \\ \Sigma_i = \mathbb{R}_i \uplus \mathbb{S}_i}} P_i(\mathbb{R}_i | \mathbb{S}_i). \tag{3.55}$$

For this factorisation to hold, the consistency condition that the probabilities coincide on the intersections of the hyperedges has to be satisfied [Mey98]:

$$P_i((\Sigma_i \cap \Sigma_j)(\omega)) = P_j((\Sigma_i \cap \Sigma_j)(\omega)) \qquad \text{for all } 1 \le i, j \le |\mathcal{E}|. \tag{3.56}$$

Example 3.51. We illustrate LEG networks with the car start example and the hypertree given in Figure 3.7 and the probability distributions given in Table 3.9 (above). We have the local event groups (Σ_1, P_1) as well as (Σ_2, P_2) which are combined to a global probability distribution by means of (3.55) in the bottom line of the table.

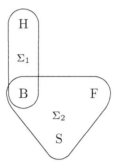

Figure 3.7: Hypergraph to the car start example in Example 3.51

Table 3.9: Probability of local event groups (above) and combination to a global probability distribution (below) in the car start example illustrating LEG networks

ω	$h\,b\,f\,s$	$h\,b\,f\,\overline{s}$	$h\,b\,\overline{f}\,s$	$h\,b\,\overline{f}\,\overline{s}$	$h\,\overline{b}\,f\,s$	$h\,\overline{b}\,f\,\overline{s}$	$h\,\overline{b}\,\overline{f}\,s$	$h\,\overline{b}\,\overline{f}\,\overline{s}$
$P_1(\Sigma_1)$	0.001	0.001	0.001	0.001	0.009	0.009	0.009	0.009
$P_2(\Sigma_2)$	0.75140307	0.00758993	0.0079894	0.0319576	0.0382014	0.1528056	0.000010053	0.010042947
$P(\mathbb{R}_2|\mathbb{S}_2)$	0.9405	0.0095	0.01	0.04	0.19	0.76	0.00005	0.04995
$P(\Sigma)$	0.0009405	0.0000095	0.00001	0.00004	0.00171	0.00684	0.00000045	0.00044955

ω	$\overline{h}\,b\,f\,s$	$\overline{h}\,b\,f\,\overline{s}$	$\overline{h}\,b\,\overline{f}\,s$	$\overline{h}\,b\,\overline{f}\,\overline{s}$	$\overline{h}\,\overline{b}\,f\,s$	$\overline{h}\,\overline{b}\,f\,\overline{s}$	$\overline{h}\,\overline{b}\,\overline{f}\,s$	$\overline{h}\,\overline{b}\,\overline{f}\,\overline{s}$
$P_1(\Sigma_1)$	0.792	0.792	0.792	0.792	0.198	0.198	0.198	0.198
$P_2(\Sigma_2)$	0.75140307	0.00758993	0.0079894	0.0319576	0.0382014	0.1528056	0.000010053	0.010042947
$P(\mathbb{R}_2|\mathbb{S}_2)$	0.9405	0.0095	0.01	0.04	0.19	0.76	0.00005	0.04995
$P(\Sigma)$	0.744876	0.007524	0.00792	0.03168	0.03762	0.15048	0.0000099	0.0098901

3.6 Ceteris Paribus Networks

The techniques to represent an epistemic state we discussed so far represent (or formalise) what the agent believes to be true. This belief is expressed in how plausible or probable the different possible worlds are believed to be. These formalisms then lead to inference relations using preferential models which are instantiated by the preferential relation imposed by the formalisms. On top of that, the approach of Bayesian Networks organises a belief state represented as probability distribution in (conditionally) independent parts.

In this section, these approaches are complemented by a representation that does not capture what the agent believes, but what it desires to be true. This means we will address preference relations where preference expresses what the agent prefers, that is, likes or desires. These preference relations will be organised by Ceteris Paribus networks [BBD$^+$04] which formalise conditional preferences where an outcome is conditionally preferred to another in a context, and will be preferred whatever additional information is learned, as long as the context is constant.

Definition 3.52 (CP-Network [BBD$^+$04]). Let $\mathcal{G} = (\Sigma, \mathcal{E})$ be a directed acyclic graph. We define by $CPT(V, pa(V))$ the *conditional preference table* (CPT) of V that assigns to V a preference relation $\prec_{\mathbf{p}}$ between the literals v and $\overline{v}$ in context of the outcome $\mathbf{p}$ of the parents of V. Let $\{CPT(V, pa(V))\}_{V \in \Sigma}$ be the set of CPT of all variables in Σ. The triple $(\Sigma, \mathcal{E}, \{CPT(V, pa(V))\}_{V \in \Sigma})$ is called a *CP-network*.

A CP network assigns to each variable which of its outcome if preferred given the configuration of the its parents. We illustrate this with the following example from the literature.

Example 3.53 (Dinner [BBD$^+$04]). Let $\Sigma = \{F, V, W\}$ be an alphabet for a very simple dinner configuration indicating whether the dinner comes with a fish course (f) or not ($\overline{f}$), a vegetable soup (v) or nor ($\overline{v}$), and whether it is accompanied by wine (w) or nor ($\overline{w}$). An agent strictly prefers to have a fish course over not having a fish course ($f \prec_{\top} \overline{f}$). If having a fish course, the agents prefers to have a vegetable soup to not having a vegetable soup ($s \prec_f \overline{s}$), but if not having a fish course, the agent prefers not to have a vegetable soup ($\overline{v} \prec_{\overline{f}} v$). Finally, having a vegetable soup the agent prefers to drink wine, while prefers not to drink wine otherwise

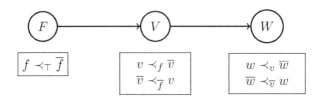

Figure 3.8: CP-network for the dinner example

$(w \prec_v \overline{w}, \overline{w} \prec_{\overline{v}} w)$. Figure 3.8 illustrated how these conditional preferences are arranged to CPTs in the network.

A preference relation $\prec_{CP}^*$ satisfies a CP-network CP if and only if each preference $\dot{v} \prec_{\mathbf{p}} \overline{\mathbf{v}}$ in a $CPT(V, pa(V))$ of CP implies that for each fixed configuration $\mathbf{p}$ of $pa(V)$ and fixed configuration $\mathbf{o}$ of $\Sigma \setminus pa(V) \cup \{V\}$ for each pair $\omega \vDash \dot{v}\mathbf{po}$, $\omega' \vDash \overline{v}\mathbf{po}$ we have

$$\dot{v} \prec_{\mathbf{p}} \overline{\mathbf{v}} \qquad \text{if and only if} \qquad \omega \prec_{CP}^* \omega'. \qquad (3.57)$$

[BBD+04] have shown that there is such a preference relation for every CP-network, that is, each CP-network is *satisfiable*.

The global preference relation of a CP-network CP is the sceptical preference of all CP-satisfying preferences, that is, a world ω is globally preferred to a world ω' in the context of CP if and only if it is preferred in every relation $\prec_{CP}^*$ that satisfies CP, formally

$$\omega \prec_{CP} \omega' \qquad \text{if and only if} \qquad \omega \prec_{CP}^* \omega' \qquad (3.58)$$

for all CP satisfying $\prec_{CP}^*$.

Example 3.54 (Dinner [BBD+04] (continued)). In the dinner example the network is satisfied by two preference relations

$$f\,v\,w \prec_{CP}^{(1)} f\,v\,\overline{w} \prec_{CP}^{(1)} f\,\overline{v}\,\overline{w} \prec_{CP}^{(1)} \underline{f\,\overline{v}\,w}$$
$$\prec_{CP}^{(1)} \underline{\overline{f}\,\overline{v}\,\overline{w}} \prec_{CP}^{(1)} \overline{f}\,\overline{v}\,w \prec_{CP}^{(1)} \overline{f}\,v\,w \prec_{CP}^{(1)} \overline{f}\,v\,\overline{w}$$

$$f\,v\,w \prec_{CP}^{(2)} f\,v\,\overline{w} \prec_{CP}^{(2)} f\,\overline{v}\,\overline{w} \prec_{CP}^{(2)} \underline{\overline{f}\,\overline{v}\,\overline{w}}$$
$$\prec_{CP}^{(2)} \underline{f\,\overline{v}\,w} \prec_{CP}^{(2)} \overline{f}\,\overline{v}\,w \prec_{CP}^{(2)} \overline{f}\,v\,w \prec_{CP}^{(2)} \overline{f}\,v\,\overline{w}$$

which differ in the preference of $f\,\overline{v}\,w$ to $\overline{f}\,\overline{v}\,\overline{w}$, only (highlighted by underlining). These two worlds are incomparable in the global preference relation but share the same neighbours. We write $\{f\,\overline{v}\,w,\overline{f}\,\overline{v}\,\overline{w}\}$ as an element of the preference relation to indicate this, which gives us the global relation

$$f\,v\,w \prec_{CP} f\,v\,\overline{w} \prec_{CP} f\,\overline{v}\,\overline{w} \prec_{CP} \{f\,\overline{v}\,w,\overline{f}\,\overline{v}\,\overline{w}\}$$
$$\prec_{CP} \overline{f}\,\overline{v}\,w \prec_{CP} \overline{f}\,v\,w \prec_{CP} \overline{f}\,v\,\overline{w}.$$

It is clear that $\prec_{CP}$ is neither reflexive not symmetric. The above example is a counterexample for $\prec_{CP}$ being total, and [BBD$^+$04] have shown that $\prec_{CP}$ is transitive. We thus can instantiate preferential models and preferential entailment with $\prec_{CP}$ to obtain a classical stopped preferential model with a respective inference relation as follows.

Definition 3.55 (CP-inference [EFKI16, Definition 4]). Let $\prec_{CP}$ be the global preference relation of a CP-network according to Definition 3.52, that is, $CP = (\Sigma, \mathcal{E}, \{CPT(V, pa(V))\}_{V \in \Sigma})$. We define the preferential model $(\Omega, \vDash, \prec_{CP})$ according to Definition 3.1 and from this obtain an inference relation $\vert\!\sim_{CP}$ by means of Definition 3.6 such that ψ follows under *CP*-preference from ϕ if and only if

$$\phi\vert\!\sim_{CP}\psi \quad \text{iff} \quad \forall\,\omega' \vDash \phi\overline{\psi} \quad \exists\,\omega \vDash \phi\psi \quad \text{such that} \quad \omega \prec_{CP} \omega'. \quad (3.59)$$

Ceteris paribus preference defines an independence property as follows:

Definition 3.56 (Conditional CP-independence [BBD$^+$04]). Let Σ be a set of variables and let $\mathbf{V}, \mathbf{P}, \mathbf{O} \subseteq \Sigma$ be mutually disjoint sets of variables. Let $\prec$ be a preference relation on the possible worlds, $\prec \subseteq \Omega \times \Omega$. $\mathbf{V}$ is *conditionally CP-independent* of $\mathbf{O}$ given $\mathbf{P}$, written as $\mathbf{V} \perp\!\!\!\perp_\prec \mathbf{O} \mid \mathbf{P}$, if and only if for all fixed outcomes $\mathbf{v}, \mathbf{v}', \mathbf{o}, \mathbf{o}', \mathbf{p}$ of $\mathbf{V}, \mathbf{P}, \mathbf{O}$, respectively, we have

$$\mathbf{vop} \prec \mathbf{v'op} \quad \text{if and only if} \quad \mathbf{vo'p} \prec \mathbf{v'o'p}. \quad (3.60)$$

[BBD$^+$04] presupposed an independence property for *CP*-networks as consequence of the satisfiability of CP-networks which is proven formally in [EFKI16]:

Lemma 3.57 ([BBD$^+$04, EFKI16]). Let *CP* be a CP-network over a set of variables Σ with a global preference $\prec_{CP}$. Every vertex $V \in \Sigma$ is conditionally CP-independent from every non-parent vertex given its parents, formally

$$\{V\} \perp\!\!\!\perp_{\prec_{CP}} (\Sigma \setminus pa(V)) \mid pa(V). \tag{3.61}$$

3.7 Interim Summary

This chapter very briefly recalls the basic techniques that provide the foundations of this thesis: From these, preferential inference will be the primary way of defining nonmonotonic inference relations in this thesis, and will be instantiated mainly by OCF, but also using conditional structures and probabilities. Nonetheless other preferential relations can be used to instantiate preferential models, as we already demonstrated for CP-networks. We recalled conditional structures as purely qualitative approach to inductive inference. We further recalled ordinal conditional functions (OCF) which are one of the major basic techniques of this thesis. We demonstrated that OCF satisfy strong formal properties, despite the fact that their algebraic structure and normalisation condition is relatively weak compared to the later recalled probabilities: The latter are taken from the semigroup $\mathbb{R}^+$ of real numbers with addition (+) and multiplication (·), whilst OCF are from the weaker semiring over $\mathbb{N}_0^\infty$ with min as addition (which is, in contrast to +, not invertible) and + as multiplication. This chapter extends the literature insofar as we showed conditional independence with OCF are not characterised by the axiomatisation of conditional independence [Pea88]: even if we showed most the axioms of conditional independence [Pea88] do hold for OCF notwithstanding the noted weaker algebraic structure, the property weak union is violated by conditional κ-independence, in general. This was followed by a brief recollection of probabilities and network approaches to probabilities and complemented with a brief reminder to CP-networks.

Note that this chapter only recalls the different inference relations, and neither discusses their relationship nor gives formal properties of these relations. This will be done as application of the following chapter dealing with properties of nonmonotonic inference relations.

4 Properties of Nonmonotonic Inference Relations

In the previous chapters we already recalled inference relations based on the consistency of knowledge bases, preference orderings, plausibilities and probabilities of the possible worlds. So far, we just juxtaposed these different inference relations, but neither compared them by means of inferential strength nor formal properties. To set up the groundwork for the latter and on this groundwork classify the inference relation presented in the previous chapters is the object of this chapter.

With syntactical inference based on axiom systems we show how the inference relations defined in the previous chapters can be classified with these systems. After that, we recall some selected inference properties from the literature to further differentiate between the different inference relations.

In addition to the groundwork in properties for inference relations, and calculi of nonmonotonic inference, this chapter recalls and elaborates on findings from the articles [KIE12, KIE14] as well as from the unpublished manual [EKIBB18].

4.1 Axiom Systems for Nonmonotonic Reasoning

In this section, we recall the established axiom systems for nonmonotonic inference. These Systems O, C, P, and R have three properties in common, which are used to illustrate the notions and formalisms of the systems as follows. The properties are selected from the more thorough collection [EKIBB18].

4.1.1 Introduction and Common Properties

In its most general way, an inference relation a relation between formulas, which we define as follows:

Definition 4.1 (Syntactical Inference Relation / Operation). An *inference relation* $\mid\sim$ is a binary relation $\cdot\mid\sim\cdot \subseteq \mathfrak{L} \times \mathfrak{L}$ that assigns formulas ψ to formulas ϕ; we write $\phi\mid\sim\psi$ to indicate that ϕ syntactically infers ψ. The associated *inference operation* $C(\cdot) \subseteq \mathfrak{L} \times \mathfrak{P}(\mathfrak{L})$ assigns to a formula ϕ the set of formulas $\mathcal{A} \subseteq \mathfrak{L}$ that can be inferred from ϕ, formally $C(\phi) = \{\psi | \phi\mid\sim\psi\}$. In this way, inference relation and inference operation mutually define each

© Springer-Verlag GmbH Germany, part of Springer Nature 2018
C. Eichhorn, *Rational Reasoning with Finite Conditional Knowledge Bases*, https://doi.org/10.1007/978-3-476-04824-0_4

other by

$$\phi\hspace{-0.5em}\sim\hspace{-0.3em}\psi \qquad\qquad \text{if and only if} \qquad\qquad \psi \in C(\phi). \qquad (4.1)$$

We lift the inference relation and inference operation to sets of formulas by conjunction of the formulas in the set, that is, by defining $\mathcal{A}\hspace{-0.5em}\sim\hspace{-0.3em}\psi$ if and only if $(\bigwedge_{\phi\in\mathcal{A}} \phi)\hspace{-0.5em}\sim\hspace{-0.3em}\psi$ and, likewise, $C(\mathcal{A}) = \{\psi|\mathcal{A}\hspace{-0.5em}\sim\hspace{-0.3em}\psi\}$.

In this way, inference relation and inference operation are defined in parallel to the mutual definition of the entailment relation ($\models$) and consequence operation (Cn) in Section 2.1, but without the entry point of the satisfaction relation between possible worlds and formulas. Thus other definitions of inference relations are needed.

Definition 4.2 (Inference Rule). Let $\mathbf{I} = \{\phi_1\hspace{-0.5em}\sim\hspace{-0.3em}\psi_1, ..., \phi_k\hspace{-0.5em}\sim\hspace{-0.3em}\psi_k\}$ be a set of (nonmonotonic) inferences and let $\iota = \phi\hspace{-0.5em}\sim\hspace{-0.3em}\psi$ be a (nonmonotonic) inference. An inference rule $\zeta = \dfrac{\mathbf{I}}{\iota}$ defines the syntactical derivation of ι from the set $\mathbf{I}$.

Such inferences rules are usually named, as the already discussed rule *Monotony* (M), which is formalised according to this definition as

$$\frac{\phi\hspace{-0.5em}\sim\hspace{-0.3em}\psi}{\phi\chi\hspace{-0.5em}\sim\hspace{-0.3em}\psi}, \qquad (M)$$

stating that with monotony, from $\phi\hspace{-0.5em}\sim\hspace{-0.3em}\psi$ it follows that $\phi\chi\hspace{-0.5em}\sim\hspace{-0.3em}\psi$ for $\phi, \psi \in \mathfrak{L}$ and any $\chi \in \mathfrak{L}$.

A set $\mathcal{C} = \{\zeta_1, ..., \zeta_o\}$ of inferences rules defines an *inference system* such that $\phi\hspace{-0.5em}\sim\hspace{-0.3em}\psi$ follows from a set of inferences $\mathbf{I} = \{\phi_1\hspace{-0.5em}\sim\hspace{-0.3em}\psi_1, ..., \phi_k\hspace{-0.5em}\sim\hspace{-0.3em}\psi_k\}$ under $\mathcal{C}$, written $\mathbf{I} \vdash^{\mathcal{C}} (\phi\hspace{-0.5em}\sim\hspace{-0.3em}\psi)$, if and only if $\phi\hspace{-0.5em}\sim\hspace{-0.3em}\psi$ follows from $\mathbf{I}$ by repeated application of the rules in $\mathcal{C}$.

The *closure of* $\mathbf{I}$ *under* $\mathcal{C}$ is the (non necessarily finite) set

$$Cl_{\mathcal{C}}(\mathbf{I}) = \{\phi\hspace{-0.5em}\sim\hspace{-0.3em}\psi \,|\, \mathbf{I} \vdash^{\mathcal{C}} (\phi\hspace{-0.5em}\sim\hspace{-0.3em}\psi)\} \qquad (4.2)$$

that contains all inferences $\phi\hspace{-0.5em}\sim\hspace{-0.3em}\psi$ that follow from $\mathbf{I}$ by repeated application of the rules in $\mathcal{C}$. Note that $\vdash^{\mathcal{C}}$ only licenses for the inference of nonmonotonic inferences $\phi\hspace{-0.5em}\sim\hspace{-0.3em}\psi$, not for formulas ϕ.

In the following section we recall concrete inference systems; we here recall inference rules that all these systems have in common.

REFLEXIVITY (REF) [Ada65]. Every formula is inferred by itself. This property is called *Reflexivity* (REF). This axiom is formally written as

$$\frac{\phi}{\phi\hspace{-0.3em}\sim\hspace{-0.3em}\phi}. \tag{REF}$$

We already noted that inference rules license to infer inferences from inferences, only. Here, (REF) bridges the gap between formulas and nonmonotonic inferences in providing an entry point such that even if the inference rules infer only nonmonotonic inferences, having (REF) licenses for inferring them from formulas.

In this dissertation, inference is a concept that is set up upon an underlying propositional logic. It is reasonable to assume that such an underlying concept is compatible with the inference set up upon it. The following two properties ensure that semantical equivalence and entailment on the object level behaves in such a way.

LEFT LOGICAL EQUIVALENCE (LLE) [KLM90] ensures that a nonmonotonic inference relation behaves "naturally" with respect to semantically equivalent premises: It states that semantically equivalent premises infer identical conclusions, that is,

$$\frac{\phi \equiv \psi \quad \text{and} \quad \psi\hspace{-0.3em}\sim\hspace{-0.3em}\chi}{\phi\hspace{-0.3em}\sim\hspace{-0.3em}\chi} \tag{LLE}$$

Note that (LLE) is valid for non-inferences, as well.

Lemma 4.3. From (LLE) it follows that $\dfrac{\phi \equiv \psi, \phi\hspace{-0.3em}\not\sim\hspace{-0.3em}\chi}{\psi\hspace{-0.3em}\not\sim\hspace{-0.3em}\chi}$.

RIGHT WEAKENING (RW) [KLM90] states that the set of formulas which can be inferred nonmonotonically from ϕ contains all formulas that are entailed classically from the nonmonotone conclusions of ϕ, formally

$$\frac{\phi\hspace{-0.3em}\sim\hspace{-0.3em}\psi, \psi \vDash \chi}{\phi\hspace{-0.3em}\sim\hspace{-0.3em}\chi}. \tag{RW}$$

In other words, an inference relation that satisfies (RW) behaves transitively with respect to classical entailment.

(REF)		For all	ϕ	it holds that	$\phi\hspace{-1pt}\mid\hspace{-5pt}\sim\hspace{-1pt}\phi$
(VCM)	$\phi\hspace{-1pt}\mid\hspace{-5pt}\sim\hspace{-1pt}\psi\chi$			implies	$\phi\psi\hspace{-1pt}\mid\hspace{-5pt}\sim\hspace{-1pt}\chi$
(RW)	$\phi\hspace{-1pt}\mid\hspace{-5pt}\sim\hspace{-1pt}\psi$	and	$\psi \vDash \chi$	imply	$\phi\hspace{-1pt}\mid\hspace{-5pt}\sim\hspace{-1pt}\chi$
(LLE)	$\phi \equiv \psi$	and	$\psi\hspace{-1pt}\mid\hspace{-5pt}\sim\hspace{-1pt}\chi$	imply	$\phi\hspace{-1pt}\mid\hspace{-5pt}\sim\hspace{-1pt}\chi$
(WAND)	$\phi\hspace{-1pt}\mid\hspace{-5pt}\sim\hspace{-1pt}\psi$	and	$\phi\overline{\chi}\hspace{-1pt}\mid\hspace{-5pt}\sim\hspace{-1pt}\chi$	imply	$\phi\hspace{-1pt}\mid\hspace{-5pt}\sim\hspace{-1pt}\psi\chi$
(WOR)	$\phi\psi\hspace{-1pt}\mid\hspace{-5pt}\sim\hspace{-1pt}\chi$	and	$\phi\overline{\psi}\hspace{-1pt}\mid\hspace{-5pt}\sim\hspace{-1pt}\chi$	imply	$\phi\hspace{-1pt}\mid\hspace{-5pt}\sim\hspace{-1pt}\chi$

Figure 4.1: Axioms of System O

4.1.2 System O

We start presenting the established axiom systems for nonmonotonic inference with the most cautious one: *System O* [KLM90, Haw07]. This system consists of the axioms recalled in Figure 4.1, these are the already discussed properties (REF), (RW) and (LLE) and three new properties (WOR), (WAND) and (VCM) which we recall in the following.

WEAK OR (WOR) [HM07] states that given both $\phi\psi$ and $\phi\overline{\psi}$ infer χ, χ can be inferred solely from ϕ, formally

$$\frac{\phi\psi\hspace{-1pt}\mid\hspace{-5pt}\sim\hspace{-1pt}\chi, \phi\overline{\psi}\hspace{-1pt}\mid\hspace{-5pt}\sim\hspace{-1pt}\chi}{\phi\hspace{-1pt}\mid\hspace{-5pt}\sim\hspace{-1pt}\chi}. \tag{WOR}$$

This property is also known by the name of *Proof by case differentiation* (DIFF) in the literature [Mak94].

WEAK AND (WAND) [HM07]. If there is a formula ϕ that, in the sense of [Haw07, Page 630] "makes a formula χ certain", that is, ϕ entails χ *even if* $\overline{\chi}$ *is added*, χ can be added to every conclusion drawn from ϕ.

$$\frac{\phi\hspace{-1pt}\mid\hspace{-5pt}\sim\hspace{-1pt}\psi, \phi\overline{\chi}\hspace{-1pt}\mid\hspace{-5pt}\sim\hspace{-1pt}\chi}{\phi\hspace{-1pt}\mid\hspace{-5pt}\sim\hspace{-1pt}\psi\chi} \tag{WAND}$$

VERY CAUTIOUS MONOTONY (VCM) [HM07] This strongly weakened scion of Monotony, also known as also known as *Conjunctive Cautious Monotony* [Boc01], states that if from a formula ϕ a conjunction $\psi\chi$ can be inferred then one of the conjuncts can still be inferred if the other is added to the premise, formally

$$\frac{\phi\hspace{1pt}\vdash\hspace{-6pt}\sim\psi\chi}{\phi\psi\hspace{1pt}\vdash\hspace{-6pt}\sim\chi}. \tag{VCM}$$

The inference relation that rises from the calculus obtained from these axioms is defined as follows:

Definition 4.4 (System O Inference). Let $\phi, \psi \in \mathfrak{L}$ be formulas, and let $\mathbf{I}$ be a set of inferences $\phi_i\hspace{1pt}\vdash\hspace{-6pt}\sim\psi_i$. The inference $\phi\hspace{1pt}\vdash\hspace{-6pt}\sim\psi$ follows from $\mathbf{I}$ by System O, written $\mathbf{I} \vdash^O (\phi\hspace{1pt}\vdash\hspace{-6pt}\sim\psi)$, if and only if ψ can be derived by from ϕ by iteratively and repeatedly applying the axioms (confer [ST12]). We further define ψ to follow from ϕ in the context of $\mathbf{I}$ under System O, written $\phi\hspace{1pt}\vdash\hspace{-6pt}\sim_{\mathbf{I}}^O \psi$, if and only if $\mathbf{I} \vdash^O (\phi\hspace{1pt}\vdash\hspace{-6pt}\sim\psi)$. Additionally, presupposing the property (DI) to hold, we define inference from the background knowledge $\Delta = \{(\psi_1|\phi_1), \ldots, (\psi_n|\phi_n)\} \subseteq (\mathfrak{L} \mid \mathfrak{L})$ such that ψ follows from ϕ in System O in the context of Δ, written $\phi\hspace{1pt}\vdash\hspace{-6pt}\sim_{\Delta}^O \psi$, if and only if given $\mathbf{I} = \{\phi_i\hspace{1pt}\vdash\hspace{-6pt}\sim\psi_i|(\phi_i|\phi_i) \in \Delta\}$ we have $\phi\hspace{1pt}\vdash\hspace{-6pt}\sim_{\mathbf{I}}^O \psi$.

In System O, two properties relevant for this dissertation can be derived:

SUPRACLASSICALITY (SCL) [Mak94], stating that the nonmonotonic inference from a premise ϕ covers all classical entailments from ϕ, formally

$$\frac{\phi \vDash \psi}{\phi\hspace{1pt}\vdash\hspace{-6pt}\sim\psi}. \tag{SCL}$$

Proposition 4.5 ([Boc01]). (SCL) can be derived from (REF) and (RW).

DEDUCTION (DED) [Boc01], introduces the so-called "tough half of the deduction theorem"[1] to nonmonotonic inferences:

$$\frac{\phi\psi\hspace{1pt}\vdash\hspace{-6pt}\sim\chi}{\phi\hspace{1pt}\vdash\hspace{-6pt}\sim(\phi \Rightarrow \chi)} \tag{DED}$$

Proposition 4.6 ([KLM90]). (DED) can be derived from (SCL), (WOR), and (RW).

Figure 4.2 illustrates the axioms of System O and the inference properties derivable in this calculus. As already mentioned, this thesis discusses only

---

[1]   In distinction to the "easy half of the deduction theorem", $\phi\hspace{1pt}\vdash\hspace{-6pt}\sim(\psi \Rightarrow \chi)$ implies $\phi\psi\hspace{1pt}\vdash\hspace{-6pt}\sim\chi$, which implies Monotony [KLM90].

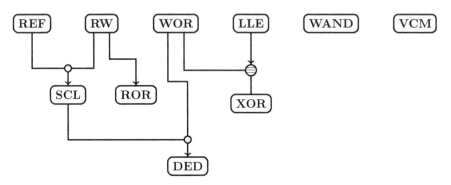

Figure 4.2: Axioms (shaded) and derived properties of System O

selected properties from the plethora of inference properties. For System O and the derivable properties, this means that we meet (SCL) and (DED) in the following, an overview over all properties of System O is given in Table 4.1.

To illustrate System O with a concrete semantic, we use threshold inference.

Proposition 4.7 ([Haw07]). Threshold inference satisfies System O.

Example 4.8. We recall Example 3.45 on behalf of illustrating the properties of System O. In the probability distribution of this example (see Table 3.7 on Page 67) we find:

$$P(p|p) = 1 \qquad\qquad \text{and therefore} \qquad\qquad p \mathbin{\vrule width0.7pt\relax\!\approx}^{P,\geq 0.5} p$$

as required by (REF), and

$$P(\overline{f}|p) \approx 0.62 \qquad \text{and therefore} \qquad p \mathbin{\vrule width0.7pt\relax\!\approx}^{P,\geq 0.5} \overline{f}$$
$$P((f \Rightarrow b)|p) \approx 0.94 \qquad \text{and therefore} \qquad p \mathbin{\vrule width0.7pt\relax\!\approx}^{P,\geq 0.5} (f \Rightarrow b)$$

so, according to (RW), from $p \mathbin{\vrule width0.7pt\relax\!\approx}^{P,\geq 0.5} \overline{f}$ and $\overline{f} \vDash (b \vee \overline{f})$ (and $(b \vee \overline{f}) \equiv (f \Rightarrow b))$ we obtain $p \mathbin{\vrule width0.7pt\relax\!\approx}^{P,\geq 0.5} (f \Rightarrow b)$. (LLE) must hold in threshold acceptance as $P(\phi) = P(\psi)$ for all $\phi \equiv \psi$. In accordance with (WOR), we have

$$P(b|p\overline{f}) \approx 0.88 \qquad \text{and therefore} \qquad p\overline{f} \mathrel{\vert\!\sim}^{P,\geq 0.5} b,$$

$$P(b|pf) \approx 0.84 \qquad \text{and therefore} \qquad pf \mathrel{\vert\!\sim}^{P,\geq 0.5} b,$$

$$P(b|p) \approx 0.87 \qquad \text{and therefore} \qquad p \mathrel{\vert\!\sim}^{P,\geq 0.5} b,$$

and, following (VCM),

$$P(b\overline{f}|p) \approx 0.54 \qquad \text{and therefore} \qquad p \mathrel{\vert\!\sim}^{P,\geq 0.5} b\overline{f}$$

$$P(b|p\overline{f}) \approx 0.88 \qquad \text{and therefore} \qquad p\overline{f} \mathrel{\vert\!\sim}^{P,\geq 0.5} b.$$

Regarding (WAND) we obtain that $P(\chi|\phi\overline{\chi}) = 0$ for all $\phi, \chi \in \mathfrak{L}$, therefore the prerequisite for the implication (WAND) is false and (WAND) holds trivially. Finally, for the selected derived properties we note that $pb \models p$ and find, in accordance with (SCL),

$$P(p|pb) = 1 \qquad \text{and therefore} \qquad pb \mathrel{\vert\!\sim}^{P,\geq 0.5} p,$$

and, finally, following the property (DED),

$$P(b|p\overline{f}) \approx 0.88 \qquad \text{and therefore} \qquad p\overline{f} \mathrel{\vert\!\sim}^{P,\geq 0.5} b,$$

$$P((\overline{f} \Rightarrow b)|p) \approx 0.93 \qquad \text{and therefore} \qquad p \mathrel{\vert\!\sim}^{P,\geq 0.5} (\overline{f} \Rightarrow b).$$

Extending the axioms of System O with the following property we obtain System O$^+$ [ST12].

NEGATION RATIONALITY (NR) [FL96] states that if a formula χ can be inferred from ϕ, then it must be possible to infer χ from at least one of the premises $\phi\psi$ or $\phi\overline{\psi}$ for any formula $\psi \in \mathfrak{L}$, formally

$$\phi \mathrel{\vert\!\sim} \chi \quad \text{implies} \quad \phi\psi \mathrel{\vert\!\sim} \chi \quad \text{or} \quad \phi\overline{\psi} \mathrel{\vert\!\sim} \chi \quad \text{for all } \phi \in \mathfrak{L}. \qquad \text{(NR)}$$

In its contrapositive form, this property can be interpreted to state that if a property cannot be inferred from any sub-population, it also cannot be inferred from the population, formally

$$\phi\psi \mathrel{\vert\!\not\sim} \chi \quad \text{and} \quad \phi\overline{\psi} \mathrel{\vert\!\not\sim} \chi \quad \text{imply} \quad \phi \mathrel{\vert\!\not\sim} \chi.$$

Proposition 4.9 ([EKIBB18, Proposition 65 / Corollary 66]). Threshold inference satisfies System O$^+$.

Note that by the proof of [Haw07] we obtain that for every $x \in (0,1]$, probabilistic threshold inference satisfies all axioms of System O and thus is a complete semantics for System O, that is, $\phi \vdash^O \psi$ implies $\phi \mathrel{\vert\!\approx}^{P, \geq x} \psi$. But this inference system is not correct for this calculus, that is, $\phi \mathrel{\vert\!\approx}^{P, \geq x} \psi$ does not necessarily imply $\phi \vdash^O \psi$, which is a direct conclusion of Proposition 4.9[2].

Corollary 4.10. Threshold inference licenses for inferences not possible in System O.

In the following section of this chapter we see that threshold inference is nonetheless useful for illustrating calculus of System O, as it is not strong enough to satisfy any calculus less cautious with respect to monotony. With the argumentation of [ST12] we therefore see that this may not be a correct semantics for this calculus, but as no correct and complete semantics is known[3], it is as close as we can get for the time being.

---

[2]   In the proof in [Haw07, p.635], this is shown by proving that threshold inference satisfies (OR) (Page 95). With Proposition 4.9, we have an additional property satisfied by this inference but not by System O.

[3]   At least not known to the author of this thesis and the literature consulted with respect to the formal properties of nonmonotonic inference relations at the time this thesis was written; this was also mentioned by [ST12].

Property	Abbrev.						Reference	
Deduction	(DED)	$\phi\psi\mathrel{|\!\sim}\chi$			implies	$\phi\mathrel{|\!\approx}(\psi\Rightarrow\chi)$	[Boc01]	
Exclusive Or	(XOR)	$\phi\mathrel{|\!\sim}\chi,\ \psi\mathrel{|\!\sim}\chi$	and	$\models\overline{(\phi\psi)}$	imply	$(\phi\vee\psi)\mathrel{|\!\sim}\chi$	[HM07]	p. 79
Left Logical Equivalence	(LLE)	$\phi\equiv\psi$	and	$\phi\mathrel{|\!\approx}\chi$	imply	$\psi\mathrel{|\!\approx}\chi$	[KLM90]	p. 79
Reflexivity	(REF) For all	ϕ			it holds that	$\phi\mathrel{|\!\approx}\phi$	[KLM90]	
Right Or	(ROR)	$\phi\mathrel{|\!\approx}\psi\chi$	implies	$\phi\mathrel{|\!\approx}\psi$	or	$\phi\mathrel{|\!\approx}\chi$	[EKIBB18]	
Right Weakening	(RW)	$\phi\mathrel{|\!\approx}\psi$	and	$\psi\models\chi$	imply	$\phi\mathrel{|\!\approx}\chi$	[KLM90]	p. 79
Supraclassicality	(SCL)	$\phi\models\psi$			implies	$\phi\mathrel{|\!\approx}\psi$	[Mak94]	p. 81
Very Cautious Monotony	(VCM)	$\phi\mathrel{|\!\sim}\psi\chi$	and	$\phi\chi\mathrel{|\!\sim}\chi$	implies	$\phi\psi\mathrel{|\!\sim}\chi$	[HM07]	p. 81
Weak And	(WAND)	$\phi\mathrel{|\!\sim}\psi$	and	$\phi\mathrel{|\!\sim}\psi$	imply	$\phi\wedge\psi\mathrel{|\!\sim}\chi$	[HM07]	p. 80
Weak Or	(WOR) (also (DIFF))	$\phi\psi\mathrel{|\!\sim}\chi$	and	$\phi\psi\mathrel{|\!\sim}\chi$	imply	$\phi\mathrel{|\!\sim}\chi$	[HM07]	p. 80

Table 4.1: Alphabetical overview over all properties of System O; as not all properties are described in this thesis, a reference to additional literature is added to each property; properties contained in this thesis are referred to by the page number of their formal definition.

4.1.3 System C

Strictly stronger with respect to monotone properties, but incomparable to System O by its lack of disjunctive property is *System C*, the system to be recalled in this section. This system is sometimes called the "basis for plausible reasoning" [Gab85] and is closely tied to the preferential relation of preferential models and thus preferential inference [Mak94, Observation 3.4.3]. The axioms of System C [KLM90] consists of the axioms recalled in Figure 4.3, these are the already defined properties (REF), (RW) and (LLE) and two properties (CM) and (CUT) which are recalled as follows.

CAUTIOUS MONOTONY (CM) [KLM90], also known under the name of *Cumulative Monotony* [Mak88] or *triangulation*[4], is, as its name implies, a weak form of (M) and states that the inference relation behaves monotone with respect to formulas that are inferable. That is, a premise ϕ can be extended by formulas that can be inferred from ϕ, without the danger of rendering other inferences impossible, according to the intuition that "learning a new fact that could have been plausibly concluded anyway should not invalidate previous conclusions" [KLM90, Page 12].

$$\frac{\phi\mid\sim\psi,\ \phi\mid\sim\chi}{\phi\psi\mid\sim\chi} \tag{CM}$$

Proposition 4.11 ([EKIBB18, Proposition 56]). Given (RW), (VCM) is a consequence of (CM).

In Section 4.1.2 we already mentioned that threshold inference is not strong enough to satisfy any calculus less cautious than System O. This statement now can be grounded with the following observation.

Observation 4.12 ([EKIBB18, Proposition 67]). Threshold inference does not satisfy (CM).

We give an example for this as follows.

Example 4.13. Let $\Sigma = \{A, B, C\}$ with a probability distribution as given in Table 4.2. Here we have $a\mid\sim^{P,\geq 0.6}b$ because $P(b|a) \approx 0.65 \geq 0.6$ and also

---

[4]   Secondary source: Judea Pearl and Hector Geffner, Probabilistic semantics for a subset of default reasoning. TR CSD 8700XX, R-93-III, Computer Science Department, UCLA, March 1988 via [KLM90].

(REF)		For all	ϕ	it holds that	$\phi \vdash\!\!\sim \phi$
(CUT)	$\phi \vdash\!\!\sim \psi$	and	$\phi\psi \vdash\!\!\sim \chi$	imply	$\phi \vdash\!\!\sim \chi$
(CM)	$\phi \vdash\!\!\sim \psi$	and	$\phi \vdash\!\!\sim \chi$	imply	$\phi\psi \vdash\!\!\sim \chi$
(RW)	$\phi \vdash\!\!\sim \psi$	and	$\psi \vDash \chi$	imply	$\phi \vdash\!\!\sim \chi$
(LLE)	$\phi \equiv \psi$	and	$\psi \vdash\!\!\sim \chi$	imply	$\phi \vdash\!\!\sim \chi$

Figure 4.3: Axioms of System C

Table 4.2: Probability distribution of Example 4.13 to show that threshold inference does not satisfy (CM)

ω	$a\,b\,c$	$a\,b\,\bar{c}$	$a\,\bar{b}\,c$	$a\,\bar{b}\,\bar{c}$	$\bar{a}\,b\,c$	$\bar{a}\,b\,\bar{c}$	$\bar{a}\,\bar{b}\,c$	$\bar{a}\,\bar{b}\,\bar{c}$
$P(\omega)$	0.24	0.28	0.26	0.02	0.04	0.13	0.01	0.02

$a \vdash\!\!\sim^{P, \geq 0.6} c$ because $P(c|a) \approx 0.63 \geq 0.6$ but $P(c|ab) \approx 0.46 < 0.6$ and thus $ab \not\vdash\!\!\sim^{P, \geq 0.6} c$ in contrast to (CM).

Hence we need another semantic to illustrate System C, for instance preferential inference with a preference relation that is stoppered [Mak94, Observation 3.4.3]. As we will see in Section 4.3, structural inference is stronger as demanded, but is the least strong of the systems presented save for threshold inference. So choosing this inference relation gives us a better insight as choosing an even stronger one.

Example 4.14. We use the formalisation of the full running example (Example 2.1) in Example 2.4 and add the conditional statements that being from the class of penguins and being from the class of chicken is mutually exclusive. So our knowledge base is

$$\Delta = \left\{ \begin{array}{llll} \delta_1 : (f|b), & \delta_2 : (w|b), & \delta_3 : (b|p), & \delta_4 : (\overline{f}|p), \\ \delta_5 : (b|c), & \delta_6 : (\overline{f}|cb), & \delta_7 : (\overline{c}|p), & \delta_8 : (\overline{p}|c) \end{array} \right\}.$$

Figure 4.4 illustrates the preference relation defined by structural preference on the worlds with this knowledge base.

With this preference relation and the resulting structural inference according to Definition 3.14 we can in the following illustrate the to be presented selected properties of System C.

Table 4.3: Verification/falsification table for the running example modelled in Example 4.14 regarding the possible worlds and conditionals in the knowledge base, and the resulting conditional structure $\sigma(\omega)$ for each world ω.

ω	verifies	falsifies	$\sigma(\omega)$
$p\,c\,b\,f\,w$	r_1,r_2,r_3,r_5	r_4,r_6,r_7,r_8	$a_1^+ a_2^+ a_3^- a_4^- a_5^- a_6^- a_7^- a_8^-$
$p\,c\,b\,f\,\bar{w}$	r_1,r_3,r_5	r_2,r_4,r_6,r_7,r_8	$a_1^+ a_2^- a_3^- a_4^- a_5^- a_6^- a_7^- a_8^-$
$p\,c\,b\,\bar{f}\,w$	r_2,r_3,r_4,r_5,r_6	r_1,r_7,r_8	$a_1^- a_2^+ a_3^+ a_4^+ a_5^+ a_6^+ a_7^- a_8^-$
$p\,c\,b\,\bar{f}\,\bar{w}$	r_3,r_4,r_5,r_6	r_1,r_2,r_7,r_8	$a_1^- a_2^- a_3^+ a_4^+ a_5^+ a_6^+ a_7^- a_8^-$
$p\,c\,\bar{b}\,f\,w$	—	r_3,r_4,r_5,r_7,r_8	$a_3^- a_4^- a_5^- a_7^- a_8^-$
$p\,c\,\bar{b}\,f\,\bar{w}$	—	r_3,r_4,r_5,r_7,r_8	$a_3^- a_4^- a_5^- a_7^- a_8^-$
$p\,c\,\bar{b}\,\bar{f}\,w$	r_4	r_3,r_5,r_7,r_8	$a_3^- a_4^+ a_5^- a_7^- a_8^-$
$p\,c\,\bar{b}\,\bar{f}\,\bar{w}$	r_4	r_3,r_5,r_7,r_8	$a_3^- a_4^+ a_5^- a_7^- a_8^-$
$p\,\bar{c}\,b\,f\,w$	r_1,r_2,r_3,r_7	r_4	$a_1^+ a_2^+ a_3^+ a_4^- a_7^+$
$p\,\bar{c}\,b\,f\,\bar{w}$	r_1,r_3,r_7	r_2,r_4	$a_1^+ a_2^- a_3^+ a_4^- a_7^+$
$p\,\bar{c}\,b\,\bar{f}\,w$	r_2,r_3,r_4,r_7	r_1	$a_1^- a_2^+ a_3^+ a_4^+ a_7^+$
$p\,\bar{c}\,b\,\bar{f}\,\bar{w}$	r_3,r_4,r_7	r_1,r_2	$a_1^- a_2^- a_3^+ a_4^+ a_7^+$
$p\,\bar{c}\,\bar{b}\,f\,w$	r_7	r_3,r_4	$a_3^- a_4^- a_7^+$
$p\,\bar{c}\,\bar{b}\,f\,\bar{w}$	r_7	r_3,r_4	$a_3^- a_4^- a_7^+$
$p\,\bar{c}\,\bar{b}\,\bar{f}\,w$	r_4,r_7	r_3	$a_3^- a_4^+ a_7^+$
$p\,\bar{c}\,\bar{b}\,\bar{f}\,\bar{w}$	r_4,r_7	r_3	$a_3^- a_4^+ a_7^+$
$\bar{p}\,c\,b\,f\,w$	r_1,r_2,r_5,r_8	r_6	$a_1^+ a_2^+ a_5^- a_6^- a_8^+$
$\bar{p}\,c\,b\,f\,\bar{w}$	r_1,r_5,r_8	r_2,r_6	$a_1^+ a_2^- a_5^- a_6^- a_8^+$
$\bar{p}\,c\,b\,\bar{f}\,w$	r_2,r_5,r_6,r_8	r_1	$a_1^- a_2^+ a_5^- a_6^+ a_8^+$
$\bar{p}\,c\,b\,\bar{f}\,\bar{w}$	r_5,r_6,r_8	r_1,r_2	$a_1^- a_2^- a_5^- a_6^+ a_8^+$
$\bar{p}\,c\,\bar{b}\,f\,w$	r_8	r_5	$a_5^- a_8^+$
$\bar{p}\,c\,\bar{b}\,f\,\bar{w}$	r_8	r_5	$a_5^- a_8^+$
$\bar{p}\,c\,\bar{b}\,\bar{f}\,w$	r_8	r_5	$a_5^- a_8^+$
$\bar{p}\,c\,\bar{b}\,\bar{f}\,\bar{w}$	r_8	r_5	$a_5^- a_8^+$
$\bar{p}\,\bar{c}\,b\,f\,w$	r_1,r_2	—	$a_1^+ a_2^+$
$\bar{p}\,\bar{c}\,b\,f\,\bar{w}$	r_1	r_2	$a_1^+ a_2^-$
$\bar{p}\,\bar{c}\,b\,\bar{f}\,w$	r_2	r_1	$a_1^- a_2^+$
$\bar{p}\,\bar{c}\,b\,\bar{f}\,\bar{w}$	—	r_1,r_2	$a_1^- a_2^-$
$\bar{p}\,\bar{c}\,\bar{b}\,f\,w$	—	—	1
$\bar{p}\,\bar{c}\,\bar{b}\,f\,\bar{w}$	—	—	1
$\bar{p}\,\bar{c}\,\bar{b}\,\bar{f}\,w$	—	—	1
$\bar{p}\,\bar{c}\,\bar{b}\,\bar{f}\,\bar{w}$	—	—	1

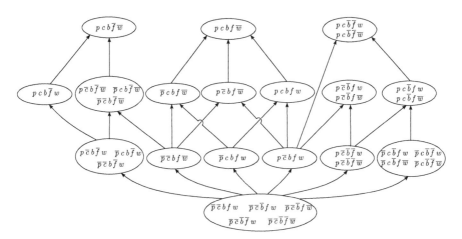

Figure 4.4: Structural preference of worlds in the extended penguin example defined in Example 4.14 (confer [EKIBB18]). Each possible worlds in a source vertex of an arrow is preferred to all possible worlds in the target vertex. Possible worlds without any connecting edge are not comparable, as are possible worlds within one vertex. Note that structural preference is transitive [KIE12].

Example 4.15 (Illustration of (CM)). In Example 4.14 we find that birds usually have wings, $b \hspace{-0.5em}\mid\sim^{\sigma}_{\Delta} w$, because for every $\omega' \models b\overline{w}$ we find a $\prec^{\sigma}_{\Delta}$-preferred world $\omega \models bw$ (for instance the world $\overline{p}\,\overline{c}\,b\,f\,w$). We also find that birds usually fly, $b \hspace{-0.5em}\mid\sim^{\sigma}_{\Delta} f$, because for every $\omega' \models b\overline{f}$ we find a $\prec^{\sigma}_{\Delta}$-preferred world $\omega \models bf$ (again, for instance, the world $\overline{p}\,\overline{c}\,b\,f\,w$). With (CM) we therefore should be able to infer that winged birds usually fly, $bw \hspace{-0.5em}\mid\sim^{\sigma}_{\Delta} f$, which is indeed the case with the same argumentation as above.

CUMULATIVE TRANSITIVITY (CUT) [KLM90, HM07] is a very weak form of transitivity, stating that inferences from a given premise and its inferables are inferable directly by the premise, formally

$$\frac{\phi \hspace{-0.5em}\mid\sim \psi, \ \phi\psi \hspace{-0.5em}\mid\sim \chi}{\phi \hspace{-0.5em}\mid\sim \chi} \qquad (\text{CUT})$$

Example 4.16 (Illustration of (CUT)). To illustrate (CUT) in Example 4.14 we find $b \hspace{-0.5em}\mid\sim^{\sigma}_{\Delta} w$ and also $bw \hspace{-0.5em}\mid\sim^{\sigma}_{\Delta} f$, and, in accordance to (CUT), also $b \hspace{-0.5em}\mid\sim^{\sigma}_{\Delta} f$ (see Example 4.15 for a detailed argumentation about the individual preferences).

The most prominent property that can be derived from the axioms of System C is the for this calculus eponymous property Cumulativity.

CUMULATIVITY (CUM) [Mak94] states that extending the premise with knowledge that can be entailed does not change the possible inferences, that is,

$$\text{Given} \quad \phi\hspace{-0.3em}\mid\hspace{-0.6em}\sim\hspace{-0.3em}\psi, \qquad \phi\hspace{-0.3em}\mid\hspace{-0.6em}\sim\hspace{-0.3em}\chi \quad \text{if and only if} \quad \phi\psi\hspace{-0.3em}\mid\hspace{-0.6em}\sim\hspace{-0.3em}\chi. \qquad \text{(CUM)}$$

This property is a direct consequence of (CM) (the "only if" part) and (CUT) (the "if" part); Examples 4.15 and 4.16 serve as examples for either direction of (CUM). With (CUM) we have a property that, according to [Mak94], licenses for drawing conclusions without loosing inferential power (CM) and at the same time not amplifying it too much (CUT), a behaviour that is called "stable" by [Mak94].

With System C, it is possible to join the conclusions of two inferences, given they are drawn from the same premise:

AND [KLM90] is a property stating that if from a formula ϕ two different formulas can be inferred, the conjunction of both formulas can also be inferred from ϕ, formally

$$\frac{\phi\hspace{-0.3em}\mid\hspace{-0.6em}\sim\hspace{-0.3em}\psi, \phi\hspace{-0.3em}\mid\hspace{-0.6em}\sim\hspace{-0.3em}\chi}{\phi\hspace{-0.3em}\mid\hspace{-0.6em}\sim\hspace{-0.3em}\psi\chi.} \qquad \text{(AND)}$$

Example 4.17 (Illustration of (AND)). We again use Example 4.14 to illustrate this property. As it has been discussed by previous examples, from birds we can structurally infer both that they have wings and that they can fly, $b\hspace{-0.3em}\approx^{\sigma}_{\Delta}w$ and $b\hspace{-0.3em}\approx^{\sigma}_{\Delta}f$. With (AND), we should also be able to infer them to be winged flyers, $b\hspace{-0.3em}\approx^{\sigma}_{\Delta}fw$, and indeed we find the world $\overline{p}\,\overline{c}\,b\,f\,w \vDash bfw$ in the $\prec^{\sigma}_{\Delta}$-minimal worlds, and no world one satisfying $b\,f\,\overline{w}$, $b\,\overline{f}\,w$, or $b\,\overline{f}\,\overline{w}$ to be $\prec^{\sigma}_{\Delta}$-minimal, so this inference holds.

As (CM) is a stronger than (VCM) one could assume that (AND) was also stronger than (WAND). We already moved preferential inference close to System O inference, and so show that every preferential inference relation satisfies (WAND) trivially, because for the inference of a classical preferential model, the second premise of (WAND) expands to

$$\text{For each } \omega' \vDash \phi\overline{\chi}\chi \text{ there is an } \omega \vDash \phi\chi \text{ such that } \omega \prec \omega'. \qquad (4.3)$$

As $\phi\overline{\chi}\chi \equiv \bot$, this is vacuously true, because $Mod(\phi\overline{\chi}\chi)$ is empty. This means even if (WAND) holds in System C, it cannot be attributed to be an implication of (AND) more than of any other property.

The inference rule Modus Ponens (MP) is an important property of classical logic and classical inference. Not least because of that, a great amount of psychological studies regarding human inference and human rationality involve (MP). We here just mention [Was68, Byr89], but this thesis will turn to this in Chapter 8. Because of that, a "Modus Ponens like" inference rule is desirable, in the main. Here, the following property introduces deduction into nonmonotonic inference relations.

MODUS PONENS IN THE CONSEQUENCE (MPC) [KLM90] licenses for a weak form of deduction into the nonmonotonic System C. (MPC) states that if from a formula both a material implication and the premise of this implication can be inferred, then the conclusion of the implication can also be inferred, formally

$$\frac{\phi\hspace{-0.5mm}\mid\hspace{-2mm}\sim (\psi \Rightarrow \chi)\,,\phi\hspace{-0.5mm}\mid\hspace{-2mm}\sim\psi}{\phi\hspace{-0.5mm}\mid\hspace{-2mm}\sim\chi}. \tag{MPC}$$

We illustrate this property with the running example.

Example 4.18. In Example 4.14 we have $b\hspace{-0.5mm}\mid\hspace{-2mm}\sim_{\Delta}^{\sigma}(\overline{c} \Rightarrow \overline{p})$ because $\overline{p}\,\overline{c}\,b\,f\,w \models (b \wedge (\overline{c} \Rightarrow \overline{p}))$ and this world is one of the $\prec_{\Delta}^{\sigma}$-minimal worlds in this example, whereas neither world ω' with $\omega' \models p\,b\,\overline{c}$ is minimal. We also have $b\hspace{-0.5mm}\mid\hspace{-2mm}\sim_{\Delta}^{\sigma}\overline{c}$ for the same reason (and minimal world). Thus by (MPC) we should have $b\hspace{-0.5mm}\mid\hspace{-2mm}\sim_{\Delta}^{\sigma}\overline{p}$, and indeed $\overline{p}\,\overline{c}\,b\,f\,w \models b\overline{p}$ is a model which is $\prec_{\Delta}^{\sigma}$-preferred to all $\omega' \models bp$.

Modus Ponens in the consequence is derivable in System C, as we formally state as follows.

Proposition 4.19 ([KLM90]). (MPC) follows from (AND) and (RW).

Finally, we recall a property which ensures that, if from a formula inconsistent conclusions can be drawn, this formula is nonmonotonically mapped to the inconsistency:

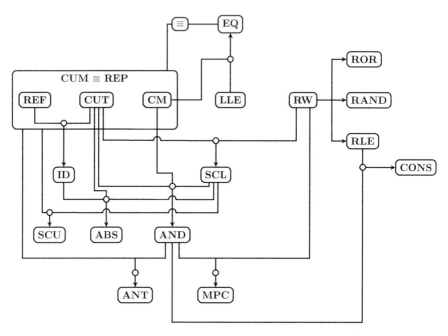

Figure 4.5: Axioms (shaded) and derived properties of System C [EKIBB18]

CONSISTENCY (CONS) [Boc01] states that if from a formula ϕ a formula ψ and its negation can be inferred, this formula should lead to $\bot$.

$$\frac{\phi\mathbin{|\!\sim}\psi, \phi\mathbin{|\!\sim}\overline{\psi}}{\phi\mathbin{|\!\sim}\bot}. \tag{CONS}$$

Proposition 4.20. (CONS) follows from (AND) and (RW).

A list of properties derivable in System C is given in Table 4.4; Figure 4.5 shows how these properties are related. We define the inference relation of this calculus in parallel to the one of System O in Definition 4.4.

Definition 4.21 (System C Inference). Let $\phi, \psi \in \mathfrak{L}$ be formulas, and let $\mathbf{I}$ be a set of inferences $\phi_i\mathbin{|\!\sim}\psi_i$. The inference $\phi\mathbin{|\!\sim}\psi$ follows from $\mathbf{I}$ by System C, written $\mathbf{I} \vdash^C (\phi\mathbin{|\!\sim}\psi)$ if and only if ψ can be derived by from ϕ by iteratively and repeatedly applying the axioms. We further define ψ to follow from ϕ in the context of $\mathbf{I}$ under System C, written $\phi\mathbin{|\!\sim}_{\mathbf{I}}^C \psi$, if and only if $\mathbf{I} \vdash^C (\phi\mathbin{|\!\sim}\psi)$.

Additionally, presupposing the property (DI) to hold, we define inference from the background knowledge $\Delta = \{(\psi_1|\phi_1), \ldots, (\psi_n|\phi_n)\} \subseteq (\mathfrak{L} \mid \mathfrak{L})$ such that ψ follows from ϕ in System C in the context of Δ, written $\phi \hspace{-0.1em}\sim^C_\Delta \psi$, if and only if given $\mathbf{I} = \{\phi_i \hspace{-0.1em}\sim \psi_i | (\phi_i|\phi_i) \in \Delta\}$ we have $\phi \hspace{-0.1em}\sim^C_\mathbf{I} \psi$.

Name							Ref.	Page
And	(AND)		$\phi\mathrel{|\!\sim}\psi$	and	$\phi\mathrel{|\!\sim}\chi$	imply	$\phi\mathrel{|\!\sim}\psi\wedge\chi$	[Boc01]	
Antecedence	(ANT)		$\phi\mathrel{|\!\sim}\psi$			implies	$\phi\mathrel{|\!\sim}\phi\wedge\psi$	[Boc01]	
Cautious Monotony	(CM)		$\phi\mathrel{|\!\sim}\psi$	and	$\phi\mathrel{|\!\sim}\chi$	imply	$\phi\wedge\psi\mathrel{|\!\sim}\chi$	[Mak88]	p. 86
Consistency	(CONS)		$\phi\mathrel{|\!\sim}\psi$	and		imply	$\phi\mathrel{|\!\sim}\bot$	[Boc01]	
Cumulativity	(CUM)	Given $\phi\mathrel{|\!\sim}\psi$,	$\phi\mathrel{|\!\sim}\psi$			if and only if	$\phi\wedge\psi\mathrel{|\!\sim}\chi$	[Mak94]	p. 90
Cut	(CUT)		$\phi\mathrel{|\!\sim}\psi$	and	$\phi\wedge\psi\mathrel{|\!\sim}\chi$	imply	$\phi\mathrel{|\!\sim}\chi$	[KLM90]	p. 89
Equivalence	(EQ)	If	$\phi\mathrel{|\!\sim}\psi$	as well as	$\psi\mathrel{|\!\sim}\phi$	then	$\phi\mathrel{|\!\sim}\chi$ implies $\psi\mathrel{|\!\sim}\chi$	[KLM90]	
Left Logical Equivalence	(LLE)		$\phi\equiv\psi$	and	$\psi\mathrel{|\!\sim}\chi$	imply	$\phi\mathrel{|\!\sim}\chi$	[KLM90]	p. 79
(MP) in the consequence	(MPC)		$\phi\mathrel{|\!\sim}(\psi\Rightarrow\chi)$	and	$\phi\mathrel{|\!\sim}\psi$	imply	$\phi\mathrel{|\!\sim}\chi$	[KLM90]	p. 91
Reflexivity	(REF)	For all ϕ				it holds that	$\phi\mathrel{|\!\sim}\phi$	[KLM90]	p. 79
Right And	(RAND)		$\phi\mathrel{|\!\sim}\psi\wedge\chi$	implies	$\phi\mathrel{|\!\sim}\psi$	and	$\phi\mathrel{|\!\sim}\chi$	[HM07]	
Right Logical Equivalence	(RLE)	If	$\phi\equiv\psi$	then	$\phi\mathrel{|\!\sim}\psi$	implies	$\phi\mathrel{|\!\sim}\psi$	[EKIBB18]	
Right Or	(ROR)		$\phi\mathrel{|\!\sim}\psi\vee\chi$	implies	$\phi\mathrel{|\!\sim}\psi$	or	$\phi\mathrel{|\!\sim}\chi$	[EKIBB18]	
Right Weakening	(RW)		$\phi\mathrel{|\!\sim}\psi$	and	$\psi\models\chi$	imply	$\phi\mathrel{|\!\sim}\chi$	[KLM90]	p. 79
Supraclassicality	(SCL)		$\phi\models\psi$			implies	$\phi\mathrel{|\!\sim}\psi$	[Mak94]	p. 81
Very Cautious Monotony	(VCM)		$\phi\mathrel{|\!\sim}\psi\wedge\chi$			implies	$\phi\wedge\psi\mathrel{|\!\sim}\chi$	[HM07]	p. 81

Table 4.4: Alphabetical overview over properties derivable in System C; as not all properties are described in this thesis, a reference to additional literature is added to each property; properties contained in this thesis are referred to by the page number of their formal definition.

4.1.4 System P

The axiom system known under the name of System P [Ada65] is probably the best known and most established of the formal inference systems. This system is set up from the axioms (REF), (RW), (LLE), (CM), (CUT), and the property (OR) (see Figure 4.6) which we recall as follows:

DISJUNCTION IN THE ANTECEDENT [KLM90, Mak94] is better known by its short name (OR). This property states that if there is a conclusion χ that can be inferred from both a premise ϕ and a premise ψ, the conclusion can also be inferred from the disjunction of the premises, formally:

$$\frac{\phi\mathrel{|\!\sim}\chi,\ \psi\mathrel{|\!\sim}\chi}{(\phi\vee\psi)\mathrel{|\!\sim}\chi.} \tag{OR}$$

Example 4.22. In Example 4.14 we both find that penguin-birds usually have wings, $pb\approx^\sigma_\Delta w$, and chicken-birds usually have wings $cb\approx^\sigma_\Delta w$. (OR) then implies that penguin-birds or chicken-birds usually have wings, $(pb\vee cb)\approx^\sigma_\Delta w$, which is valid in the example: For every $\omega'\in Mod((pb\vee cb)\overline{w})$ there is a world from the set from $\omega\in Mod((pb\vee cb)w)$ with $\omega\prec^\sigma_\Delta\omega'$ (see Figure 4.4).

With the axioms of System C being a proper subset of the axioms of System P, it is clear that inference with System P contains inference with System C. The following proposition also ensures that inference with System P contains all inferences possible with System O.

Proposition 4.23 ([Mak94]). (OR) implies (WOR).

We define the inference relation of this calculus in parallel to the one of System O in Definition 4.4.

Definition 4.24 (System P Inference). Let $\phi,\phi\in\mathfrak{L}$ be formulas, and let **I** be a set of inferences $\phi_i\mathrel{|\!\sim}\psi_i$. The inference $\phi\mathrel{|\!\sim}\psi$ follows from **I** by System P, written $\mathbf{I}\vdash^P(\phi\mathrel{|\!\sim}\psi)$, if and only if ψ can be derived by from ϕ by iteratively and repeatedly applying the axioms. We further define ψ to follow from ϕ in the context of **I** under System P, written $\phi\mathrel{|\!\sim}^P_{\mathbf{I}}\psi$, if and only if $\mathbf{I}\vdash^P(\phi\mathrel{|\!\sim}\psi)$. Additionally, presupposing the property (DI) to hold, we define inference from the background knowledge $\Delta=\{(\psi_1|\phi_1),\ldots,(\psi_n|\phi_n)\}\subseteq(\mathfrak{L}\mid\mathfrak{L})$ such that ψ follows from ϕ in System P in the context of Δ, written $\phi\mathrel{|\!\sim}^P_\Delta\psi$, if and only if given $\mathbf{I}=\{\phi_i\mathrel{|\!\sim}\psi_i|(\phi_i|\phi_i)\in\Delta\}$ we have $\phi\mathrel{|\!\sim}^P_{\mathbf{I}}\psi$.

(REF)		For all	ϕ	it holds that	$\phi\mathrel{\vdash\!\!\!\sim}\phi$
(CUT)	$\phi\mathrel{\vdash\!\!\!\sim}\psi$	and	$\phi\psi\mathrel{\vdash\!\!\!\sim}\chi$	imply	$\phi\mathrel{\vdash\!\!\!\sim}\chi$
(CM)	$\phi\mathrel{\vdash\!\!\!\sim}\psi$	and	$\phi\mathrel{\vdash\!\!\!\sim}\chi$	imply	$\phi\psi\mathrel{\vdash\!\!\!\sim}\chi$
(RW)	$\phi\mathrel{\vdash\!\!\!\sim}\psi$	and	$\psi\vDash\chi$	imply	$\phi\mathrel{\vdash\!\!\!\sim}\chi$
(LLE)	$\phi\equiv\psi$	and	$\psi\mathrel{\vdash\!\!\!\sim}\chi$	imply	$\phi\mathrel{\vdash\!\!\!\sim}\chi$
(OR)	$\phi\mathrel{\vdash\!\!\!\sim}\chi$	and	$\psi\mathrel{\vdash\!\!\!\sim}\chi$	imply	$(\phi\vee\psi)\mathrel{\vdash\!\!\!\sim}\chi$

Figure 4.6: Axioms of System P

We already discussed that (WAND) ins true, vacuously, in the context of preferential inference (see (4.3)), so together with Proposition 4.11, this proposition gives us that every inference drawn with System O can also be drawn with System P.

Corollary 4.25. Let $\phi, \psi \in \mathfrak{L}$ be formulas, and let $\mathbf{I}$ be a set of inferences $\phi_i\mathrel{\vdash\!\!\!\sim}\psi_i$. If ψ is inferable from ϕ with System O or with System C, then it is also inferable with System P, formally

$$\mathbf{I}\vdash^O (\phi\mathrel{\vdash\!\!\!\sim}\psi) \qquad \text{implies} \qquad \mathbf{I}\vdash^P (\phi\mathrel{\vdash\!\!\!\sim}\psi)$$

$$\mathbf{I}\vdash^C (\phi\mathrel{\vdash\!\!\!\sim}\psi) \qquad \text{implies} \qquad \mathbf{I}\vdash^P (\phi\mathrel{\vdash\!\!\!\sim}\psi)$$

The inference relation $\mathrel{\approx}_\Delta$ [Pea88, DP96], already introduced in the preliminaries in Definition 2.11 (see Page 30) provides a sound and complete semantic for System P:

Proposition 4.26 ([Pea88, DP96]). Let $\Delta = \{(\psi_1|\phi_1), \dots, (\psi_n|\phi_n)\}$ be a conditional knowledge base and let $\phi, \psi \in \mathfrak{L}$ be formulas. We have $\phi\mathrel{\approx}_\Delta\psi$ if and only if $\phi\mathrel{\vdash\!\!\!\sim}^P_\Delta\psi$.

Apart from this semantic, preferential inference, which was responsible for this system being named "System P" in the first place (confer [Ada65, Mak94]), provides a sound and complete semantic for System P.

Theorem 4.27 (Representation Theorem for System P [KLM90, Thm. 3]). An inference relation $\mathrel{\approx}$ satisfies System P, that is, $\phi\mathrel{\vdash\!\!\!\sim}^P\psi$ implies $\phi\mathrel{\approx}\psi$, if and only if $\mathrel{\approx}$ is defined by a classical stoppered preferential model.

In Section 3.3.2 we recalled inference with Δ-admissible OCF. We now recall an inference over all of OCF that are Δ-admissible. Thus we have an additional sound and complete semantic for System P:

Definition 4.28 (Sceptical Inference over All Δ-Admissible κ, $\mathrel{\vicurlyvee^{\kappa}_{\Delta}}$ [GP96]). Let ϕ and ψ be formulas and let $\Delta = \{(\psi_1|\phi_1), \ldots, (\psi_n|\phi_n)\} \subseteq (\mathfrak{L} \mid \mathfrak{L})$ be a conditional knowledge base. ψ follows sceptically with all Δ-admissible κ from ϕ, written $\phi \mathrel{\vicurlyvee^{\kappa}_{\Delta}} \psi$ if and only if $\phi \mathrel{\vicurlyvee_{\kappa_\Delta}} \psi$ for all Δ-admissible OCF κ_Δ.

Proposition 4.29 ([GP96]). The inference relation $\mathrel{\vicurlyvee^{\kappa}_{\Delta}}$ coincides with the inference relation $\mathrel{\vicurlyvee_{\Delta}}$, that is, we have

$$\phi \mathrel{\vicurlyvee^{\kappa}_{\Delta}} \psi \qquad \text{if and only if} \qquad \phi \mathrel{\vicurlyvee_{\Delta}} \psi. \qquad (4.4)$$

From this proposition we directly obtain

Corollary 4.30 ([GP96]). The inference relation $\mathrel{\vicurlyvee^{\kappa}_{\Delta}}$ is a sound and complete semantics for System P.

A list of properties derivable in System P is given in Table 4.5; Figure 4.7 shows how these properties are related. It has been tested empirically whether the rules of System P are used by human reasoners for their inferences. [DBR02] showed that in situations where Monotony (M) is not applicable human test persons tend to use (among others) the rules (REF), (CM), (RW) and (OR). Additionally, [BDDP06, PK05] showed (CUT) and (LLE) to be used by human reasoners in situations where (M) is not applicable. But even if these properties could be found to be used one at a time, recent work [KR14] challenges the idea that human reasoners use System P as an inference calculus.

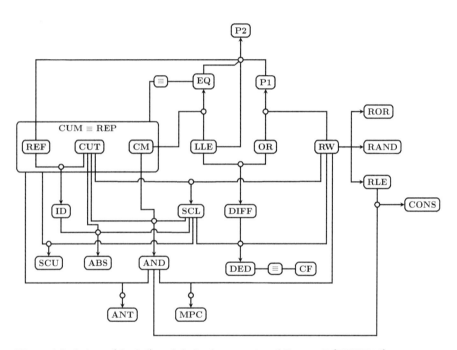

Figure 4.7: Axioms (shaded) and derived properties of System P [EKIBB18]

Name							Reference	
And	(AND)	$\phi\!\mid\!\sim\!\psi$	and	$\phi\!\mid\!\sim\!\chi$	imply	$\phi\!\mid\!\approx\!\psi\wedge\chi$	[Boc01]	
Antecedence	(ANT)	$\phi\!\mid\!\sim\!\psi$	and	$\phi\!\mid\!\sim\!\chi$	implies	$\phi\!\mid\!\approx\!\phi\wedge\psi$	[Boc01]	
Cautious Monotony	(CM)	$\phi\!\mid\!\sim\!\psi$	and	$\phi\!\mid\!\sim\!\chi$	imply	$\phi\psi\!\mid\!\approx\!\chi$	[Mak88]	p. 86
Confirmation	(CF)	$\phi\!\mid\!\sim\!\psi$			implies	$(\phi\vee\chi)\!\mid\!\approx\!(\psi\vee\chi)$	[Boc01]	
Consistency	(CONS) Given	$\phi\!\mid\!\sim\!\overline{\bot}$			imply	$\phi\!\mid\!\approx\!\bot$	[Boc01]	
Cumulativity	(CUM)	$\phi\!\mid\!\sim\!\psi,\ \phi\wedge\psi\!\mid\!\sim\!\chi$	as well as	$\phi\equiv\psi$	if and only if	$\phi\!\mid\!\approx\!\chi$	[Mak94]	p. 90
Cut	(CUT)	$\phi\wedge\psi\!\mid\!\sim\!\chi$	and	$\phi\!\mid\!\sim\!\psi$	implies	$\phi\!\mid\!\approx\!\chi$	[KLM90]	p. 89
Deduction	(DED) If	$\phi\wedge\psi\!\mid\!\sim\!\chi$			then	$\phi\!\mid\!\approx\!(\psi\Rightarrow\chi)$	[Boc01]	
Equivalence	(EQ) If	$\phi\equiv\psi,\ \psi\!\mid\!\approx\!\phi$	as well as	$\psi\!\mid\!\approx\!\phi$	then	$\phi\!\mid\!\approx\!\chi$ implies $\psi\!\mid\!\approx\!\chi$	[KLM90]	
Exclusive Or	(XOR)	$\phi\!\mid\!\sim\!\chi,\ \psi\!\mid\!\sim\!\chi$	and	$\models\overline{(\phi\psi)}$	imply	$\psi\!\mid\!\approx\!\phi$	[HM07]	
Left Logical Equivalence	(LLE)	$\phi\equiv\psi$	and	$\phi\!\mid\!\sim\!\chi$	imply	$\psi\!\mid\!\approx\!\chi$	[KLM90]	p. 79
(MP) in the consequence	(MPC)	$\phi\!\mid\!\approx\!(\psi\Rightarrow\chi)$	and	$\phi\!\mid\!\sim\!\psi$	imply	$\phi\!\mid\!\approx\!\chi$	[KLM90]	p. 91
Or	(OR)	$\phi\!\mid\!\sim\!\chi$	and	$\psi\!\mid\!\sim\!\psi$	imply	$\phi\!\mid\!\approx\!\chi$	[KLM90]	p. 95
P1	(P1)	$\phi\wedge\psi\!\mid\!\sim\!\chi$	and	$(\phi\vee\psi)\!\mid\!\sim\!\xi$	imply	$\phi\psi\!\mid\!\approx\!\chi$	[KLM90]	
P2	(P2)	$(\psi\vee\chi)\!\mid\!\sim\!\phi$			imply	$(\phi\vee\psi)\!\mid\!\approx\!\phi$	[KLM90]	
Reflexivity	(REF) For all	ϕ			it holds that	$\phi\!\mid\!\approx\!\phi$	[HM07]	p. 79
Right And	(RAND)	$\phi\!\mid\!\sim\!\psi\wedge\chi$	implies		and	$\phi\!\mid\!\approx\!\psi$	[HM07]	
Right Logical Equivalence	(RLE) If	$\phi\equiv\psi$	then		implies	$\phi\!\mid\!\approx\!\chi$	[EKIBB18]	
Right Or	(ROR)	$\phi\!\mid\!\sim\!\psi\wedge\chi$	implies		or	$\phi\!\mid\!\approx\!\chi$	[EKIBB18]	
Right Weakening	(RW)	$\phi\!\mid\!\sim\!\psi$	and	$\psi\models\chi$	implies	$\phi\!\mid\!\approx\!\psi$	[KLM90]	p. 79
Supraclassicality	(SCL)	$\phi\models\psi$			implies	$\phi\!\mid\!\approx\!\chi$	[Mak94]	p. 81
Very Cautious Monotony	(VCM)	$\phi\!\mid\!\sim\!\psi\wedge\chi$			implies	$\phi\psi\!\mid\!\sim\!\chi$	[HM07]	p. 81
Weak And	(WAND)	$\phi\!\mid\!\sim\!\psi$	and	$\phi\overline{\chi}\!\mid\!\sim\!\chi$	imply	$\phi\!\sim\!\psi$	[HM07]	p. 80
Weak Or	(WOR) (also (DIFF))	$\phi\psi\!\mid\!\sim\!\chi$	and	$\phi\psi\!\mid\!\sim\!\chi$	imply	$\phi\!\mid\!\sim\!\chi$	[HM07]	p. 80

Table 4.5: Alphabetical overview over properties derivable in System P; as not all properties are described in this thesis, a reference to additional literature is added to each property; properties contained in this thesis are referred to by the page number of their formal definition.

4.1.5 System R

The axiom system called *System R* [LM92] uses most of the axioms of System P, but swaps (CM) for the following property:

RATIONAL MONOTONY (RM) [LM92, Boc01] states that we can add formulas to the premise of an inference for which we cannot infer the opposite, formally

$$\frac{\phi\mathrel{|\!\sim}\chi, \phi\mathrel{|\!\not\sim}\overline{\psi}}{\phi\psi\mathrel{|\!\sim}\chi}.\tag{RM}$$

The contrapositive formulation of this property that can be interpreted as (CUT) for non-entailments, that is,

$$\frac{\phi\mathrel{|\!\not\sim}\overline{\psi}, \phi\psi\mathrel{|\!\not\sim}\chi}{\phi\mathrel{|\!\not\sim}\chi}.$$

This property is stronger than the property (CM) that it was swapped for.

Proposition 4.31 ([EKIBB18, Proposition 74]). (CM) can be derived in System R using (CONS) and (RM).

By this proposition we obtain that System R contains System P and thus transitively System C and System O. As for the other axiom systems, we define a syntactic inference for System R as follows.

Definition 4.32 (System R Inference). Let $\phi, \psi \in \mathcal{L}$ be formulas, and let **I** be a set of inferences $\phi_i\mathrel{|\!\sim}\psi_i$. The inference $\phi\mathrel{|\!\sim}\psi$ follows from **I** by System R, written $\mathbf{I} \vdash^R (\phi\mathrel{|\!\sim}\psi)$ if and only if ψ can be derived by from ϕ by iteratively and repeatedly applying the axioms. We further define ψ to follow from ϕ in the context of **I** under System R, written $\phi\mathrel{|\!\sim}^R_{\mathbf{I}}\psi$, if and only if $\mathbf{I} \vdash^R (\phi\mathrel{|\!\sim}\psi)$. Additionally, presupposing the property (DI) to hold, we define inference from the background knowledge $\Delta = \{(\psi_1|\phi_1), \ldots, (\psi_n|\phi_n)\} \subseteq (\mathcal{L} \mid \mathcal{L})$ such that ψ follows from ϕ in System R in the context of Δ, written $\phi\mathrel{|\!\sim}^R_{\Delta}\psi$, if and only if given $\mathbf{I} = \{\phi_i\mathrel{|\!\sim}\psi_i|(\phi_i|\phi_i) \in \Delta\}$ we have $\phi\mathrel{|\!\sim}^R_{\mathbf{I}}\psi$.

We recall modular orderings and ranked models to obtain a representation theorem for System R.

Definition 4.33 (Modular Ordering [LM92]). A partial ordering $\prec$ on a set of states $\mathcal{M}$ is called *modular* if and only if for any totally ordered set $\mathfrak{X}$

with $\leq$ ($<$) being the (strict) ordering on $\mathfrak{X}$ there is a function $f : \mathcal{M} \to \mathfrak{X}$ with the property that for any pair of states $m, m' \in \mathcal{M}$ we have $m \prec m'$ if and only if $f(m) < f(m')$.

Modular orderings can be used as preferential relation in preferential models, thus generating ranked models:

Definition 4.34 (Ranked Model [LM92]). A preferential model (see Definition 3.1) $\mathfrak{M} = (\mathcal{M}, \models, \prec)$ is called a *ranked model* if and only if $\prec$ is modular.

With these definitions we can now recall the representation theorem for rational entailment.

Theorem 4.35 (Representation Theorem for Rational Inference [LM92]). An inference relation $\approx$ satisfies System R (and henceforth is called *rational inference*) if and only if it is based on a ranked model by means of Definition 3.6.

As the inference relation $\approx_\kappa$ of an OCF is set up by means of preferential models (see Definition 3.25), and $<_\kappa$ is modular according to Definition 4.33 with the function κ, we obtain:

Proposition 4.36 (confer [KIE14]). Let κ be an OCF. The inference relation $\approx_\kappa$ satisfies System R.

So we can use κ-inference to illustrate the properties of System R.

Example 4.37. To illustrate (RM) and the following properties in this section, we use the OCF of the running example (Example 2.1) given in Table 4.6. This OCF was generated on the knowledge base from Example 4.14 using System Z. In this OCF we can infer that penguins do not fly ($p \approx_\kappa \overline{f}$) since $\kappa(p\overline{f}) = 1 < 2 = \kappa(pf)$ and we can neither infer that penguins do not have wings ($p \not\approx_\kappa \overline{w}$) because $\kappa(p\overline{w}) = 1 = \kappa_\Delta(pw)$. By (RM) from these preliminaries we obtain that winged penguins do not fly ($pw \approx_\kappa \overline{f}$), which is verified by the example since here we have $\kappa(p\overline{f}w) = 1 < 2 = \kappa(pfw)$.

In the following we show that System R also contains System O^+ by showing that (NR) is entailable from System R. This is done with a slight detour via the following property:

Table 4.6: OCF to illustrate Example 4.37

ω	$pcbfw$	$pcbf\overline{w}$	$pcb\overline{f}w$	$pcb\overline{f}\,\overline{w}$	$pc\overline{b}fw$	$pc\overline{b}f\overline{w}$	$pc\overline{b}\,\overline{f}w$	$pc\overline{b}\,\overline{f}\,\overline{w}$
$\kappa(\omega)$	2	2	2	2	2	2	2	2
ω	$p\overline{c}bfw$	$p\overline{c}bf\overline{w}$	$p\overline{c}b\overline{f}w$	$p\overline{c}b\overline{f}\,\overline{w}$	$p\overline{c}\,\overline{b}fw$	$p\overline{c}\,\overline{b}f\overline{w}$	$p\overline{c}\,\overline{b}\,\overline{f}w$	$p\overline{c}\,\overline{b}\,\overline{f}\,\overline{w}$
$\kappa(\omega)$	2	2	1	1	2	2	2	2
ω	$\overline{p}cbfw$	$\overline{p}cbf\overline{w}$	$\overline{p}cb\overline{f}w$	$\overline{p}cb\overline{f}\,\overline{w}$	$\overline{p}c\overline{b}fw$	$\overline{p}c\overline{b}f\overline{w}$	$\overline{p}c\overline{b}\,\overline{f}w$	$\overline{p}c\overline{b}\,\overline{f}\,\overline{w}$
$\kappa(\omega)$	2	2	1	1	2	2	2	2
ω	$\overline{p}\,\overline{c}bfw$	$\overline{p}\,\overline{c}bf\overline{w}$	$\overline{p}\,\overline{c}b\overline{f}w$	$\overline{p}\,\overline{c}b\overline{f}\,\overline{w}$	$\overline{p}\,\overline{c}\,\overline{b}fw$	$\overline{p}\,\overline{c}\,\overline{b}f\overline{w}$	$\overline{p}\,\overline{c}\,\overline{b}\,\overline{f}w$	$\overline{p}\,\overline{c}\,\overline{b}\,\overline{f}\,\overline{w}$
$\kappa(\omega)$	0	1	1	1	0	0	0	0

DISJUNCTIVE RATIONALITY (DR) [KLM90] is, in a way, the inverse of (OR), because it licenses for distributing the inferences of a disjunction to the disjoint parts of the premise, formally

$$\frac{(\phi \vee \psi)\mathrel|\joinrel\sim\chi}{\phi\mathrel|\joinrel\sim\chi \quad \text{or} \quad \psi\mathrel|\joinrel\sim\chi.} \tag{DR}$$

This property is usually given in its contrapositive formulation which reads

$$\frac{\phi\mathrel|\joinrel\not\sim\chi,\ \psi\mathrel|\joinrel\not\sim\chi}{(\phi \vee \psi)\mathrel|\joinrel\not\sim\chi}.$$

Example 4.38. We illustrate (DR) by continuing Example 4.37: Here cannot infer that penguins have wings ($p\mathrel|\joinrel\not\sim_\kappa w$), because we have $\kappa(pw) = 1 = \kappa(p\overline{w})$, neither can we infer that chicken have wings ($c\mathrel|\joinrel\not\sim_\kappa w$), because we have $\kappa(cw) = 1 = \kappa(c\overline{w})$. Given this prerequisites, (DR) infers $(p \vee c)\mathrel|\joinrel\not\sim_\kappa w$, which we also find in the example, since here we have $\kappa((p \vee c) \wedge w) = 1 = \kappa((p \vee c) \wedge \overline{w})$ and thus $\kappa((p \vee c) \wedge w) \not< \kappa((p \vee c) \wedge \overline{w})$.

Proposition 4.39 ([LM92]). (DR) is derivable in System R using (RM), (RW), (LLE), and (CUT).

Proposition 4.40 ([EKIBB18, Proposition 78]). (DR) implies (NR) given (LLE).

Both propositions then directly lead to the following conclusion.

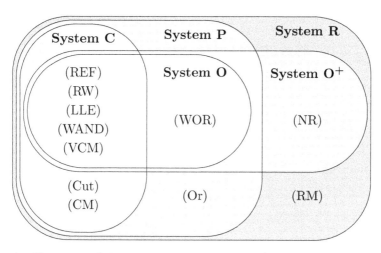

Figure 4.8: Illustration of the axiom systems System O, O$^+$, C, P, and R and how they are (partially) included in each other

Corollary 4.41 ([EKIBB18, Corollary 79]). (RM) implies (NR) given the properties (RW), (LLE), and (CUT).

Figure 4.8 summarises the findings about the relationships between the axiom systems and their inference in this chapter. An overview of properties derivable in System R is given in Table 4.7; Figure 4.9 shows how these properties are related.

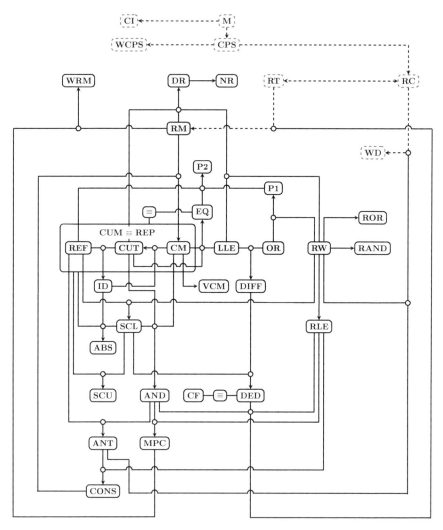

Figure 4.9: Axioms (shaded) and derived properties of System R; dotted properties do not belong to System R

Name	Abbrev.							Reference	Page
And	(AND)	$\phi\mid\!\sim\psi$	and	$\phi\mid\!\sim\chi$	imply	$\phi\mid\!\sim\psi\wedge\chi$		[Boc01]	
Antecedence	(ANT)	$\phi\mid\!\sim\psi$	and	$\phi\mid\!\sim\chi$	implies	$\phi\mid\!\approx\phi\wedge\psi$		[Boc01]	
Cautious Monotony	(CM)	$\phi\mid\!\sim\psi$	and	$\phi\mid\!\sim\chi$	imply	$\phi\psi\mid\!\sim\chi$		[Mak88]	p. 86
Confirmation	(CF)	$\phi\mid\!\sim\psi$	and	$\phi\mid\!\sim\bar{\psi}$	implies	$(\phi\wedge\chi)\mid\!\approx(\psi\vee\chi)$		[Boc01]	
Consistency	(CONS)	$\phi\mid\!\sim\psi$	and		imply	$\phi\mid\!\approx\bot$		[Boc01]	
Cumulativity	(CUM) *Given*	$\phi\mid\!\sim\psi,$	and	$\phi\mid\!\sim\chi$	if and only if	$\phi\psi\mid\!\sim\chi$		[Mak94]	p. 90
Cut	(CUT) *Given*	$\phi\mid\!\sim\psi$	and	$\phi\psi\mid\!\sim\chi$	imply	$\phi\mid\!\sim\chi$		[KLM90]	p. 89
Deduction	(DED)	$\phi\mid\!\sim\psi$	and	$\phi\vee\psi\mid\!\sim\chi$	implies	$\phi\mid\!\approx(\psi\Rightarrow\chi)$		[Boc01]	
Disjunctive Rationality	(DR)	$\phi\mid\!\not\approx\chi$	and	$\psi\mid\!\not\approx\chi$	imply	$(\phi\vee\psi)\mid\!\not\approx\chi$		[KLM90]	p. 102
Equivalence	(EQ) *If*	$\phi\equiv\psi$	as well as	$\psi\mid\!\approx\phi$	then	$\phi\mid\!\sim\chi$	implies $\psi\mid\!\approx\chi$	[KLM90]	
Exclusive Or	(XOR)	$\phi\mid\!\sim\chi,\ \psi\mid\!\sim\chi$	and	$\models(\phi\chi)$	imply	$\phi\mid\!\sim\chi$		[HM07]	
Left Logical Equivalence	(LLE)	$\phi\equiv\psi$	and	$\psi\mid\!\sim\chi$	imply	$\phi\mid\!\sim\chi$		[KLM90]	p. 79
(MP) in the consequence	(MPC)	$\phi\mid\!\approx(\psi\Rightarrow\chi)$	implies	$\phi\mid\!\sim\psi$	imply	$\phi\mid\!\sim\chi$		[KLM90]	p. 91
Negation Rationality	(NR)	$\phi\mid\!\sim\chi$	implies	$\phi\psi\mid\!\sim\chi$	or	$\overline{\phi\psi}\mid\!\sim\chi$	for all $\psi\in\mathcal{L}$	[FL96]	p. 83
Or	(OR)	$\phi\mid\!\sim\chi$	and	$\psi\mid\!\sim\chi$	imply	$(\phi\vee\psi)\mid\!\sim\chi$		[KLM90]	p. 95
P1	(P1)	$\phi\mid\!\sim\chi$	and	$\psi\mid\!\approx\xi$	imply	$(\phi\vee\psi)\mid\!\sim\chi$		[KLM90]	
P2	(P2)	$(\phi\vee\psi)\mid\!\sim\phi$	and	$(\psi\vee\chi)\mid\!\sim\psi$	imply	$(\phi\vee\psi)\mid\!\sim(\chi\vee\xi)$		[KLM90]	
Rational Monotony	(RM) *Given*	$\phi\mid\!\sim\psi$		$\phi\mid\!\not\approx\chi$	implies	$\phi\psi\mid\!\sim\chi$		[Boc01, LM92]	p. 100
Reflexivity	(REF) *For all*	ϕ			it holds that	$\phi\mid\!\sim\phi$		[KLM90]	p. 79
Right And	(RAND)	$\phi\mid\!\sim\psi\chi$	implies	$\phi\mid\!\sim\psi$	and	$\phi\mid\!\sim\chi$		[HM07]	
Right Logical Equivalence	(RLE) *If*	$\phi\equiv\psi$	then	$\phi\models\psi$	implies	$\phi\mid\!\sim\chi$		[EKIBB18]	
Right Or	(ROR)	$\phi\mid\!\sim\psi\vee\chi$	implies	$\psi\mid\!\sim\chi$	or	$\phi\mid\!\sim\chi$		[EKIBB18]	
Right Weakening	(RW)	$\phi\mid\!\sim\psi$	and	$\psi\models\chi$	imply	$\phi\mid\!\sim\chi$		[KLM90]	p. 79
Supraclassicality	(SCL)	$\phi\models\psi$			implies	$\phi\mid\!\sim\psi$		[Mak94]	p. 81
Very Cautious Monotony	(VCM)	$\phi\mid\!\sim\psi\chi$	and	$\phi\mid\!\sim\chi$	implies	$\phi\psi\mid\!\sim\chi$		[HM07]	p. 81
Weak And	(WAND)	$\phi\mid\!\sim\chi$	and	$\phi\mid\!\sim\chi$	imply	$\phi\mid\!\sim\chi$		[HM07]	p. 80
Weak Or	(WOR) *(also (DIFF))*	$\phi\psi\mid\!\sim\chi$	and	$\phi\psi\mid\!\sim\chi$	imply	$\phi\mid\!\sim\chi$		[HM07]	p. 80
Weak Rational Monotony	(WRM)	$\top\mid\!\approx\phi\Rightarrow\psi$	and	$\top\mid\!\not\approx\phi$	imply	$\phi\mid\!\sim\psi$		[Boc01]	

Table 4.7: Alphabetical overview over properties derivable in System R; as not all properties are described in this thesis, a reference to additional literature is added to each property.

4.2 Selected Formal Properties of Nonmonotonic Inference

In the previous section we recalled the well established axiom systems of nonmontonic inference. With threshold inference and the Systems O and C, we demonstrated that apart from providing a syntactic inference mechanism, these systems are useful for classifying semantical inference relations with respect to their inferential power.

In this section we recall selected properties of nonmonotonic inference that do not belong to any of the calculi presented and also extend these properties. To illustrate how these properties can be used to further differentiate between inference relation we use preferential inference as example relation for the properties and show whether this relation is satisfied them, or not.

As first property we translate the principle of explosion to nonmontonic inference.

EX FALSO (SEQUITUR) QUODLIBET (NMEFQ) states that from a contradiction, everything can be inferred.

$$\bot \mathrel{\rvert\!\approx} \psi \qquad \text{for all} \qquad \psi \in \mathfrak{L}. \qquad \text{(NMEFQ)}$$

Proposition 4.42. Preferential inference satisfies (NMEFQ).

INTEGRITY (INT) constraints the inference relation to infer contradictions from contradictory premises, only.

$$\phi \mathrel{\rvert\!\not\approx} \bot \qquad \text{if and only if} \qquad \phi \not\equiv \bot. \qquad \text{(INT)}$$

Proposition 4.43. Preferential inference satisfies (INT).

(STRONG) REGULARITY [Boc01]. An inference relation is *regular* if formulas that infer formulas which on their part infer the contradiction directly infer to contradictions. An inference relation is *strongly regular* if the negation of a formula that infers the contradiction can be added conjunctively to the conclusion of any inference.

$$\frac{\phi \mathrel{\rvert\!\sim} \psi,\ \psi \mathrel{\rvert\!\sim} \bot}{\phi \mathrel{\rvert\!\sim} \bot} \qquad \text{(REG)}$$

$$\frac{\phi \mathrel{\rvert\!\sim} \chi,\ \psi \mathrel{\rvert\!\sim} \bot}{\phi \mathrel{\rvert\!\sim} \overline{\psi}\chi} \qquad \text{(SREG)}$$

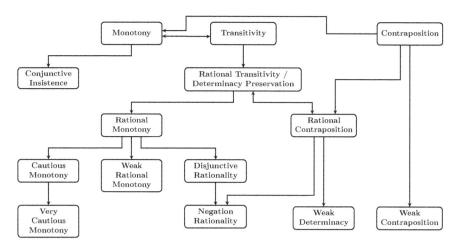

Figure 4.10: Properties implied by (M), (T), and (CPS) given System P, in extension of [BMP97]

Lemma 4.44. Preferential inference satisfies (REG) and (SREG).

Figure 4.10 shows a selection of properties that can be inferred from the classical properties Monotony, Transitivity, and Contraposition using the rules of System P. This dissertation does not recall all proofs for the relationships; the interested reader is referred to [KLM90, Mak94, BP96, BMP97, EKIBB18] for proofs of implications not given in the dissertation.

WEAK DETERMINACY (WD) [BMP97]. This property states that if a formula ϕ is exceptional, that is, if its negation follows nonmonotonically from the tautologies, this formula cannot be indifferent with respect to the entailment of any other formula $\psi \in \mathfrak{L}$.

$$\frac{\top \vdash\!\sim \overline{\phi}}{\phi \vdash\!\sim \psi \quad \text{or} \quad \phi \vdash\!\sim \overline{\psi}.} \tag{WD}$$

Observation 4.45. There are preference relations such that preferential inference violates (WD).

We give an example for this as follows.

Figure 4.11: Example for a preference relation such that preferential inference violate (WD), $\omega \to \omega'$ indicates $\omega \prec \omega'$

Example 4.46. Figure 4.11 shows a reference relation with this property: Here we have $\top \mathrel{\vert\!\approx} \bar{a}$ and $a \mathrel{\vert\!\not\approx} b$, but also $a \mathrel{\vert\!\not\approx} \bar{b}$ contrary to (WD), as neither $ab \prec a\bar{b}$ nor $\bar{a}\bar{b} \prec ab$.

WEAK CONTRAPOSITION (WCPS) [FL96]. If a formula χ can be inferred from a conjunction but not from one of the conjuncts alone, from one conjunct and $\overline{\chi}$ the negation of the other follows.

$$\frac{\phi\psi \mathrel{\vert\!\sim} \chi \quad \text{and} \quad \phi \mathrel{\vert\!\not\sim} \chi}{\psi\overline{\chi} \mathrel{\vert\!\sim} \overline{\phi}} \qquad \text{(WCPS)}$$

As the name indicates, (WCPS) is a weak form of (CPS)

Proposition 4.47. (CPS) implies (WCPS) under (DED), (LLE), and (RW).

Observation 4.48. There are preference relations such that preferential inference violates (WCPS).

We illustrate this observation with the following example.

Example 4.49. Let $\prec$ be the preference relation defined by Figure4.12. Then the inference relation $\mathrel{\vert\!\approx}$ licenses for the inference $ab \mathrel{\vert\!\approx} c$ because $abc \prec ab\bar{c}$ and $a \mathrel{\vert\!\not\approx} c$ because, for instance, there is no model of ac that is preferred to $a\bar{b}c$, but also $b\bar{c} \mathrel{\vert\!\not\approx} \bar{a}$ because $ab\bar{c} \not\prec \bar{a}b\bar{c}$, in contrast to (WCPS) which from these prerequisites would infer $b\bar{c} \mathrel{\vert\!\approx} \bar{a}$.

Observations 4.45 and 4.48 together with the implications given in Figure 4.10 result in:

Corollary 4.50. Preferential inference neither satisfies (RC) nor (CPS).

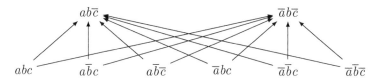

Figure 4.12: Example for a preference relation which results in an preferential inference that violates (WCPS); $\omega \to \omega'$ indicates $\omega \prec \omega'$

In System P, the property (AND) licenses for joining the conclusions of identical premises, conjunctively, and (P 1) (in Table 4.5) to join them, disjunctively; the property (OR) disjunctively joins the premises of identical conclusions. The following property closes the gap left open by these properties.

CONJUNCTIVE INSISTENCE (CI) [BMP97]. If a formula can be inferred by two different premises, this property states that both can be extended with the respective other without rendering the inference invalid.

$$\frac{\phi \hspace{0.1em}\vdash\hspace{-0.5em}\sim\hspace{0.1em} \chi \quad \text{and} \quad \psi \hspace{0.1em}\vdash\hspace{-0.5em}\sim\hspace{0.1em} \chi}{\phi\psi \hspace{0.1em}\vdash\hspace{-0.5em}\sim\hspace{0.1em} \chi.} \tag{CI}$$

Hereby this weakening of (M) (which licenses to infer $\phi\psi \hspace{0.1em}\vdash\hspace{-0.5em}\sim\hspace{0.1em} \chi$ from $\phi \hspace{0.1em}\vdash\hspace{-0.5em}\sim\hspace{0.1em} \chi$ alone) defines a conjunctive property for the premises of inferences.

Observation 4.51. There are preference relations $\prec$ such that $\hspace{0.1em}\vdash\hspace{-0.5em}\approx_{\prec}$ violates (CI).

Example 4.52. Figure 4.13 is a counterexample for $\hspace{0.1em}\vdash\hspace{-0.5em}\approx_{\prec}$ satisfying (CI), as here we find $a \hspace{0.1em}\vdash\hspace{-0.5em}\approx_{\prec} c$ and $b \hspace{0.1em}\vdash\hspace{-0.5em}\approx_{\prec} c$, but not $ab \hspace{0.1em}\vdash\hspace{-0.5em}\approx_{\prec} c$ because $abc \not\prec ab\overline{c}$ in contrast to (CI).

We finalise this enumeration of properties by examining preferential inference with respect to the already defined (RM) and the results thereof.

Observation 4.53. There are preference relations $\prec$ such that $\hspace{0.1em}\vdash\hspace{-0.5em}\approx_{\prec}$ violates (RM).

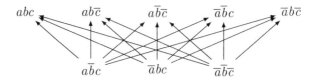

Figure 4.13: Example for a preference relation $\prec$ such that $\approx$ violates (CI); $\omega \to \omega'$ indicates $\omega \prec \omega'$

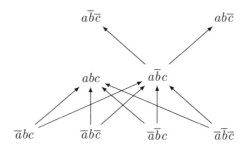

Figure 4.14: Example for a preference relation $\prec$ such that $\approx$ violates (RM)[5]; $\omega \to \omega'$ indicates $\omega \prec \omega'$

Example 4.54. Let $\prec$ be the preference relation given in Figure 4.14[5]. The respective inference gives us $a\approx c$ as well as $a\not\approx b$, but also, in contrast to (RM), $ab\not\approx\bar{c}$ because the world abc is not $\prec$-preferred to the world $ab\bar{c}$.

Together with the implications from Figure 4.10 from this observation we conclude:

Corollary 4.55. Preferential inference does not satisfy (RT) in general.

In this section we presented and recalled properties of nonmonotonic inference relations that are no elements of System O, C, P, and R. We demonstrated how these properties can be used to assess an inference relation using the example of preferential inference. The insights support the representation theorem 4.27 in such a way that we found counterexamples for all properties outside System P.

---

5   The structure of this example has been pointed out by Hans Rott in a discussion.

In the following sections we put the properties to further use and apply them to classify inference relations presented in Section 3.

4.3 Properties of Structural Inference

We recalled conditional structures and the thereupon defined structural inference in Section 3.2. In this section we will, based on and extending the articles [KIE12, EKI14], research this inference relation with respect to the formal inference properties presented in the previous sections of this chapter.

We recalled structural inference to be defined upon the preferential model $(\Omega, \vDash, \prec_\Delta^\sigma)$, thus we start our investigations with a closer study of this model.

Lemma 4.56 ([KIE12, Lemma 1]). The preferential model $\mathfrak{M}^\Delta = (\Omega, \vDash, \prec_\Delta^\sigma)$ with $\prec_\Delta^\sigma$ set up from structural preference is a classical stoppered preferential model.

With the representation theorem (Theorem 4.27) and the inclusions of the inference systems shown in the previous chapters and summarised in Figure 4.8 (see Page 103) from this we directly obtain:

Corollary 4.57 ([KIE12, Proposition 3]). Structural inference satisfies System O, C, and P.

It is usually assumed that an inference relation set up upon a knowledge base Δ retrieves the knowledge encoded into the conditionals. That this is not always the case is demonstrated by structural inference:

Observation 4.58 ([KIE12]). There are knowledge bases such that structural inference does not satisfy (DI).

Example 4.59 ([KIE12, confer Example 6]). The excerpt of the running example used in Example 3.15 is an example for structural inference violating (DI). For the knowledge base $\Delta_{pbf} = \{\delta_1 : (b|f), \delta_3 : (b|p), \delta_4 : (\overline{f}|p)\}$ the verification/falsification given in Table 3.1 (see Page 44) leads to the structural preference pictured in Figure 3.2 (see Page 44). Here we have $b \approx_\Delta^\sigma f$ because the world $\overline{p}bf$ is a $\prec_\Delta^\sigma$-minimal world and no $\omega \vDash b\overline{f}$ is $\prec_\Delta^\sigma$-minimal, and so the conditional δ_1 is retrieved. For δ_3 we find no $\prec_\Delta^\sigma$-preferred world to any world satisfying $p\overline{b}f$, and thus $p \not\approx_\Delta^\sigma b$, even if $\delta_3 \in \Delta_{pbf}$ The same holds for δ_4. There is no $\prec_\Delta^\sigma$-preferred world to pbf, so in this example we have $p \not\approx_\Delta^\sigma f$, despite δ_4 being in the knowledge base.

Being set up as preferential inference, structural inference inherits properties from this formalism. So from Propositions 4.42, 4.43, and 4.44 we obtain the following corollary.

Corollary 4.60. Structural inference $\approx_\Delta^\sigma$ satisfies the properties (NMEFQ), (INT), (REG), and (SREG).

Observation 4.61. There are knowledge bases such that structural inference violates (WCPS).

Example 4.62. The knowledge base $\Delta = \{\delta_1 : (c|ab), \delta_2 : (c|\overline{a}b)\}$ is an example for Observation 4.61. Here, $fal(ab\overline{c}) = \mathbf{a}_1^-$, $fal(\overline{a}b\overline{c}) = \mathbf{a}_2^-$, and $fal(\omega) = \varnothing$ for all other worlds. Therefore the resulting preference structure is identical to the one depicted in Figure 4.12. Then, arguing as in Example 4.49, the inference relation $\approx_\Delta^\sigma$ licenses for the inference $ab \approx_\Delta^\sigma c$ as well as $a \not\approx_\Delta^\sigma c$, but we have also $b\overline{c} \not\approx_\Delta^\sigma \overline{a}$, in contrast to (WCPS) which from this prerequisites would infer $b\overline{c} \approx_\Delta \overline{a}$.

Observation 4.63. There are knowledge bases such that structural inference violates (WD).

Example 4.64. This can be observed with the knowledge base $\Delta = \{(\overline{a}|\top)\}$ which generates a preferential structure given in Figure 4.11 for Observation 4.45. Thus we can use the same argumentation of the observed Example 4.46 to show that we have $\top \approx_\Delta \overline{a}$ and $a \not\approx_\Delta b$, but also $a \not\approx_\Delta \overline{b}$ contrary to (WD).

Together with the implications given in Figure 4.10 (see Page 107) from Observations 4.61 and 4.63 we conclude:

Corollary 4.65. Structural inference does neither satisfy (RC) nor (CPS) in general.

From the System P satisfaction of structural inference we obtain that the inference relation $\approx_\Delta^\sigma$ satisfies (CM). In the following we observe that the stronger property (RM) is not valid in this inference.

Observation 4.66. There are knowledge bases such that structural inference violates (RM).

We give an example for such a knowledge base.

Example 4.67. Let $\Delta = \{\delta_1 : (\overline{a}|bc), \delta_2 : (bc|a), \delta_3 : (\overline{a}|\overline{bc}), \delta_4 : (\overline{a}|b\overline{c})\}$ be a knowledge base. Δ results in the verification/falsification behaviour shown in Table 4.8 and in the preference relation given in Figure 4.14 (see Page 110). In parallel to Example 4.54 for preferential inference, the inference $\approx_\Delta^\sigma$ gives us $a\approx_\Delta^\sigma c$ as well as $a\not\approx_\Delta^\sigma \overline{b}$, but also, in contrast to (RM), $ab\not\approx_\Delta^\sigma \overline{c}$.

With the satisfaction of System P we obtain that for structural inference it is possible to join two premises of the same conclusion disjunctively with the property (OR). We examine whether the inverse, splitting a disjunctive premise into its elements and keeping the inference for at least one of the elements as postulated by the property (DR), is also valid for structural inference.

Example 4.68. Let $\Delta = \{\delta_1 : (\overline{a}|\top), \delta_2 : (\overline{b}|\top), \delta_3 : (c|a \Leftrightarrow \overline{b})\}$ be a knowledge base. Δ gives us the conditional structures and structural preferences shown in Figure 4.15. We use the formulas $\phi = (a \Leftrightarrow \overline{b}) \wedge \neg(\overline{a}bc)$ and $\psi = (a \Leftrightarrow \overline{b}) \wedge \neg(\overline{a}bc)$ with $Mod(\phi) = \{a\overline{b}\overline{c}, \overline{a}bc, \overline{a}b\overline{c}\}$ and $Mod(\psi) = \{a\overline{b}c, \overline{a}bc, \overline{a}b\overline{c}\}$ as premises[6]. We obtain that $\phi\not\approx_\Delta^\sigma c$ because there the only model of $\phi \wedge c$, $\overline{a}bc$, is not $\prec_\Delta^\sigma$-preferred to $a\overline{b}\overline{c} \in Mod(\phi \wedge \overline{c})$. Likewise, we obtain that $\psi\not\approx_\Delta^\sigma c$ because $\overline{a}bc$, the only model of $\psi \wedge c$, is not $\prec_\Delta^\sigma$-preferred to $a\overline{b}\overline{c} \in Mod(\psi \wedge \overline{c})$. The disjunction $\phi \vee \psi$ is equivalent to $a \Leftrightarrow \overline{b}$, as one can be seen, for instance, on the model sets, as $Mod(\phi) \cup Mod(\psi) = \{a\overline{b}\overline{c}, a\overline{b}c, \overline{a}bc, \overline{a}b\overline{c}\} = Mod(a \Leftrightarrow \overline{b})$. On this knowledge base, we have $\phi \vee \psi\approx_\Delta^\sigma c$, because for every world $\omega' \in Mod((a \Leftrightarrow \overline{b}) \wedge \overline{c}) = \{a\overline{b}\overline{c}, \overline{a}b\overline{c}\}$ there is a world $\omega \in Mod((a \Leftrightarrow \overline{b}) \wedge c) = \{a\overline{b}c, \overline{a}bc\}$ with the property that $\omega \prec_\Delta^\sigma \omega'$, as can be seen in Figure 4.15(b). Overall we have $\phi \vee \psi\approx_\Delta^\sigma c$ but both $\phi\not\approx_\Delta^\sigma c$ and $\psi\not\approx_\Delta^\sigma c$ in contrast to (DR).

From this example we obtain:

---

[6]   The structure of this example arose in discussions involving the author of this thesis, Gabriele Kern-Isberner, and Hans Rott.

ω	verifies	falsifies	$\sigma_\Delta(\omega)$
abc	—	δ_1, δ_2	$\mathbf{a}_1^- \mathbf{a}_2^-$
$ab\overline{c}$	—	δ_1, δ_2	$\mathbf{a}_1^- \mathbf{a}_2^-$
$a\overline{b}c$	δ_2, δ_3	δ_1	$\mathbf{a}_1^- \mathbf{a}_2^+ \mathbf{a}_3^+$
$a\overline{b}\overline{c}$	δ_2	δ_1, δ_3	$\mathbf{a}_1^- \mathbf{a}_2^+ \mathbf{a}_3^-$
$\overline{a}bc$	δ_1, δ_3	δ_2	$\mathbf{a}_1^+ \mathbf{a}_2^- \mathbf{a}_3^+$
$\overline{a}b\overline{c}$	δ_1	δ_2, δ_3	$\mathbf{a}_1^+ \mathbf{a}_2^- \mathbf{a}_3^-$
$\overline{a}\overline{b}c$	δ_1, δ_2	—	$\mathbf{a}_1^+ \mathbf{a}_2^+$
$\overline{a}\overline{b}\overline{c}$	δ_1, δ_2	—	$\mathbf{a}_1^+ \mathbf{a}_2^+$

(a)

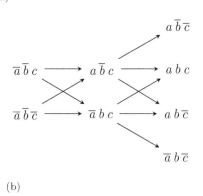

(b)

Figure 4.15: Conditional structures (a) and structural preference (b) for Example 4.68 with $\Delta = \{\delta_1 : (\overline{a}|\top), \delta_2 : (\overline{b}|\top), \delta_1 : (c|a \Leftrightarrow \overline{b})\}$ illustrating that (DR) does not hold for structural inference, in general.

Table 4.8: Verification/falsification behaviour for Example 4.67 to show that structural inference does not satisfy (RM) in general.

ω	$a\,b\,c$	$a\,b\,\overline{c}$	$a\,\overline{b}\,c$	$a\,\overline{b}\,\overline{c}$	$\overline{a}\,b\,c$	$\overline{a}\,b\,\overline{c}$	$\overline{a}\,\overline{b}\,c$	$\overline{a}\,\overline{b}\,\overline{c}$
verifies	δ_2	—	—	—	δ_1	δ_4	—	δ_3
falsifies	δ_1	δ_2, δ_4	δ_2	δ_2, δ_3	—	—	—	—
$\sigma_\Delta(\omega)$	$\mathbf{a}_1^-\,\mathbf{a}_2^+$	$\mathbf{a}_2^-\,\mathbf{a}_4^-$	$\mathbf{a}_2^-$	$\mathbf{a}_2^-\,\mathbf{a}_3^-$	$\mathbf{a}_1^+$	$\mathbf{a}_4^+$	1	$\mathbf{a}_3^-$

Observation 4.69. There are knowledge bases Δ such that the inference relation $\mathrel{|\!\approx_\Delta^\sigma}$ based on Δ does not satisfy Disjunctive Rationality (DR).

But not only it is not possible for structural inference to disentangle an explicit disjunction in the premise, but also to disentangle (implicit) conjunctions:

Observation 4.70. There are knowledge bases Δ such that the inference relation $\mathrel{|\!\approx_\Delta^\sigma}$ based on Δ violates Negation Rationality (NR).

This can be seen in the following example.

Example 4.71. We illustrate Observation 4.70 with a counterexample to the opposite using $\Delta = \{\delta_1 : (b \Leftrightarrow c|b \vee c), \delta_2 : (b \,\overline{\vee}\, c|a), \delta_3 : (b|ac), \delta_4 : (\overline{a}|\overline{b}\overline{c})\}$ as knowledge base. From Δ we obtain the conditional structures and preference relation shown in Figure 4.16. Here we have $a\mathrel{|\!\approx_\Delta^\sigma}b$, because for each world $\omega' \in \{a\overline{b}c, a\overline{b}\overline{c}\} = Mod(a\overline{b})$ we find a $\prec_\Delta^\sigma$-preferred world $\omega \in \{abc, ab\overline{c}\} = Mod(ab)$. But neither is $abc \prec_\Delta^\sigma$-preferred to $a\overline{b}c$ nor $ab\overline{c} \prec_\Delta^\sigma$-preferred to $a\overline{b}\overline{c}$, therefore we have $ac\mathrel{|\!\not\approx_\Delta^\sigma}b$ as well as $a\overline{c}\mathrel{|\!\not\approx_\Delta^\sigma}b$ in contradiction to (NR).

We use the implications shown in Figure 4.10 (see Page 107) and from this observation further obtain:

Corollary 4.72. Structural inference neither satisfies (RT), (T), nor (M) in general.

In Observation 4.51 we found that the property (CI) is not satisfied for preferential inference; the same holds for structural inference.

ω	verifies	falsifies	$\sigma_\Delta(\omega)$
abc	δ_1, δ_3	δ_2	$\mathbf{a}_1^+ \mathbf{a}_2^- \mathbf{a}_3^+$
$ab\overline{c}$	δ_2	δ_1	$\mathbf{a}_1^- \mathbf{a}_2^+$
$a\overline{b}c$	δ_2	δ_1, δ_3	$\mathbf{a}_1^- \mathbf{a}_2^+ \mathbf{a}_3^-$
$a\overline{b}\overline{c}$	—	δ_2, δ_4	$\mathbf{a}_2^- \mathbf{a}_4^-$
$\overline{a}bc$	δ_1	—	$\mathbf{a}_1^+$
$\overline{a}b\overline{c}$	—	δ_1	$\mathbf{a}_1^-$
$\overline{a}\overline{b}c$	—	δ_1	$\mathbf{a}_1^-$
$\overline{a}\overline{b}\overline{c}$	δ_4	—	$\mathbf{a}_4^+$

(a)

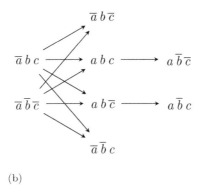

(b)

Figure 4.16: Conditional structures (a) and structural preference (b) for Example 4.71 with $\Delta = \{\delta_1 : (b \Leftrightarrow c | b \vee c), \delta_2 : (b \overline{\vee} c | a), \delta_3 : (b | ac), \delta_4 : (\overline{a} | \overline{b}\overline{c})\}$ illustrating that structural inference does not satisfy (NR), in general.

Table 4.9: Verification/falsification behaviour for Example 4.74 to show that structural inference does not satisfy (CI) in general.

ω	$a\,b\,c$	$a\,b\,\bar{c}$	$a\,\bar{b}\,c$	$a\,\bar{b}\,\bar{c}$	$\bar{a}\,b\,c$	$\bar{a}\,b\,\bar{c}$	$\bar{a}\,\bar{b}\,c$	$\bar{a}\,\bar{b}\,\bar{c}$
verifies	—	—	δ_1	—	δ_2	—	—	δ_3
falsifies	δ_1	δ_1	—	δ_1	—	δ_3	δ_2	—
$\sigma_\Delta(\omega)$	$\mathbf{a}_1^-$	$\mathbf{a}_1^-$	$\mathbf{a}_1^+$	$\mathbf{a}_1^-$	$\mathbf{a}_2^+$	$\mathbf{a}_3^-$	$\mathbf{a}_2^-$	$\mathbf{a}_3^+$

Observation 4.73. There are knowledge bases such that structural inference violates (CI).

Example 4.74. The knowledge base $\Delta = \{\delta_1 : (\bar{b}c|a), \delta_2 : (b|\bar{a}c), \delta_3 : (\bar{b}|\bar{a}\,\bar{c})\}$ is an example for such a knowledge base. For this knowledge base we obtain the verification/falsification behaviour and conditional structures as given in Table 4.9, which leads to the structural preference relation given Figure 4.13 (see Page 110). This is the same preferential relation as in Example 4.52, and so we likewise have $a\!\mathop{\approx}\limits^{\sigma}_{\Delta}c$ and $b\!\mathop{\approx}\limits^{\sigma}_{\Delta}c$, but not $ab\!\mathop{\approx}\limits^{\sigma}_{\Delta}c$ because $abc \not\prec^{\sigma}_{\Delta} ab\bar{c}$ in contrast to (CI).

Corollary 4.57 gave us that structural inference is complete with respect to System P. From this section we obtain that apart from the properties inherited from structural inference, structural inference does not satisfy formal properties outside System P; Figure 4.19 gives an overview over the properties satisfied and violated by structural inference. This covering kindles the conjecture that structural inference also is sound with respect to System P, but this conjecture still lacks a formal proof.

Conjecture 4.75. Structural inference is a sound and complete semantic for System P.

Structural inference is an inductive inference in that it is set up upon a knowledge base which, from which a complete epistemic state represented by structural preference $\prec^{\sigma}_{\Delta}$ is induced. Therefore this inference relation is tied closely to knowledge bases, and we have to analyse how this relationship impacts the inference apart from the formal properties of the inference relation alone.

ω	verifies	falsifies	$\sigma_\Delta(\omega)$
ab	δ_1	δ_2	$\mathbf{a_1^+ a_2^-}$
$a\bar{b}$	δ_2	δ_1	$\mathbf{a_1^- a_2^+}$
$\bar{a}b$	—	—	1
$\bar{a}\bar{b}$	—	—	1

(a)

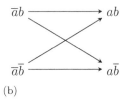

(b)

Figure 4.17: Conditional structures (a) and structural preference (b) for Example 4.76 with $\Delta = \{\delta_1 : (b|a), \delta_2 : (\bar{b}|a)\}$, illustrating that structural inference draws meaningful inferences from inconsistent knowledge bases.

In comparison to Δ-inference $\mathrel{|\!\approx}_\Delta$ (Definition 2.11, see Page 30) we already found a difference with respect to (DI) which is satisfied by $\mathrel{|\!\approx}_\Delta$ (Proposition 2.15) but violated by $\mathrel{|\!\approx}_\Delta^\sigma$ (Observation 4.58).

As we see in the following paragraph. the relation $\mathrel{|\!\approx}_\Delta^\sigma$ does not satisfy the property (MExp). Instead of licensing arbitrary inferences from inconsistent knowledge bases, or not being able to infer anything at all based on an inconsistent knowledge base, even in this case this inference relation licenses for meaningful inferences, as we show in the following example.

Example 4.76. Let $\Delta = \{\delta_1 : (b|a), \delta_2 : (\bar{b}|a)\}$ be a knowledge base. Figure 4.17 gives us the conditional structures and structural preference for this knowledge base. Here we have $\top \mathrel{|\!\approx}_\Delta^\sigma \bar{a}$ because for every model of a there is a structurally preferred model of $\bar{a}$. But we also have, for instance, $\top \mathrel{|\!\not\approx}_\Delta^\sigma a$ for the same reasons, illustrating that no arbitrary inferences are possible.

Observation 4.77. Structural inference does not satisfy (MExp).

With the violation of (MExp) also (SM) is at risk, and this property is indeed is not valid for structural inference.

Observation 4.78. Structural inference does not satisfy (SM).

Example 4.79. We illustrate Observation 4.78 with the knowledge base Δ from Example 4.76 and the knowledge base $\Delta' = \{\delta_1 : (\bar{b}|a)\} \subsetneq \Delta$ with the conditional structures and structural preference given in Figure 4.18. Here we have $a \mathrel{|\!\approx}_{\Delta'}^\sigma b$ but $a \mathrel{|\!\not\approx}_\Delta^\sigma b$, so adding $(\bar{b}|a)$ to Δ' renders the inference impossible in violation of (SM).

ω	verifies	falsifies	$\sigma_\Delta(\omega)$
ab	δ_1	—	$\mathbf{a}_1^+$
$a\bar{b}$	—	δ_1	$\mathbf{a}_1^-$
$\bar{a}b$	—	—	1
$\bar{a}\bar{b}$	—	—	1

(a)

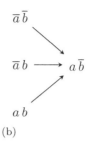

(b)

Figure 4.18: Conditional structures (a) and structural preference (b) for Example 4.79

When setting up conditional structures, every conditional in the knowledge base is taken into account. In this, every conditional in the knowledge base exerts an influence on the resulting inference relations, even if not every conditional can be retrieved in the inference relation. This effect of every conditional in the knowledge base influencing the inference relation was formalised as property for belief revision in [KIK11]. We recall the formulation of this property for OCF:

INDUCTIVE ENFORCEMENT (Ind-Enf) (confer [KIK11, KIE12, EKI14]). An epistemic state Ψ satisfies (Ind-Enf) if given $\Delta = \{(\psi_1|\phi_1),\dots,(\psi_n|\phi_n)\}$ as fixed background knowledge, for every pair $\omega,\omega' \in \Omega$ we have $\omega \prec_\Delta^\sigma \omega'$ implies $\omega \prec_\Psi \omega'$.

As discussed when introducing preferential models and their inference, given than we keep the set of models and the satisfaction relation of a preferential model constant, the resulting preferential inference depends on the preferential relation, only. So under the prerequisite of a classical preferential model over the set of possible worlds from the definition of (Ind-Enf) we directly conclude:

Corollary 4.80. Let $\Delta = \{(\psi_1|\phi_1),\dots,(\psi_n|\phi_n)\} \subseteq (\mathfrak{L} \mid \mathfrak{L})$ be a knowledge base and let $\mathrel{\vert\!\approx}_\Delta^\circ$ be a preferential inference based on Δ. The epistemic state Ψ_Δ° satisfies (Ind-Enf) if and only if $\phi \mathrel{\vert\!\approx}_\Delta^\sigma \psi$ implies $\phi \mathrel{\vert\!\approx}_\Delta^\circ \psi$ for all $\phi, \psi \in \mathfrak{L}$.

4.4 Properties of Ranking Inference

We recalled κ-inference as an instantiation of preferential inference where the preference relation was instantiated by the relation $<_\kappa$ induced by the

OCF κ on the set of possible worlds in Section 3.3. In this section, we examine the formal properties of this inference relation and also point out relationships between κ-inference and Δ-inference.

The preferential model induced by an OCF is $(\Omega, \vDash, <_\kappa)$. As $<_\kappa$ is defined on the ranks $\kappa(\omega)$ of the possible worlds $\omega \in \Omega$ which are non negative integers we directly obtain that $<_\kappa$ is strict and transitive. This gives us:

Corollary 4.81 ([KIE12]). The preferential model $(\Omega, \vDash, <_\kappa)$ is classical and stoppered.

With Proposition 4.36 we already noted that κ-inference satisfies System R. Therefore with this corollary, Theorem 4.27 and the inclusions between the axiom systems in Sections 4.1.3, 4.1.4, and 4.1.5 directly give us the following corollary.

Corollary 4.82 ([Pea90, KIE12]). κ-inference satisfies System O, O$^+$ C, P, and R.

With the same argumentation used for structural inference, κ-inference inherits properties from preferential inference (Propositions 4.42, 4.43, and 4.44).

Corollary 4.83. κ-inference satisfies (NMEFQ), (INT), (REG), and (SREG).

These corollaries cover most of the properties discussed in the first sections of this chapter and leave us with inspecting the properties discussed in Section 4.2. As κ-inference satisfies (RM), from the implications in Figure 4.10 (Page 107) we obtain:

Corollary 4.84. κ-inference satisfies (WRM).

Observation 4.85. There are OCF such that $\vDash_\kappa$ does not satisfy (WD).

Example 4.86. The OCF in Table 4.11a is an example for such an OCF: Here we have $\top \hspace{-0.2em}\vDash_\kappa \overline{a}$ because $\kappa(\overline{a}) = 0 < 1 = \kappa(a)$ and $a \hspace{-0.2em}\not\vDash_\kappa b$ because $\kappa(ab) = 1 = \kappa(a\overline{b})$. However, we also have $a \hspace{-0.2em}\not\vDash_\kappa \overline{b}$ for the same reason.

Together with the implications from Figure 4.10 (Page 107), this observation gives us directly:

Table 4.10: Examples for OCF that do not satisfy (WD) (a), (CI) (b), (WCPS) (c), (RC) (d), (CPS) (e), and (RT) (f)

ω	ab	$a\overline{b}$	$\overline{a}b$	$\overline{a}\,\overline{b}$
$\kappa(\omega)$	1	1	0	0

(a) OCF for Example 4.86.

ω	abc	$ab\overline{c}$	$a\overline{b}c$	$a\overline{b}\overline{c}$	$\overline{a}bc$	$\overline{a}b\overline{c}$	$\overline{a}\,\overline{b}c$	$\overline{a}\,\overline{b}\overline{c}$
$\kappa(\omega)$	1	1	0	1	0	1	1	0

(b) OCF for Example 4.94.

ω	abc	$ab\overline{c}$	$a\overline{b}c$	$a\overline{b}\overline{c}$	$\overline{a}bc$	$\overline{a}b\overline{c}$	$\overline{a}\,\overline{b}c$	$\overline{a}\,\overline{b}\overline{c}$
$\kappa(\omega)$	0	1	0	0	0	1	0	0

(c) OCF for Example 4.92.

ω	ab	$a\overline{b}$	$\overline{a}b$	$\overline{a}\,\overline{b}$
$\kappa(\omega)$	0	1	0	1

(d) OCF for Example 4.88.

ω	ab	$a\overline{b}$	$\overline{a}b$	$\overline{a}\,\overline{b}$
$\kappa(\omega)$	0	1	0	0

(e) OCF for Example 4.91.

ω	$abcd$	$abc\overline{d}$	$ab\overline{c}d$	$ab\overline{c}\overline{d}$	$\overline{a}bcd$	$\overline{a}bc\overline{d}$	$\overline{a}b\overline{c}d$	$\overline{a}b\overline{c}\overline{d}$
$\kappa(\omega)$	2	2	1	1	2	2	2	2
ω	$a\overline{b}cd$	$a\overline{b}c\overline{d}$	$a\overline{b}\overline{c}d$	$a\overline{b}\overline{c}\overline{d}$	$\overline{a}\,\overline{b}cd$	$\overline{a}\,\overline{b}c\overline{d}$	$\overline{a}\,\overline{b}\overline{c}d$	$\overline{a}\,\overline{b}\overline{c}\overline{d}$
$\kappa(\omega)$	0	1	1	1	0	0	0	0

(f) OCF for Example 4.89.

Corollary 4.87. κ-inference does neither satisfy (RC) nor (RT) in general.

Examples for OCF not satisfying (RC) nor (RT) are given as follows.

Example 4.88. The OCF given in Table 4.11d is an example for an OCF that does not satisfy (RC): Here we have $a\,\mid\!\approx_\kappa b$, and $\overline{b}\,\mid\!\not\approx_\kappa a$ but also $\overline{b}\,\mid\!\not\approx_\kappa \overline{a}$.

Example 4.89. Table 4.11f gives an example for an OCF that does not satisfy (RT). For this OCF we have $a\,\mid\!\approx_\kappa b$, $b\,\mid\!\approx_\kappa c$ and $a\,\mid\!\not\approx_\kappa \overline{c}$, but also $a\,\mid\!\not\approx_\kappa c$.

We further examine contrapositive properties in the following proposition.

Observation 4.90. There are OCF κ such that the respective κ-inference neither satisfies (CPS) not (WCPS).

This is illustrated with the next to examples:

Example 4.91. For the OCF in Table 4.11e we have $a\,\mid\!\approx_\kappa b$ but $\overline{b}\,\mid\!\not\approx_\kappa \overline{a}$, contradicting CPS.

Example 4.92. The OCF κ given in Table 4.11c licenses for the inferences $ab\,\mid\!\approx_\kappa c$ and $a\,\mid\!\not\approx_\kappa c$, but we also have $b\overline{c}\,\mid\!\not\approx_\kappa \overline{a}$ in contrast to (WCPS).

By using System P rules it is possible to join the consequences of identical premises for κ-inference using the property (AND). This is not possible for the premises of identical conclusions, formally:

Observation 4.93. There are OCF κ such that $\mathrel{\vcenter{\hbox{$\approx$}}}_\kappa$ does not satisfy (CI).

Example 4.94. The OCF in Table 4.11b is an example for such an OCF: Here we have $a\mathrel{\vcenter{\hbox{$\approx$}}}_\kappa c$ and $b\mathrel{\vcenter{\hbox{$\approx$}}}_\kappa c$, but also $ab\mathrel{\not\vcenter{\hbox{$\approx$}}}_\kappa c$.

We summarise these findings for ranking functions in general in Figure 4.20.

In Section 4.3 we recalled the property (Ind-Enf) which formalises whether an inference relation takes all conditionals in a knowledge base into account. It is clear that ranking inference does not satisfies (Ind-Enf), in general, because it is defined as generic inference upon ranking functions that do not necessarily have any relationship with knowledge bases. We restrict ourselves to ranking functions that are admissible with respect to knowledge bases and we use the symbol $\mathrel{\vcenter{\hbox{$\approx$}}}_{\kappa_\Delta}$ for the inference relation of an OCF κ_Δ that is admissible with respect to a knowledge base $\Delta = \{(\psi_1|\phi_1), \ldots, (\psi_n|\phi_n)\} \subseteq (\mathfrak{L} \mid \mathfrak{L})$. However, even with this restriction, this property is not ensured to hold, as we show in the following example.

Observation 4.95 ([KIE14]). There are ranking functions κ_Δ which are admissible with respect to a knowledge base $\Delta = \{(\psi_1|\phi_1), \ldots, (\psi_n|\phi_n)\}$ such that the ranking inference $\mathrel{\vcenter{\hbox{$\approx$}}}_{\kappa_\Delta}$ violates (Ind-Enf).

The following example is a counterexample for $\mathrel{\vcenter{\hbox{$\approx$}}}_{\kappa_\Delta}$ satisfying (Ind-Enf).

Example 4.96. We use the knowledge base of Example 4.14 (Page 87) and the ranking function for Example 4.37 (Table 4.6, Page 101) as example. The ranking function κ is admissible with respect to

$$\Delta = \left\{ \begin{array}{llll} \delta_1 : (f|b), & \delta_2 : (w|b), & \delta_3 : (b|p), & \delta_4 : (\overline{f}|p), \\ \delta_5 : (b|c), & \delta_6 : (\overline{f}|cb), & \delta_7 : (\overline{c}|p), & \delta_8 : (\overline{c}|p) \end{array} \right\}$$

because

$$\kappa(bf) = 0 < 1 = \kappa(b\overline{f}) \qquad \kappa(bw) = 0 < 1 = \kappa(b\overline{w})$$
$$\kappa(pb) = 1 < 2 = \kappa(p\overline{b}) \qquad \kappa(p\overline{f}) = 1 < 2 = \kappa(pf)$$
$$\kappa(cb) = 1 < 2 = \kappa(c\overline{b}) \qquad \kappa(cb\overline{f}) = 1 < 2 = \kappa(cbf)$$
$$\kappa(p\overline{c}) = 1 < 2 = \kappa(pc) \qquad \kappa(c\overline{p}) = 1 < 2 = \kappa(cp).$$

Here we have $\sigma(p\overline{c}\,\overline{b}\,\overline{f}w) = \mathbf{a}_3^- \mathbf{a}_4^+ \mathbf{a}_7^+ \prec_\Delta^\sigma \mathbf{a}_3^- \mathbf{a}_4^- \mathbf{a}_7^+ = \sigma(p\overline{c}\,\overline{b}fw)$ for structural preference, but $\kappa_\Delta^Z(p\overline{c}\,\overline{b}\,\overline{f}w) = 2 = \kappa_\Delta^Z(p\overline{c}\,\overline{b}fw)$ with the OCF κ, so κ violates (Ind-Enf).

In Section 3.3 we argued that an OCF is admissible with respect to a knowledge base if and only if it is a model of the knowledge base (and canonically overloaded the symbol $\models$ for this relation). This means that there is no admissible OCF to an inconsistent knowledge base and this directly gives us that the inference relation $\approx_{\kappa_\Delta}$ cannot satisfy (MExp) nor (SM).

Observation 4.97. There are knowledge bases $\Delta = \{(\psi_1|\phi_1), \ldots, (\psi_n|\phi_n)\}$ and conditionals $(\psi|\phi)$ such that $\approx_{\kappa_\Delta}$ violates (MExp) and (SM).

4.5 Properties of Inference with System Z

In Section 3.3.3 we recalled two approaches to inductively generate an admissible OCF to consistent knowledge bases. From these two approaches, System Z generates a unique, Pareto-minimal OCF. In this section we further examine inference with OCF generated by System Z, and narrow down the formal properties of this relation. We refer to this inference relation as $\approx_{\kappa_\Delta^Z}$. Being set up upon OCF, $\approx_{\kappa_\Delta^Z}$ inherits the properties of $\approx_\kappa$.

Corollary 4.98 (see [KIE12]). $\approx_{\kappa_\Delta^Z}$ satisfies Systems O, O$^+$, C, P, and R and the formal properties (NMEFQ), (INT), (REG), and (SREG).

By construction, κ_Δ^Z is an OCF that is admissible with respect to the knowledge base Δ, which means that it accepts all conditionals in the knowledge base which by (3.26) is equivalent to the property (DI). Therefore we conclude:

Corollary 4.99 ([EKIBB18, Corollary 103]). Inference with System Z satisfies (DI).

Originating from the consistency test algorithm, System Z needs a consistent knowledge base to be set up. Thus there are no inferences possible for any inconsistent knowledge base, which gives us:

Observation 4.100. There are knowledge bases $\Delta = \{(\psi_1|\phi_1), \ldots, (\psi_n|\phi_n)\}$ and conditionals $(\psi|\phi)$ such that $\approx_{\kappa_\Delta^Z}$ violates (MExp) and (SM).

Observation 4.101 ([EKIBB18, Proposition 104]). There are knowledge bases $\Delta = \{(\psi_1|\phi_1), \ldots, (\psi_n|\phi_n)\}$ such that $\approx_{\kappa_\Delta^Z}$ violates (WD).

This can be observed with the following example.

Example 4.102. As already noted the OCF given in Table 4.6 (Page 102) is generated on the knowledge base from Example 4.14 using System Z. Here we have $\top \hspace{-0.3em}\mid\hspace{-0.6em}\approx_{\kappa_\Delta^Z} \overline{c}$ and, because of $\kappa_\Delta^Z(cw) = 1 = \kappa_\Delta^Z(c\overline{w})$, $c \hspace{-0.3em}\mid\hspace{-0.6em}\not\approx_{\kappa_\Delta^Z} \overline{w}$. For the same reason we also have $c \hspace{-0.3em}\mid\hspace{-0.6em}\not\approx_{\kappa_\Delta^Z} w$, contrasting (WD).

Applying the inference chain in Figure 4.10 (Page 107) this directly gives us

Corollary 4.103 ([EKIBB18, Corollary 106]). There are knowledge bases Δ such that $\approx_{\kappa_\Delta^Z}$ violates (RC) and (CPS).

For any $\phi, \psi \in \mathcal{L}$ we call $\phi\psi$ a *subclass* of ϕ if from ψ we can infer ϕ, that is, we believe that every ψ is a ϕ. With subclass inheritance we can frame a weaker form of monotony called *subclass inheritance*.

SUBCLASS INHERITANCE. [ST12] Let $\psi \approx_\kappa \phi$, that is, let ψ be a subclass of ϕ. $\phi\psi$ *inherits* the properties of ϕ if and only if $\phi \hspace{-0.1em}\mid\hspace{-0.6em}\sim \chi$ and $\psi \hspace{-0.1em}\mid\hspace{-0.6em}\sim \overline{\chi}$ imply $\phi\psi \hspace{-0.1em}\mid\hspace{-0.6em}\sim \chi$ for all $\chi \in \mathcal{L}$. It is clear that in this generic way, Subclass Inheritance is (RT) in alternative formulation.

The literature describes two variants of subclass inheritance: Subclass inheritance for usual subclasses and subclass inheritance for exceptional subclasses. A subclass is called *exceptional* with respect to χ if and only if $\phi \hspace{-0.1em}\mid\hspace{-0.6em}\sim \chi$ and $\psi \hspace{-0.1em}\mid\hspace{-0.6em}\sim \overline{\chi}$. The running example serves as an example for exception subclasses, as there we find, for instance, penguins which are a subclass of birds that are exceptional with respect to their property of not being able to fly.

Proposition 4.104 ([ST12]). System Z licenses for subclass inheritance for usual subclasses.

This, however, is not conveyed to inheritance for exceptional subclasses, as the following example shows.

Example 4.105. The ranking function in Table 4.6 (Page 101) for the knowledge base of Example 4.14 (Page 87) used in Example 4.96 is indeed the System Z OCF for this knowledge base. Here penguins are an exceptional subclass of birds as they are birds $(p \mathrel{\vcenter{\hbox{$\approx$}}}_{\kappa^Z_\Delta} b)$ that cannot fly $(p \mathrel{\vcenter{\hbox{$\approx$}}}_{\kappa^Z_\Delta} \overline{f})$ in contrast to the superclass $(b \mathrel{\vcenter{\hbox{$\approx$}}}_{\kappa^Z_\Delta} f)$. With System Z we here cannot infer whether penguin-birds have wings, or not $(pb \mathrel{\vcenter{\hbox{$\not\approx$}}}_{\kappa^Z_\Delta} w,\ pb \mathrel{\vcenter{\hbox{$\not\approx$}}}_{\kappa^Z_\Delta} \overline{w})$.

This violation of subclass inheritance for exceptional subclasses was noticed by [Pea90] and is also called the *Drowning Problem* [BCD+93]. From this example we obtain:

Observation 4.106 ([Pea90, BCD+93, EKI15a]). System Z inference suffers from the Drowning Problem.

With the above remark on the relationship between the Drowning Problem and (RT), it follows directly that $\mathrel{\vcenter{\hbox{$\approx$}}}_{\kappa^Z_\Delta}$ cannot satisfy (RT).

Corollary 4.107 ([EKIBB18, Proposition 103]). There are knowledge bases Δ such that $\mathrel{\vcenter{\hbox{$\approx$}}}_{\kappa^Z_\Delta}$ violates (RT).

We used Example 4.96 to illustrate that System Z does suffer from the Drowning Problem. As we used this example with the very same OCF to illustrate that OCF do not satisfy (Ind-Enf), in general, with the same Example and argumentation we conclude as follows.

Observation 4.108 ([KIE12]). There are knowledge base Δ such that $\mathrel{\vcenter{\hbox{$\approx$}}}_{\kappa^Z_\Delta}$ violates (Ind-Enf).

As $\mathrel{\vcenter{\hbox{$\approx$}}}_{\kappa^Z_\Delta}$ satisfies System R, it is only to be expected that inferences with this relation exceed the inferences with System P. This was confirmed experimentally in [ST12, TEKIS15a, TEKIS15b], which also showed that even if this relation licenses for additional inferences, the possible inferences are still significantly fewer than using classical logic, so this inference is more cautious as the "classical reasoner".

4.6 Properties of Inference with c-Representations

In the previous section we inspected the formal properties of inference with System Z. In this section we do the very same for inference with single c-representations. The inference with a c-representation κ_Δ^c defined according to Definition 3.33 is, as all ranking inference, inference based on a preferential model with a preferential relation instantiated with $<_{\kappa_\Delta^c}$. We write $\mathrel{\v\!\sim}_{\kappa_\Delta^c}$ to indicate the inference with κ_Δ^c. Thus, like for System Z, for $\mathrel{\v\!\sim}_{\kappa_\Delta^c}$ we inherit a set of formal properties from these inference relations. Additionally, like inference with any ranking function admissible with respect to a knowledge base, a consistent knowledge base is necessary to make any inference at all.

Corollary 4.109. $\mathrel{\v\!\sim}_{\kappa_\Delta^z}$ satisfies Systems O, O$^+$, C, P, and R and the formal properties (NMEFQ), (INT), (REG), and (SREG). There are knowledge bases Δ and conditionals $(\psi|\phi)$ such that $\mathrel{\v\!\sim}_{\kappa_\Delta^c}$ violates (MExp) and (SM).

In contrast to System Z, the sum (3.29) that constitutes the OCF sums up the impact of every falsified conditional and not only takes the most exceptional one into account. Due to this, we can observe inference with c-representations not to suffer from the Drowning Problem in the running example.

Example 4.110. We use the knowledge base of Example 4.14 (Page 87). For this knowledge base, a minimal c-representation can be achieved with the solution

$$\kappa_1^- = 1 \qquad \kappa_2^- = 1 \qquad \kappa_3^- = 2 \qquad \kappa_4^- = 2$$
$$\kappa_5^- = 2 \qquad \kappa_6^- = 2 \qquad \kappa_7^- = 0 \qquad \kappa_8^- = 1,$$

which leads to the OCF given in Table 4.11. Here, for instance, penguin-birds inherit the property of having wings from their superclass birds even if they are exceptional birds as they cannot fly:

$$pb\mathrel{\v\!\sim}_{\kappa_\Delta^c} w \qquad\qquad \text{because} \qquad\qquad \kappa(pbw) = 1 < 2 = \kappa(pb\overline{w}).$$

Table 4.11: c-Representation for the running example in Example 4.110

ω	$pcbfw$	$pcbf\overline{w}$	$pcb\overline{f}w$	$pcb\overline{f}\overline{w}$	$pc\overline{b}fw$	$pc\overline{b}f\overline{w}$	$pc\overline{b}\overline{f}w$	$pc\overline{b}\overline{f}\overline{w}$
$\kappa(\omega)$	5	6	2	3	7	7	5	5

ω	$p\overline{c}bfw$	$p\overline{c}bf\overline{w}$	$p\overline{c}b\overline{f}w$	$p\overline{c}b\overline{f}\overline{w}$	$p\overline{c}\overline{b}fw$	$p\overline{c}\overline{b}f\overline{w}$	$p\overline{c}\overline{b}\overline{f}w$	$p\overline{c}\overline{b}\overline{f}\overline{w}$
$\kappa(\omega)$	2	3	1	2	2	4	2	2

ω	$\overline{p}cbfw$	$\overline{p}cbf\overline{w}$	$\overline{p}cb\overline{f}w$	$\overline{p}cb\overline{f}\overline{w}$	$\overline{p}c\overline{b}fw$	$\overline{p}c\overline{b}f\overline{w}$	$\overline{p}c\overline{b}\overline{f}w$	$\overline{p}c\overline{b}\overline{f}\overline{w}$
$\kappa(\omega)$	2	2	1	2	2	2	2	2

ω	$\overline{p}\overline{c}bfw$	$\overline{p}\overline{c}bf\overline{w}$	$\overline{p}\overline{c}b\overline{f}w$	$\overline{p}\overline{c}b\overline{f}\overline{w}$	$\overline{p}\overline{c}\overline{b}fw$	$\overline{p}\overline{c}\overline{b}f\overline{w}$	$\overline{p}\overline{c}\overline{b}\overline{f}w$	$\overline{p}\overline{c}\overline{b}\overline{f}\overline{w}$
$\kappa(\omega)$	0	1	1	2	0	0	0	0

But even if we have subclass inheritance for exceptional subclasses, $\approx_{\kappa_{\Delta}^c}$ does not satisfy (RT) in general, which we show as follows.

Example 4.111. Let $\Sigma = \{A, B, C\}$ be the alphabet of a knowledge base $\Delta = \{\delta_1 : (\overline{a}|\top), \delta_2 : (c|b\overline{a}), \delta_3 : (\overline{a}|\overline{b}c), \delta_4 : (\overline{a}|\overline{b}\overline{c})\}$ with a verification/-falsification behaviour shown in Table 4.12 (above). This gives a minimal solution

$$\kappa_1^- > 0 \qquad \kappa_2^- > 0 \qquad \kappa_3^- > 0 \qquad \kappa_4^- > 0$$

for the system of inequalities (3.30), which result in the c-representation given in Table 4.12 (below). Here we have

$$a\approx_{\kappa_{\Delta}^c} b \qquad \text{because} \qquad \kappa_{\Delta}^c(ab) = 1 < 3 = \kappa_{\Delta}^c(a\overline{b}),$$
$$b\approx_{\kappa_{\Delta}^c} c \qquad \text{because} \qquad \kappa_{\Delta}^c(bc) = 0 < 1 = \kappa_{\Delta}^c(b\overline{c}), \text{and}$$
$$a\not\approx_{\kappa_{\Delta}^c} \overline{c} \qquad \text{because} \qquad \kappa_{\Delta}^c(a\overline{c}) = 1 = \kappa_{\Delta}^c(ac), \qquad (4.5)$$

so the prerequisited of (RT) as satisfies, but (4.5) also gives us $a\not\approx_{\kappa_{\Delta}^c} c$ in contrast to (RT).

Observation 4.112. There are knowledge base $\Delta = \{(\psi_1|\phi_1), \dots, (\psi_n|\phi_n)\}$ with c-representations that lead to inference relations $\approx_{\kappa_{\Delta}^c}$ which violate (RT).

Table 4.12: Example for a c-representation such that $\mathrel{\mkern-3mu\vrule height 1.6ex depth 0pt width 0pt}\!\approx_{\kappa_\Delta^c}$ violates (RT)

ω	$a\,b\,c$	$a\,b\,\overline{c}$	$a\,\overline{b}\,c$	$a\,\overline{b}\,\overline{c}$	$\overline{a}\,b\,c$	$\overline{a}\,b\,\overline{c}$	$\overline{a}\,\overline{b}\,c$	$\overline{a}\,\overline{b}\,\overline{c}$
verifies	—	—	—	δ_1,δ_2	δ_1	δ_1,δ_3	δ_1,δ_4
falsifies	δ_1	δ_1	δ_1,δ_3	δ_1,δ_3	—	δ_2	—	—
κ_Δ^c	1	1	3	3	0	1	0	0

Each c-representation is an OCF that is admissible with respect to the knowledge base, this means that it accepts all conditionals in the knowledge base which by (3.26) is equivalent to the property (DI). Therefore we conclude:

Corollary 4.113 ([EKIBB18, Corollary 109],[KIE12]). Inference with any c-representation satisfies (DI).

For the rank of each world, c-representations sum up the impact of every conditional falsified (3.29). This means that, other as for System Z, every conditional is taken into account, if its impact is positive. Nonetheless the possibility of impacts with a value of 0 renders c-representations to violate the property (Ind-Enf) in general.

Example 4.114 ([KIE14, Example 9]). Let $\Delta = \{\delta_1 : (\psi|\phi), \delta_2 : (\psi\chi|\phi)\}$. A minimal solution to the system of inequalities (3.30) is obtained by setting $\kappa_1^- = 0$ and $\kappa_2^- = 1$. This results in an OCF κ as given in Table 4.13, which also contains the conditional structures for this knowledge base. Here we find $a\,b\,\overline{c} \prec_\Delta^\sigma a\,\overline{b}\,c$ but $\kappa_\Delta^c(a\,b\,\overline{c}) = 1 = \kappa_\Delta^c(a\,\overline{b}\,c)$ in contrast to (Ind-Enf).

In this example we observe:

Observation 4.115. There are knowledge bases with c-representations that violate (Ind-Enf).

We already argued that this violation stems from the minimal c-representation assigning an impact of 0 to some conditionals, and these conditionals then do not have an impact on the preferential relation imposed by the c-representation. Based on these deliberations, [KIE14] gives a sufficient condition for c-representations to satisfy (Ind-Enf).

Table 4.13: Verification/falsification behaviour, conditional structures and minimal c-representation for the knowledge base $\Delta = \{\delta_1 : (\psi|\phi), \delta_2 : (\psi\chi|\phi)\}$ in Example 4.114

ω	$a\,b\,c$	$a\,b\,\bar{c}$	$a\,\bar{b}\,c$	$a\,\bar{b}\,\bar{c}$	$\bar{a}\,b\,c$	$\bar{a}\,b\,\bar{c}$	$\bar{a}\,\bar{b}\,c$	$\bar{a}\,\bar{b}\,\bar{c}$
verifies	δ_1,δ_2	δ_1	—	—	—	—	—	—
falsifies	—	δ_2	δ_1,δ_2	—	—	—	—	—
$\sigma_\Delta(\omega)$	$a_1^+ a_2^+$	$a_1^+ a_2^-$	$a_1^- a_2^-$	$a_1^- a_2^-$	1	1	1	1
$\kappa_\Delta^c(\omega)$	0	1	1	1	0	0	0	0

Lemma 4.116 ([KIE14, Proposition 6]). A c-representation κ_Δ^c for a knowledge base $\Delta = \{(\psi_1|\phi_1), \ldots, (\psi_n|\phi_n)\} \subseteq (\mathfrak{L} \mid \mathfrak{L})$ satisfies (Ind-Enf) if in the solution to the system of inequalities (3.30) constituting κ_Δ^c by means of Equation (3.29) the impacts κ_i^- are strictly positive for all $(\psi_i|\phi_i) \in \Delta$.

4.7 Interim Summary

This chapter recalls the major axiom systems of nonmonotonic reasoning, Systems O, C, P, and R. These systems are illustrated with different inference relations defined in the previous chapters as semantics. In this we simultaneously illustrate the properties of the axiom systems and their ability to rate semantical inference relations. The chapter extends the literature by formally defining generic syntactic inferences based on inference rules, which we instantiated with the axiom systems recalled. This is followed by recalling additional selected formal properties not covered by the axiom systems. Here we recalled properties of interest for this dissertation and showed how they relate to preferential inference.

The chapter is based on the findings of [KIE12, KIE14, EKIBB18]. The manual [EKIBB18] is still an unpublished manuscript at the time this dissertation is written, and is being compiled under the direction of the author of this thesis. Results given in this thesis which are referenced to this manual do appear in this thesis for the first time and in this extend the literature regarding formal properties of nonmonotonic inference relations. My own contributions to the articles [KIE12, KIE14] has been to show that structural inference does not satisfy (DI) and that inference with a c-representation with strictly positive impacts κ_i^- satisfies (Ind-Enf).

This chapter extends the literature by defining the properties (NMEFQ) and (INT), formally; we illustrated how the given properties can be applied by a thorough examination of preferential inference with respect to these properties. It further extends the literature in showing that (LLE) can be used for non-inferences, (CONS) follows from (AND) and (RW), and (CPS) implies (WCPS). The chapter thoroughly examines the inference relations discussed in the previous chapter with respect to their formal properties and extends the literature in the following findings:

- Showing that preferential inference satisfies (NMFQ), (INT), (REG) and (SREG), but violates (WD), (WCPS), (RC), (CPS), (CI), (RM), and (RT).

- Showing that structural inference satisfies (NMFQ), (INT), (REG), and (SREG), but falsifies (WD), (WCPS), (RC), (CPS), (DR), (NR), (CI), (RM), and (RT) in extension of [KIE12, KIE14]. Also showing that structural inference does neither satisfy (MExp) nor (SM) in general, but licenses for meaningful inferences from inconsistent knowledge bases.

- Showing that, in extension of [Spo88, GP96, Spo12, KIE12, KIE14], κ-inference satisfies (NMFQ), (INT), (REG), and (SREG), but violates the properties (WD), (WCPS), (RC), (CPS), (DR), (NR), (CI), (RM), and (RT), as well as (MExp) and (SM).

- Showing that, in extension of [Pea90, KIE12, KIE14], inference with System Z satisfies (NMFQ), (INT), (REG), and (SREG), but violates (MExp) and (SM).

- Showing that, in extension of [KI01, KIE12, KIE14], inference with any c-representation satisfies (NMFQ), (INT), (REG), and (SREG), but violates (MExp) and (SM).

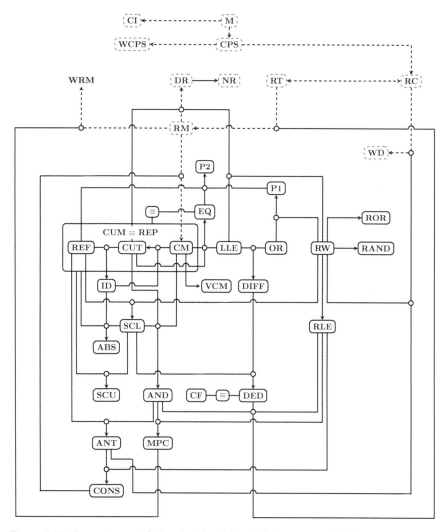

Figure 4.19: Properties satisfied and violated (dashed) by structural inference; properties unknown are given in grey

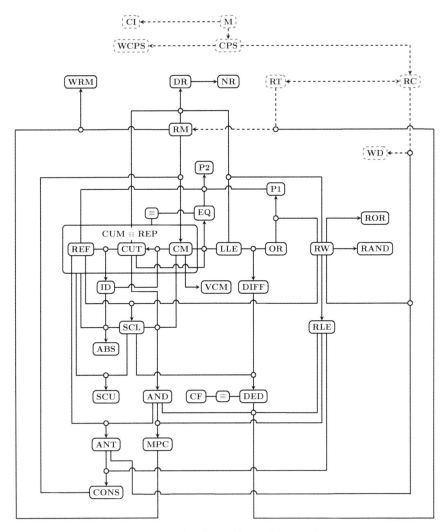

Figure 4.20: Properties satisfied and violated (dashed) by κ-inference

5 Reasoning with Sets of c-Representations

In Section 3.3.3.3 we recalled c-representations [KI01] as a technique to inductively obtain ranking models for a given conditional knowledge base. We also already discussed that other than ranking models obtained by System Z [Pea90], which are the (with respect to the ranking of the worlds) unique Pareto minimal ranking models of the knowledge base, the approach of c-representations gives us a schema for ranking models of the knowledge base defined by a system of inequalities.

We already discussed properties and merits of the approach of c-representation with respect to inference and implementations based on single c-representations of the knowledge base in previous chapters. In this chapter, which is based on and extends the articles [BEK16, BEKI16, BEKIK16, BEKIK18], we turn to inferences with all c-representations or subsets thereof. We characterise inference with sets of c-representations as constraint satisfaction problems in Section 5.1 and discuss the relationships between these inference and properties thereof in Section 5.2.

5.1 c-Representations as Constraint Satisfaction Problems and Solutions Thereof

We first take another look at the definition of c-representations (Definition 3.33) via the system of inequalities (3.30) and show how this can be understood as constraint satisfaction problem and use this to characterise inference with sets of c-representations. In Section 3.3.3.3 we recalled a c-representation of a knowledge base $\Delta = \{(\psi_1|\phi_1), \ldots, (\psi_n|\phi_n)\}$ to be an OCF κ^c_Δ that is composed from a set of non negative impacts κ^-_i for each conditional $(\psi_i|\phi_i) \in \Delta$ such that the rank of every world $\omega \in \Omega$ is the sum of the impacts of the conditionals the worlds, and the impacts satisfy the inequality (3.30) (Definition 3.33).

Definition 5.1 (*CSP*(Δ), *Sol*(*CSP*(Δ)) [BEK16]). Let Δ be a knowledge base, $\Delta = \{(\psi_1|\phi_1), \ldots, (\psi_n|\phi_n)\}$. By *CSP*($\Delta$) we define the *constraint satisfaction problem* that captures the constraints the system of inequalities (3.30) imposes on the impacts κ^-_i of the conditionals, as well as the

© Springer-Verlag GmbH Germany, part of Springer Nature 2018
C. Eichhorn, *Rational Reasoning with Finite Conditional
Knowledge Bases*, https://doi.org/10.1007/978-3-476-04824-0_5

domain of these impacts, formally, for all $1 \leq i \leq n$, with the constraints

$$\kappa_i^- \geq 0 \tag{5.1}$$

$$\kappa_i^- > \min_{\omega \models \phi_i \psi_i} \left\{ \sum_{\substack{j \neq i \\ \omega \models \phi_j \overline{\psi_i}}} \kappa_i^- \right\} - \min_{\omega \models \phi_i \overline{\psi_i}} \left\{ \sum_{\substack{j \neq i \\ \omega \models \phi_j \overline{\psi_i}}} \kappa_i^- \right\}. \tag{5.2}$$

A *solution* to this system is a n-tuple $(\kappa_i^-)_{i=1}^n$ of nonnegative integers; the set of all solutions to $CSP(\Delta)$ is denoted as $Sol(CSP(\Delta))$.

The constraint satisfaction problem $CSP(\Delta)$ is set up to capture the inequalities of c-representations, and contains neither more nor less then the domain definition (5.1) and the defining inequality (5.2) for each impact κ_i^- of a c-representation for a conditional knowledge base Δ. So $CSP(\Delta)$ is a correct and complete modelling of c-representations.

Corollary 5.2 ([BEKI16, Propositions 3 and 4]). Let Δ be a conditional knowledge base, $\Delta = \{(\psi_1|\phi_1), \ldots, (\psi_n|\phi_n)\} \subseteq (\mathfrak{L} \mid \mathfrak{L})$ with $CSP(\Delta)$ according to Definition 5.1. For every solution $\vec{\eta} := (\kappa_i^-)_{i=1}^n \in Sol(CSP(\Delta))$ there is a c-representation κ_Δ^c such that $(\kappa_i^-)_{i=1}^n$ is a correct configuration of the conditional impacts in the system (3.30), and for every c-representation κ_Δ^c of Δ with a correct configuration of the conditional impacts in the system (3.30) $(\kappa_i^-)_{i=1}^n$, this tuple is an element of $Sol(CSP(\Delta))$.

From this equivalence and Proposition 3.39 we directly obtain:

Corollary 5.3 ([BEKI16, Propositions 3 and 4]). A conditional knowledge base $\Delta = \{(\psi_1|\phi_1), \ldots, (\psi_n|\phi_n)\}$ is consistent if and only if $CSP(\Delta)$ is solvable, that is, if and only if $Sol(CSP(\Delta)) \neq \varnothing$.

So by Corollary 5.2 we obtain that we can use solutions $\vec{\eta}$ to the $CSP(\Delta)$ and OCF $\kappa_{\vec{\eta}}$ thereof interchangeable with c-representations κ_Δ^c of Δ. We put this result to use by writing $\kappa_{\vec{\eta}}$ to denote the c-representation obtained from $\vec{\eta} \in Sol(CSP(\Delta))$ by means of formula (3.29). As each solution generates exactly one c-representations by means of Formula (3.29), we sometimes abbreviate the statement "$\vec{\eta} \in Sol(CSP(\Delta))$ constituting a c-representation $\kappa_{\vec{\eta}}$ according to Formula (3.29)" by simply stating $\kappa_{\vec{\eta}} \in Sol(CSP(\Delta))$ where this abbreviation leads to shorter and more legible statements. With these insights, we now have a language to reason about single c-representations and sets thereof.

We use τ_{Δ}^{c} as a *generic c-representation* where each rank if given as a sum of the abstract symbols for the impacts that constitute the rank to argue about the different sets of OCF $\kappa_{\vec{\eta}}$ as a generic function of the tuple $\vec{\eta}$.

With $\mathrel{\vert\!\approx_{\kappa_{\Delta}^{c}}}$ we already framed the inference relation of a single c-representation. We use this formalisation as a base for inference with sets of c-representations, as follows.

Definition 5.4 (Credulous/Sceptical Inference with c-Representations [BEKI16]). Let $\Delta = \{(\psi_1|\phi_1), \ldots, (\psi_n|\phi_n)\} \subseteq (\mathfrak{L} \mid \mathfrak{L})$ be a conditional knowledge base and let $\phi, \psi \in \mathfrak{L}$ be formulas. ψ can be *credulously c-inferred* from ϕ in the context of Δ, written $\mathrel{\vert\!\approx_{\Delta}^{\cup,c}}$, if and only if there is a c-representation $\kappa_{\vec{\eta}}$ with $\vec{\eta} \in Sol(CSP(\Delta))$ such that $\phi \mathrel{\vert\!\approx_{\kappa_{\vec{\eta}}}} \psi$. ψ can be *sceptically c-inferred* from ϕ in the context of Δ, written $\mathrel{\vert\!\approx_{\Delta}^{\cap,c}}$, if and only if for every c-representation $\kappa_{\vec{\eta}}$ with $\vec{\eta} \in Sol(CSP(\Delta))$ such that $\phi \mathrel{\vert\!\approx_{\kappa_{\vec{\eta}}}} \psi$.

In addition to these classical ways of defining inference, we recall that κ-inference in general is set up upon inequalities, that is, for any κ-inference we have $\phi \mathrel{\vert\!\approx_{\kappa}} \psi$ if and only if $\kappa(\phi\psi) < \kappa(\phi\overline{\psi})$ (see 3.26). With this equivalence between acceptance of a conditional and inference between formulas, Definition 5.4 leads to $\phi \mathrel{\vert\!\approx_{\Delta}^{\cup,c}} \psi$ if and only if $\kappa_{\vec{\eta}}(\phi\psi) < \kappa_{\vec{\eta}}(\phi\overline{\psi})$ for any $\vec{\eta} \in Sol(CSP(\Delta))$ and $\phi \mathrel{\vert\!\approx_{\Delta}^{\cap,c}} \psi$ if and only if $\kappa_{\vec{\eta}}(\phi\psi) < \kappa_{\vec{\eta}}(\phi\overline{\psi})$ for all $\vec{\eta} \in Sol(CSP(\Delta))$. This insight leads us to another possible definition of inference, where we infer ϕ from ψ if and only if we find c-representations of Δ that licenses for this inference, but none that licenses for the inference of the inverse, that is, ψ can be credulously inferred from ϕ in the context of Δ, but $\overline{\psi}$ cannot.

Definition 5.5 (Weakly Sceptical Inference with c-Representations [BEKI16]). Let $\Delta = \{(\psi_1|\phi_1), \ldots, (\psi_n|\phi_n)\} \subseteq (\mathfrak{L} \mid \mathfrak{L})$ be a conditional knowledge base and let $\phi, \psi \in \mathfrak{L}$ be formulas. ψ is *weakly sceptical c-inferred* from ϕ in the context of Δ, written $\mathrel{\vert\!\approx_{\Delta}^{ws,c}}$, if and only if there is a c-representation $\kappa_{\vec{\eta}}$ with $\vec{\eta} \in Sol(CSP(\Delta))$ such that $\phi \mathrel{\vert\!\approx_{\kappa_{\vec{\eta}}}} \psi$ and we have $\phi \mathrel{\not\vert\!\approx_{\kappa_{\vec{\eta}'}}} \overline{\psi}$ for all c-representations $\kappa_{\vec{\eta}'} \in Sol(CSP(\Delta))$.

We illustrate these three inference relations based on all c-representations with the following examples:

Example 5.6 (confer [BEKIK16]). Let $\Sigma = \{P, B, A\}$ be a variation of the running Example 3.34 with variables that encode our knowledge about (not) being a $\underline{P}$enguin, (not) being a $\underline{B}$ird and (not) living in $\underline{A}$ntarctica. We here use the knowledge that penguins usually are birds $\delta_1 : (b|p)$, penguins usually live in Antarctica $\delta_2 : (a|p)$, and that penguin living in the Antarctica usually are birds $\delta_3 : (b|pa)$ as knowledge base $\Delta = \{\delta_1, \delta_2, \delta_3\}$. This knowledge base has a verification / falsification behaviour as shown in Table 5.1 (upper part), which, applying the technique of c-representations, results in the inequalities

$$\kappa_1^- > -\min\{\kappa_2^-, \kappa_3^-\}$$
$$\kappa_2^- > 0$$
$$\kappa_3^- > -\kappa_1^-, \qquad\qquad\qquad (5.3)$$

which give us the generic ranks given in Table 5.1 (middle); in Table 5.1 (below) we given three concrete instances from the solutions $\vec{\eta}_1 = (1, 1, 0)$, $\vec{\eta}_2 = (0, 1, 1)$, and $\vec{\eta}_2 = (1, 1, 1)$. Note that we usually assume each impact to be strictly positive because of the system of inequalities (3.30), and thus this inequality would usually be strict . Nonetheless for the impacts of this knowledge base we have $\kappa_2^- \leq \kappa_1^- + \kappa_2^-$ because there are valid solutions with $\kappa_1^- = 0$. Therefore there are solutions $\vec{\eta} \in Sol(CSP(\Delta))$ resulting in ranking functions $\kappa_{\vec{\eta}}$ where $\kappa_{\vec{\eta}}(p\,b\,\overline{a}) < \kappa_{\vec{\eta}}(p\,\overline{b}\,\overline{a})$, as, for instance, $\vec{\eta}_1$, and solutions $\vec{\eta}' \in Sol(CSP(\Delta))$ resulting in ranking functions $\kappa_{\vec{\eta}'}$ where $\kappa_{\vec{\eta}'}(p\,b\,\overline{a}) = \kappa_{\vec{\eta}'}(p\,\overline{b}\,\overline{a})$, as, for instance, $\vec{\eta}_2$, but for neither solution we find $p\,b\,\overline{a}$ to be strictly less plausible as $p\,\overline{b}\,\overline{a}$. This means we can credulously and weakly sceptically infer that penguins that do not live in Antarctica are birds ($\overline{pa}\,\approx_{\Delta}^{\cup,c}b$ and $\overline{pa}\,\approx_{\Delta}^{ws,c}b$), but not sceptically ($\overline{pa}\,\not\approx_{\Delta}^{\cap,c}b$). In this example we can additionally from penguin birds infer that they live in Antarctica, that is $pb\,\approx_{\Delta}^{\bullet},c$ for any $\bullet \in \{\cap, ws, \cup\}$, because $\tau_{\Delta}^c(p\,b\,a) = 0 < \kappa_2^- = \tau_{\Delta}^c(p\,b\,\overline{a})$ as $\kappa_2^- > 0$.

With the following example we show that credulous and weakly sceptical inference do not, in general, coincide, but license for different inferences.

Example 5.7 (confer [BEKI16]). Let $\Delta = \{\delta_1 : (b|a), \delta_2 : (b|\overline{a})\}$ be a knowledge base over an alphabet $\Sigma = \{A, B\}$. Applying the approach of

Table 5.1: Verification / falsification behaviour (upper part), generic ranks (middle) and three solutions ($\vec{\eta}_1 = (1,1,0)$, $\vec{\eta}_2 = (0,1,1)$, and $\vec{\eta}_2 = (1,1,1)$, bottom) for the c-representations in Example 5.6

ω	$p\,b\,a$	$p\,b\,\bar{a}$	$p\,\bar{b}\,a$	$p\,\bar{b}\,\bar{a}$	$\bar{p}\,b\,a$	$\bar{p}\,b\,\bar{a}$	$\bar{p}\,\bar{b}\,a$	$\bar{p}\,\bar{b}\,\bar{a}$
verifies	$\delta_1,\delta_2,\delta_3$	δ_1	δ_2	—	—	—	—	—
falsifies	—	δ_2	δ_1,δ_3	δ_1,δ_2	—	—	—	—
$\tau^c_\Delta(\omega)$	0	κ^-_2	$\kappa^-_1 + \kappa^-_3$	$\kappa^-_1 + \kappa_2$	0	0	0	0
$\kappa_{\vec{\eta}_1}(\omega)$	0	1	1	2	0	0	0	0
$\kappa_{\vec{\eta}_2}(\omega)$	0	1	1	1	0	0	0	0
$\kappa_{\vec{\eta}_3}(\omega)$	0	1	2	2	0	0	0	0

c-representations gives us the inequalities

$$\kappa^-_1 > 0$$
$$\kappa^-_2 > 0,$$

and therefore the set $Sol(CSP(\Delta))$ of all solutions to the respective CSP can be partitioned into the three disjoint sets $\mathcal{S}_1 = \{(\kappa^-_1, \kappa^-_2) | \kappa^-_1 < \kappa^-_2\}$, $\mathcal{S}_2 = \{(\kappa^-_1, \kappa^-_2) | \kappa^-_1 > \kappa^-_2\}$, and $\mathcal{S}_3 = \{(\kappa^-_1, \kappa^-_2) | \kappa^-_1 = \kappa^-_2\}$. So with $\kappa_{\vec{\eta}_1} \in \mathcal{S}_1$ (for instance $\vec{\eta}_1 = (1,2)$ as given in Table 5.2), $\kappa_{\vec{\eta}_2} \in \mathcal{S}_2$ (for instance $\vec{\eta}_2 = (2,1)$), and $\kappa_{\vec{\eta}_3} \in \mathcal{S}_3$ (for instance $\vec{\eta}_2 = (1,1)$), we obtain $\bar{b} \not\hspace{-0.3em}\sim^{\cap,c}_\Delta a$, $\bar{b} \not\hspace{-0.3em}\sim^{ws,c}_\Delta a$, but $\bar{b} \hspace{0.1em}|\!\!\sim^{\cup,c}_\Delta a$ as well as $\bar{b} \hspace{0.1em}|\!\!\sim^{\cup,c}_\Delta \bar{a}$.

So we obtain that weakly sceptical c-inference prevents the inference of contradictory formulas without the strict restriction that a formulas inferred under this semantic has to be inferred in every c-representation of the knowledge base.

5.2 Formal Properties of and Relations among Inference Relations over Sets of c-Representations

In the previous section we recalled the inference relations of sceptical, credulous, and weakly sceptical c-inference. For these relations, even small and not-notorious examples (as, for instance, Example 5.7) revealed that credulous c-inference easily licenses contradictory inferences. Therefore, in the following we concentrate on determining the properties of sceptical and

Table 5.2: Verification / falsification behaviour (upper part), generic ranks (middle) and three solutions for the c-representations (bottom) in Example 5.7 where $\vec{\eta}_1 = (1, 2) \in \mathcal{S}_1$, $\vec{\eta}_2 = (2, 1) \in \mathcal{S}_2$, and $\vec{\eta}_3 = (1, 1) \in \mathcal{S}_3$.

ω	$a\,b$	$a\,\overline{b}$	$\overline{a}\,b$	$\overline{a}\,\overline{b}$
verifies	δ_1	—	δ_2	—
falsifies	—	δ_1	—	δ_2
$\tau_\Delta^c(\omega)$	0	κ_1^-	0	κ_2^-
$\kappa_{\vec{\eta}_1}(\omega)$	0	1	0	2
$\kappa_{\vec{\eta}_2}(\omega)$	0	2	0	1
$\kappa_{\vec{\eta}_3}(\omega)$	0	1	0	1

weakly sceptical c-inference, but will come back to credulous c-inference as upper bound of possible inferences with sets of c-representations.

Every c-representation satisfies System P, as showed in Corollary 4.109. This gives us that also the sceptical inference over all c-representation of a knowledge base satisfies this inference system.

Proposition 5.8 ([BEKI16, Proposition 5]). Let $\Delta = \{(\psi_1|\phi_1), \ldots, (\psi_n|\phi_n)\}$ be a knowledge base and $\psi, \phi \in \mathfrak{L}$ be formulas. If, in the context of Δ, ψ can be inferred from ϕ with System P, then ψ can also be sceptically c-inferred from ϕ.

So every inference valid for System P is also valid for sceptical c-inference. The converse is not true in general, which we see in the following example.

Example 5.9 (confer [BEKI16]). We use an excerpt of the penguin example, namely the knowledge base

$$\Delta = \{\delta_1 \ : \ (f|b), \delta_2 \ : \ (w|b), \delta_3 \ : \ (b|p), \delta_4 \ : \ (\overline{f}|p)\}$$

with a verification / falsification behaviour as shown in Table 5.3. We solve the inequalities (3.30) and obtain

$$\kappa_1^- > 0$$

$$\kappa_2^- > 0$$

$$\kappa_3^- > \min\{\kappa_1^-, \kappa_4^-\} \tag{5.4}$$

$$\kappa_4^- > \min\{\kappa_1^-, \kappa_3^-\} \tag{5.5}$$

We further inspect (5.4) and (5.5). Assume $\kappa_4^- \leq \kappa_1^-$. Then in (5.4) we had $\kappa_4 = \min\{\kappa_1^-, \kappa_4^-\}$ and therefore $\kappa_3^- > \kappa_4^-$, which clashes with (5.5). Therefore $\kappa_1^- < \kappa_4^-$, which gives us $\kappa_3^- > \kappa_1^-$ by (5.4), and this gives us $\kappa_4^- > \kappa_1^-$ by (5.5), and we obtain

$$\kappa_1^- > 0, \qquad \kappa_2^- > 0, \qquad \kappa_3^- > \kappa_1^-, \qquad \kappa_4^- > \kappa_1^- \tag{5.6}$$

as constraints for solutions of $CSP(\Delta)$. We illustrate the weak monotone property of default inheritance by showing that given $b \mathrel{\approx}_\Delta^{\cap,c} w$ we obtain $bp \mathrel{\approx}_\Delta^{\cap,c} w$ given $p \mathrel{\not\approx}_\Delta^{\cap,c} \overline{w}$. We consult Table 5.3 to obtain the necessary generic ranks:

$$\tau_\Delta^c(bw) = \min\{\tau_\Delta^c(\,p\,b\,f\,w\,), \tau_\Delta^c(\,p\,b\,\overline{f}\,w\,), \tau_\Delta^c(\,\overline{p}\,b\,f\,w\,), \tau_\Delta^c(\,\overline{p}\,b\,\overline{f}\,w\,)\}$$
$$= 0$$

$$\tau_\Delta^c(b\overline{w}) = \min\{\tau_\Delta^c(\,p\,b\,f\,\overline{w}\,), \tau_\Delta^c(\,p\,b\,\overline{f}\,\overline{w}\,), \tau_\Delta^c(\,\overline{p}\,b\,f\,\overline{w}\,), \tau_\Delta^c(\,\overline{p}\,b\,\overline{f}\,\overline{w}\,)\}$$
$$= \min\{\kappa_1^-, \kappa_2^-\}$$

$$\tau_\Delta^c(pw) = \min\{\tau_\Delta^c(\,p\,b\,f\,w\,), \tau_\Delta^c(\,p\,b\,\overline{f}\,w\,), \tau_\Delta^c(\,p\,\overline{b}\,f\,w\,), \tau_\Delta^c(\,p\,\overline{b}\,\overline{f}\,w\,)\} \tag{5.7}$$
$$= \min\{\kappa_1^-, \kappa_4^-, \kappa_3^- + \kappa_4^-, \kappa_3^-\}$$
$$= \kappa_1^-$$

$$\tau_\Delta^c(p\overline{w}) = \min\{\tau_\Delta^c(\,p\,b\,f\,\overline{w}\,), \tau_\Delta^c(\,p\,b\,\overline{f}\,\overline{w}\,), \tau_\Delta^c(\,p\,\overline{b}\,f\,\overline{w}\,), \tau_\Delta^c(\,p\,\overline{b}\,\overline{f}\,\overline{w}\,)\} \tag{5.8}$$
$$= \min\{\kappa_2^- + \kappa_3^-, \kappa_1^- + \kappa_2^-, \kappa_3^- + \kappa_4^-, \kappa_3^-\}$$
$$= \min\{\kappa_1^- + \kappa_2^-, \kappa_3^-\}$$

$$\tau_\Delta^c(pbw) = \min\{\tau_\Delta^c(p\,b\,f\,w), \tau_\Delta^c(p\,b\,\overline{f}\,w)\}$$
$$= \min\{\kappa_1^-, \kappa_4^-\}$$

$$\tau_\Delta^c(pb\overline{w}) = \min\{\tau_\Delta^c(p\,b\,f\,\overline{w}), \tau_\Delta^c(p\,b\,\overline{f}\,\overline{w})\}$$
$$= \min\{\kappa_2^- + \kappa_3^-, \kappa_1^- + \kappa_2^-\}$$
$$= \kappa_2^- + \min\{\kappa_1^-, \kappa_3^-\}$$

And so we find

$$\tau_\Delta^c(bw) = 0 < \min\{\kappa_1^-, \kappa_2^-\} = \tau_\Delta^c(b\overline{w}) \qquad \text{and thus} \quad b\approx_\Delta^{\cap,c} w \qquad (5.9)$$
$$\tau_\Delta^c(p\overline{w}) = \min\{\kappa_1^- + \kappa_2^-, \kappa_3^-\} \not< \kappa_1^- = \tau_\Delta^c(p\overline{w}) \quad \text{and thus} \quad p\not\approx_\Delta^{\cap,c}\overline{w}, \quad (5.10)$$

that is, the prerequisites for default inheritance for exceptional subclasses, as well as

$$\tau_\Delta^c(pbw) = \min\{\kappa_1^-, \kappa_4^-\} = \kappa_1^-$$
$$< \kappa_2^- + \kappa_1^- = \min\{\kappa_1^- + \kappa_2^-, \kappa_2^- + \kappa_3^-\} = \tau_\Delta^c(pb\overline{w})$$

and thus $pb\approx_\Delta^{\cap,c} w$ as predicted by default inheritance for exceptional subclasses.

We further illustrate the weak transitive property of rule chaining by showing that given $p\approx_\Delta^{\cap,c} b$ and $b\approx_\Delta^{\cap,c} w$ we obtain $p\approx_\Delta^{\cap,c} w$ given $p\not\approx_\Delta^{\cap,c}\overline{w}$. We consult Table 5.3 and obtain

$$\tau_\Delta^c(pb) = \min\{\tau_\Delta^c(p\,b\,f\,w), \tau_\Delta^c(p\,b\,f\,\overline{w}), \tau_\Delta^c(p\,b\,\overline{f}\,\overline{w}), \tau_\Delta^c(p\,\overline{b}\,f\,w)\}$$
$$= \min\{\kappa_4^-, \kappa_2^- + \kappa_3^-, \kappa_1^-, \kappa_1^- + \kappa_2^-\}$$
$$= \min\{\kappa_1^-, \kappa_2^-\}$$

$$\tau_\Delta^c(p\overline{b}) = \min\{\tau_\Delta^c(p\,\overline{b}\,f\,\overline{w}), \tau_\Delta^c(p\,\overline{b}\,\overline{f}\,w), \tau_\Delta^c(p\,\overline{b}\,\overline{f}\,\overline{w}), \tau_\Delta^c(\overline{p}\,b\,f\,w)\}$$
$$= \min\{\kappa_3^- + \kappa_4^-, \kappa_3^-\}$$
$$= \kappa_3^-.$$

From (5.6) we have $\kappa_1^- < \kappa_3^-$ and therefore either $\min\{\kappa_1^-, \kappa_2^-\} = \kappa_1^- < \kappa_3^-$ or $\min\{\kappa_1^-, \kappa_2^-\} = \kappa_2^- < \kappa_1^- < \kappa_3^-$ and overall we have $\tau_\Delta^c(pb) < \tau_\Delta^c(p\overline{b})$ and therefore $p\approx_\Delta^{\cap,c} b$. By (5.9) we have $p\approx_\Delta^{\cap,c} b$ and by (5.10) $p\not\approx_\Delta^{\cap,c}\overline{w}$. From these prerequisites, default rule chaining predicts $p\approx_\Delta^{\cap,c} w$ which indeed holds because of (5.7) and (5.8).

Table 5.3: Verification / falsification behaviour of the excerpt of the penguin example used in Example 5.9 (upper part) and generic c-representation for this knowledge base (lower part)

ω	$p\,b\,f\,w$	$p\,b\,f\,\bar{w}$	$p\,b\,\bar{f}\,w$	$p\,b\,\bar{f}\,\bar{w}$	$\bar{p}\,b\,f\,w$	$\bar{p}\,b\,f\,\bar{w}$	$\bar{p}\,b\,\bar{f}\,w$	$\bar{p}\,b\,\bar{f}\,\bar{w}$
verifies	$\delta_1,\delta_2,\delta_3$	δ_1,δ_3	$\delta_2,\delta_3,\delta_4$	δ_3,δ_4	—	—	δ_4	δ_4
falsifies	δ_4	δ_2,δ_4	δ_1	δ_1,δ_2	δ_3,δ_4	δ_3,δ_4	δ_3	δ_3
$\tau_\Delta^c(\omega)$	κ_4^-	$\kappa_2^-+\kappa_4^-$	κ_1^-	$\kappa_1^-+\kappa_2^-$	$\kappa_3^-+\kappa_4^-$	$\kappa_3^-+\kappa_4^-$	κ_3^-	κ_3^-

ω	$\bar{p}\,b\,f\,w$	$\bar{p}\,b\,f\,\bar{w}$	$\bar{p}\,b\,\bar{f}\,w$	$\bar{p}\,b\,\bar{f}\,\bar{w}$	$\bar{p}\,\bar{b}\,f\,w$	$\bar{p}\,\bar{b}\,f\,\bar{w}$	$\bar{p}\,\bar{b}\,\bar{f}\,w$	$\bar{p}\,\bar{b}\,\bar{f}\,\bar{w}$
verifies	δ_1,δ_2	δ_1	δ_2	—	—	—	—	—
falsifies	—	δ_2	δ_1	δ_1,δ_2	—	—	—	—
$\tau_\Delta^c(\omega)$	0	κ_2^-	κ_1^-	$\kappa_1^-+\kappa_2^-$	0	0	0	0

This example illustrates:

Proposition 5.10 ([BEKI16, Proposition 6]). There are formulas $\psi, \phi \in \mathfrak{L}$ and knowledge bases $\Delta = \{(\psi_1|\phi_1), \ldots, (\psi_n|\phi_n)\} \subseteq (\mathfrak{L} \mid \mathfrak{L})$ such that in the context of Δ, ψ can also be sceptically c-inferred from ϕ, but not by means of System P.

From Propositions 5.8 and 5.10 we directly obtain that sceptical c-inference is stronger than System P inference.

Corollary 5.11 ([BEKI16]). Every System P inference based on a conditional knowledge base $\Delta = \{(\psi_1|\phi_1), \ldots, (\psi_n|\phi_n)\}$ is also a sceptical c-inference based on Δ, the converse is not true in general.

We identified c-representations of a knowledge base Δ with solutions to the constraint satisfaction problem $CSP(\Delta)$ in Section 5.1. Following [BEKI16] we extend on this identification and characterise sceptical c-inference, that is, sceptical inference over all c-representations of Δ, as a constraint satisfaction problem.

For this we recall Proposition 4.26 that characterises System P inference based on Δ such that ϕ infers ψ under System P in the context of Δ if and only if $\Delta \cup \{(\bar{\psi}|\phi)\}$ is inconsistent. This characterisation is not sufficient for characterising c-inference, as stated in Corollary 5.11, but we use the basic idea of this to devise the CSP characterisation of sceptical c-inference.

Definition 5.12 (Acceptance Constraint [BEKIK18, Definition 6]). Let the vector $(\kappa_1^-, \ldots, \kappa_n^-) = \vec{\eta}$ be a solution to the constraint satisfaction problem $CSP(\Delta)$ for a knowledge base $\Delta = \{(\psi_1|\phi_1), \ldots, (\psi_n|\phi_n)\} \subseteq (\mathfrak{L} \mid \mathfrak{L})$. The c-representation $\kappa_{\vec{\eta}}$ accepts a conditional $(\psi|\phi)$ and therefore infers ψ from ϕ under Δ if and only if

$$\kappa_{\vec{\eta}}(\phi\psi) = \min_{\omega \models \phi\psi} \left\{ \sum_{\omega \models \phi\psi} \right\} < \min_{\omega \models \phi\psi} \left\{ \sum_{\omega \models \phi\overline{\psi}} \right\} = \kappa_{\vec{\eta}}(\phi\overline{\psi}). \quad (5.11)$$

$$\underbrace{\phantom{\min_{\omega \models \phi\psi} \left\{ \sum_{\omega \models \phi\psi} \right\} < \min_{\omega \models \phi\psi} \left\{ \sum_{\omega \models \phi\overline{\psi}} \right\}}}_{\overset{\text{def}}{=\!=}: \; CSP_\Delta(\psi|\phi)}$$

We call $CSP_\Delta(\psi|\phi)$ the *acceptance constraint* of $(\psi|\phi)$. Likewise, we have $\phi \not\hspace{-0.3em}\models_{\kappa_\Delta^c} \psi$ if and only if $\kappa_\Delta^c \not\models (\psi|\phi)$ if and only if

$$\kappa_{\vec{\eta}}(\phi\psi) = \min_{\omega \models \phi\psi} \left\{ \sum_{\omega \models \phi\psi} \right\} \geq \min_{\omega \models \phi\psi} \left\{ \sum_{\omega \models \phi\overline{\psi}} \right\} = \kappa_{\vec{\eta}}(\phi\overline{\psi}), \quad (5.12)$$

$$\underbrace{\phantom{\min_{\omega \models \phi\psi} \left\{ \sum_{\omega \models \phi\psi} \right\} \geq \min_{\omega \models \phi\psi} \left\{ \sum_{\omega \models \phi\overline{\psi}} \right\}}}_{\overset{\text{def}}{=\!=}: \; \neg CSP_\Delta(\psi|\phi)}$$

and by $\neg CSP_\Delta(\psi|\phi)$ we denote the negation of the acceptance constraint.

Note that neither the acceptance constraint $CSP_\Delta(\psi|\phi)$ nor the negation of this constraint, $\neg CSP_\Delta(\psi|\phi)$, introduce any new variables to the solution $\vec{\eta}$, but range over the impacts already present.

Based on a c-representation of Δ an inference can be drawn if and only if the c-representation $\kappa_{\vec{\eta}}$ satisfies the respective acceptance constraint for the conditional in addition to the CSP which results in $\vec{\eta}$ that constitutes $\kappa_{\vec{\eta}}$. In the following proposition, we formalise this as a CSP.

Theorem 5.13 ([BEKIK18, Proposition 10]). Let Δ be be a consistent knowledge base $\Delta = \{(\psi_1|\phi_1), \ldots, (\psi_n|\phi_n)\} \subseteq (\mathfrak{L} \mid \mathfrak{L})$ and let $\phi, \psi \in \mathfrak{L}$ be formulas. ψ is sceptically c-inferred from ϕ in the context of Δ if and only if

$$\phi \hspace{0.2em}\mid\!\approx_\Delta^{\cap,c} \psi \quad \text{iff} \quad CSP(\Delta) \cup \{\neg CSP_\Delta(\psi|\phi)\} \quad \text{is not solvable.} \quad (5.13)$$

Together with the findings in Corollary 5.11 this theorem gives us directly:

Corollary 5.14 ([BEKIK18, Corollary 3]). Let $\Delta = \{(\psi_1|\phi_1), \ldots, (\psi_n|\phi_n)\}$ be a conditional knowledge base and let $\phi, \psi \in \mathfrak{L}$ be formulas. If $CSP(\Delta \cup \{(\overline{\psi}|\phi)\})$ is not solvable, then $CSP(\Delta) \cup \{\neg CSP_\Delta(\psi|\phi)\}$ is not solvable; the converse is not true in general.

As we have shown above, c-inference extends System P. So we examine whether sceptical c-inference satisfies selected formal properties of inference relations not included in System P, like (NR), (DR), and (CI).

Proposition 5.15. Sceptical c-inference satisfies (NR).

From the proof of Proposition 5.15 we also see that this property is valid for weakly sceptical c-inference, as well.

Proposition 5.16. Sceptical c-inference satisfies (NR).

Proposition 5.17. Sceptical c-inference satisfies (DR).

The proof of this proposition also gives us that (DR) is valid for weakly sceptical c-inference.

Proposition 5.18. Weakly sceptical c-inference satisfies (DR).

Observation 5.19 ([BEKIK18, Proposition 7]). There are knowledge bases Δ such that sceptical c-inference violates (CI).

We give an example for such a knowledge base.

Example 5.20. We use the knowledge base

$$\Delta = \{\delta_1 : (a\bar{b} \vee \bar{a}b \vee \bar{c} | \top), \ \delta_2 : (c | \top)\} \tag{5.14}$$

with the verification/falsification behaviour shown in Table 5.4. The system of inequalities (3.30) for this knowledge base directly gives us $\kappa_1^- > 0$ and $\kappa_2^- > 0$. With generic ranks calculated as given in the last line in Table 5.4. Regardless of the concrete values for κ_1^- and κ_2^- this gives us for every c-representation $\kappa_{\vec{\eta}}$ of the knowledge base Δ

$$\tau_\Delta^c(a\bar{b}c) = 0 < \kappa_1^- = \tau_\Delta^c(abc),$$
$$\tau_\Delta^c(a\bar{b}c) = 0 < \kappa_2^- = \tau_\Delta^c(a\bar{b}\bar{c}),$$
$$\tau_\Delta^c(a\bar{b}c) = 0 < \kappa_2^- = \tau_\Delta^c(ab\bar{c}).$$

From this we obtain

$$\kappa_{\vec{\eta}}(a\bar{b}c) = \underbrace{\min\{\kappa_{\vec{\eta}}(abc), \kappa_{\vec{\eta}}(a\bar{b}c)\}}_{(5.15.a)} < \min\{\kappa_{\vec{\eta}}(ab\bar{c}), \kappa_{\vec{\eta}}(a\bar{b}\bar{c})\} \tag{5.15}$$

Table 5.4: Verification/falsification and (generic) c-representation in Example 5.20

ω	$a\,b\,c$	$a\,b\,\overline{c}$	$a\,\overline{b}\,c$	$a\,\overline{b}\,\overline{c}$	$\overline{a}\,b\,c$	$\overline{a}\,b\,\overline{c}$	$\overline{a}\,\overline{b}\,c$	$\overline{a}\,\overline{b}\,\overline{c}$
verifies	δ_2	δ_1	δ_1,δ_2	δ_1	δ_1,δ_2	δ_1	δ_2	δ_1
falsifies	δ_1	δ_2	—	δ_2	—	δ_2	δ_1	δ_2
$\tau_\Delta^c(\omega)$	κ_1^-	κ_2^-	0	κ_2^-	0	κ_2^-	κ_1^-	κ_2^-
$\kappa_\Delta^c(\omega)$	2	1	0	1	0	1	2	1

for all c-representations $\kappa_{\vec{\eta}}$ of Δ. Additionally (5.15) gives us that $\kappa_{\vec{\eta}}(ac) < \kappa_{\vec{\eta}}(a\overline{c})$ for all c-representations $\kappa_{\vec{\eta}}$ of Δ because of the definition of the rank of formulas in (3.10). And therefore we also have $a\!\!\mid\!\approx_\Delta^{\cap,c} c$. We likewise obtain

$$\tau_\Delta^c(\overline{a}bc) = 0 < \kappa_1^- = \tau_\Delta^c(abc)$$
$$\tau_\Delta^c(\overline{a}bc) = 0 < \kappa_1^- = \tau_\Delta^c(\overline{a}b\overline{c})$$
$$\tau_\Delta^c(\overline{a}bc) = 0 < \kappa_1^- = \tau_\Delta^c(ab\overline{c})$$

from Table 5.4, and therefore

$$\tau_\Delta^c(\overline{a}bc) = \underbrace{\min\{\tau_\Delta^c(abc), \tau_\Delta^c(\overline{a}bc)\} < \min\{\tau_\Delta^c(ab\overline{c}), \tau_\Delta^c(\overline{a}b\overline{c})\}}_{(5.16.b)}, \qquad (5.16)$$

and with the same argumentation as above, (5.16.b) gives us $b\!\!\mid\!\approx_\Delta^{\cap,c} c$. If sceptical c-inference would satisfy (CI), then from these preliminaries we also had $ab\!\!\mid\!\approx_\Delta^{\cap,c} c$, that is, $\tau_\Delta^c(abc) < \tau_\Delta^c(ab\overline{c})$ but, as we obtain from the table, we have $\tau_\Delta^c(abc) = \kappa_1^-$ and $\tau_\Delta^c ab\overline{c} = \kappa_2^-$. So both values can be set independently, and there are solutions to $CSP(\Delta)$ such that $\kappa_1^- > \kappa_2^-$, for instance the vector $(2,1)$, for which the OCF κ_Δ^c is given in Table 5.4 (lower row). Here we have $ab\!\!\mid\!\approx_{\kappa_\Delta^c} \overline{c}$, therefore we obtain that $ab\!\!\not\mid\!\approx_\Delta^{\cap,c} c$ by Definition 5.4, in contrast to (CI).

From the same example we directly obtain:

Observation 5.21. Weakly sceptical c-inference violates (CI).

By satisfaction of System P we know that sceptical c-inference satisfies the property (REF), that is, every formula can be inferred from itself. With the following property we ensure that every conditional in the knowledge base is accepted, as well.

Lemma 5.22 ([BEKIK16, Proposition 15]). Sceptical c-inference satisfies (DI).

From the proof of Lemma 5.22 we also obtain

Lemma 5.23. Weakly sceptical c-inference satisfies (DI).

We now consider additional challenges to inference relations, default inheritance for exceptional subclasses and rule chaining, and default rule chaining, illustrating that sceptical c-inference handles these challenges, whereas the more general property of Rational Transitivity (RT) is violated by sceptical c-inference. We recall Example 5.9 for the first two properties and obtain:

Observation 5.24 ([BEKIK18]). Sceptical c-inference licenses for default inheritance for exceptional subclasses, that is, it does not suffer from the Drowning Problem, and licenses for default rule chaining.

But even if we can observe these properties to hold for sceptical c-inference, and so it is possible to connect explicitly stated knowledge under sceptical c-inference, this is not the case for the more general Rational Transitivity, as we show with the following example.

Example 5.25. Let $\Delta = \{\delta_1 : (\overline{a}|\top), \delta_2 : (b|a), \delta_3 : (\overline{b} \vee c|\overline{a})\}$ be a knowledge base over the alphabet $\Sigma = \{A, B, C\}$ with a verification/falsification behaviour shown in Table 5.5. The constraint satisfaction problem $CSP(\Delta)$ for Δ reduces to $\kappa_1^- > 0$, $\kappa_2^- > 0$, and $\kappa_3^- > 0$, with no further constraints on the impacts, so that they can be set independently. From these results we obtain that for all c-representations $\kappa_{\vec{\eta}}$ of Δ we have the inferences $a \mid\!\approx_\Delta^{\cap,c} b$ since $\kappa(ab) = \kappa_1^- < \kappa_1^- + \kappa_2^- = \kappa(a\overline{b})$, $b \mid\!\approx_\Delta^{\cap,c} c$ since $\kappa(bc) = 0 < \min\{\kappa_1^-, \kappa_3^-\} = \kappa(b\overline{c})$, and $a \mid\!\not\approx_\Delta^{\cap,c} \overline{c}$ because $\kappa(a\overline{c}) = \kappa_1^- = \kappa(ac)$. But because of this equality we also have $a \mid\!\not\approx_\Delta^{\cap,c} c$, violating (RT).

We capture the results of this example in the following observation.

Observation 5.26 ([BEKIK18, Proposition 8]). There are knowledge bases for which sceptical c-inference violates (RT).

Table 5.5: Verification/falsification and (generic) c-representation for the knowledge base in Example 5.25

ω	$a\,b\,c$	$a\,b\,\bar{c}$	$a\,\bar{b}\,c$	$a\,\bar{b}\,\bar{c}$	$\bar{a}\,b\,c$	$\bar{a}\,b\,\bar{c}$	$\bar{a}\,\bar{b}\,c$	$\bar{a}\,\bar{b}\,\bar{c}$
verifies	δ_2	δ_2	—	—	δ_1,δ_3	δ_1	δ_1,δ_3	δ_1,δ_3
falsifies	δ_1	δ_1	δ_1,δ_2	δ_1,δ_2	—	δ_3	—	—
$\tau_\Delta^c(\omega)$	κ_1^-	κ_1^-	$\kappa_1^- + \kappa_2^-$	$\kappa_1^- + \kappa_2^-$	0	κ_3^-	0	0

We elaborate on Example 5.25 to demonstrate that it is also a counter-example against weakly sceptical c-inference satisfying (RT).

Example 5.27. The example gives us the preliminaries for (RT), because these are also valid in sceptical c-inference. However, as $\tau_\Delta^c(a\bar{c}) = \kappa_1^- = \tau_\Delta^c(ac)$, we do not find any c-representation $\kappa_{\vec{\eta}} \in Sol(CSP(\Delta))$ such that $a\!\mid\!\approx_{\kappa_{\vec{\eta}}} c$, so $a\!\mid\!\not\approx_\Delta^{ws,c} b$ in contrast to (RT).

Observation 5.28. There are knowledge bases for which weakly sceptical c-inference violates (RT).

The example also gives us the following result for the two weaker inference relations: We ascertain that all three inferences handle irrelevance of variables to further assess these inference relations. We here safely assume that variables that do not appear in any conditional in the knowledge base are not relevant for the outcome of an inference based on this knowledge base.

Proposition 5.29 ([BEKIK18, Proposition 9]). Variables that do not appear in the knowledge base do not change the outcome of the inferences drawn with sceptical, weakly sceptical, or credulous c-inference: Let $\Delta = \{(\psi_1|\phi_1), \ldots, (\psi_n|\phi_n)\}$ be a knowledge base, let

$$\Sigma_\Delta = \{V\,|\,V \in \phi_i\psi_i \text{ for all } (\psi_i|\phi_i) \in \Delta\}, \qquad (5.17)$$

and let $\Sigma \supseteq \Sigma_\Delta$. Then $\phi\!\mid\!\approx_\Delta^{\bullet,c}\psi$ implies $(\phi \wedge \dot{a})\!\mid\!\approx_\Delta^{\bullet,c}\psi$ for any outcome $\dot{a}$ of variables $A \in \Sigma \setminus \Sigma_\Delta$ and $\bullet \in \{\cup, \cap, ws\}$.

Note that even if this is a sensible assumption for formal systems, humans not always adhere to this assumption, as we will see in Chapter 8. We illustrate Proposition 5.29 with the following example.

Table 5.6: Verification / falsification behaviour of the excerpt of the penguin example used in Example 5.30 (upper part) and generic c-representation for this knowledge base (lower part). Note that W is irrelevant, because $\tau_\Delta^c(\dot{p}\dot{b}\dot{f}w) = \tau_\Delta^c(\dot{p}\dot{b}\dot{f}\overline{w})$ for all outcomes $\dot{p}, \dot{b}, \dot{f}$ of the variables P, B, F, respectively.

ω	$pbfw$	$pbf\overline{w}$	$pb\overline{f}w$	$pb\overline{f}\,\overline{w}$	$p\overline{b}fw$	$p\overline{b}f\overline{w}$	$p\overline{b}\,\overline{f}w$	$p\overline{b}\,\overline{f}\,\overline{w}$
verifies	δ_1,δ_3	δ_1,δ_3	δ_3,δ_4	δ_3,δ_4	—	—	δ_4	δ_4
falsifies	δ_4	$,\delta_4$	δ_1	$\delta_1,$	δ_3,δ_4	δ_3,δ_4	δ_3	δ_3
$\tau_\Delta^c(\omega)$	κ_4^-	κ_4^-	κ_1^-	κ_1^-	$\kappa_3^- + \kappa_4^-$	$\kappa_3^- + \kappa_4^-$	κ_3^-	κ_3^-

ω	$\overline{p}bfw$	$\overline{p}bf\overline{w}$	$\overline{p}b\overline{f}w$	$\overline{p}b\overline{f}\,\overline{w}$	$\overline{p}\,\overline{b}fw$	$\overline{p}\,\overline{b}f\overline{w}$	$\overline{p}\,\overline{b}\,\overline{f}w$	$\overline{p}\,\overline{b}\,\overline{f}\,\overline{w}$
verifies	$\delta_1,$	δ_1	—	—	—	—	—	—
falsifies	—	—	δ_1	$\delta_1,$	—	—	—	—
$\tau_\Delta^c(\omega)$	0		κ_1^-	κ_1^-	0	0	0	0

Example 5.30 (confer [BEKIK18]). To illustrate irrelevance for sceptical, weakly sceptical, and credulous c-inference, we recall Example 5.9, but use the even more reduced knowledge base

$$\Delta = \{\delta_1 \ : \ (f|b), \delta_3 \ : \ (b|p), \delta_4 \ : \ (\overline{f}|p)\}. \tag{5.18}$$

which give us the alphabet $\Sigma_\Delta = \{P, B, F\} \subsetneq \Sigma = \{P, B, F, W\}$. Here, W is irrelevant for $\phi \mathrel{\vmathbb{\sim}}_\Delta^{\bullet,c} \psi$ with $\bullet \in \{\cup, \cap, ws\}$ because $\tau_\Delta^c(\dot{p}\dot{b}\dot{f}w) = \tau_\Delta^c(\dot{p}\dot{b}\dot{f}\overline{w})$ for all outcomes $\dot{p}, \dot{b}, \dot{f}$ of the variables in Σ_Δ, respectively, as can be observed in Table 5.6.

In the following we examine further formal properties of weakly sceptical c-inference. Using weakly sceptical c-inference, it is possible to infer every formula already known:

Proposition 5.31 ([BEKIK16, Proposition 20]). Weakly sceptical c-inference satisfies (REF).

Weakly sceptical c-inference licenses for using classical operations on the object level, namely both semantic equivalence in the premise of an inference, and classical entailment in its conclusion.

Proposition 5.32 ([BEKIK16, Proposition 21]). Weakly sceptical c-inference satisfies (LLE).

Proposition 5.33 ([BEKIK16, Proposition 22]). Weakly sceptical c-inference satisfies (RW).

Proposition 5.34. Weakly sceptical c-inference satisfies (OR).

We will now examine the relationship between the three inferences sceptical, weakly sceptical, and credulous c-inference and their relationship to single c-representations. For this, we first recall the inference operation for these inferences.

Definition 5.35 (Inference Operation $C_\Delta^{\bullet,c}$ [BEKIK16]). The inference operation $C_\Delta^{\bullet,c} : \mathfrak{L} \to \mathfrak{P}(\mathfrak{L})$ is a function that, in the context of a conditional knowledge base $\Delta = \{(\psi_1|\phi_1), \ldots, (\psi_n|\phi_n)\} \subseteq (\mathfrak{L} \mid \mathfrak{L})$, assigns to each formula ϕ the set of formulas that are $\approx_\Delta^{\bullet,c}$-inferable from ϕ with $\bullet \in \{\cup, \cap, ws\}$, that is

$$C_\Delta^{\bullet,c}(\phi) = \{\psi | \phi \approx_\Delta^{\bullet,c} \psi\} \qquad \text{for } \bullet \in \{\cup, \cap, ws\} \qquad (5.19)$$

Proposition 5.36 (Closure of $C_\Delta^{\cap,c}(\phi)$ [BEKIK16, Proposition 13]). The inference operation $C_\Delta^{\cap,c}(\phi)$ is deductively closed for every $\Delta \in (\mathfrak{L}|\mathfrak{L})$ and every $\phi \in \mathfrak{L}$.

In classical logic, the inferences of a formula are inconsistent if and only if the formula is inconsistent. This is not the case for sceptical c-inference, where inference of inconsistent formulas result in consistent (but trivial) inferences, and only inconsistent knowledge bases lead to inconsistent inferences.

Proposition 5.37 ([BEKIK16, Proposition 14]). Let Δ be a knowledge base, $\Delta = \{(\psi_1|\phi_1), \ldots, (\psi_n|\phi_n)\} \subseteq (\mathfrak{L} \mid \mathfrak{L})$, let $\phi \in \mathfrak{L}$ be a formula, and let $\bullet \in \{\cap, \cup, ws\}$. For consistent Δ, $\phi \equiv \bot$ implies $C_\Delta^{\bullet,c}(\phi) = \varnothing$. The set $C_\Delta^{\bullet,c}(\phi)$ is inconsistent if and only if Δ is inconsistent.

For credulous inference, Example 5.6 gives us directly:

Observation 5.38 ([BEKIK16]). There are formulas $\phi \in \mathfrak{L}$ and knowledge bases $\Delta = \{(\psi_1|\phi_1), \ldots, (\psi_n|\phi_n)\} \subseteq (\mathfrak{L} \mid \mathfrak{L})$ such that $C_\Delta^{\cup,c}(\phi) \supset \{\psi, \overline{\psi}\}$.

With these preliminary considerations, we can now determine the relationship between the three inferences.

Proposition 5.39 ([BEKIK16, Proposition 25]). Let $\phi \in \mathfrak{L}$ be a formula and $\Delta = \{(\psi_1|\phi_1), \ldots, (\psi_n|\phi_n)\} \subseteq (\mathfrak{L} \mid \mathfrak{L})$ be a knowledge base. We have

$$C_\Delta^{\cap,c}(\phi) \subsetneq C_\Delta^{sk,c}(\phi) \subsetneq C_\Delta^{\cup,c}(\phi) \qquad \text{respectively} \qquad (5.20)$$

$$\vDash_\Delta^{\cap,c} \subsetneq \vDash_\Delta^{sk,c} \subsetneq \vDash_\Delta^{\cup,c}. \qquad (5.21)$$

So the three inference relations of this chapter are proper inclusions of each other, and, as intended, weakly sceptical c-inference is less strict than sceptical c-inference. But this relation is strictly more strict than credulous c-inference, not licensing for the inference of inconsistent conclusions.

5.3 Reasoning with Sets of Preferred c-Representations

Up to this point, this chapter has dealt with different inference relations defined on the set of all c-representations. In the following, we recall that every c-representation is a model of the knowledge base, and model based reasoning is highly successful when not reasoning over *all*, but a set of *preferred* models, as realised in reasoning based preferential models which provides most of the inference methods of this thesis.

In this section we report the findings of [BEKIK16, BEK16, BEKIK18] and recall notions of preference over c-representations and inference relations based on (with respect to these notions) preferred c-representations. As a c-representation is a model that is composed from a tuple of impacts of conditionals, we do not expect the ordering to be total, thus the resulting relations are not preference relations in the definition of such relations to be total preorders. Nonetheless the relations will be reflexive and transitive, and thus we will keep the label *preference* to indicate the proximity of this idea to the idea of preferential relation on models and model preference.

All of the notions of preference for c-representations in this section will use the solution vector $\vec{\eta}$ for identifying c-representations, ordering the c-representations by the sum of the impacts, componentwise-minimality and the induced OCF, and reasoning with the minimal c-representations of the respective notion. We start by recalling the three preferences.

Definition 5.40 (Minimal c-Representations [BEKIK16]). Let $Sol(CSP(\Delta))$ be the solutions to the constraint satisfaction problem imposed by c-representations (Definition 5.1) based on the conditional knowledge base $\Delta = \{(\psi_1|\phi_1), \ldots, (\psi_n|\phi_n)\}$. Let the solutions $\vec{\eta} = (\kappa_1^-, \ldots, \kappa_n^-)$, and $\vec{\eta}' =$

$(\eta_1^-, \ldots, \eta_n^-) \in Sol(CSP(\Delta))$ constitute the c-representations $\kappa_{\vec{\eta}}$ and $\kappa_{\vec{\eta}'}$. A c-representation $\kappa_{\vec{\eta}}$ is *sum-preferred* to $\kappa_{\vec{\eta}'}$ if and only if the sum of the sum of the impacts in $\vec{\eta}$ is smaller or equal than the sum of the impacts in $\vec{\eta}'$, formally

$$\kappa_{\vec{\eta}} \preceq_c^+ \kappa_{\vec{\eta}'} \qquad \text{if and only if} \qquad \sum_{i=1}^n \kappa_i^- \leq \sum_{i=1}^n \eta_i^-, \qquad (5.22)$$

and is *strictly sum-preferred* to $\vec{\eta}'$ if and only if the sum of the sum of the impacts in $\vec{\eta}$ is strictly smaller than the sum of the impacts in $\vec{\eta}'$, formally

$$\kappa_{\vec{\eta}} \prec_c^+ \kappa_{\vec{\eta}'} \qquad \text{if and only if} \qquad \sum_{i=1}^n \kappa_i^- < \sum_{i=1}^n \eta_i^-. \qquad (5.23)$$

A c-representation $\kappa_{\vec{\eta}}$ is *componentwise preferred* to $\kappa_{\vec{\eta}'}$ if and only if each impact of $\vec{\eta}$ is smaller than the respective impact of $\vec{\eta}'$

$$\kappa_{\vec{\eta}} \preceq_c^{cw} \kappa_{\vec{\eta}'} \qquad \text{if and only if} \qquad \kappa_i^- \leq \eta_i^- \qquad \text{for all } 1 \leq i \leq n \qquad (5.24)$$

and is *strictly componentwise preferred* to $\kappa_{\vec{\eta}'}$ if and only if is componentwise preferred and there is at least one impact in $\vec{\eta}$ that is strictly smaller than the respective impact in $\vec{\eta}'$, formally

$$\kappa_{\vec{\eta}} \prec_c^{cw} \kappa_{\vec{\eta}'} \qquad \text{iff} \qquad \kappa_i^- \leq \eta_i^- \qquad \text{for all } 1 \leq i \leq n \qquad (5.25)$$
$$\text{and } \exists\, 1 \leq i \leq n \text{ s.t. } \quad \kappa_i^- < \eta_i^-. \qquad (5.26)$$

Finally, a c-representation $\kappa_{\vec{\eta}}$ is *inductively preferred* to $\kappa_{\vec{\eta}}$ if and only if the ranking on the worlds $\omega \in \Omega$ induced by $\kappa_{\vec{\eta}}$ on Ω is Pareto smaller to the ranking induced by $\kappa_{\vec{\eta}'}$, formally

$$\kappa_{\vec{\eta}} \preceq_c^\kappa \kappa_{\vec{\eta}'} \qquad \text{if and only if} \qquad \kappa_{\vec{\eta}}(\omega) \leq \kappa_{\vec{\eta}'}(\omega) \qquad (5.27)$$

and is *strictly inductively preferred* to $\kappa_{\vec{\eta}'}$ if and only if is inductively preferred and there is at least one world for which $\kappa_{\vec{\eta}}(\omega)$ is smaller than $\kappa_{\vec{\eta}'}(\omega)$.

$$\kappa_{\vec{\eta}} \prec_c^\kappa \kappa_{\vec{\eta}'} \qquad \text{if and only if} \qquad \kappa_{\vec{\eta}}(\omega) \leq \kappa_{\vec{\eta}'}(\omega) \qquad (5.28)$$
$$\text{and } \exists\, \omega \in \Omega \text{ such that} \qquad \kappa_{\vec{\eta}}(\omega) < \kappa_{\vec{\eta}'}(\omega). \qquad (5.29)$$

The set of *minimal c-representations* of Δ with respect to a preference $\circ \in \{+, cw, \kappa\}$ is

$$Min_c^\circ(\Delta) = \{\kappa_{\vec{\eta}} | \vec{\eta} \in Sol(CSP(\Delta)), \nexists \vec{\eta}'\, Sol(CSP(\Delta)) \text{ such that } \kappa_{\vec{\eta}'} \prec_c^\circ \kappa_{\vec{\eta}}\}. \qquad (5.30)$$

Example 5.41 (confer [BEKIK18]). We illustrate these notions of preference with Example 5.7 where we have the solutions $\vec{\eta}_1 = (1, 1, 0)$, $\vec{\eta}_2 = (0, 1, 1)$, and $\vec{\eta}_3 = (1, 1, 1)$ with induced ranking functions $\kappa_{\vec{\eta}_1}$, $\kappa_{\vec{\eta}_2}$, and $\kappa_{\vec{\eta}_3}$ as given in Table 5.2. Here, $\kappa_{\vec{\eta}_1}$ and $\kappa_{\vec{\eta}_2}$ are sum-preferred and componentwise preferred to $\kappa_{\vec{\eta}_3}$. Furthermore, we have $\kappa_{\vec{\eta}_2} \prec_c^\kappa \kappa_{\vec{\eta}_1} \prec_c^\kappa \kappa_{\vec{\eta}_3}$. There are no smaller solutions to the system of inequalities (5.3), so the minimal sets are

$$Min_c^+(\Delta) = \{\kappa_{\vec{\eta}_1}, \kappa_{\vec{\eta}_2}\}$$
$$Min_c^{cw}(\Delta) = \{\kappa_{\vec{\eta}_1}, \kappa_{\vec{\eta}_2}\}$$
$$Min_c^\kappa(\Delta) = \{\kappa_{\vec{\eta}_2}\}.$$

Having recalled these three notions of preference we need proper semantics for using them for inference. We use the inference relations on sets of c-representations defined in Section 5.1 using different degrees of scepticism to infer from the set of all c-representations:

Definition 5.42 ([BEKIK16, Definition 30]). Let $\Delta = \{(\psi_1|\phi_1), \ldots, (\psi_n|\phi_n)\}$ be a knowledge base, let $\bullet \in \{\cap, ws, \cup\}$ denote the scepticism of an inference relation according to Definitions 5.4 and 5.5, and let $\circ \in \{+, cw, \kappa, all\}$ denote the set of minimal c-representations according to Definition 5.40 where we use the indicator *all* for the set of all c-representations of Δ. The inference relation $\approx_\Delta^{\circ, \bullet}$ is the inference relation over the set $\circ$ of c-representation using the $\bullet$ semantics, whilst $C_\Delta^{\circ, \bullet}(\phi) = \{\psi | \phi \approx_\Delta^{\circ, \bullet} \psi\}$, as usual.

This gives us the twelve inference relations shown in Table 5.7. To put these inference relation to a proper use, we capture the mutual relations and the properties of these inference relations as follows. From the findings of the previous sections we obtain:

Corollary 5.43 ([BEKIK16, Proposition 32]). Let $\Delta = \{(\psi_1|\phi_1), \ldots, (\psi_n|\phi_n)\}$ be a consistent knowledge base, let $\phi \in \mathfrak{L}$ be a formula, and let $\circ \in \{+, cw, \kappa, all\}$ be an arbitrary but fixed notion of preference. We have

$$C_\Delta^{\circ, \cap}(\phi) \subsetneq C_\Delta^{\circ, sk}(\phi) \subsetneq C_\Delta^{\circ, \cup}(\phi) \qquad \text{respectively} \qquad (5.31)$$
$$\approx_\Delta^{\circ, \cap} \subsetneq \approx_\Delta^{\circ, sk} \subsetneq \approx_\Delta^{\circ, \cup}. \qquad (5.32)$$

Lemma 5.44 ([BEKIK16, Proposition 33]). Let $\Delta = \{(\psi_1|\phi_1), \ldots, (\psi_n|\phi_n)\}$ be a consistent knowledge base, let $\phi \in \mathfrak{L}$ be a formula, and let $\circ \in$

Table 5.7: Inference relations based on sets of preferred c-representations and the degree of scepticism

	all c-representations	componentwise minimal	sum-minimal	inductively minimal
sceptical	$\models_\Delta^{all,\cap}$	$\models_\Delta^{cw,\cap}$	$\models_\Delta^{+,\cap}$	$\models_\Delta^{\kappa,\cap}$
weakly sceptical	$\models_\Delta^{all,ws}$	$\models_\Delta^{cw,ws}$	$\models_\Delta^{+,ws}$	$\models_\Delta^{\kappa,ws}$
credulous	$\models_\Delta^{all,\cup}$	$\models_\Delta^{cw,\cup}$	$\models_\Delta^{+,\cup}$	$\models_\Delta^{\kappa,\cup}$

$\{+, cw, \kappa, all\}$. We have

$$C_\Delta^{\cap,c}(\phi) :\overset{\text{def}}{=} C_\Delta^{all,\cap}(\phi) \subseteq C_\Delta^{\circ,\cap}(\phi) \qquad \text{respectively} \qquad (5.33)$$

$$\models_\Delta^{\cap} :\overset{\text{def}}{=} \models_\Delta^{all,\cap} \subseteq \models_\Delta^{\circ,\cap} \qquad\qquad\qquad (5.34)$$

and

$$C_\Delta^{\cup,c}(\phi) :\overset{\text{def}}{=} C_\Delta^{all,\cup}(\phi) \supseteq C_\Delta^{\circ,\cup}(\phi) \qquad \text{respectively} \qquad (5.35)$$

$$\models_\Delta^{\cup} :\overset{\text{def}}{=} \models_\Delta^{all,\cap} \supseteq \models_\Delta^{\circ,\cap}. \qquad\qquad\qquad (5.36)$$

We first inspect the relationships between the sets of minimal c-representations with respect to these notions for examining the relationship between the inferences of different notions of preference.

Lemma 5.45 ([BEK16, Proposition 2]). Let Δ be a knowledge base. Every sum-minimal c-representations of Δ is a componentwise minimal c-representation of Δ, formally

$$Min_c^+ \subseteq Min_c^{cw}. \qquad\qquad\qquad (5.37)$$

Lemma 5.46 ([BEK16, Proposition 2]). Let Δ be a knowledge base without self-fulfilling conditionals. Every minimal inductively preferred c-representations of Δ is a componentwise minimal c-representation of Δ, formally

$$Min_c^\kappa \subseteq Min_c^{cw}. \qquad\qquad\qquad (5.38)$$

This cannot be ensured for knowledge bases in general.

Lemma 5.46 indicates that for ordering minimal c-representations, self-fulfilling conditionals are problematic, because they have an impact on the componentwise preference, while having to impact on the resulting OCF, as they cannot be falsified and thus never impose their impact on the possible worlds. The motivation for ordering the sets of c-representations to infer on (a given definition of) minimal models. As the impact of such a self-fulfilling conditional is irrelevant for the OCF and it therefore also is for the inferences to be drawn. Hence it seems reasonable to consider knowledge bases which do not contain self-fulfilling conditionals or are cleared of self-fulfilling conditionals. If this is not desirable in a given application, another way to overcome this problem is to partition the knowledge base into sets of self-fulfilling conditionals and not self-fulfilling conditionals, and taking only the latter set into account when determining the most preferred models. Chapter 6 discusses how to process knowledge bases such that the resulting knowledge base only contains the inferentially meaningful conditionals. So a third option it to apply these notions of preference to knowledge bases normalised with respect to the methods propose in Chapter 6.

We further obtain for the relationship of the inference relations according to Definition 5.42 using the findings of the above lemmata:

Corollary 5.47 ([BEKIK16, Proposition 34]). For every consistent knowledge base $\Delta = \{(\psi_1|\phi_1), \ldots, (\psi_n|\phi_n)\} \subseteq (\mathfrak{L} \mid \mathfrak{L})$ we have

$$\approx_{\Delta}^{cw,\cap} \subseteq \approx_{\Delta}^{+,\cap} \tag{5.39}$$

$$\approx_{\Delta}^{cw,\cup} \supseteq \approx_{\Delta}^{+,\cup} \tag{5.40}$$

and, given Δ does not contain self-fulfilling conditionals,

$$\approx_{\Delta}^{cw,\cap} \subseteq \approx_{\Delta}^{\kappa,\cap} \tag{5.41}$$

$$\approx_{\Delta}^{cw,\cup} \supseteq \approx_{\Delta}^{\kappa,\cup} \tag{5.42}$$

Using the following example of [BEKIK16] we strengthen (5.39) to strict inclusion:

Example 5.48 ([BEKIK16, Example 35]). Let $\Delta = \{\delta_1, \delta_2, \delta_3, \delta_4, \delta_5\}$ be a knowledge base composed from the following set of conditionals:

$\delta_1 : (b|p)$ *penguins are birds*
$\delta_2 : (b|\overline{p})$ *non-penguins are birds*
$\delta_3 : (b|\overline{p}sf)$ *flying strange non-penguins are birds*
$\delta_4 : (s|\overline{b}f)$ *flying things that do not are birds are strange*
$\delta_5 : (p|\overline{f})$ *things that do not fly are likely penguins*

Table 5.8: Ranks of the worlds $\omega \models \overline{p}\overline{f}$ in Example 5.48

$\omega \models \overline{p}\overline{f}$	$\overline{p}\,b\,s\,\overline{f}$	$\overline{p}\,b\,\overline{s}\,\overline{f}$	$\overline{p}\,\overline{b}\,s\,\overline{f}$	$\overline{p}\,\overline{b}\,\overline{s}\,\overline{f}$
$\kappa^c_{\vec{\eta}}(\omega)$	1	1	1	1
$\kappa^c_{\vec{\eta}'}(\omega)$	1	1	2	2

For $CSP(\Delta)$, the impact vector $\vec{\eta} = (1, 0, 1, 2, 1)$ inducing the OCF $\kappa_{\vec{\eta}}$ is both cw- and ind-minimal while $\vec{\eta}' = (1, 1, 0, 1, 1)$ inducing $\kappa_{\vec{\eta}'}$ is cw-, ind- and sum-minimal; there are no other minimal solutions. We concentrate on the four worlds satisfying $\overline{p}\overline{f}$ with ranks given in Table 5.8 their assigned ranks under both solutions. For the conditional $(b|\overline{p}\overline{f})$ observe that $\kappa^c_{\vec{\eta}} \not\models (b|\overline{p}\overline{f})$ since $\kappa^c_{\vec{\eta}}(\overline{p}b\overline{f}) = 1 = \kappa^c_{\vec{\eta}}(\overline{p}\overline{b}\overline{f})$, but $\kappa^c_{\vec{\eta}'} \models (b|\overline{p}\overline{f})$ since $\kappa^c_{\vec{\eta}'}(\overline{p}b\overline{f}) = 1 < 2 = \kappa^c_{\vec{\eta}'}(\overline{p}\overline{b}\overline{f})$. Thus $\overline{p}\overline{f}\approx^{cw,\cap}_{\Delta}b$ and $\overline{p}\overline{f}\not\approx^{cw,\cap}_{\Delta}b$, but $\overline{p}\overline{f}\approx^{+,\cap}_{\Delta}b$. This shows that sceptical inference over all c-representations induced by sum-minimal impact vectors differs both from inference over cw-minimal and over ind-minimal models in general.

We summarise the findings about the relationship between the twelve inference relations of Definition 5.42 in Figure 5.1.

5.4 Interim Summary and Discussion

This chapter recalls inference with sets of c-representations as defined in the articles [BEK16, BEKI16, BEKIK16, BEKIK18]. It recalls that it is possible to correctly and completely represent the system of inequalities of c-representations as constraint satisfaction problem and all c-representations of a knowledge base as the set of solutions to this problem. With this, we not only recalled a generic c-representation which captures the sceptical inferences over all c-representations, but also, mimicking the characterisation of System P inference by [GP96], characterises sceptical inference over all c-representations as a constraint satisfaction problem.

These inference can be instantiated in three different degrees of sceptical inference on sets of c-representations, credulous, weakly sceptical and sceptical inference. From these inferences, credulous c-inference over all c-representations of a knowledge base easily leads to contradictory inferences, which reduces its usability as inference relation in reasoning tasks,

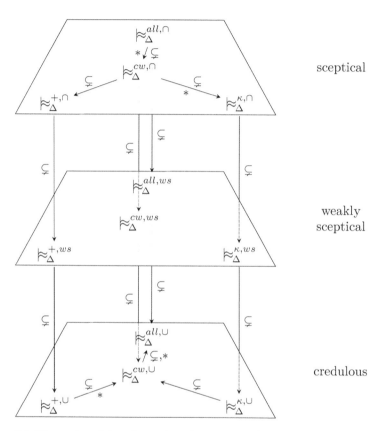

Figure 5.1: Illustration of the relationships (set inclusions) between the inferences drawn based on sets of c-representations and the degree of scepticism of the inference relations (Definition 5.42), in direction of the arrow, that is $\approx \xrightarrow{\dagger} \approx'$ with $\dagger \in \{\subseteq \subsetneq\}$ means that $\approx$ is a $\dagger$ subset of $\approx'$ (confer [BEKIK16]). These relationships have been investigated further in [BKO17], the additional results show some relations being strict and are included in the graphic (denoted with an asterisk $*$ on the edge). These results are added to this graphic to provide an overview which is as complete as possible, but not included further into this thesis as the author was not part of the authors of this publication.

but renders it to be a baseline for the maximum of formulas that can be sensibly inferred. Another perspective to this, following the argumentation of [Poo88], is that a formula ψ which can be credulously c-inferred from a formula ϕ in the context of Δ is *explainable* by ϕ given the background knowledge Δ. By this, credulous inference also proves its usefulness for abductive inference. Sceptical c-inference over all c-representations of a knowledge base is the most strict of the three, licensing for inferences of formulas ψ that are strictly more plausible that their negation in the context of ϕ under Δ. This inference licenses for the least inferences, but satisfies strong formal properties like System P, (NR), (DR), as well as classical benchmarks like default rule chaining and subclass inheritance for exceptional subclasses. The third degree of scepticism, weakly sceptical c-inference over all c-representations of a knowledge base, is recalled as well as demonstrated to be in between these two extremes of sceptical and credulous inference, and licenses for the inference of ψ from ϕ given Δ if ψ, but $\overline{\psi}$ can be explained by ϕ. Preferential inference defines inference relations with respect to the most plausible models of formulas. Recalling inference with preferred c-representations we apply this principle to models of knowledge bases. This gives us another dimension to determine inference relations that differ from inferring with all c-representations of a knowledge base. We recalled three different relations that prefer c-representations with respect to their individual impacts, the sum of their impacts, and on the rankings of the worlds and with these inference with minimal c-representations using degrees of scepticism already established in this thesis. We finally recalled how the resulting twelve inference relations relate to each other.

The inferences reported in this section are implemented using CSP-solvers at the Lehrgebiet Intelligente Systeme of FernUniversität in Hagen, documented in [BEKIK16, BEK16, BEKIK18]. The idea of formalising c-representations as CSP is to be attributed to Christoph Beierle, the implementation is to be attributed to Steven Kutsch. Most of the formal results regarding sets of preferred c-representations and their relationships are to be attributed to these co-authors, too. The closure property as well as the definition of the c-inference as CSP was the result of discussions of all authors of the abovementioned articles. The contribution of the author of this thesis to this topic lies mainly in the examination of the formal properties of the defined inference relations. This thesis extends the cited literature in that it condenses the definitions as relations over all and certain sets of c-representations, as well as showing that sceptical c-inference satisfies (NR) and (DR) and that weakly sceptical c-inference satisfies (NR), (DR), (OR) and (DI), but violates (CI) and (RT).

6 Normal Forms of Conditional Knowledge Bases

Conditionals are logical entities composed from the set of propositional formulas, and conditional knowledge bases are composed from sets of conditionals. Therefore it is possible to encode information in very different and even unclear or confusing ways. Conditional knowledge bases serve as base for the inductive inference approaches from Section 3.3.3 and background knowledge of reasoning systems. In the complexity estimations of the said approaches to inductive inference and algorithms thereof we always found the size of the knowledge base to be an important factor, so having a small knowledge base results in faster computation of these algorithms. Also it may also be necessary to compare the information stored in different knowledge bases, or several knowledge bases have to be merged. Both tasks are easier to perform and less prone to error if the information presented is clear and unconvoluted.

In this chapter we recall and summarise the articles [BEKI17a, BEKI17b] and in this transformation systems for conditional knowledge bases with the goal to achieve a normal form for these sets. As a first step, we recall equivalences for conditional knowledge bases so we can ensure that steps undertaken to normalise and minimise the knowledge base do not change the stored information. Based on these equivalences we then recall transformation systems for conditional knowledge bases and show whether these are terminating, confluent and minimising and finally lead to normal forms of conditional knowledge bases.

6.1 Equivalences for Conditional Knowledge Bases

As noted in the introduction of this chapter, before defining rules to transform a knowledge base into a more normal(ised) one, we need a way to assess whether the knowledge bases before and after the application of the rule are equivalent. We here follow [BEKI17a, BEKI17b] and recall both a modelwise and an elementwise equivalence on this behalf.

Using propositional logic as starting point, the relation $\equiv$ for semantical equivalence defines two formulas $\phi, \psi \in \mathcal{L}$ to be equivalent if and only if they share the same propositional models, that is, are satisfied by the same possible worlds (see Page 17 in Section 2.1). When introducing conditionals we already stated that the evaluation between conditionals and worlds is not sufficient to provide an appropriate semantic for conditionals

© Springer-Verlag GmbH Germany, part of Springer Nature 2018
C. Eichhorn, *Rational Reasoning with Finite Conditional Knowledge Bases*, https://doi.org/10.1007/978-3-476-04824-0_6

(see Page 2.2 in Section 2.2). A possible semantic was given when introducing OCF with the notion of *admissibility* (Formula (3.22), Page 52). For modelwise equivalence of conditional knowledge bases we use this admissibility relation and overload the operation *Mod* such that for a conditional $(\psi|\phi)$ the set of models is the set of OCF that accept the conditional, formally $Mod((\psi|\phi)) = \{\kappa|\kappa \vDash (\psi|\phi)\}$. Furthermore for a knowledge base $\Delta = \{(\psi_1|\phi_1), \ldots, (\psi_n|\phi_n)\} \subseteq (\mathfrak{L} \mid \mathfrak{L})$, $Mod(\Delta)$ is the set of OCF that are admissible with respect to Δ, formally

$$Mod(\Delta) = \{\kappa|\kappa \vDash \Delta\}. \tag{6.1}$$

With this operation, we recall modelwise equivalence of knowledge bases as follows.

Definition 6.1 (Modelwise Equivalence [BEKI17a, Definition 2]). Let both $\Delta, \Delta' \subseteq (\mathfrak{L}|\mathfrak{L})$ be knowledge bases. Δ and Δ' are *modelwise equivalent*, if and only if their model sets are identical, formally

$$\Delta \equiv_{mod} \Delta' \qquad \text{if and only if} \qquad Mod(\Delta) = Mod(\Delta'). \tag{6.2}$$

We illustrate this notion with the following example.

Example 6.2. Let $\Delta = \{(b|a)\}$ and let $\Delta' = \{(ab|a)\}$. We have $\kappa \vDash \Delta$ if and only if $\kappa \vDash (b|a)$ if and only if $\kappa(ab) < \kappa(a\overline{b})$. We also have $\kappa \vDash \Delta'$ if and only if $\kappa \vDash (ab|a)$ if and only if $\kappa(ab) < \kappa(a\overline{b})$. Thus $Mod(\Delta) = Mod(\Delta')$ and therefore $\Delta \equiv_{mod} \Delta'$.

Every inconsistent knowledge base has an empty model set, therefore all inconsistent knowledge bases are modelwise equivalent. We recall the special knowledge base $\Delta^{\perp}$ as inclusion minimal inconsistent knowledge base, with, for instance, $\{(\perp|\top)\} \equiv_{mod} \Delta^{\perp}$ [BEKI17a].

Elementwise equivalence examines the individual conditionals in the knowledge bases, following the idea that a knowledge base Δ is equivalent to another one (Δ'), if for every conditional in Δ there is a corresponding conditional in Δ', and vice versa. For this we first recall the concept of elementwise sub knowledge bases.

Definition 6.3 (Elementwise Sub Knowledge Base [BEKI17a, Definition 3]). Let $\Delta, \Delta' \subseteq (\mathfrak{L}|\mathfrak{L})$ be knowledge bases. Δ is an *elementwise sub knowledge base* of Δ', written $\Delta \sqsubseteq_{ew} \Delta'$ if and only if for every not self-fulfilling conditional $(\xi|\chi) \in \Delta'$ there is a conditional $(\psi|\phi) \in \Delta$ with the property that $Mod((\psi|\phi)) = Mod((\xi|\chi))$.

Definition 6.4 (Elementwise Equivalence [BEKI17a, Definition 3]). Let both $\Delta, \Delta' \subseteq (\mathfrak{L}|\mathfrak{L})$ be knowledge bases. Δ and Δ' are *strictly elementwise equivalent* if and only if $\Delta \sqsubseteq_{\text{ew}} \Delta'$ and $\Delta' \sqsubseteq_{\text{ew}} \Delta$. The knowledge bases Δ and Δ' are *elementwise equivalent*, written $\Delta \equiv_{\text{ew}} \Delta'$, if and only if Δ and Δ' are strictly elementwise equivalent or both knowledge bases are inconsistent, that is, $\Delta \equiv_{\text{mod}} \Delta^\perp$ and $\Delta' \equiv_{\text{mod}} \Delta^\perp$.

Defining all inconsistent knowledge bases to be elementwise equivalent is done following [BEKI17a] for avoiding the special case distinctions when dealing with sets of knowledge bases containing consistent and inconsistent knowledge bases. We illustrate modelwise equivalence with a variation of running example.

Example 6.5 ([BEKI17b, Example 1]). We add four rules to the excerpt of the running example in Example 3.31, namely "non-flying penguins usually are penguins" (δ_9), "penguins usually are non-flying penguins" (δ_{10}), "usually individuals are no penguins" (δ_{11}), and "individuals that are no penguins usually are birds that can fly or are not birds but can fly" (δ_{10}). This means for this example we deal with the conditionals

$$\delta_1 : (f|b), \qquad \delta_3 : (b|p), \qquad \delta_4 : (\overline{b}|b), \qquad \delta_9 : (p|p\overline{f}),$$
$$\delta_{10} : (p\overline{f}|p), \qquad \delta_{11} : (\overline{p}|\top), \qquad \delta_{12} : (bf \vee \overline{b}f|pb \vee \overline{p}b).$$

We define $\Delta = \{\delta_1, \delta_3, \delta_4, \delta_{12}\}$ and $\Delta' = \{\delta_1, \delta_3, \delta_4\}$. As $(bf \vee \overline{b}f) \equiv f$ and $(pb \vee \overline{p}b) \equiv b$ we have $\kappa(bf) = \kappa((pb \vee \overline{p}b) \wedge (bf \vee \overline{b}f))$ as well as $\kappa(b\overline{f}) = \kappa((pb \vee \overline{p}b) \wedge \neg(bf \vee \overline{b}f))$ and hence $\kappa \vDash \delta_1$ if and only if $\kappa \vDash \delta_{12}$. So $Mod(\delta_1) = Mod(\delta_{12})$ and we have $\Delta \sqsubseteq_{\text{ew}} \Delta'$ as well as $\Delta' \sqsubseteq_{\text{ew}} \Delta$ and therefore $\Delta \equiv_{\text{ew}} \Delta'$.

6.2 Transformation Systems for Knowledge Bases

With the equivalences of the previous section we now can recall transformation rules that transform a knowledge base into an equivalent knowledge base. For determining consistency we use Algorithm 2.1, denoting $\text{CTA}(\Delta)$ for the outcome of the consistency test algorithm.

There are various ways for normalising propositional formulas, for instance conjunctive normal form (CNF) or disjunctive normal form (DNF). For the following rules we use the function norm(ϕ) as propositional normal form of a formula $\phi \in \mathfrak{L}$ and leave the concrete instantiation of this propositional normalisation to the user of the system.

With these to additional notions, the transformation system $\mathcal{T}$ is set up from the following rules formalised in Figure 6.1. These rules formalise the following intuitions about transforming conditionals (see [BEKI17a, BEKI17b]):

(SF) Remove a conditional from the knowledge base if it is self-fulfilling.

(DP) Remove one conditional out of a pair of conditionals which are duplicates under propositional equivalence of premise and conclusion.

(CE) Remove a conditional from the knowledge base that is equivalent to another in the knowledge base with respect to the evaluation function $[\![(\cdot|\cdot)]\!]_\omega$ (defined in (2.1), Page 20).

(PN) Normalise premise and conclusion of the conditionals propositionally.

(CN) Transform the conditionals into their conditional normal form.

(CC) Replace the knowledge base with the inconsistent knowledge base given it contains a conditional and its negation (which renders the knowledge base inconsistent but can be checked for, syntactically).

(SC) Replace the knowledge base with the inconsistent knowledge base given it includes a conditional that cannot be verified (which renders the knowledge base inconsistent but can be checked for, locally).

(IC) replaces the knowledge base with the inconsistent knowledge base given it is inconsistent.

We illustrate $\mathcal{T}$ with the following example.

Example 6.6 (confer [BEKI17b, Example 2]). Let Δ be the knowledge base set up from the conditionals given in Example 6.5, that is,

$$\Delta = \{\delta_1, \delta_3, \delta_4, \delta_9, \delta_{10}, \delta_{11}, \delta_{12}\}.$$

(SF) removes δ_9 because $p\overline{f} \models p$.

(SF)	self fulfilling	$\dfrac{\Delta \cup \{(\psi\|\phi)\}}{\Delta}$	$\phi \vDash \psi, \phi \not\equiv \bot$
(DP)	duplicate	$\dfrac{\Delta \cup \{(\psi\|\phi),(\xi\|\chi)\}}{\Delta \cup \{(\psi\|\phi)\}}$	$\phi \equiv \chi, \psi \equiv \xi$
(CE)	conditional equivalence	$\dfrac{\Delta \cup \{(\psi\|\phi),(\xi\|\chi)\}}{\Delta \cup \{(\psi\|\phi)\}}$	$\phi\psi \equiv \chi\xi,\ \phi\overline{\psi} \equiv \chi\overline{\xi},$ $\phi\overline{\psi} \equiv \chi\overline{\xi}$
(PN)	propositional normal form	$\dfrac{\Delta \cup \{(\psi\|\phi)\}}{\Delta \cup \{(\mathrm{norm}(\psi)\|\mathrm{norm}(\phi))\}}$	$\phi \neq \mathrm{norm}(\phi),$ $\psi \neq \mathrm{norm}(\psi)$
(CN)	conditional normal form	$\dfrac{\Delta \cup \{(\psi\|\phi)\}}{\Delta \cup \{(\phi\psi\|\phi)\}}$	$\psi \not\equiv \phi\psi$
(CC)	counter conditional	$\dfrac{\Delta \cup \{(\psi\|\phi),(\overline{\psi}\|\phi)\}}{\Delta^\bot}$	
(SC)	self-contradictory	$\dfrac{\Delta \cup \{(\psi\|\phi)\}}{\Delta^\bot}$	$\phi\psi \equiv \bot$
(IC)	inconsistency	$\dfrac{\Delta}{\Delta^\bot}$	$\Delta \neq \Delta^\bot$ $\mathrm{CTA}(\Delta) = \mathrm{NULL}$

Figure 6.1: Transformation rules $\mathcal{T}$ for conditional knowledge bases [BEKI17a]

(DP) removes either δ_1 or δ_{12} because (as argued in Example 6.5) these conditionals are duplicates.

(CE) removes either δ_4 or δ_{10} because $p\overline{f} \equiv pp\overline{f}$ and $pf \equiv (p \wedge \neg(p\overline{f}))$.

(PN) removes δ_{12} because premise and conclusion of δ_1 are equivalent to δ_{12}, respectively, but shorter (which we here assume to be a propositional normal form).

(CN) transforms, for instance, δ_1 to $(bf|b)$. We write δ'_i as outcome of (CN) applied on δ_i for easier legibility of the example.

(CC) is not applicable as there is no such pair.

(SC) is not applicable as there is no such conditional.

(IC) is not applicable as the knowledge base is consistent.

The exhaustive application of $\mathcal{T}$ on Δ results in the knowledge base $\Delta^{\mathcal{T}} = \mathcal{T}(\Delta) = \{\delta'_1, \delta'_3, \delta'_4, \delta'_{11}\}$.

The transformation system $\mathcal{T}$ is not a minimal set of rules, for instance (CC), (SC), and (IC) are all covered by (IC), and in Example 6.6 the effect of (DP) could have been covered by (PN), which would have mapped both conditionals to the identical normal form. However, the objective in [BEKI17a, BEKI17b] has not been to present a minimal transformation system, but a comprehensive transformation system which is composed from rules that arise more or less naturally when normalising knowledge bases by hand.

In the following we examine formal properties of this transformation system.

Proposition 6.7 ([BEKI17a, Proposition 2]). The transformation system $\mathcal{T}$ is terminating.

Proposition 6.8 ([BEKI17a, Proposition 3]). Let $\Delta = \{(\psi_1|\phi_1), \ldots, (\psi_n|\phi_n)\}$ be a knowledge base and let $\mathcal{T}(\Delta)$ be the knowledge base obtained by exhaustively applying the rules of $\mathcal{T}$ to Δ. Then $\Delta \equiv_{\text{mod}} \mathcal{T}(\Delta)$.

With the above proposition we have shown correctness with respect to modelwise equivalence; we continue the correctness examination with respect to elementwise equivalence.

Proposition 6.9 ([BEKI17a, Proposition 4]). Let $\Delta = \{(\psi_1|\phi_1), \ldots, (\psi_n|\phi_n)\}$ be a knowledge base and let $\mathcal{T}(\Delta)$ be the knowledge base obtained by exhaustively applying the rules of $\mathcal{T}$ to Δ. Then $\Delta \equiv_{\text{ew}} \mathcal{T}(\Delta)$.

Proposition 6.10 ([BEKI17a, Proposition 5]). The transformation system $\mathcal{T}$ is confluent.

Even more the system $\mathcal{T}$ is not only confluent with respect to modelwise equivalence, but also with respect to elementwise equivalence:

Proposition 6.11 ([BEKI17a, Proposition 6]). Let $\Delta = \{(\psi_1|\phi_1), \ldots, (\psi_n|\phi_n)\}$ be a knowledge base. If Δ is inconsistent, we have $\mathcal{T}(\Delta) = \Delta^\perp$. Otherwise

$$\Delta' \subsetneq \mathcal{T}(\Delta) \qquad\qquad \text{implies} \qquad\qquad \Delta' \not\equiv_{\text{ew}} \Delta. \qquad (6.3)$$

So by Propositions 6.7 to 6.11 we obtain that by application of $\mathcal{T}$ to a knowledge base Δ we yields the unique knowledge base $\mathcal{T}(\Delta)$ that is elementwise equivalent to Δ and minimal with respect to set inclusion. Therefore from these propositions we conclude:

Corollary 6.12 (Normal Form of Conditional Knowledge Bases [BEKI17a, Definition 4]). A knowledge base $\Delta = \{(\psi_1|\phi_1), \ldots, (\psi_n|\phi_n)\} \subseteq (\mathfrak{L} \mid \mathfrak{L})$ is in normal form if and only if $\Delta = \mathcal{T}(\Delta)$.

Using this normal form we can test knowledge bases for their equivalence with respect to elementwise equivalence:

Corollary 6.13 ([BEKI17a, Proposition 7]). Two knowledge bases Δ, Δ' are elementwise equivalent if and only if they share the same normal form, formally

$$\Delta \equiv_{\mathrm{ew}} \Delta' \qquad \text{if and only if} \qquad \mathcal{T}(\Delta) = \mathcal{T}(\Delta'). \qquad (6.4)$$

We obtained that $\mathcal{T}$ is correct with respect to model equivalence as well as elementwise equivalence. The transformation system is also minimising with respect to elementwise equivalence. The following example shows that this is not always the case for modelwise equivalence.

Example 6.14 (confer [BEKI17a, Example 4]). We recall the knowledge bases Δ and $\mathcal{T}(\Delta)$ of example 6.6, in this example we demonstrated that $\mathcal{T}(\Delta)$ is the normal form of Δ. We define an additional knowledge base $\Delta' = \{\delta_1, \delta_3, \delta_4\}$. Here, $\Delta' \cup (p|\top)$ is inconsistent and thus $\Delta' \approx_\Delta \overline{p}$ by Definition 2.11 and therefore with Definition 4.28 we obtain that for $\kappa \models \Delta'$ we also have $\kappa \models (\overline{p}|\top)$. Thus $Mod(\mathcal{T}(\Delta)) = Mod(\Delta')$ and we have $\mathcal{T}(\Delta) \equiv_{\mathrm{mod}} \Delta'$, even if $\Delta' \subsetneq \mathcal{T}(\Delta)$.

We formalise this in the following observation:

Observation 6.15 ([BEKI17a]). There are knowledge bases where the normal form is not inclusion minimal with respect to modelwise equivalence.

The example showed that it is possible that the transformation system $\mathcal{T}$ does not remove conditionals from the knowledge base which follow from the remainder knowledge base under System P. The following extension of this system is motivated by this and removes inferable conditionals.

Definition 6.16 ($\mathcal{T}_2$ [BEKI17a, Definition 5]). The transformation system $\mathcal{T}_2$ is the transformation system $\mathcal{T}$ extended by the rule

(RC) $\begin{array}{c} \text{redundant} \\ \text{conditional} \end{array}$ $\dfrac{\Delta \cup \{(\psi|\phi)\}}{\Delta}$ $\mathrm{CTA}(\Delta \cup \{(\overline{\psi}|\phi)\}) = \mathtt{NULL}.$

As we see by the definition as well as the motivating example, this rule removes every System P entailable conditional from the knowledge base. We already argued that by Definitions 2.11 and 4.28, the ranking models of a knowledge base joined with the conditionals which are System P inferable from the knowledge base and the ranking models of the remainder knowledge base must be identical. The additional rule removes at most a conditional from the knowledge base, so together with Propositions 6.7 and 6.8 we directly conclude:

Corollary 6.17 ([BEKI17a, Proposition 8]). The transformation system $\mathcal{T}_2$ is terminating and for all knowledge bases $\Delta = \{(\psi_1|\phi_1), \dots, (\psi_n|\phi_n)\}$ we have $\Delta \equiv_{\text{mod}} \mathcal{T}(\Delta)$.

Example 6.18 ([BEKI17a, Example 5]). Let $\Delta = \{\delta_1 : (b|a), \delta_2 : (a|c), \delta_3 : (\overline{b}|c), \delta_4 : (\overline{b}|ac), \}$. We define $\Delta_1 = \{\delta_1, \delta_2, \delta_3\}$ and obtain $ac \hspace{1pt} \|{\approx}_{\Delta_1} \overline{b}$, thus applying (RC) to Δ on δ_4 yields Δ_1. But for $\Delta_2 = \{\delta_1, \delta_2, \delta_3\}$ we obtain $e \hspace{1pt} \|{\approx}_{\Delta_2} \overline{b}$, and therefore applying (RC) to Δ on δ_3 yields Δ_2. This means that applying $\mathcal{T}_2$ to Δ yields two different normal forms.

Observation 6.19 ([BEKI17a]). The transformation System $\mathcal{T}_2$ is not confluent.

But it could be shown that $\mathcal{T}_2$ is minimising with respect to model equivalence.

Proposition 6.20 ([BEKI17a, Proposition 9]). The transformation system $\mathcal{T}_2$ produces $\mathcal{T}_2(\Delta) = \Delta^\perp$ if and only if Δ is inconsistent for any conditional knowledge base $\Delta = \{(\psi_1|\phi_1), \dots, (\psi_n|\phi_n)\}$. If Δ is consistent, $\mathcal{T}_2$ is minimising, that is for any knowledge base Δ' we have

$$\Delta' \subsetneq \mathcal{T}_2(\Delta) \qquad \text{implies} \qquad \Delta' \not\equiv_{\text{mod}} \Delta. \qquad (6.5)$$

So even if $\mathcal{T}_2(\Delta)$ is not a normal form of Δ because it is not unique, the system yields at least a minimal knowledge base and thus succeeds in reducing the workload of algorithms to work on the resulting knowledge bases.

6.3 Interim Summary

This chapter, which is based on the articles [BEKI17a, BEKI17b], recalls notions of equivalence for conditional knowledge bases. These equivalences are the base for transformation systems which transform knowledge bases into (with respect to these notions) equivalent forms. For modelwise equivalence, the result of this transformation is a unique minimal knowledge base, that is, a normalised form of the original knowledge base. This is not the case for elementwise equivalence, where the transformation yields a minimal but not unique knowledge base. However, this "normalised form" still succeeds in being a minimal knowledge base, and the transformation steps remove unnecessary conditionals and transform the remaining conditionals into a standardised form. So the original goal of having a slim and unconvoluted knowledge base is achieved for both notions of equivalence.

The idea of transforming knowledge bases in such a way was brought up by Christoph Beierle, as well as the formalisation as transformation system and most of the formal proofs, whereas the different transformation rules are the result of discussions among the authors of the articles cited.

7 Compact Representations of Conditional Knowledge and Implementational Aspects: Network Approaches to Ordinal Conditional Functions

From the definition of ordinal conditional functions in Section 3.3 we obtained that storing an OCF means to store the ranking value of every possible world, and therefore the space needed to store an OCF is exponentially large in the number of variables. Additionally, generating such an OCF from a conditional knowledge base with the presented inductive approaches of System Z or c-representations has exponential computational time in the size of the propositional alphabet (see Section 3.3.3). Both is unsatisfactory, because both exponential time and space needed for the approaches restricts the problems to which these semantics can be applied in the field, hugely.

This chapter recalls two approaches that use graph structures which we borrow from approaches to probabilistic networks. These structures divide the alphabet and the knowledge base into smaller, more feasible components. This allows us to conquer the problems of computing and storing the ranks for applications, and so to use larger alphabets and knowledge bases with more conditionals as are practicable when applying the approaches in the plain, undivided case. We will see that by the approaches of OCF-networks in Section 7.1 (based on and extending the articles [KIE13a, KIE13b, EKI15b]) and OCF-LEG networks in Section 7.3 (based on and extending the article [EKI14]), the mentioned problems of time and space complexity are eased to such an extent that the application of OCF and the respective inductive methods to real-world problems is conceivable.

But even more than the benefits in computational and space complexity, breaking down global knowledge to small(er) components also makes sense, cognitively: Assume we want to reason whether a given bird can fly, or not. In this case, we usually do not consult our knowledge about the influences the headlights and the fuel tank of our car have on the plausibility that the car starts after we twist the ignition key. Using network approaches we can use inductive methods, represent knowledge and belief, and reason in the local components containing the variables of our interest, rather than taking every single variable and conditional of the knowledge into account, even the ones not relevant to the question asked.

© Springer-Verlag GmbH Germany, part of Springer Nature 2018
C. Eichhorn, *Rational Reasoning with Finite Conditional Knowledge Bases*, https://doi.org/10.1007/978-3-476-04824-0_7

Breaking down a global representation into smaller, local components is not only popular in formal approaches to representing what is probable or plausible, but also to what is (more or less) preferred. We compare OCF-networks with CP-networks [BBD⁺04], a formalisation of said distributed preferences, in Section 7.2, which is based on and extends the article [EFKI16].

As each of the sections is rather long, we apply the idea of this chapter, that is, to divide knowledge and information into smaller parts, to the chapter itself and conclude each section its own interim summary. This allows us to sum up and discuss the contents of the different sections, locally, rather than mentioning all of the points raised, in a global summary and discussion at the end of this chapter.

7.1 OCF-Networks

The assuredly most established approach of networks in reasoning is the one of Bayesian networks, which we summarised in Section 3.5 (see also [Pea88]). In this approach, the vertices of directed, acyclic networks store probabilistic information, so it is possible to make local calculations and combine the local information to a global probability function over the alphabet when needed. *OCF-networks*, which are presented in this chapter, adopt techniques of Bayesian networks for OCF. To be more precise, this technique uses local ranking tables, that is, a notion of local plausibility, rather than the notion of local probability used in the Bayesian approach. This section is based on and extends the articles [KIE13a, KIE13b, EKI15b, EFKI16].

We recall OCF-networks in Section 7.1.1 and examine the static properties of these networks, showing that they inherit decomposability (factorisation), coincidence of global and local values and the local directed Markov properties from Bayesian networks. After these statical properties, we turn towards inductive properties, namely generating an OCF-network inductively from a conditional knowledge base in Section 7.1.2. We split up this generation into three major parts: Generating the graph component from a conditional knowledge base in Section 7.1.2.1, generating the local ranking tables from a semi-qualitative knowledge base in Section 7.1.2.2. Generating the local ranking table from a purely qualitative conditional knowledge base is the topic of Section 7.1.2.5. We discuss time and space complexity of the algorithms in Section 7.1.2.3. After that, we show that even if it is possible to generate an OCF-network both from a qualitative and semi-quantitative knowledge base, the algorithms fail to generate an OCF-network with a global OCF that accepts the knowledge base, in general (Section 7.1.2.4). We then illustrate that this failure is a general problem of the approach in inductively setting up OCF-networks and cannot be overcome by local means.

7.1.1 Structure and Properties

Roughly speaking, an OCF-network is a Bayesian network (see Section 3.5) where the local probability tables are exchanged with local ranking tables. In this section we recall the formal definition of OCF-networks and present the properties these networks have.

Definition 7.1 (OCF-Network [GP96, BT10, KIE13a, KIE13b, EKI15b]).
An *OCF-network* $\Gamma = \langle \Sigma, \mathcal{E}, \{\kappa_V\}_{V \in \Sigma} \rangle$ is a directed acyclic graph (DAG) over a set of propositional atoms Σ as set of vertices and a set of edges $\mathcal{E} \subseteq \Sigma \times \Sigma$ where every vertex $V \in \Sigma$ is annotated with local rankings $\kappa_V(\dot{v}|\mathbf{p}_V) \in \mathbb{N}_0$ for the outcomes $\dot{v} \in \{v, \overline{v}\}$ and every configuration $\mathbf{p}_V$ of $pa(V)$ that satisfy the normalisation condition

$$\min_{\dot{v} \in \{v, \overline{v}\}} \{\kappa_V(\dot{v}|\mathbf{p}_V)\} = 0 \quad \text{for every configuration } \mathbf{p}_V \text{ of } pa(V). \quad (7.1)$$

We recall that by $V(\omega)$ we indicate the outcome $\dot{v}$ of V with $\omega \vDash \dot{v}$ and by $pa(V)(\omega)$ the configuration $\mathbf{p}_V$ of $pa(V)$ with $\omega \vDash \mathbf{p}_V$. By applying the idea of stratification [GP96], the local ranking information stored at the vertices of an OCF-network can be used to constructively define a global function κ_Γ over Σ: A ranking function κ_Γ is *stratified* relatively to an OCF-network [GP96] if and only if

$$\kappa_\Gamma(\omega) = \sum_{V \in \Sigma} \kappa_V\big(V(\omega)|pa(V)(\omega)\big) \quad (7.2)$$

for every world $\omega \in \Omega$.

The global function κ_Γ of an OCF-network Γ is an ordinal conditional function (see Section 3.3), which is formalised in the following lemma.

Lemma 7.2 ([EKI15b]). Let $\Gamma = \langle \Sigma, \mathcal{E}, \{\kappa_V\}_{V \in \Sigma} \rangle$ be an OCF-network. The function κ_Γ defined by (7.2) is an OCF.

Conversely an OCF κ_Γ over the variables Σ can be stratified or *decomposed* according to a graph $\mathcal{G} = \{\Sigma, \mathcal{E}\}$ provided that each vertex $V \in \Sigma$ is κ-independent of its non-descendants given its parents. This decomposition, which is in accordance with the conditional independence properties of OCF (see Section 3.3, Page 46ff), is formalised in the following proposition.

Proposition 7.3 (Decomposability [GP96, BT10, EKI15b]). Let $\mathcal{G} = \{\Sigma, \mathcal{E}\}$ be a DAG over a propositional alphabet $\Sigma = \{V_1, ..., V_m\}$, the latter enumerated in breadth-first ordering according to $\mathcal{G}$ such that for each $V_i \in \Sigma$ we have $pa(V_i) \subseteq \{V_1, ..., V_{i-1}\}$, and edges $\mathcal{E} \subseteq \Sigma \times \Sigma$. Let κ be an OCF over Σ with the property that $\{V\} \perp\!\!\!\perp_\kappa nd(V) \mid pa(V)$. Then κ can be decomposed such that

$$\kappa(V_1, ..., V_m) = \sum_{i=1}^{m} \kappa(V_i | pa(V_i)) = \sum_{V \in \Sigma} \kappa(V | pa(V)). \qquad (7.3)$$

Like the whole approach of OCF-networks, this decomposability-property originates from Bayesian Networks, where the combination operation is the product and therefore decomposability is also known as *factorisation*, even if, in the case of OCF-networks, it not a decomposition in factors but into addends. So with Formula 7.2 we can construct a global, stratified OCF κ_Γ relative to an OCF-network Γ by Lemma 7.2. Proposition 7.3 hereby ensures that an OCF which satisfies the independence properties presupposed by the graphical structure of a DAG can be decomposed according to the graph structure. Still, it is unclear whether the local ranks $\kappa_V(V | pa(V))$ of the network and the global conditional ranks $\kappa_\Gamma(V | pa(V))$ coincide. This issue is solved by the following theorem.

Theorem 7.4 (Local / Global Coincidence [EKI15b]). Let W be a variable in Σ with a fixed value $\dot{w}$ of W, let $\mathbf{p}_w$ be a fixed configuration of the variables in $pa(W)$. For a ranking function κ stratified according to Equation (7.2) the conditional ranking values $\kappa(\dot{w} | \mathbf{p}_w)$ are identical to the local ranking values $\kappa_W(\dot{w} | \mathbf{p}_w)$:

$$\kappa(\dot{w} | \mathbf{p}_w) = \kappa_W(\dot{w} | \mathbf{p}_w) \qquad (7.4)$$

The local/global coincidence gives us that the conditional ranking tables of an OCF-network are the ranks of the conditionals encoded by the graph structures of the global OCF. Therefore alternatively to storing these conditional ranks in tables we also can store them using firmness annotated conditionals. So the ranking tables of an OCF-network Γ can be represented as a semi-quantitative conditional knowledge base Δ_Γ in a way such $\Delta_\Gamma = \{(\dot{v}|\mathbf{p}_V)[f] \mid \kappa_V(\overline{v}|\mathbf{p}_V) = f, f > 0\}$ for all configuration of the variables in $pa(V)$ denoted as $\mathbf{p}_V$. Such a knowledge base Δ_Γ contains a conditional for every non-zero local ranking value in Γ and is therefore called *complete* with respect to Γ (or Γ-complete for short). Note that the conclusions in the local conditional rank given in the network and in the firmness annotated conditional in the knowledge base are inverse, that is, if $\kappa_V(\dot{v}|\mathbf{p}) = m$, then $(\overline{v}|\mathbf{p})[m] \in \Delta_\Gamma$. The reason for this is that the syntax in both representations express inverse concepts: The local conditional rank in the network states the implausibility of this configuration of the variable given its parents. The conditional in the knowledge base represents how firmly the conditional is believed, this is defined by [Spo12] as the disbelief, that is, implausibility of the inverse.

Example 7.5 (confer [KIE13a]). We illustrate the basic definitions and properties of OCF-networks with the car start example ([GP96, BT10], see Example 3.21). So let the vertices be the set $\Sigma = \{H, B, F, S\}$ and let the set $\mathcal{E} = \{(H, B), (B, S), (F, S)\}$ be the edges of the network. As values for the local ranking tables we define $\kappa_H(h) = 15$, $\kappa_B(b|h) = 4$, $\kappa_B(\overline{b}|\overline{h}) = 4$, $\kappa_F(\overline{f} = 10)$, $\kappa_S(\overline{s}|bf) = 3$, $\kappa_S(s|b\overline{f}) = 13$, $\kappa_S(s|\overline{b}f) = 11$, $\kappa_S(s|\overline{b}\,\overline{f}) = 3$; all other local values are 0 due to the normalisation condition (7.1). Figure 7.1 depicts this graph $\Gamma = \langle \Sigma, \mathcal{E}, \{\kappa_H, \kappa_B, \kappa_F, \kappa_S\}\rangle$ and Table 7.1 shows how the global OCF κ_Γ is calculated from the local ranking tables. In this table we can see that the global function is normalised, because we have $\kappa_\Gamma(\overline{h}bfs) = 0$ and that the local and global ranks coincide, we have, for instance,

$$\kappa_\Gamma(s|b\overline{f}) = \kappa_\Gamma(b\overline{f}s) - \kappa_\Gamma(b\overline{f}) = \min\{\kappa_\Gamma(hb\overline{f}s), \kappa_\Gamma(\overline{h}b\overline{f}s)\}$$
$$- \min\{\kappa_\Gamma(hb\overline{f}s), \kappa_\Gamma(hb\overline{f}\,\overline{s})\kappa_\Gamma(\overline{h}b\overline{f}s), \kappa_\Gamma(\overline{h}b\overline{f}\,\overline{s})\}$$
$$= \min\{42, 23\} - \min\{42, 29, 23, 10\} = 13 = \kappa_S(s|b\overline{f}).$$

The Γ-complete knowledge base for this OCF-network is the set

$$\Delta_\Gamma = \left\{ \begin{array}{l} (\overline{h}|\top)[15], (\overline{b}|h)[4], (h|\overline{h})[8], (f|\top)[10], \\ (a|bf)[3], (\overline{s}|b\overline{f})[13], (\overline{s}|\overline{b}s)[11], (\overline{s}|\overline{b}\,\overline{f})[27] \end{array} \right\}$$

Until now, the decomposability/stratification (and hence also Proposition 7.3) presupposes that each vertex is independent from its non-descendants given its parents, which is known as the *local directed Markov Property*

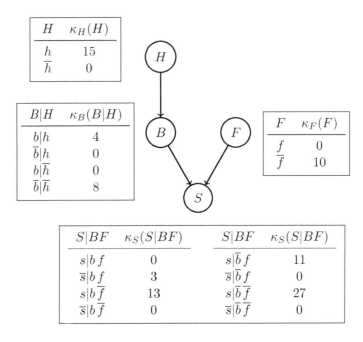

Figure 7.1: OCF-network of the car start example

and also is a vital property of Bayesian Networks. The following theorem ensures that a global OCF κ_Γ of an OCF-network Γ that is generated according to (7.2) always satisfies this property.

Theorem 7.6 (Markov Property for OCF-Networks [KIE13b, Theorem 2]). Let $\Gamma = \langle \Sigma, \mathcal{E} \rangle$ be an OCF-network where for each vertex $V \in \Sigma$ we have the local ranking tables $\kappa_V(V|pa(V))$. Let κ be an OCF stratified with respect to Γ according to (7.2). Then the local directed Markov property holds, that is,

$$\{V\} \perp\!\!\!\perp_\kappa nd(V) \mid pa(V) \qquad \text{for each vertex } V \in \Sigma. \qquad (7.5)$$

We have seen that the approach of OCF-networks shares the central properties with Bayesian Networks, namely (de-)composability, coincidence of local and global values, and the local directed Markov Property. So overall we obtain that OCF-networks are in no way inferior to Bayesian networks when it comes to storing or representing static knowledge.

7.1.2 Inductive Generation of OCF-Networks

The definition of Γ-complete knowledge bases on Page 173 foreshadows that not only there is a way to construct semi-quantitative conditional knowledge bases from OCF-networks, but also a way in the opposite direction, that is, to construct an OCF-network inductively from a knowledge base. In this section we use single-elementary conditionals (see Definition 2.5), that is, conditionals where the premise is a conjunction of literals and the conclusion is a literal, and knowledge bases thereof as base for constructing OCF-networks, inductively.

To construct the graph component of an OCF-network, only the structural information of the knowledge base is needed, so this part of the generation is identical both for qualitative and semi-quantitative knowledge bases. To take account for these, in substance mutually independent, steps, we split this section of how to generate an OCF-network inductively from a conditional knowledge base in three parts: We start by describing the construction of the network, then proceed to the generation of local ranking tables in case the knowledge base is semi-quantitative. Finally we describe

Table 7.1: Calculation of the global OCF from the local ranking tables in Example 7.5

	$hbfs$	$hbf\bar{s}$	$hb\bar{f}s$	$hb\bar{f}\bar{s}$	$h\bar{b}fs$	$h\bar{b}f\bar{s}$	$h\bar{b}\bar{f}s$	$h\bar{b}\bar{f}\bar{s}$
$\kappa_H(H(\omega))$	15	15	15	15	15	15	15	15
$+\,\kappa_B(B(\omega)\|H(\omega))$	4	4	4	4	0	0	0	0
$+\,\kappa(F(\omega))$	0	0	10	10	0	0	10	10
$+\,\kappa(S(\omega)\|BF(\omega))$	0	3	13	0	11	0	27	0
$=\kappa_\Gamma(\omega)$	19	22	42	29	26	15	52	25

	$\bar{h}bfs$	$\bar{h}bf\bar{s}$	$\bar{h}b\bar{f}s$	$\bar{h}b\bar{f}\bar{s}$	$\bar{h}\bar{b}fs$	$\bar{h}\bar{b}f\bar{s}$	$\bar{h}\bar{b}\bar{f}s$	$\bar{h}\bar{b}\bar{f}\bar{s}$
$\kappa_H(H(\omega))$	0	0	0	0	0	0	0	0
$+\,\kappa_B(B(\omega)\|H(\omega))$	0	0	0	0	8	8	8	8
$+\,\kappa(F(\omega))$	0	0	10	10	0	0	10	10
$+\,\kappa(S(\omega)\|BF(\omega))$	0	3	13	0	11	0	27	0
$=\kappa_\Gamma(\omega)$	0	3	23	10	19	8	45	18

the generation of the local ranking tables in the case the knowledge base is purely qualitative in a separate section, each.

7.1.2.1 Inductive Generation of the Network Component for an OCF-Network

The graph component of an OCF-network is constructed from the qualitative information stored in the knowledge base, whereas potentially present quantitative information is disregarded. Therefore in the following we refer to knowledge bases $\Delta = \{(\psi_1|\phi_1), \ldots, (\psi_n|\phi_n)\} \subseteq (\mathfrak{L} \mid \mathfrak{L})$. If the knowledge base of interest is a semi-quantitative knowledge base of the form $\mathcal{R} = \{(\psi_1|\phi_1)[f_1], \ldots, (\psi_n|\phi_n)[f_n]\}$, this section refers to the qualitative part $\Delta_\mathcal{R} = \{(\psi|\phi)|(\psi|\phi)[f] \in \mathcal{R}\}$ of the knowledge base (see Section 2.2)

Definition 7.7 (Single-Elementary Knowledge Base). A conditional knowledge base $\Delta = \{(\psi_1|\phi_1), \ldots, (\psi_n|\phi_n)\}$ with the property that that each $(\psi|\phi) \in \Delta$ is a single-elementary conditional is called a *single-elementary knowledge base*. We sharpen the definition of a single-elementary knowledge base such that the conclusion of each conditional is a literal and keep in mind that the premise is not an arbitrary formula but a conjunction of literals writing $\Delta = \{(\psi_1|\phi_1), \ldots, (\psi_n|\phi_n)\} \subseteq (\mathcal{L} \mid \mathfrak{L})$ with $\mathcal{L}$ being the set of literals over Σ.

We recall the method from [GP96] for creating a DAG from a single-elementary knowledge base Δ. Again, and as for OCF-networks in general, we use the propositional alphabet Σ as set of vertices. We compose the edges from the conditionals such that $(V, W) \in \mathcal{E}$ if and only if there is a conditional $(\psi|\phi) \in \Delta$ with the property that $\{W\} = cons(\psi|\phi)$ and $V \in ant(\psi|\phi)$ as shown in Algorithm 7.1, illustrated in Figure 7.2.

Example 7.8. We illustrate Algorithm 7.1 with the running car start example (see Example 3.48), so let

$$\Delta = \left\{ \begin{array}{cccccc} (s|b), & (\overline{s}|\overline{b}), & (s|f), & (\overline{s}|\overline{f}), & (\overline{s}|b\overline{f}), \\ (\overline{s}|\overline{b}f), & (\overline{h}|\top), & (f|\top), & (\overline{b}|h), & (b|\overline{h}) \end{array} \right\}$$

be the input knowledge base of the algorithm. The conditionals $(s|b)$ and $(\overline{s}|\overline{b})$ give us edges (B, S), from the conditionals $(s|f)$ and $(\overline{s}|\overline{f})$ we generate edges (F, S), $(\overline{s}|b\overline{f})$ and $(\overline{s}|\overline{b}f)$ give us (B, S) and (F, S), neither $(\overline{h}|\top)$ nor $(f|\top)$ generate any edge and finally from $(\overline{b}|h)$ and $(b|\overline{h})$ we generate edges

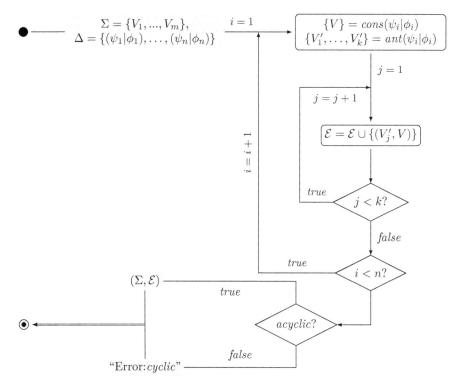

Figure 7.2: Network generation procedure for single-elementary knowledge bases (Algorithm 7.1)

Listing 7.1: Generate a directed graph $(\Sigma, \mathcal{E})$ from a qualitative single-elementary conditional knowledge base $\Delta = \{(\psi_1|\phi_1), \ldots, (\psi_n|\phi_n)\} \subseteq (\mathcal{L} \mid \mathfrak{L})$ (confer [GP96, EKI15b]).

```
INPUT  : Conditional knowledge base Δ = {(ψ₁|φ₁),...,(ψₙ|φₙ)} ⊆ (ℒ | 𝔏)
         over propositional alphabet Σ
OUTPUT: Directed graph (Σ,ℰ)

BEGIN
  ℰ:=∅;
  FOR-EACH((ψ|φ) ∈ Δ)
    W:=cons(ψ|φ)
    FOR-EACH(V∈ ant(ψ|φ))
      ℰ:=ℰ∪(V,W)
    END FOR-EACH
  END FOR-EACH
  RETURN (Σ,ℰ)
END
```

(H, B). Since $\mathcal{E}$ is a set, each of the generated edges are contained once, therefore from Δ we obtain the graph $(\{B, F, H, S\}, \{(H, B), (B, S), (F, S)\})$ which is drawn in Figure 7.3.

Graphs generated by Algorithm 7.1 are not guaranteed to be acyclic, which is already mentioned in [GP96, Definition 30]; also, Algorithm 7.1 is not affected by the consistence or inconsistency of the knowledge base. In the following example we illustrate that we can construct a DAG from an inconsistent knowledge base, as well as that there are consistent knowledge bases which by Algorithm 7.1 result in a cyclic graph.

Example 7.9 ([EKI15b, Example 6]). Let $\Sigma = \{A, B\}$ be the set of variables and $\Delta = \{(b|a), (\overline{b}|a)\}$. It is clear that Δ is inconsistent, but using Algorithm 7.1, the DAG $\mathcal{G}_\Delta = (\{A, B\}, \{(A, B)\})$ can be constructed, nevertheless. On the other hand, for $\Delta' = \{(b|a), (a|b)\}$ Algorithm 7.1 construct the graph $\mathcal{G}_{\Delta'} = (\{A, B\}, \{(A, B), (B, A)\})$ which is cyclic, but the knowledge base is consistent and there are admissible OCF to this knowledge base: Let $\kappa(ab) = 0, \kappa(a\overline{b}) = 1, \kappa(\overline{a}b) = 1, \kappa(\overline{a}\overline{b}) = 2$, then we have $\kappa(ab) = 0 < 1 = \kappa(a\overline{b})$ and $\kappa(ab) = 0 < 1 = \kappa(\overline{a}b)$ and thus $\kappa \vDash \Delta'$. Figure 7.4 shows both graphs for this example.

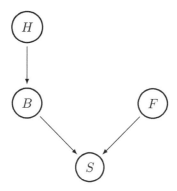

Figure 7.3: Network component generated from the car start example in Example 7.8

(a) Graph of $\{(b|a), (\bar{b}|a)\}$ (b) Graph of $\{(b|a), (a|b)\}$

Figure 7.4: Illustration of both graphs from Example 7.9

So both the consistency of Δ and the acyclicity of the generated graph $\mathcal{G}_\Delta$ have to be tested for generating an OCF-network inductively from a knowledge base Δ, individually, and no OCF-network can be constructed for Δ if either test fails. In the following, we assume the graph to be acyclic and keep in mind that we have to check for acyclicity after invoking Algorithm 7.1.

7.1.2.2 Inductive Generation of the OCF Component of an OCF-Network Using Semi-Quantitative Knowledge Bases

After having described the construction of the graph component of an OCF-network from a knowledge base we here show how to set up the local ranking tables inductively from a semi-quantitative knowledge base. We here extent the literature [KIE13a, KIE13b, EKI15b] by introducing the LS-constraint (Definition 7.10), and further commenting on the correctness result (see page 189). In particular, we present a formal property that allows us to check whether the global OCF of the hereby constructed OCF-network is admissible with respect to the knowledge base by just taking local information into account.

To determine whether a given knowledge base contains all information necessary to set up the OCF-component of an OCF-network, directly, and without the need of an inductive approach like System Z or c-representations, we use the following constraint for the knowledge base serving as local storage for an OCF-network.

Definition 7.10 (LS-Constraint). Let $\Delta = \{(\psi_1|\phi_1), \ldots, (\psi_n|\phi_n)\} \subseteq (\mathcal{L} \mid \mathfrak{L})$ be a consistent single-elementary knowledge base. Δ satisfies the *LS-constraint* if and only if for every pair $(\psi|\phi), (\xi|\chi) \in \Delta$ of conditionals, the equality $cons(\psi|\phi) = cons(\xi|\chi)$ implies $ant(\psi|\phi) = ant(\xi|\chi)$.[1]

This constraint is satisfied if all conditionals in the knowledge base which share the same consequence have antecedences ranging over the same set of variables. As proposed, this constraint can be used to determine whether an inductive approach is necessary, or not.

Lemma 7.11. Let $\mathcal{R} = \{(\psi_1|\phi_1)[f_1], \ldots, (\psi_n|\phi_n)[f_n]\}$ be a consistent single-elementary knowledge base. There is an OCF-Network Γ such that Δ is complete with respect to Γ if and only if the qualitative part of $\mathcal{R}$ satisfies the LS-constraint.

Lemma 7.11 gives us Algorithm 7.2 to construct OCF-networks given that Δ satisfies the LS-constraint; Figure 7.5 illustrates this algorithm. The LS-constraint is very rigorous and cannot be assumed to be satisfied, generally. For instance, none of the running examples satisfies the LS-constraint.

Example 7.12. In the running example (see Example 2.1) for F we have the conditionals $(\overline{f}|cb), (f|b)$, and $(\overline{f}|p) \in \Delta$ and $\{C, B\} \neq \{P\} \neq \{B\}$. Even an easier variant without chickens fails (Example 3.15) satisfies the LS-constraint because of the conditionals $(f|b)$ and $(\overline{f}|p)$, F has two parents, $pa(F) = \{B, P\}$ and we have, for instance, $ant(f|b) = \{B\} \neq \{B, P\} = pa(F)$. In Example 3.48 dealing with (not) starting cars there are several conditionals where either s or $\overline{s}$ is the conclusion, whereas the variables used in the premises vary (e.g. $(s|b)$ and $(s|f)$).

---

[1]   Note that *ant* and *cons* are the sets of the variables involved in the antecedence or consequence of the conditional, respectively, not the formula in the antecedence or consequence itself (see Section 2.2).

Listing 7.2: Construct an OCF-network from a knowledge base given Δ satisfies the LS-constraint. The steps annotated with $*$ are in the following referred to as Procedure 7.2.a

```
INPUT  : Semi-quantitative single-elementary knowledge base that
         satisfies the LS-constraint R = {(ψ₁|φ₁)[f₁],...,(ψₙ|φₙ)[fₙ]}
OUTPUT : OCF-network ⟨(Σ,ε),{κ_V}_{V∈Σ}⟩

BEGIN
  // Construct graph component
  invoke Algorithm 7.1 on Δ_R to construct DAG (Σ,ε)

  // Initialise all local OCF with empty OCF (*)
  FOR-EACH(V∈ Σ)
    FOR-EACH(v̇ ∈ dom(V))
      FOR-EACH(configuration p_V of pa(V))
        κ_V(v̇|p_v):=0
      END FOR-EACH
    END FOR-EACH
  END FOR-EACH

  // Construct OCF from knowledge base (*)
  FOR-EACH((v̇|φ)[f] ∈ R)
    κ_V(v̄|φ):=f
  END FOR-EACH
  RETURN ⟨(Σ,ε),{κ_V}_{V∈Σ}⟩
END
```

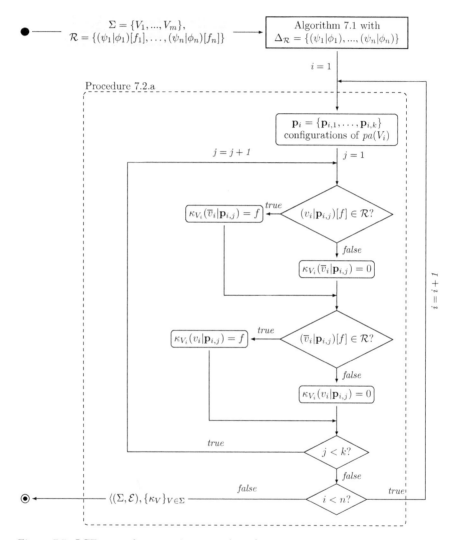

Figure 7.5: OCF-network generation procedure for semi-quantitative single-elementary knowledge bases $\mathcal{R}$ that satisfy the LS-constraint (Algorithm 7.2). The shaded box illustrates the procedure that in the following will be referred to as *Procedure 7.2.a*

Listing 7.3: Split up the knowledge base according [EKI15b].

```
INPUT   : Semi-quantitative consistent single-elementary
          knowledge base R = {(ψ₁|φ₁)[f₁],...,(ψₙ|φₙ)[fₙ]}
OUTPUT  : Set of local knowledge bases {R_V}_{V∈Σ}

BEGIN
  // Initialisation
  FOR-EACH(V ∈ Σ)
    R_V := ∅
  END FOR-EACH

  // Splitting procedure
  FOR-EACH((ψᵢ|φᵢ)[fᵢ] ∈ R)
    V := cons(ψᵢ|φᵢ)
    R_V := R_V ∪ {(ψᵢ|φᵢ)[fᵢ]}
  END FOR-EACH
  RETURN {R_V}_{V∈Σ}
END
```

So if the ranking tables of the OCF-networks cannot be taken from the knowledge base directly because they does not satisfy the LS-constraint, the local information has been generated inductively from the conditionals using the inductive approaches System Z^+ or c-representations (see Section 3.3.3.3). For this, we partition the knowledge base into local components $\mathcal{R}_V = \{(\psi|\phi)[f] \mid cons(\psi|\phi) = \{V\}, (\psi|\phi)[f] \in \mathcal{R}\}$ with the following procedure: For every variable V there is a unique set of conditionals $\mathcal{R}_V$, because for single-elementary conditionals, the conclusion consists of exactly one literal. Therefore, the different local knowledge bases are disjoint, and every conditional in the knowledge base is associated to exactly one variable, formally

$$\mathcal{R} = \bigcup_{V \in \Sigma} \mathcal{R}_V \quad \text{and} \quad \mathcal{R}_V \cap \mathcal{R}_W = \varnothing \quad \text{for each pair} \quad V, W \in \Sigma. \quad (7.6)$$

We shape this partitioning of $\mathcal{R}$ into Algorithm 7.3, illustrated by Figure 7.6.

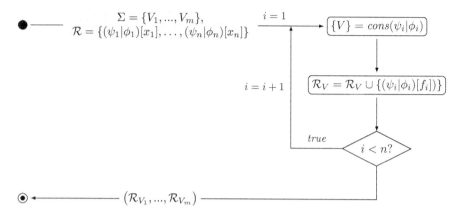

Figure 7.6: Procedure for splitting up the (global) knowledge base into local knowledge
bases (Algorithm 7.3)

Example 7.13. We apply Algorithm 7.3 to the car start example (see Example 3.48), so we use the knowledge base

$$\mathcal{R} = \left\{ \begin{array}{cccccc} (s|b)[2], & (\overline{s}|\overline{b})[12], & (s|f)[1], & (\overline{s}|\overline{f})[15], & (\overline{s}|b\overline{f})[13], \\ (\overline{s}|\overline{b}f)[11], & (\overline{h}|\top)[15], & (f|\top)[10], & (\overline{b}|h)[4], & (b|\overline{h})[8] \end{array} \right\}$$

over the variables $\Sigma = \{B, F, H, S\}$. Algorithm 7.3 partitions the knowledge base into the components

$$\mathcal{R}_H = \{(\overline{h}|\top)[15]\}$$
$$\mathcal{R}_B = \{(\overline{b}|h)[4], (b|\overline{h})[8]\}$$
$$\mathcal{R}_F = \{(f|\top)[10]\}$$
$$\mathcal{R}_S = \left\{ \begin{array}{ccc} (s|b)[2], & (\overline{s}|\overline{b})[12], & (s|f)[1], \\ (\overline{s}|\overline{f})[15], & (\overline{s}|b\overline{f})[13], & (\overline{s}|\overline{b}f)[11] \end{array} \right\}.$$

Based on these partitions, the local ranking tables κ_V can then obtained by inductively generating local ranking functions $\kappa_{\mathcal{R}_V}$ with System Z^+ or c-representations and condition the local rankings on the variables $pa(V)$.

Example 7.13 shows that even if the global knowledge base does not satisfy the LS-constraint, there may be local knowledge bases $\mathcal{R}_V$ such that $ant(\psi|\phi) = pa(V)$ for all $(\psi|\phi) \in \mathcal{R}_V$, which satisfies the LS-constraint for the subgraph $(\{V\} \cup pa(V), \{(V', V) | (V', V) \in \mathcal{E}, V' \in pa(V)\})$. This

Listing 7.4: Generate an OCF-network from a knowledge base ([EKI15b]).

```
INPUT   : Semi-quantitative consistent single-elementary
          knowledge base  R = {(ψ₁|φ₁)[f₁],...,(ψₙ|φₙ)[fₙ]}
OUTPUT  : OCF-network ⟨(Σ,ℰ),{κ_V}_{V∈Σ}⟩

BEGIN
   invoke Algorithm 7.1 to generate DAG (Σ,ℰ)
   invoke Algorithm 7.3 to partition R into {R_V}_{V∈Σ}
   FOR-EACH(V ∈ Σ)
     IF(R_V satisfies the LS-constraint)
        invoke Procedure 7.2.a to obtain κ_V
     ELSE
        invoke System˜Z⁺ or c-representations on R_V
        condition resulting local OCF on pa(V) to obtain κ_V
     END IF
   END FOR-EACH
   RETURN ⟨(Σ,ℰ),{κ_V}_{V∈Σ}⟩
END
```

property is in the following referred to as *local LS-constraint*. For these subgraphs defined by $(\{V\} \cup pa(V), \{(W|V)|W \in pa(V)\})$, the knowledge bases $\mathcal{R}_V$ are complete, therefore, there is no need of invoking an inductive OCF-method on every $\mathcal{R}_V$, $V \in \Sigma$, because there are cases where the local ranking table can be taken directly from $\mathcal{R}_V$ by applying Procedure 7.2.a.

Algorithm 7.4 joins the single steps from this and the previous section in one process which generates an OCF-network from a semi-quantitative consistent, single-elementary knowledge base; Figure 7.7 illustrates this algorithm.

Example 7.14. We apply Algorithm 7.4 to the car start example (see Example 3.48), continuing Examples 7.8 and 7.13 in this way. The graph component (Figure 7.3) has been constructed in Example 7.8, the local knowledge bases have been computed in Example 7.13 to be

$$\mathcal{R}_H = \{(\overline{h}|\top)[15]\}$$

$$\mathcal{R}_B = \{(\overline{b}|h)[4], (b|\overline{h})[8]\}$$

$$\mathcal{R}_F = \{f|\top)[10]\}$$

$$\mathcal{R}_S = \left\{ \begin{array}{lll} r_1 = (s|b)[2], & r_2 = (\overline{s}|\overline{b})[12], & r_3 = (s|f)[1], \\ r_4 = (\overline{s}|\overline{f})[15], & r_5 = (\overline{s}|b\overline{f})[13], & r_6 = (\overline{s}|\overline{b}f)[11] \end{array} \right\}.$$

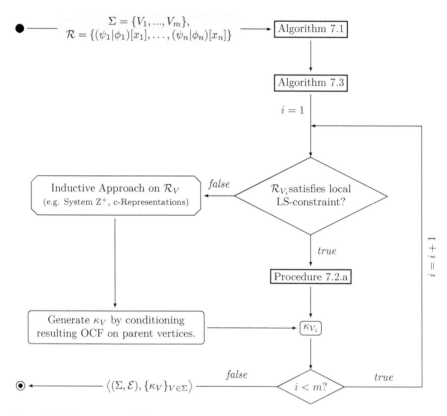

Figure 7.7: Illustration of Algorithm 7.4 to generate an OCF-network from a conditional knowledge base

Table 7.2: Verification/falsification behaviour of local worlds of $\{B, F, S\}$ given the local car start knowledge base $\mathcal{R}_S$ from Example 7.14

BFS	verifies	falsifies	$\kappa^Z_{\mathcal{R}_S}(BFS)$	$\kappa^Z_{\mathcal{R}_S}(BF)$	$\kappa^Z_S(S\|BF)$	$\kappa^c_{\mathcal{R}_S}(BFS)$	$\kappa^c_{\mathcal{R}_S}(BF)$	$\kappa^c_S(S\|BF)$
$b\,f\,s$	r_1, r_3	—	0	0	0	0	0	0
$b\,f\,\bar{s}$	—	r_1, r_3	2	0	2	3	0	3
$b\,\bar{f}\,s$	r_1	r_4, r_5	16	2	14	15	2	13
$b\,\bar{f}\,\bar{s}$	r_4, r_5	r_1	2	2	0	2	2	0
$\bar{b}\,f\,s$	r_3	r_2, r_6	13	1	12	12	1	11
$\bar{b}\,f\,\bar{s}$	r_2, r_6	r_3	1	1	0	1	1	0
$\bar{b}\,\bar{f}\,s$	—	r_2, r_4	15	0	15	27	0	27
$\bar{b}\,\bar{f}\,\bar{s}$	r_2, r_4	—	0	0	0	0	0	0

Here $\mathcal{R}_H$, $\mathcal{R}_B$ and $\mathcal{R}_F$ satisfy the local LS-constraint so by applying Procedure 7.2.a we can construct the local ranking tables at the vertices H, B, and F, directly from the knowledge bases $\mathcal{R}_H$, $\mathcal{R}_B$, and $\mathcal{R}_F$. The knowledge base $\mathcal{R}_S$ violates the LS-constraint because it contains, for instance, the conditionals $(s|f)[1]$ and $(s|b)[2]$ for which $cons(s|f) = \{S\} = cons(s|b)$ but $ant(s|f) = \{F\} \neq \{B\} = ant(s|b)$ and so we have to invoke an inductive approach on this knowledge base. To illustrate the differences, we here invoke both System Z and c-representations on this knowledge base, which give us the ranking values given in Table 7.2. With these values, we can construct the OCF-network as given in Figure 7.8 for either inductive approach.

Up to this point we have shown that OCF-networks not only have desirable formal properties, but there also are algorithms to construct these networks inductively from a semi-quantitative consistent single-elementary conditional knowledge base. In the following, we analyse the time and space complexity of this approach to compare it with the approach of applying inductive approaches to the knowledge base directly. As a final step we check the results of this approach for correctness.

7.1.2.3 Complexity Results

The *time complexity* of Algorithm 7.4 is the combined complexity of the components:

- For each $(\psi|\phi)[x] \in \mathcal{R}$, the network generation procedure (that is, Algorithm 7.1) adds $|ant(\psi|\phi)|$ edges to the graph. Since the input is constraint to single-elementary knowledge bases, the largest ante-

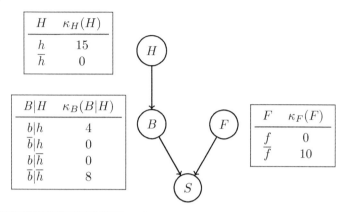

H	$\kappa_H(H)$
h	15
$\overline{h}$	0

$B\|H$	$\kappa_B(B\|H)$
$b\|h$	4
$\overline{b}\|h$	0
$b\|\overline{h}$	0
$\overline{b}\|\overline{h}$	8

F	$\kappa_F(F)$
f	0
$\overline{f}$	10

$S\|BF$	$\kappa_S^Z(S\|BF)$	$\kappa_S^c(S\|BF)$	$S\|BF$	$\kappa_S^Z(S\|BF)$	$\kappa_S^c(S\|BF)$
$s\|b\,f$	0	0	$s\|\overline{b}\,f$	12	11
$\overline{s}\|b\,f$	2	3	$\overline{s}\|\overline{b}\,f$	0	0
$s\|b\,\overline{f}$	14	13	$s\|\overline{b}\,\overline{f}$	15	27
$\overline{s}\|b\,\overline{f}$	0	0	$\overline{s}\|\overline{b}\,\overline{f}$	0	0

Figure 7.8: Solutions for the car starting problem in Example 7.14 using both System Z^+ and c-representations

cedence of a conditional with respect to variable count consists of $\bigwedge_{i=1}^{|\Sigma|} V_i$, therefore this number is bounded by $|\Sigma|$, hence the graph can be constructed in less or equal $|\mathcal{R}| \cdot |\Sigma|$ steps.

- The graph then has to be checked for acyclicity, which is bounded by $|\Sigma|^2$ steps (confer, for instance, [Die00]).

- Algorithm 7.3 to split up the knowledge base into local components needs to inspect every conditional once, so this can be done in $|\mathcal{R}|$ steps.

- Checking whether a local knowledge base satisfies the local LS-constraint can be done in the same step, so no additional calculation time is needed. If invoked separately it can be computed by inspecting every conditional once, hence again in $|\mathcal{R}|$ steps.

- Computation time for setting up the local ranking tables depends on the method to be invoked:

  - If the the local LS-constraint is satisfied, the local ranking table can be set up from the knowledge base directly by visiting every conditional once, so this can be done in $\sum_{V \in \Sigma} |\mathcal{R}_V|$ steps.

  - Otherwise, one of the inductive approaches has to be invoked. The calculation time here is bounded by the number of configurations of the set $\Sigma_V = \{V\} \cup pa(V)$, thus this step is bounded exponentially in the number of variables in the local alphabets $\mathcal{O}(2^{|\Sigma_V|})$ (confer Section 3.3.3).

  This has to be repeated for each V, so the worst case complexity here is $\sum_{V \in \Sigma} \mathcal{X}_V$ where $\mathcal{X}_V$ is the computation time for either System Z^+ or c-representations at vertex V, which gives us, asymptotically, a computational time of $\mathcal{O}(\max\{2^{|\Sigma_V|}|V \in \Sigma\})$ for setting up all local ranking tables.

Combining these values we obtain that an OCF-network can be set up from a consistent single-elementary knowledge base has a computational complexity of $\mathcal{O}(\max\{2^{|\Sigma_V|}|V \in \Sigma\})$.

The *space complexity* for storing an OCF-network is the sum of the space needed for each local ranking table which are bounded by $\mathcal{O}(2^{|\Sigma_V|})$, so again for storing an OCF encoded in an OCF-network we have an asymptotic space complexity of $\mathcal{O}(\max\{2^{|\Sigma_V|}|V \in \Sigma\})$.

Overall we obtain that given the cardinality of the local alphabets is significantly smaller than the cardinality of the global alphabet, that is $\max\{\Sigma_V | V \in \Sigma\} \ll |\Sigma|$, both time and space complexity for the OCF-network are significantly smaller than the complexity for generating and storing an OCF, which are both bounded by $\mathcal{O}(2^{|\Sigma|})$ (confer Section 3.3).

7.1.2.4 Correctness Results

We have seen that Algorithm 7.4 needs an exponential number of steps to compute the resulting OCF-network, nonetheless it traverses the alphabet and the knowledge base sequentially, and each of the inductive methods has been proven to be finite, so the algorithm is finite. The algorithm is *correct* if and only if it generates a ranking model of the knowledge base, that is, if and only if the global ranking function obtained from the network is admissible with respect to the knowledge base used to set it up [EKI15b].

For this definition, Algorithm 7.4 is not correct: the car start example is a knowledge base where the inductively generated global OCF κ_Γ is not admissible with respect to the knowledge base Δ which was used to set up the network.

Example 7.15 ([EKI15b, Example 7]). We continue Example 7.14 on this behalf. The global OCF κ_Γ^Z and κ_Γ^c of the OCF-network in Figure 7.8 obtained by both filling-in approaches are given in Table 7.3. Here we see, for example, that $\kappa_\Gamma^Z \not\models \mathcal{R}$ since we have $\kappa_\Gamma^Z(s|\overline{f}) = \kappa_\Gamma^Z(s\overline{f}) - \kappa_\Gamma^Z(\overline{f}) = 24 - 10 = 14$, and also $\kappa_\Gamma^c \not\models \mathcal{R}$ since $\kappa_\Gamma^c(s|\overline{f}) = \kappa_\Gamma^c(s\overline{f}) - \kappa_\Gamma^c(\overline{f}) = 23 - 10 = 13$ which both are smaller than 15, violating the admissibility condition for $(\overline{s}|\overline{f})[15]$ given in (3.22). We examine this failure of admissibility more thoroughly following [EKI15b, Example 7]: We have $\kappa_{\mathcal{R}_S}^Z \models \mathcal{R}_S$ due to construction (confer Example 7.14 and Table 7.2), for example it is $\kappa_{\mathcal{R}_S}^Z(s|\overline{f}) = 15$. The OCF κ_Γ^Z is obtained via stratification from the local tables, in this, also from the local table κ_S^Z is added to the value. This table was filled inductively from the local knowledge base. By Lemma 3.17 (total conditional rank), $\kappa_\Gamma^Z(s|\overline{f})$ is calculated as follows:

$$\kappa_\Gamma^Z(s|\overline{f}) \overset{\text{Lem. 3.17}}{=\!=\!=\!=\!=} \min\{\kappa_\Gamma^Z(s|b\overline{f}) + \kappa_\Gamma^Z(b|\overline{f}), \kappa_\Gamma^Z(s|\overline{b}\,\overline{f}) + \kappa_\Gamma^Z(\overline{b}|\overline{f})\}$$

$$\overset{\text{Thm. 7.4}}{=\!=\!=\!=\!=} \min\{\underbrace{\kappa_S^Z(s|b\overline{f}) + \kappa_\Gamma^Z(b|\overline{f})}_{=14}, \underbrace{\kappa_S^Z(s|\overline{b}\,\overline{f}) + \kappa_\Gamma^Z(\overline{b}|\overline{f})}_{=15}\}$$

Note that the conditional $(s|\overline{f})[15]$ is realised locally by $\kappa_S^Z(s|\overline{b}\,\overline{f}) = 15$. The ranks $\kappa_S^Z(s|b\overline{f})$ and $\kappa_S^Z(s|\overline{b}\,\overline{f})$ are obtained via Procedure 7.2.a. The conditional $(b|\overline{f})$ is not represented by the network, but its global rank can be computed from the global OCF κ_Γ^Z as follows:

$$\kappa_\Gamma^Z(b|\overline{f}) = \kappa_\Gamma^Z(b\overline{f}) - \kappa_\Gamma^Z(\overline{f})$$

$$= \min_{\omega \models b\overline{f}}\{\kappa_\Gamma^Z(\omega)\} - \min_{\omega \models \overline{f}}\{\kappa_\Gamma^Z(\omega)\}$$

$$= \min_{\omega \models b\overline{f}}\left\{\sum_{V \in \Sigma} \kappa_V(V(\omega)|pa(V)(\omega))\right\}$$

$$- \min_{\omega \models \overline{f}}\left\{\sum_{V \in \Sigma} \kappa_V(V(\omega)|pa(V)(\omega))\right\}$$

$$= \min_{\omega \models b\overline{f}}\left\{\begin{array}{l} \kappa_H(H(\omega)) + \kappa_B(B(\omega)|H(\omega)) \\ + \kappa_F(F(\omega)) + \kappa_S^Z(S(\omega)|BF(\omega)) \end{array}\right\}$$

$$- \min_{\omega \models \overline{f}}\left\{\begin{array}{l} \kappa_H(H(\omega)) + \kappa_B(B(\omega)|H(\omega)) \\ + \kappa_F(F(\omega)) + \kappa_S^Z(S(\omega)|BF(\omega)) \end{array}\right\}$$

The first minimum is computed as follows:

$$\min\left\{\begin{array}{l} \kappa_H(h) + \kappa_B(b|h) + \kappa_F(\overline{f}) + \kappa_S^Z(s|b\,\overline{f}) \\ \kappa_H(h) + \kappa_B(b|h) + \kappa_F(\overline{f}) + \kappa_S^Z(\overline{s}|b\,\overline{f}) \\ \kappa_H(\overline{h}) + \kappa_B(b|\overline{h}) + \kappa_F(\overline{f}) + \kappa_S^Z(s|b\,\overline{f}) \\ \kappa_H(\overline{h}) + \kappa_B(b|\overline{h}) + \kappa_F(\overline{f}) + \kappa_S^Z(\overline{s}|b\,\overline{f}) \end{array}\right\}$$

$$= \min\left\{\begin{array}{l} 15 + 4 + 10 + 14 \\ 15 + 4 + 10 + 0 \\ 0 \ + 0 + 10 + 14 \\ 0 \ + 0 + 10 + 0 \end{array}\right\} = 10.$$

The second minimum is computed to be 10, so $\kappa_\Gamma^Z(b|\overline{f}) = 0$. With the same steps for $(\overline{b}|\overline{f})$ we obtain $\kappa_\Gamma^Z(\overline{b}|\overline{f}) = 4$ and hence calculate the rank for $(s|\overline{f})$ to be $\kappa_\Gamma^Z(s|\overline{f}) = \min\{14 + 0, 15 + 4\} = 14 < 15$, so κ_Γ^Z fails to be admissible with respect to $\mathcal{R}$. So in the stepwise calculation we have seen that the information of having a conditional rank of 15 is present, it is not taken into account when calculating $\kappa_\Gamma^Z(s|\overline{f})$ due to the focus on the minimum.

This example gives us that even if the algorithm generates an OCF-network, this network does not, in general, represent the information (the knowledge base) used to set it up.

This problem is a consequence of the conditioning of the local ranking function in step three of Algorithm 7.4 (confer Table 7.2). Here, a posit-

Table 7.3: Stratified ranking functions for the car start OCF-network given in Figure 7.8

ω	$bfhs$	$bfh\overline{s}$	$bf\overline{h}s$	$bf\overline{h}\,\overline{s}$	$b\overline{f}hs$	$b\overline{f}h\overline{s}$	$b\overline{f}\,\overline{h}s$	$b\overline{f}\,\overline{h}\,\overline{s}$
$\kappa^Z_\Gamma(\omega)$	23	25	0	2	47	33	24	10
$\kappa^c_\Gamma(\omega)$	23	26	0	3	46	33	23	10
ω	$\overline{b}fhs$	$\overline{b}fh\overline{s}$	$\overline{b}f\overline{h}s$	$\overline{b}f\overline{h}\,\overline{s}$	$\overline{b}\,\overline{f}hs$	$\overline{b}\,\overline{f}h\overline{s}$	$\overline{b}\,\overline{f}\,\overline{h}s$	$\overline{b}\,\overline{f}\,\overline{h}\,\overline{s}$
$\kappa^Z_\Gamma(\omega)$	27	15	16	4	40	25	29	14
$\kappa^c_\Gamma(\omega)$	26	15	15	4	52	25	41	14

ive rank of a configuration of the variables in $pa(V)$ reduces the rank of an instance $(V|pa(V))$ in the conditioning. Since for every world the rank of the *conditioned* local ranking table is summed up to obtain the global OCF (7.2). This may lead to the global ranking function no longer being admissible with respect to the knowledge base because there may be conditionals not accepted, as seen in Example 7.15, even if the (local, unconditioned) ranking function obtained from the local knowledge base accepts the conditional.

This effect can occur only if an inductive approach is used to calculate the local ranking tables. It does not occur if the local knowledge base satisfies the local LS-constraint and the table therefore can be obtained from the knowledge base, directly. In the following we introduce a way of detecting whether this failure of correctness occurs.

Definition 7.16 (λ-Function). Let $\Gamma = \langle \Sigma, \mathcal{E}, \{\kappa_V\}_{V\in\Sigma}\rangle$ be an OCF-network. For each $V \in \Sigma$ we define by $\lambda_V : \Omega(\{V\} \cup pa(V)) \to \mathbb{N}_0$ the function that assigns to each local world $\omega^V \in \Omega(\{V\} \cup pa(V))$ the value $\kappa((V(\omega^V)|pa(V)(\omega^V))$.

Lemma 7.17. The λ-function is an OCF.

Note that constructing an OCF with values from the local conditional tables is possible for OCF because the combination function is the minimum. This is, however, not possible for probabilities: Assume $\langle \Sigma, \mathcal{E}, \{P_V\}_{V\in\Sigma}\rangle$ would be a Bayesian network. The canonical function λ^P then would be defined as $\lambda^P(\omega^V) = P((V(\omega^V)|pa(V)(\omega^V))$. The normalisation condition of conditional probabilities (see Section 3.4) gives us $P(v|\mathbf{p}_V)+P(\overline{v}|\mathbf{p}_V) = 1$

for each configuration $\mathbf{p}_V$ of $pa(V)$, and since $\Omega(\{V\} \cup pa(V))$ contains $2^{pa(V)}$ of such pairs, we had $\sum_{\omega^V} \lambda_V(\omega^V) = 2^{pa(V)}$ in contrast to the normalisation condition of probability functions.

Further note that since λ_V is defined by a projection into $\kappa((V|pa(V))$, anyway, we drop the constraint of the domain to $\Omega(\{V\} \cup pa(V))$ and overload λ_V such that for each $\omega \in \Omega$ with $\omega \vDash \omega^V$ we define $\lambda_V(\omega) = \lambda_V(\omega^V)$. This function is still an OCF because $\lambda_V(\omega) = 0$ for all $\omega \vDash \omega^V$ where $\lambda_V(\omega^V) = 0$ and therefore the normalisation condition is satisfied[2].

The following proposition gives us that from having local λ functions that are admissible with respect to the respective knowledge bases we can conclude that the global OCF of the network is admissible with respect to the global knowledge base.

Proposition 7.18. Let $\Gamma = \langle \Sigma, \mathcal{E}, \{\kappa_V\}_{V \in \Sigma} \rangle$ be an OCF-network originating from a conditional knowledge base $\mathcal{R} = \{(\psi_1|\phi_1)[f_1], \ldots, (\psi_n|\phi_n)[f_n]\}$ by means of the algorithms presented in this section. The global OCF κ_Γ obtained via (7.2) is admissible with respect to $\mathcal{R}$ if $\lambda_V \vDash \mathcal{R}_V$ for each $V \in \Sigma$.

On the other hand, given the global OCF is admissible with respect to the global knowledge base, we obtain that all local λ-functions are admissible with respect to their respective local knowledge bases.

Proposition 7.19. Let $\Gamma = \langle \Sigma, \mathcal{E}, \{\kappa_V\}_{V \in \Sigma} \rangle$ be an OCF-network originating from a conditional knowledge base $\mathcal{R} = \{(\psi_1|\phi_1)[f_1], \ldots, (\psi_n|\phi_n)[f_n]\}$ by means of the algorithms presented in this section with a global OCF $\kappa_\Gamma \vDash \mathcal{R}$. Every function λ_V, $V \in \Sigma$, is admissible with respect to the respective local knowledge base $\mathcal{R}_V$.

From Propositions 7.18 and 7.19 we directly conclude:

Corollary 7.20. Let $\Gamma = \langle \Sigma, \mathcal{E}, \{\kappa_V\}_{V \in \Sigma} \rangle$ be an OCF-network originating from a conditional knowledge base $\mathcal{R} = \{(\psi_1|\phi_1)[f_1], \ldots, (\psi_n|\phi_n)[f_n]\}$. The

---

[2]   Again, changing the domain and keeping codomain of the function untouched at the same time is possible for OCF because the combination operation (see Section 3.3) is the minimum. This easy transferral from a local to a global domain would, for instance, not be possible for probabilities. If there was a probability function λ_V^P the canonical way would be to equally distribute $\lambda_V^P(\omega^V)$ equally over all $\omega \vDash \omega^V$ such that $\lambda_V^P(\omega) = \frac{\lambda_V^P(\omega^V)}{|\{\omega | \omega \vDash \omega^V\}|}$.

global function κ_Γ is admissible with respect to $\mathcal{R}$ if and only if every function λ_V, $V \in \Sigma$, is admissible with respect to the respective local knowledge base $\mathcal{R}_V$.

Example 7.21. We illustrate this property using the car start example with values from Example 7.15. We noted that $\kappa_\Gamma \nvDash (\overline{s}|\overline{f})[15]$. Locally we have $\lambda_S \nvDash (\overline{s}|\overline{f})[15]$ since $\lambda(\overline{f}s) = \min\{\lambda(b\overline{f}s), \lambda(\overline{b}\,\overline{f}s)\} = \min\{11, 13\} = 11 < 15$ as predicted by Corollary 7.20.

So with Corollary 7.20 we can examine locally whether the global ranking function of an OCF-network generated inductively from a semi-quantitative conditional knowledge base will be admissible with respect to this knowledge base. Apart from its practical use, this corollary reveals that the failure of correctness is a local problem that propagates to the global function. This gives hope that the problem may be overcome locally, as well, by adjusting the local ranking tables. Such a "repairing" procedure cannot be used for System Z^+ which generates unique local ranking functions, but may be applicable using c-representations. This may be because the latter provides a schema of OCF rather than a unique OCF, so this method leaves room for changing some ranks, or to be more precise, swap one c-representation for another. For this approach, the idea would be to adjust the impacts such that the resulting ranking tables themselves result in functions λ_V that are admissible to the respective local knowledge base. In the following example we see that such an approach, in general, is bound to fail.

Example 7.22. We again use the values from Example 7.15. Here, the only conditional in the local knowledge base $\mathcal{R}_S$ that is not accepted by λ_S is $(\overline{s}|\overline{f})$. To overcome this we had to adjust κ_4^- or κ_5^- and κ_2^- or κ_3^- such that both $\lambda_S(b\overline{f}s) - \lambda_S(b\overline{f})$ and $\lambda_S(\overline{b}\,\overline{f}s) - \lambda_S(\overline{b}\,\overline{f})$ would be greater or equal 15. But from Table 7.2 we obtain that every increase on one of these impacts would also increase the impacts κ_1^- and κ_3^- which would increase $\lambda_S(b\overline{f})$ and because of the conditionalisation the increase would not be carried over to the local ranking table. Therefore we cannot "repair" the OCF-network such that its global function is admissible with respect to $\mathcal{R}$, even if we clearly identified the reason for the failure.

A final resort could be the hope that this correctness result may be an effect of using semi-quantitative knowledge bases. In the following section we examine qualitative knowledge bases instead of semi-quantitative knowledge bases and show that they share the same problems on this behalf. So the failure in correctness is not an effect of the firmness annotation at the conditionals, but a general problem of the approach.

7.1.2.5 Generating the OCF-component with qualitative knowledge base

Generating the OCF-component of an OCF-network inductively from a qualitative knowledge base is similar to generating the component from a semi-quantitative knowledge bases, with small changes, only. As we have already discussed in Section 2.2, a qualitative conditional knowledge base $\Delta = \{(\psi_1|\phi_1), \ldots, (\psi_n|\phi_n)\}$ can be seen as a semi-quantitative knowledge base where the firmness of each conditional is 1. We use this equivalence in Algorithm 7.4 if for any V, Δ_V satisfies the local LS-constraint, that is, if Δ_V satisfies the local LS-constraint in V we set $\kappa_V(\dot{v}|\mathbf{p}_V) = 1$ if and only if $(\bar{v}|\mathbf{p}_V) \in \Delta$. For cases where Δ_V does not satisfy the local LS-constraint, it would be possible to invoke the inductive methods already discussed in Section 7.1.2.2 using the equivalence between qualitative and semi-quantitative knowledge bases. But since there are specialised inductive methods to deal with with qualitative knowledge bases, namely System Z and c-representations, the major change in Algorithm 7.4 is to exchange the inductive approaches with the qualitative ones. For every other step, the algorithm is executed as discussed in Section 7.1.2.2, the change noted does not change the complexity of the algorithm.

We still have to examine whether the problem of correctness does occur for qualitative knowledge bases, which we do with the following example.

Example 7.23 ([EKI15b, Example 8]). Let $\Sigma = \{A, B, C\}$ be a propositional alphabet with a respective set of possible worlds. For this example we use the qualitative knowledge base $\Delta = \{(c|b), (\bar{c}|\bar{b}), (c|a), (\bar{c}|\bar{a}), (\bar{c}|\bar{a}b), (\bar{c}|a\bar{b})\}$. From this knowledge base, Algorithm 7.1 gives us the graph shown in Figure 7.9. There are no conditionals with a conclusion $\dot{a}$ or $\dot{b}$, so Procedure 7.2.a gives us that the local rankings at vertices A and B are 0 for all configurations of A and B. For vertex C we have to use an inductive method, in this example we use qualitative c-representations on the local knowledge base $\Delta_C = \{r_1 = (c|b), r_2 = (\bar{c}|\bar{b}), r_3 = (c|a), r_4 = (\bar{c}|\bar{a}), r_5 = (\bar{c}|\bar{a}b), r_6 = (\bar{c}|a\bar{b})\} = \Delta$. The respective system of inequalities (3.30) can be solved minimally with the solution

$$\kappa_1^- = 1 \qquad \kappa_2^- = 1 \qquad \kappa_3^- = 1 \qquad \kappa_4^- = 0 \qquad \kappa_5^- = 2 \qquad \kappa_6^- = 1,$$

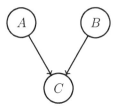

Figure 7.9: Generated graph from Example 7.23

from which with Equation (3.29) we generate the local table κ_C^c as given in Table 7.4. Overall we obtain the OCF-network given in Figure 7.10 with the a global ranking function also given in Table 7.5. Note that since $\kappa_A(A(\omega)) = \kappa_B(B(\omega)) = 0$ for all $\omega \in \Omega$, the global OCF κ coincides with κ_C, that is $\kappa(\omega) = \kappa_C(C(\omega)|AB(\omega))$ for all $\omega \in \Omega$. To check this OCF for admissibility with respect to Δ we use (7.2) to calculate the respective ranks and obtain

$$\kappa(bc) = \min_{\omega \models bc} \left\{ \sum_{V \in \Sigma} \kappa_V(V(\omega)|pa(V)(\omega)) \right\}$$

$$= \min\{\kappa_A(a) + \kappa_B(b) + \kappa_C(c|ab), \kappa_A(\overline{a}) + \kappa_B(b) + \kappa_C(c|\overline{a}b)\}$$

$$= \min\{0 + 0 + 0, 0 + 0 + 1\} = 0 \qquad (= \min\{\kappa_C(c|ab), \kappa_C(c|\overline{a}b)\})$$

$$\kappa(b\overline{c}) = \min_{\omega \models b\overline{c}} \left\{ \sum_{V \in \Sigma} \kappa_V(V(\omega)|pa(V)(\omega)) \right\}$$

$$= \min\{\kappa_A(a) + \kappa_B(b) + \kappa_C(\overline{c}|ab), \kappa_A(\overline{a}) + \kappa_B(b) + \kappa_C(\overline{c}|\overline{a}b)\}$$

$$= \min\{0 + 0 + 2, 0 + 0 + 0\} = 0 \qquad (= \min\{\kappa_C(\overline{c}|ab), \kappa_C(\overline{c}|\overline{a}b)\}),$$

which means that for this OCF-networks we have $\kappa(bc) = 0 \not< 0 = \kappa(b\overline{c})$ which means that $\kappa \not\models \Delta$.

Overall we obtain that the hope that the problems regarding the correctness of the algorithms of these sections could be overcome by a purely qualitative approach to storing knowledge was in vain: Even if we can set up an OCF-network for a conditional knowledge base inductively, we cannot guarantee that this network recovers all knowledge of the knowledge base used as starting point.

Table 7.4: Calculating the local ranking table $\kappa^c_{\Delta_C}$ for Example 7.23

ABC	verifies	falsifies	$\kappa^c_{\Delta_C}(ABC)$	$\kappa^c_{\Delta_C}(AB)$	$\kappa^c_C(C|AB)$
$a\,b\,c$	r_1, r_3	—	0	0	0
$a\,b\,\overline{c}$	—	r_1, r_3	2	0	2
$a\,\overline{b}\,c$	r_3	r_2, r_6	2	1	1
$a\,\overline{b}\,\overline{c}$	r_2, r_6	r_3	1	1	0
$\overline{a}\,b\,c$	r_1	r_4, r_5	2	1	1
$\overline{a}\,b\,\overline{c}$	r_4, r_5	r_1	1	1	0
$\overline{a}\,\overline{b}\,c$	—	r_2, r_4	1	0	1
$\overline{a}\,\overline{b}\,\overline{c}$	r_2, r_4	—	0	0	0

Table 7.5: Global OCF for Example 7.23

ω	$a\,b\,c$	$a\,b\,\overline{c}$	$a\,\overline{b}\,c$	$a\,\overline{b}\,\overline{c}$	$\overline{a}\,b\,c$	$\overline{a}\,b\,\overline{c}$	$\overline{a}\,\overline{b}\,c$	$\overline{a}\,\overline{b}\,\overline{c}$
$\kappa_A(A(\omega))$	0	0	0	0	0	0	0	0
$\kappa_B(B(\omega))$	0	0	0	0	0	0	0	0
$\kappa_C(C(\omega)|AB(\omega))$	0	2	1	0	1	0	1	0
$\kappa(\omega)$	0	2	1	0	1	0	1	0

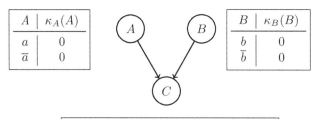

Figure 7.10: OCF-network of Example 7.23

7.1.3 Discussion

OCF-networks are, as shown in this section, a lightweight representation of OCF. With local/global coincidence (Theorem 7.4) and the local directed Markov Property (Theorem 7.6), they share crucial properties with Bayesian Networks. This relatedness is deeper, still: For instance Elena Bernshteyn showed in her (unpublished) diploma thesis [Ber16][3] that the algorithm of Lauritzen and Spiegelhalter[4] [LS88] can be canonically adapted to OCF-networks.

We have recalled that representing an OCF in the form of an OCF-network significantly reduces the space needed to represent the OCF, as well as the time needed to calculate ranks in connected subgraphs, for OCF-network that are not "notorious". Additionally to setting up the networks inductively from a knowledge base, this structure may also be used to set up OCF manually, that is, by an expert setting the local plausibility values by hand: In scenarios where the dependency of the variables, that is, the structure of the network, is known, experts can assign the local conditional ranks to the vertices. This means that we replace the assignment of plausibilities to global possible worlds to the assignment of plausibilities to local possible worlds. This is an improvement as assigning plausibility globally can be difficult or even misleading because the worlds are composed from literals of all variables, regardless of their context. By concentrating on a single variable in the context of its parents, we assume it to be easier for the expert to assign the ranks, and the global OCF can then be computed by means recalled in this section. Other than setting an an OCF via iterated contraction, as proposed by [Spo12, Section 8.3], where in every step the entirety of the non-assigned worlds have to be put into account, in this way the conditional ranks have to be set only in their related contexts.

Nevertheless, the presented results show that is is, in general, not successful to set up an OCF-network inductively from a conditional knowledge base. This failure can, if it happens, be noticed locally, so it is not necessary to complete the algorithms if the generation will not be successful. But it is still not possible to predict this on base of the knowledge base, and in the worst case it occurs in the last vertex to be set up. A workaround is to set up the graph by means of Algorithm 7.1, generate the global OCF with one of the standard inductive approaches like System Z or c-representations, and then set up the local ranking values by means of local/global coincid-

---

3   Supervised by the author of this thesis and Gabriele Kern-Isberner.
4   Also known as the "forward–backward algorithm".

ence of the global OCF. In this way, the advantages of the representation of OCF-networks can be used for inductively computed OCF for knowledge bases. So even if this method of setting up the network does not benefit from the advantages of partitioning, it overcomes the failure of correctness, and thus this method can be used safely.

7.1.4 Interim Summary

Using a network with the set of variables as vertices and local ranking tables as defined in Definition 7.1 had already be done in [GP96]. However, this article the independence properties as well as the composition of the global OCF from the local OCF tables in direct succession from Bayesian networks has been used without proofs. One contribution of the articles [KIE13a, KIE13b, EKI15b] to the field was to proof that the properties presupposed by [GP96] are valid for OCF-networks, that is:

- The global OCF generated by the composition of the local OCF tables is an OCF (Lemma 7.2) and the global OCF can be decomposed to the local ranking tables (Proposition 7.3).

- The local ranking values coincide with the respective conditional ranking values of the global function (Theorem 7.4).

- The local directed Markov property holds (Theorem 7.6).

Another contribution of these papers was to define algorithms to set up an OCF network inductively from a single-elementary conditional knowledge base. For this, the graph generation step (Algorithm 7.1), the partitioning of the knowledge base (Algorithm 7.3) and the usage of the inductive approaches to set up the local ranking tables (as done in Algorithm 7.4) have been proposed.

The idea of researching OCF-networks originated from Gabriele Kern-Isberner. My own contribution to the articles [KIE13a, KIE13b, EKI15b] has been to show that the global OCF of an OCF-network is indeed an OCF and, following the respective proof for probabilities in [Pea88] that the decomposition of the global OCF (Proposition 7.3) is valid, as was the partitioning of the global knowledge base into local ones. An additional contribution of me was to observe that the step of inductive generation of OCF-networks from a conditional knowledge base may lead to an OCF-network where the global function is no ranking model of the knowledge base.

In this area, this dissertation extends the cited literature on various points: First of all in the definition of Γ-completeness and the LS-constraint. These two allow us to determine locally whether it is necessary to invoke an inductive approach, or the ranking can be taken from the knowledge base, directly (Lemma 7.11).

Secondly, this thesis also structures the algorithms from the literature more clearly, so it is easier to see how the individual parts work and how they intertwine, and includes the insights from Lemma 7.11. The analysis of the time and space complexity of the algorithms is another contribution of this dissertation regarding the algorithms.

It has already been noted in [EKI15b] that the inductive generation of OCF-networks does not generate an OCF which is admissible with respect to the original knowledge base, in general. This thesis extends the article in examining the problem more thoroughly: We define the λ function and show that this function taken from the local ranking tables is an OCF (Lemma 7.17). We prove that the global OCF is admissible to the original knowledge base if and only if for each variable V of the alphabet, every function λ_V is admissible to the local knowledge base $\mathcal{R}_V$ (Propositions 7.18, 7.19 and Corollary 7.20). This gives us a criterion to check whether the global OCF of an OCF-network is admissible to the global knowledge base, locally. So in addition to knowing that the approach generates incorrect results for some knowledge bases, we now can isolate the problematic partition of the knowledge base, but it is still not possible to use this insight to modify the approach such that it results in guaranteed correct results.

Finally, the thesis extends the articles with the discussion in the previous section; this discussion proposes a method for generating an OCF-network without the risk of violating correctness exploiting the local/global coincidence, which benefits from the spatial merits of the network approach, but not from the benefits with respect to time complexity.

7.2 Comparing OCF- and CP-networks

Ceteris Paribus (CP-) networks, recalled in Section 3.6, use directed acyclic networks to represent preferences. So the underlying graph structure of CP- and OCF-networks is identical, but the knowledge encoded in the local tables differs: CP-networks carry information about preferences, and OCF-networks carry information about (im-)plausibility. In this section we compare both network approaches on the formal site and demonstrate that OCF-networks are strictly stronger than CP-networks, that is, every CP-network can be represented by an OCF-network, but not vice versa. We complete this comparison with a discussion about whether it is sensible to encode information about preference as plausibility ranks (or the converse). This section is based on and extends the article [EFKI16].

We start the comparison with the relations that provide the local information in the networks. This is followed by a presentation of plain approaches to generate OCF-networks from CP-networks and vice versa. We investigate why these plain approaches fail and use these insights to set up a procedure to generate an OCF-network from a CP-network, thus representing the preference information in OCF. We also show that it is not possible to generate a CP-network from an OCF-network in general.

7.2.1 Plain Mutual Generation of OCF-Networks from CP-Networks

In CP-networks, local representations are preference relations, which can be combined to a global preference relation. Examining these relations (see Section 3.6) we see that the global preference relation of a CP-network licenses for indifference, that is, there may be worlds $\omega, \omega' \in \Omega$ such that $\omega \preccurlyeq_{CP} \omega'$, $\omega' \preccurlyeq_{CP} \omega$, $\omega \not\preccurlyeq_{CP} \omega'$ and $\omega' \not\preccurlyeq_{CP} \omega$, this is ruled out for the local representation: By Definition 3.52 each vertex $V \in \Sigma$ is annotated with a conditional preference table (CPT) that assigns the (strict) preference of either $v \prec_{\mathbf{p}_V} \overline{v}$ or $\overline{v} \prec_{\mathbf{p}_V} v$ in context of each outcome $\mathbf{p}_V$ of the variables in $pa(V)$. For OCF-networks, on the other hand, both local ranking tables as well as global ranking functions may contain indifference, that is, we may have $\kappa_\Gamma(\omega) = \kappa_\Gamma(\omega')$ as well as $\kappa_V(v|\mathbf{p}_V) = \kappa_V(\overline{v}|\mathbf{p}_V)$. So it is clear that the local CPTs cannot represent the local ranking information of an OCF-network, in general. We henceforth restrict the following examination to *strict* OCF-networks, that is, OCF-network without local indifference.

Definition 7.24 (Strict OCF-Network [EFKI16, Definition 11]). A *strict OCF-network* $\Gamma = \langle \Sigma, \mathcal{E}, \{\kappa_V\}_{V \in \Sigma} \rangle$ is an OCF-network where $\kappa_V(\dot{v}|\mathbf{p}_V) = 0$ implies $\kappa_V(\overline{v}|\mathbf{p}_V) \neq 0$ for all $V \in \Sigma$ and all configurations $\mathbf{p}_V$ of $pa(V)$.

With this restriction we start formally comparing the two network types: In a CP-networks, the vertices are annotated with local conditional tables, whereas in an OCF-network, the vertices are annotated with local ranking tables. We transfer the concept of local preference to OCF networks by defining preference relations from the local ranking tables of each vertex, with respect to the possible outcomes of the vertices parents:

Definition 7.25 (Local κ-preference [EFKI16, Definition 10]). Let Γ be a strict OCF-network $\Gamma = \langle \Sigma, \mathcal{E}, \{\kappa_V\}_{V \in \Sigma} \rangle$. For all $V \in \Sigma$ and all configurations $\mathbf{p}_V$ of $pa(V)$ the local ranking tables κ_V generate a preference relation $\prec^\kappa_{\mathbf{p}_V}$ on $\{v, \overline{v}\}$ such that $\dot{v} \prec^\kappa_{\mathbf{p}_V} \overline{v}$ if and only if $\kappa_V(\dot{v}|\mathbf{p}_V) \leq \kappa_V(\overline{v}|\mathbf{p}_V)$.

If the OCF-network Γ is strict, then for each vertex V for each outcome $\mathbf{p}_V$ of the variables in $pa(V)$, there is one outcome $\dot{v}$ of V such that $\kappa_V(\dot{v}|\mathbf{p}_V) = 0$ and $\kappa_V(\overline{v}|\mathbf{p}_V) > 0$. Thus given the OCF-network is strict, the induced local κ-preference is strict, as well, which we formalise in the following lemma.

Lemma 7.26 ([EFKI16, Lemma 2]). Let $\Gamma = \langle \Sigma, \mathcal{E}, \{\kappa_V\}_{V \in \Sigma} \rangle$ be a strict OCF-network. The local κ-preference on Γ obtained by means of Definition 7.25 is a strict preference relation, that is $\dot{v} \prec^\kappa_{\mathbf{p}_V} \overline{v}$ implies $\overline{v} \not\prec^\kappa_{\mathbf{p}_V} \dot{v}$ for all $V \in \Sigma$.

This local preference relation generated by the local conditional ranking tables allows us to transfer the concept of CPTs to OCF-networks by defining local preference tables that are based on the local ranking tables.

Definition 7.27 (Local κ-preference table [EFKI16, Definition 12]). Let Γ be a strict OCF-network $\Gamma = \langle \Sigma, \mathcal{E}, \{\kappa_V\}_{V \in \Sigma} \rangle$. For all $V \in \Sigma$ and all configurations $\mathbf{p}_V$ of $pa(V)$ the local κ-preference tables $CPT^\kappa(V, pa(V))$ encode the local κ-preference $\prec^\kappa_{\mathbf{p}_V}$.

This definition provides a common ground for CP- and OCF-networks, namely a directed acyclic graph with local (κ-) preference tables. We show

Listing 7.5: Plainly generate a CP-network from an OCF-network (confer [EFKI16]).

```
INPUT   : Strict OCF-network Γ = ⟨Σ, ℰ, {κ_V}_{V∈Σ}⟩
OUTPUT  : CP-network  CP = ⟨Σ, ℰ, {CPT(V, pa(V))}_{V∈Σ}⟩

BEGIN
  // Initialisation
  FOR-EACH(V ∈ Σ)
    CPT(V, pa(V)):=∅
  END FOR-EACH

  // Generate CPTs
  FOR-EACH(V ∈ Σ)
    FOR-EACH(p_V ∈ Ω(pa(V)))
      IF(κ_V(v|p_C)<κ_V(v̄|p_C))
        CPT(V, pa(V)):=CPT(V, pa(V)) ∪ {v ≺_{p_V} v̄}
      ELSE
        CPT(V, pa(V)):=CPT(V, pa(V)) ∪ {v̄ ≺_{p_V} v}
      END IF
    END FOR-EACH
  END FOR-EACH
  RETURN  CP = ⟨Σ, ℰ, {CPT(V, pa(V))}_{V∈Σ}⟩
END
```

how, using the defined local κ-preference table, an OCF-network defines a CP-network.

Lemma 7.28 ([EFKI16, Proposition 1]). Let $\Gamma = \langle \Sigma, \mathcal{E}, \{\kappa_V\}_{V\in\Sigma}\rangle$ be a strict OCF-network with local κ-preference tables $CPT^\kappa(V, pa(V))$ obtained from κ_V for each $V \in \Sigma$ and all configurations $\mathbf{p}_V$ of $pa(V)$ by means of Definition 7.27. The network $\langle \Sigma, \mathcal{E}, \{CPT^\kappa(V, pa(V))\}_{V\in\Sigma}\rangle$ is a CP-network.

So as a first step in the mutual generation of the network types we obtain that the preferential relation induced by the local ranking tables in an OCF-network can be used to generate a CP-network directly from an OCF-network. This result is used to set up the Algorithm 7.5, which we illustrate in Figure 7.11.

However, even if this algorithm does generate valid CP-networks, the original and the generated network networks may be different with respect to their inferences, which we formalise in the following observation.

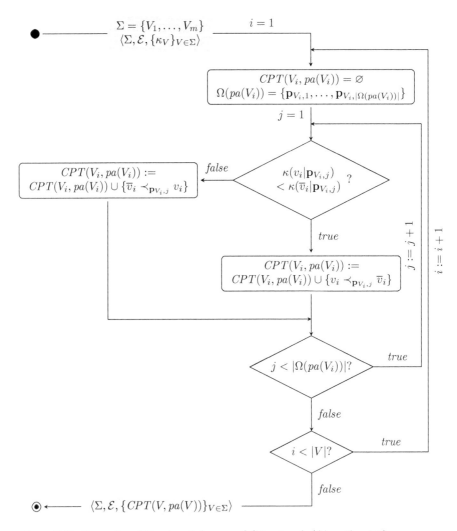

Figure 7.11: Generate a CP-network from an OCF-network (Algorithm 7.5)

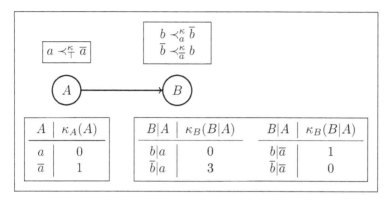

Figure 7.12: OCF-network with induced CP-network of Example 7.30 (see [EFKI16])

Observation 7.29 ([EFKI16, Observation 1]). Let $\phi, \psi \in \mathfrak{L}$ be formulas. There are strict OCF-networks $\Gamma = \langle \Sigma, \mathcal{E}, \{\kappa_V\}_{V \in \Sigma} \rangle$ such that for the induced CP-networks $CP = \langle \Sigma, \mathcal{E}, \{CPT^\kappa(V, pa(V))\}_{V \in \Sigma} \rangle$ we have $\phi \approx_\kappa \psi$ but $\phi \not\approx_{CP} \psi$.

We illustrate Algorithm 7.5 and this observation in the following example.

Example 7.30 (confer [EFKI16, Example 5]). In Figure 7.6 we have the graphical illustration of the OCF network $\Gamma = \langle \{A, B\}, \{(A, B)\}, \{\kappa_A, \kappa_B\} \rangle$ with κ_A and κ_B annotated below the respective vertices. Here, κ_A induces the local preference $a \prec_\top^\kappa \overline{a}$ (since $\kappa_A(a) = \kappa_A(a|\top) = 0 < 1 = \kappa_A(\overline{a}|\top) = \kappa_A(\overline{a})$) and κ_B induces the local preferences $b \prec_a^\kappa \overline{b}$ (since $\kappa_B(b|a) = 0 < 3 = \kappa(\overline{b}|a)$) and $\overline{b} \prec_{\overline{a}}^\kappa b$ (since $\kappa_B(\overline{b}|\overline{a}) = 0 < 1 = \kappa(b|\overline{a})$), the local κ-CPTs are give in Figure above the respective vertices. Table 7.6 sums up the local ranking tables to the global OCF κ_Γ of the OCF-network; the unique preference relation that satisfies the induces CP-network is

$$ab \prec_{CP} a\overline{b} \prec_{CP} \overline{a}\overline{b} \prec_{CP} \overline{a}b.$$

Here we have $\kappa_\Gamma(\overline{a}\overline{b}) = 1 < 3 = \kappa_\Gamma(a\overline{b})$ and thus $\overline{b} \approx_{\kappa_\Gamma} \overline{a}$, but also $a\overline{b} \prec_{CP} \overline{a}\overline{b}$ and therefore $\overline{b} \not\approx_{CP} \overline{a}$. So we see that both networks are different, inferentially.

Following the ideas of this algorithm, we turn towards the opposite direction, that is, generating an OCF-network from a CP-network. This is done

Table 7.6: Global OCF for OCF-network of Figure 7.12

ω	$a\,b$	$a\,\overline{b}$	$\overline{a}\,b$	$\overline{a}\,\overline{b}$
$\kappa_A(A(\omega))$	0	0	1	1
$\kappa_B(B(\omega)|A(\omega))$	0	3	1	0
$\kappa_\Gamma(\omega)$	0	3	2	1

locally, in such a way, that we set the rank of the preferred literal of the variable given the configuration of its parents to 0, and the inverse literal of the variable to 1. Applying this approach to every vertex, we obtain an OCF network.

Lemma 7.31 ([EFKI16, Proposition 2]). Let CP be a CP-network defined as $CP = \langle \Sigma, \mathcal{E}, \{CPT(V, pa(V))\}_{V \in \Sigma} \rangle$. Let $\kappa_V(\overline{v}|\mathbf{p}_V) = 0$ for $\overline{v} \prec_{\mathbf{p}_V} v$ in $CPT(V, pa(V))$ and $\kappa_V(\overline{v}|\mathbf{p}_V) = 1$, otherwise, for all $V \in \Sigma$ and every configuration $\mathbf{p}_V$ of $pa(V)$. The network $\Gamma = \langle \Sigma, \mathcal{E}, \{\kappa_V\}_{V \in \Sigma} \rangle$ is a strict OCF-network.

Algorithm 7.6, illustrated in Figure 7.13, puts this lemma to practical use. So, again, we can generate a network of the designated type by local computations. But, as well as we found for the other direction, an OCF-network generated by this plain approach is not necessarily identical with the CP-network used to set it up, with respect to inference, which we formalise in the following observation.

Observation 7.32 ([EFKI16, Observation 2]). Let $\phi, \psi \in \mathfrak{L}$ be formulas. There are CP-networks $CP = \langle \Sigma, \mathcal{E}, \{CPT(V, pa(V))\}_{V \in \Sigma} \rangle$ such that for the induced OCF-networks $\Gamma = \langle \Sigma, \mathcal{E}, \{\kappa_V\}_{V \in \Sigma} \rangle$ we have $\phi \hspace{-0.3em}\sim_{CP} \psi$ but $\phi \hspace{-0.3em}\not\sim_{\kappa_\Gamma} \psi$ for the global OCF κ_Γ of Γ.

We illustrate the generation of OCF-networks from CP-networks and this observation with the following example.

Example 7.33 (confer [EFKI16, Example 5]). Let $\Sigma = \{A, B, C\}$ be a propositional alphabet and let $(\Sigma, \{(A, B), (B, C)\}$ be a DAG on Σ with conditional preference tables as given in Figure 7.14 below the vertices. With Algorithm 7.13 we obtain $\kappa_A(a) = 0$ and $\kappa_A(\overline{a}) = 1$ since $a \prec_\top \overline{a}$. We similarly

Listing 7.6: Generate an OCF-network from an CP-network with the plain approach (confer [EFKI16]).

```
INPUT   : CP-network  CP = ⟨Σ, E, {CPT(V, pa(V))}_{V∈Σ}⟩
OUTPUT  : Strict OCF-network  Γ = ⟨Σ, E, {κ_V}_{V∈Σ}⟩

BEGIN
  // Initialisation
  FOR-EACH(V ∈ Σ)
    FOR-EACH(p_V ∈ Ω(pa(V)))
      κ_V(v̇|p_V):=0
    END FOR-EACH
  END FOR-EACH

  // Generate local OCF tables
  FOR-EACH(V ∈ Σ)
    FOR-EACH(p_V ∈ Ω(pa(V)))
      IF((v ≺_{p_V} v̄) ∈ CPT(V, pa(V)))  // i.e. if  v ≺_{p_V} v̄
        κ_V(v|p_V):=0
        κ_V(v̄|p_V):=1
      ELSE                              // i.e. if  v̄ ≺_{p_V} v
        κ_V(v|p_V):=1
        κ_V(v̄|p_V):=0
      END IF
    END FOR-EACH
  END FOR-EACH
  RETURN  Γ = ⟨Σ, E, {κ_V}_{V∈Σ}⟩
END
```

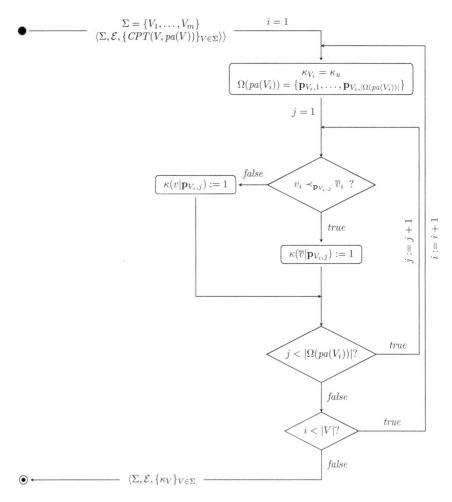

Figure 7.13: Generate an OCF-network from an CP-network (Algorithm 7.6)

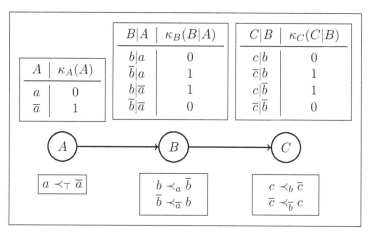

Figure 7.14: CP-network with induced OCF-network of Example 7.33 (see [EFKI16])

obtain $\kappa_B(b|a) = 0$ and $\kappa_B(\bar{b}|a) = 1$ because $b \prec_a \bar{b}$, and likewise $\kappa_B(\bar{b}|\bar{a}) = 0$ and $\kappa_B(b|\bar{a}) = 1$ because $\bar{b} \prec_{\bar{a}} b$ as well as $\kappa_C(c|b) = 0$ and $\kappa_C(\bar{c}|b) = 1$ because $c \prec_b \bar{c}$, $\kappa_C(\bar{c}|\bar{b}) = 0$ and $\kappa_C(c|\bar{b}) = 1$ because $\bar{c} \prec_{\bar{b}} c$, and therefore we get the local ranking tables given in Figure 7.14 given above the vertices. It can be seen that the OCF-network $\langle \Sigma, \{(A,B),(B,C)\}, \{\kappa_A, \kappa_B, \kappa_C\}\rangle$ is strict. There are two preference relations that satisfy the CP-network from Figure 7.14, these are (the underlined worlds are the one on which both preference relations differ)

$$a\,b\,c \prec_{cp}^{(1)} a\,b\,\bar{c} \prec_{cp}^{(1)} a\,\bar{b}\,\bar{c} \prec_{cp}^{(1)} \underline{a\,\bar{b}\,c} \prec_{cp}^{(1)} \underline{\bar{a}\,\bar{b}\,\bar{c}} \prec_{cp}^{(1)} \bar{a}\,\bar{b}\,c \prec_{cp}^{(1)} \bar{a}\,b\,c \prec_{cp}^{(1)} \bar{a}\,b\,\bar{c}$$

$$a\,b\,c \prec_{cp}^{(2)} a\,b\,\bar{c} \prec_{cp}^{(2)} a\,\bar{b}\,\bar{c} \prec_{cp}^{(2)} \underline{\bar{a}\,\bar{b}\,\bar{c}} \prec_{cp}^{(2)} \underline{a\,\bar{b}\,c} \prec_{cp}^{(2)} \bar{a}\,\bar{b}\,c \prec_{cp}^{(2)} \bar{a}\,b\,c \prec_{cp}^{(2)} \bar{a}\,b\,\bar{c}$$

Here we have $\bar{c}\hspace{-0.3em}\sim_{CP}b$ because there is a world $\omega \models b\bar{c}$, namely $ab\bar{c}$, which is cp-preferred both every model of $\bar{b}\bar{c}$ (which are $a\bar{b}\bar{c}$ and $\bar{a}\bar{b}\bar{c}$). The generated OCF-network induces the global ranking function shown in Table 7.7, and here we find $\kappa(b\bar{c}) = 1 = \kappa(\bar{b}\bar{c})$ and therefore $\bar{c}\hspace{-0.3em}\not\sim_{\kappa_\Gamma}b$ as witness for Observation 7.32.

Complexity and Correctness Results to Algorithms 7.5 and 7.6

Both algorithms are constructed in a similar way, thus we discuss the complexity for both algorithms simultaneously. For each algorithm traverses the

Table 7.7: Global OCF for the OCF-network of Example 7.33

ω	$a\,b\,c$	$a\,b\,\overline{c}$	$a\,\overline{b}\,c$	$a\,\overline{b}\,\overline{c}$	$\overline{a}\,b\,c$	$\overline{a}\,b\,\overline{c}$	$\overline{a}\,\overline{b}\,c$	$\overline{a}\,\overline{b}\,\overline{c}$
$\kappa(\omega)$	0	1	1	1	2	3	2	2

original network and calls every vertex, once. In this call, the designated, either CPT or κ, table has to be constructed by inspecting the configurations of the parent vertices of the vertex. The overall time complexity is thus the sum of the cardinality of the respective parent configurations and bounded by the maximal number of parent vertices a vertex in the graph has, formally $\mathcal{O}\left(\max\left\{2^{|pa(V)|} \mid V \in \Sigma\right\}\right)$. For each of these configurations, a line in the local table has to be stored, thus the overall space complexity is likewise bounded by $\mathcal{O}\left(\max\left\{2^{|pa(V)|} \mid V \in \Sigma\right\}\right)$.

With respect to correctness, we find that both algorithms traverse the graph vertexwise in one pass, so the algorithms terminate. However, as shown in Lemmata 7.28 and 7.31, both algorithm generate a network of the designated type, but, as seen in Observations 7.29 and 7.32, these networks do not encode the same inferential information, thus the algorithms are not correct in generating a structure that preserves the information used to set it up.

So far we showed that it is, in principle, possible to generate an OCF-network from a CP-network and a CP-network from an OCF-network, but the resulting network is not identical to the one it originates from, inferentially. Surprisingly, this difference is not always prone to information loss. In the next paragraphs, we will show that we can recover the original network type from the generated one, and, under certain preconditions, without loss of any information.

By generating a CP-network from an OCF-network using Lemma 7.28, the firmness in which the preferred outcome is believed is dropped, that is, the semi-quantitative property of the local OCF-tables is lost and a strictly qualitative representation, the local CPTs, is generated. If we generate an OCF-network from a CP-network using Lemma 7.31, this semi-quantitative notion has to be induced by a strictly qualitative relation, which we realise by setting the local conditional ranks to be as normal (plausible, least implausible) as possible, that is, setting the local conditional ranks of the not-preferred outcomes to 1.

This means we can restore the original CP-network from an OCF-network generated by this CP-network using Lemma 7.31 by applying Lemma 7.28. The other direction, that is, restoring the original OCF-network by the application of Lemma 7.31 to a CP-network that was generated from this OCF-network by means of Lemma 7.28, is possible only if in the original OCF-network no local conditional rank is greater than 1. This is formalised in the following two Lemmata:

Lemma 7.34. Let $CP = \langle \Sigma, \mathcal{E}, \{CPT(V, pa(V))\}_{V \in \Sigma} \rangle$ be a CP-network. Let $\Gamma^{CP} = \langle \Sigma, \mathcal{E}, \{\kappa_V\}_{V \in \Sigma} \rangle$ be the OCF-network generated from CP by means of Lemma 7.31. The CP-network $(CP^\Gamma)^{CP}$ generated from Γ^{CP} with of Lemma 7.28 is identical to CP.

Lemma 7.35. Let $\Gamma = \langle \Sigma, \mathcal{E}, \{\kappa_V\}_{V \in \Sigma} \rangle$ be a strict OCF-network. Let $CP^\Gamma = \langle \Sigma, \mathcal{E}, \{CPT(V, pa(V))\}_{V \in \Sigma} \rangle$ be the CP-network generated from Γ by means of Lemma 7.28. The OCF-network $(\Gamma^{CP})^\Gamma$ generated from CP^Γ by application of Lemma 7.31 is identical to Γ if and only if for the local OCF κ_V, of Γ we have $\kappa_V(\dot{v}|\mathbf{p}) \leq 1$ for each $V \in \Sigma$ and each configuration $\mathbf{p}$ of $pa(V)$.

So we obtain that the inferential difference is a indeed result of the different formalisms, but not of a possible information loss in the transferral process, because Lemmata 7.34 and 7.35 show that the information stored in the original networks is preserved.

From the previous findings and examples in this section we obtain that the difference in the inferences based on the original and generated network and is a result of different global preferences of the worlds in the different network types. This is formalised in the following observation.

Observation 7.36. [EFKI16, Observation 3] There are strict OCF-networks $\Gamma = \langle \Sigma, \mathcal{E}, \{\kappa_V\}_{V \in \Sigma} \rangle$ where the relation $<_\kappa \subseteq \Omega \times \Omega$ induced by the global OCF κ_Γ does not satisfy the local preference relations $\prec_{\mathbf{p}}^\kappa$.

We illustrate this observation with an example.

Example 7.37. We continue Example 7.33. Here, the global OCF κ_Γ (see Table 7.7) gives us $\kappa(a\bar{b}) = 3 > 1 = \kappa(\bar{a}\bar{b})$ and thus $a\bar{b} \not\prec_\kappa \bar{a}\bar{b}$, whereas the

κ-preference table in A requires us $a \prec_T^\kappa \overline{a}$, that is, $a\dot{b} <_\kappa \overline{a}\dot{b}$ for all fixed $\dot{b} \in \{b, \overline{b}\}$.

This observation proceeds to OCF-networks that are generated from CP-networks, that is, the global OCF of an OCF-network that is derived from a CP-network does not implement the local preference is the CPTs of the CP-network:

Observation 7.38. [EFKI16, Observation 4] There are CP-networks CP such that the preference relation induced by the global OCF κ_Γ generated from CP by means of Algorithm 7.6 does not implement the local preferences in CP.

This can also be observed in the abovementioned example:

Example 7.39. In Example 7.33 we have $b \prec_a \overline{b}$ hence the satisfiability condition for CP requires that we globally have $ab\dot{c} \prec_{cp} \overline{a}b\dot{c}$ for all fixed outcomes $\dot{c}$ of C, thus especially $ab\overline{c} \prec_{cp} \overline{a}b\overline{c}$. In the global OCF (see Table 7.7) we have $\kappa(ab\overline{c}) = 1 = \kappa(\overline{a}b\overline{c})$, hence $ab\overline{c} \not\prec_\kappa \overline{a}b\overline{c}$ which contradicts the requirement.

7.2.2 Bottom-Up Induction of OCF-Networks

In the previous section we have observed that the inferences drawn from CP- and OCF-networks differ, even if they are mutually generated from each other. With Observation 7.38 we could track down the cause of this difference to an incompatibility between the local preferences of the CP-network and the global preferences of the OCF-network.

The following property ensures that these two relations are compatible, globally, as follows:

Definition 7.40 (*CP-compatibility* [EFKI16, Definition 13]). Let κ be an OCF $\kappa : \Omega \to \mathbb{N}_0$ and let CP be a CP-network over Σ. κ is *compatible* to CP if and only if for all $\omega, \omega' \in \Omega$ the global preference $\omega \prec_{cp} \omega'$ implies $\omega <_\kappa \omega'$.

This *CP-compatibility*, which is an embedding of $\prec_{cp}$ into $<_\kappa$, guarantees that the global κ-preference of an OCF-network satisfies the local CP-preferences of the CPTs. The satisfaction relation of CP-networks ensures that the global preference relation satisfies the local CPTs. If the global

OCF is *CP*-compatible, then the preference relation $\prec_{CP}$ is embedded in the relation $<_{\kappa_\Gamma}$, and thus the latter respects the preferences of the prior, that is, the satisfaction of the local CPTs is preserved by the embedding.

Corollary 7.41. Let $CP = \langle \Sigma, \mathcal{E}, \{CPT(V, pa(V))\}_{V \in \Sigma} \rangle$ be a CP-network and let $\Gamma = \langle \Sigma, \mathcal{E}, \{\kappa_V\}_{V \in \Sigma} \rangle$ be a strict OCF-network. If Γ is compatible to *CP*, then we have $\omega <_{\kappa_\Gamma} \omega'$ for every $\omega \models \dot{v}\mathbf{p}_V$, $\omega' \models \overline{\dot{v}}\mathbf{p}_V$ where $\dot{v} \prec_{\mathbf{p}_V} \overline{\dot{v}}$ in every $CPT(V, pa(V))$ in *CP*.

The embedding also ensures that every inference drawn preferentially using a relation $\prec_{cp}$ can also be drawn using any OCF κ that embeds this relation, that is, is *CP*-compatible to the relation:

Lemma 7.42. Let $\prec_{cp}$ be a global preference relation of a CP-network *CP* and let κ be a *CP*-compatible OCF to $\prec_{cp}$. Then $\phi \vdash_{CP} \psi$ implies $\phi \approx_\kappa \psi$.

So with *CP*-compatibility, we have a property that ensures that an OCF satisfies the local preferences and global inferences of a CP-network. Using this embedding we find a *CP*-compatible OCF for every preference relation $\prec_{cp}$. What remains to show that it is possible to have an OCF-network with a *CP*-compatible global OCF generated locally.

Theorem 7.43 ([EFKI16, Theorem 1]). Let $\Gamma = \langle \Sigma, \mathcal{E}, \{\kappa_V\}_{V \in \Sigma} \rangle$ be a strict OCF-network with a global OCF κ_Γ. κ_Γ is *CP*-compatible to the CP-network CP^κ generated by means of Algorithm 7.5 if the inequality

$$\max_{\dot{v} \in \{v, \overline{v}\}} \left\{ \kappa_V(\dot{v}|\mathbf{p}_V) \right\} > \sum_{C \in ch(V)} \max_{\substack{\dot{c} \in \{c, \overline{c}\} \\ \mathbf{p}_C \in \Omega(pa(C))}} \left\{ \kappa_V(\dot{c}|\mathbf{p}_C) \right\} \qquad (7.7)$$

holds for all variables $V \in \Sigma$ and all fixed configurations $\mathbf{p}_V$ of $pa(V)$.

We recall that due to the local normalisation of OCF-networks (Equation (7.1) in Definition 7.1), for all $V \in \Sigma$ and all fixed configurations $\mathbf{p}_V \in \Omega(pa(V))$ of the parents of V we have $\min \{\kappa_V(\dot{v}|\mathbf{p}_V) \mid \dot{v} \in \{v, \overline{v}\}\} = 0$. The inequality (7.7) ensures that for each configuration of the parent vertices $pa(V)$ of each variable V, the implausible outcome of V is less plausible as the combined implausibility of the least plausible outcome of each of the children $C \in ch(V)$, regardless of the configuration of the parents of $pa(C)$ (that is, the configuration of V and and siblings of V), and at least 1 if V is a leaf vertex and has no children.

Theorem 7.43 ensures that if the local ranking tables of an OCF-network Γ satisfy the inequalities (7.7), then the global OCF of Γ is *CP*-compatible to a CP-network which is be obtained by applying Algorithm 7.5 to Γ. We use this theorem to devise an algorithm that induces an OCF-network from a CP-network such that the generated OCF-network is *CP*-compatible. As noted, the rank of the least plausible outcome of the configuration of the leafs is greater or equal one, and the ranks of the outcomes of each vertex can be determined when the ranking tables of the children vertices are known. Hence we induce the ranking tables in a bottom-up fashion with Algorithm 7.7, illustrated in Figure 7.15. For easier reading, we recall the assignment of ranks to local ranking tables in a more general fashion given, without loss of generality, $\mathbf{p}$ is a configuration of $pa(V)$ and $\dot{v}$ be the preferred outcome of V, that is, $\dot{v} \prec_{\mathbf{p}} \bar{v}$

$$
\kappa_V(\bar{v}|\mathbf{p}) := \begin{cases} 1 & \text{iff} \quad ch(V) = \varnothing \\ \displaystyle\sum_{C \in ch(V)} \max_{\substack{\dot{c} \in \{c, \bar{c}\} \\ [\mathbf{p}_C \in \Omega(pa(C))]}} \left\{ \kappa_V(\dot{c}|\mathbf{p}_C) \right\} + 1 & \text{o/w}. \end{cases} \tag{7.8}
$$

Complexity and Correctness Results to Algorithm 7.7

To compute the derived OCF-network using Algorithm 7.7, the algorithm calls every $V \in \Sigma$, once, and has to look up the local ranking tables of all children of V, thus we have an overall worst-time complexity of $\mathcal{O}(|\Sigma|^2)$ for graphs with one root vertex and all other vertices being children of this root vertex.

As already stated in the discussion of the space complexity of the inductive approach for OCF-networks, the *space complexity* for storing an OCF-network is the sum of the space needed for each local ranking table which are bounded by $\mathcal{O}(2^{|pa(V)|})$ for each $V \in \Sigma$. Therefore the space needed to store the generated OCF-network has an asymptotic complexity of $\mathcal{O}\left(\max\left\{2^{|pa(V)|} \mid V \in \Sigma\right\}\right)$.

With respect to correctness we obtain that the algorithm calls every vertex in the graph, once, and therefore terminates. As the algorithm implements Theorem 7.43, the resulting OCF-network is correct in that the generated OCF-network is *CP*-compatible to the original *CP*-network (confer [EFKI16, Theorem 2]).

Listing 7.7: Bottom-up induction of an OCF-network from a CP-network (confer [EFKI16]).

```
INPUT    : CP-network  CP = ⟨Σ, ℰ, {CPT(V, pa(V))}_{V∈Σ}⟩
OUTPUT   : Strict OCF-network  Γ = ⟨Σ, ℰ, {κ_V}_{V∈Σ}⟩

BEGIN
  // Initialisation
  FOR-EACH(V ∈ Σ)
    FOR-EACH(p_V ∈ Ω(pa(V)))
      κ_V(v̇|p_V):=0
    END FOR-EACH
  END FOR-EACH

  𝒥:= reverse Breadth-First iteration of Σ wrt. (Σ,ℰ)

  // Generate local OCF tables
  WHILE((V:= NEXT-ITEM(𝒥)) ≠ EMPTY)
    FOR-EACH(p_V ∈ Ω(pa(V)))
      IF((v ≺_{p_V} v̄) ∈ CPT(V, pa(V)))  // i.e. if v ≺_{p_V} v̄
        κ_V(v|p_V):=0
        IF(ch(V) = ∅)
          κ_V(v̄|p_V):=1
        ELSE
```
$$\kappa_V(\overline{v}|\mathbf{p}_V):= \sum_{C\in ch(V)} \max_{\substack{\dot{c}\in\{c,\overline{c}\} \\ \mathbf{p}_C\in\Omega(pa(C))}} \left\{\kappa_V(\dot{c}|\mathbf{p}_C)\right\} + 1$$
```
        END IF
      ELSE                    // i.e. if v̄ ≺_{p_V} v
        κ_V(v̄|p_V):=0
        IF(ch(V) = ∅)
          κ_V(v|p_V):=1
        ELSE
```
$$\kappa_V(v|\mathbf{p}_V):= \sum_{C\in ch(V)} \max_{\substack{\dot{c}\in\{c,\overline{c}\} \\ \mathbf{p}_C\in\Omega(pa(C))}} \left\{\kappa_V(\dot{c}|\mathbf{p}_C)\right\} + 1$$
```
        END IF
      END IF
    END FOR-EACH
  END FOR-EACH
  RETURN  Γ = ⟨Σ, ℰ, {κ_V}_{V∈Σ}⟩
END
```

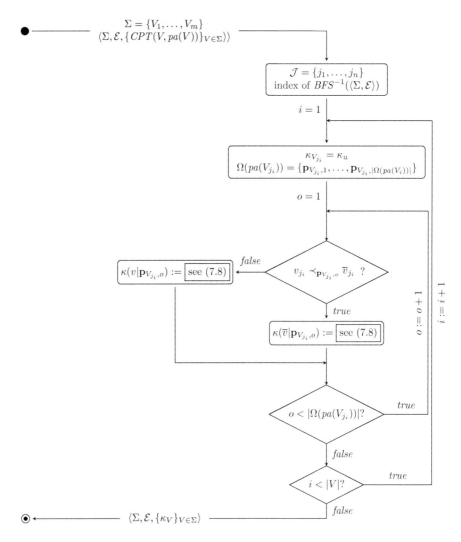

Figure 7.15: Generate an OCF-network from a CP-network using bottom-up induction (Algorithm 7.7) where the local ranks are set according to Formula (7.8)

The strategy of the bottom-up approach of Theorem 7.43 does not work for generating CP-networks that are compatible to OCF-networks: In the global preference relation of a CP-network worlds are always preferred with respect to the outcome of vertices with a lower depth in the network. Variables which vertices have a higher depth in the networks are subordinate to variables with lower depth, not only in their position in the graph, but also with respect to their impact on the ordering of the worlds in the global preference relation.

It is not to far to seek to overcome this by relaxing the constraint that the global preference relation of a CP-network has to be strict, thus extending $\prec_{CP}$. In doing so for each $\omega \in \Omega$ we obtain the sets $\Omega^{\succ}_{CP}(\omega) = \{\omega'' | \omega \prec_{CP} \omega''\}$ of worlds for which ω is preferred and the set of worlds preferred to ω, $\Omega^{\prec}_{CP}(\omega) = \{\omega'' | \omega'' \prec_{CP} \omega\}$ and define the non-strict total preference relation $\preccurlyeq_{CP} \subseteq \Omega \times \Omega$ such that for two worlds $\omega, \omega' \in \Omega$ we have $\omega \preccurlyeq_{CP} \omega'$ if and only if $\omega \prec_{CP} \omega'$ or $\Omega^{\succ}_{CP}(\omega) = \Omega^{\succ}_{CP}(\omega')$ and $\Omega^{\prec}_{CP}(\omega) = \Omega^{\prec}_{CP}(\omega')$.

This relaxation overcomes some of the noted difficulties, namely the problem with worlds with identical ranks, but still the summation in (7.2) may lead to a global κ-preference relation that is not compatible to any global CP-preference relation.

Example 7.33 is a witness for this finding, as we here find that the worlds $\omega \vDash (a \wedge (\bar{b} \vee \bar{c}))$ as well as the worlds $\omega \vDash (\bar{a} \wedge \bar{c})$ share the same ranks (see Table 7.7). In this example we also witness the (lack of) dominance from vertices of lower depth: The CP-network implies that in the global CP-preference, worlds $\omega \vDash ab$ are to be preferred to worlds $\omega' \vDash a\bar{b}$, which is not the case for the global OCF, where, for instance, $ab\bar{c}$ is not preferred to $a\bar{b}\bar{c}$.

We summarise this in the following corollary, formalising that OCF-networks are strictly more expressible than CP-networks:

Corollary 7.44 ([EFKI16, Corollary 2]). For every CP-network there is a compatible OCF-network, the converse is not true in general.

OCF-networks satisfy the local directed Markov property, that is, every vertex is κ-independent from its non-descendants given its parents, as shown in Theorem 7.6. In CP-networks, every vertex is conditionally CP-independent from the whole graph given its parents, as shown in Lemma 3.57.

Proposition 7.45 (confer [EFKI16]). Let $\mathcal{G} = \{\Sigma, \mathcal{E}\}$ be a DAG over a propositional alphabet Σ defining the graphical structure for an OCF-network

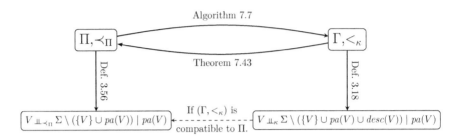

Figure 7.16: Relationship between Markov Property and CP-independence for OCF- and CP-networks [EFKI16]

$\Gamma = \{\mathcal{G}, \{\kappa_V\}_{V \in \Sigma}\}$ and a CP-network $CP = \{\mathcal{G}, \{CPT_V\}_{V \in \Sigma}\}$ in such a way that Γ is *CP*-compatible to *CP*. The local directed Markov property and the *CP*-independence are different in general.

But, as *CP*-independence is based on the global *CP*-preference of a CP-network and *CP*-compatibility of OCF-networks with global κ-preference $<_\kappa$ ensures that $\prec_{CP} \subseteq <_\kappa$, we directly obtain:

Corollary 7.46. An OCF-network Γ which is *CP*-compatible to a CP-network *CP* satisfies the global properties of *CP*, including but not limited to *CP*-independence

Figure 7.16 illustrates how the independence relations of the two network types are related.

We further inspect the implementation of Theorem 7.43 into Algorithm 7.7: The theorem is correct for any inequality (7.7), whilst the algorithm, with the +1 increment in (7.8), assigns each local conditional ranking table the minimal values such that inequality (7.7) is satisfied. This is not the only option for setting up the local OCF values, and there is an infinite number of possible allocations of numbers to the local ranking tables that the algorithm is still correct, as a direct result of Theorem 7.43, formalised in the following.

Corollary 7.47 ([EFKI16, Corollary 3]). Let *CP* be a CP-network with a global preference $\prec_{CP}$. There are ranking functions κ such that for the relation $<_\kappa$ based on κ, $\omega \prec_{CP} \omega'$ implies $\omega <_\kappa \omega'$ and thus $<_\kappa$ is compatible to CP.

The set $\mathfrak{K}(\prec_{CP})$ is the set of all OCF that are CP-compatible. With the property local/global coincidence of OCF-networks we can generate an OCF-network to any OCF, thus also any CP-compatible OCF to a CP-network. To generate these OCF, we use the global preference relation induced by the CP-network to partition the worlds Ω into a tuple $(\Omega_0, \ldots, \Omega_k)$ such that $\omega \in \Omega_i$ if and only if $\omega \prec_{CP} \omega'$ for all $\omega' \in \Omega \setminus \bigcup_{j=1}^{i} \Omega_j$ and then set up a ranking function κ by assigning ranking values to the worlds such that $\omega <_\kappa \omega'$, thus ensuring that the preference relation induced by CP is preserved by κ, and thus κ is CP-compatible. Algorithm 7.8, illustrated in Figure 7.17, realises this.

Complexity and Correctness Results for Algorithm 7.8

To set up the respective OCF-network, Algorithm 7.8 needs to set up the global preference of the CP-network, which can be done by traversing the network once per possible world, which is bounded by the number of worlds, $\mathcal{O}(2^{|\Sigma|})$. These worlds then have to be ordered with respect to their preference, which, when done by an efficient algorithm, can be done in $\mathcal{O}(2^{|\Sigma|} \cdot \log(2^{|\Sigma|}))$. Then a rank for each world has to be determined, which is, again, possible by calling each world, once, thus in $\mathcal{O}(2^{|\Sigma|})$ steps. Finally, the local OCF-values have to be computed, which is bounded by the maximal number of parent vertices a vertex in the graph has, formally $\mathcal{O}\left(\max\left\{2^{|pa(V)|} \mid V \in \Sigma\right\}\right)$. So asymptotically, the algorithm can be executed in an asymptotic time of $\mathcal{O}(2^{|\Sigma|} \cdot \log(2^{|\Sigma|}))$. In this process, the complete set of worlds has to be provided in a two lookup-tables, thus the space complexity is $\mathcal{O}(2^{|\Sigma|})$.

With respect to correctness we obtain that the algorithm sorts the set of worlds and then assigns a ranking value to each world, thus calling each world three times, and then sets up an OCF-network by means of the local/global coincidence, which means to call every vertex, that is, variable, once. Therefore, the algorithm terminates. It uses the definition of CP-compatibility (Definition 7.40) with property local/global coincidence of OCF-networks (Theorem 7.4) to set up the OCF-network, thus ensuring that the resulting ranking function is CP-compatible, and setting the worlds

Listing 7.8: Generate members of the family of CP-compatible OCF-networks $\mathfrak{K}(\prec_{CP})$ according to Corollary 7.47 (confer [EFKI16]).

```
INPUT   : CP-network  CP = ⟨Σ,ℰ,{CPT(V,pa(V))}_{V∈Σ}⟩ with
          global preference ≺_CP
OUTPUT  : Strict OCF-network Γ = ⟨Σ,ℰ,{κ_V}_{V∈Σ}⟩
          compatible to CP

/* Let  CP  be a CP-network with a global preference ≺_CP which
 * is shown to generate a schema for CP-compatible OCF-networks.
 *
 * Let Ω_0,...,Ω_m be a partitioning of Ω such that
 * Ω_0 = {ω|∄ ω' ∈ Ω : ω' ≺_CP ω} and
 * For each 1 ≤ i ≤ m
 * Set Ω_i = {ω|∄ ω' ∈ Ω \ ⋃_{j=0}^{i-1} Ω_j : ω' ≺_CP ω}.
 */

BEGIN
  // Initialisation
  FOR-EACH(ω^{(0)} ∈ Ω_0)
    κ(ω^{(0)}):=0 to all
  END FOR-EACH

  // Assign local ranking values
  FOR(i=1, i<=m, i++)
    FOR-EACH(ω^{(i)} ∈ Ω_i)
      SET f TO SATISFY f> max{κ(ω^{(i-1)}) | ω^{(i-1)} ∈ Ω_{i-1}}
      κ(ω^{(i)}):=f
    END FOR-EACH
    κ_V(V(ω)|pa(V)(ω)):=κ(({V} ∪ pa(V))(ω)) − κ(pa(V)(ω))
  END FOR
  RETURN Γ = ⟨Σ,ℰ,{κ_V}_{V∈Σ}⟩
END
```

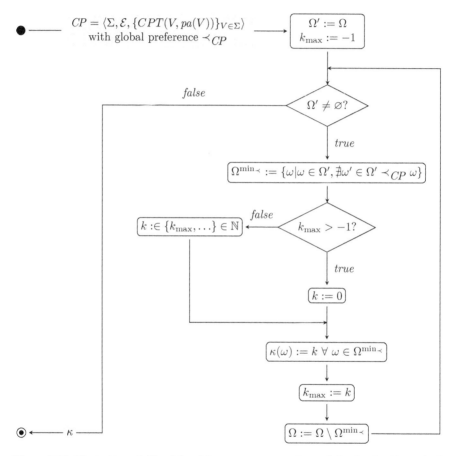

Figure 7.17: Illustration of Algorithm 7.8 to generate members of the family $\mathfrak{K}(\prec_{CP})$ of CP-compatible OCF to the CP-network CP

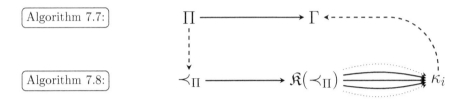

Figure 7.18: Relations between Algorithm 7.7 and Algorithm 7.8

$\omega \in \Omega_0$ to a ranking value of 0 ensures that the resulting κ is indeed an OCF. Therefore, the algorithm is correct.

In contrast to generating a single, unique OCF, Algorithm 7.8 generates a family $\mathfrak{K}(\prec_{CP})$ of OCF that are *CP*-compatible to a CP-network, from which one that is the "best" with respect to given criteria of the usage scenario can be chosen under additional constraints on the local OCF imposed by the user of the system; Figure 7.18 shows how Algorithm 7.7 and 7.8 are related.

7.2.3 Interim Summary and Discussion

This section, discusses how CP-networks and OCF-networks are related; to be more precise, we recalled that OCF-networks are strictly more expressible than CP-networks. We recalled an algorithm to generate an OCF-network from a CP-network, preserving the property of the CP-network in this process. With Algorithm 7.8 we reported a further extension of this findings to generate not a single, but a family of OCF-networks that simulate the original network, properties and stored information.

Corollary 7.44 states that OCF-networks are strictly more expressible than CP-networks, and with the Algorithms 7.7 and 7.8 we recalled procedures to encode the information of CP-networks into OCF-networks. This leaves us with the questions whether using CP-networks is a sensible way to encode preferences, in general, or whether it would be sensible to switch to OCF-networks to encode preferences altogether. We discuss this question with respect to the area the approaches are to be used in.

On the conceptual side, both plausibility and preference are fundamentally different concepts. There may be situations where an intelligent agent believes an outcome or a possible world to be simultaneously more plausible as and preferable to all or some other outcomes, but this is not always the case. Often the most desired or preferred outcome is implausible, and, vice versa, the most plausible outcome is undesired. For instance, an agent might prefer to win the lottery, but may it (correctly) assume this to be quite implausible. As example for the other direction, contracting lung cancer is probably not a desired outcome for an intelligent agent, nonetheless it is plausible given the agent smokes. This possible conflict of plausibility and preference is a desired property, as it may lead the agent to take steps for the preferred outcome to become more plausible, for instance buying additional lottery tickets or quitting smoking. Nonetheless this is not an issue of representation, but on the semantics and usage of the networks. If the usage of OCF-networks in their own semantics and the semantics of preferences is strictly kept apart, this should not become a problem.

On the formal side, simulating the strictly qualitative approach of CP-networks with the semi-quantitative of OCF-networks bears the risk of undesired side-effects. Example 7.30, for instance, showed that using summation as combination operation for the local information is the key problem for simulating CP-networks with OCF-networks. Theorem 7.43 and the resulting Algorithm 7.7 overcome this problem for statical information, but how to ensure the necessary property (7.8) under information change is still an open question. Thus for dynamical environments, using these different approaches with the same representation is prone to risks and undesired outcomes of a system.

On the practical, that is, programming side, it stands to reason to minimise the technologies introduced to a system, thus reducing the complexity of a system to the bare necessity. In this, the risk for flaws and errors in the implementation, and even security risks is reduced for a lightweight system. So if a system, for instance a multi-agent framework, using both plausibility and preference as decision machinery in the agents, was to be implemented, this argument vouches for implementing both representations as OCF-networks, which should be possible as long as the Inequalities (7.8) are adhered to. This approach, however, bears the risk of mixing both fundamentally different concepts, and should not be undertaken lightly, as discussed for conceptual and formal questions.

This topic was examined in the bachelor thesis of Matthias Fey [Fey12] under supervision of the author of this thesis and Gabriele Kern-Isberner. This has been the base of the article [EFKI16], in which we streamlined the findings of [Fey12], further formalised the groundwork that resulted in Theorem 7.43, the resulting corollaries and finally Algorithm 7.8.

This thesis extends these prior works in showing that, even if the approaches do not ensure that the semantics of the prior networks are preserved in the generated networks, the transformation steps are not always prone to information loss (Lemmata 7.34 and 7.35), discussing the complexity of the presented algorithms, and extending the discussion about representing CP-networks into OCF-networks (or the converse) from the aforementioned article.

7.3 OCF-LEG Networks

Even equipped with promising properties like the local directed Markov property, local/global coincidence and factorisation, OCF-networks have shown to bear problems with being generated inductively. This renders this approach to be problematic if the networks are to be constructed from knowledge bases incomplete with respect to a directed graph. Another weakness is that the inductive approach restricts the knowledge base to single-elementary conditionals. Nonetheless, the general principle of dividing the alphabet and the knowledge base into significantly smaller parts for reducing computational time and space for generating the local representations proved to be successful. In this section we recall another network approach to storing OCF: OCF-LEG networks. In contrast to OCF-networks, these networks are set up upon hypergraphs as graphical components. We show that this approach leads to slightly larger local alphabets and knowledge bases in comparison to OCF-networks. However, under a certain consistency condition, OCF-LEG networks can be constructed inductively from arbitrary knowledge bases, and this can be done with neither the need for a notion of completeness nor a restriction to a special kind of conditionals. This section is based on and extends the article [EKI14].

7.3.1 Basic Definition and Properties

Roughly speaking, an OCF-LEG network is a LEG network (see Section 3.5) where the local probability tables are exchanged with local ranking tables.

Definition 7.48 (OCF-LEG Network [EKI14, Definition 7]). Let $\Sigma_1, \ldots, \Sigma_m$ be a set of variables covering subsets an alphabet Σ such that $\Sigma_i \subseteq \Sigma$, $1 \leq i \leq m$, and $\Sigma = \bigcup_{i=1}^{m} \Sigma_i$; for each $1 \leq i \leq m$. Let $\kappa_1, \ldots, \kappa_m$ be OCF over local possible worlds $\Omega_i = \Omega(\Sigma_i)$, respectively. We call a tuple $\langle \Sigma_i, \kappa_i \rangle$ a *local event group (LEG)*. The system $\langle (\Sigma_1, \kappa_1), \ldots, (\Sigma_m, \kappa_m) \rangle$, abbreviated as $\langle (\Sigma_i, \kappa_i) \rangle_{i=1}^{m}$, is a *ranking network of local event groups (OCF-LEG network)* if and only if there is a global function κ on Ω with κ_i being the marginal of κ on Ω_i, that is, for all $1 \leq i \leq m$ and all $\omega^i \in \Omega_i$ we have

$$\kappa(\omega^i) = \kappa_i(\omega^i). \tag{7.9}$$

We illustrate this definition using the car start example.

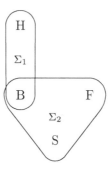

Figure 7.19: Hypergraph to the car start example in Example 7.49

Table 7.8: Local OCF for the car start example

ω^1	$b\,h$	$b\,\overline{h}$	$\overline{b}\,h$	$\overline{b}\,h$
$\kappa_1(\omega^1)$	2	0	1	1

ω^2	$b\,f\,s$	$b\,f\,\overline{s}$	$b\,\overline{f}\,s$	$b\,\overline{f}\,\overline{s}$	$\overline{b}\,f\,s$	$\overline{b}\,f\,\overline{s}$	$\overline{b}\,\overline{f}\,s$	$\overline{b}\,\overline{f}\,\overline{s}$
$\kappa_2(\omega^2)$	0	1	2	1	2	1	2	1

Example 7.49. Let $\Sigma = \{H, B, F, S\}$ be the variables from the car start example (see Example 3.21). We distribute these variables into the sets $\Sigma_1 = \{H, B\}$ and $\Sigma_2 = \{B, F, S\}$, giving us the hypergraph shown in Figure 7.19. The two subsets induce the local worlds

$$\Omega_1 = \{\,h\,b,\, h\,\overline{b},\, \overline{h}\,b,\, \overline{h}\,\overline{b}\,\},$$
$$\Omega_2 = \{\,b\,f\,s,\, b\,f\,\overline{s},\, b\,\overline{f}\,s,\, b\,\overline{f}\,\overline{s},\, \overline{b}\,f\,s,\, \overline{b}\,f\,\overline{s},\, \overline{b}\,\overline{f}\,s,\, \overline{b}\,\overline{f}\,\overline{s}\,\}.$$

Following the definition of hypergraphs, this gives us the separators $\mathbb{S}_1 = \varnothing$, $\mathbb{R}_1 = \Sigma_1$, $\mathbb{S}_2 = \{B\}$, and $\mathbb{R}_2 = \{F, S\}$. The local OCF κ_1 and κ_2 are defined in Table 7.8.

The following consistency condition (7.10) has to be satisfied for a system $\langle(\Sigma_i, \kappa_i)\rangle_{i=1}^m$ to have a global ranking function as defined above

Proposition 7.50 (Consistency Condition for OCF-LEG Networks [EKI14, Proposition 1]). A global ordinal conditional function for the system of

Table 7.9: Local OCF for Example 7.51

	abc	$ab\overline{c}$	$a\overline{b}c$	$a\overline{b}\overline{c}$	$\overline{a}bc$	$\overline{a}b\overline{c}$	$\overline{a}\overline{b}c$	$\overline{a}\overline{b}\overline{c}$
κ_1	0	0	0	0	1	1	0	0
κ_2	0	1	0	1	0	0	0	0
κ_3	1	0	0	0	1	0	0	0

OCF-LEGs $\langle(\Sigma_i, \kappa_i)\rangle_{i=1}^m$ for which the local OCF are marginals on the respective local worlds exists only if

$$\kappa_i((\Sigma_i \cap \Sigma_j)(\omega)) = \kappa_j((\Sigma_i \cap \Sigma_j)(\omega)) \tag{7.10}$$

for all pairs $1 \leq i, j \leq m$ and all worlds $\omega \in \Omega$.

The above consistency condition (7.10) is necessary, but not sufficient for the existence of a global OCF, as can be seen in the following example

Example 7.51 ([EKI14, Example 5]). Let $\Sigma = \{A, B, C\}$ be a propositional alphabet with subsets $\Sigma_1 = \{A, B\}$, $\Sigma_2 = \{A, C\}$ and $\Sigma_3 = \{B, C\}$ which constructs the hypergraph shown in Figure 7.20. Let further κ_1, κ_2 and κ_3 be OCF as given in Table 7.9 These local OCF satisfy the consistency condition (7.10) because

$$\kappa_\bullet(a) = \kappa_\bullet(\overline{a}) = \kappa_\bullet(b) = \kappa_\bullet(\overline{b}) = \kappa_\bullet(c) = \kappa_\bullet(\overline{c}) = 0 \quad \text{for all } \bullet \in \{1, 2, 3\}.$$

If there was a global κ satisfying $\kappa(\omega^i) = \kappa_i(\omega^i)$ then

$$\kappa_2(a\overline{c}) = 1 = \kappa(a\overline{c}) = \min\{\kappa(ab\overline{c}), \kappa(a\overline{b}\overline{c})\} \qquad \text{and} \tag{7.11}$$

$$\kappa_1(ab) = 0 = \kappa(ab) = \min\{\kappa(abc), \kappa(ab\overline{c})\}. \tag{7.12}$$

Equation (7.11) implies that both $\kappa(ab\overline{c}) \neq 0$ and $\kappa(a\overline{b}\overline{c}) \neq 0$, so by (7.12) we obtain that $\kappa(abc) = 0$. But then $\kappa(bc) = \min\{\kappa(abc), \kappa(\overline{a}bc)\} = 0 \neq 1 = \kappa_3(bc)$, and we see that according to Definition 7.48, κ can be no global OCF for $\langle(\Sigma_1, \kappa_1), (\Sigma_2, \kappa_2), (\Sigma_3, \kappa_3)\rangle$ in contradiction to the assumption. Hence even if κ_1, κ_2 and κ_3 satisfy the consistency condition, there is no global ranking function for this system of OCF-LEGs and thus $\langle(\Sigma_i, \kappa_i)\rangle_{i=1}^3$ is no OCF-LEG network.

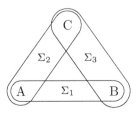

Figure 7.20: Hypergraph for Example 7.51 to show that the consistency condition alone is not sufficient for the hypergraph with local OCF to be an OCF-LEG network

This example for the consistency condition (7.10) not being sufficient for an OCF-LEG network yields that we need additional constraints on the system of OCF-LEGs which ensure that there is a global ranking function to the local OCF such that (7.9) is satisfied and the system to be an OCF-LEG network. The following theorem shows that that the consistency condition (7.10) is sufficient for the existence of a global OCF according to (7.9) given the network of hyperedges form a hypertree.

Theorem 7.52 ([EKI14, Theorem 1]). Let $\Sigma_1, \ldots, \Sigma_m$ be a set of variables covering the propositional alphabet $\Sigma_i \subseteq \Sigma$ s.t. the separators $\mathbb{S}_1, \ldots, \mathbb{S}_m$ satisfy the RIP, that is, $\langle \Sigma, \{\Sigma_1, \ldots, \Sigma_m\}\rangle$ is a hypertree (see Section 2.4). Let $\kappa_1, \ldots, \kappa_m$ be a set of OCF on the local worlds $\Omega_1, \ldots, \Omega_m$, respectively, satisfying the consistency condition (7.10). Then

$$\kappa(\omega) = \sum_{i=1}^{m} \kappa_i(\Sigma_i(\omega)) - \sum_{i=1}^{m} \kappa_i(\mathbb{S}_i(\omega)) \tag{7.13}$$

is a global ranking function for the system $\langle(\Sigma_i, \kappa_i)\rangle_{i=1}^{m}$, that is, $\kappa(\omega^i) = \kappa_i(\omega^i)$ for all $\omega^i \in \Omega_i$, for all $1 \leq i \leq m$.

With $\mathbb{R}_i = \Sigma_i \setminus \mathbb{S}_i$, $1 \leq i \leq m$ (see Section 2.4) and the rank of conditionals being defined by (3.13), Equation (7.13) can be rewritten to

$$\kappa(\omega) = \sum_{i=1}^{m} \kappa_i(\mathbb{R}_i(\omega)|\mathbb{S}_i(\omega)). \tag{7.14}$$

We illustrate Theorem 7.52 with the car start example.

Table 7.10: Calculating a global OCF κ for Example 7.53

ω	$h\,b\,f\,s$	$h\,b\,f\,\overline{s}$	$h\,b\,\overline{f}\,s$	$h\,b\,\overline{f}\,\overline{s}$	$h\,\overline{b}\,f\,s$	$h\,\overline{b}\,f\,\overline{s}$	$h\,\overline{b}\,\overline{f}\,s$	$h\,\overline{b}\,\overline{f}\,\overline{s}$
$\kappa_1(\Sigma_1(\omega))$	2	2	2	2	1	1	1	1
$+\,\kappa_2(\Sigma_2(\omega))$	0	1	2	1	2	1	2	1
$-\,\kappa_2(\mathbb{S}_2(\omega))$	0	0	0	0	1	1	1	1
$=\quad \kappa(\omega)$	2	3	4	3	2	1	2	1
ω	$\overline{h}\,b\,f\,s$	$\overline{h}\,b\,f\,\overline{s}$	$\overline{h}\,b\,\overline{f}\,s$	$\overline{h}\,b\,\overline{f}\,\overline{s}$	$\overline{h}\,\overline{b}\,f\,s$	$\overline{h}\,\overline{b}\,f\,\overline{s}$	$\overline{h}\,\overline{b}\,\overline{f}\,s$	$\overline{h}\,\overline{b}\,\overline{f}\,\overline{s}$
$\kappa_1(\Sigma_1(\omega))$	0	0	0	0	1	1	1	1
$+\,\kappa_2(\Sigma_2(\omega))$	0	1	2	1	2	1	2	1
$-\,\kappa_2(\mathbb{S}_2(\omega))$	0	0	0	0	1	1	1	1
$=\quad \kappa(\omega)$	0	1	2	1	2	1	2	1

Example 7.53 ([EKI14, Example 6]). We continue Example 7.49 on this behalf. The network satisfies the running intersection property, because we have $\mathbb{S}_2 \subseteq \Sigma_1$. κ_1 and κ_2 have already be given in Table 7.8. These local ranking functions satisfy the consistency condition (7.10) on $\Sigma_1 \cap \Sigma_2 = \{B\}$ because we find $\kappa_1(b) = 0 = \kappa_2(b)$ and $\kappa_1(\overline{b}) = 1 = \kappa_2(\overline{b})$. The calculation of the global OCF κ according to Equation (7.13) is explicated in Table 7.10. These values also verify that κ is an OCF with $\kappa(\overline{h}bfs) = 0$; it is easily checked that κ_1 and κ_2 are marginals of κ on Ω_1 and Ω_2, respectively.

So Theorem 7.52 ensures that a system $\langle \Sigma_i, \kappa_i \rangle_{i=1}^{m}$ which satisfies the consistency condition (7.10) is an OCF-LEG network given the underlying hypergraph is a hypertree. This is formalised as the following corollary.

Corollary 7.54 ([EKI14, Corollary 1]). Let $\langle \Sigma, \langle \Sigma_i, \kappa_i \rangle_{i=1}^{m} \rangle$ be a covering hypertree with local OCF on an alphabet Σ such that each pair κ_i, κ_j, $1 \leq i, j \leq m$, satisfies the consistency condition (7.10). Then $\langle \Sigma_i, \kappa_i \rangle_{i=1}^{m}$ is an OCF-LEG network with a global ranking function κ obtained by (7.13). Moreover, due to the coincidence of κ with the local OCF κ_i on respective Ω_i, local and global inferences coincide, that is, for ϕ, ψ being formulas out of the language composed by Σ_i, we have

$$\phi \mathrel{\vert\!\approx_\kappa} \psi \quad \text{iff} \quad \kappa \vDash (\psi|\phi) \quad \text{iff} \quad \kappa_i \vDash (\psi|\phi) \quad \text{iff} \quad \phi \mathrel{\vert\!\approx_{\kappa_i}} \psi. \tag{7.15}$$

The motivation for using network approaches was to obtain independence properties like the ones found in Bayesian Networks, and to utilise these properties to make algorithms more efficient, especially to shift storage and calculation with a high global complexity to local areas. OCF-LEG networks have been defined such that the global function of the network coincides with the local ones, and Theorem 7.52 shows how a global OCF can be calculated given an OCF-network. The following proposition ensures that two succeeding hyperedges are independent given their separator.

Proposition 7.55 ([EKI14, Proposition 2]). Let $\langle \Sigma_i, \kappa_i \rangle_{i=1}^m$ be an OCF-LEG network with a global ranking function according to formula (7.13). Let $\mathbb{S}_i$ be a separator between two succeeding hyperedges Σ_i, Σ_j with Σ_i being the child of Σ_j. The sets $\Sigma_i \setminus \mathbb{S}_i$ and $\Sigma_j \setminus \mathbb{S}_i$ are conditionally independent given $\mathbb{S}_i$, formally $(\Sigma_i \setminus \mathbb{S}_i) \perp\!\!\!\perp_\kappa (\Sigma_j \setminus \mathbb{S}_i) \mid \mathbb{S}_i$.

Together, Theorem 7.52 and Proposition 7.55 give us the local storage and computation which we searched for. In the following, we propose a method for inductively setting up an OCF-LEG network from a conditional knowledge base.

7.3.2 Inductive Generation

We have already shown that OCF-LEG networks can be used to efficiently store ranking functions by means of local OCF-LEGs. In this section, we will propose an algorithm to generate OCF-LEG networks from conditional knowledge bases. In this we follow the route paved in Section 7.1.2 in that we first show how to generate the graph component. We then use the so obtained subsets of the alphabet to generate local knowledge bases for the hyperedges. On these local knowledge bases we then invoke inductive methods to generate ranking functions, which then pose as local OCF. We already demonstrated in Section 7.1.2 that using firmness-annotated or purely qualitative knowledge bases makes little difference. Therefore in this section we only demonstrate the technique with purely qualitative knowledge bases for reasons of clarity in presentation. If for a given application it was necessary to have firmness-annotated conditional, the only thing to be changed in the proposed approach is to replace the qualitative inductive OCF approaches with semi-qualitative variants thereof.

So we first generating the hypertree using established techniques of techniques of [Pea88, Mey98] which form Algorithm 7.9 (illustrated in Figure 7.3). This is done we generate a variable set for every conditional such that the set contains all variables of which literals appear the conditional, and then reducing this set of variable sets to a minimal covering hypertree. Here, the first which is different to the approach of OCF-networks is that this algorithm accepts any conditional knowledge base as input, not only a special subset.

Complexity and Correctness Results to Algorithm 7.9

The algorithm can, as indicated in Figure 7.21, be split into four parts. The first part generates subsets of variables for the conditional knowledge bases by calling every conditional, once, so this part needs $\mathcal{O}(|\Delta|)$ steps.

In the next part, the MCS is calculated for the graph. Here, every subset generated in the previous step is called, once, and every variable $V \in \Sigma$ is numbered, once. The time complexity of the actual enumeration of vertices then is in $\mathcal{O}(|\Delta| \cdot |\Sigma|)$ (see [TY84]). In the worst case, every variable has to be inspected for being numbered in every call to a subset because it is possible that the subsets share lots of variables. Therefore we obtain that this step needs no more than $\mathcal{O}(|\Delta| \cdot |\Sigma|)$ steps.

The cutgraph generation then traverses through the sets of variables and adds an edge for every pair of variables in the set, this step can be computed in $\mathcal{O}(|\Delta| \cdot |\mathcal{E}|)$ (see [HS09]). The hypertree generation part of the algorithm can again be split into two parts, the fill in and the hypertree generation.

For the fill-in, we call every vertex and add an edge to set of smaller neighbours for every connected vertex with smaller MCS-number. Here the set up of the sets of smaller neighbours needs, in the worst case, a call to every MCS-smaller vertex, thus $\mathcal{O}(2|\Sigma|)$ calls, and for each of these sets all pairs of elements have to be computed to fill in the cutgraph. This is bounded by $\mathcal{O}(|\Delta| \cdot |\Sigma|^2)$. The hypertree generation step detects all cliques in $\mathcal{H}_S$. The fill-in ensures that $\mathcal{H}_S$ is chordal (see [Pea88, Chapter 3.2]) and hence the clique problem can be solved in $\mathcal{O}(|\Delta| \cdot |\Sigma|)$ steps [HS09].

Overall, the generation of the hypergraph is bounded by the alphabet size, the number of conditionals in the knowledge base, and the number of literals used in the conditionals, that is, the graph generation has an asymptotic time complexity of $\mathcal{O}(|\Delta| \cdot |\Sigma|^2)$.

The algorithm traverses through the conditionals, the respective sets, and the variables in a linear fashion, thus every loop only calls each of the sets, once. In the fill-in step, the set of edges $\mathcal{E}$ is modified during the loop, but as only edges between variables with a lover MCS enumeration are added,

Listing 7.9: Generate a hypertree based on a conditional knowledge base [TY84, Pea88, Mey98, EKI14].

```
INPUT   : Conditional knowledge base \KBdef over alphabet Σ
OUTPUT  : Hypertree 𝓗 = ⟨Σ, {Σᵢ}ᵢ₌₁ᵐ ⊆ 𝔓(Σ)⟩

BEGIN
  // Initialisation
  MCS:=TABLE[V->INT]
  FOR-EACH(V ∈ Σ)
    MCS(V)=NULL;
  END FOR-EACH
  // Maximum Cardinality Search
  FOR-EACH((Bᵢ|Aᵢ) ∈ Δ)
    Σ'ᵢ:={V|V ⊨ AᵢBᵢ}
  END FOR-EACH
  SET c:=0
  WHILE(∃ V ∈ Σ : MCS(V)==NULL)
    Σ'ₖ:=unmarked set Σ'ᵢ with the most numbered variables,
                       select arbitrarily if this is not unique.
    MARK Σ'ₖ
    FOR-EACH(V ∈ Σ'ᵢ : MCS(V)==NULL)
      MCS(V):=c
      c++
    END FOR-EACH
  END WHILE
  // Generate Cutgraph
  FOR(i=1; i<=m; i++)
    FOR-EACH({V,V'} ⊆ Σᵢ)
      𝓔:=𝓔 ∪ {{V,V'}}
    END FOR-EACH
  END FOR
  // Connect smaller neighbours in the cutgraph
  FOR(i=1; i<=c; i++)
    FOR-EACH(V: MCS(V)=i)
      FOR-EACH(\{V;V'\}: {V} ∪ ⋃ⱼ = 0ⁱ⁻¹MCS(V'))
        𝓔:=𝓔 ∪ {{V,V'}}
      END FOR-EACH
    END FOR-EACH
  END FOR
  // Define cliques in cutgraph as edges of the hypertree
  FOR-EACH(CLIQUE V in (Σ,𝓔)){
    𝓗':=𝓗' ∪ V
  END FOR-EACH
  RETURN 𝓗 = ⟨Σ,𝓗'⟩
END
```

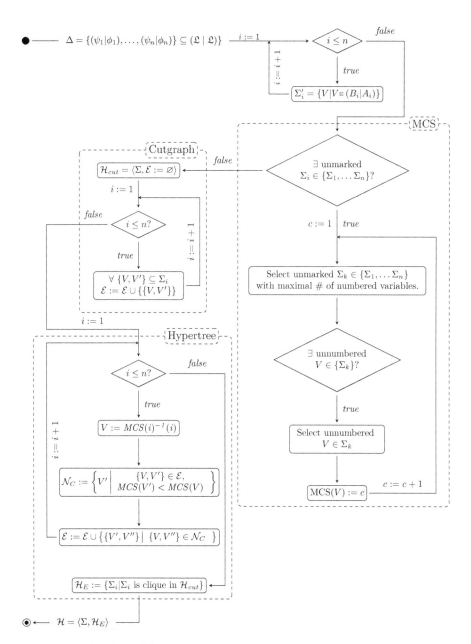

Figure 7.21: Flowchart of Algorithm 7.9

this does not change the edges relevant for the following steps regarding variables with higher MCS ranks. Therefore, the algorithm terminates. As for correctness, the MCS and cutgraph generation steps define the respective data structures they generate, thus they are inherently correct. The fill-in ensures that the resulting graph is chordal [TY84], and the hypergraph generated from the cliques of a chordal graph is a hypertree [Pea88], therefore, the algorithm correctly generates a hypertree from a conditional knowledge base; see [Pea88, Mey98] for a more thoroughly analysis of this graph generation.

We illustrate Algorithm 7.9 with the car start example.

Example 7.56. We use the car start example to illustrate this generation of hypertrees, so we have an alphabet of $\Sigma = \{H, B, F, S\}$ and use the knowledge base defined in Example 7.8 as input[5], that is,

$$\Delta = \left\{ \begin{array}{lllll} (s|b), & (\overline{s}|\overline{b}), & (s|f), & (\overline{s}|\overline{f}), & (\overline{s}|b\overline{f}), \\ (\overline{s}|\overline{b}f), & (\overline{h}|\top), & (f|\top), & (\overline{b}|h), & (b|\overline{h}) \end{array} \right\}. \tag{7.16}$$

The first step of the algorithms leads to the sets

$$\begin{array}{llll} \Sigma_1' = \{B, S\}, & \Sigma_2' = \{B, S\}, & \Sigma_3' = \{F, S\}, & \Sigma_4' = \{F, S\}, \\ \Sigma_5' = \{B, F, S\} & \Sigma_6' = \{B, F, S\}, & \Sigma_7' = \{H\}, & \Sigma_8' = \{F\}, \\ \Sigma_9' = \{H, B\}, & \Sigma_{10}' = \{H, B\}. \end{array}$$

The MCS part then enumerates the variables, for instance in this ordering:

1. All sets have the same number of numbered variables. We choose and mark Σ_7', and therefore set $MCS(H) := 1$.

2. The sets Σ_9' and Σ_{10}' both have the maximal count of numbered elements (one, namely the variable H), all other unmarked sets of none. We choose and mark Σ_7', and hence set $MCS(B) := 1$.

3. The set Σ_{10}' has the maximal count of numbered variables (two, H and B), so we have to select and mark Σ_{10}', there are no unnumbered variables, thus there is nothing else to do in this step.

---

[5]   Note that eve if we do not need to restrict the input to single-elementary knowledge bases we use the same knowledge base to be able to compare the inductive steps of OCF-networks and OCF-LEG networks, afterwards.

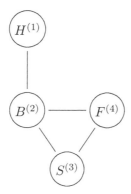

Figure 7.22: Cutgraph to Example 7.56 with the MCS-number of each variable is given
as superscript and cliques $\{H, B\}$ and $\{B, F, S\}$

4. The sets Σ_1', Σ_2', Σ_5', and Σ_6' both have one numbered element (B); we
   choose and mark Σ_1' and subsequently assign to S the MCS-number
   3.

   In the following, we must select Σ_2' with has no effect on the MCS-
   numbering, then are free to choose between Σ_5' and Σ_6', either choice
   leads to F being MCS-numbered to 4.

   After this step, we traverse through the other sets, but as all variables
   are numbered, the MCS stays unchanged.

Table2 7.11 illustrates these steps; we obtain the MCS given in the right-
most column (Step 7). In the next step of the algorithm, the cutgraph is
set up, with edges $\{B, S\}$ (as both variables are elements of Σ_1', Σ_2', Σ_5',
and Σ_6'), $\{F, S\}$ (as both variables are elements of Σ_3', Σ_4', Σ_5', and Σ_6')
and $\{H, B\}$ (from Σ_9' and Σ_{10}'), Figure 7.22 shows this graph. Table 7.12
shows the smaller neighbours of each vertex. The fill-in step is unnecessary,
because the only edge the algorithm would fill-in was $\{S, B\}$, but this edge
is already present. The cliques in the graph are $\{H, B\}$ and $\{B, F, S\}$, so
the resulting hypertree is $\langle \Sigma, \{\Sigma_1 = \{H, B\}, \Sigma_2 = \{B, F, S\}\rangle$ with $\mathbb{S}_1 = \varnothing$,
$\mathbb{R}_1 = \Sigma_1$, $\mathbb{S}_2 = \{B\}$, and $\mathbb{R}_2 = \{F, S\}$.

Now, as the the graph component of the OCF-LEG network is complete,
we turn towards generating the local OCF. We first set up local knowledge
bases Δ_i for each hyperedge Σ_i $1 \leq i \leq m$ of the hypertree. This is done by

Table 7.11: First seven steps of the MCS part of Algorithm 7.9, the actual selection is highlighted, sets with superscript • are marked as called

Set → # numbered	Step 1	Step 2	Step 3	Step 4	Step5	Step 6	Step 7
$\Sigma'_1 = \{B,S\}$	0	0	1	1	2•	2•	2•
$\Sigma'_2 = \{B,S\}$	0	0	1	1	2	2•	2•
$\Sigma'_3 = \{F,S\}$	0	0	0	0	1	1	2
$\Sigma'_4 = \{F,S\}$	0	0	1	1	1	1	2
$\Sigma'_5 = \{B,F,S\}$	0	0	1	1	2	2	3•
$\Sigma'_6 = \{B,F,S\}$	0	0	1	1	2	2	3
$\Sigma'_7 = \{H\}$	0	1•	1•	1•	1•	1•	1•
$\Sigma'_8 = \{F\}$	0	0	0	0	0	0	1
$\Sigma'_9 = \{H,B\}$	0	1	2•	2•	2•	2•	2•
$\Sigma'_{10} = \{H,B\}$	0	1	2	2•	2•	2•	2•

Variable → MCS-number	Step 1	Step 2	Step 3	Step 4	Step5	Step 6	Step 7
H	—	1	1	1	1	1	1
B	—	—	2	2	2	2	2
F	—	—	—	—	—	—	4
S	—	—	—	—	3	3	3

Table 7.12: Smaller neighbours in the graph of Figure 7.22

Variable	H	B	S	F
Smaller neighbours	$\varnothing$	$\{H\}$	$\{B\}$	$\{S, B\}$

Listing 7.10: Setting up local knowledge bases for a hypertree (confer [EKI14]).

```
INPUT   : Conditional knowledge base Δ = {(ψ₁|φ₁),...,(ψₙ|φₙ)} ⊆ (𝔏 | 𝔏)
          and Hypertree ℋ = ⟨Σ, {Σᵢ}ᵢ₌₁ᵐ ⊆ 𝔓(Σ)⟩
          generated by Algorithm 7.9
OUTPUT  : Local knowledge bases {Δⱼ}ⱼ₌₁ᵐ

BEGIN
   // Initialisation
   FOR-EACH(Σⱼ ∈ ℋ)
     Δⱼ:=∅
   END FOR-EACH

   // Distribution of variables
   FOR-EACH((ψᵢ|φᵢ) ∈ Δ)
     FOR-EACH(Σⱼ ∈ ℋ)
       IF({V|V∈ AᵢBᵢ} ⊆ Σᵢ)
         Δⱼ:=Δⱼ ∪ (ψᵢ|φᵢ)
       END IF
     END FOR-EACH
   END FOR-EACH
   RETURN {Δⱼ}ⱼ₌₁ᵐ
END
```

assigning a conditional of the global knowledge base to a local knowledge base if and only if all variables covered by the conditional are elements of the hyperedge. This means that the resulting set of local knowledge bases is no partitioning of the knowledge base, and some conditionals may be used in more than one local contexts. Algorithm 7.10 implements this distribution of conditionals and is illustrated in Figure 7.23.

Complexity and Correctness Results to Algorithm 7.10

The algorithms calls every conditional in Δ, once, and each hyperedge in $\mathcal{H}$ once per conditional, thus it has an asymptotic complexity of $\mathcal{O}(m \cdot |\Delta|)$ where m is the number of hyperedges of $\mathcal{H}$.

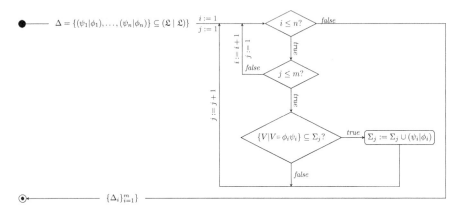

Figure 7.23: Illustration of Algorithm 7.10 to distribute the conditionals of a global knowledge base into local knowledge bases

As noted for complexity, the algorithm calls every conditional in Δ once, and each hyperedge in $\mathcal{H}$ not more than once per conditional, therefore the algorithm terminates. Each hyperedge either was generated from a conditional of Δ, or is a covering hyperedge of a hyperedge generated by a conditional of Δ. Thus for every conditional $(B_i|A_i) \in \Delta$ there is at least one hyperedge Σ_i such that $\{V|V \models A_i B_i\} \subseteq \Sigma_i$. For the same reasons, for every hyperedge Σ_j in the hypertree there is at least one conditional in $(B_i|A_i) \in \Delta$ such that $(B_i|A_i)$ is associated to Σ_i. Therefore, the algorithm assigns all conditionals of the global knowledge base to a local knowledge base, and there are no empty local knowledge bases.

The distribution of conditionals into more than one local knowledge base is demonstrated as follows.

Example 7.57. Let $\Delta = \{(A|\top), (B|A), (C|A)\}$ be a conditional knowledge base over an alphabet of $\Sigma = \{A, B, C\}$. For this knowledge base, Algorithm 7.3 generates the hypertree $\langle \Sigma, \{\Sigma_1 = \{A, B\}, \Sigma_2 = \{A, C\}\}\rangle$. The local knowledge base generation of Algorithm 7.10 then sets up the knowledge bases $\Delta_1 = \{(A|\top), (B|A)\}$, because $\{A\} \subseteq \Sigma_1$ and $\{A, B\} \subseteq \Sigma_1$, and $\Delta_1 = \{(A|\top), (C|A)\}$, because $\{A\} \subseteq \Sigma_2$ and $\{A, C\} \subseteq \Sigma_2$. So we see that (Δ_1, Δ_2) is no partitioning of Δ.

Table 7.13: Local OCF for the hypertree generated from the knowledge base of the car start example using System Z and c-representations for local worlds $\omega^{(1)} \in \Omega_1 = \Omega(\{H, B\})$ and $\omega^{(2)} \in \Omega_2 = \Omega(\{B, F, S\})$

$\omega^{(1)}$	$h\,b$	$h\,\overline{b}$	$\overline{h}\,b$	$\overline{h}\,\overline{b}$
$\kappa^Z_{\Delta_1}(\omega^{(1)})$	1	1	0	1
$\kappa^c_{\Delta_1}(\omega^{(1)})$	2	1	0	1

(a) $\Delta_1 = \{(\overline{h}|\top), (b|\overline{h}), (\overline{b}|h)\}$.

$\omega^{(2)}$	$b\,f\,s$	$b\,f\,\overline{s}$	$b\,\overline{f}\,s$	$b\,\overline{f}\,\overline{s}$	$\overline{b}\,f\,s$	$\overline{b}\,f\,\overline{s}$	$\overline{b}\,\overline{f}\,s$	$\overline{b}\,\overline{f}\,\overline{s}$
$\kappa^Z_{\Delta_2}(\omega^{(1)})$	0	1	2	2	2	1	2	2
$\kappa^c_{\Delta_2}(\omega^{(1)})$	0	1	1	1	2	1	2	1

(b) $\Delta_2 = \{(s|b), (\overline{s}|\overline{b}), (s|f), (\overline{s}|\overline{f}), (\overline{s}|b\overline{f}), (\overline{s}|\overline{b}f), (f|\top)$.

The local knowledge bases set up this way are then used with inductive approaches to generating ranking functions like System Z [Pea90] or c-representations [KI01] to obtain the OCF-component of the OCF-LEGs. We illustrate this by applying the methods recalled in Section 3.3.3.

Example 7.58. We continue Example 7.56 on this behalf, so we have the knowledge base (7.16) and the hypertree $\langle \Sigma, \{\Sigma_1 = \{H, B\}, \Sigma_2 = \{B, F, S\}\rangle$ with $\mathbb{S}_1 = \varnothing$, $\mathbb{R}_1 = \Sigma_1$, $\mathbb{S}_2 = \{B\}$, and $\mathbb{R}_2 = \{F, S\}$. Algorithm 7.10 splits Δ into the subsets

$$\Delta_1 = \{(\overline{h}|\top), (b|\overline{h}), (\overline{b}|h)\} \tag{7.17}$$

$$\Delta_2 = \{(s|b), (\overline{s}|\overline{b}), (s|f), (\overline{s}|\overline{f}), (\overline{s}|b\overline{f}), (\overline{s}|\overline{b}f), (b|\overline{h})\}. \tag{7.18}$$

On these we apply System Z and minimal c-representations to obtain the local OCF given in Table 7.13.

After having set up the local OCF, the next-to-last step is to check for the consistency condition (7.10) to hold, after which the generation of the OCF-LEG network is finished. As final step, the global OCF for the network can be calculated using 7.13.

So the complete generation of an OCF-network can be combined in a single algorithm given as Algorithm 7.11 which we illustrate in Figure 7.24.

Listing 7.11: Generate an OCF-LEG network from a conditional knowledge base Δ (confer [EKI14]).

```
INPUT   : Conditional knowledge base Δ = {(ψ₁|φ₁),...,(ψₙ|φₙ)} ⊆ (𝔏 | 𝔏)
OUTPUT  : OCF-LEG network ⟨(Σᵢ,κᵢ)⟩ᵢ₌₁ᵐ

BEGIN
  // Generate Hypergraph
  ℋ = ⟨Σ,{Σᵢ}ᵢ₌₁ᵐ:=ALGORITHM_7.9(Δ)

  // Split Δ into system of local knowledge bases
  {Δᵢ}ᵢ₌₁ᵐ:=ALGORITHM_7.10(Δ,ℋ)

  // Check local knowledge bases for consistency
  FOR(i=1;i<=m; i++)
    IF(ALGORITHM_2.1(Δ)==NULL)
      RETURN "Δ INCONSISTENT"
    END IF
  END FOR

  // Generate local OCF with inductive method from Section 3.3.3
  // referred to as IND(Δ)
  FOR(i=1;i<=m; i++)
    κᵢ:=IND(Δᵢ)
  END FOR

  // Check consistency condition (7.10)
  FOR(i=1;i<=m; i++)
    FOR(j=i;j<=m; j++)
      FOR-EACH(ω ∈ Ω(Σᵢ ∩ Σⱼ))
        IF(κᵢ(ω) ≠ κⱼ(ω))
          RETURN "CONSISTENCY CONDITION NOT MET"
        END IF
      END FOR-EACH
    END FOR
  END FOR

  // Checks passed,
  // the generated network of OCF-LEGs is an OCF-LEG network
  RETURN ⟨(Σᵢ,κᵢ)⟩ᵢ₌₁ᵐ
END
```

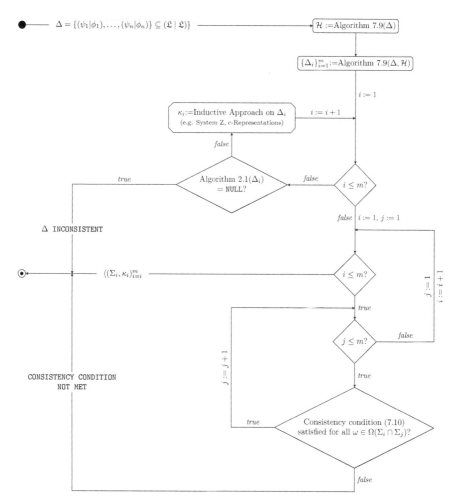

Figure 7.24: Illustration of Algorithm 7.11 to generate an OCF-LEG network from a conditional knowledge base Δ

Complexity and Correctness Results to Algorithm 7.11

The time complexity of Algorithm 7.11 is the sum of the time complexity of
the individual steps. Here, the summand with the largest impact is the step
of generating local OCF for the local knowledge bases, because the inductive
OCF-approaches are bounded polynomially in the cardinality of the knowledge base, and exponentially in the cardinality of the alphabet (see Section 3.3.3). We have shown that the time-complexity of the other steps are
bounded polynomially in the cardinality of the alphabet and the knowledge
base. So the worst case time complexity is $\mathcal{O}\left(\max\left\{2^{|\Sigma_i|} \mid 1 \leq i \leq n\right\}\right)$, and
the algorithm is bounded exponentially in the number of the vertices in
the cardinality maximal hyperedge. This gives us a worst-case time com-
plexity of $\mathcal{O}(2^{|\Sigma|})$ for the case where all variables are contained in only one
hyperedge of the tree.

As for OCF-networks, the space complexity for storing an OCF-LEG
network is the sum of the space needed for each local ranking representa-
tion. For OCF-LEG networks, this is in $\mathcal{O}\left(\max\left\{2^{|\Sigma_i|} \mid 1 \leq i \leq n\right\}\right)$ with a
worst-case space complexity of $\mathcal{O}(2^{|\Sigma|})$ for the case where all variables are
contained in only one hyperedge of the tree.

We have discussed that for every step of the algorithm to terminate, as
these steps are executed in a linear fashion, the complete algorithm terminates. Each step of the algorithm is correct in itself: We recalled that the hypertree generation indeed generate hypertrees (confer [TY84, Pea88, Mey98]
for a formal proof thereof) and discussed that the generation of local knowledge base splits the global knowledge base as designated. Furthermore
given that the knowledge bases are consistent the inductive approaches yield
OCF for the local knowledge bases. So as long as the local knowledge bases
are consistent, which is the case if and only if the global knowledge base is
consistent; the algorithm returns an OCF-LEG network of the knowledge
base given the consistency condition (7.10) is met, and an error, otherwise.
So the algorithm may fail to generate an OCF-LEG network. If it does not,
the OCF-LEG network is correct in that its global OCF accepts all conditionals in Δ, as direct result of the local/global coincidence (7.9) of the
OCF-LEG network, and the properties of the inductive ranking approaches.
We combine the these results regarding the correctness of Algorithm 7.11
formally as follows.

Corollary 7.59 (Inductive OCF-LEG Network Generation [EKI14, Theorem
2]). Let $\Delta = \{(\psi_1|\phi_1), \ldots, (\psi_n|\phi_n)\} \subseteq (\mathfrak{L} \mid \mathfrak{L})$ be a consistent conditional

Table 7.14: Calculating a global OCF κ' for System Z in Example 7.14

ω	$hbfs$	$hbf\overline{s}$	$hb\overline{f}s$	$hb\overline{f}\,\overline{s}$	$h\overline{b}fs$	$h\overline{b}f\overline{s}$	$h\overline{b}\,\overline{f}s$	$h\overline{b}\,\overline{f}\,\overline{s}$
$\kappa^Z_{\Delta_1}(\Sigma_1(\omega))$	1	1	1	1	1	1	1	1
$+\,\kappa^Z_{\Delta_2}(\Sigma_2(\omega))$	0	1	2	2	2	1	2	2
$-\,\kappa^Z_{\Delta_2}(\mathbb{S}_2(\omega))$	0	0	0	0	1	1	1	1
$=\quad \kappa'(\omega)$	1	2	3	3	3	2	2	2

ω	$\overline{h}bfs$	$\overline{h}bf\overline{s}$	$\overline{h}b\overline{f}s$	$\overline{h}b\overline{f}\,\overline{s}$	$\overline{h}\,\overline{b}fs$	$\overline{h}\,\overline{b}f\overline{s}$	$\overline{h}\,\overline{b}\,\overline{f}s$	$\overline{h}\,\overline{b}\,\overline{f}\,\overline{s}$
$\kappa^Z_{\Delta_1}(\Sigma_1(\omega))$	0	0	0	0	1	1	1	1
$+\,\kappa^Z_{\Delta_2}(\Sigma_2(\omega))$	0	1	2	2	2	1	2	2
$-\,\kappa^Z_{\Delta_1}(\mathbb{S}_2(\omega))$	0	0	0	0	1	1	1	1
$=\quad \kappa'(\omega)$	0	1	2	1	2	1	2	1

knowledge base. Let $\Delta_1,\ldots,\Delta_m$ be a covering system of subsets of Δ obtained by Algorithm 7.9 on a hypertree $\langle \Sigma, \{\mathbb{C}_1,\ldots,\mathbb{C}_m\}\rangle$. Let $\kappa_1,\ldots,\kappa_m$ be ranking functions $\kappa_i \models \Delta_i$ resulting from an inductive reasoning approach on Δ_i for all $1 \leq i \leq m$ that satisfy the consistency condition (7.10). Let κ be the global ranking function obtained by Equation (7.13) on the system $\langle(\Sigma_i,\kappa_i)\rangle_{i=1}^{m}$. Then the global ranking function is admissible with respect to Δ, that is, $\kappa \models \Delta$.

Example 7.60. We continue Example 7.58 to illustrate the whole Algorithm 7.11. For the approach of c-representations, Example 7.53 already shows the this approach satisfies the consistency condition (7.10) and sums up the local OCF-values to obtain a global OCF. For System Z, the ranking values in 7.58 satisfy the consistency condition (7.10), as $\kappa^Z_{\Delta_1}(\dot{b}) = \kappa^Z_{\Delta_2}(\dot{b})$ for $\dot{b} \in \{b,\overline{b}\}$. We sum up the local values to obtain a global OCF for the OCF-LEG network in Table 7.14.

We discussed that different inductive approaches to generating OCF can be used to set up the local OCF. However, the resulting global OCF is not necessarily of the type of the ones generated by the inductive approaches. For instance, System Z uses the most exceptional rule falsified by the world to determine the rank of a world. Thus conditionals in a knowledge base that cover disjoint variable sets will never have a mutual impact on the exceptionality of each other. In the network approach, falsifying both con-

Table 7.15: Comparison of the global OCF obtained by the OCF-LEG approach using System Z ($\kappa_{\mathcal{H}}^Z$) and the OCF obtained by System Z on the global knowledge base (κ_{Δ}^Z). Worlds where the global System Z rank and the global rank of the network differ are highlighted.

ω	$h\,b\,f\,s$	$h\,b\,f\,\overline{s}$	$h\,b\,\overline{f}\,s$	$h\,b\,\overline{f}\,\overline{s}$	$h\,\overline{b}\,f\,s$	$h\,\overline{b}\,f\,\overline{s}$	$h\,\overline{b}\,\overline{f}\,s$	$h\,\overline{b}\,\overline{f}\,\overline{s}$
$\kappa_{\mathcal{H}}^Z$	1	2	3	3	3	2	2	2
κ_{Δ}^Z	2	2	2	2	2	1	2	1
ω	$\overline{h}\,b\,f\,s$	$\overline{h}\,b\,f\,\overline{s}$	$\overline{h}\,b\,\overline{f}\,s$	$\overline{h}\,b\,\overline{f}\,\overline{s}$	$\overline{h}\,\overline{b}\,f\,s$	$\overline{h}\,\overline{b}\,f\,\overline{s}$	$\overline{h}\,\overline{b}\,\overline{f}\,s$	$\overline{h}\,\overline{b}\,\overline{f}\,\overline{s}$
$\kappa_{\mathcal{H}}^Z$	0	1	2	1	2	1	2	1
κ_{Δ}^Z	0	1	2	1	2	1	2	1

ditionals of such a pair will result in a positive rank in the local event group, which is an addend in the calculation of the global rank of a world. Thus, falsifying two conditionals that might be ranked with identical exceptionality might result in both having an impact on the rank of a world, other than intended by the approach. This results in the following observation:

Observation 7.61. Using the approach of System Z for generating local OCF in OCF-LEG networks will, in general, result in a global function that is no System Z representation of Δ.

Example 7.62. We illustrate Observation 7.61 by comparing the the ranking values calculated in Example 7.60 with the ranks generated on the global knowledge base Δ using System Z in Table 7.15 and highlighted the worlds where the global System Z rank and the global rank of the network differ.

Other than that, using c-representations the rank of a world is calculated by a sum. Therefore it is possible that the global OCF is a c-representation of an OCF-LEG network is the OCF yield by a c-representation of the global knowledge base, but only if the conditionals are distributed to the local knowledge bases such that the combined solutions of the local systems of inequalities constitute a solution to the system of inequalities for the global knowledge base. Formalising and elaborating on this idea is, however, left for future research,

7.3.3 Further Reflections on the Consistency Condition

We have shown that the consistency condition (7.10) is sufficient for a hypertree of OCF-LEGs to be an OCF-LEG network. In this section we show that using c-representations for generating local OCF in the inductive approach can, under certain preconditions, ensure that this condition is met. This is done by adjusting the impacts of the local c-representations such that the ranking value coincides.

We realise that the consistency condition is a trivially satisfied for hyperedges with an empty intersection: As $\kappa(\varnothing) = \kappa(\top) = 0$, for all pairs Σ_i, Σ_j with $1 \leq i, j \leq m$ of a system of OCF-LEGs $\langle(\Sigma_i, \kappa_i)_{i=1}^m\rangle$ with $\Sigma_i \cap \Sigma_j = \varnothing$, the ranking values are $\kappa_i(\Sigma_i \cap \Sigma_j) = \kappa_j(\Sigma_i \cap \Sigma_j) = 0$ for all outcomes of the variables $\Sigma_i \cap \Sigma_j$. This means we have to concentrate our on hyperedges with a nonempty intersections, only. But if two hyperedges have a nonempty intersection, then the variables are in the separator between the hyperedges, therefore in the following we only discuss how it is possible to ensure the consistency condition (7.10) on separators.

A ranking value of a (local) world is 0 if and only if it does not falsify any conditionals in the (local) knowledge base. If for a separator $\mathbb{S}_j$ between Σ_j and Σ_i, without loss of generality, $2 \leq j \leq n, j < i$ a configuration $\mathbf{s} \in \Omega(\Sigma_i)$ has a ranking value $\kappa_i = 0$ and $\kappa_j > 0$, then $\mathbf{s}$ falsifies conditionals in Δ_j but none in Δ_i. In this case, the consistency condition cannot be met, because it is impossible to raise the ranking value of $\kappa_i(\mathbf{s})$ by adjusting the local impacts, because the impacts are not applicable to $\mathbf{s}$ by means of (3.29), which we formalise in the following observation:

Observation 7.63. Let $\Delta = \{(\psi_1|\phi_1), \ldots, (\psi_n|\phi_n)\}$ be a knowledge base with a system of OCF-LEGs $\langle(\Sigma_i, \kappa_i)_{i=1}^m\rangle$ obtained by Algorithm 7.11. If for any separator $\mathbb{S}_j$ between hyperedges Σ_i and Σ_j there is an outcome $\mathbf{s} \in \Omega(\mathbb{S}_j)$ such that $\kappa_i(\mathbf{s}) = 0$ and $\kappa_j(\mathbf{s}) > 0$, or $\kappa_i(\mathbf{s}) > 0$ and $\kappa_j(\mathbf{s}) > 0$, then $\langle(\Sigma_i, \kappa_i)_{i=1}^m\rangle$ is no OCF-LEG network.

We give an example for this observation:

Example 7.64. Let $\{(c|b), (\bar{c}|a), (b|a), (c|a)\}$ be a knowledge base. Invoking the algorithms of the OCF-LEG approach on this knowledge base yields the OCF-LEG network

$$(\{A, B, C, D\}, \langle(\{A, B, C\}, \kappa_1), (\{A, D\}, \kappa_2)\rangle)$$

Figure 7.25: Hypergraph of Example 7.64

Table 7.16: Ranking functions of Example 7.64

ω^1	abc	$ab\bar{c}$	$a\bar{b}c$	$a\bar{b}\bar{c}$	$\bar{a}bc$	$\bar{a}b\bar{c}$	$\bar{a}\bar{b}c$	$\bar{a}\bar{b}\bar{c}$
$\kappa_1(\omega^{(1)})$	2	1	4	2	0	1	0	0

(a) κ_1.

$\omega^{(2)}$	ac	$a\bar{c}$	$\bar{a}c$	$\bar{a}\bar{c}$
$\kappa_2(\omega^{(2)})$	0	1	0	0

(b) κ_2.

with a hypergraph given in Figure 7.25 and local OCF given in Tables 7.16. Here, the consistency condition is violated, because $\kappa_1(a) = 1 \neq 0 = \kappa_2(a)$ and hence there is no global OCF for this network of OCF-LEGs.

So the failure of the consistency condition (7.10) cannot be overcome if for some separators outcomes are, in one adjacent local OCF, maximally plausible, and implausible to any degree in others. In the following, we turn our focus towards cases where the outcomes of the variables in the separators outcomes are implausible to different degrees.

Proposition 7.65. Let $\mathbb{C}_i, \mathbb{C}_j$ be to subsets over an alphabet Σ, $\mathbb{C}_i \subseteq \Sigma$ with c-representations κ_i according to Definition 3.33 and separators $\mathbb{S}_j = \mathbb{C}_i \cap \mathbb{C}_j$. Let $\kappa_i(\mathbf{s}) > 0$ if and only if $\kappa_j > 0$ for all configurations of $\mathbf{s}$. Then there are local c-representations that satisfy the consistency condition.

We illustrate this approach of "repairing" a failure in the consistency condition (7.10) with the following example.

Example 7.66. Let $\Delta = \{\delta_1 : (a|\top), \delta_2 : (c|\top), \delta_3 : (b|a), \delta_4 : (b|c)\}$. Algorithm 7.9 gives us the graph shown in Figure 7.26, and the knowledge bases are split up into $\Delta_1 = \{\delta_1, \delta_3\}$, $\Delta_1 = \{\delta_2, \delta_4\}$. The approach of

Figure 7.26: Hypergraph for $\Delta = \{\delta_1 \; : \; (a|\top), \delta_2 \; : \; (c|\top), \delta_3 \; : \; (b|a), \delta_4 \; : \; (b|c)\}$ in Example 7.66

Table 7.17: Local ranking tables obtained by c-representations for Example 7.66

$\omega^{(1)}$	$a\,b$	$a\,\overline{b}$	$\overline{a}\,b$	$\overline{a}\,\overline{b}$
$\kappa_1^c(\omega^{(1)})$	0	1	1	1

(a) κ_1^c

$\omega^{(1)}$	$b\,c$	$b\,\overline{c}$	$\overline{b}\,c$	$\overline{b}\,\overline{c}$
$\kappa_1^c(\omega^{(1)})$	0	2	2	2

(b) κ_2^c

$\omega^{(1)}$	$a\,b$	$a\,\overline{b}$	$\overline{a}\,b$	$\overline{a}\,\overline{b}$
$\kappa_1^{c\prime}(\omega^{(1)})$	0	2	2	2

(c) $\kappa_1^{c\prime}$

c-representations yields

$$\kappa_1^- > 0 \qquad\qquad \kappa_3^- > 0$$

for the first, and

$$\kappa_2^- > 0 \qquad\qquad \kappa_4^- > 0$$

for the second system of inequalities. The values

$$\kappa_1^- = 1 \qquad\qquad \kappa_3^- = 1$$
$$\kappa_2^- = 2 \qquad\qquad \kappa_4^- = 2$$

are a valid solution for these system and result in the ranking functions shown in Tables 7.18a and 7.18b. These local OCF violate the consistency condition (7.10) as $\kappa_1^c(\overline{b}) = 1 \neq 2 = \kappa_c^2(\overline{b})$. But by adjusting the impacts in the first c-representations to 2, each, we obtain the ranking function shown in Table 7.18c, and here $\kappa_1^{c\prime}(\dot{b}) = 2 = \kappa_c^2(\dot{b})$ for all outcomes $\dot{b}$ of B, so $\langle\{\Delta_1, \Delta_2\}, \{\kappa_1^{c\prime}, \kappa_2^c\}\rangle$ is an OCF-LEG network.

So there are knowledge bases where a failure of the consistency condition (7.10) can be overcome. Therefore for these knowledge bases an OCF-LEG network can be constructed, even if it violated this condition after the application of Algorithm 7.11 in the first place.

In Section 7.1.3 we proposed an approach to safely use OCF-networks inductively without the risk for the global OCF not being applicable to the original knowledge base. This involved setting up the global OCF inductively by techniques discussed in Section 3.3.3 and exploiting the local/global coincidence to set the local values. The same method can be used for OCF-LEG networks: We can generate the hypertree component of the OCF-LEG network using Algorithm 7.9, generate the global OCF with inductive approaches to OCF (Section 3.3.3), and set the local OCF to the hyperedges as marginals of the global OCF according to Definition 7.48. This will safely result in a correct OCF-LEG network which benefits from the spatial merits of the network, but not from the benefits with respect to time complexity.

7.3.4 Discussion and Comparison to OCF-Networks

OCF-networks split the variable set into vertices with a single variable, each, resulting in small local sets of a variable and its parents, only. In OCF-LEG networks, the local sets of variables are larger, as here sets of variables are joined to form hyperedges. Therefore the number of local contexts is larger in the OCF-network approach and lower in the OCF-LEG network approach – directly comparing the car start example gives us four local OCF-tables in the OCF-network approach, and two local OCF in the OCF-LEG approach. But this does not necessarily result in larger space complexity, as the interconnectivity of the networks is an additional factor in the space complexity. This can, for instance, be observed with the different representations of the car start example. The OCF-network in Example 7.5 with three edges needs to store sixteen local worlds, coincidently the same number as are needed to store the global OCF for this example, while the OCF-LEG network representation, as illustrated in Example 7.49, needs to store only twelve ranking values, and thus only 75 % of the ones needed for the OCF-network.

While OCF-networks store tables of conditional ranking values, the OCF-LEG networks store local ranking functions. This effects the effort of calculating either the local from the global, or the global from the local values: To set up the local tables in an OCF-network from a global OCF κ, for each entry in each local table and for each $V \in \Sigma$, the ranks $\kappa(\{V\} \cup pa(V))$

and $\kappa(pa(V))$ have to be calculated. In contrast, given an OCF-network the global function can be calculated by a mere summation of the local values (see Proposition 7.3). The complexity of these steps are somehow reversed for OCF-LEG networks: The local OCF are marginals of the global κ (see Definition 7.48) and can thus be read from this function directly. For the calculation of the global κ from the local values the ranks of the separators must be calculated, too (see (7.14)).

For calculating ranks and inferences in local contexts, there is no clear "better" approach, either: In OCF-networks, the local contexts are smaller, consisting only of a variable in the given its parents, or sets of conditionally independent variables with respect to the Markov property (see Theorem 7.6). On the one hand, this reduces the set of variables that have to be considered when applying semantical methods, significantly, and as semantical methods have an exponential time complexity dependent on the cardinality of the variable set, thus the computation of these methods is way faster than for larger sets. On the other hand, local calculations may not be possible because the variables of interest may not be in the same context, and then the global OCF has to be consulted for the calculation: In the car start example, for instance, we need to consult the global OCF to make statements about the fuel tank and the battery. Comparing this with OCF-LEG networks, we obtain that the contexts are larger, thus the efficiency of the local computations is lower compared to OCF-networks. However, variables that are connected by appearing in conditionals together are also connected in the network, thus the wider context. In the car start example, for instance, this leads to the possibility to reason locally over the battery and the fuel tank.

When it comes to inductive methods, OCF-LEG networks outperform OCF-networks. As discussed for Algorithm 7.4, the inductive generation of OCF-networks is not guaranteed to be correct and this failure cannot be overcome easily. For inductive generation of OCF-LEG networks, the consistency condition (7.10) must be satisfied. This condition seems to be more benign than the acceptance of the local knowledge bases by the λ-function, and, as we discussed in Section 7.3.3, that violation of the consistency condition (7.10) may be overcome by adjusting the impacts of the conditionals in the local c-representations. A major difference is the input of both approaches of inductive generation: While OCF-network can only be set up from single-elementary conditionals, which is a major restriction on the language of the background knowledge, OCF-LEG networks accept any conditional knowledge base, making it the more versatile approach.

Overall the vote of this discussion goes towards OCF-LEG networks, because they provide a good trade off between reduction of complexity on the one, and stability in the application on the other hand.

7.3.5 Interim Summary

After encountering the problem of OCF-networks failing to ensure that the generated OCF is a model of the initial knowledge base, in this section we turn towards local event groups to represent local contexts. This is originally a tool for in generating the graphical structure for calculating the MaxEnt probability distribution over a set of variables (see, for instance, [Mey98]). Recalling OCF-LEG networks, we followed [EKI14] and canonically translated the generation of the global probability distribution into a method for calculating the global OCF, and that this stratification yields correct results, which was done for Theorem 7.52. We recalled that the consistency condition (7.10) is a sufficient and necessary condition for a system of OCF-LEGs to be an OCF-LEG network, given the underlying hypergraph is a hypertree For establishing the possibility of local computations, we recalled an independence property between adjacent hyperedges.

As the graph generation in both the MaxEnt and the ranking approach deal with conditionals which then define the hypergraph, we adopted the hypertree generation in an unchanged way. We then devised the distribution of the conditionals into local knowledge bases to ensure that every conditional is put into the hypertree that covers its variables completely. However, the consistency condition (7.10) of OCF-LEG networks may fail and it may not be possible to overcome this failure by adjusting the local ranks.

This chapter is based on the article [EKI14]. My contribution to this article has been to elaborate on the idea of using LEG-networks to overcome the problems found in OCF-networks, as showing (following the proofs of [LB82, Mey98] for probabilistic environments) that the consistency condition is necessary but not sufficient for a system of OCF-LEGs being an OCF-LEG network, and the distribution of the global knowledge base into local knowledge bases. Proving that the consistency condition (7.9) is sufficient given the underlying hypergraph is a hypertree ([EKI14, Theorem 1]) was the joint work of Gabriele Kern-Isberner and me.

This thesis recalls and extends the description of the inductive approach towards OCF-LEG networks to such an extend that it canonises, further formalises and illustrates algorithms that result from the method described in [EKI14], as well as discusses time and space complexity and correctness of the algorithms. In [EKI14], this technique was only demonstrated for c-representations as generator for the local OCF. We here extended the cited literature by demonstrating that also System Z can be used for these steps. We observed that the global OCF of an OCF-LEG network is, in general, no System Z representation of the global knowledge base, and that this is a structural contradiction of representations raised by the different combination operations (maximum for System Z, and sum for OCF-LEG networks).

The time complexity result to Algorithm 7.11 gives us an overall time complexity of $\mathcal{O}\left(\max\left\{2^{|\Sigma_i|} \mid 1 \leq i \leq n\right\}\right)$ which, if $\max\{|\Sigma_i| \mid 1 \leq i \leq n\}$ is smaller than $|\Sigma|$ results in a significant improvement in comparison to applying the inductive OCF methods to knowledge bases. All other steps of the algorithm are of polynomial time complexity. Therefore the overhead generated by the approach is manageable. So even for a degenerate hypertree with only one hyperedge containing all variables the additional complexity for setting up the OCF is drowned by the exponential time complexity for setting up the ranking function from the conditionals by means of Section 3.3.3. Furthermore, we have seen in the car start example that even for knowledge bases with redundant conditionals and thus highly interconnected variables, the variables are decomposed in more than one hyperedge. We assume the decomposition to be even more effective for more realistic examples.

The approach proposed in [EKI14] can fail because of the consistency condition (7.10), this is already stated in the paper, but no means of overcoming this failure is given. The results of Section 7.3.3 extend the literature on this behalf, but are only are first steps on work on this open end, whilst a more thorough examination of structural properties of the original or the local knowledge bases are necessary to decide on the knowledge bases directly, whether the LEG-approach can be applied successfully. We also sketched an approach to generating OCF-LEG networks safely without the risk for this failure that benefits from the network approach with respect to storing information, but not with respect to the computation time needed to set up the OCF. This thesis also extends the cited literature with a discussion about the relationship between OCF-networks and OCF-LEG networks as well as unifying presentation of algorithms and discussion of the correctness and complexity of these algorithms.

7.4 Interim Summary of the Chapter

In this chapter we recalled two different network approaches to OCF and compared them to established approaches to representing probabilities (that is, Bayesian networks and LEG networks) and preference (that is, ceteris paribus networks). With these techniques we demonstrated that even if conditional independence for OCF is not axiomatised by the same strong properties as conditional independence in probabilistics, the properties of the networks with respect to independence, (de-)composition and coincidence with the global function are equally strong as the respective ones for probabilities. We also recalled that OCF-networks are strictly stronger than ceteris paribus networks. As signalised in the introduction of this section, we discussed the individual benefits and problems of the techniques in the respective local context, that is, in the sections this discussion is concerned with. The same has been done for the contributions of this thesis to the field.

Summarising these findings we obtain that network approaches to OCF are beneficial when it comes to storing OCF, but when it comes to inductively generating OCF and networks, only the technique of OCF-LEG is a potential candidate.

Following the idea of this chapter, that information is used most efficiently when kept in its proper context, my contributions to the articles [KIE13a, KIE13b, EKI15b] are mentioned in the summary of Section 7.1, my contributions to the article [EFKI16] is mentioned in the summary of Section 7.2, and my contributions to the article [EKI14] is mentioned in the summary of Section 7.3.

8 Formal Inferences and Commonsense Reasoning: Connections to Psychology and Cognition

Humans reasoning about a single rule, presented with an additional fact and sometimes additional background information, are an objects of investigation in the disciplines of psychology and cognition, especially since the studies [Was68, Byr89]. In these studies, usually a rule δ in the form "if A then B" is presented to the participants, together with a fact related to the premise or conclusion, that is, either A, $\neg A$, B, or $\neg B$[1]. Given the general rule and A or $\neg A$, the participants are asked whether B holds, or not; given the general rule and B or $\neg B$, the participants are asked whether A holds, or not. In addition to this, additional facts or a whole cover story is presented. The answers of the participants can the be formalised to be the result of them having applied the classically valid inference rules Modus Ponens (MP) (answering B given δ and A) or Modus Tollens (MT) (answering $\neg A$ given δ and $\neg B$), or the classically invalid inference rules Affirmation of the Consequent (AC) (answering A given δ and B) or Denial of the Antecedent (DA) (answering $\neg B$ given δ and $\neg A$). A familiar example for these studies is the Suppression Task:

Example 8.1 (Suppression Task). In [Byr89], the participants were given the rule "If Lisa has an essay to write, she will (usually) study late in the library". This general rule was accompanied with one of the facts "Lisa has an essay to write" (a), "Lisa does not have an essay to write" (b), "Lisa studies late in the library" (c), or "Lisa does not study late in the library" (d). The participants where then asked about the outcome of the variable not given in the fact: In the cases where (a) or (b) were given, they were asked whether "Lisa studies late in the library", and in the cases where (c) or (d) were given, they were asked whether "Lisa has an essay to write". In this experiment, the variation between the tested groups was additional information, which was either (α) no additional information, (β) the rule "Is Lisa has a textbook to read, she will study late in the library", or (γ) "If the library is open, Lisa will study late in the library". The inference rules applied to this scenario yield the following answers:

---

[1] Note that these experiments in their tasks usually use literals respectively propositional atoms rather than complex formulas. For this reason, in this chapter we deliberately use the symbols for variables A, B, ..., rather than symbols for formulas ϕ, ψ, ..., to indicate that the formalisations range over atomic rather than more complex formulas.

© Springer-Verlag Gmbh Germany, part of Springer Nature 2018
C. Eichhorn, *Rational Reasoning with Finite Conditional Knowledge Bases*, https://doi.org/10.1007/978-3-476-04824-0_8

- "Lisa will study late in the library." (a, MP)

- "Lisa has no essay to write." (d, MT)

- "Lisa has an essay to write." (c, AC)

- "Lisa will not study late in the library." (b, DA)

We formalise the different statements with E indicating whether Lisa has an essay to write (e) or not ($\bar{e}$), T indicating whether Lisa has a textbook to read (t) or not ($\bar{t}$), O indicating whether the library is open (o) or not ($\bar{o}$), and L indicating whether Lisa studies late in the library (l) or not ($\bar{l}$).

In this chapter we approach these studies and their result by formalising human inference in the suppression task with different approaches to and systematic variation of the represented information (Section 8.1), recalling, summarising and extending the articles [REKI16, REB$^+$17, ERKI18]. In this, we examine which, and to what extend, successful approaches to formal nonmonotonic reasoning are capable of modelling the common sense of human reasoners. This section turns over the classical perception of formalisms being the normative standard for human reasoners to be measured with, using human reasoners as norm for the formalisms to be classified. In Section 8.2 we recall the notion of *inference patterns* [ERKI18] and how they can be used to classify experimental studies, show how these patterns give rise to a measure of nonmonotonic rationality and finally use the patterns to reverse engineer hypotheses for the background knowledge of the participants of the studies.

8.1 Simulating Human Inference in the Suppression Task

One goal of knowledge representation and reasoning, and in particular non-monotonic inference, is to define inference processes and formalisms that, given identical information, come to the same conclusions as human reasoners. To examine whether this goal is reached, we use the human reasoner as normative model for the formalisms. We concentrate on the Suppression Task, which kindled research about nonmonotonic reasoning in the are of cognition. In this case using the human reasoner as normative model means that we inspect whether established approaches of nonmonotonic inference mimic the inferences drawn (or not drawn) by the participants in the Suppression Task.

8.1.1 Modelling the Suppression Task

In this section we follow [REKI16] and concentrate on the experiments focussing on the participants applying or not applying Modus Ponens (MP), that is, the information given to the participants is a conditional sentence, the premise of the conditional as fact and, as variation, none (α) or one additional conditional sentence (β) or (γ). In the seminal study [Byr89], and others to follow (for instance [TB02]), it became obvious that human reasoners do not apply classical, monotone logic, because in this case there should have not been a difference between the cases (α), (β), and (γ). However, the results differ: In setup (α) and (β) most of the the participants apply MP, whereas most of the participants do not apply MP in setup (γ). To explain this result, [Byr89] argued that the conditional (γ) *suppresses* the valid inference, hence the appellation *Suppression Task*.

We systematically vary the Suppression Task (a, γ) in that we use the original conditional statement (γ), reverting the relationship between premise and conclusion, that is, the inverse of the conditional statement (γ'), and a variant where we negate both premise and conclusion (γ''). Note that in an understanding of conditional statements as material implication, (γ'') is equivalent to (γ'), whilst in an understanding of conditional statements as conditionals, the falsification sets of (γ') and (γ'') are identical, that is, both conditionals are falsified by the same worlds. This means that both conditionals are indistinguishable for semantics based on falsification of conditionals as, for instance, System Z and c-representations.

Example 8.2. In the Suppression Task, this variation leads to the following conditional statements:

(γ) "If the library is open, Lisa will study late in the library."
(γ') "If Lisa studies late in the library, the library is open."
(γ'') "If the library is not open, Lisa will not study late in the library."

Logic Programs

We start our examinations with logic programming approaches. Here, conditional statements "if A then B" are interpreted as "licenses for implications" [SvL08, HKR09, DHR13] and thus encoded as logical rule with an additional conjunct $\overline{ab}$ in the premise, $B \leftarrow A \wedge \overline{ab}$, indicating that A licenses for B given that nothing *ab*normal is happening. Applying weak-completion semantics [HKR09], that is:

1. Replacing all clauses sharing the same head by a disjunction of the body elements ($A \leftarrow B_1, \ldots, A \leftarrow B_n$ by $A \leftarrow B_1 \vee \ldots \vee B_n$).

2. Replacing all occurrences of $\leftarrow$ with the coimplication $\Leftrightarrow$.

we obtain the trivalent Łukasiewicz logic [Łuk20]. With its model intersection property [HKR09], that is, the property that the intersection of two models is a model itself, this property guarantees the existence of least models.

We model the Suppression Task in logic programs following [SvL08, DHR13] and compare the results with the results of the study in [Byr89].

Example 8.3 (confer [REKI16]). We follow the modelling of [SvL08, HKR09, DHR13] to apply logic programming to the suppression task. The conditional statements are modelled as follows:

(α)   "If Lisa has an essay to write, she will study late in the library." $l \leftarrow e \wedge \overline{ab_1}$

(β)   "If Lisa has textbook to read, she will study late in the library." $l \leftarrow t \wedge \overline{ab_2}$

(γ)   "If the library is open, Lisa will study late in the library." $l \leftarrow o \wedge \overline{ab_3}$

(γ')   "If Lisa studies late in the library, the library is open." $o \leftarrow l \wedge \overline{ab_4}$

(γ'')   "If the library is not open, Lisa will not study late in the library." $\overline{l} \leftarrow \overline{o} \wedge \overline{ab_5}$

Again following the already cited literature, the abnormalities are defined as follows: In the (α) and (β) case, no abnormal situation is mentioned, therefore in these cases we model

$$ab_1 \leftarrow \bot$$
$$ab_2 \leftarrow \bot.$$

In the (γ) case, the library not being open is an abnormality both for being in the library and having an essay to write, and not having an essay to write is an abnormality for being in the library and the library being open. Finally, having an essay to write is modelled to be an exception for not being in the library if the library is not open, that is we model

$$ab_1 \leftarrow \overline{o}$$
$$ab_3 \leftarrow \overline{e}$$
$$ab_4 \leftarrow \overline{e}.$$

For all cases, we add the fact the Lisa has an essay to write, that is, the license

$$e \leftarrow \top.$$

This leads to a modelling for the given tasks (α), (β), (γ) and (γ') as given in Table 8.1 (upper row). Application of weak completion semantics (middle row) leads to the least models given in the same table (bottom row). Note that, as argued above, (γ'') is equivalent to (γ) under weak completion semantics.

We obtain that for this example, the logic programs yield the same inferences as the majority of the human reasoners, that is, in the (α) and (β) case, we can infer l, whereas this is suppressed in the (γ) case. Also in our variations (γ') and (γ''), l cannot be derived.

This example (and additional work done in this area by, for instance, [SvL08, HKR09, DHR13]) acts as a proof of concept that logic programs can be used to model the results of the human reasoners in experiments. However, as we see in the (γ) modelling, it is necessary to include the suppression directly in the program. Then the weak completion step of replacing all $\leftarrow$ with $\Leftrightarrow$, the weakly completed program licenses for substitution such that we, for instance, get $l \Leftrightarrow (e\overline{o})$.

Reiter Default Logic

Logic programming models the conditional assertions as licenses for implications with the technique of rules with explicitly stated exceptions. With Reiter Default Logic [Rei80], we follow keep this general route and formalise the conditional assertions as default rules with justifications which are accepted if their inverse cannot be proven to hold.

Table 8.1: Modelling of the Suppression Task cases (α), (β), (γ) and (γ'), weak completion of the programs and least models, adapted from [DHR13]. Note that (γ'') is equivalent to (γ) under weak completion semantics (confer [REKI16]).

Task	(α)	(β)	(γ)	(γ')
Logic Program	$l \leftarrow e \wedge \overline{ab}_1$ $ab_1 \leftarrow \bot$ $e \leftarrow \top$	$l \leftarrow e \wedge \overline{ab}_1$ $l \leftarrow t \wedge \overline{ab}_2$ $ab_1 \leftarrow \bot$ $ab_2 \leftarrow \bot$ $e \leftarrow \top$	$l \leftarrow e \wedge \overline{ab}_1$ $l \leftarrow o \wedge \overline{ab}_3$ $ab_1 \leftarrow \overline{o}$ $ab_3 \leftarrow \overline{e}$ $e \leftarrow \top$	$l \leftarrow e \wedge \overline{ab}_1$ $l \leftarrow o \wedge \overline{ab}_4$ $ab_1 \leftarrow \overline{o}$ $ab_4 \leftarrow \overline{e}$ $e \leftarrow \top$
Weak Completion	$l \Leftrightarrow (e \wedge \overline{ab}_1)$ $ab_1 \Leftrightarrow \bot$ $e \Leftrightarrow \top$	$l \Leftrightarrow (e \wedge \overline{ab}_1)$ $(\vee t \wedge \overline{ab}_2)$ $ab_1 \Leftrightarrow \bot$ $ab_2 \Leftrightarrow \bot$ $e \Leftrightarrow \top$	$l \Leftrightarrow (e \wedge \overline{ab}_1)$ $(\vee o \wedge \overline{ab}_3)$ $ab_1 \Leftrightarrow \overline{o}$ $ab_3 \Leftrightarrow \overline{e}$ $e \Leftrightarrow \top$	$l \Leftrightarrow e \wedge \overline{ab}_1$ $o \Leftrightarrow o \wedge \overline{ab}_4$ $ab_1 \Leftrightarrow \overline{o}$ $ab_4 \Leftrightarrow \overline{e}$ $e \Leftrightarrow \top$
Least Model	$(\{e, l\}, \{ab_1\})$	$(\{e, l\}, \{ab_1, ab_2\})$	$(\{e\}, \{ab_3\})$	$(\{e\}, \{ab_4\})$

Definition 8.4 (Reiter Defaults and Reiter Default Theory [Rei80]). Let ϕ, ψ, and $\chi_1, \ldots, \chi_k$, be formulas in $\mathcal{L}$. A *Reiter Default*

$$\mu = \frac{\phi \; : \; \chi_1, \ldots, \chi_k}{\psi} \tag{8.1}$$

connects the precondition $pre(\mu) = \phi$ with the consequence $cns(\mu) = \psi$ over the justifications $just(\mu) = \chi_1, \ldots, \chi_k$ in such a way that it licenses for concluding ψ from ϕ given the justifications $\chi_1, \ldots, \chi_k$ can be consistently assumed to hold, that is, neither $\overline{\chi}_1, \ldots, \overline{\chi}_k$ can be proven. A *Reiter Default Theory* $\mathfrak{R} = (\mathcal{F}, \mathcal{D})$ is a tuple containing the strict knowledge of an agent, represented as set of (strict / classical) formulas $\mathcal{F} \subseteq \mathcal{L}$, and the defaults (default / defeasible rules) $\mathcal{D} = \{\mu_1, \ldots, \mu_n\}$ the agents believes in.

The semantics of Reiter Default Logic is set upon the notion of *extensions* of a Reiter Default Theory $\mathfrak{R}$; extensions are deductively closed sets of formulas containing the knowledge of the agent and are closed under default application. The set of all extensions $Ext(\mathfrak{R})$ of a Reiter Default Theory can be calculated using process trees [Ant97]: Let $\Pi = (\mu_{\Pi_1}, \ldots, \mu_{\Pi_m})$ be a finite sequence of defaults $\mu_{\Pi_i} \in \mathcal{D}$, $1 \leq i \leq m$; and let $\Pi[i] = (\mu_{\Pi_1}, \ldots, \mu_{\Pi_i})$, $1 \leq i \leq n$, a sub-sequence of Π. To each sub-sequence $\Pi[i]$, $1 \leq i \leq n$, we assign a two sets

$$In(\Pi[i]) = Cn(\mathcal{F} \cup \{\psi|\psi \in cns(\mu) \text{ for all } \mu \text{ in } \Pi[i]\}) \qquad (8.2)$$

$$Out(\Pi[i]) = \{\chi|\chi \in just(\mu) \text{ for all } \mu \text{ in } \Pi[i]\}, \qquad (8.3)$$

and additionally determine $In(\Pi[0]) = Cn(\mathcal{F})$ and $Out(\Pi[0]) = \varnothing$.

A Default μ is *applicable* to a sequence Π of defaults if and only if $pre(\mu) \in In(\Pi)$ and $\overline{\chi} \notin In(\Pi)$ for all $\chi \in just(\mu)$. A sequence Π is called a *(Reiter default) process* if and only if every μ_i, $1 \leq i \leq n$, in the sequence is applicable to the sub-sequence $\Pi[i-1]$. A process Π is successful if and only if $In(\Pi) \cap Out(\Pi) = \varnothing$ and failed, otherwise. A process Π is closed if and only if every $\mu \in \mathcal{D}$ that is applicable to Π is an element of the process. Processes are closely tied to extensions, as has been shown by [Ant97]:

Theorem 8.5 (Extensions of Reiter Default Theories / Processes [Ant97]). The set $ext \subseteq \mathfrak{L}$ is an extension of the Reiter Default Theory $\mathfrak{R}$ if and only if there is a successful process Π in $\mathfrak{R}$ such that $ext = In(\Pi)$.

The set of all processes of a Reiter Default Theory $\mathfrak{R} = (\mathcal{F}, \mathcal{D})$ can be captured by a process tree [Ant97]. Let $\mathcal{E}$ be the set of edges of this tree. Every edge $E \in \mathcal{E}$ is annotated with a default $\mu \in \mathcal{D}$ such that $default(E) = \mu$. The root of the tree represents the empty process $In(()) = In(\Pi[0]) = Cn(\mathcal{F})$ and $Out(()) = Out(\Pi[0]) = \varnothing$. For every (non-root) vertex V in the tree $path(V)$ is the sequence of edges defined by the path from the root vertex the V. So $path(V)$ represents the process $\Pi(path(V))$. $\mathcal{E}$ contains an edge $V \xrightarrow{\mu} V'$ if and only if μ is applicable to $\Pi(path(V))$. Every leaf V' in the tree is either a failed process, that is, $In(\Pi(path(V'))) \cap Out(\Pi(path(V'))) \neq \varnothing$, or a successful process, then $In(\Pi(path(V')))$ is an extension of $\mathfrak{R}$.

With process trees we have an algorithmic approach to calculate all extensions of a Reiter Default Theory. Inference with these extensions can be realised as sceptical or credulous inference, as usual:

Definition 8.6 (Sceptical/Credulous Inference in Reiter Default Logic [Rei80]). A formula ψ can be *sceptically inferred* from a set of formulas $\mathcal{F}$ in Reiter Default Theory $\mathfrak{R} = (\mathcal{F}, \mathcal{D})$, written $\mathcal{F} \mathrel{|\!\approx}_{\mathcal{D}}^{\text{Reiter},\cap} \psi$, if and only if $\psi \in ext$ for all $ext \in Ext(\mathfrak{R})$. A formula ψ can be *credulously inferred* from a set of formulas $\mathcal{F}$ in Reiter Default Theory $\mathfrak{R} = (\mathcal{F}, \mathcal{D})$, written $\mathcal{F} \mathrel{|\!\approx}_{\mathcal{D}}^{\text{Reiter},\cup} \psi$, if and only if $\psi \in ext$ for any $ext \in Ext(\mathfrak{R})$.

Following [REKI16] we apply the ideas of the modelling of the Suppression Task in Logic Programs ([SvL08, DHR13]) to Reiter Default Theory, and to inspect whether inference with Reiter Default Logic models the suppression effect found in [Byr89].

Example 8.7 (confer [REKI16]). We formalise the conditional assertions of the suppression task with justifications derived from the exceptions in the logic programming approach (see Example 8.3) in Table 8.2. Note that in this case, there is no need to explicitly negate the abnormalities, because they do not need to be set to be consistently assumed not to hold.

In this example we have $\mathcal{F} = \{e\}$ for all theories, the sets of defaults are as follows (with indices according to the cases):

$$
\begin{aligned}
\mathcal{R}_\alpha &= (\mathcal{F} = \{e\}, \mathcal{D}_\alpha = \{\mu_1\}) \\
\mathcal{R}_\beta &= (\mathcal{F} = \{e\}, \mathcal{D}_\beta = \{\mu_1, \mu_2\}) \\
\mathcal{R}_\gamma &= (\mathcal{F} = \{e\}, \mathcal{D}_\gamma = \{\mu_1, \mu_3, \mu_6, \mu_7\}) \\
\mathcal{R}_{\gamma'} &= (\mathcal{F} = \{e\}, \mathcal{D}_{\gamma'} = \{\mu_1, \mu_4, \mu_6, \mu_8\}) \\
\mathcal{R}_{\gamma''} &= (\mathcal{F} = \{e\}, \mathcal{D}_{\gamma''} = \{\mu_1, \mu_5, \mu_6, \mu_9\})
\end{aligned}
$$

Applying the technique of process trees we obtain the trees illustrated in Figure 8.1a for all cases except for (γ') and 8.1b for (γ'). There is exactly one extension for every of the default theories, so credulous and sceptical inference coincide. This means we can infer l from every theory $\mathcal{R}_\bullet$, $\bullet \in \{\alpha, \beta, \gamma, \gamma', \gamma''\}$ that is we have $\mathcal{F} \mathrel{|\!\approx}_{\mathcal{D}_\bullet}^{\mathrm{Reiter}, \cup} l$ as well as $\mathcal{F} \mathrel{|\!\approx}_{\mathcal{D}_\bullet}^{\mathrm{Reiter}, \cap} l$. Therefore no suppression occurs for either variant or degree of scepticism of the different modellings of the suppression task.

System P

Following [REKI16] we started the formalisation of the conditional assertions in the Suppression Task with explicitly stated exceptions in logic programming. This was followed by a less strict formalisation using (the negation of) these exceptions as justifications for default rules in Reiter Default Logic. We here proceed another step in the direction of weakening the explicitness in the formalisation of the exceptions, and use conditionals to formalise the task, that is, a formalisation that already contains the possibility of the rules to have exceptions. In this, we no longer need to explicitly

Table 8.2: Realisation of the conditional assertions in the Suppression Task as Reiter
Defaults [REB$^+$17]

(α) "If Lisa has an essay to write,
she will study late in the library." $\mu_1 = \dfrac{e \; : \; \overline{ab}_1}{l}$

(β) "If Lisa has textbook to read,
she will study late in the library." $\mu_2 = \dfrac{t \; : \; \overline{ab}_2}{l}$

(γ) "If the library is open,
Lisa will study late in the library." $\mu_3 = \dfrac{o \; : \; \overline{ab}_3}{l}$

(γ') "If Lisa studies late in the library,
the library is open." $\mu_4 = \dfrac{l \; : \; \overline{ab}_4}{o}$

(γ'') "If the library is not open,
Lisa will not study late in the library." $\mu_5 = \dfrac{\overline{o} \; : \; \overline{ab}_5}{\overline{l}}$

$$\mu_6 = \dfrac{\overline{o} \; : \; ab_1}{ab_1}$$

$$\mu_7 = \dfrac{\overline{e} \; : \; ab_3}{ab_3}$$

$$\mu_8 = \dfrac{\overline{e} \; : \; ab_4}{ab_4}$$

$$\mu_9 = \dfrac{\overline{e} \; : \; ab_5}{ab_5}$$

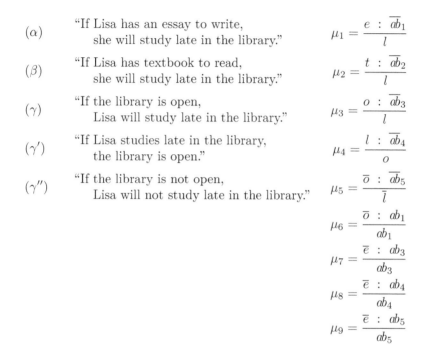

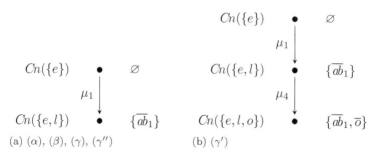

(a) (α), (β), (γ), (γ'') (b) (γ')

Figure 8.1: Process trees for the Reiter Default Theories formalising the different variants
of the Suppression Task in Example 8.7

state the exceptions. Based on these conditionals, we apply inference with System P (confer the formal introduction of System P and the respective inference in Section 4.1.4) to examine whether we will find a suppression effect, or not.

Example 8.8 (confer [REKI16]). We formalise the conditional assertions of the Suppression Task in form of conditionals as follows:

	"Lisa has an essay to write."	$\delta_0 = (e\|\top)$
(α)	"If Lisa has an essay to write, she will study late in the library."	$\delta_1 = (l\|e)$
(β)	"If Lisa has textbook to read, she will study late in the library."	$\delta_2 = (l\|t)$
(γ)	"If the library is open, Lisa will study late in the library."	$\delta_3 = (l\|o)$
(γ')	"If Lisa studies late in the library, the library is open."	$\delta_4 = (o\|l)$
(γ'')	"If The library is not open, Lisa will not study late in the library."	$\delta_5 = (\bar{l}\|\bar{o})$

With these conditionals we obtain the following knowledge bases for the different tasks:

$$\Delta_\alpha = \{\delta_0, \delta_1\}$$
$$\Delta_\beta = \{\delta_0, \delta_1, \delta_2\}$$
$$\Delta_\gamma = \{\delta_0, \delta_1, \delta_3\}$$
$$\Delta_{\gamma'} = \{\delta_0, \delta_1, \delta_4\}$$
$$\Delta_{\gamma''} = \{\delta_0, \delta_1, \delta_5\}$$

We apply the System P semantics Δ-inference of [GP91a, DP96] (see Definition 2.11) stating that $\phi\hspace{-0.5em}\underset{\Delta}{\mid\sim}^P\psi$ if and only if $\Delta \cup \{(\overline{\psi}|\phi)\}$ inconsistent to the so formalised conditional assertions to obtain the System P inferences of the modellings.

Example 8.9 (confer [REKI16]). For the suppression task, we are interested in whether the system derives Lisa to study late in the library, that it, whether $\top \models_{\Delta_\bullet} l$ for the tasks $\bullet \in \{\alpha, \beta, \gamma, \gamma', \gamma''\}$. We obtain that $\Delta_\alpha \cup (\bar{l}|\top)$ is inconsistent. System P is semi-monotone (see (SM) (see Page 31)), thus, since $\Delta_\alpha \subseteq \Delta_\bullet$, we obtain $\top \models_{\Delta_\bullet^P} l$ for all $\bullet \in \{\alpha, \beta, \gamma, \gamma', \gamma''\}$, which means that using System P, no suppression effect occurs for any variation of the original task.

Inductive OCF Based Inference Systems

We use the modelling of the Suppression Task as conditional knowledge base in Example 8.8 for applying the inductive approaches System Z and c-representations to the Suppression Task. As all inferences based on a single OCF satisfy System R, which properly contains System P (see Proposition 4.31 in Section 4.1.5), by Example 8.9 we directly obtain that we will find no suppression effect for both systems. The same holds for inference with all c-representations, which satisfies System P, as shown in Section 5.2. We nonetheless illustrate the modelling of the tasks in the inductive approaches as follows.

Example 8.10 (confer [REKI16]). The consistency test algorithm (Algorithm 2.1) partitions the knowledge bases $\Delta_\bullet$, $\bullet \in \{\alpha, \beta, \gamma, \gamma'\}$, of Example 8.8 into one partition, only, and $\Delta_{\gamma''}$ into the partitions $(\{\delta_0, \delta_1\}, \{\delta_5\})$, which results in the System Z generated OCF shown in Table 8.3 (left). Applying the approach of c-representations yields that for every impact of every conditional in every of the knowledge bases the minimum value is 1, save for κ_5^- in $\Delta_{\gamma''}$ where the minimum value is 2. This gives us the OCF shown in Table 8.3 (right). For all of these OCF, all $\bullet \in \{\alpha, \beta, \gamma, \gamma', \gamma''\}$ and all $\circ \in \{Z, c\}$ we find $\kappa_{\Delta_\bullet}^\circ(l) = 0 < 1 = \kappa_{\Delta_\bullet}^\circ(\bar{l})$, and thus can infer e, that is, no suppression occurs.

From the different modellings and semantics in this section, only logic programming with weak completion semantics succeeds in mimicking the suppression effect we find in the experiment in [Byr89].

Table 8.3: OCF generated by System Z and minimal c-representations for the knowledge bases formalising the Suppression Task in Example 8.10

ω	System Z					c-Representations				
	$\kappa^Z_{\Delta_\alpha}$	$\kappa^Z_{\Delta_\beta}$	$\kappa^Z_{\Delta_\gamma}$	$\kappa^Z_{\Delta_{\gamma'}}$	$\kappa^Z_{\Delta_{\gamma''}}$	$\kappa^c_{\Delta_\alpha}$	$\kappa^c_{\Delta_\beta}$	$\kappa^c_{\Delta_\gamma}$	$\kappa^c_{\Delta_{\gamma'}}$	$\kappa^c_{\Delta_{\gamma''}}$
$e\,l\,o\,t$	0	0	0	0	0	0	0	0	0	0
$e\,l\,o\,\bar{t}$	0	0	0	0	0	0	0	0	0	0
$e\,l\,\bar{o}\,t$	0	0	0	1	2	0	0	0	2	3
$e\,l\,\bar{o}\,\bar{t}$	0	0	0	1	2	0	0	0	2	3
$e\,\bar{l}\,o\,t$	1	1	1	1	1	1	2	2	1	1
$e\,\bar{l}\,o\,\bar{t}$	1	1	1	1	1	1	1	2	1	1
$e\,\bar{l}\,\bar{o}\,t$	1	1	1	1	1	1	2	1	1	1
$e\,\bar{l}\,\bar{o}\,\bar{t}$	1	1	1	1	1	1	1	1	1	1
$\bar{e}\,l\,o\,t$	1	1	1	1	1	1	1	1	1	1
$\bar{e}\,l\,o\,\bar{t}$	1	1	1	1	1	1	1	1	1	1
$\bar{e}\,l\,\bar{o}\,t$	1	1	1	1	2	1	1	1	2	3
$\bar{e}\,l\,\bar{o}\,\bar{t}$	1	1	1	1	2	1	1	1	2	3
$\bar{e}\,\bar{l}\,o\,t$	1	1	1	1	1	1	2	2	1	1
$\bar{e}\,\bar{l}\,o\,\bar{t}$	1	1	1	1	1	1	1	2	1	1
$\bar{e}\,\bar{l}\,\bar{o}\,t$	1	1	1	1	1	1	2	1	1	1
$\bar{e}\,\bar{l}\,\bar{o}\,\bar{t}$	1	1	1	1	1	1	1	1	1	1

8.1.2 Modelling Background Knowledge in the Suppression Task

As shown in [REKI16] and the previous sections, modelling the Suppression Task as conditional knowledge base does not yield the suppression effect found in the experiments, whereas this was educible with logic programming under weak completion semantics. As already discussed, we can ascribe the suppression in logic programming to the modelling making the implicit connections between the variables explicit with the abnormality predicates. Having such a connection is standing to reason: Even if the variables might not be connected in the cover story nor necessarily in the logic, they may be nonetheless be connected in the background knowledge of the participants. The Suppression Task (Example 8.1) serves as prominent example for this implicit connection: Here, the variables L (studying late in the library) and O (the library being open) are connected in the background knowledge[2]. In this section we follow [REB^{+}17] and systematically investigate how to implement this connection in approaches to nonmonotonic reasoning including, Logic Programming, Reiter Default Logic, and conditional knowledge bases with the semantics System P, System Z and c-representations.

The *plain approach* is the baseline in this investigation and uses the modellings from Section 8.1.1. The *connecting premise* connects the additional information with the premise of the modelling of the conditional. This follows the modelling in logic programming via the abnormality predicates and introducing coimplications in the rules: $l \Leftrightarrow e \wedge \overline{ab}_1$ and $ab_1 \Leftrightarrow \overline{o}$ can be joined to the single statement $l \Leftrightarrow eo$. So in this we do not use the coimplication, but the idea of connecting the two statements. The *necessary condition* formalises the idea of an abductive quality of both statements, rather than the deductive one, that is, for instance, "Lisa studies late in the library, *because* she has an essay to write". Therefore, both premises are necessary conditions for her being in the library. This means that from "Lisa being in the library" we can conclude both "Lisa has an essay to write" and "the library is open." Finally, with the *weak completion* modelling we connect both approaches, mimicking the coimplication of the weak completion semantics, by adding both formalisations of the connecting premise and the necessary condition case.

---

[2] Scenarios where someone studies in a closed library are thinkable, but pretty weird: For instance being (deliberately or by accident) locked in in the library, as well as scenarios including a crowbar and brute force.

Example 8.11 ([REB$^+$17]). Modelling the suppression task in these ways as Reiter Default Theory, we obtain $\mathcal{D}_P = \mathcal{D}_\gamma$ from Example 8.7 and for the other sets of defaults, $\mathcal{D}_\bullet$, $\bullet \in \{CP, NC, WC\}$ as given in Table 8.5 (left) for the connecting premise, necessary condition and weak completion cases, respectively. For the modelling as conditional knowledge base we obtain we model the different cases as given in Table 8.5 (right).

Here, the Reiter Default Theory $\mathcal{D}_P$ together with the strict knowledge $\{e\}$ licenses for the inference of l (see Example 8.7). In the other MP cases setting, no default is applicable to the knowledge e, thus the only extension is $Cn(\{e\})$, which does yield neither l nor $\bar{l}$, so this system is undecided with respect to whether Lisa studies late in the library, or not. In the MT cases with the strict knowledge $\{\bar{l}\}$, no default of the theories is applicable, and thus the only extension is $Cn(\{\bar{l}\})$. Therefore, neither e nor $\bar{e}$ can be inferred from $\{\bar{l}\}$. This means that in all but the plain case of MP, suppression occurs.

For the conditional knowledge base modelling we inspect whether the inference from e to l for MP and $\bar{l}$ to $\bar{e}$ is valid in the semantics System P, System Z and c-representations, that is, we inspect whether $e \vdash^\circ_{\Delta_\bullet} l$ with $\bullet \in \{P, CP, NC, WC\}$ and $\circ \in \{P, Z, c\}$ is valid. For System P, we therefore test whether $\Delta_\bullet$ is inconsistent when extended with $(\bar{l}|e)$ or $(e|\bar{l})$. Here, only $\Delta_{PL} \cup \{(\bar{l}|e)\}$ is inconsistent, all other in this matter extended knowledge bases are consistent. Therefore we find a suppression effect for the non-plain modellings. The rankings in System Z and c-representations for the different knowledge bases are given in Table 8.4. We obtain that $e \vdash^\circ_{\Delta_P} l$ for $\circ \in \{Z, c\}$, and $e \not\vdash^\circ_{\Delta_\bullet} l$ with $\bullet \in \{CP, NC, WC\}$, so we have a suppression effect for the non-plain modellings and MP. The same behaviour can be found for the MT case, that is, we have $\bar{l} \vdash^\circ_{\Delta_P} \bar{e}$ for $\circ \in \{Z, c\}$, and $\bar{l} \not\vdash^\circ_{\Delta_\bullet} \bar{e}$ with $\bullet \in \{CP, NC, WC\}$.

Overall we obtain that explicitly including the implicit background knowledge in the modellings leads to Reiter Default Logic as well as the approaches to reasoning upon a conditional knowledge base to show the suppression effect also observed in the logic programming formalisation under weak completion.

Table 8.4: Rankings induced from the different conditional knowledge bases in Example 8.11 using System Z (upper half) and c-representations (lower half)

Ranking function	$e\,l\,o$	$e\,l\,\bar{o}$	$e\,\bar{l}\,o$	$e\,\bar{l}\,\bar{o}$	$\bar{e}\,l\,o$	$\bar{e}\,l\,\bar{o}$	$\bar{e}\,\bar{l}\,o$	$\bar{e}\,\bar{l}\,\bar{o}$
$\kappa^Z_{\Delta_{PL}}$	0	0	1	1	0	0	0	0
$\kappa^Z_{\Delta_{CP}}$	0	0	1	0	0	0	0	0
$\kappa^Z_{\Delta_{NC}}$	0	1	0	0	1	1	0	0
$\kappa^Z_{\Delta_{WC}}$	0	1	1	0	1	1	0	0
$\kappa^c_{\Delta_{PL}}$	0	0	2	1	0	0	1	0
$\kappa^c_{\Delta_{CP}}$	0	0	1	0	0	0	0	0
$\kappa^c_{\Delta_{NC}}$	0	1	0	0	1	1	0	0
$\kappa^c_{\Delta_{WC}}$	0	1	1	0	1	1	0	0

Table 8.5: Realisation of the different modellings of background knowledge in the Suppression Task as Reiter Default Logic and as conditional knowledge base for the plain approach PL, connecting premise CP, necessary condition NC, and weak completion WC [REB$^+$17]

Modelling	Reiter Default Theory
Plain (PL)	$\mathcal{D}_{PL} = \left\{ \xi_1 = \dfrac{e : \overline{ab_1}}{l},\ \xi_3 = \dfrac{o : \overline{ab_3}}{l},\ \xi_5 = \dfrac{\overline{o} : ab_1}{ab_1},\ \xi_7 = \dfrac{\overline{e} : ab_3}{ab_3} \right\}$
Connecting premise (CP)	$\mathcal{D}_{CP} = \left\{ \xi_{10} = \dfrac{eo : l}{l} \right\}$
Necessary condition (NC)	$\mathcal{D}_{NC} = \left\{ \xi_{11} = \dfrac{l : eo}{eo} \right\}$
Weak completion (WC)	$\mathcal{D}_{WC} = \left\{ \xi_{10} = \dfrac{eo : l}{l},\ \xi_{11} = \dfrac{l : eo}{eo} \right\}$

Modelling	Conditional knowledge base
Plain (PL)	$\Delta_{PL} = \{ \delta_1 = (l|e), \delta_3 = (l|o) \}$
Connecting premise (CP)	$\Delta_{CP} = \{ \delta_6 = (l|eo) \}$
Necessary condition (NC)	$\Delta_{NC} = \{ \delta_7 = (eo|l) \}$
Weak completion (WC)	$\Delta_{WC} = \{ \delta_6 = (l|eo), \delta_7 = (eo|l) \}$

8.1.3 Strengthening / Weakening the Statements in the Suppression Task

In Section 8.1.1 we already modelled the conditional assertions as conditionals. In this section we broaden our view to such an extent that we model these assertions either as conditionals or in classical logic, that is, as material implication or strict respectively facts. In this, experiments in the form of [Byr89] lead four possible modellings of knowledge bases for each inference rule used. We follow [REB⁺17] in concentrating on Modus Ponens and Modus Tollens in our examinations.

Formalising inference studies with a single conditional statement and one fact in this way, we obtain representations with variations in the two dimensions: The first one is $\circ \in \{MP, MT\}$, indicating whether the knowledge base models the Modus Ponens (MP) or the Modus Tollens (MT) task. The second dimension is $\bullet \in \{CC, CW, FW, CFW\}$, indicating whether we implement the statements in classical logic (material implication and strict fact, CC), weaken the conditional assertion (CW), the fact (FW), or weaken both (CFW). For syntax and semantics of the formalisations, we use the approaches to nonmonotonic reasoning in general and modelling the Suppression Task in particular which we already discussed in Section 8.1.1. For each of the approaches, the weakening has to be carried out differently, as the representation of the task in the different logic itself differs.

We use classical logic as baseline. For this modelling, there is no weakening possible, so the only modelling is the one where the fact is a strict fact and the conditional is the material implication.

Example 8.12 ([REB⁺17]). We formalise the Suppression Task in classical logic by using the material implication $e \Rightarrow l$ for the conditional assertion "If Lisa has an essay to write, she will study late in the library", and e respectively $\bar{l}$ for the facts "Lisa has an essay to write." and "Lisa does not study late in the library". Here unsurprisingly $l \in \mathit{Cn}(e, e \Rightarrow l)$ and $\bar{e} \in \mathit{Cn}(\bar{l}, e \Rightarrow l)$, that is, the classical modelling satisfies the classical inference rules.

The implementation of a defeasible rule in logic programming is achieved by adding an *ab*normality predicate to a strict rule [SvL08], as demonstrated in the previous sections of this chapter.

Example 8.13 (Logic Programming [REB⁺17]). As already discussed, for this approach we model the conditional assertions in the Suppression Task

Table 8.6: Logic programs formalising the Suppression Task in Example 8.13 [REB$^+$17], least model of the programs and inference with respect to the variables L respectively E

Program		Least model	Inference
LP_{CC}^{MP}	$= \{l \leftarrow e, e \leftarrow \top\}$	$(\{e, l\}, \varnothing)$	l
LP_{CW}^{MP}	$= \{l \leftarrow e \wedge \overline{ab}_1, e \leftarrow \top, ab_1 \leftarrow \bot\}$	$(\{e, l\}, \{ab_1\})$	l
LP_{FW}^{MP}	$= \{l \leftarrow e, e \leftarrow \overline{ab}_6, ab_6 \leftarrow \bot\}$	$(\{e, l\}, \{ab_6\})$	l
LP_{CFW}^{MP}	$= \{l \leftarrow e \wedge \overline{ab}_1, e \leftarrow \overline{ab}_6, ab_1 \leftarrow \bot, ab_6 \leftarrow \bot\}$	$(\{e, l\}, \{ab_1, ab_6\})$	l
LP_{CC}^{MT}	$= \{l \leftarrow e, l \leftarrow \bot\}$	$(\varnothing, \{e, l\})$	$\overline{e}$
LP_{CW}^{MT}	$= \{l \leftarrow e \wedge \overline{ab}_1, l \leftarrow \bot, ab_1 \leftarrow \bot\}$	$(\varnothing, \{e, l, ab_1\})$	$\overline{e}$
LP_{FW}^{MT}	$= \{l \leftarrow e, l \leftarrow ab_7, ab_7 \leftarrow \bot\}$	$(\varnothing, \{e, l, ab_7\})$	$\overline{e}$
LP_{CFW}^{MT}	$= \{l \leftarrow e \wedge \overline{ab}_1, l \leftarrow ab_7, ab_1 \leftarrow \bot, ab_7 \leftarrow \bot\}$	$(\varnothing, \{e, l, ab_1, ab_7\})$	$\overline{e}$

as logical rules with an abnormality constraint in the rule if the conditional assertion is weakened. This means that, for instance the conditional assertion "If Lisa has an essay to write, she will study late in the library" is modelled as the rule $l \leftarrow e$ if the rule is strong and $l \leftarrow e \wedge \overline{ab}_1$, otherwise. Facts are weakened similarly, that is, a strong fact as, for instance, "Lisa has an essay to write" is a conclusion from $\top$, that is, $e \leftarrow \top$, and a weak fact a conclusion from a negated abnormality, that is, $e \leftarrow \overline{ab}_6$. Table 8.6 lists the different programs, their least models, and inferences with respect to the variables L and E. Here we see that both rules MP and MT are valid for all modellings of the task, that is, l follows for all MP modellings, and $\overline{e}$ for all MT modellings, regardless of the weakening.

Reiter Default Logic differentiates between strict and defeasible knowledge with the two sets $\mathcal{F}$ and $\mathcal{D}$. We utilise this distinction for the weakening / strengthening process and add a material implication to $\mathcal{F}$ if the conditional assertion is modelled to be strong, and a default in the form used in Section 8.1.1 to $\mathcal{D}$ if the assertion is modelled to be weak. Likewise we add a formula to $\mathcal{F}$ if the fact is strong, and a normal default to $\mathcal{D}$ if the fact is weak.

Example 8.14 ([REB$^+$17]). We model the conditional assertion "If Lisa has an essay to write, she will study late in the library" as formula $e \Rightarrow l \in \mathcal{F}$ if it is modelled to be strong, and as default $\dfrac{e \; : \; \overline{ab}_1}{l} \in \mathcal{D}$ if it is modelled

Table 8.7: Reiter Default Logic modellings for formalising the Suppression Task in Example 8.14 [REB$^+$17], extensions and inference with respect to the variables L respectively E

Default Theory		Extensions	Inference
$\mathfrak{R}_{CC}^{\mathrm{MP}}$	$= \left(\mathcal{W}_{CC}^{\mathrm{MP}} = \{e \Rightarrow l, e\}, \mathcal{D}_{CC}^{\mathrm{MP}} = \varnothing \right)$	$Cn(\{e, e \Rightarrow l\})$	l
$\mathfrak{R}_{CW}^{\mathrm{MP}}$	$= \left(\mathcal{W}_{CW}^{\mathrm{MP}} = \{e\}, \mathcal{D}_{CW}^{\mathrm{MP}} = \left\{ \dfrac{e \; : \; ab_1}{l} \right\} \right)$	$Cn(\{e, l\})$	l
$\mathfrak{R}_{FW}^{\mathrm{MP}}$	$= \left(\mathcal{W}_{FW}^{\mathrm{MP}} = \{e \Rightarrow l\}, \mathcal{D}_{FW}^{\mathrm{MP}} = \left\{ \dfrac{\top \; : \; ab_6}{e} \right\} \right)$	$Cn(\{e, l\})$	l
$\mathfrak{R}_{CFW}^{\mathrm{MP}}$	$= \left(\mathcal{W}_{CFW}^{\mathrm{MP}} = \varnothing, \mathcal{D}_{CFW}^{\mathrm{MP}} = \left\{ \dfrac{e \; : \; ab_1}{l}, \dfrac{\top \; : \; ab_6}{e} \right\} \right)$	$Cn(\{e, l\})$	l
$\mathfrak{R}_{CC}^{\mathrm{MT}}$	$= \left(\mathcal{W}_{CC}^{\mathrm{MT}} = \{e \Rightarrow l, \bar{l}\}, \mathcal{D}_{CC}^{\mathrm{MT}} = \varnothing \right)$	$Cn(\{\bar{l}, e \Rightarrow l\})$	$\bar{e}$
$\mathfrak{R}_{CW}^{\mathrm{MT}}$	$= \left(\mathcal{W}_{CW}^{\mathrm{MT}} = \{\bar{l}\}, \mathcal{D}_{CW}^{\mathrm{MT}} = \left\{ \dfrac{e \; : \; ab_1}{l} \right\} \right)$	$Cn(\bar{l})$	—
$\mathfrak{R}_{FW}^{\mathrm{MT}}$	$= \left(\mathcal{W}_{FW}^{\mathrm{MT}} = \{e \Rightarrow l\}, \mathcal{D}_{FW}^{\mathrm{MT}} = \left\{ \dfrac{\top \; : \; ab_7}{\bar{l}} \right\} \right)$	$Cn(\{\bar{l}, e \Rightarrow l\})$	$\bar{e}$
$\mathfrak{R}_{CFW}^{\mathrm{MT}}$	$= \left(\mathcal{W}_{CFW}^{\mathrm{MT}} = \varnothing, \mathcal{D}_{CFW}^{\mathrm{MT}} = \left\{ \dfrac{e \; : \; ab_1}{l}, \dfrac{\top \; : \; ab_7}{\bar{l}} \right\} \right)$	$Cn(\{\bar{l}\})$	—

to be weak. Likewise, the fact "Lisa has an essay to write" is modelled as strict fact $e \in \mathfrak{L}$ in the strong, and as default $\dfrac{\top \; : \; e}{e}$, otherwise. Table 8.7 lists the different default theories of the weakenings, their extensions, and inferences with respect to E and L. We here obtain that we are able to infer with respect to MP in all of the weakenings, but with respect to MT only where the fact, but not the conditional is weakened.

For applying System P and ranking models, we use formalisations as conditional knowledge base, like the ones used in Section 8.1.1. For having both weak and strong conditionals and facts, we use knowledge bases with strict and conditional knowledge, as we did for Reiter Default Logic. In this, the the strong modelling of conditional assertions and facts are placed in the strict part of the knowledge base, and the weakened forms are represented as conditionals or conditional facts in the conditional part of the knowledge base. Note that strict knowledge in a knowledge base restricts the possible worlds to worlds that satisfy all strict formulas (confer Section 2.2).

Example 8.15 (The Suppression Task in Conditional Knowledge Bases [REB$^+$17, Example 1]). In the Suppression Task, the conditional assertion "If Lisa has an essay to write, she will study late in the library" can be modelled to be the material implication $e \Rightarrow l$ or the conditional $(l|e)$. The additional factual statement can for MP either be the strict fact e or the conditional fact $(e|\top)$, and likewise for MT either the strict fact $\bar{l}$ or the conditional fact $(\bar{l}|\top)$. This yields the knowledge bases given in Table 8.8. The different sets of strict knowledge constraints the set of possible worlds, as worlds that violate the strict knowledge are impossible, the worlds possible for the different knowledge bases are also listed in this table. Here, $\mathcal{R}_{CW}^{MT}$ is inconsistent because there is no possible world $\omega \in \Omega_{CW}^{MT} = \{e\bar{l}, \bar{e}\bar{l}\}$ that verifies the conditional $(l|e)$, all other knowledge bases are consistent. Table 8.8 lists the inferences of the semantics System P, System Z, and c-representations for these knowledge bases and worlds. We obtain that can infer according to MP in all MP-cases, and according to MT in all MT-cases save for the CW-case where the knowledge base is inconsistent. In this case we have to differentiate between the approaches to inference, as System P licenses for the inference via the property (NMEFQ), while System Z and c-representations do not license for any inference, as no ranking models exist.

Overall we obtain that all approaches of formalising the plain Suppression Task, that is, the variant (α) without suppressing information, license for the usage of the inferences rules MP and MT in the case of CC, that is, where the tasks are modelled as strict knowledge. Even more, all least models, extensions or possible worlds support these inferences, that is, when using a classical modelling, there is not only not even the remotest doubt that the classical inference rules are to be applied, but there even are no other results possible. Using weak completion semantics on logic programming, this behaviour is stable for the weakenings, that is, regardless of the weakening of the conditional or the fact, MP and MT hold because the respective inferences are valid in all models. The same goes for Reiter Default Logic, at least in the MP case. Here, MP is valid for all weakenings and the respective inference holds in all extensions. In the MT case, either the inference can be inferred sceptically, that is holds all extensions, holds in neither extension, that is, the inference can not even be inferred credulously. The approaches to nonmonotonic reasoning set up upon a conditional knowledge base all show a nearly identical behaviour in that the results of the MP, MT

Table 8.8: Knowledge bases $\mathcal{R} = (\mathcal{S}, \Delta)$ with strict ($\mathcal{S}$) and defeasible (Δ) knowledge formalising the Suppression Task in Example 8.15, possible worlds for these knowledge bases and inferences with respect to E and L in System P, System Z and c-representations from these knowledge bases [REB+17]

Knowledge Base	Possible Worlds	Inference		
		System P	System Z	c-representations
$\mathcal{R}_{CC}^{MP} = (\{e \Rightarrow l, e\}, \varnothing)$	$\Omega_{CC}^{MP} = \{el\}$	l	l	l
$\mathcal{R}_{CW}^{MP} = (\{e\}, \{(l|e)\})$	$\Omega_{CW}^{MP} = \{el, e\bar{l}\}$	l	l	l
$\mathcal{R}_{FW}^{MP} = (\{e \Rightarrow l\}, \{(e|\top)\})$	$\Omega_{FW}^{MP} = \{el, \bar{e}l, \bar{e}\bar{l}\}$	l	l	l
$\mathcal{R}_{CFW}^{MP} = (\varnothing, \{(l|e), (e|\top)\})$	$\Omega_{CFW}^{MP} = \{el, \bar{e}l, \bar{e}l, \bar{e}\bar{l}\}$	l	l	l
$\mathcal{R}_{CC}^{MT} = (\{e \Rightarrow l, \bar{l}\}, \varnothing)$	$\Omega_{CC}^{MT} = \{\bar{e}\bar{l}\}$	$\bar{e}$	$\bar{e}$	$\bar{e}$
$\mathcal{R}_{CW}^{MT} = (\{\bar{l}\}, \{(l|e)\})$	$\Omega_{CW}^{MT} = \{el, \bar{e}l\}$	—	Inconsistent	—
$\mathcal{R}_{FW}^{MT} = (\{e \Rightarrow l\}, \{(\bar{l}|\top)\})$	$\Omega_{FW}^{MT} = \{el, \bar{e}l, \bar{e}\bar{l}\}$	$\bar{e}$	$\bar{e}$	$\bar{e}$
$\mathcal{R}_{CFW}^{MT} = (\varnothing, \{(l|e), (\bar{l}|\top)\})$	$\Omega_{CFW}^{MT} = \{el, \bar{e}l, \bar{e}l, \bar{e}\bar{l}\}$	$\bar{e}$	$\bar{e}$	$\bar{e}$

Table 8.9: Inferences for the implementation of the Suppression Task in Section 8.1.3 (one conditional assertion and one fact, no additional information) in the different semantics. Notation: ⟨empty cell⟩ not applicable; − cannot be inferred, ○: can be inferred (i.e. holds in all preferred possible worlds / models / extensions / ...); ◖: can be inferred and holds in most possible worlds; ●: can be inferred and holds in all possible worlds; ɬ: inconsistent (confer [REB+17]).

Inference	CC		FW		CFW		CW	
System	MP	MT	MP	MT	MP	MT	MP	MT
Weak completion semantics	●	●	●	●	●	●	●	●
Reiter Default Logic	●	●	●	●	●	−	●	−
System P	●	●	◖	○	○	○	○	ɬ
System Z	●	●	◖	○	○	○	○	ⓩ
c-representations	●	●	◖	○	○	○	○	ɬ
Propositional Logic	●	●						

inferences hold in all worlds for the classical modelling, most of the worlds for *FW* and some, but the most preferred worlds for the *CFW* case. This is true for *CW*, as well, but only for MP, whilst for MT the knowledge base is inconsistent. Here the results differ, because for an inconsistent knowledge base, by (NMEFQ) (see (NMEFQ), Page 106) System P licenses for any inference, whilst since there are no ranking models for the knowledge base, System Z and c-representations license for no inferences. Finally, for propositional logic, there are no inferences for any weakened modellings, as the language does not support the weakening of the knowledge. Table 8.9 summarises these results (see [REB+17]).

To sum up the results of this section, we obtain that the strength of the conditionals and facts, represented by their strictness or defeasibility, play a major role in determining the possible inferences, valid inference rules, and even possible alternatives. Even more, choosing the wrong weakening may render a whole knowledge base inconsistent. Given the results shown in Table 8.9 it seems that the MP-task is more robust against changing strength of the modellings than the MT-task – this is an interesting finding as human reasoners tend to perceive MT-tasks to be more difficult than MP-tasks.

8.2 Inference Patterns

In studies about human reasoning behaviour, like the ones already cited in this chapter, the focus of the discussion usually lies on single inference rules. That is, the reasoner examines whether the participants applied, for instance, Modus Ponens, or not. In the previous sections of this chapter, we adapted this approach[3]. In this section, however, we broaden the view to simultaneously taking all four inference rules MP, MT, AC, and DA, and their usage or not-usage by the participants into account. The resulting *inference patterns* provide us with a formalisation and classification of the qualitative results of inference studies, resulting in a novel way of systematise inference studies in the form of [Byr89, TB02]. Traditionally, the application of classically invalid rules is seen as fallacies, and the not-application of classically valid rules is seen as errors of the participants. The approach recalled in this section, follows [ERKI18] and inspects the inferences from a preferential reasoning, that is, nonmonotonic view. In this, the formalisation in inference pattern provides a novel notion of rationality. Inducing an epistemic state in the sense of [Hal05], the patterns also reveal the implicit assumptions of the participants as deductively closed set of formulas. Finally, using c-representations, the inference patterns can be used to reverse-engineer conditional knowledge bases that would license for the observed inferences. In this, the patterns can be used to generate hypotheses for the background knowledge of the participants of the inference studies.

To set up the inference patterns, we start with the single inference rules used or not used. If the participants concluded B from A, we assume this to be the case because the inference $A \hspace{-0.4em}\vert\!\!\sim\!\! B$ is valid for the participants. The close connection between drawing a conclusion from a premise and believing a nonmonotonic inference was already referred to as Ramsey test for nonmonotonic logic (see Page 30). This holds, preferentially, if and only if in the context of A, B is more plausible as A, that is $A\,B$ is more plausible as $A\,\overline{B}$. Other rules are modelled in parallel, that is, if the participants concluded $\neg A$ from $\neg B$, they believed in the inference $\overline{B} \hspace{-0.4em}\vert\!\!\sim\!\! \overline{A}$, that is, we assume that in their epistemic state the formula $\overline{A}\,\overline{B}$ is more plausible as $A\,\overline{B}$. If the participants concluded A from B, they believed in the inference $B \hspace{-0.4em}\vert\!\!\sim\!\! A$, so in their epistemic state the formula $A\,B$ is more plausible as $\overline{A}\,B$.

---

[3] In this formally mimicking the approach of human sciences to formally model the inferences of human reasoners.

Table 8.10: Belief for using or not using inference rules (confer [REB$^+$17])

Fact given	Conclusion drawn	Inference rule	Inference believed	Plausibility constraint
A	B	MP	$A\!\approx\!B$	$A\,B \prec A\,\overline{B}$
$\overline{B}$	$\overline{A}$	MT	$\overline{B}\!\approx\!\overline{A}$	$\overline{A}\,\overline{B} \prec A\,\overline{B}$
B	A	AC	$B\!\approx\!A$	$A\,B \prec \overline{A}\,B$
$\overline{A}$	$\overline{B}$	DA	$\overline{A}\!\approx\!\overline{B}$	$\overline{A}\,\overline{B} \prec \overline{A}\,B$

(a) Given fact, drawn conclusion, inference rule applied, believed inference, and constraint on plausibility relation for inferences drawn in reasoning experiments.

Inference rule	Inference believed	Plausibility constraint
$\neg$MP	$A\!\not\approx\!B$	$A\,\overline{B} \preccurlyeq A\,B$
$\neg$MT	$\overline{B}\!\not\approx\!\overline{A}$	$A\,\overline{B} \preccurlyeq \overline{A}\,\overline{B}$
$\neg$AC	$B\!\not\approx\!A$	$\overline{A}\,B \preccurlyeq A\,B$
$\neg$DA	$\overline{A}\!\not\approx\!\overline{B}$	$\overline{A}\,B \preccurlyeq \overline{A}\,\overline{B}$

(b) Believed non-inferences and constraints on plausibility relation for rules not being used in reasoning experiments.

If the participants concluded $\neg B$ from $\neg A$, they believed in the inference $\overline{A}\!\approx\!\overline{B}$, so in their epistemic state the formula $\overline{A}\,\overline{B}$ is more plausible as $\overline{A}\,B$. In this, each pair of a given fact with an answer of the participants form a constraint on the plausibility relation that forms the epistemic state of the reasoning agent. Table 8.11a summarizes these constraints in compact form.

However, in these experiments, participants cannot only draw an inference according to these rules, they also may *not* draw an inference with respect to these inference rules. We write MP, MT, AC, and DA to indicate the usage of the respective rule, and $\neg$MP, $\neg$MT, $\neg$AC, and $\neg$DA to indicate the not usage of the respective rule.

With this notation, we capture the qualitative result of an inference study according to the usage or not usage of the inferences by a given proportion of the participants. For this dissertation, we follow [ERKI18] by defining the participants to have used an inference rule if at least half of the participants drew inferences according to Table 8.11a, and not having used an inference rule, otherwise. In this we capture the qualitative results of an inference study with a binary quadruple denoting whether the participants used (or did not use) the four inference rules.

Definition 8.16 (Inference Pattern (confer[ERKI18, Definition 4])). An *inference pattern* $\varrho \subseteq \{true, false\} \times \{true, false\} \times \{true, false\} \times \{true, false\}$ is a quadruple that at each position indicates whether the inference rules of MP (first position), MT (second position), AC (third), and DA (fourth) are used by at least 50 % of the participants of an inference study (or not). The set of all 16 inference patterns is called $\mathcal{I}$.

For easier reading we use the indicators of using or not using a rule as introduced above instead of truth values. This means that we instance denote the inference pattern $(true, false, false, true)$ as $(MP, \neg MT, \neg AC, DA)$.

Example 8.17. The Suppression Task ([Byr89], Example 8.1) leads to the following pattern:

38 % of the participants applied Modus Ponens, which gives us $\neg MP$.

33 % of the participants reasoned according to Modus Tollens, yielding $\neg MT$.

63 % of the participants applied Affirmation of the Consequent, yielding AC.

54 % of the participants reasoned according to Denial of the Antecedent, which gives us DA.

This results in the pattern $\varrho_{B89} = (\neg MP, \neg MT, AC, DA)$.

Table 8.11a already lists the constraints imposed to the epistemic state for believing the inference if a given inference rule is applied. We extend these constraints with Table 8.11b, listing the believed non-inference and respective constraint on the plausibility relation. As each of the believed inferences or not believed inferences (that is, believed non-inferences) imposes a constraint on the plausibility relation representing the epistemic state, an inference pattern imposes four constraints on the epistemic state. We call a pattern rational if and only if its imposed plausibility constraints are jointly satisfiable.

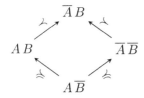

(a) Plausibility ordering imposed by the pattern.

ω	$\kappa_{B89}(\omega)$	$\kappa'_{B89}(\omega)$
AB	0	1
$A\overline{B}$	0	0
$\overline{A}B$	1	2
$\overline{A}\,\overline{B}$	0	1

(b) Ranking functions meeting these constraints.

Figure 8.2: Illustration of the constraints imposed on the epistemic state of an agent by the reasoning pattern $\varrho_{B89} = (\neg\mathrm{MP}, \neg\mathrm{MT}, \mathrm{AC}, \mathrm{DA})$

Definition 8.18 (Rationality for Inference Patterns [ERKI18]). An inference pattern $\varrho \in \mathcal{I}$ is *rational* if and only if the constraints imposed by ϱ are jointly satisfiable if and only if there is a stoppered preferential relation $\preccurlyeq$ that meets all constraints imposed by ϱ.

In the Suppression Task, where participants did use the (with respect to classical logic) invalid inference rules and rejected the (with respect to classical logic) valid inference ones, this definition determines the inferences of the participants to be rational:

Example 8.19. We captured the results of the Suppression Task (Example 8.17) as inference pattern $\varrho_{B89} = (\neg\mathrm{MP}, \neg\mathrm{MT}, \mathrm{AC}, \mathrm{DA})$. This imposes the constraints $A\overline{B} \preccurlyeq AB$, $A\overline{B} \preccurlyeq \overline{A}\,\overline{B}$, $AB \prec \overline{A}B$, and $\overline{A}\,\overline{B} \prec \overline{A}B$ on the epistemic state. Figure 8.2a illustrates these constraints. This pattern is rational, the ranking functions κ_{B89} and κ'_{B89} in Figure 8.2b are plausibility relations that meet all these constraints.

Preferential relations $\prec \subseteq \Omega \times \Omega$ can be expressed as graphs where each vertex represents a possible world, and en edge $\omega \to \omega'$ indicates $\omega \prec \omega'$. In her Bachelor's thesis [Tay17], Tayyem pointed out that the rationality of a pattern can be checked on the graph of the plausibility ordering imposed by the pattern.

Lemma 8.20 (Graph-Based Rationality for Inference Patterns [Tay17]). An inference pattern $\varrho \in \mathcal{I}$ is rational if and only if the imposed plausibility ordering does not contain any cycles.

There are 16 different patterns in $\mathcal{I}$; Figure 8.3 lists the illustrations of the joint constraints imposed by each of the patterns. From these patterns, only the patterns (MP, ¬MT, ¬AC, DA), which imposes the unrealisable ordering $\overline{A}\,\overline{B} \prec \overline{A}\,B \preccurlyeq A\,B \prec A\,\overline{B} \preccurlyeq \overline{A}\,B$, and its inverse (¬MP, MT, AC, ¬DA), which imposes the unrealisable ordering $\overline{A}\,\overline{B} \prec A\,\overline{B} \preccurlyeq A\,B \prec \overline{A}\,B \preccurlyeq \overline{A}\,B$, are irrational. This means that except for the two mentioned patterns, all inference patterns conceivable in inference studies are to be called rational with respect to Definition 8.18, because there are epistemic states in which the inferences drawn are believed.

This definition of rationality provides a formal nonmonotonic notion of the abstract concept of rationality. This nonmonotonic rationality includes the "classical" understanding of rationality which uses classical logic as normative theory of rationality as the pattern (MP, MT, ¬AC, ¬DA), which describes a reasoner who uses only classically valid rules for drawing inferences, is rational. Concurrently it extends this definition in that it also rates other combination of inference rules to be rational.

Using a preferential definition of rationality directly gives us formal properties of these inference processes: Being set up upon a preferential model, each inference based on an epistemic state satisfying a rational pattern satisfies the properties of System P. Additionally, the pattern (MP, MT, AC, DA) imposes a total strict ordering of the worlds, therefore inferences based on an epistemic state satisfying this pattern satisfy System R. So Definition 8.18 captures a rationality based on nonmonotonic structures that are widely accepted as benchmarks for inference relations as well as agreed to license for inferences of high quality.

Until now, we can rate the answers of participants in inference studies to be rational or irrational with respect to epistemic states according to Definition 8.18. In the following, we use the constraints on the epistemic states to not only rate the answers that constructed the patterns, but also to reverse engineer knowledge bases that inductively generate these epistemic states. In this, we generate a hypothesis of the background knowledge necessary for having an epistemic state on which basis the inferences constructing the patterns are drawn. This knowledge bases serve as an explanation for the results of the studies being as they are. Thus the knowledge bases can are hypotheses for the background knowledge the participants activated when giving the answers in the tasks.

As a first step we realise that each usage of a positive rule constraints the epistemic state Ψ to such an extent that in Ψ a respective inference is

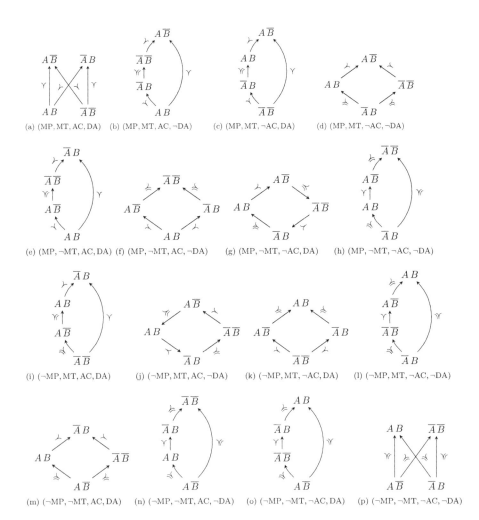

Figure 8.3: Preference relations that result on the constraints imposed on the epistemic state by all sixteen inference patterns.

Table 8.11: Overview over the inference rules and conditionals that are to be accepted by the epistemic state in order to believe the inference according to Tables 8.11a and 8.11b

Inference rule	Resulting conditional	Inference rule	Resulting conditional
MP	$(B\|A)$	$\neg$MP	$(\overline{B}\|A)$
MT	$(\overline{A}\|\overline{B})$	$\neg$MT	$(A\|\overline{B})$
AC	$(A\|B)$	$\neg$AC	$(\overline{A}\|B)$
DA	$(\overline{B}\|\overline{A})$	$\neg$DA	$(B\|\overline{A})$

believed. If we use OCF for formalising the epistemic state, Definition 3.29 closely connects the belief into an inference with the belief into a conditional in such a way that an inference $\phi \approx_\kappa \psi$ is valid if and only if the strong conditional $(\psi|\phi)$ is accepted by κ. For negative rules we obtain that a non-entailment $\phi \not\approx_\kappa \psi$ is valid in the epistemic state κ if and only if $\kappa(\phi\overline{\psi}) \leq \kappa(\phi\psi)$, which is the case if and only if κ accepts the weak conditional $(\overline{\psi}|\phi)$ (see Section 3.3). So the constraints imposed by an inference pattern are realised by ranking functions and, basically, the Ramsey Test for nonmonotonic logic. This produces a set of conditionals which are to be accepted if and only if the OCF is to meet the constraints. Table 8.11 gives an overview of the rules and the resulting conditionals.

Each pattern defines four requirements for the epistemic states in the form of a set of four conditionals that are accepted by the epistemic state if and only if it licenses for the inferences represented by the pattern. On this set of conditionals, we now can use approaches like System Z or c-representations to inductively obtain an epistemic state that satisfies the constraints. Even more, the system of inequalities for a mixed knowledge base (Proposition 3.40, Inequality (3.38)) of c-representations can be used to minimise the set of conditionals by removing the ones which are not informative, that is, which do not yield additional information to the basic definitions and conditionals already present.

This is the case if for any conditional the inequalities yield a semi-positive impact, which is already required by the definition of the impacts. With this approach we obtain a set of inclusion minimal knowledge bases. If we apply c-representations to one of these knowledge bases, we obtain a ranking function that satisfies all constraints imposed by the inference patterns.

Thus we call each of the generated knowledge bases an *explanation* for the pattern. These explanations also are hypotheses for the background knowledge the participants in the studies activated when given their answers, as already discussed.

Example 8.21 ([REB$^+$17]). We further develop Example 8.19. According to Table 8.11 the pattern $\varrho_{B89} = (\neg MP, \neg MT, AC, DA)$ yields the conditionals $\Delta^*_{B89} = \{\delta_1 : (\overline{l}|e), \delta_2 : (e|\overline{l}), \delta_3 : (e|l), \delta_4 : (\overline{l}|\overline{e})\}$, substituting the generic literals A and B by the variables E to indicate whether Lisa has an essay to write (or not), and L to indicate whether Lisa studies late in the library (or not), respectively. The verification / falsification behaviour of the worlds given in Table 8.12 in this example together with the definition of the system of inequalities in (3.38) results in the following system of inequalities:

$$\kappa_1^- \geq 0 \tag{8.4}$$

$$\kappa_2^- \geq 0 \tag{8.5}$$

$$\kappa_3^- > \kappa_1^- - \kappa_4^- \tag{8.6}$$

$$\kappa_4^- > \kappa_2^- - \kappa_3^- \tag{8.7}$$

Here we see that (8.4) and (8.5) do not yield additional information to the definitions of the impacts. Also, (8.6) and (8.7) can be joined to give us the inequality $\kappa_3^- + \kappa_4^- > \min\{\kappa_1^-, \kappa_2^-\}$. As either of the impacts in the minimum can be 0, only one of the impacts κ_3^- or κ_4^- has to be strictly positive to provide a valid solution to the system, only one of these lines yields additional information, whereas the other conditional does not. Thus either $(e|l)$ or $(\overline{l}|\overline{e})$ are informative, while the other is not. Therefore there are two inclusion minimal knowledge bases $\Delta_{B89} = \{(e|l)\}$ and $\Delta'_{B89} = \{(\overline{l}|\overline{e})\}$ which both generate the minimal c-representation κ_{B89} in Table 8.12. This c-representation satisfies the constraints imposed by the pattern ϱ_{B89}:

$$\kappa(e\,\overline{l}) = 0 \leq 0 = \kappa(e\,l) \quad \text{thus} \quad e\,\overline{l} \leq_{\kappa_{B89}} e\,l \quad \text{as imposed by} \quad \neg MP$$

$$\kappa(e\,\overline{l}) = 0 \leq 0 = \kappa(\overline{e}\,\overline{l}) \quad \text{thus} \quad e\,\overline{l} \leq_{\kappa_{B89}} \overline{e}\,\overline{l} \quad \text{as imposed by} \quad \neg MT$$

$$\kappa(e\,l) = 0 < 1 = \kappa(\overline{e}\,l) \quad \text{thus} \quad e\,l <_{\kappa_{B89}} \overline{e}\,l \quad \text{as imposed by} \quad AC$$

$$\kappa(\overline{e}\,\overline{l}) = 0 < 1 = \kappa(\overline{e}\,l) \quad \text{thus} \quad \overline{e}\,\overline{l} <_{\kappa_{B89}} \overline{e}\,l \quad \text{as imposed by} \quad DA.$$

The resulting hypothesis is that the participants either activated the background knowledge "If Lisa studies late in the library, then she has an essay to write", or "If Lisa does not have an essay to write, she will not study late in the library".

Table 8.12: Verification / falsification behaviour and one c-representation for the knowledge base Δ^*_{B89} of Example 8.21

ω	$e\,l$	$e\,\overline{l}$	$\overline{e}\,l$	$\overline{e}\,\overline{l}$
verifies	δ_3	δ_1,δ_2	—	δ_4
falsifies	δ_1	—	δ_3,δ_4	δ_2
$\kappa_{B89}(\omega)$	0	0	1	0

Listing 8.1: Explanation Generator [ERKI18].

```
INPUT   : Inference Pattern ϱ
OUTPUT  : Set of knowledge bases {Δ_ϱ^(1),...};
          Δ_ϱ^(i) ⊆ (ℒ|ℒ) ∪ (ℒ|ℒ) for all i.

BEGIN
  // Preprocessing
  Set up Δ* according to Table 8.11
  Set up the system of inequalities (3.38) for Δ*

  // Simplify system of inequalities:
  FOR(i:=1, i<=4; i++)
    IF(line i of the system is implied by other inequalities)
      Remove line i from the system
      Remove conditional (B_i|A_i) from Δ*
    END IF
  END FOR
  RETURN {Δ_ϱ^(1),...}
END
```

We formalise the procedure discussed above as Algorithm 8.1, additionally illustrated in Figure 8.4 and demonstrate Algorithm 8.1 with another example, that is, another reasoning study from the literature.

Example 8.22 (Counterfactual Study [TB02] (confer [REB+17])). In [TB02, Experiment 2, reasoning about nonnecessary/causal] the participants had to reason about counterfactual statements like "If the car had been out of $g$as, then it would have $\underline{s}$talled" with possible worlds $\{gs, g\overline{s}, \overline{g}s, \overline{g}\,\overline{s}\}$. In this study the majority of the participants, introductory students of psychology, applied MP (78%) and MT (85%), and did not apply AC (41%). They were

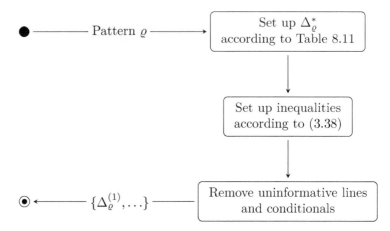

Figure 8.4: Illustration of the Algorithm 8.1 "Explanation Generator" to obtain a inclusion minimal knowledge base for an inference pattern as explanation for
the epistemic state and as hypothesis for the background knowledge of the
participants in the inference study that resulted in the pattern

on the fence with respect to DA (50%); we here decide to model this as DA
(other than ¬DA), see [Tay17] for an analysis about "better" thresholds.
So this study can be covered by the pattern $\varrho_{TB02} = (\mathrm{MP}, \mathrm{MT}, \neg\mathrm{AC}, \mathrm{DA})$,
which yields the constraints in Tables 8.11a and 8.11b. Algorithm 8.1 sets
up the knowledge base $\Delta^*_{TB02} = \{\delta_1 : (s|g), \delta_2 : (\overline{g}|\overline{s}), \delta_3 : (\overline{g}|s), \delta_4 : (\overline{s}|\overline{g})\}$,
which, according to (3.38) and the verification / falsification behaviour given
in Table 8.13, yields the following system of inequalities

$$\kappa_1^- > \kappa_3^- - \kappa_2^-$$
$$\kappa_2^- > 0 - \kappa_1^-$$
$$\kappa_3^- \geq \kappa_4^- - 0 \qquad\qquad (8.8)$$
$$\kappa_4^- > 0 - 0.$$

Here the impact of δ_2 (8.8) is covered by the other conditionals, so the sys-
tem can be simplified to $\kappa_1^- > \kappa_3^-$, $\kappa_3^- \geq \kappa_4^-$, and $\kappa_4^- > 0$, which gives us the
minimal explaining knowledge base $\Delta_{TB02} = \{\delta_1 : (s|g), \delta_3 : (\overline{g}|s), \delta_4 : (\overline{s}|\overline{g})\}$
and the minimal c-representation given in Table 8.13. This example illus-

Table 8.13: Verification / falsification behaviour and minimal c-representation for Example 8.22

ω	$g\,s$	$g\,\overline{s}$	$\overline{g}\,s$	$\overline{g}\,\overline{s}$
verifies	δ_1	—	δ_3	δ_4,δ_4
falsifies	δ_3	δ_1,δ_2	δ_4	—
$\kappa_{TB02}(\omega)$	1	2	1	0

trates that that the constraints imposed by ϱ_{TB02} on κ_{TB02} are satisfied:

$\kappa(g\,s) = 1 < 2 = \kappa(g\,\overline{s})$ thus $g\,s <_{\kappa_{TB02}} g\,\overline{s}$ as imposed by MP

$\kappa(\overline{g}\,\overline{s}) = 0 < 2 = \kappa(g\,\overline{s})$ thus $\overline{g}\,\overline{s} <_{\kappa_{TB02}} g\,\overline{s}$ as imposed by MT

$\kappa(\overline{g}\,s) = 1 \leq 1 = \kappa(g\,s)$ thus $\overline{g}\,s \leq_{\kappa_{TB02}} g\,s$ as imposed by $\neg$AC

$\kappa(\overline{g}\,\overline{s}) = 0 < 1 = \kappa(\overline{g}\,s)$ thus $\overline{g}\,\overline{s} <_{\kappa_{TB02}} \overline{g}\,s$ as imposed by DA.

From Δ_{TB02} we read the hypothesis for the background knowledge to be:

δ_1 "If the car had been out of gas, then (usually) it would have stalled."

δ_3 "If the car had stalled, then it possibly would not have been out of gas"[4]

δ_4 "If the car had not been out of gas, then (usually) it would not have stalled."

Additionally to the hypotheses for the activated background knowledge of the participants, we also obtain the belief state of the participants from the epistemic states. We recall Definition 3.9 that the belief of an OCF is the set of formal theories of the worlds that are maximally plausible. As the system of inequalities in Algorithm 8.1 yields a c-representation κ_Δ^c, we also can determine the belief of the agents as $Bel(\kappa_\Delta^c) = Th(\{\omega | \kappa_\Delta^c(\omega) = 0\})$.

Example 8.23. We continue Examples 8.21 and 8.22 on behalf of pointing out the belief set of the participants. In the Suppression Task, the participants reasoned according to the pattern $(\neg$MP$, \neg$MT$, AC, DA)$. Table 8.12 shows a minimal c-representation, here the belief is $Th(\{e\,l, e\,\overline{l}, \overline{e}\,l\}) = Ch(l \Rightarrow e)$, that is, in the case where the participants reasoned using only

---

[4]   Alternatively: "It is not true that if the car had stalled, it would (usually) have been out of gas."

classically invalid rules and reject classically valid rules, they believe the material implication encoding the inverse of the conditional presented to then ("If Lisa studies late in the library, then she has an essay to write" instead of "If Lisa has an essay to write, she will study late in the library"). As AC and DA are the rules MP and MT for the inverse conditional, this indicates that the participants reasoned in accordance with classical logic, but proceedings from and believing in the inverse of the conditional presented to them. In the counterfactual task of Example 8.22, the belief set is $\mathit{Th}(\{\,\overline{g}\,\overline{s}\,\}) = \mathit{Cn}(\overline{g}\,\overline{s})$, that is, based on the knowledge base Δ_{TB02} the participants believe that the car is neither out of gas nor stalls. This is in accordance with the task being a counterfactual task, that is, a task of reasoning about what is not true (or believed): Even if the participants do not believe the car neither to have stalled nor being out of gas, they reason hypothetically about a situation where the prior occured.

As there are only fourteen inference patterns, the calculations, that is, the algorithm can be run beforehand; Table 8.14 lists the generic patterns, resulting knowledge bases Δ^* and minimal explanations according to Algorithm 8.1, where the variables can be substituted with the variables of the respective experiment that is to be explained with this method.

Overall we have shown that inference patterns can be used to formally capture the qualitative result of inference studies, and in this are a useful tool to classify these studies. We have seen that the satisfiability of the plausibility constraints imposed by the patterns provides a novel notion of rationality. Additionally, each epistemic state satisfying a pattern reveals a set of deductively closed formulas as implicit assumptions of the reasoners tested. Finally, we have seen that inference patterns together with the technique of c-representations can be used to generate conditional knowledge bases that inductively generate the respective epistemic state and thus can be used as hypotheses for the background knowledge of the participants.

Table 8.14: Overview over the inference patterns, initial knowledge bases Δ^*, minimal explanations according to Algorithm 8.1, minimal c-representation and belief set induced by the patterns

Pattern	Δ^* δ_1	δ_2	δ_3	δ_4	Minimal explanations $\{\Delta^{(1)}, \dots\}$	$\kappa^c_{\Delta}(\omega)$ AB	$A\overline{B}$	$\overline{A}B$	$\overline{A}\,\overline{B}$	Belief Set Ψ
(MP, MT, AC, DA)	$(B\|A)$	$(\overline{A}\|\overline{B})$	$(A\|B)$	$(\overline{B}\|\overline{A})$	$\{\delta_1,\delta_3\},\ \{\delta_1,\delta_4\},\ \{\delta_2,\delta_3\},\ \{\delta_2,\delta_4\}$	0	1	1	0	$Ch(A \Leftrightarrow B)$
(MP, MT, AC, ¬DA)	$(B\|A)$	$(\overline{A}\|\overline{B})$	$(A\|B)$	$(B\|\overline{A})$	$\{\delta_2,\delta_3,\delta_4\}$	0	2	2	1	$Ch(AB)$
(MP, MT, ¬AC, DA)	$(B\|A)$	$(\overline{A}\|\overline{B})$	$(\overline{A}\|B)$	$(\overline{B}\|\overline{A})$	$\{\delta_1,\delta_3,\delta_4\}$	1	2	1	0	$Ch(\overline{A}\,\overline{B})$
(MP, MT, ¬AC, ¬DA)	$(B\|A)$	$(\overline{A}\|\overline{B})$	$(\overline{A}\|B)$	$(B\|\overline{A})$	$\{\delta_1\},\ \{\delta_2\}$	0	1	0	0	$Ch(A \Rightarrow B)$
(MP, ¬MT, AC, DA)	$(B\|A)$	$(A\|\overline{B})$	$(A\|B)$	$(\overline{B}\|\overline{A})$	$\{\delta_1,\delta_2,\delta_4\}$	0	1	2	1	$Ch(AB)$
(MP, ¬MT, AC, ¬DA)	$(B\|A)$	$(A\|\overline{B})$	$(A\|B)$	$(B\|\overline{A})$	$\{\delta_1,\delta_2,\delta_3\},\ \{\delta_1,\delta_3,\delta_4\}$	0	1	1	1	$Ch(AB)$
(MP, ¬MT, ¬AC, DA)	$(B\|A)$	$(A\|\overline{B})$	$(\overline{A}\|B)$	$(\overline{B}\|\overline{A})$	irrational pattern					
(MP, ¬MT, ¬AC, ¬DA)	$(B\|A)$	$(A\|\overline{B})$	$(\overline{A}\|B)$	$(B\|\overline{A})$	$\{\delta_1,\delta_2\}$	0	1	0	1	$Ch(B)$
(¬MP, MT, AC, DA)	$(\overline{B}\|A)$	$(\overline{A}\|\overline{B})$	$(A\|B)$	$(\overline{B}\|\overline{A})$	$\{\delta_1,\delta_2,\delta_3\}$	1	2	1	0	$Ch(\overline{A}\,\overline{B})$
(¬MP, MT, AC, ¬DA)	$(\overline{B}\|A)$	$(\overline{A}\|\overline{B})$	$(A\|B)$	$(B\|\overline{A})$	irrational pattern					
(¬MP, MT, ¬AC, DA)	$(\overline{B}\|A)$	$(\overline{A}\|\overline{B})$	$(\overline{A}\|B)$	$(\overline{B}\|\overline{A})$	$\{\delta_1,\delta_2,\delta_4\},\ \{\delta_2,\delta_3,\delta_4\}$	1	1	1	0	$Ch(\overline{A}\,\overline{B})$
(¬MP, MT, ¬AC, ¬DA)	$(\overline{B}\|A)$	$(\overline{A}\|\overline{B})$	$(\overline{A}\|B)$	$(B\|\overline{A})$	$\{\delta_1,\delta_2\}$	1	1	0	0	$Ch(\overline{A})$
(¬MP, ¬MT, AC, DA)	$(\overline{B}\|A)$	$(A\|\overline{B})$	$(A\|B)$	$(\overline{B}\|\overline{A})$	$\{\delta_3\},\ \{\delta_4\}$	0	0	1	0	$Ch(B \Rightarrow A)$
(¬MP, ¬MT, AC, ¬DA)	$(\overline{B}\|A)$	$(A\|\overline{B})$	$(A\|B)$	$(B\|\overline{A})$	$\{\delta_3,\delta_4\}$	0	0	1	1	$Ch(A)$
(¬MP, ¬MT, ¬AC, DA)	$(\overline{B}\|A)$	$(A\|\overline{B})$	$(\overline{A}\|B)$	$(\overline{B}\|\overline{A})$	$\{\delta_3,\delta_4\}$	1	0	1	0	$Ch(\overline{B})$
(¬MP, ¬MT, ¬AC, ¬DA)	$(\overline{B}\|A)$	$(A\|\overline{B})$	$(\overline{A}\|B)$	$(B\|\overline{A})$	$\varnothing$	0	0	0	0	$Ch(\varnothing)$

8.3 Interim Conclusion and Discussion

Summing up the results of all parts of this chapter we see that it is possible to mimic the behaviour of human reasoners found in psychological inference studies. This holds regardless of the used formalism, be it logic programming, as already shown by [SvL08, HKR09], Reiter Default Logic, System P, System Z and c-representations. But for all approaches it is necessary to model the knowledge of the agent carefully: In Section 8.1.1 we saw that a plain modelling into the designated formalism is prone to not follow the human reasoners inferences [REKI16]. We demonstrated in Section 8.1.2 that making the connections between the variables in the experiment explicit yields the designated effect, but to achieve this, the knowledge engineer has to be aware of these connections. This is not always the case. When, for instance, an expert system is to be designed, the knowledge engineer does not know all the details of the area to be modelled. As additional challenge, the tuning of defeasibility and strictness has to be carefully balanced. Section 8.1.3 shows that strengthening or weakening the "wrong" part of the knowledge may lead to inconsistent knowledge bases. But, in the same way, this risk bears the possibility to implicitly include exceptions not mentioned in the modelling: Having models that infer the designated test-cases but are leave room for other inferences apart the specified are, in our way, preferable [REB+17].

With inference patterns in Section 8.2 we recalled a way of capturing the result of inference experiment in a holistic fashion from [ERKI18], and not only with respect to a single inference rule. With this technique, proposed by the author of this dissertation, we recalled a nonmonotonic notion of rationality based on the Ramsey test for nonmonotonic logic and preferential inference that contains and extends the definition of rationality via accordance with classical logic. These inference patterns open the door to classifying and comparing inference studies with each other, and may even be used to classify different cover stories of experiments. This thesis extends [ERKI18] with a compete analysis of the preferences and explanations induced from the patterns by the explanation generator for every consistent inference pattern.

Overall in this chapter we demonstrated that it is possible to model human reasoning with formal inference methods given the background knowledge is sufficiently formalised. We also demonstrated that a differentiation between strict and defeasible knowledge is a crucial step in modelling human reasoning, as the formalised knowledge can become inconsistent if this is not done thoroughly. Finally, with inference patterns we demonstrated that there is an algorithmic method to make the implicit assumptions in an inference task explicit when the answers of the human reasoners can be taken into account.

The modelling of the Suppression Task into logic programming is to be attributed to Marco Ragni, the modellings into other logics in [REKI16, REB+17] was contributed by the author of this thesis. The basic idea of the holistic view of the inference patterns in [ERKI18] originated from the author of this thesis, whilst applying weak conditionals to the non-inferences is to be attributed to Gabriele Kern-Isberner. The other cited results are mainly the results of discussions of all the authors of the respective papers.

9 Summary and Final Remarks

In this chapter we sum up the thesis, comment on the research questions raised and indicate starting points for further work in the areas of this thesis.

9.1 Summary

To sum up this thesis, we refer again to Figure 1.1 (Page 12) and see that this thesis has come to a full circle: We showed that approaches to nonmonotonic reasoning like conditional structures, System Z, and c-representations inductively realise epistemic states based on knowledge bases. These epistemic states instantiate preferential inference, thus each of these methods is tied closely to its own inference relation. We demonstrated that formal properties of nonmonotonic inference relations are useful in classifying and comparing different inference relations in that we applied these properties to these inductive methods. We also demonstrated that these (and other) approaches to knowledge representation and reasoning can model human reasoning given the representation of the knowledge captures all necessary relationships between the variables. With inference patterns we also recalled that preferential inference, together with c-representations, is capable of making the implicit relationships between the variables, that it, the hidden assumptions of the human reasoner, explicit.

With OCF- and OCF-LEG networks we recalled methods of making inductive inference with OCF computationally feasible. The formulation of the consistency conditions and the examples provided violating these, however, indicate that setting up these network types inductively is not always successful.

9.2 Further and Future Work

Working on the topics of this thesis has left few loose threads which provide good starting points for future and further work:

By showing that structural inference satisfies all properties of System P but none of the selected properties outside System P, we already conjectured that structural inference could be a complete semantic for System P. Proving or disproving this formally provides a starting point for further research in the area of strictly qualitative nonmonotonic inference.

© Springer-Verlag GmbH Germany, part of Springer Nature 2018
C. Eichhorn, *Rational Reasoning with Finite Conditional Knowledge Bases*, https://doi.org/10.1007/978-3-476-04824-0_9

This thesis mainly relies on ordinal conditional functions to represent epistemic states. On finite sets of worlds, OCF and inference therewith bear great similarity to possibility functions and the respective inference. Future work includes to research if and where these two approaches are different with respect to formalising, storing and inducing epistemic states. A starting point is set by the violation of the consistency condition of OCF-networks which may be overcome when using the real-valued approach of possibility theory instead of the integer-valued approach of OCF.

We demonstrated that the construction of an OCF-LEG network is possible, even if the initial consistency check fails for the local c-representations, by swapping local c-representations for other ones. This thesis gives a very strong condition for this to be possible in general, but also a weaker condition may be sufficient. Further work includes more thorough research in this area to provide constraints which ensure that OCF-LEG networks can be generated safely.

In this thesis and the article [ERKI18] the respective chapter is based upon, we use a threshold of 50% of the participants to decide whether an inference rule is to be formalised as *used* or *not used*. As the relatively weak properties of threshold inference (see Section 3.4) and indicate, choosing a fixed value may not be the best choice. In her Bachelor's Thesis [Tay17] under supervision of the author of this thesis and Gabriele Kern-Isberner, Tayyem discusses having a floating threshold. This work provides a starting point for further research into how to determine whether a rule in an experiment is to be classified as used or not used.

Inference patterns have been devised to classify the results of inference studies. It would be interesting to use them not on averaged results on many cover stories, but on the results of the task under each story, separately. By this it could be possible to determine similarities and dissimilarities between the different experiments.

In this thesis, the reverse-engineering step on inference patterns is made using OCF. It has already been shown[1] that it is possible to use conditional structures for this step, as well, showing that using the weaker inductive approach (conditional structures instead of c-representations) yields stronger explanations (knowledge bases without weak conditionals versus knowledge bases with weak conditionals).

---

[1]   Christian Eichhorn and Gabriele Kern-Isberner: *Explaining Rational Reasoning by Symbolic Conditional Knowledge Bases Using Strictly Qualitative Structural Inference*; submitted manuscript, 2018.

9.3 Conclusion

This thesis gives an overview of qualitative rational reasoning with finite conditional knowledge bases by commenting on conceptual, implementational and applicational aspects of this topic.

With respect to conceptual aspects, we answered the research question of how to realise qualitative and semi-quantitative reasoning with the semantics of conditional structures and ordinal conditional functions. The preferential inferences constructed on these representations and thus also the inductive approaches to generating them, provided formal inference of high quality. This was ensured by answering and applying the results of the research question regarding how to classify formal approaches to non-monotonic reasoning. We recalled approaches to reasoning with sets of c-representations, thus providing a baseline for inference with any single c-representation. This also overcomes the problem that arbitrary choices in solving the respective systems of inequalities may lead to different inferences. Additionally, with the transformation systems for conditional knowledge bases recalled a method to get rid of "notorious" conditionals in the knowledge base.

With respect to implementation aspects our analysis of networks approaches to OCF resulted in OCF-networks and OCF-LEG networks are, statically, in no way inferior to their probabilistic counterparts and provide a significant reduction of space complexity to the global OCF. However, if they are to be constructed inductively, failure is possible. We presented algorithms to construct the networks and check them for consistency by local computations.

With respect to the application of methods from the area of qualitative rational reasoning we recalled how to model human inference and how to use the result of humans reasoning to make the hidden assumptions of the reasoners explicit.

A Proofs of Technical Findings

This appendix contains the proofs for the technical findings contained in this thesis, be it novel or reported ones, ordered by chapter of their occurrence. Note that references to formal environments are numbered with numbers, only, if they refer to the main part of the thesis, and start with an A is they refer to formal environments in the appendix.

Some results reported in this thesis are not proven in this appendix. There mainly are two reasons for this: Firstly, no proof is needed in the appendix because it was already shown in the main part of the thesis that the result is valid. This is the case for most corollaries as it is discussed how they follow from their prerequisites in the text introducing the corollary. This is also the case for the observations because they are accompanied by an example supporting the observation. Secondly, the finding is a result from the literature (without involvement of the author of this thesis) and it is a well-established result (like, for instance, the representation theorem for System P (Theorem 4.27 from [KLM90, Theorem 3]) or the actual proof needs additional background which is not needed elsewhere in this thesis (as, for instance, the proof for Proposition 4.29 in [GP96]).

A.1 Proofs for Chapter 2

The first five proofs of this section are for well-known findings from the literature (see, for instance, [Tar30, GS69]) which are used in the beginning of the preliminaries of this thesis. They are proven for the sake of completeness of this thesis; the author explicitly does not claim these to be novel findings or proofs.

Proof that classical entailment satisfies (M): Let $\phi \vDash \chi$. We show that from this we obtain $\phi\psi \vDash \chi$. By definition of $\vDash$ we have $\phi \vDash \chi$ if and only if $Mod(\phi) \subseteq Mod(\chi)$. We also have $Mod(\phi\psi) = \{\omega | \omega \vDash \phi\psi\} = \{\omega | \omega \vDash \phi \text{ and } \omega \vDash \psi\} = \{\omega | \omega \vDash \phi\} \cap \{\omega | \omega \vDash \psi\} = Mod(\phi) \cap Mod(\psi)$ and trivially $Mod(\phi) \cap Mod(\psi) \subseteq Mod(\phi)$. Thus we obtain $Mod(\phi) \cap Mod(\psi) \subseteq Mod(\phi) \subseteq Mod(\chi)$. By transitivity of $\subseteq$ we further obtain $Mod(\phi) \cap Mod(\psi) \subseteq Mod(\chi)$ which gives us $\phi\psi \vDash \chi$, as proposed. $\qquad\square$

Proof that classical entailment satisfies (T): We show that $\phi \vDash \psi$ and $\psi \vDash \chi$ imply $\phi \vDash \chi$. By definition of $\vDash$ the prerequisites give us $Mod(\phi) \subseteq Mod(\psi)$ and $Mod(\psi) \subseteq Mod(\chi)$. We chain these relations on $Mod(\psi)$ and obtain

© Springer-Verlag GmbH Germany, part of Springer Nature 2018
C. Eichhorn, *Rational Reasoning with Finite Conditional Knowledge Bases*, https://doi.org/10.1007/978-3-476-04824-0

$Mod(\phi) \subseteq Mod(\psi) \subseteq Mod(\chi)$ and therefore $Mod(\phi) \subseteq Mod(\chi)$ which gives us $\phi \vDash \chi$ as proposed.   □

Proof that classical entailment satisfies (DThm): We show that we have $\phi \vDash \psi$ if and only if $\top \vDash (\phi \Rightarrow \psi)$; note that $\Omega = Mod(\top) = Mod(\phi \vee \overline{\phi}) = Mod(\phi) \cup Mod(\overline{\phi})$ ⋆.

For the "only if"-part we show that $\phi \vDash \psi$ implies $\top \vDash (\phi \Rightarrow \psi)$. From $\phi \vDash \psi$ then the definition of $\vDash$ gives us $Mod(\phi) \subseteq Mod(\psi)$ and hence ⋆ gives us $Mod(\overline{\phi}) \cup Mod(\psi) = \Omega$. Therefore $\Omega \subseteq Mod(\phi \Rightarrow \psi)$, which gives us $\top \vDash (\phi \Rightarrow \psi)$.

For the "if"-part we show $\top \vDash (\phi \Rightarrow \psi)$ implies $\phi \vDash \psi$. $\top \vDash (\phi \Rightarrow \psi)$ this gives us $\Omega \subseteq Mod(\overline{\phi}) \cup Mod(\psi)$. But then also $\Omega \setminus Mod(\overline{\phi}) \subseteq (Mod(\overline{\phi}) \cup Mod(\psi)) \setminus Mod(\overline{\phi})$, which gives us $Mod(\phi) \subseteq (Mod(\overline{\phi}) \setminus (Mod(\overline{\phi}) \cup (Mod(\psi) \setminus Mod(\overline{\phi})))$ and thus $Mod(\phi) \subseteq (Mod(\psi) \setminus Mod(\overline{\phi}))$ and therefore $Mod(\phi) \subseteq Mod(\psi)$ which, by the definition of $\vDash$ gives us $\phi \vDash \psi$, and that completes the proof.   □

Proof that classical entailment satisfies (CPS): Let $\phi \vDash \psi$, we show that this implies $\overline{\psi} \vDash \overline{\phi}$. By (DThm), $\phi \vDash \psi$ is equivalent to $\top \vDash (\phi \Rightarrow \psi)$. We have

$$(\phi \Rightarrow \psi) \equiv (\overline{\phi} \vee \psi) \equiv (\overline{\psi} \Rightarrow \overline{\phi})$$

and thus an obtain $\top \vDash (\overline{\psi} \Rightarrow \overline{\phi})$ which is, again by (DThm), equivalent to $\overline{\psi} \vDash \overline{\phi}$, which we wanted to show.   □

Proof that classical entailment satisfies (EFQ).: We have $Mod(\bot) = \varnothing$ and $\varnothing \subseteq \mathcal{A}$ for any set $\mathcal{A}$. Therefore $Mod(\bot) \subseteq Mod(\psi)$ for all $\psi \in \mathfrak{L}$ and hence $\bot \vDash \psi$ for all $\psi \in \mathfrak{L}$, as proposed.   □

Proof of Proposition 2.15 that Δ-inference satisfies (DI) (confer [Luk05]): Let $\Delta = \{(\psi_1|\phi_1), \ldots, (\psi_n|\phi_n)\}$ be a knowledge base, we show that Δ-inference satisfies (DI). For every conditional $(\psi|\phi) \in \Delta$ the extended knowledge base $\Delta \cup \{(\overline{\psi}|\phi)\}$ has a subset $\{(\psi|\phi), (\overline{\psi}|\phi)\}$ which is inconsistent because the conditionals directly contradict each other and thus the whole set $\Delta \cup \{(\overline{\psi}|\phi)\}$ is inconsistent. Therefore Definition 2.11 gives us $\phi \mathrel{\vcenter{\hbox{$\not\hspace{-0.3em}\approx$}}}_\Delta \psi$ for every $(\psi|\phi) \in \Delta$ as proposed.   □

Proof of Proposition 2.16 that Δ-inference satisfies (MExp): Let $\Delta = \{(\psi_1|\phi_1), \ldots, (\psi_n|\phi_n)\} \subseteq (\mathfrak{L} \mid \mathfrak{L})$ be a conditional knowledge base, we show that Δ-inference satisfies (MExp). By Definition 2.11 we have

$\phi\mathrel{|\!\approx}_\Delta \psi$ if and only if $\Delta\cup\{(\overline{\psi}|\phi)\}$ is inconsistent. If Δ is already inconsistent, then $\Delta\cup\{(\overline{\psi}|\phi)\}$ is inconsistent for every conditional $(\overline{\psi}|\phi)\in(\mathfrak{L}|\mathfrak{L})$ and therefore we have $\phi\mathrel{|\!\approx}_\Delta \psi$ for all $\phi,\psi\in\mathfrak{L}$, as we wanted to show. □

Proof of Proposition 2.17 that Δ-inference satisfies (SM) (confer [ST12]):
Let $\Delta=\{(\psi_1|\phi_1),\ldots,(\psi_n|\phi_n)\}\subseteq(\mathfrak{L}\mid\mathfrak{L})$ be a conditional knowledge base, we show that Δ-inference satisfies (SM). By Definition 2.11 we have $\phi\mathrel{|\!\approx}_\Delta \psi$ if and only if $\Delta\cup\{(\overline{\psi}|\phi)\}$ is inconsistent. If $\Delta\cup\{(\overline{\psi}|\phi)\}$ is inconsistent, then the set $\Delta'\cup\{(\overline{\psi}|\phi)\}$ is inconsistent for every $\Delta'\supseteq\Delta$, and then also $\phi\mathrel{|\!\approx}_{\Delta'}\psi$ as proposed. □

A.2 Proofs for Chapter 3

Proof of Lemma 3.3 (confer [Mak94]): This is clear because the behaviour of the satisfaction relation postulated in 3.2 is satisfied by $\vDash$, directly. ☐

Proof of Lemma 3.5 (confer [Mak94]): Let $\mathcal{M}$ be a finite set of states and let $\prec$ be a strict and transitive preference relation $\prec \subseteq \mathcal{M} \times \mathcal{M}$. If $\prec$ is transitive and strict, $\prec$ does not contain circles. So, since $\mathcal{M}$ is finite, every path defined in $\prec$ is finite, and thus there are $\prec$-minimal states in every subset of $\mathcal{M}$. ☐

Proof of basic properties of OCF (confer [Spo88, Spo12]):
We recall the proofs for basic properties of OCF in Section 3.3:
(3.11) Rank of a disjunction:

$$\kappa(\phi \vee \psi) \stackrel{(3.10)}{=\!=\!=} \min\{\kappa(\omega)|\omega \vDash (\phi \vee \psi)\}$$
$$= \min\{\kappa(\omega)|(\omega \vDash \phi) \vee (\omega \vDash \psi)\}$$
$$= \min\{\min\{\kappa(\omega)|(\omega \vDash \phi)\}, \min\{\kappa(\omega)|(\omega \vDash \psi)\}\}$$
$$\stackrel{(3.10)}{=\!=\!=} \min\{\kappa(\phi), \kappa(\psi)\}$$

(3.12) Rank of a conjunction: The rank of a conjunction cannot be smaller than the rank of any of the conjuncts, thus the rank of a conjunction is bounded by the maximum rank of any conjunct, which themselves are the rank of the minimum world satisfying the respective conjunct by (3.10). ☐

Proof of Lemma 3.17 (confer [EKI15b, Lemma 2]): For (3.14) we have to show that

$$\kappa(\phi) = \min\{\kappa(\phi|\psi) + \kappa(\psi), \kappa(\phi|\overline{\psi}) + \kappa(\overline{\psi})\}$$

By (3.13) from this we obtain

$$\kappa(\phi) = \min\{\kappa(\phi\psi) - \kappa(\psi) + \kappa(\psi), \kappa(\phi\overline{\psi}) - \kappa(\overline{\psi}) + \kappa(\overline{\psi})\}$$
$$\Leftrightarrow \quad \kappa(\phi) = \min\{\kappa(\phi\psi), \kappa(\phi\overline{\psi})\}$$

and this holds due to the definition of the rank of formulas (3.10). For (3.15) we have to show that

$$\kappa(\phi|\chi) = \min\{\kappa(\phi|\psi\chi) + \kappa(\phi|\chi), \kappa(\phi|\overline{\psi}\chi) + \kappa(\overline{\psi}|\chi)\}.$$

In parallel to the proof in [EKI15b, Lemma 2] we have

$$\kappa(\phi|\chi) = \kappa(\phi\chi) - \kappa(\chi)$$
$$= \min\left\{\kappa(\phi\psi\chi), \kappa(\phi\overline{\psi}\chi)\right\} - \kappa(\chi)$$
$$= \min\left\{\kappa(\phi\psi\chi) - \kappa(\chi), \kappa(\phi\overline{\psi}\chi) - \kappa(\chi)\right\}$$
$$= \min\left\{\begin{array}{l}\kappa(\phi\psi\chi) - \kappa(\psi\chi) + \kappa(\psi\chi) - \kappa(\chi),\\ \kappa(\phi\overline{\psi}\chi) - \kappa(\overline{\psi}\chi) + \kappa(\overline{\psi}\chi) - \kappa(\chi)\end{array}\right\}$$
$$= \min\left\{\kappa(\phi|\psi\chi) + \kappa(\psi|\chi), \kappa(\phi|\overline{\psi}\chi) + \kappa(\overline{\psi}|\chi)\right\}$$

which is (3.15). $\qquad\square$

Proof of Lemma 3.20 [EKI15b]: Let $\mathbf{A}$, $\mathbf{B}$, and $\mathbf{C}$ be sets of propositional variables $\mathbf{A}, \mathbf{B}, \mathbf{C} \subseteq \Sigma$. Let further $\mathbf{A} \perp\!\!\!\perp_\kappa \mathbf{B} \mid \mathbf{C}$. Then, by Definition 3.19, for all complete conjunctions of $\mathbf{a}$, $\mathbf{b}$ and $\mathbf{c}$ of $\mathbf{A}$, $\mathbf{B}$ and $\mathbf{C}$, respectively, we have

$$\kappa(\mathbf{ab}|\mathbf{c}) = \kappa(\mathbf{a}|\mathbf{c}) + \kappa(\mathbf{b}|\mathbf{c})$$

which, be the definition of conditional ranks, gives us

$$\kappa(\mathbf{abc}) - \kappa(\mathbf{c}) = \kappa(\mathbf{a}|\mathbf{c}) + \kappa(\mathbf{bc}) - \kappa(\mathbf{c})$$
$$\Leftrightarrow \quad \kappa(\mathbf{abc}) - \kappa(\mathbf{bc}) = \kappa(\mathbf{a}|\mathbf{c}) + \kappa(\mathbf{c}) - \kappa(\mathbf{c})$$
$$\Leftrightarrow \quad \kappa(\mathbf{a}|\mathbf{bc}) = \kappa(\mathbf{a}|\mathbf{c}),$$

which completes the proof. $\qquad\square$

Proof of Proposition 3.22 (Symmetry for conditional κ-inference):
This symmetry follows directly from the symmetry of the underlying summation on natural numbers and the symmetry of the conjunction junctor: Let $\mathbf{A} \perp\!\!\!\perp_\kappa \mathbf{B} \mid \mathbf{C}$, then, by Definition 3.19, for all complete conjunctions of $\mathbf{a}$, $\mathbf{b}$ and $\mathbf{c}$ of $\mathbf{A}$, $\mathbf{B}$ and $\mathbf{C}$, respectively, we have

$$\kappa(\mathbf{ab}|\mathbf{c}) = \kappa(\mathbf{a}|\mathbf{c}) + \kappa(\mathbf{b}|\mathbf{c})$$

this is equivalent to

$$\kappa(\mathbf{b}|\mathbf{c}) + \kappa(\mathbf{a}|\mathbf{c}) = \kappa(\mathbf{ba}|\mathbf{c})$$

and thus we also have $\mathbf{B} \perp\!\!\!\perp_\kappa \mathbf{A} \mid \mathbf{C}$, as proposed. $\qquad\square$

Proof of Proposition 3.23 (Intersection for conditional κ-inference): Let $\mathbf{A}$,
$\mathbf{B}$, $\mathbf{C}$, $\mathbf{D} \subseteq \Sigma$ be sets of variables, and let $\mathbf{a}$, $\mathbf{b}$, $\mathbf{c}$ and $\mathbf{d}$ be complete conjunctions of $\mathbf{A}$, $\mathbf{B}$, $\mathbf{C}$ and $\mathbf{D}$, respectively. We show that $\mathbf{A} \perp\!\!\!\perp_\kappa \mathbf{B} \mid (\mathbf{C} \cup \mathbf{D})$
and $\mathbf{A} \perp\!\!\!\perp_\kappa \mathbf{D} \mid (\mathbf{B} \cup \mathbf{C})$ imply $\mathbf{A} \perp\!\!\!\perp_\kappa (\mathbf{B} \cup \mathbf{D}) \mid \mathbf{C}$. By Lemma 3.20 this can
be proven by showing that $\kappa(\mathbf{a}|\mathbf{bcd}) = \kappa(\mathbf{a}|\mathbf{cd})$ and $\kappa(\mathbf{a}|\mathbf{bcd}) = \kappa(\mathbf{a}|\mathbf{bc})$
imply $\kappa(\mathbf{a}|\mathbf{bcd}) = \kappa(\mathbf{a}|\mathbf{c})$. We start by rearranging the prerequisites and
obtain

$$\kappa(\mathbf{a}|\mathbf{bcd}) = \kappa(\mathbf{a}|\mathbf{bc})$$

$$\overset{(3.13)}{\Longleftrightarrow} \quad \kappa(\mathbf{abcd}) - \kappa(\mathbf{bcd}) = \kappa(\mathbf{abc}) - \kappa(\mathbf{bc})$$

$$\Leftrightarrow \quad \kappa(\mathbf{abc}) = \kappa(\mathbf{abcd}) - \kappa(\mathbf{bcd}) + \kappa(\mathbf{bc}) \quad (A.2.1)$$

for the first prerequisite, and for the second

$$\kappa(\mathbf{a}|\mathbf{bcd}) = \kappa(\mathbf{a}|\mathbf{cd})$$

$$\overset{(3.13)}{\Longleftrightarrow} \quad \kappa(\mathbf{abcd}) - \kappa(\mathbf{bcd}) = \kappa(\mathbf{acd}) - \kappa(\mathbf{cd})$$

$$\Leftrightarrow \quad \kappa(\mathbf{abcd}) = \kappa(\mathbf{bcd}) + \kappa(\mathbf{acd}) - \kappa(\mathbf{cd}). \quad (A.2.2)$$

We combine (A.2.1) with (A.2.2) and obtain

$$\kappa(\mathbf{abc}) = \kappa(\mathbf{bcd}) + \kappa(\mathbf{acd}) - \kappa(\mathbf{cd}) - \kappa(\mathbf{bcd}) + \kappa(\mathbf{bc})$$

$$\Leftrightarrow \quad \kappa(\mathbf{abc}) = \kappa(\mathbf{acd}) - \kappa(\mathbf{cd}) + \kappa(\mathbf{bc}) \quad (A.2.3)$$

We now turn towards the equation to be proven and inspect the term
$\kappa(\mathbf{a}|\mathbf{c})$. Here we obtain

$$\kappa(\mathbf{a}|\mathbf{c}) = \kappa(\mathbf{ac}) - \kappa(\mathbf{c})$$

$$\overset{(3.10)}{=\!=\!=} \min_{\mathbf{b}} \{\kappa(\mathbf{abc})\} - \kappa(\mathbf{c}).$$

$$\overset{(A.2.3)}{=\!=\!=} \min_{\mathbf{b}} \{\underbrace{\kappa(\mathbf{acd})}_{(A.2.4.a)} - \underbrace{\kappa(\mathbf{cd})}_{(A.2.4.b)} + \kappa(\mathbf{bc})\} - \kappa(\mathbf{c}). \quad (A.2.4)$$

The two summands $(A.2.4.a)$ and $(A.2.4.b)$ do not contain $\mathbf{b}$ and thus can be excluded from the minimum, by which we obtain

$$
(A.2.4) = \min_{\mathbf{b}}\{\kappa(\mathbf{bc})\} + \kappa(\mathbf{acd}) - \kappa(\mathbf{cd}) - \kappa(\mathbf{c})
$$

$$
\overset{(3.10)}{=\!=\!=} \kappa(\mathbf{c}) + \kappa(\mathbf{acd}) - \kappa(\mathbf{cd}) - \kappa(\mathbf{c})
$$

$$
= \kappa(\mathbf{acd}) - \kappa(\mathbf{cd})
$$

$$
\overset{(3.13)}{=\!=\!=} \kappa(\mathbf{a}|\mathbf{cd}).
$$

So we have $\kappa(\mathbf{a}|\mathbf{cd}) = \kappa(\mathbf{a}|\mathbf{c})$. Combining this with the prerequisite

$$
\kappa(\mathbf{a}|\mathbf{bcd}) = \kappa(\mathbf{a}|\mathbf{bc})
$$

we obtain $\kappa(\mathbf{a}|\mathbf{bcd}) = \kappa(\mathbf{a}|\mathbf{c})$ and thus $\mathbf{A} \perp\!\!\!\perp_\kappa (\mathbf{B} \cup \mathbf{D}) \mid \mathbf{C}$, which we wanted to show. $\qquad\square$

Proof of Proposition 3.26 (Decomposition for conditional κ-inference): Let $\mathbf{A}, \mathbf{B}, \mathbf{C}, \mathbf{D} \subseteq \Sigma$ be sets of variables, and let $\mathbf{a}, \mathbf{b}, \mathbf{c}$ and $\mathbf{d}$ be complete conjunctions of $\mathbf{A}, \mathbf{B}, \mathbf{C}$ and $\mathbf{D}$, respectively. Let further be $\mathbf{A} \perp\!\!\!\perp_\kappa (\mathbf{B} \cup \mathbf{D}) \mid \mathbf{C}$. We show that this implies $\mathbf{A} \perp\!\!\!\perp_\kappa \mathbf{B} \mid \mathbf{C}$. Applying Lemma 3.20 we have to show that $\kappa(\mathbf{a}|\mathbf{bcd}) = \kappa(\mathbf{a}|\mathbf{c})$ implies $\kappa(\mathbf{a}|\mathbf{bc}) = \kappa(\mathbf{a}|\mathbf{c})$. The prerequisite can be rearranged as follows.

$$
\kappa(\mathbf{a}|\mathbf{bcd}) = \kappa(\mathbf{a}|\mathbf{c})
$$

$$
\Leftrightarrow \qquad \kappa(\mathbf{abcd}) - \kappa(\mathbf{bcd}) = \kappa(\mathbf{a}|\mathbf{c})
$$

$$
\Leftrightarrow \qquad \kappa(\mathbf{abcd}) = \kappa(\mathbf{bcd}) + \kappa(\mathbf{a}|\mathbf{c}) \qquad (A.2.5)
$$

Furthermore, turning to the implicant, we have

$$
\kappa(\mathbf{a}|\mathbf{bc}) = \kappa(\mathbf{abc}) - \kappa(\mathbf{bc})
$$

$$
\overset{(3.10)}{=\!=\!=} \min_{\mathbf{d}}\{\kappa(\mathbf{abcd})\} - \kappa(\mathbf{bc})
$$

$$
\overset{(A.2.5)}{=\!=\!=} \min_{\mathbf{d}}\{\kappa(\mathbf{bcd}) + \underbrace{\kappa(\mathbf{a}|\mathbf{c})}_{(A.2.6.a)}\} - \kappa(\mathbf{bc}). \qquad (A.2.6)
$$

The term $(A.2.6.a)$ does not contain $\mathbf{d}$ and thus can be excluded from the minimum and therefore

$$(A.2.6) = \min_{\mathbf{d}}\{\kappa(\mathbf{bcd})\} + \kappa(\mathbf{a}|\mathbf{c}) - \kappa(\mathbf{bc})$$

$$\stackrel{(3.10)}{=\!=\!=\!=} \kappa(\mathbf{bc}) + \kappa(\mathbf{a}|\mathbf{c}) - \kappa(\mathbf{bc})$$

$$= \kappa(\mathbf{a}|\mathbf{c}),$$

and this completes the proof.   □

Proof of Proposition 3.27 (Contraction for conditional κ-inference): Let $\mathbf{A}$, $\mathbf{B}$, $\mathbf{C}$, $\mathbf{D} \subseteq \Sigma$ be sets of variables, and let $\mathbf{a}$, $\mathbf{b}$, $\mathbf{c}$ and $\mathbf{d}$ be complete conjunctions of $\mathbf{A}$, $\mathbf{B}$, $\mathbf{C}$ and $\mathbf{D}$, respectively. Let further $\mathbf{A} \perp\!\!\!\perp_\kappa \mathbf{B} \mid \mathbf{C}$ and $\mathbf{A} \perp\!\!\!\perp_\kappa \mathbf{D} \mid (\mathbf{C} \cup \mathbf{B})$. We show that these prerequisites imply $\mathbf{A} \perp\!\!\!\perp_\kappa (\mathbf{B} \cup \mathbf{D}) \mid \mathbf{C}$. With Lemma 3.20 the prerequisites can be written as

$$\kappa(\mathbf{a}|\mathbf{bc}) = \kappa(\mathbf{a}|\mathbf{c})$$
$$\kappa(\mathbf{a}|\mathbf{bcd}) = \kappa(\mathbf{a}|\mathbf{bc})$$

From these formulas we obtain

$$\kappa(\mathbf{a}|\mathbf{bcd}) = \kappa(\mathbf{a}|\mathbf{bc}) = \kappa(\mathbf{a}|\mathbf{c})$$
$$\Rightarrow \quad \kappa(\mathbf{a}|\mathbf{bcd}) = \kappa(\mathbf{a}|\mathbf{c}),$$

which by Lemma 3.20 gives us $\mathbf{A} \perp\!\!\!\perp_\kappa (\mathbf{B} \cup \mathbf{D}) \mid \mathbf{C}$, as proposed.   □

Proof of Lemma 3.28 [EKI15b]: Let κ be an OCF and let $(\psi|\phi)[f]$ be a conditional with $\phi, \psi \in \mathfrak{L}$ and $f \in \mathbb{N}$. Let $\kappa \models (\psi|\phi)[f]$ then for each $f \in \mathbb{N}$ we have

$$\kappa(\phi\psi) < \kappa(\phi\psi) + 1 \leq \kappa(\phi\psi) + f \leq \kappa(\phi\overline{\psi})$$

and this gives us $\kappa \models (\psi|\phi)$. The converse is not true in general, because we could have an OCF such that $\kappa(\phi\psi) = 0$ and $\kappa(\phi\overline{\psi}) = 1$, which gave us $\kappa \models (\psi|\phi)$ but not $\kappa \models (\psi|\phi)[f]$ for any $f > 1$ since we had

$$0 = \kappa(\phi\psi) < \kappa(\phi\psi) + f \nleq \kappa(\phi\overline{\psi}) = 1 \qquad \text{for } f > 1.$$

□

Proof of Proposition 3.29 (confer [KIE14]): Let κ be an OCF and let $\phi, \psi \in \mathfrak{L}$ be formulas. We show that ϕ infers ψ with κ preferentially with respect to (3.25), $\phi\approx_\kappa\psi$, if and only if $\kappa \vDash (\psi|\phi)$. By (3.20) we have $\kappa \vDash (\psi|\phi)$ if and only if $\kappa(\phi\psi) < \kappa(\phi\overline{\psi})$ and by the definition of the rank of a formula in (3.10) this is equivalent to $\min\{\kappa(\omega) \mid \omega \vDash \phi\psi\} < \min\{\kappa(\omega) \mid \omega \vDash \phi\overline{\psi}\}$. Since an OCF is, by definition, a function $\kappa : \Omega \to \mathbb{N}_0^\infty$, each of the sets in the minima is totally ordered, and hence there is a set $\Omega^{\min(\psi\phi)} \subseteq \Omega$ such that $\Omega^{\min(\psi\phi)} = \operatorname{argmin}\{\kappa(\omega)|\omega \vDash \phi\psi\}$. So by (3.20) for each $\omega' \vDash \phi\overline{\psi}$ there is an $\omega \in \Omega^{\min(\psi\phi)}$ with the property that $\omega < \omega'$ and $\omega \vDash \phi\psi$. For the other direction we obtain that, if $\phi\approx_\kappa\psi$ in the sense of (3.25), for each $\omega' \vDash \phi\psi$ there is a world $\omega \vDash \phi\psi$ with the property $\omega <_\kappa \omega'$. The total ordering of $\mathbb{N}_0^\infty$ then gives us that there is a world $\omega \vDash \phi\psi$ with the property that $\omega <_\kappa \omega'$ for all $\omega' \vDash \psi\overline{\psi}$ and thus by (3.10) we obtain $\kappa(\phi\psi) < \kappa(\phi\overline{\psi})$. $\square$

Proof of Proposition 3.41 (confer [BKI14]): Both equations follow from the definition of the probability of a conditional. For (3.44) we have

$$P(\phi|\psi) \cdot P(\psi) + P(\phi|\overline{\psi}) \cdot P(\overline{\psi}) = \frac{P(\phi\psi)}{P(\psi)} \cdot P(\psi) + \frac{P(\phi\overline{\psi})}{P(\overline{\psi})} \cdot P(\overline{\psi})$$

$$= P(\phi\psi) + P(\phi\overline{\psi}) = P(\phi)$$

and, likewise, for (3.45) we have

$$P(\chi|\phi\psi) \cdot P(\psi|\phi) + P(\chi|\phi\overline{\psi}) \cdot P(\overline{\psi}|\phi) =$$

$$= \frac{P(\phi\psi\chi)}{P(\phi\psi)} \cdot \frac{P(\phi\psi)}{P(\phi)} + \frac{P(\phi\overline{\psi}\chi)}{P(\phi\overline{\psi})} \cdot \frac{P(\phi\overline{\psi})}{P(\phi)}$$

$$= \frac{P(\phi\psi\chi)}{P(\phi)} + \frac{P(\phi\overline{\psi}\chi)}{P(\phi)} = \frac{P(\phi\chi)}{P(\phi)} = P(\chi|\phi)$$

$\square$

Proof of Lemma 3.42: Let $\phi, \psi, \chi \in \mathfrak{L}$ be formulas and let P be a probability function such that $P(\phi) > 0$ and $P(\chi) = 0$. If $P(\phi) > 0$ then Formulas (3.46) and (3.47) are equivalent transformations of each other, that is

$$x = \frac{P(\phi\psi)}{P(\phi)} \qquad \text{if and only if} \qquad x \cdot P(\phi) = P(\phi\psi), \qquad \text{(A.2.7)}$$

giving us that $P \vDash (\psi|\phi)[x]$ if and only if $P \vDash^0 (\psi|\phi)[x]$, as proposed. For χ with $P(\chi) = 0$, $P(\psi|\chi)$ is undefined and thus $P(\psi|\chi) \neq x$ for any $x \in [0, 1]$. By finite additivity any formula χ is always at least as probable as a conjunction of χ and any other formula $\psi \in \mathfrak{L}$. So we have $P(\psi\chi) \leq P(\chi) = 0$, which with the semipositive definition of P gives us $P(\psi\chi) = 0$, and thus (3.47) yields $x \cdot 0 = 0$ which holds for any $x \in [0,1]$, and this closes the proof. $\qquad\square$

Proof of Lemma 3.57, we recall the proof of [EFKI16]: Let $\mathbf{V}, \mathbf{O}, \mathbf{P} \subseteq \Sigma$ be disjoint sets of vertices. $\mathbf{V}$ is conditionally CP-independent from $\mathbf{O}$ in the context of $\mathbf{P}$ given $\mathbf{vo\hat{p}} \prec \mathbf{v'o\hat{p}}$ if and only if $\mathbf{vo'\hat{p}} \prec \mathbf{v'o'\hat{p}}$ (Definition 3.56) for any configuration $\mathbf{v}, \mathbf{v}', \mathbf{o}, \mathbf{o}', \hat{\mathbf{p}}$ of $\mathbf{V}, \mathbf{O}, \mathbf{P}$, respectively. Let now $V \in \Sigma$ be a vertex in the CP-network CP with parent vertices $\hat{\mathbf{p}} = pa(V)$ and $\mathbf{O} = \Sigma \setminus (\{V\} \cup pa(V))$ be the remainder graph. The relation $\prec_{CP}$ is defined as sceptical preference over all CP-satisfying preference relations. The satisfiability condition (Definition 3.57) then requires that we have $\dot{v} \prec_{\hat{\mathbf{p}}} \bar{v}$ if and only if $\dot{v}\mathbf{o}\hat{\mathbf{p}} \prec_{CP} \bar{v}\mathbf{o}\hat{\mathbf{p}}$ for all outcomes $\mathbf{o}$ of $\mathbf{O}$ given a fixed outcome $\hat{\mathbf{p}}$ of $\mathbf{P}$ and all CP-satisfying relations $\prec_{CP}^*$. Therefore the definition of $\prec_{CP}$ gives us $\dot{v}\mathbf{o}\hat{\mathbf{p}} \prec_{CP} \bar{v}\mathbf{o}\hat{\mathbf{p}}$ for all outcomes of $\mathbf{o}$ of $\mathbf{O}$ given a fixed outcome $\hat{\mathbf{p}}$ of $\mathbf{P}$ if and only if $\dot{v} \prec_{\hat{\mathbf{p}}} \bar{v}$. Therefore for any two outcomes $\mathbf{o}, \mathbf{o}'$ we have $\dot{v}\mathbf{o}\hat{\mathbf{p}} \prec_{CP} \bar{v}\mathbf{o}\hat{\mathbf{p}}$ if and only if $\dot{v}\mathbf{o}'\hat{\mathbf{p}} \prec_{CP} \bar{v}\mathbf{o}'\hat{\mathbf{p}}$ if and only if $\dot{v} \prec_{\hat{\mathbf{p}}} \bar{v}$. So by Definition 3.56 we obtain $\{V\} \perp\!\!\!\perp_{\prec_{CP}} \mathbf{O} \mid \hat{\mathbf{p}}$, as proposed. $\quad\square$

A.3 Proofs for Chapter 4

Proof of Lemma 4.3 ((LLE) for non-inferences): The validity of (LLE) for non-inferences follows directly from the definition of (LLE):

$$(\phi \equiv \psi \quad \text{and} \quad \psi \hspace{-2pt}\mid\hspace{-6pt}\sim\hspace{-2pt} \chi) \qquad \text{imply} \qquad (\phi \hspace{-2pt}\mid\hspace{-6pt}\sim\hspace{-2pt} \chi)$$

if and only if $\quad \neg(\phi \equiv \psi \quad \text{and} \quad \psi \hspace{-2pt}\mid\hspace{-6pt}\sim\hspace{-2pt} \chi) \vee (\phi \hspace{-2pt}\mid\hspace{-6pt}\sim\hspace{-2pt} \chi)$

if and only if $\quad (\phi \not\equiv \psi) \vee (\psi \hspace{-2pt}\mid\hspace{-7pt}\not\sim\hspace{-2pt} \chi) \vee (\phi \hspace{-2pt}\mid\hspace{-6pt}\sim\hspace{-2pt} \chi)$

if and only if $\quad \neg(\phi \equiv \psi \quad \text{and} \quad \phi \hspace{-2pt}\mid\hspace{-7pt}\not\sim\hspace{-2pt} \chi) \vee (\psi \hspace{-2pt}\mid\hspace{-7pt}\not\sim\hspace{-2pt} \chi)$

if and only if $\quad \phi \equiv \psi \quad \text{and} \quad \phi \hspace{-2pt}\mid\hspace{-7pt}\not\sim\hspace{-2pt} \chi \qquad \text{imply} \qquad \psi \hspace{-2pt}\mid\hspace{-7pt}\not\sim\hspace{-2pt} \chi.$

$\square$

Proof of Proposition 4.5 (confer [Boc01]): We show that $\phi \vDash \psi$ implies $\phi \hspace{-2pt}\mid\hspace{-6pt}\sim\hspace{-2pt} \psi$ given (REF) and (RW): By (REF) we have $\phi \hspace{-2pt}\mid\hspace{-6pt}\sim\hspace{-2pt} \phi$, and thus

$$\frac{\phi \hspace{-2pt}\mid\hspace{-6pt}\sim\hspace{-2pt} \phi, \ \phi \vDash \psi}{\phi \hspace{-2pt}\mid\hspace{-6pt}\sim\hspace{-2pt} \psi.} \quad \text{(RW)}$$

$\square$

Proof of Proposition 4.6: We elaborate on on the proof of [KLM90, p.26] and show that by (SCL), (WOR), and (RW) from $\phi\psi \hspace{-2pt}\mid\hspace{-6pt}\sim\hspace{-2pt} \chi$ it follows that $\phi \hspace{-2pt}\mid\hspace{-6pt}\sim\hspace{-2pt} (\psi \Rightarrow \chi)$. Using classical logic, we have $\chi \vDash \chi \vee \overline{\psi}$ and thus $\chi \vDash (\psi \Rightarrow \chi)$, and also $\phi\overline{\psi} \vDash \overline{\psi} \vee \chi$ and thus $\phi\overline{\psi} \vDash (\psi \Rightarrow \chi)$. Using these preliminaries we have:

$$\text{(RW)} \ \frac{\dfrac{\phi\psi \hspace{-2pt}\mid\hspace{-6pt}\sim\hspace{-2pt} \chi, \ \ \chi \vDash (\psi \Rightarrow \chi)}{\phi\psi \hspace{-2pt}\mid\hspace{-6pt}\sim\hspace{-2pt} (\psi \Rightarrow \chi)} \quad \dfrac{\phi\overline{\psi} \vDash (\psi \Rightarrow \chi)}{\phi\overline{\psi} \hspace{-2pt}\mid\hspace{-6pt}\sim\hspace{-2pt} (\psi \Rightarrow \chi)} \ \text{(SCL)}}{\phi \hspace{-2pt}\mid\hspace{-6pt}\sim\hspace{-2pt} (\psi \Rightarrow \chi)} \ \text{(WOR)}$$

which completes the proof. $\square$

Proof of Proposition 4.7: To prove that probabilistic threshold inference satisfies System O, we recall and elaborate on the proof of [Haw07] and show that each axiom is satisfied by threshold inference, individually. Let $\phi, \psi, \chi \in \mathfrak{L}$ be propositional formulas, for an economic usage of symbols and readable proofs, we further assume additional prelimiaries for each of the properties, separately.

For (REF) to be satisfied, we have to proof that for any formula $\phi \in \mathfrak{L}$ it holds that $\phi \hspace{-2pt}\mid\hspace{-6pt}\sim\hspace{-2pt}^{P, \geq x} \phi$. By Definition 3.44 we have $\phi \hspace{-2pt}\mid\hspace{-6pt}\sim\hspace{-2pt}^{P, \geq x} \phi$ if and only if

$P(\phi|\phi) \geq x$. We have $P(\phi|\phi) = \frac{P(\phi)}{P(\phi)} = 1$ and hence $P(\phi|\phi) \geq x$ for all $x \in (0,1]$.

To show that (LLE) is satisfied, we have to show that $\psi\mid\!\sim^{P,\geq x}\chi$ given $\phi\mid\!\sim^{P,\geq x}\chi$ and $\phi \equiv \psi$. We have $\phi \equiv \psi$ if and only if $Mod(\phi) = Mod(\psi)$ and therefore by (3.41) we have $P(\phi) = P(\psi)$. Likewise we have $Mod(\phi\chi) = Mod(\psi\chi)$ and hence $P(\phi\chi) = P(\psi\chi)$. This results in

$$x \leq P(\chi|\phi) = \frac{P(\phi\chi)}{P(\phi)} = \frac{P(\psi\chi)}{P(\psi)} = P(\chi|\phi),$$

and therefore $P(\chi|\phi) \geq x$ and hence $\psi\mid\!\sim^{P,\geq x}\chi$ as proposed.

To show the satisfaction of (RW) we show that from $\phi\mid\!\sim^{P,\geq x}\psi$ and $\psi \vDash \chi$ it follows that $\phi\mid\!\sim^{P,\geq x}\chi$: We have $\psi \vDash \chi$ and therefore also $\phi\psi \vDash \phi\chi$. This implies that for all probability distributions P we have $P(\phi\psi) \leq P(\phi\chi)$, and therefore

$$P(\psi|\phi) = \frac{P(\phi\psi)}{P(\phi)} \leq \frac{P(\phi\chi)}{P(\phi)} = P(\chi|\phi).$$

So we have $P(\chi|\phi) \geq P(\psi|\phi) \geq x$ which by transitivity gives us $P(\chi|\phi) \geq x$ and hence $\phi\mid\!\sim^{P,\geq x}\chi$ as proposed.

For (WAND), we have to show that $\phi\mid\!\sim^{P,\geq x}\psi$ and $\phi\overline{\chi}\mid\!\sim^{P,\geq x}\chi$ imply $\phi\psi\mid\!\sim^{P,\geq x}\chi$. The second preliminary $\phi\overline{\chi}\mid\!\sim^{P,\geq x}\chi$ is unaccomplishable, since $P(\phi\overline{\chi}\chi) = P(\bot) = 0$ and hence $P(\chi|\phi\overline{\chi}) = 0 < x$ for all $x \in (0,1]$ and all $\phi, \chi \in \mathfrak{L}$ Therefore, the implication is vacuously true and (WAND) is satisfied by probabilistic threshold inference.

To show that (WOR) is satisfied by probabilistic threshold inference, we have to show that from $\phi\psi\mid\!\sim^{P,\geq x}\chi$ and $\phi\overline{\psi}\mid\!\sim^{P,\geq x}\chi$ we obtain $\phi\mid\!\sim^{P,\geq x}\chi$. So according to Definition 3.44 we have to show that $P(\chi|\phi\psi) \geq x$ and $P(\chi|\phi\overline{\psi}) \geq x$ implies $P(\chi|\phi) \geq x$. By the law of total conditional probability (see Proposition 3.41) we have

$$P(\chi|\phi) = P(\chi|\phi\psi) \cdot P(\psi|\phi) + P(\chi|\phi\overline{\psi}) \cdot P(\overline{\psi}|\phi).$$

By the prerequisites we have both $P(\chi|\phi\psi) \geq x$ and $P(\chi|\phi\overline{\psi}) \geq x$, and since both $P(\psi|\phi)$ and $P(\overline{\psi}|\phi)$ are probabilities and hence from the interval $[0,1]$ we obtain the lower estimate

$$P(\chi|\phi) \geq x \cdot P(\psi|\phi) + x \cdot P(\overline{\psi}|\phi)$$
$$= x \cdot (P(\psi|\phi) + P(\overline{\psi}|\phi)) = x,$$

and so $P(\chi|\phi) \geq x$ and hence $\phi \hspace{-2pt}\mid\hspace{-5pt}\sim^{P, \geq x}\chi$, as proposed.

This leaves us with showing that (VCM) is satisfied by probabilistic threshold inference, that is, we have to show that from $\phi \hspace{-2pt}\mid\hspace{-5pt}\sim^{P, \geq x}\psi\chi$ it follows that $\phi\psi \hspace{-2pt}\mid\hspace{-5pt}\sim^{P, \geq x}\chi$. This means we have to show that $P(\psi\chi|\phi) \geq x$ implies $P(\chi|\psi\phi) \geq x$. We recall that $P(\phi) \geq P(\phi\psi)$ for any formulas $\phi, \psi \in \mathfrak{L}$ and by this it follows directly

$$x \leq P(\psi\chi|\phi) = \frac{P(\phi\psi\chi)}{P(\phi)} \leq \frac{P(\phi\psi\chi)}{P(\phi\psi)} = P(\chi|\phi\psi),$$

and so, $P(\chi|\phi\psi) \geq x$ as proposed.

Overall we could show that probabilistic threshold inference satisfies all axioms of System O and hence licenses for inferences by System O, as proposed. $\qquad\square$

Proof of Proposition 4.9 (confer [EKIBB18]): With the proof of Proposition 4.7 we have already shown that threshold inference satisfies System O, so we only have to show that it also satisfies (NR) to prove the proposition. We show that given $\phi \hspace{-2pt}\mid\hspace{-5pt}\sim^{P, \geq x}\chi$, $\phi\psi \hspace{-2pt}\mid\hspace{-5pt}\not\sim^{P, \geq x}\chi$ implies $\phi\overline{\psi} \hspace{-2pt}\mid\hspace{-5pt}\sim^{P, \geq x}\chi$ using threshold inference, so we show that $P(\chi|\phi) \geq x$ and $P(\chi|\phi\psi) < x$ implies $P(\chi|\phi\overline{\psi}) \geq x$. We recall the law of total conditional probability (see Proposition 3.41) to be

$$P(\chi|\psi) = P(\chi|\phi\psi) \cdot P(\psi|\phi) + P(\chi|\phi\overline{\psi}) \cdot P(\overline{\psi}|\phi)$$

iff $\quad P(\chi|\phi\overline{\psi}) \cdot P(\overline{\psi}|\phi) = P(\chi|\psi) - P(\chi|\phi\psi) \cdot P(\psi|\phi).$

We insert the prerequisites in this equation and obtain

$$P(\chi|\phi\overline{\psi}) \cdot P(\overline{\psi}|\phi) \geq x - x \cdot P(\psi|\phi)$$
$$= x \cdot (1 - P(\psi|\phi)) = x \cdot P(\overline{\psi}|\phi)$$

iff $\quad\quad\quad P(\chi|\phi\overline{\psi}) \geq x,$

which gives us $\phi\overline{\psi} \hspace{-2pt}\mid\hspace{-5pt}\sim^{P, \geq x}\chi$, as proposed. $\qquad\square$

Proof of Proposition 4.11 that (CM) implies (VCM) (confer [EKIBB18]): Let ϕ, ψ, and $\chi \in \mathfrak{L}$ be formulas. We show that from $\phi \hspace{-2pt}\mid\hspace{-5pt}\sim\psi\chi$ we can infer $\phi\psi \hspace{-2pt}\mid\hspace{-5pt}\sim\psi$ given (REF) and (CM): As for any pair of formulas ψ, χ its holds that $\psi\chi \vDash \psi$ and $\psi\chi \vDash \chi$ we obtain

$$(\text{RW}) \quad \frac{\phi \hspace{-2pt}\mid\hspace{-5pt}\sim\psi\chi, \ \psi\chi \vDash \psi}{\phi \hspace{-2pt}\mid\hspace{-5pt}\sim\psi} \quad\quad \frac{\phi \hspace{-2pt}\mid\hspace{-5pt}\sim\psi\chi, \ \psi\chi \vDash \chi}{\phi \hspace{-2pt}\mid\hspace{-5pt}\sim\chi} \ (\text{RW})$$
$$\frac{}{\phi\psi \hspace{-2pt}\mid\hspace{-5pt}\sim\chi} \ (\text{CM})$$

as proposed. □

Proof of Proposition 4.19 that (MPC) is valid in System C [KLM90]: Let ϕ, ψ, and $\chi \in \mathfrak{L}$ be formulas. We show that $\phi\hspace{-0.2em}\mid\hspace{-0.5em}\sim(\psi \Rightarrow \chi)$ and $\phi\hspace{-0.2em}\mid\hspace{-0.5em}\sim\psi$ implies $\phi\hspace{-0.2em}\mid\hspace{-0.5em}\sim\chi$ given (AND) and (RW).

$$\frac{\dfrac{\phi\hspace{-0.2em}\mid\hspace{-0.5em}\sim(\psi \Rightarrow \chi),\ \phi\hspace{-0.2em}\mid\hspace{-0.5em}\sim\psi}{\phi\hspace{-0.2em}\mid\hspace{-0.5em}\sim(\psi \wedge (\psi \Rightarrow \chi))}\ \text{(AND)}}{\phi\hspace{-0.2em}\mid\hspace{-0.5em}\sim\chi}\ \text{(RW)}$$

□

Proof of Proposition 4.20 that (CONS) is valid in System C: Let ϕ, ψ, and $\chi \in \mathfrak{L}$ be formulas. We show that $\phi\hspace{-0.2em}\mid\hspace{-0.5em}\sim\psi$ and $\phi\hspace{-0.2em}\mid\hspace{-0.5em}\sim\overline{\psi}$ implies $\phi\hspace{-0.2em}\mid\hspace{-0.5em}\sim\bot$ given (AND) and (RW).

$$\frac{\dfrac{\phi\hspace{-0.2em}\mid\hspace{-0.5em}\sim\psi,\ \phi\hspace{-0.2em}\mid\hspace{-0.5em}\sim\overline{\psi}}{\phi\hspace{-0.2em}\mid\hspace{-0.5em}\sim\psi \wedge \overline{\psi}}\ \text{(AND)}}{\phi\hspace{-0.2em}\mid\hspace{-0.5em}\sim\bot}\ \text{(RW)}$$

□

Proof of Proposition 4.23 that (OR) implies (WOR) [Mak94]:
Let ϕ, ψ, and $\chi \in \mathfrak{L}$ be formulas. We show that $\phi\psi\hspace{-0.2em}\mid\hspace{-0.5em}\sim\chi$ and $\phi\overline{\psi}\hspace{-0.2em}\mid\hspace{-0.5em}\sim\chi$ implies $\phi\hspace{-0.2em}\mid\hspace{-0.5em}\sim\chi$ given (OR) and (LLE).

$$\frac{\dfrac{\phi\psi\hspace{-0.2em}\mid\hspace{-0.5em}\sim\chi,\ \phi\overline{\psi}\hspace{-0.2em}\mid\hspace{-0.5em}\sim\chi}{\phi\psi \vee \phi\overline{\psi}\hspace{-0.2em}\mid\hspace{-0.5em}\sim\chi}\ \text{(OR)}}{\phi\hspace{-0.2em}\mid\hspace{-0.5em}\sim\chi}\ \text{(LLE)}$$

□

Proof of Proposition 4.31 that (RM) implies (CM) [EKIBB18]: Let ϕ, ψ, and $\chi \in \mathfrak{L}$ be formulas. We show that $\phi\hspace{-0.2em}\mid\hspace{-0.5em}\sim\psi$ and $\phi\hspace{-0.2em}\mid\hspace{-0.5em}\sim\chi$ imply $\phi\psi\hspace{-0.2em}\mid\hspace{-0.5em}\sim\chi$ given (RM) and (CONS).

$$\frac{\phi\hspace{-0.2em}\mid\hspace{-0.5em}\sim\chi,\ \dfrac{\phi\hspace{-0.2em}\mid\hspace{-0.5em}\sim\psi}{\phi\hspace{-0.2em}\mid\hspace{0.2em}\not\sim\overline{\psi}}\ \text{(CONS)}}{\phi\psi\hspace{-0.2em}\mid\hspace{-0.5em}\sim\chi}\ \text{(RM)}$$

□

Proof of Proposition 4.36 that $\hspace{-0.2em}\mid\hspace{-0.4em}\approx_{\kappa}$ satisfies System R: $\hspace{-0.2em}\mid\hspace{-0.4em}\approx_{\kappa}$ satisfies System P by being set up upon a classical stoppered preferential model (see Corollary 4.81), thus to show that $\hspace{-0.2em}\mid\hspace{-0.4em}\approx_{\kappa}$ satisfies System R we only need to show that $\hspace{0.15em}\vdash_\kappa$ satisfies (RM). By definition, an OCF maps the set of possible worlds to the totally ordered set $\mathbb{N}$. Therefore, κ is *modular* in the sense of [LM92, Lemma 14], and thus $\langle \Omega, \vDash, <_\kappa \rangle$ is a *ranked model* in the sense of [LM92, Definition 14], which is rational by [LM92, Lemma 15] and thus the resulting preferential entailment $\hspace{0.15em}\vdash_\kappa$ satisfies Rational Monotony (RM).

Apart from this structural proof it can also be shown that $\hspace{0.15em}\vdash_\kappa$ satisfies (RM) by inspecting the ranking function itself; we recall the proof in [KI10] on this behalf. Let $\phi, \psi, \chi \in \mathfrak{L}$ be formulas, and let $\phi \hspace{0.15em}\vdash_\kappa \chi$ and $\phi \hspace{0.15em}\not\vdash_\kappa \overline{\psi}$. We show that $\phi\psi \hspace{0.15em}\vdash_\kappa \chi$ via reductio ad absurdum:

$$
\begin{aligned}
\phi \hspace{0.15em}\vdash_\kappa \chi \quad &\text{iff} & \kappa(\phi\chi) &< \kappa(\phi\overline{\chi}) \\
&\text{iff} & \min\{\kappa(\phi\psi\chi), \kappa(\phi\overline{\psi}\chi)\} &< \min\{\kappa(\phi\psi\overline{\chi}), \kappa(\phi\overline{\psi}\,\overline{\chi})\} & \text{(A.3.1)} \\
\phi \hspace{0.15em}\not\vdash_\kappa \overline{\psi} \quad &\text{iff} & \kappa(\phi\overline{\psi}) &\not< \kappa(\phi\psi) \\
&\text{iff} & \kappa(\phi\psi) &\leq \kappa(\phi\overline{\psi}) \\
&\text{iff} & \min\{\kappa(\phi\psi\chi), \kappa(\phi\psi\overline{\chi})\} &\leq \min\{\kappa(\phi\overline{\psi}\chi), \kappa(\phi\overline{\psi}\,\overline{\chi})\} & \text{(A.3.2)}
\end{aligned}
$$

We assume that $\phi\psi \hspace{0.15em}\not\vdash_\kappa \chi$:

$$\phi\psi \hspace{0.15em}\not\vdash_\kappa \chi \quad \text{iff} \quad \kappa(\phi\psi\chi) \not< \kappa(\phi\psi\overline{\chi}) \quad \text{iff} \quad \kappa(\phi\psi\overline{\chi}) \leq \kappa(\phi\psi\chi), \quad \text{(A.3.3)}$$

then we would have

$$
\begin{aligned}
&\kappa(\phi\psi\overline{\chi}) = \min\{\kappa(\phi\psi\chi), \kappa(\phi\psi\overline{\chi})\} = \kappa(\phi\psi) \\
\xrightarrow{\text{(A.3.2)}} \quad &\kappa(\phi\psi\overline{\chi}) \leq \min\{\kappa(\phi\overline{\psi}\chi), \kappa(\phi\overline{\psi}\,\overline{\chi})\} \\
\xrightarrow{\text{(A.3.3)}} \quad &\kappa(\phi\psi\overline{\chi}) \leq \min\{\kappa(\phi\psi\chi), \kappa(\phi\overline{\psi}\chi), \kappa(\phi\overline{\psi}\,\overline{\chi})\},
\end{aligned}
$$

which gave us

$$
\begin{aligned}
\kappa(\phi\psi\overline{\chi}) &= \min\{\kappa(\phi\psi\overline{\chi}), \kappa(\phi\overline{\psi}\,\overline{\chi})\} = \kappa(\phi\overline{\chi}) \\
\kappa(\phi\psi\overline{\chi}) &= \min\{\kappa(\phi\psi\chi), \kappa(\phi\psi\overline{\chi})\} = \kappa(\phi\psi),
\end{aligned}
$$

and hence $\kappa(\phi\psi) = \kappa(\phi\overline{\chi})$, contrary to (A.3.1). So given the prerequisites we have $\phi\psi \hspace{0.15em}\vdash_\kappa \chi$, which we wanted to show. $\qquad\square$

Proof of Proposition 4.39 that System R contains (DR): We recall and extend the proof in [LM92, p. 16] to show that $\overline{(DR)}$ can be derived in System R. For this proof we use (LLE) for non-inferences, which is shown to be valid for Lemma 4.3. We show that $\phi \hspace{0.15em}\not\vdash \chi$ and $\psi \hspace{0.15em}\not\vdash \chi$ imply $(\phi \vee \psi) \hspace{0.15em}\not\vdash \chi$. It holds that $\phi \equiv ((\phi \vee \psi) \wedge \phi)$, so (LLE) gives $(\phi \wedge (\phi \vee \psi)) \hspace{0.15em}\not\vdash \chi$ from the prerequisites. Now we differentiate between the (exhaustive) cases

(4.39.a) $\phi \vee \psi \mathrel{\not\approx} \overline{\phi}$

(4.39.b) $\phi \vee \psi \mathrel{\approx} \overline{\phi}$

In the case of (4.39.a), we use the contrapositive form of (RM) and obtain

$$\frac{(\phi \vee \psi) \mathrel{\not\approx} \overline{\phi} \quad , \quad \dfrac{\phi \mathrel{\not\approx} \chi}{((\phi \vee \psi) \wedge \phi) \mathrel{\not\approx} \chi} \text{ (LLE)}}{(\phi \vee \psi) \mathrel{\not\approx} \chi.} \text{ (RM)}$$

So for (4.39.a), the proposition holds. For (4.39.b), we assume $(\phi \vee \psi) \mathrel{\approx} \chi$ in contrast to the proposition and show that this leads to a contradiction. We recall that classically it holds that $\psi \vDash \phi \vee \psi$ and obtain

$$\text{(RW)} \quad \frac{\dfrac{\psi \vDash \phi \vee \psi, \quad \phi \vee \psi \mathrel{\approx} \overline{\phi}}{\psi \mathrel{\approx} \overline{\phi}} \quad , \quad \dfrac{\dfrac{\phi \vee \psi \mathrel{\approx} \overline{\phi}, \quad \phi \vee \psi \mathrel{\approx} \chi}{(\phi \vee \psi) \wedge \overline{\phi} \mathrel{\approx} \chi} \text{ (CM)}}{\overline{\phi}\psi \mathrel{\approx} \chi} \text{ (LLE)}}{\psi \mathrel{\approx} \chi} \text{ (CUT)}$$

So for (4.39.b), the assumption $(\phi \vee \psi) \mathrel{\approx} \chi$ leads to $\psi \mathrel{\approx} \chi$ which contradicts the prerequisites, therefore for case (4.39.b) we also have to have $(\phi \vee \psi) \mathrel{\not\approx} \chi$ in accordance with the proposition, which completes the proof. $\qquad \square$

Proof of Proposition 4.40 that (DR) implies (NR) [EKIBB18]: Let ϕ, ψ, and χ be formulas. Let $\phi\psi \mathrel{\not\approx} \chi$ and $\phi\overline{\psi} \mathrel{\not\approx} \chi$. We show that from these prerequisites we can infer $\phi \mathrel{\not\approx} \chi$ using (DR) and (LLE).

$$\frac{\dfrac{\phi\psi \mathrel{\not\approx} \chi, \quad \phi\overline{\psi} \mathrel{\not\approx} \chi}{(\phi\psi \vee \phi\overline{\psi}) \mathrel{\not\approx} \chi} \text{ (DR)}}{\phi \mathrel{\not\approx} \chi} \text{ (LLE)}$$

$\qquad \square$

Proof of Proposition 4.42 that preferential inference satisfies (EFQ): We instantiate Definition 3.6 of preferential inference with a contradictory premise and obtain

$$\bot \mathrel{\approx}_{\preceq} \psi \quad \text{iff} \quad \forall \underbrace{\omega' \vDash \bot \wedge \psi}_{(A.3.4.a)} \quad \exists \omega \vDash \bot \wedge \overline{\psi} \quad \text{s.t.} \quad \omega \prec \omega'. \quad (A.3.4)$$

As the set $(A.3.4.a)$ is empty this statement is vacuously true, and thus holds for any $\psi \in \mathfrak{L}$. $\qquad \square$

Proof of Proposition 4.43 that preferential inference satisfies (INT): We instantiate Definition 3.6 of preferential inference with the premise and obtain

$$\phi\kappa_\leq\bot \quad \text{iff} \quad \underbrace{\forall\,\omega' \vDash \phi \wedge \top \quad \exists\,\omega \vDash \phi \wedge \bot}_{(A.3.5.a)} \quad \text{s.t.} \quad \underbrace{\omega \prec \omega'}_{(A.3.5.b)}. \quad (A.3.5)$$

If $\phi \not\equiv \bot$, then the set $(A.3.5.a)$ is empty and therefore $(A.3.5.b)$ cannot be met, thus for any $\phi \not\equiv \bot$, $\phi\not\kappa_\leq\bot$. If $\phi \equiv \bot$, by Proposition 4.42, $\phi\kappa_\leq\psi$ for any $\psi \in \mathfrak{L}$, which includes $\psi \equiv \bot$. Therefore $\phi\kappa_\leq\bot$ if and only if $\phi \equiv \bot$, as proposed. □

Proof of Lemma 4.44: preferential inference satisfies (REG) and (SREG): Both regularity properties follow directly from Proposition 4.43. As $\psi\kappa_\leq\bot$ if and only if $\psi \equiv \bot$ we obtain (REG) directly from (RW). For (SREG) we realise that this means that $\overline{\psi} \equiv \top$ which can added conjunctively to any formula without effect, so again (RW) gives us that (SREG) □

Proof of Proposition 4.47 that (CPS) implies (WCPS): Let ϕ, ψ, and $\chi \in \mathfrak{L}$ be formulas. We show that given $\phi\psi\kappa_\sim\chi$ and $\phi\kappa_\sim\chi$ we can infer $\psi\overline{\chi}\kappa_\sim\overline{\phi}$ using (CPS), (DED), (LLE), and (RW).

$$\frac{\dfrac{\dfrac{\dfrac{\phi\psi\kappa_\sim\chi}{\phi\kappa_\sim(\psi \Rightarrow \chi)}\,(\text{DED})}{\phi\kappa_\sim(\overline{\psi} \vee \chi)}\,(\text{RW})}{\neg(\overline{\psi} \vee \chi)\kappa_\sim\overline{\phi}}\,(\text{CPS})}{\psi\overline{\chi}\kappa_\sim\overline{\phi}.}\,(\text{LLE})$$

□

Proof of Lemma 4.56 [KIE12, Lemma 1]: We show that $\mathfrak{M}_\sigma^\Delta = (\Omega, \vDash, \prec_\Delta^\sigma)$ is a classical stoppered preferential model. Lemma 3.3 gives us that that $\mathfrak{M}_\sigma^\Delta$ is classical as the model uses the classical entailment as entailment relation. The set of states is the (finite) set of models, so Lemma 3.5 gives us that $\mathfrak{M}_\sigma^\Delta$ is stoppered if $\prec_\Delta^\sigma$ is strict and transitive. As this was already shown in Corollary 3.13, we overall obtain that $\mathfrak{M}_\sigma^\Delta$ is a classical stoppered preferential model, as proposed. □

Proof of Lemma 4.116: We recall and elaborate on the proof in [KIE14]. Let $\Delta = \{(\psi_1|\phi_1), \dots, (\psi_n|\phi_n)\}$ be a knowledge base and let κ_Δ^c be a c-representation of Δ with a solution $(\kappa_1^-, \dots, \kappa_n^-)$ to the system of inequalities (3.30). We have $\omega \prec_\Delta^\sigma \omega'$ for any pair of $\omega, \omega' \in \Omega$ if and only if ω

falsifies, ceteris paribus, less conditionals than ω', that is $fal_\Delta(\omega) \subsetneq fal_\Delta(\omega')$ (see (3.7)). For the rank of the worlds we have

$$\kappa_\Delta^c(\omega) = \sum_{\omega \vDash \phi_i \overline{\psi}_i} \kappa_i^- = \sum_{(\psi_i|\phi_i) \in fal_\Delta(\omega)} \kappa_i^- \qquad (A.3.6)$$

and likewise

$$\kappa_\Delta^c(\omega') = \sum_{\omega' \vDash \phi_i \overline{\psi}_i} \kappa_i^- = \sum_{(\psi_i|\phi_i) \in fal_\Delta(\omega')} \kappa_i^- . \qquad (A.3.7)$$

The sum can be split into

$$\kappa_\Delta^c(\omega') = \underbrace{\sum_{(\psi_i|\phi_i) \in (fal_\Delta(\omega') \cap fal_\Delta(\omega))} \kappa_i^-}_{(A.3.8.a)} + \sum_{(\psi_i|\phi_i) \in (fal_\Delta(\omega') \setminus fal_\Delta(\omega))} \kappa_i^- , \qquad (A.3.8)$$

and as $fal_\Delta(\omega) \subsetneq fal_\Delta(\omega')$, we have $fal_\Delta(\omega') \cap fal_\Delta(\omega) = fal_\Delta(\omega)$, and thus the sum $(A.3.8.a)$ is identical to (A.3.6), which gives us

$$\kappa_\Delta^c(\omega') = \kappa_\Delta^c(\omega) + \underbrace{\sum_{(\psi_i|\phi_i) \in (fal_\Delta(\omega') \setminus fal_\Delta(\omega))} \kappa_i^-}_{(A.3.9.a)} . \qquad (A.3.9)$$

The prerequisite $\omega \prec_\Delta^\sigma \omega'$ ensures that $fal_\Delta(\omega') \setminus fal_\Delta(\omega) \neq \varnothing$ and therefore the condition $\kappa_i^- > 0$ for all $1 \leq i \leq n$ ensures that $(A.3.9.a) > 0$ and hence $\kappa_\Delta^c(\omega) < \kappa_\Delta^c(\omega')$, as proposed. $\qquad\square$

A.4 Proofs for Chapter 5

Proof of Proposition 5.8 that $\mathrel{\approx}_\Delta^{\cap,c}$ satisfies System P [BEKI16, Prop. 6]:
We recall the characterisation of System P (Definition 4.28 respectively Proposition 4.29), that ψ can be System P inferred from ϕ in the context of Δ if and only if $\Delta \cup \{(\psi|\overline{\phi})\}$ is inconsistent if and only if every Δ-admissible OCF accepts the conditional $(\psi|\phi)$. The set of all c-representations of Δ is a subset of all Δ-admissible OCF, therefore $(\psi|\phi)$ is accepted by every c-representation. By Proposition 3.29 and the relationship between acceptance of conditionals and ranking inference we have $\phi \mathrel{\approx}_{\kappa_\Delta^c} \psi$ for every c-representation of Δ. Overall, this combined with Definition 5.4 of sceptical c-inference gives us that $\phi \mathrel{\vert\!\sim}^P \psi$ implies $\phi \mathrel{\approx}_\Delta^{\cap,c} \psi$, as proposed. □

Proof of Proposition 5.10 that $\mathrel{\approx}_\Delta^{\cap,c}$ exceeds System P [BEKI16, Prop. 6]:
The sceptical inference $pb \mathrel{\approx}_\Delta^{\cap,c} w$ found in Example 5.9 is a witness for sceptical c-inference to license for inferences not possible in System P: This inference valid for sceptical c-inference but is no System P inference because $\Delta \cup \{(\overline{w}|p)\}$ is consistent. □

Proof of Theorem 5.13 characterising sceptical c-inference as CSP: We extend the proof in [BEKIK18, Proposition 10] and show this equivalence in two steps. First we show that $\phi \mathrel{\approx}_\Delta^{all,\cap} \psi$ implies $CSP(\Delta) \cup \{\neg CSP_\Delta(\psi|\phi)\}$ to be unsolvable by reductio ad absurdum. If $\phi \mathrel{\approx}_\Delta^{all,\cap} \psi$, then for all c-representations $\kappa_{\vec{\eta}}$ of solutions $\vec{\eta} \in Sol(CSP(\Delta))$ we have

$$\kappa_{\vec{\eta}}(\phi\psi) < \kappa_{\vec{\eta}}(\phi\overline{\psi}). \tag{A.4.1}$$

We assume $CSP \cup \{\neg CSP_\Delta(\psi|\phi)\}$ was solvable, then by (5.12) we also had

$$\kappa_{\vec{\eta}}(\phi\psi) \geq \kappa_{\vec{\eta}}(\phi\overline{\psi}). \tag{A.4.2}$$

This is a direct contradiction, hence $\phi \mathrel{\approx}_\Delta^{all,\cap} \psi$ implies that the CSP $CSP(\Delta) \cup \{\neg CSP_\Delta(\psi|\phi)\}$ is not solvable. Secondly we show that $\phi \mathrel{\not\approx}_\Delta^{all,\cap} \psi$ implies $CSP \cup \{\neg CSP_\Delta(\psi|\phi)\}$ to be solvable. From $\phi \mathrel{\not\approx}_\Delta^{all,\cap} \psi$ we obtain that there are c-representations $\kappa_{\vec{\eta}}$ in the set of solutions $\vec{\eta} \in Sol(CSP(\Delta))$ with the property that

$$\kappa_{\vec{\eta}}(\phi\psi) \geq \kappa_{\vec{\eta}}(\phi\overline{\psi}); \tag{A.4.3}$$

this is the definition of the constraint $\neg CSP_\Delta(\psi|\phi)$, so $\kappa_{\vec{\eta}}$ is a c-representation (and thus solves $CSP(\Delta)$) and satisfies $\neg CSP_\Delta(\psi|\phi)$. So the vector of values for the impact that constitutes $\kappa_{\vec{\eta}}$ is a solution to $CSP(\Delta) \cup \{\neg CSP_\Delta(\psi|\phi)\}$, therefore this CSP is solvable. Overall we obtain $\phi \mathrel{\vcenter{\hbox{$\approx$}}}^{all,\cap}_\Delta \psi$ if and only if $CSP(\Delta) \cup \{\neg CSP_\Delta(\psi|\phi)\}$, as proposed. □

Proof of Proposition 5.15 that sceptical c-inference satisfies (NR):

We show that from $\phi \mathrel{\vcenter{\hbox{$\approx$}}}^{\cap,c}_\Delta \psi$ we can infer $\phi\chi \mathrel{\vcenter{\hbox{$\approx$}}}^{\cap,c}_\Delta \psi$ or $\phi\overline{\chi} \mathrel{\vcenter{\hbox{$\approx$}}}^{\cap,c}_\Delta \psi$. Using (3.26) we have to show that if $\phi \mathrel{\vcenter{\hbox{$\approx$}}}_{\kappa^c_\Delta} \psi$ holds for all $\kappa_{\vec{\eta}} \in Sol(CSP(\Delta))$, it also holds that $\phi\chi \mathrel{\vcenter{\hbox{$\approx$}}}_{\kappa^c_\Delta} \psi$ or $\phi\overline{\chi} \mathrel{\vcenter{\hbox{$\approx$}}}_{\kappa^c_\Delta} \psi$ for all c-representations $\kappa_{\vec{\eta}} \in Sol(CSP(\Delta))$. With (3.26) the prerequisite is equivalent to

$$\kappa_{\vec{\eta}}(\phi\psi) < \kappa_{\vec{\eta}}(\phi\overline{\psi}) \qquad \text{for all } \kappa_{\vec{\eta}} \in Sol(CSP(\Delta)). \qquad (A.4.4)$$

With the general properties of ranking functions this gives us

$$\min\{\kappa_{\vec{\eta}}(\phi\psi\chi), \kappa_{\vec{\eta}}(\phi\psi\overline{\chi})\} < \min\{\kappa_{\vec{\eta}}(\phi\overline{\psi}\chi), \kappa_{\vec{\eta}}(\phi\overline{\psi}\overline{\chi})\} \qquad (A.4.5)$$

for all $\kappa_{\vec{\eta}} \in Sol(CSP(\Delta))$, and thus

$$\min\{\kappa_{\vec{\eta}}(\phi\psi\chi), \kappa_{\vec{\eta}}(\phi\psi\overline{\chi})\} < \kappa_{\vec{\eta}}(\phi\overline{\psi}\chi) \quad \text{and} \qquad (A.4.6)$$

$$\min\{\kappa_{\vec{\eta}}(\phi\psi\chi), \kappa_{\vec{\eta}}(\phi\psi\overline{\chi})\} < \kappa_{\vec{\eta}}(\phi\overline{\psi}\overline{\chi}) \quad \text{for all } \kappa_{\vec{\eta}} \in Sol(CSP(\Delta)). \qquad (A.4.7)$$

We have to show that this implies

$$\kappa_{\vec{\eta}}(\phi\psi\chi) < \kappa_{\vec{\eta}}(\phi\overline{\psi}\chi) \qquad \text{or} \qquad\qquad (A.4.8)$$

$$\kappa_{\vec{\eta}}(\phi\psi\overline{\chi}) < \kappa_{\vec{\eta}}(\phi\overline{\psi}\,\overline{\chi}) \qquad \text{for all } \kappa_{\vec{\eta}} \in Sol(CSP(\Delta)). \qquad (A.4.9)$$

With a complete case analysis we obtain:

- If $\kappa_{\vec{\eta}}(\phi\psi\chi) \leq \kappa_{\vec{\eta}}(\phi\psi\overline{\chi})$ then by (A.4.6) we have $\kappa_{\vec{\eta}}(\phi\psi\chi) < \kappa_{\vec{\eta}}(\phi\overline{\psi}\chi)$ in accordance to (A.4.8).

- If $\kappa_{\vec{\eta}}(\phi\psi\overline{\chi}) < \kappa_{\vec{\eta}}(\phi\psi\chi)$ then by (A.4.7) we have $\kappa_{\vec{\eta}}(\phi\psi\overline{\chi}) < \kappa_{\vec{\eta}}(\phi\overline{\psi}\overline{\chi})$ in accordance to (A.4.9).

Therefore from $\phi \mathrel{\vcenter{\hbox{$\approx$}}}^{\cap,c}_\Delta \psi$ we obtain $\phi\chi \mathrel{\vcenter{\hbox{$\approx$}}}^{\cap,c}_\Delta \psi$ or $\phi\overline{\chi} \mathrel{\vcenter{\hbox{$\approx$}}}^{\cap,c}_\Delta \psi$, as proposed. □

Proof of Proposition 5.16 that weakly sceptical c-inference satisfies (NR):

For the existence of a c-representation $\kappa_{\vec{\eta}} \in Sol(CSP(\Delta))$ that gives us the prerequisites, the property that κ-inference satisfies System R (Corollary 4.82) and System R contains (NR) (Corollary 4.41) gives us that from $\phi \hspace{-2pt}\mid\hspace{-6pt}\approx_{\kappa_{\vec{\eta}}} \psi$ we can infer $\phi\chi \hspace{-2pt}\mid\hspace{-6pt}\approx_{\kappa_{\vec{\eta}}} \psi$ or $\phi\overline{\chi} \hspace{-2pt}\mid\hspace{-6pt}\approx_{\kappa_{\vec{\eta}}} \psi$. So the existence of a c-representation which is a witness for (NR) is ensured. To show that $\phi\chi \hspace{-2pt}\mid\hspace{-8pt}\not\approx_{\Delta}^{\cup,c} \psi$ and $\phi\overline{\chi} \hspace{-2pt}\mid\hspace{-8pt}\not\approx_{\Delta}^{\cup,c} \psi$ we recall the proof of Proposition 5.15: The argumentation in this proof is equivalently valid for $\leq$ instead of $<$, which gives us there is no c-representation $\kappa_{\vec{\eta}} \in Sol(CSP(\Delta))$ such that $\phi\psi \hspace{-2pt}\mid\hspace{-6pt}\approx_{\kappa_{\vec{\eta}}} \overline{\chi}$ and $\phi\overline{\psi} \hspace{-2pt}\mid\hspace{-6pt}\approx_{\kappa_{\vec{\eta}}} \overline{\chi}$, given the prerequisite $\phi \hspace{-2pt}\mid\hspace{-6pt}\approx_{\Delta}^{ws,c} \psi$, which completes the proof. $\square$

Proof of Proposition 5.17 that sceptical c-inference satisfies (DR):

We show that from $\phi \vee \chi \hspace{-2pt}\mid\hspace{-6pt}\approx_{\Delta}^{\cap,c} \psi$ we obtain that $\phi \hspace{-2pt}\mid\hspace{-6pt}\approx_{\Delta}^{\cap,c} \psi$ or $\chi \hspace{-2pt}\mid\hspace{-6pt}\approx_{\Delta}^{\cap,c} \psi$. Applying the definitions of c-inference and κ-inference, the prerequisite gives us for all c-representations $\kappa_{\vec{\eta}} \in Sol(CSP(\Delta))$,

$$\kappa_{\vec{\eta}}((\phi \vee \chi) \wedge \psi) < \kappa_{\vec{\eta}}((\phi \vee \chi) \wedge \overline{\psi}) \tag{A.4.10}$$

$$\Leftrightarrow \quad \kappa_{\vec{\eta}}(\phi\psi \vee \chi\psi) < \kappa_{\vec{\eta}}(\phi\overline{\psi} \vee \chi\overline{\psi})$$

$$\overset{(3.11)}{\Longleftrightarrow} \quad \min\{\kappa_{\vec{\eta}}(\phi\psi), \kappa_{\vec{\eta}}(\chi\psi)\} < \min\{\kappa_{\vec{\eta}}(\phi\overline{\psi}), \chi\overline{\psi})\}$$

$$\Rightarrow \quad \min\{\kappa_{\vec{\eta}}(\phi\psi), \kappa_{\vec{\eta}}(\chi\psi)\} < \kappa_{\vec{\eta}}(\phi\overline{\psi}) \qquad \text{and} \qquad \tag{A.4.11}$$

$$\min\{\kappa_{\vec{\eta}}(\phi\psi), \kappa_{\vec{\eta}}(\chi\psi)\} < \kappa_{\vec{\eta}}(\chi\overline{\psi}). \tag{A.4.12}$$

By a complete case differentiation we obtain that if we have $\kappa_{\vec{\eta}}(\phi\psi) \leq \kappa_{\Delta}^{c}(\chi\psi)$ then (A.4.11) results in $\kappa_{\vec{\eta}}(\phi\psi) \leq \kappa_{\vec{\eta}}(\phi\overline{\psi})$ for all $\kappa_{\vec{\eta}} \in Sol(CSP(\Delta))$ and thus $\phi \hspace{-2pt}\mid\hspace{-6pt}\approx_{\Delta}^{\cap,c} \psi$. If, in the contrary, $\kappa_{\vec{\eta}}(\chi\psi) < \kappa_{\vec{\eta}}(\phi\psi)$ then (A.4.12) results in $\kappa_{\vec{\eta}}(\chi\psi) \leq \kappa_{\vec{\eta}}(\chi\overline{\psi})$ for all $\kappa_{\vec{\eta}} \in Sol(CSP(\Delta))$ and thus $\chi \hspace{-2pt}\mid\hspace{-6pt}\approx_{\Delta}^{\cap,c} \psi$, which completes the proof. $\square$

Proof of Proposition 5.18: weakly sceptical c-inference satisfies (DR):

Inference with OCF satisfies (DR), because κ-inference satisfies System R (Corollary 4.82) and System R contains (DR) (Proposition 4.39) therefore from the existence of a c-representation $\kappa_{\vec{\eta}} \in Sol(CSP(\Delta))$ that satisfies the prerequisite $\phi \vee \chi \hspace{-2pt}\mid\hspace{-6pt}\approx_{\kappa_{\vec{\eta}}} \psi$ we directly obtain $\phi \hspace{-2pt}\mid\hspace{-6pt}\approx_{\kappa_{\vec{\eta}}} \psi$ or $\chi \hspace{-2pt}\mid\hspace{-6pt}\approx_{\kappa_{\vec{\eta}}} \psi$. To show that the non-strict condition of weakly sceptical c-inference is satisfied, we recall the proof of Proposition 5.17. Here the argumentation is valid for this proof by simply exchanging the strict relation $<$ with the relation $\leq$. Therefore weakly sceptical c-inference satisfies (DR), as proposed. $\square$

Proof of Lemma 5.22 that $\approx_\Delta^{\cap,c}$ satisfies (DI) (cf. [BEKIK16, Prop. 15]):

Every c-representation κ_Δ^c of Δ satisfies (DI), that is, for each conditional $(\psi|\phi) \in \Delta$ implies $\phi \approx_{\kappa_\Delta^c} \psi$ for every c-representation of Δ. So with Definition 5.35 we directly conclude $\phi \approx_\Delta^{\cap,c} \psi$ for every $(\psi|\phi) \in \Delta$. $\quad\square$

Proof of Lemma 5.23 that weakly sceptical c-inference satisfies (DI):

We follow the proof of Lemma 5.22. As $\phi \approx_\Delta^{\cap,c} \psi$ for every $(\psi|\phi) \in \Delta$, we directly obtain $\phi \not\approx_{\kappa_{\vec{\eta}}} \overline{\psi}$ for every $(\psi|\phi) \in \Delta$ and any $\kappa_{\vec{\eta}} \in Sol(CSP(\Delta))$. Also, because $\phi \approx_{\kappa_{\vec{\eta}}} \psi$ for every $(\psi|\phi) \in \Delta$ and every $\kappa_{\vec{\eta}} \in Sol(CSP(\Delta))$, the existence of at least one of $\kappa_{\vec{\eta}}$ with this property is ensured. $\quad\square$

Proof of Proposition 5.29, confer [BEKIK16, Prop. 9]: For a knowledge base $\Delta = \{(\psi_1|\phi_1), \ldots, (\psi_n|\phi_n)\} \subseteq (\mathfrak{L} \mid \mathfrak{L})$ let Σ_Δ be $\Sigma_\Delta = \{V|V \models \phi_i\psi_i$ for all $(\psi_i|\phi_i) \in \Delta\}$ and let further $\Sigma \supseteq \Sigma_\Delta$ be a set of variables. As $\tau_\Delta^c(\omega) = \sum_{\omega \models \phi_i\overline{\psi}_i} \kappa_i^-$, the (generic) rank of a world is dependent on the conditionals in Δ. Furthermore, being a generic ranking function, the rank of a formula $\tau_\Delta^c(\phi) = \min\{\tau_\Delta^c(\omega)|\omega \models \phi\}$ is the minimum of the ranks of all ϕ satisfying worlds. Let $\omega \in \Omega(\Sigma_\Delta)$, and let $A \in \Sigma \setminus \Sigma_\Delta$ be an arbitrary variable not in Σ_Δ, then neither a nor $\overline{a}$ is a member of any conjunction $\phi_i\psi_i$, $1 \leq i \leq n$. Therefore the sets of conditionals falsified by $\omega \wedge a$ and $\omega \wedge \overline{a}$ are identical, thus the rank of $\tau_\Delta^c(\omega \wedge a)$ and $\tau_\Delta^c(\omega \wedge \overline{a})$ are identical, too. But then $\tau_\Delta^c(\omega) = \tau_\Delta^c(\omega \wedge a) = \tau_\Delta^c(\omega \wedge \overline{a})$ and thus $\tau_\Delta^c(\phi \wedge a) = \tau_\Delta^c(\phi) = \tau_\Delta^c(\phi \wedge \overline{a})$, which gives us $\phi \approx_\Delta^{\bullet,c} \psi$ implies $(\phi \wedge \dot{a}) \approx_\Delta^{\bullet,c} \psi$ for any outcome $\dot{a}$ of variables $A \in \Sigma \setminus \Sigma_\Delta$ and $\bullet \in \{\cup, \cap, ws\}$, as proposed. $\quad\square$

Proof of Proposition 5.31, confer [BEKIK16, Proposition 20]:

To show that the property (REF) holds for $\approx_\Delta^{ws,c}$, we have to show that for every ϕ we have $\phi \approx_\Delta^{ws,c} \phi$. As $\kappa_\Delta^c(\bot) = \infty$ for every non contradictory formula $\bot \not\equiv \phi \in \mathfrak{L}$ and every c-representation κ_Δ^c of Δ we have $\kappa_\Delta^c(\phi) = \kappa_\Delta^c(\phi\phi) < \kappa_\Delta^c(\phi\overline{\phi}) = \kappa_\Delta^c(\bot)$. Therefore there are c-representations that draw the inference, and none that infer $\overline{\phi}$ from ϕ, so by Definition 5.5 we have $\phi \approx_\Delta^{ws,c} \phi$ for every non-contradictory $\phi \in \mathfrak{L}$. $\quad\square$

Proof of Proposition 5.32 that weakly sceptical c-inference satisfies (LLE):

Following [BEKIK16, Proposition 21] this can be shown by general properties of ranking functions. By having recalled the rank of a formula as the minimal rank of all worlds that satisfy the formula in (3.10), given $\phi \equiv \chi$ we have $\{\omega|\omega \models \phi\} = \{\omega|\omega \models \chi\}$ and therefore $\kappa(\phi) = \min\{\kappa(\omega)|\omega \models \phi\} = \min\{\kappa(\omega)|\omega \models \chi\} = \kappa(\chi)$. With the same argumentation an again $\phi \equiv \chi$ we have $\kappa(\phi\psi) = \kappa(\chi\psi)$ and $\kappa(\phi\overline{\psi}) = \kappa(\chi\overline{\psi})$ given $\phi \equiv \chi$. Thus if $\phi \equiv \chi$ it is $\kappa(\phi\psi) < \kappa(\phi\overline{\psi})$ if and only if $\kappa(\chi\psi) < \kappa(\chi\overline{\psi})$ and therefore $\phi\mathrel{\vnmid}_{\Delta}^{ws,c}\psi$ if and only if $\chi\mathrel{\vnmid}_{\Delta}^{ws,c}\psi$. $\qquad\square$

Proof of Proposition 5.33 that weakly sceptical c-inference satisfies (RW):

Following [BEKIK16, Proposition 22] we show that $\phi\mathrel{\vnmid}_{\Delta}^{ws,c}\psi$ and $\psi \vDash \chi$ imply $\phi\mathrel{\vnmid}_{\Delta}^{ws,c}\chi$. That is, that we have

$$\kappa_{\Delta}^{c}(\phi\psi) < \kappa_{\Delta}^{c}(\phi\overline{\psi}) \qquad\qquad \text{for any } \kappa_{\Delta}^{c} \text{ of } \Delta, \text{ and}$$
$$\kappa_{\Delta}^{c\,\prime}(\phi\psi) \leq \kappa_{\Delta}^{c\,\prime}(\phi\overline{\psi}) \qquad\qquad \text{all } \kappa_{\Delta}^{c\,\prime} \text{ of } \Delta$$

from the first prerequisite, and $Mod(\psi) \subseteq Mod(\chi)$ from the second. The latter gives us $Mod(\overline{\chi}) \subseteq Mod(\overline{\psi})$ and subsequently $Mod(\phi\psi) \subseteq Mod(\phi\chi)$ and $Mod(\phi\overline{\chi}) \subseteq Mod(\phi\overline{\psi})$. From the definition of ranks of formulas in (3.10) we have $\kappa(\phi\psi) = \min\{\omega | \omega \in Mod(\phi\psi)\}$ and $\kappa(\phi\overline{\psi}) = \min\{\omega | \omega \in Mod(\phi\overline{\psi})\}$, this gives us

$$\kappa_{\Delta}^{c}(\phi\chi) = \min_{\omega\in Mod(\phi\chi)}\{\omega\} \leq \min_{\omega\in Mod(\phi\psi)}\{\omega\} = \kappa_{\Delta}^{c}(\phi\psi)$$
$$\kappa_{\Delta}^{c}(\phi\overline{\chi}) = \min_{\omega\in Mod(\phi\overline{\chi})}\{\omega\} \geq \min_{\omega\in Mod(\phi\overline{\psi})}\{\omega\} = \kappa_{\Delta}^{c}(\phi\overline{\psi})$$

and hence

$$\kappa_{\Delta}^{c}(\phi\chi) \leq \kappa_{\Delta}^{c}(\phi\psi) < \kappa_{\Delta}^{c}(\phi\overline{\psi}) \leq \kappa_{\Delta}^{c}(\phi\overline{\chi}),$$

and with the same argumentation

$$\kappa_{\Delta}^{c\,\prime}(\phi\chi) \leq \kappa_{\Delta}^{c\,\prime}(\phi\psi) < \kappa_{\Delta}^{c\,\prime}(\phi\overline{\psi}) \leq \kappa_{\Delta}^{c\,\prime}(\phi\overline{\chi}) \qquad \text{for all } \kappa_{\Delta}^{c\,\prime} \text{ of } \Delta.$$

Which, with Definition 5.5, gives us $\phi\mathrel{\vnmid}_{\Delta}^{ws,c}\chi$, as proposed. $\qquad\square$

Proof of Proposition 5.34 that weakly sceptical c-inference satisfies (OR):

Let $\Delta = \{(\psi_1|\phi_1), \ldots, (\psi_n|\phi_n)\}$ be a conditional knowledge base and let $\phi\mathrel{\vnmid}_{\Delta}^{ws,c}\chi$ and $\psi\mathrel{\vnmid}_{\Delta}^{ws,c}\chi$. We show that from these prerequisites $(\phi\vee\psi)\mathrel{\vnmid}_{\Delta}^{ws,c}\chi$ follows. Applying Definition 5.5, (3.26), and (3.10) the prerequisites expand to

$$\phi\mathrel{\vnmid}_{\Delta}^{ws,c}\chi \tag{A.4.13}$$

iff
$$\kappa_{\vec{\eta}}(\phi\chi) \leq \kappa_{\vec{\eta}}(\phi\overline{\chi}) \tag{A.4.14}$$

iff
$$\min\{\kappa_{\vec{\eta}}(\phi\psi\chi), \kappa_{\vec{\eta}}(\phi\overline{\psi}\chi)\} \leq \min\{\kappa_{\vec{\eta}}(\phi\psi\overline{\chi}), \kappa_{\vec{\eta}}(\phi\overline{\psi}\overline{\chi})\} \tag{A.4.15}$$

for all $\kappa_{\vec{\eta}} \in Sol(CSP(\Delta))$, and there is at least one c-representation for which these inequalities are strict, and

$$\psi \approx_{\Delta}^{ws,c} \chi \tag{A.4.16}$$

iff $$\kappa_{\vec{\eta}}(\psi\chi) \leq \kappa_{\vec{\eta}}(\psi\overline{\chi}) \tag{A.4.17}$$

iff $$\min\{\kappa_{\vec{\eta}}(\phi\psi\chi), \kappa_{\vec{\eta}}(\overline{\phi}\psi\chi)\} \leq \min\{\kappa_{\vec{\eta}}(\phi\psi\overline{\chi}), \kappa_{\vec{\eta}}(\overline{\phi}\psi\overline{\chi})\} \tag{A.4.18}$$

for all $\kappa_{\vec{\eta}} \in Sol(CSP(\Delta))$, and there is at least one c-representation for which these inequalities are strict. For $(\phi \vee \psi) \approx_{\Delta}^{ws,c} \chi$ to hold we have to show that

$$\min\{\kappa_{\vec{\eta}}(\phi\psi\chi), \kappa_{\vec{\eta}}(\phi\overline{\psi}\chi), \kappa_{\vec{\eta}}(\overline{\phi}\psi\chi)\} \leq \min\{\kappa_{\vec{\eta}}(\phi\psi\overline{\chi}), \kappa_{\vec{\eta}}(\phi\overline{\psi}\overline{\chi}), \kappa_{\vec{\eta}}(\overline{\phi}\psi\overline{\chi})\} \tag{A.4.19}$$

for all $\kappa_{\vec{\eta}} \in Sol(CSP(\Delta))$, and there is at least one c-representation for which this inequality is strict. We start by showing that the non-strict inequalities hold by a complete case differentiation:

(i) $\kappa_{\vec{\eta}}(\phi\psi\chi) < \kappa_{\vec{\eta}}(\phi\overline{\psi}\chi)$ and $\kappa_{\vec{\eta}}(\phi\psi\chi) < \kappa_{\vec{\eta}}(\overline{\phi}\psi\chi)$. Then (A.4.15) and (A.4.18) directly yield (A.4.19).

(ii) $\kappa_{\vec{\eta}}(\phi\psi\chi) < \kappa_{\vec{\eta}}(\phi\overline{\psi}\chi)$ and $\kappa_{\vec{\eta}}(\phi\psi\chi) \geq \kappa_{\vec{\eta}}(\overline{\phi}\psi\chi)$. Then $\kappa_{\vec{\eta}}(\overline{\phi}\psi\chi) \leq \kappa_{\vec{\eta}}(\phi\psi\chi)$ by transitivity gives us (A.4.19) from (A.4.15) and (A.4.18).

(iii) $\kappa_{\vec{\eta}}(\phi\psi\chi) \geq \kappa_{\vec{\eta}}(\phi\overline{\psi}\chi)$ and $\kappa_{\vec{\eta}}(\phi\psi\chi) < \kappa_{\vec{\eta}}(\overline{\phi}\psi\chi)$. In this case we have to further differentiate between the cases $\kappa_{\vec{\eta}}(\phi\psi\chi) \leq \kappa_{\vec{\eta}}(\phi\psi\chi)$ and $\kappa_{\vec{\eta}}(\phi\psi\chi) < \kappa_{\vec{\eta}}(\phi\psi\chi)$, but in either case transitivity in combination with (A.4.15) and (A.4.18) yield (A.4.19) .

(iv) $\kappa_{\vec{\eta}}(\phi\psi\chi) \geq \kappa_{\vec{\eta}}(\phi\overline{\psi}\chi)$ and $\kappa_{\vec{\eta}}(\phi\psi\chi) \geq \kappa_{\vec{\eta}}(\overline{\phi}\psi\chi)$. As in case (iii) we have to differentiate between the cases $\kappa_{\vec{\eta}}(\phi\overline{\psi}\chi) < \kappa_{\vec{\eta}}(\overline{\phi}\psi\chi)$ and $\kappa_{\vec{\eta}}(\overline{\phi}\psi\chi) \leq \kappa_{\vec{\eta}}(\phi\overline{\psi}\chi)$, but again in either case we obtain (A.4.19).

So for all $\kappa_{\vec{\eta}} \in Sol(CSP(\Delta))$, (A.4.19) holds. To show that there have to be solutions such that (A.4.19) is strict, we assume the opposite and directly obtain that this would contradict the prerequisites. So assume there was no c-representation $\kappa_{\vec{\eta}'} \in Sol(CSP(\Delta))$ satisfying

$$\min\{\kappa_{\vec{\eta}'}(\phi\psi\chi), \kappa_{\vec{\eta}'}(\phi\overline{\psi}\chi), \kappa_{\vec{\eta}'}(\overline{\phi}\psi\chi)\}$$
$$< \min\{\kappa_{\vec{\eta}'}(\phi\psi\overline{\chi}), \kappa_{\vec{\eta}'}(\phi\overline{\psi}\overline{\chi}), \kappa_{\vec{\eta}'}(\overline{\phi}\psi\overline{\chi})\}. \tag{A.4.20}$$

Then, because (A.4.19) holds for all $\kappa_{\vec{\eta}} \in Sol(CSP(\Delta))$, for all c-representations $\kappa_{\vec{\eta}} \in Sol(CSP(\Delta))$ we had

$$\min\{\kappa_{\vec{\eta}}(\phi\psi\chi), \kappa_{\vec{\eta}}(\phi\overline{\psi}\chi), \kappa_{\vec{\eta}}(\overline{\phi}\psi\chi)\} = \min\{\kappa_{\vec{\eta}}(\phi\psi\overline{\chi}), \kappa_{\vec{\eta}}(\phi\overline{\psi}\overline{\chi}), \kappa_{\vec{\eta}}(\overline{\phi}\psi\overline{\chi})\}$$

and therefore

$$\min\{\kappa_{\vec{\eta}}(\phi\psi\chi), \kappa_{\vec{\eta}}(\phi\overline{\psi}\chi), \kappa_{\vec{\eta}}(\overline{\phi}\psi\chi)\} \geq \kappa_{\vec{\eta}}(\phi\psi\overline{\chi})$$
$$\min\{\kappa_{\vec{\eta}}(\phi\psi\chi), \kappa_{\vec{\eta}}(\phi\overline{\psi}\chi), \kappa_{\vec{\eta}}(\overline{\phi}\psi\chi)\} \geq \kappa_{\vec{\eta}}(\phi\overline{\psi}\overline{\chi})$$
$$\min\{\kappa_{\vec{\eta}}(\phi\psi\chi), \kappa_{\vec{\eta}}(\phi\overline{\psi}\chi), \kappa_{\vec{\eta}}(\overline{\phi}\psi\chi)\} \geq \kappa_{\vec{\eta}}(\overline{\phi}\psi\overline{\chi})$$

By a complete case analysis we obtain for any $\kappa_{\vec{\eta}'} \in Sol(CSP(\Delta))$:

If $\quad\quad\quad\quad \kappa_{\vec{\eta}'}(\phi\psi\chi) = \min\{\kappa_{\vec{\eta}'}(\phi\psi\chi), \kappa_{\vec{\eta}'}(\phi\overline{\psi}\chi), \kappa_{\vec{\eta}'}(\overline{\phi}\psi\chi)\}$

then $\quad \min\{\kappa_{\vec{\eta}'}(\phi\psi\chi), \kappa_{\vec{\eta}'}(\phi\overline{\psi}\chi)\} \geq \min\{\kappa_{\vec{\eta}'}(\phi\psi\overline{\chi}), \kappa_{\vec{\eta}'}(\phi\overline{\psi}\overline{\chi})\}$

contradicting (A.4.15).

If $\quad\quad\quad\quad \kappa_{\vec{\eta}'}(\phi\overline{\psi}\chi) = \min\{\kappa_{\vec{\eta}'}(\phi\psi\chi), \kappa_{\vec{\eta}'}(\phi\overline{\psi}\chi), \kappa_{\vec{\eta}'}(\overline{\phi}\psi\chi)\}$

then $\quad \min\{\kappa_{\vec{\eta}'}(\phi\psi\chi), \kappa_{\vec{\eta}'}(\phi\overline{\psi}\chi)\} \geq \min\{\kappa_{\vec{\eta}'}(\phi\psi\overline{\chi}), \kappa_{\vec{\eta}'}(\phi\overline{\psi}\overline{\chi})\}$

contradicting (A.4.15).

If $\quad\quad\quad\quad \kappa_{\vec{\eta}'}(\overline{\phi}\psi\chi) = \min\{\kappa_{\vec{\eta}'}(\phi\psi\chi), \kappa_{\vec{\eta}'}(\phi\overline{\psi}\chi), \kappa_{\vec{\eta}'}(\overline{\phi}\psi\chi)\}$

then $\quad \min\{\kappa_{\vec{\eta}'}(\phi\psi\chi), \kappa_{\vec{\eta}'}(\overline{\phi}\psi\chi)\} \geq \min\{\kappa_{\vec{\eta}'}(\phi\psi\overline{\chi}), \kappa_{\vec{\eta}'}(\overline{\phi}\psi\overline{\chi})\}$

contradicting (A.4.18).

Therefore there is a c-representation $\kappa_{\vec{\eta}'} \in Sol(CSP(\Delta))$ satisfying A.4.20, and this completes the proof. $\qquad\square$

Proof of Proposition 5.36, confer [BEKIK16, Proposition 13]:
We distinguish the cases where Δ is consistent and where Δ is inconsistent. If Δ is inconsistent, then there are no c-representations of Δ. This means $\phi \approx_{\Delta}^{\cap,c} \psi$ holds trivially for all pairs $\phi, \psi \in \mathfrak{L}$ as Definition 5.4 is a proposition over the empty set and trivially true, therefore $C_{\Delta}^{\cap,c}(\phi) = \mathfrak{L}$ for all $\phi \in \mathfrak{L}$ given Δ is inconsistent, and this is trivially deductively closed. For the case where Δ is consistent, we first consider the inference operation for single c-representations κ_{Δ}^{c} of Δ (see (3.37)), $C_{\Delta}^{c}(\phi)$. Let $\psi \in \mathfrak{L}$ be a formula such that $\psi \in C_{\Delta}^{c}(\phi)$. Due to the compactness of propositional logic, there is a finite set $\{\psi_1, \ldots, \psi_m\} \subseteq C_{\Delta}^{c}(\phi)$ such that $(\psi_1 \wedge \cdots \wedge \psi_m) \vDash \psi$. Being

a ranking inference, $\mathrel{\mathop{\approx}\limits_{\kappa_\Delta^c}}$ satisfies System P (see Corollary 4.109), and so satisfies the property (AND), which means that from $\phi\mathrel{\mathop{\approx}\limits_{\kappa_\Delta^c}}\psi_1$ and $\phi\mathrel{\mathop{\approx}\limits_{\kappa_\Delta^c}}\psi_2$ we obtain $\phi\mathrel{\mathop{\approx}\limits_{\kappa_\Delta^c}}(\psi_1\psi_2)$, which by iterative application gives us $\phi\mathrel{\mathop{\approx}\limits_{\kappa_\Delta^c}}(\psi_1\wedge\cdots\wedge\psi_m)$. Being a System P inference means $\mathrel{\mathop{\approx}\limits_{\kappa_\Delta^c}}$ also satisfies (RM), so from $\phi\mathrel{\mathop{\approx}\limits_{\kappa_\Delta^c}}(\psi_1\wedge\cdots\wedge\psi_m)$ we obtain $\phi\mathrel{\mathop{\approx}\limits_{\kappa_\Delta^c}}\psi$, and thus overall we obtain that $C_\Delta^c(\phi)$ is deductively closed. As the intersection of deductive closed sets is again a deductively closed set, and $C_\Delta^{\cap,c}(\phi)$ being the intersection of the sets $C_\Delta^c(\phi)$ for all c-representations κ_Δ^c of Δ, we finally obtain that given Δ is consistent, $C_\Delta^{\cap,c}(\phi)$ is deductively closed, which completes the proof $\square$

Proof of Proposition 5.37, confer [BEKIK16, Proposition 14]:
We prove the two propositions separately.

If $\phi\equiv\bot$ then $\kappa_\Delta^c(\phi)=\infty$ and therefore $\kappa_\Delta^c(\phi\psi)=\infty$ for all $\psi\in\mathfrak{L}$ and all κ_Δ^c of Δ. But then there is no formula ψ such that $\kappa(\phi\psi)<\kappa(\phi\overline{\psi})$ and therefore $C_\Delta^c(\phi)=\varnothing$ for all κ_Δ^c of Δ, which then gives us that $C_\Delta^{\bullet,c}(\phi)=\varnothing$ for $\bullet\in\{\cap,\cup,ws\}$.

In the proof of Proposition 5.36 we already showed that $C_\Delta^{\cap,c}(\phi)=\mathfrak{L}$ for all $\phi\in\mathfrak{L}$ given Δ is inconsistent. For consistent Δ, $\bot\in C_\Delta^{\cap,c}(\phi)$ would imply that $\kappa_\Delta^c(\phi\bot)=\infty<\kappa_\Delta^c(\phi\top)$ which is a contradiction. Therefore for consistent Δ there is no formula which infers $\bot$ and thus no consistent Δ can result in $\bot\in C_\Delta^{\bullet,c}(\phi)$, $\bullet\in\{\cap,\cup,ws\}$, for any $\phi\in\mathfrak{L}$, which completes the proof. $\square$

Proof of Proposition 5.39, confer [BEKIK16, Proposition 25]: The inclusions of this proposition follow directly from the respective definitions:
- (5.39.a) For $\phi\mathrel{\mathop{\approx}\limits_\Delta^{\cap,c}}\psi$ to hold, every c-representation of Δ has to satisfy the inequality $\kappa_\Delta^c(\phi\psi)<\kappa_\Delta^c(\psi\overline{\psi})$.
- (5.39.b) For $\phi\mathrel{\mathop{\approx}\limits_\Delta^{ws,c}}\psi$ to hold, every c-representation of Δ has to satisfy the inequality $\kappa_\Delta^c(\phi\psi)\leq\kappa_\Delta^c(\psi\overline{\psi})$, with one c-representation where the inequality is strict.
- (5.39.c) For $\phi\mathrel{\mathop{\approx}\limits_\Delta^{\cup,c}}\psi$ to hold, any c-representation of Δ has to satisfy the inequality $\kappa_\Delta^c(\phi\psi)<\kappa_\Delta^c(\psi\overline{\psi})$

In this enumeration we directly have (5.39.a) implies (5.39.b) implies (5.39.c), but not the other way round. To prove that these subset relations are proper, we refer to examples where formulas are inferable with one, but not the other relation: For $\mathrel{\mathop{\approx}\limits_\Delta^{ws,c}}\not\subset\mathrel{\mathop{\approx}\limits_\Delta^{\cap,c}}$ we find a knowledge base in Example 5.6 where there are formulas inferable by $\phi\mathrel{\mathop{\approx}\limits_\Delta^{ws,c}}\psi$ but not by $\mathrel{\mathop{\approx}\limits_\Delta^{\cap,c}}$;

for $\mathrel{|\!\approx}_\Delta^{\cup,c} \not\subset \mathrel{|\!\approx}_\Delta^{ws,c}$ we find a knowledge base in Example 5.7 where there are formulas inferable by $\mathrel{|\!\approx}_\Delta^{\cup,c}$ but not by $\mathrel{|\!\approx}_\Delta^{ws,c}$. □

Proof of Corollary 5.43, confer [BEKIK16, Proposition 32]: The set inclusions follow the same argumentation as for the proof of Proposition 5.39 with the additional constraint that (5.39.a), (5.39.b), and (5.39.c) range over certain sets of, and not all, c-representations of Δ. To show that these are proper set-inclusions, we refer to the examples also used in the mentioned proof, as the solutions given in Example 5.6 and 5.7 are the minimal ones (already mentioned in Example 5.41). □

Proof of Lemma 5.44, confer [BEKIK16, Proposition 33]: Each of the minimal sets is a subset of the set of all c-representations of Δ. Therefore, inferring with a minimal set of c-representations of Δ takes less models into account than inferring with the set of all c-representations of Δ. Regarding sceptical inference, we obtain that if ψ follows from ϕ in every c-representation of Δ, then also in every subset of the c-representation of Δ, which gives us (5.33). Regarding credulous inference, we obtain that given ψ credulously follows from ϕ follows in a subset of the c-representations of Δ, then this c-representations are also present in the set of all c-representations of Δ, and therefore ψ can be credulously inferred from ϕ given the set of all c-representations of Δ, which gives us (5.35). □

Proof of Lemma 5.45 [BEK16, Proposition 2]: We show this by reduction ad absurdum:

Assume that for $CSP(\Delta)$ of a knowledge base $\Delta = \{(\psi_1|\phi_1), \ldots, (\psi_n|\phi_n)\}$ there was a c-representation $\kappa_{\vec{\eta}}$ constituted from a $\vec{\eta} = (\kappa_1^-, \ldots, \kappa_n^-)$ out of $Sol(CSP(\Delta))$ which was sum-minimal, but not componentwise minimal, that is, $\vec{\eta} \in Min_c^+$, $\vec{\eta} \notin Min_c^{cw}$. Then there was a solution $((\kappa_1^-)', \ldots, (\kappa_n^-)') = \vec{\eta}' \in Min_c^{cw}$ with the property that $(\kappa_i^-)' \leq \kappa_i^-$ for all $1 \leq i \leq n$ and there was an index j, $1 \leq j \leq n$, such that $(\kappa_j)^- < \kappa_j^-$. But then we had

$$\sum_{i=1}^n (\kappa_i^-)' < \sum_{i=1}^n \kappa_i^-,$$

and therefore $\vec{\eta}' \prec_c^+ \vec{\eta}$. But then there was a strictly sum-preferred solution to $\vec{\eta}$ and by (5.30), $\vec{\eta} \notin Min_c^+$ in contradiction to the assumption. Therefore $\vec{\eta} \in Min_c^+$ implies $\vec{\eta} \in Min_c^{cw}$ which is equivalent to stating $Min_c^+ \subseteq Min_c^{cw}$, as proposed. □

Proof of Lemma 5.46 [BEK16, Proposition 2]: We show this by reduction ad absurdum:

Assume that for $CSP(\Delta)$ of a knowledge base $\Delta = \{(\psi_1|\phi_1), \ldots, (\psi_n|\phi_n)\}$ without self-fulfilling conditionals there was a c-representation $\kappa_{\vec{\eta}}$ constituted from $\vec{\eta} = (\kappa_1^-, \ldots, \kappa_n^-) \in Sol(CSP(\Delta))$ that was ind-minimal, but not componentwise minimal, that is, $\vec{\eta} \in Min_c^{\kappa}$, $\vec{\eta} \notin Min_c^{cw}$. Then there was a solution $((\kappa_1^-)', \ldots, (\kappa_n^-)') = \vec{\eta}' \in Min_c^{cw}$ with the property that $(\kappa_i^-)' \leq \kappa_i^-$ for all $1 \leq i \leq n$ and there was an index j, $1 \leq j \leq n$, such that $(\kappa_j^-)' < \kappa_j^-$. But then for all $\omega \in \Omega$ we had

$$\kappa_{\vec{\eta}'}(\omega) = \Big(\sum_{\omega \models (\phi_i \overline{\psi_i}} (\kappa_i^-)' \Big) \leq \Big(\sum_{\omega \models (\phi_i \overline{\psi_i}} \kappa_i^- \Big) = \kappa_{\vec{\eta}}(\omega)$$

and there was at least one $\omega' \in \Omega$ such that

$$\kappa_{\vec{\eta}'}(\omega') = \Big(\sum_{\omega' \models (\phi_i \overline{\psi_i}} (\kappa_i^-)' \Big) < \Big(\sum_{\omega' \models (\phi_i \overline{\psi_i}} \kappa_i^- \Big) = \kappa_{\vec{\eta}}(\omega')$$

which gave us $\vec{\eta}' \prec_c^{\kappa} \vec{\eta}$ in contradiction to the assumption.

If $\Delta = \{(\psi_1|\phi_1), \ldots, (\psi_n|\phi_n)\} \subseteq (\mathfrak{L} \mid \mathfrak{L})$ had self-fulfilling conditionals, for simplicity of the proof we, without loss of generality, assume that there is exactly one index j, $1 \leq j \leq n$, such that $(\kappa_j^-)' < \kappa_j^-$ and for all $1 \leq i \leq n$, $i \neq j$ we had $(\kappa_i^-)' = \kappa_i^-$. If $(\psi_j|\phi_j)$ was not a self-fulfilling conditional, then, with the same argumentation as above, we had $\vec{\eta}' \prec_c^{\kappa} \vec{\eta}$ in contradiction to the assumption. If $(\psi_j|\phi_j)$ was a self-fulfilling conditional, then $\kappa_{\vec{\eta}'}(\omega) = \kappa_{\vec{\eta}}(\omega)$ for all $\omega \in \Omega$, which means that both $\kappa_{\vec{\eta}'}$ and $\kappa_{\vec{\eta}}$ are equivalent with respect to inductive preference and thus if $\vec{\eta} \in Min_c^{\kappa}$ then also $\vec{\eta}' \in Min_c^{\kappa}$.

Overall we obtain that for knowledge bases without self-fulfilling conditionals we have $\vec{\eta} \in Min_c^{\kappa}$ implies $\vec{\eta} \in Min_c^{cw}$ which is equivalent to stating $Min_c^{\kappa} \subseteq Min_c^{cw}$, as proposed, whilst for knowledge bases with self-fulfilling conditionals this cannot be guaranteed. $\quad\square$

Proof of Corollary 5.47: We here use the findings of the chapter so far and with these present a more compact proof as the original proof in [BEKIK16, Proposition 34]. We recall the argumentation for the proof of Proposition 5.39, where we obtained that for two sets $\mathcal{A}, \mathcal{B}$ of c-representations $\mathcal{A} \subseteq \mathcal{B} \subseteq Sol(CSP(\Delta))$ such that the sceptical inferences based on $\mathcal{B}$ are included in the sceptical inferences based on $\mathcal{A}$, and the credulous inferences based on $\mathcal{A}$ are included in the credulous inferences based on $\mathcal{B}$ (see (5.39.a) and (5.39.b). Together with Lemma 5.45 this, without further ado, gives us (5.39) and (5.40); Together with Lemma 5.46, and the additional constraint of Δ not to contain self-fulfilling conditionals, this gives us (5.41) and (5.42). □

A.5 Proofs for Chapter 6

Proof of Proposition 6.7 that $\mathcal{T}$ is terminating [BEKI17a, Proposition 2]:
We recall the proof in. To be terminating, we have to show that there is no infinite chain of rule applications. The rules (SF), (DP), (CE), and (IC) all remove at least one conditional, the same holds for (CC), (SC), and (IC), none of which are applicable to an empty knowledge base. The rules (PN) and (CN) can be applied at most once for every conditional. Therefore the system is terminating.   □

Proof of Proposition 6.8 [BEKI17a, Proposition 3]: Following the proof of [BEKI17a, Proposition 3] we show that each rule is correct, individually.

(SF)   is correct: If $\phi \vDash \psi$ then $\kappa(\phi\psi) < \infty = \kappa(\phi\overline{\psi})$ for any OCF.

(DP)   is correct because $\phi \equiv \chi$ and $\psi \equiv \xi$ implies $\kappa(\phi\psi) = \kappa(\chi\xi)$ and $\kappa(\phi\overline{\psi}) = \kappa(\chi\overline{\xi})$ by (3.10) and thus $\kappa \vDash (\psi|\phi)$ if and only if $\kappa \vDash (\xi|\chi)$.

(CE)   is correct because if $\phi\psi \equiv \chi\xi$ then $\kappa(\phi\psi) = \kappa(\chi\xi)$, and likewise if $\phi\overline{\psi} \equiv \chi\overline{\xi}$ then $\kappa(\phi\overline{\psi}) = \kappa(\chi\overline{\xi})$ which results in $\kappa \vDash (\psi|\phi)$ if and only if $\kappa \vDash (\xi|\chi)$.

(PN)   is correct for the same reasons as (DP) by definition of norm().

(CN)   is correct for the same reasons as (CE) because $\phi\psi \equiv \phi\phi\psi$ and $\phi\overline{\psi} \equiv (\phi \wedge \neg(\phi\psi))$.

(CC), **(SC)**, and **(IC)** are correct because in either case Δ is inconsistent and thus has the same empty model set as $Mod(\Delta^{\perp})$.   □

Proof of Proposition 6.9 [BEKI17a, Proposition 4]: Like in the proof of Proposition 6.8 we inspect the rules individually. For (CC), (SC), and (IC), $\mathcal{T}$ is correct because the definition of modelwise equivalence explicitly covers inconsistent knowledge bases and defines them to be elementwise equivalent. Also, for self-fulfilling conditionals no counterpart is needed so (SF) is correct. (PN), (CN) preserve elementwise equivalence because the model sets of the conditionals the rules are applied to are unchanged. Finally, from a pair of conditionals with identical models, (DP) and (CE) remove one, so the other is still present in the knowledge base, preserving elementwise equivalence.   □

Proof of Proposition 6.10 [BEKI17a, Proposition 5]: Proposition 6.7 shows that $\mathcal{T}$ is terminating, thus local confluence of the system implies global confluence. By [KB83, BN98] this means we have to show that for every critical pair obtained from superpositioning two left hand sides of rules in $\mathcal{T}$ we obtain the same knowledge base. It is clear that for (CC), (SC), and (IC), every critical pair and a rule in $\mathcal{T}$ reduces to $\Delta^{\perp}$, as all rules keep the consistency of a knowledge base unchanged. As every self-fulfilling conditional replaced by any rule in $\{(\text{DP}), (\text{CE}), (\text{PN}), (\text{CN})\}$ is still self-fulfilling, any critical pair obtained from (SF) and $\mathcal{T} \setminus \{(\text{CC}), (\text{SC}), (\text{IC})\}$ reduces to the same knowledge base. For the rules transforming conditionals into normal forms, (CN) and (PN), every critical pair is reduced to the same knowledge base. This leaves us with the critical pairs obtained from (DP) and (CE). We consider the knowledge base $\Delta_0 = \Delta \cup \{(\psi|\phi), (\psi'|\phi'), (\psi''|\phi'')\}$ If (DP) can be applied to Δ_0 at $\{(\psi|\phi), (\psi'|\phi')\}$ we get $\Delta_1 = \Delta \cup \{(\psi|\phi), (\psi''|\phi'')\}$, and if (CE) can be applied to Δ_0 at $\{(\psi'|\phi'), (\psi''|\phi'')\}$ we get $\Delta_2 = \Delta \cup \{(\psi|\phi), (\psi'|\phi')\}$. As (DP) is applicable to Δ_0 we have $\phi \equiv \phi', \psi \equiv \psi'$; therefore (DP) can be applied to Δ_2, resulting in $\Delta_3 = \Delta \cup \{(\psi|\phi)\}$. As (CE) was applicable to Δ_0 we have $\phi'\psi' \equiv \phi''\psi'', \phi'\overline{\psi'} \equiv \phi''\overline{\psi''}$; and therefore we also have $\phi\psi \equiv \phi''\psi'', \phi\overline{\psi} \equiv \phi''\overline{\psi''}$ so that (CE) can be applied to Δ_1. This results in $\Delta \cup \{(\psi|\phi)\} = \Delta_3$, so $\mathcal{T}$ reduces both Δ_1 and Δ_2 to Δ_3. The other critical pairs obtained from (DP) and (CE) are reducible to the same knowledge base, similarly. □

Proof of Proposition 6.11 [BEKI17a, Proposition 6]: For inconsistent knowledge bases, this follows directly from Proposition 6.9. Proposition 6.9 also shows that $\Delta \equiv_{\text{ew}} \mathcal{T}(\Delta)$, so for consistent knowledge bases we have to show $\Delta' \not\equiv_{\text{ew}} \Delta$. We show this by reductio ad absurdum and assume that $\Delta' \equiv_{\text{ew}} \Delta$. Then by the prerequisite $\Delta \subsetneq \mathcal{T}(\Delta)$ we obtain that there must be two different conditionals $(\psi_1|\phi_1), (\psi_2|\phi_2) \in \mathcal{T}(\Delta)$ and a conditional $(\psi|\phi) \in \Delta'$ such that $Mod\{(\psi_1|\phi_1)\} = Mod\{(\psi|\phi)\}$ and $Mod\{(\psi_1|\phi_1)\} = Mod\{(\psi|\phi)\}$. This gives us $Mod\{(\psi_1|\phi_1)\} = Mod\{(\psi_2|\phi_2)\}$. But for this we need to have $\phi_1 \equiv \phi_2$, $\phi_1\psi_1 \equiv \phi_2\psi_2$, and $\phi_1\overline{\psi_1} \equiv \phi_2\overline{\psi_2}$. In this case, (CE) could have been applied to $(\psi_1|\phi_1), (\psi_2|\phi_2)$ in contrast to the assumption. So we finally obtain that $\Delta' \not\equiv_{\text{ew}} \Delta$. □

Proof of Proposition 6.20 [BEKI17a, Proposition 9]: Following the referred proof we only show the case for consistent knowledge bases, as $\Delta^{\perp}$ is minimal by definition. Let $\Delta = \{(\psi_1|\phi_1), \ldots, (\psi_n|\phi_n)\}$ be a consistent knowledge base and let $\Delta' \subsetneq \mathcal{T}_2(\Delta)$ be a strict subset of the knowledge base obtained from $\mathcal{T}_2$. As $\Delta \equiv_{\text{mod}} \mathcal{T}_2(\Delta)$ to show that $\Delta' \not\equiv_{\text{mod}} \Delta$ with Corollary 6.17 it suffices to show that $\Delta' \not\equiv_{\text{mod}} \mathcal{T}_2(\Delta)$. We show the latter by reduction ad absurdum. So we assume that $\Delta' \not\equiv_{\mathrm{mod}} T_2(\Delta)$. But then the prerequisite $\Delta' \subsetneq T_2(\Delta)$ gives us that there must be a set of conditionals $\Delta'' = \{(\xi_1|\chi_1), \ldots, (\xi_m|\chi_m)\}$ such that $\Delta' \cap \Delta'' = \varnothing$ and $\Delta' \cup \Delta'' = T_2(\Delta)$. But then the application of (RC) to $T_2(\Delta)$ should have removed all conditionals in Δ'' from $T_2(\Delta)$. Therefore, $\Delta' \equiv_{\mathrm{mod}} T_2(\Delta)$ and $\Delta \equiv_{\mathrm{mod}} T_2(\Delta)$ lead to a contradiction, which gives us $\Delta' \not\equiv_{\mathrm{mod}} T_2(\Delta)$ and therefore $\Delta' \not\equiv_{\mathrm{mod}} \Delta$ as proposed. $\qquad\square$

A.6 Proofs for Chapter 7

Proof of Lemma 7.2 [EKI15b, Lemma 3]: To show that the function κ_Γ defined by Equation (7.2) is an OCF we have to show that κ_Γ is function $\Omega \to \mathbb{N}_0$ and that the preimage $\kappa_\Gamma^{-1}(0)$ is a non-empty set. The first follows direct from the definition, because every summand in (7.2) contributes a non-negative integer to the sum and so the closure property of the semigroup $(\mathbb{N}, +)$ gives us that for every $\omega \in \Omega$, $\kappa_\Gamma(\omega)$ is a non-negative integer. To show that $\kappa_\Gamma^{-1}(0) \neq \varnothing$ we follow the proof in [EKI15b, Lemma 3]: By the normalisation condition (7.1) for every vertex $V \in \Sigma$ and for every configuration $\mathbf{p}_V$ of the vertex's parents variables $pa(V)$ there is an outcome $\dot{v}$, such that $\kappa_V(\dot{v}|\mathbf{p}_V) = 0$. We inspect the configuration of all variables with respect to the direction of the edges, starting by the network's root vertices and traversing the network in breadth-first order. We obtain an enumeration $V_1, \dots, V_t \in \Sigma$ of the vertices such that $pa(V_i) \subseteq \{V_1, \dots, V_{i-1}\}$. In this enumeration, V_1 is a root vertex, and so, $pa(V_1) = \varnothing$. By the normalisation constraint (7.1) there is a configuration $\dot{v}_1 \in \{v_1, \overline{v}_1\}$ of V such that $\kappa_{V_1}(\dot{v}_1) = 0$. For each following vertex V_i, the $\dot{v}_j$, $1 \leq j < i$ we define a unique configuration $\mathbf{p}_{V_i}$ of $pa(V_i)$ such that $\dot{v}_1 \cdots \dot{v}_{i-1} \vDash \mathbf{p}_{V_i}$ (with $\mathbf{p}_{V_i} = \top$ for root vertices V_i). For this configuration $\mathbf{p}_{V_i}$, we choose $\dot{v}_i$ such that $\kappa_{V_i}(\dot{v}_i|\mathbf{p}_{V_i}) = 0$ which is guaranteed to exist because of (7.1). We now calculate the global rank for the world $\dot{v}_1 \wedge \cdots \wedge \dot{v}_p$, which by (7.2) is $\kappa_\Gamma(\dot{v}_1 \cdots \dot{v}_p) = \sum_{i=1}^{t} \kappa_{V_i}(\dot{v}_i|\mathbf{p}_{V_i}) = \sum_{V \in \Sigma} \kappa_V\big(V(\dot{v}_1 \cdots \dot{v}_p)|pa(V)(\dot{v}_1 \cdots \dot{v}_p)\big) = 0$. This completes the proof. $\square$

Proof of Proposition 7.3 [EKI15b, Proposition 1]: Let $\mathcal{G} = \{\Sigma, \mathcal{E}\}$ be a DAG over a propositional alphabet $\Sigma = \{V_1, \dots, V_m\}$, enumerated in breadth-first ordering according to $\mathcal{G}$ such that $pa(V_i) \subseteq \{V_1, \dots, V_{i-1}\}$ for each $V_i \in \Sigma$. For this proof we us the trivial property that for all numbers i, j it is $i = i - j + j$, which gives us

$$\kappa_\Gamma(V_1, \dots, V_m) = \kappa_\Gamma(V_1, \dots, V_m) - \kappa_\Gamma(V_1, \dots, V_{m-1}) + \kappa_\Gamma(V_1, \dots, V_{m-1}).$$

We continue this until we reach, by which we finally obtain

$$\begin{aligned}
\kappa_\Gamma(V_1, \dots, V_m) = {}& \kappa_\Gamma(V_1, \dots, V_m) - \kappa_\Gamma(V_1, \dots, V_{m-1}) \\
& + \kappa_\Gamma(V_1, \dots, V_{m-1}) - \kappa_\Gamma(V_1, \dots, V_{m-2}) \\
& + \dots + \kappa_\Gamma(V_1, V_2) - \kappa_\Gamma(V_1) + \kappa_\Gamma(V_1).
\end{aligned}$$

With the definition of conditional ranks in (3.13) this can be rewritten to

$$\kappa_\Gamma(V_1, ..., V_m) = \kappa_\Gamma(V_m|V_1, ..., V_{m-1}) + \kappa_\Gamma(V_{m-1}|V_1, ..., V_{m-2})$$
$$+ ... + \kappa_\Gamma(V_2|V_1) + \kappa_\Gamma(V_1).$$

We presupposed the vertices to be ordered such that $pa(V_i) \subseteq \{V_1, ..., V_{i-1}\}$. This ordering also ensures that $desc(V) \cap \{V_1, ..., V_{i-1}\} = \varnothing$ and thus for each $V_i \in \Sigma$ we have $\{V_1, ..., V_{i-1}\} \subseteq pa(V_i) \cup nd(V_i)$, which gives us $\{V_1, ..., V_{i-1})\} \setminus pa(V_i) \subseteq nd(V_i)$.

Therefore Lemma 3.20 gives us $\kappa_\Gamma(V_i|V_i, ..., V_{i-1}) = \kappa_\Gamma(V_i|pa(V_i))$ and with $\kappa(V|pa(V)) = \kappa(V|\varnothing) = \kappa(V|\top) = \kappa(V)$ for root vertices (that is, vertices V with $pa(V) = \varnothing$) the above equation rewrites to

$$\kappa_\Gamma(V_1, ..., V_m) = \kappa_\Gamma(V_1) + \sum_{i=2}^{m} \kappa_\Gamma(V_i|pa(V_i)).$$

As last step we rewrite $\kappa_\Gamma(V_1) = \kappa_\Gamma(V_1|\top) = \kappa_\Gamma(V_1|\varnothing)$ to $\kappa_\Gamma(V_1|pa(V_1))$ and extend the sum to the whole set of variables to obtain

$$\kappa_\Gamma(V_1, ..., V_m) = \sum_{V \in \Sigma} \kappa_\Gamma(V|pa(V))$$

which completes the proof.   □

Proof of Theorem 7.4 [EKI15b, Theorem 1]: Let W be a variable in Σ with a fixed value $\dot{w}$ of W, let $\mathbf{p}_w$ be a fixed configuration of the variables in $pa(W)$. To show that Theorem 7.4 holds we first apply the definition of ranking functions and conditional ranking functions from Section 3.3 and obtain

$$\kappa(\dot{w}|\mathbf{p}_w) = \kappa(\dot{w}\mathbf{p}_w) - \kappa(\mathbf{p}_w)$$
$$= \min_{\omega \models \dot{w}\mathbf{p}_w} \{\kappa(\omega)\} - \min_{\omega \models \mathbf{p}_w} \{\kappa(\omega)\}.$$

where $\mathbf{p}_w$ is an arbitrary but fixed configuration of $pa(W)$, $W \in \Sigma$, and $\dot{w} \in \{w, \overline{w}\}$. With the stratification defined in Equation (7.2), this can be rewritten to

$$\kappa(\dot{w}|\mathbf{p}_w) = \underbrace{\min_{\omega \models \dot{w}\mathbf{p}_w} \left\{ \sum_{V \in \Sigma} \kappa_V \left(V(\omega)|pa(V)(\omega) \right) \right\}}_{(A.6.1.a)} \qquad (A.6.1)$$
$$- \min_{\omega \models \mathbf{p}_w} \left\{ \sum_{V \in \Sigma} \kappa_V \left(V(\omega)|pa(V)(\omega) \right) \right\}.$$

Because of the condition of the min-term in $(A.6.1.a)$, the value of $\kappa_W(\dot{w}|\mathbf{p}_w)$ appears in every respective sum, therefore the equation is equivalent to

$$\kappa(\dot{w}|\mathbf{p}_w) = \min_{\omega \models \dot{w}\mathbf{p}_w} \left\{ \sum_{V \in \Sigma \setminus \{W\}} \kappa_V\left(V(\omega)|pa(V)(\omega) + \kappa_W(\dot{w}|\mathbf{p}_w)\right) \right\}$$
$$- \min_{\omega \models \mathbf{p}_w} \left\{ \sum_{V \in \Sigma} \kappa_V\left(V(\omega)|pa(V)(\omega)\right) \right\}.$$

And since $\kappa_W(\dot{w}|\mathbf{p}_w)$ therefore is a summand of every minimum it can be extracted from the min-term, hence we obtain

$$\kappa(\dot{w}|\mathbf{p}_w) = \min_{\omega \models \dot{w}\mathbf{p}_w} \left\{ \sum_{V \in \Sigma \setminus \{W\}} \kappa_V\left(V(\omega)|pa(V)(\omega)\right) \right\}$$
$$- \min_{\omega \models \mathbf{p}_w} \left\{ \sum_{V \in \Sigma} \kappa_V\left(V(\omega)|pa(V)(\omega)\right) \right\} + \kappa_W(\dot{w}|\mathbf{p}_w).$$

We further inspect the first min-term and split $\Sigma \setminus \{W\}$ into the set of descendants of W and the joint set of parents and non-descendants of W, thus rewriting the formula to

$$\kappa(\dot{w}|\mathbf{p}_w) = \min_{\omega \models \dot{w}\mathbf{p}_w} \left\{ \begin{array}{l} \displaystyle\sum_{V \in pa(W) \cup nd(W)} \kappa_V\left(V(\omega)|pa(V)(\omega)\right) \\ + \displaystyle\sum_{V \in desc(W)} \kappa_V\left(V(\omega)|pa(V)(\omega)\right) \end{array} \right\}$$
$$- \min_{\omega \models \mathbf{p}_w} \left\{ \sum_{V \in \Sigma} \kappa_V\left(V(\omega)|pa(V)(\omega)\right) \right\} + \kappa_W(\dot{w}|\mathbf{p}_w).$$

The normalisation condition (7.1) gives us that that for every vertex C in the set of children of W there is a configuration $\dot{c}$ of C such that $\kappa_C(\dot{c}|\dot{w}\mathbf{p}_c^*) = 0$, with $\mathbf{p}_c^*$ being a configuration of $pa(C) \setminus \{W\}$; this holds iteratively for the children of C, so in the above formula, we have

$$\min_{\omega \models \dot{w}\mathbf{p}_w} \left\{ \sum_{V \in desc(W)} \kappa_V(V(\omega)|pa(V)(\omega)) \right\} = 0.$$

Since the configuration of each vertex apart from W and the parents of W is not fixed and the configuration of each variable is independent from the others, the actual *minimum* is obtained when a configuration as sketched above is chosen, hence the descendants of W can be ignored for the first min-term. So we have

$$\kappa(\dot{w}|\mathbf{p}_w) = \min_{\omega\models\dot{w}\mathbf{p}_w} \left\{ \sum_{V\in pa(W)\cup nd(W)} \kappa_V\left(V(\omega)|pa(V)(\omega)\right) \right\}$$
$$- \min_{\omega\models\mathbf{p}_w} \left\{ \sum_{V\in\Sigma} \kappa_V\left(V(\omega)|pa(V)(\omega)\right) \right\} + \kappa_W(\dot{w}|\mathbf{p}_w).$$

The value of vertices $V \in (nd(W) \cup pa(W))$ can be chosen independently of the value W, while $\mathbf{p}_w$ is fixed, hence the minimum of the sum over these values is constant for the term. Therefore it can be extracted and will be termed *Const* in the following, so the equation can be written as

$$\kappa(\dot{w}|\mathbf{p}_w) = \kappa_W(\dot{w}|\mathbf{p}_w) + Const - \min_{\omega\models\mathbf{p}_w} \left\{ \sum_{V\in\Sigma} \kappa_V\left(V(\omega)|pa(V)(\omega)\right) \right\}.$$
$$(A.6.2)$$

We now look at the second min-term. Here W is not fixed so the outcomes of the variables affected an be chosen without further constraints. We recall Lemma 3.10 and obtain that the minimum of this min-term is the minimal sum with W fixed either to w or to $\overline{w}$. So we can rewrite this min-term to

$$\min_{\omega\models\mathbf{p}_w} \left\{ \sum_{V\in\Sigma} \kappa_V\left(V(\omega)|pa(V)(\omega)\right) \right\} \qquad (A.6.3)$$

$$= \min \left\{ \begin{array}{c} \underbrace{\min_{\omega\models w\mathbf{p}_w} \left\{ \sum_{V\in\Sigma} \kappa_V\left(V(\omega)|pa(V)(\omega)\right) \right\}}_{(A.6.4.b)}, \\ \underbrace{\min_{\omega\models\overline{w}\mathbf{p}_w} \left\{ \sum_{V\in\Sigma} \kappa_V\left(V(\omega)|pa(V)(\omega)\right) \right\}}_{(A.6.4.c)} \end{array} \right\}. \qquad (A.6.4)$$

Comparing the terms $(A.6.4.b)$ and $(A.6.4.c)$ with $(A.6.1.a)$ from above we see that these are similar with the only limitation that in $(A.6.1.a)$, W is fixed to an undetermined value w or $\overline{w}$, whereas in $(A.6.4.b)$ the value W is fixed to w and in $(A.6.4.c)$ the value of W is fixed to $\overline{w}$. So we apply the same steps to $(A.6.4.b)$ and $(A.6.4.c)$ which we have applied to $(A.6.1.a)$ and obtain

$$(A.6.4.b) = \kappa_W(w|\mathbf{p}_w) + Const \qquad (A.6.4.c) = \kappa_W(\overline{w}|\mathbf{p}_w) + Const$$

and therefore

$$(A.6.3) = \min_{\omega \models \mathbf{p}_w} \left\{ \kappa_W(w|\mathbf{p}_w) + Const, \kappa_W(\overline{w}|\mathbf{p}_w) + Const \right\}.$$

Here, *Const* is a summand of every part of the minimum and can be extracted, which gives us

$$\min_{\omega \models \mathbf{p}_w} \left\{ \sum_{V \in \Sigma} \kappa_V \left(V(\omega)|pa(V)(\omega) \right) \right\}$$

$$= \underbrace{\min_{\omega \models \mathbf{p}_w} \left\{ \kappa_W(w|\mathbf{p}_w), \kappa_W(\overline{w}|\mathbf{p}_w) \right\}}_{(A.6.5.d)} + Const. \tag{A.6.5}$$

From the normalisation condition (7.1) we obtain $(A.6.5.d) = 0$, thus

$$\min_{\omega \models \mathbf{p}_w} \left\{ \sum_{V \in \Sigma} \kappa_V \left(V(\omega)|pa(V)(\omega) \right) \right\} = Const.$$

Together with (A.6.2) this gives ua

$$\kappa(\dot{w}|\mathbf{p}_w) = \kappa_W(\dot{w}|\mathbf{p}_w) + Const - Const,$$

that is, $\kappa(\dot{w}|\mathbf{p}_w) = \kappa_W(\dot{w}|\mathbf{p}_w)$, and thus the local and global ranking values coincide, which we wanted to show. □

Proof of Theorem 7.6 [KIE13b, Theorem 2]: Let $\Gamma = \langle \Sigma, \mathcal{E} \rangle$ be an OCF-network and let κ be an OCF stratified with respect to Γ according to (7.2). For each vertex $V \in \Sigma$, $\mathbf{n}_v$ is an arbitrary but fixed configuration of the variables $nd(V)$ and $\mathbf{p}_v$ is an arbitrary but fixed configuration of the variables $pa(V)$. Let further $W \in \Sigma$ be an arbitrary but fixed variable. We show that

$$\kappa(\mathbf{wn}_w|\mathbf{p}_w) = \kappa(\mathbf{w}|\mathbf{p}_w) + \kappa(\mathbf{n}_w|\mathbf{p}_w) \tag{A.6.6}$$

holds for every configuration of $\mathbf{w}$, $\mathbf{n}_w$ and $\mathbf{p}_w$ which establishes the local Markov property as claimed. Theorem 7.4 gives us $\kappa(\mathbf{w}|\mathbf{p}_w) = \kappa_W(\mathbf{w}|\mathbf{p}_w)$. We begin the proof by including this into (A.6.6), so we obtain

$$\kappa(\mathbf{wn}_w|\mathbf{p}_w) = \kappa(\mathbf{w}|\mathbf{p}_w) + \kappa(\mathbf{n}_w|\mathbf{p}_w) \tag{A.6.7}$$

$$\Leftrightarrow \qquad \kappa(\mathbf{wn}_w|\mathbf{p}_w) = \kappa_W(\mathbf{w}|\mathbf{p}_w) + \kappa(\mathbf{n}_w|\mathbf{p}_w) \tag{A.6.8}$$

$$\overset{(3.13)}{\Longleftrightarrow} \quad \kappa(\mathbf{wn}_w\mathbf{p}_w) - \kappa(\mathbf{p}_w) = \kappa_W(\mathbf{w}|\mathbf{p}_w) + \kappa(\mathbf{n}_w\mathbf{p}_w) - \kappa(\mathbf{p}_w) \tag{A.6.9}$$

$$\Leftrightarrow \qquad \kappa(\mathbf{wn}_w\mathbf{p}_w) = \kappa_W(\mathbf{w}|\mathbf{p}_w) + \kappa(\mathbf{n}_w\mathbf{p}_w). \tag{A.6.10}$$

We continue with the left-hand side of this equation.

$$\kappa(\mathbf{wn}_w\mathbf{p}_w) = \min_{\omega \vDash \mathbf{wn}_w\mathbf{p}_w} \left\{ \sum_V \kappa_V(V(\omega)|pa(V)(\omega)) \right\}$$

$$= \min_{\omega \vDash \mathbf{wn}_w\mathbf{p}_w} \left\{ \begin{array}{l} \kappa_W(\mathbf{w}|\mathbf{p}_w) + \\ \displaystyle\sum_{V \in nd(W) \cup pa(W)} \kappa_V(V(\omega)|pa(V)(\omega)) + \\ \displaystyle\sum_{V \in desc(W)} \kappa_V(V(\omega)|pa(V)(\omega)). \end{array} \right\}$$

The first sum here is fixed by the chosen configuration $\mathbf{n}_w, \mathbf{p}_w$, the minimum over the second sum is 0, as discussed in the proof of Theorem 7.4:

$$\sum_{V \in nd(W) \cup pa(W)} \kappa_V(V(\omega)|pa(V)(\omega)) \quad =: \quad Const(\mathbf{n}_w, \mathbf{p}_w),$$

$$\min_{\omega \vDash \mathbf{wn}_w\mathbf{p}_w} \left\{ \sum_{V \in desc(W)} \kappa_V(V(\omega)|pa(V)(\omega)) \right\} \quad = \quad 0,$$

and therefore $\kappa(\mathbf{wn}_w\mathbf{p}_w) = \kappa_W(\mathbf{w}|\mathbf{p}_w) + Const(\mathbf{n}_w, \mathbf{p}_w)$. For the right-hand side of the equation, we similarly obtain

$$\kappa(\mathbf{n}_w\mathbf{p}_w) = \min_{\omega \vDash \mathbf{n}_w\mathbf{p}_w} \left\{ \sum_V \kappa_V(V(\omega)|pa(V)(\omega)) \right\}$$

$$= \min_{\omega \vDash \mathbf{n}_w\mathbf{p}_w} \left\{ \begin{array}{l} \kappa_W(W(\omega)|\mathbf{p}_w) + \\ \displaystyle\sum_{V \in nd(W) \cup pa(W)} \kappa_V(V(\omega)|pa(V)(\omega)) + \\ \displaystyle\sum_{V \in desc(W)} \kappa_V(V(\omega)|pa(V)(\omega)). \end{array} \right\}$$

$$= Const(\mathbf{n}_w, \mathbf{p}_w) + \min_{\omega \vDash \mathbf{n}_w\mathbf{p}_w} \left\{ \begin{array}{l} \kappa_W(W(\omega)|\mathbf{p}_w) + \\ \displaystyle\sum_{V \in desc(W)} \kappa_V(V(\omega)|pa(V)(\omega)) \end{array} \right\}$$

$$= Const(\mathbf{n}_w, \mathbf{p}_w) + \min_{\omega \vDash \mathbf{n}_w\mathbf{p}_w} \left\{ \kappa_W(W(\omega)|\mathbf{p}_w) \right\} = Const(\mathbf{n}_w, \mathbf{p}_w),$$

since $\min_{\omega \vDash \mathbf{n}_w\mathbf{p}_w} \left\{ \sum_{V \in desc(W)} \kappa_V(V(\omega)|pa(V)(\omega)) \right\} = 0$, independently of W being chosen to be w or $\overline{w}$, and one of $\kappa_W(w|\mathbf{p}_w), \kappa_W(\overline{w}|\mathbf{p}_w)$ again has to be 0.

So we obtain

$$\kappa(\mathbf{wn}_w\mathbf{p}_w) = \kappa_W(\mathbf{w}|\mathbf{p}_w) + Const(\mathbf{n}_w, \mathbf{p}_w)$$
$$= \kappa_W(\mathbf{w}|\mathbf{p}_w) + \kappa(\mathbf{n}_w\mathbf{p}_w),$$

and this completes the proof. □

Proof of Lemma 7.11: Let $\mathcal{R}$ be a consistent single elementary knowledge base with the property that $\Delta_{\mathcal{R}}$, the qualitative part of $\mathcal{R}$, satisfies the LS-constraint, that is, for every pair $(\psi|\phi), (\xi|\chi) \in \Delta$ we have $cons(\psi|\phi) = cons(\psi|\chi)$ implies $ant(\psi|\phi) = ant(\psi|\chi)$. We show that this implies that $\mathcal{R}$ is complete with respect to the graph generated by Algorithm 7.1. If $\Delta_{\mathcal{R}}$ satisfies the LS-constraint then all conditionals $(\psi|\phi)$ with $\{W\} = cons(\psi|\phi)$, that is, all conditionals $(\dot{w}|\phi)$ share the same set $ant(\dot{w}|\phi)$ and by then by the graph construction with Algorithm 7.1 we hence have $pa(W) = ant(\dot{w}|\phi)$. Then we can construct the local ranking tables directly from the knowledge base such that $\kappa_V(\bar{\dot{v}}|\phi) = f$ if and only if $(\dot{v}|\phi)[f] \in \mathcal{R}$ and $\kappa_V(\bar{\dot{v}}|\phi) = 0$ otherwise. By construction and the definition of completeness with respect to an OCF-network Γ we obtain directly that Δ is Γ-complete. For the "only if" part we recall the definition of complete conditional knowledge bases in Section 7.1.1 and obtain directly that if Γ is an OCF-network we can construct a complete knowledge base form the network that contains the conditional ranking tables in form of conditionals and allows us to reconstruct the graph-component using by Algorithm 7.1. □

Proof of Lemma 7.17: To show that the λ-function is an OCF, we have to prove that the normalisation condition holds for λ_V for all $V \in \Sigma$, that is, for every $V \in \Sigma$ there is at least one local world $\omega^V \in \Omega(\{V\} \cup pa(V))$ with the property that $\lambda_V(\omega^V) = 0$. By the normalisation condition, for each $V \in \Sigma$ and each configuration $\mathbf{p}_V$ of $pa(V)$ we have $\min\{\kappa_V(v|\mathbf{p}_V), \kappa_V(\bar{v}|\mathbf{p}_V)\} = 0$. Each world $\omega^V \in \Omega(\{V\} \cup pa(V))$ is a conjunction of an outcome of V and a configuration $\mathbf{p}_V$ of $pa(V)$, therefore $\Omega(\{V\} \cup pa(V))$ contains all pairs $(v\mathbf{p}_V, \bar{v}\mathbf{p}_V)$. By the normalisation condition, from these pairs at least one has a local conditional rank of 0. Henceforth the preimage $\lambda_V^{-1}(0)$ cannot be empty and therefore for every $V \in \Sigma$, λ_V is an OCF, as proposed. □

Proof of Proposition 7.18: To prove this proposition we have to show that from $\lambda_V \models \mathcal{R}_V$ for each $V \in \Sigma$ it follows that $\kappa_\Gamma(\phi\bar{\psi}) \geq f$ for all $(\psi|\phi)[f] \in \mathcal{R}$. By definition, $\lambda_V(\omega) = \kappa_V(V(\omega)|pa(V)(\omega))$, so with local/global coincidence (Theorem 7.4) we can rewrite formula (7.2) to

$$\kappa_\Gamma(\omega) = \sum_{V \in \Sigma} \kappa_V(V(\omega)|pa(V)(\omega)) = \sum_{V \in \Sigma} \lambda_V(\omega).$$

We want to show that $\kappa_\Gamma \vDash \mathcal{R}$. Since the presented algorithm partitions $\mathcal{R}$ into $\mathcal{R}_V$, we here can concentrate on the local knowledge bases $\mathcal{R}_V$. We show that $\kappa_\Gamma \vDash \mathcal{R}_V$ for all $V \in \Sigma$ which then implies $\kappa_\Gamma \vDash \mathcal{R}$, directly. For each $V \in \Sigma$ and each $(\psi|\phi)[f] \in \mathcal{R}_V$ we have

$$\kappa_\Gamma(\phi\overline{\psi}) = \min_{\omega \vDash \phi\overline{\psi}} \left\{ \sum_{V \in \Sigma} \lambda_V(\omega) \right\}.$$

Here we differentiate exhaustingly between the cases $ant(\psi|\phi) = pa(V)$ and $ant(\psi|\phi) \subsetneq pa(V)$ (note that $ant(\psi|\phi) \not\subseteq pa(V)$ is excluded by construction):

Case $ant(\psi|\phi) = pa(V)$: If we have $ant(\psi|\phi) = pa(V)$ then every variable in $\lambda_V(\overline{\psi}\phi)$ is fixed and hence $\lambda_V(\overline{\psi}\phi)$ is a constant in the minimum and thus can be extracted. This gives us

$$\kappa_\Gamma(\phi\overline{\psi}) = \min_{\omega \vDash \phi\overline{\psi}} \left\{ \sum_{V \in \Sigma \setminus \{V\}} \lambda_V(\omega) \right\} + \lambda_V(\phi\overline{\psi}).$$

We split the sum into the ancestors, descendants and non-descendants of V.

$$\kappa_\Gamma(\phi\overline{\psi}) = \min_{\omega \vDash \phi\overline{\psi}} \left\{ \sum_{V \in anc(V)} \lambda_V(\omega) + \sum_{V \in desc(V)} \lambda_V(\omega) + \sum_{V \in nd(V)} \lambda_V(\omega) \right\}$$
$$+ \lambda_V(\phi\overline{\psi}).$$

The proof of Theorem 7.4 gives us that for an arbitrary but fixed configuration of a vertex V, which here is encoded as the formula ψ, the normalisation condition (7.1) enforces the sum of the ranks of the descendants to be 0 in the minimum. The rank of the non-descendants can be minimised without considering the configuration of V and $pa(V)$, hence regardless of the actual values for ϕ and ψ, the minimum sum over the non-descendants is 0 again due to the normalisation condition (7.1). This leaves the sum of the ancestors as only summand that is not necessarily 0 in the minimum. Hence we have

$$\kappa_\Gamma(\phi\overline{\psi}) = \min_{\omega \vDash \phi\overline{\psi}} \left\{ \sum_{V \in anc(V)} \lambda_V(\omega) \right\} + \lambda_V(\phi\overline{\psi}).$$

In this minimum the constraint of $\overline{\psi}$ can be omitted since $\overline{\psi}$ is an outcome of V and this variable do not appear in $anc(V)$.

$$\kappa_\Gamma(\phi\overline{\psi}) = \min_{\omega \models \phi} \left\{ \sum_{V \in anc(V)} \lambda_V(\omega) \right\} + \lambda_V(\phi\overline{\psi}). \tag{A.6.11}$$

To show that $\kappa_\Gamma \models (\psi|\phi)[f]$ we still have to show that $\kappa_\Gamma(\phi\overline{\psi}) \geq f + \kappa_\Gamma(\phi)$, so we concentrate on $\kappa_\Gamma(\phi)$, next, which is

$$\kappa_\Gamma(\phi) = \min_{\omega \models \phi} \left\{ \sum_{V \in \Sigma} \lambda_V(\omega) \right\}$$

according to Formula (7.2). We again split the minimum into V, $anc(V)$, $desc(V)$ and $nd(V)$:

$$\kappa_\Gamma(\phi) = \min_{\omega \models \phi} \left\{ \begin{array}{c} \displaystyle\sum_{V \in anc(V)} \lambda_V(\omega) + \sum_{V \in desc(V)} \lambda_V(\omega) \\ + \displaystyle\sum_{V \in nd(V)} \lambda_V(\omega) + \lambda_V(\phi) \end{array} \right\}.$$

With the same argumentation as above, regardless of the actual value of ϕ the minimum of the sum over $nd(V)$ and $desc(V)$ is 0 by the the normalisation condition (7.1), the same holds for λ_V because now ψ can be chosen freely, too, which simplifies this formula to

$$\kappa_\Gamma(\phi) = \min_{\omega \models \phi} \left\{ \sum_{V \in anc(V)} \lambda_V(\omega) \right\}. \tag{A.6.12}$$

So overall we still have to show that $\kappa_\Gamma(\phi\overline{\psi}) > f + \kappa_\Gamma(\phi)$. Substituting (A.6.11) and (A.6.12) into this inequality can be rewritten to

$$\min_{\omega \models \phi} \left\{ \sum_{V \in anc(V)} \lambda_V(\omega) \right\} + \lambda_V(\phi\overline{\psi}) \geq f + \min_{\omega \models \phi} \left\{ \sum_{V \in anc(V)} \lambda_V(\omega) \right\}$$

iff

$$\lambda_V(\phi\overline{\psi}) \geq f \tag{A.6.13}$$

By the preliminaries we have $\lambda_V \models \mathcal{R}_V$ and therefore $\lambda_V(\phi\overline{\psi}) \geq f + \lambda_V(\phi)$. In this case ϕ is a configuration of $pa(V)$. By the normalisation condition and the definition of ranks for formulas we obtain $\lambda_V(\phi) = \min\{\lambda_V(\psi\phi), \lambda_V(\overline{\psi}\phi)\} = 0$ which gives us $\lambda_V(\phi\overline{\psi}) \geq f$, so the inequality holds and we have $\kappa_\Gamma \models (\psi|\phi)$, as proposed.

Case $ant(\psi|\phi) \subsetneq pa(V)$: We define by $\mathbf{o}$ a configuration of $pa(V)\backslash ant(\psi|\phi)$ and by $\mathbf{O}$ the set of all such configurations. The definition of ranks of formulas gives us

$$\kappa_\Gamma(\phi\overline{\psi}) = \min_{\mathbf{o}\in\mathbf{O}}\{\kappa_\Gamma(\mathbf{o}\phi\overline{\psi})\} = \min_{\mathbf{o}\in\mathbf{O}}\Big\{\min_{\omega\models\mathbf{o}\phi\overline{\psi}}\Big\{\sum_{V\in\Sigma}\lambda_V(\omega)\Big\}\Big\}.$$

Again, for the second min-term, every variable in $\lambda_V(\psi\phi)$ is fixed and hence $\lambda_V(\psi\phi)$ is a constant for this term and can be extracted, which gives us

$$\kappa_\Gamma(\phi\overline{\psi}) = \min_{\mathbf{o}\in\mathbf{O}}\Big\{\min_{\omega\models\mathbf{o}\phi\overline{\psi}}\Big\{\sum_{V\in\Sigma\backslash\{V\}}\lambda_V(\omega)\Big\} + \lambda_V(\mathbf{o}\phi\overline{\psi})\Big\}.$$

For the rank of the premise we likewise obtain

$$\kappa_\Gamma(\phi) = \min_{\mathbf{o}\in\mathbf{O}}\Big\{\min_{\omega\models\mathbf{o}\phi}\Big\{\sum_{V\in\Sigma}\lambda_V(\omega)\Big\}\Big\}.$$

With identical deliberations as above we transform these formulas to

$$\kappa_\Gamma(\phi\overline{\psi}) = \min_{\mathbf{o}\in\mathbf{O}}\Big\{\min_{\omega\models\mathbf{o}\phi}\Big\{\sum_{V\in pa(V)\}}\lambda_V(\omega)\Big\} + \lambda_V(\mathbf{o}\phi\overline{\psi})\Big\}.$$

$$\kappa_\Gamma(\phi) = \min_{\mathbf{o}\in\mathbf{O}}\Big\{\min_{\omega\models\mathbf{o}\phi}\Big\{\sum_{V\in pa(V)}\lambda_V(\omega)\Big\}\Big\}.$$

We combine both formulas with the condition $\kappa_\Gamma(\phi\overline{\psi}) - \kappa_\Gamma(\phi) \geq f$ to obtain

$$\min_{\mathbf{o}\in\mathbf{O}}\Big\{\min_{\omega\models\mathbf{o}\phi}\Big\{\sum_{V\in pa(V)\}}\lambda_V(\omega)\Big\} + \lambda_V(\mathbf{o}\phi\overline{\psi})\Big\}$$

$$- \min_{\mathbf{o}\in\mathbf{O}}\Big\{\min_{\omega\models\mathbf{o}\phi}\Big\{\sum_{V\in pa(V)}\lambda_V(\omega)\Big\}\Big\} \geq f$$

Both outer minima range over the same variables, so we combine them to getting

$$\min_{\mathbf{o}\in\mathbf{O}}\Big\{\min_{\omega\models\mathbf{o}\phi}\Big\{\sum_{V\in pa(V)\}}\lambda_V(\omega)\Big\} + \lambda_V(\mathbf{o}\phi\overline{\psi}) - \min_{\omega\models\mathbf{o}\phi}\Big\{\sum_{V\in pa(V)}\lambda_V(\omega)\Big\}\Big\} \geq f$$

$$\text{if and only if} \qquad \min_{\mathbf{o}\in\mathbf{O}}\Big\{\lambda_V(\mathbf{o}\phi\overline{\psi})\Big\} \geq f$$

$$(A.6.14)$$

By the preliminary $\lambda_V \vDash \mathcal{R}_V$ we have $\lambda_V(\phi\overline{\psi}) \geq f$ thus $\min\{\lambda_V(\omega) \mid \omega \vDash \phi\overline{\psi}\} \geq 0$ and therefore for all $\mathbf{o} \in \mathbf{O}$ we have $\lambda_V(\mathbf{o}\phi\overline{\psi}) > f$, so this inequality holds and we have $\kappa_\Gamma \vDash (\psi|\phi)$, as proposed. So for both cases we have $\kappa_\Gamma \vDash (\psi|\phi)[f]$ for all $V \in \Sigma$ and all $(\psi|\phi)[f] \in \mathcal{R}_V$, which completes the proof. $\qquad\qquad\square$

Proof of Proposition 7.19: We show this by reductio ad absurdum, so assume we have $\kappa_\Gamma \vDash (\psi|\phi)[f]$ for all $(\psi|\phi)[f] \in \mathcal{R}_V$ for all $V \in \Sigma$ but there was a conditional $(\psi|\phi)[f]$ of a knowledge base $\mathcal{R}_V$ for any $V \in \Sigma$ such that $\lambda_V \nvDash (\psi|\phi)[f]$. We have $\lambda_V \nvDash (\psi|\phi)[f]$ if and only if $\lambda_V(\phi\overline{\psi}) - \lambda_V(\phi) < f$. By the normalisation condition (7.1) and the argumentation in the proof of Proposition 7.18 we have $\lambda_V(\phi) = 0$, hence $\lambda_V \nvDash (\psi|\phi)[f]$ gave us $\lambda_V(\phi\overline{\psi}) < f$. In the proof of Proposition 7.18 only equivalent transformations were used, since $\lambda_V(\phi\overline{\psi}) < f$ dissatisfies Formula (A.6.13) respectively Formula (A.6.14) we therefore obtain $\kappa_\Gamma \nvDash (\psi|\phi)[f]$ in contradiction to the assumption. Therefore it is impossible to have $\kappa_\Gamma \vDash (\psi|\phi)[f]$ for all $(\psi|\phi)[f]$ in all $\mathcal{R}_V$ for all $V \in \Sigma$ such that for any V and any $(\psi|\phi) \in \mathcal{R}_V$ we have $\lambda_V \nvDash (\psi|\phi)[f]$. $\qquad\qquad\square$

Proof of Lemma 7.26 [EFKI16, Lemma 2]: We show this by reductio ad absurdum and assume there would be a $V \in \Sigma$ with $\mathbf{p} \in \Omega_{pa(V)}$ such that $\dot{v} \preccurlyeq_{\mathbf{p}_V}^\kappa \overline{v}$ and $\overline{v} \preccurlyeq_{\mathbf{p}_V}^\kappa \dot{v}$. By Definition of $\leq_\kappa$ in Section 3.3.2 this would imply $\kappa_V(\dot{v}|\mathbf{p}_V) \leq \kappa_V(\overline{v}|\mathbf{p}_V)$ and $\kappa_V(\overline{v}|\mathbf{p}_V) \leq \kappa_V(\dot{v}|\mathbf{p}_V)$ which is equivalent to $\kappa_V(\dot{v}|\mathbf{p}_V) = \kappa_V(\overline{v}|\mathbf{p}_V)$. By the normalisation condition this implies $\kappa_V(\dot{v}|\mathbf{p}_V) = \kappa_V(\overline{v}|\mathbf{p}_V) = 0$, but this contradicts Definition 7.24 of strict OCF-networks. Therefore the local κ-preference $\preccurlyeq_{\mathbf{p}_V}^\kappa$ in strict OCF-networks is strict for all $V \in \Sigma$ as well. $\qquad\qquad\square$

Proof of Lemma 7.28 [EFKI16, Proposition 1]: The lemma follows directly from the definition of CP-networks (see Definition 3.52): If Γ is an OCF-network then $(\Sigma, \mathcal{E})$ is a DAG, hence the underlying graph structure matches the definition of the one used for CP-networks. The preferences given in the κ-preference tables match the definition of CPTs since for every V and every configuration $\mathbf{p}_V$ of $pa(V)$ they encode a strict preference relation $\dot{v} \prec_{\mathbf{p}_V}^\kappa \overline{v}$. Therefore $\Pi = \langle\Sigma, \mathcal{E}, \{CPT^\kappa(V, pa(V))\}_{V \in \Sigma}\rangle$ is a CP-network as proposed. $\qquad\qquad\square$

Proof of Lemma 7.31 [EFKI16, Proposition 2]: We show that a network $\Gamma = \langle\Sigma, \mathcal{E}, \{\kappa_V\}_{V \in \Sigma}\rangle$ generated as result of Lemma 7.31 is a strict OCF-network. By definition of CP-networks, $(\Sigma, \mathcal{E})$ is a DAG, which is necessary for an OCF-network, so the structure of the graph is of the correct type. The possible local ranking values are $\{0,1\} \subseteq \mathbb{N}_0$ obtained by means of this lemma, hence the tables $\{\kappa_V\}_{V \in \Sigma}$ have a valid range of for OCF. For each $V \in \Sigma$ and each interpretation $\mathbf{p}_V$ of $pa(V)$ in a CP-network we either have $\overline{v} \prec_{\mathbf{p}_V} \dot{v}$ or $\dot{v} \prec_{\mathbf{p}_V} \overline{v}$, therefore this lemma either sets $\kappa_V(\dot{v}|\mathbf{p}_V) = 0$ or $\kappa_V(\overline{v}|\mathbf{p}_V) = 0$ and the local ranking tables are normalised. Therefore, $\Gamma = \langle \Sigma, \mathcal{E}, \{\kappa_V\}_{V \in \Sigma} \rangle$ is an OCF-network. Because of the strictness in the relations encoded in the CPTs, for each V we have *either* $\kappa_V(\dot{v}|\mathbf{p}_V) = 0$ or $\kappa_V(\overline{v}|\mathbf{p}_V) = 0$, the OCF-network is strict.   □

Proof of Lemma 7.34: By applying Algorithm 7.6 and then Algorithm 7.5 to a CP-network, neither the set of vertices nor the set of edges is changed, hence the resulting network has only to be checked with respect to whether the conditional preference tables are identical. Both approaches are local approaches, only, and therefore it suffices to inspect whether each CPT is identical to the original one. Here, by Algorithm 7.6 for each variable V we obtain a local ranking table where $\kappa(\dot{v}|\mathbf{p}) < \kappa(\overline{v}|\mathbf{p})$ if and only if $\dot{v} \prec_{\mathbf{p}} \overline{v}$ for each configuration $\mathbf{p}$ of $pa(V)$. In the next transformation step, Algorithm 7.5 constructs CPTs such that for each variable V and each configuration $\mathbf{p}$ of $pa(V)$ we obtain $\dot{v} \prec'_{\mathbf{p}} \overline{v}$ if and only if $\kappa(\dot{v}|\mathbf{p}) < \kappa(\overline{v}|\mathbf{p})$. So overall we have

$$\dot{v} \prec_{\mathbf{p}} \overline{v} \qquad \text{iff} \qquad \kappa(\dot{v}|\mathbf{p}) < \kappa(\overline{v}|\mathbf{p}) \qquad \text{iff} \qquad \dot{v} \prec'_{\mathbf{p}} \overline{v}$$

and therefore for each variable V and each configuration $\mathbf{p}$ of $pa(V)$ it is $\dot{v} \prec'_{\mathbf{p}} \overline{v}$ if and only if $\dot{v} \prec_{\mathbf{p}} \overline{v}$, which completes the proof.   □

Proof of Lemma 7.35: As already discussed in the proof of Lemma 7.34, the network components of all three networks in question are identical, so in this proof we only inspect the ranking tables of the OCF-networks before and after the transferral. By application of Algorithm 7.5, for each local ranking function κ_V, we obtain the conditional preference table $CPT^\kappa(V, pa(V))$ according to Definition 7.27. Here $\dot{v} \prec^\kappa_{\mathbf{p}_V} \overline{v}$ if and only if $\kappa(\dot{v}|\mathbf{p}_V) < \kappa(\overline{v}|\mathbf{p}_V)$. The application of Algorithm 7.6 then generates local ranking tables $\widehat{\kappa}_V$ such that $\widehat{\kappa}_V(\dot{v}|\mathbf{p}_V) = 0$ and $\widehat{\kappa}_V(\overline{v}|\mathbf{p}_V) = 1$. Hence $\kappa_V(\dot{v}|\mathbf{p}_V) = \widehat{\kappa}_V(\dot{v}|\mathbf{p}_V) = 0$ holds regardless of the other ranking values in the table and $\kappa_V(\overline{v}|\mathbf{p}_V) = \widehat{\kappa}_V(\overline{v}|\mathbf{p}_V)$ if and only if $\kappa_V(\overline{v}|\mathbf{p}_V) = 1$, as proposed.   □

Proof of Lemma 7.42: It is $\phi \vdash_{CP} \psi$ if and only if for each world $\omega' \models \phi\overline{\psi}$ there is a world $\omega \models \phi\psi$ with the property that $\omega \prec_{cp} \omega'$ (Definition 3.55).

If κ is *CP*-compatible, then $\omega \prec_{cp} \omega'$ implies $\omega <_\kappa \omega'$ for all pairs $\omega, \omega' \in \Omega$, and therefore especially for pairs $\omega' \vDash \phi\overline{\psi}$ and $\omega \vDash \phi\psi$.   □

Proof of Theorem 7.43 [EFKI16, Theorem 1]: Let $\Gamma = \langle \Sigma, \mathcal{E}, \{\kappa_V\}_{V \in \Sigma} \rangle$ be an OCF-network with a global OCF κ and local preferences $\prec^\kappa_\mathbf{p}$ for every $V \in \Sigma$ and every $\mathbf{p} \in \Omega_{pa(V)}$ which we capture in the preference tables $CPT^\kappa(V, pa(V))$ (confer Section 3.3.2 / Definition 7.27). Let $\Pi = \langle \Sigma, \mathcal{E}, \{CPT^\kappa(V, pa(V))\}_{V \in \Sigma} \rangle$ be the CP-network generated of Γ by means of Lemma 7.28. Then we have $\kappa_V(\dot{v}|\mathbf{p}) < \kappa_V(\overline{v}|\mathbf{p})$ if and only if $\dot{v} \prec^\kappa_\mathbf{p} \overline{v}$ if and only if $\dot{v} \prec_\Pi \overline{v}$. We follow the proof of [EFKI16, Theorem 1] and prove this theorem in two steps, which are illustrated in Figure 7.43: The first step is to show that (7.7) enforces the OCF to have a ranking where the local κ-preference of a variable in the context of its parents models ceteris paribus preference in the network. In the second step we show that this is indeed the global preference of the original *CP*-network.

As a first step of the proof we show that for every $V \in \Sigma$, every fixed $\mathbf{p} \in \Omega_{pa(V)}$ and every outcome $\mathbf{r}$ of the variables of $\Sigma \setminus (\{V\} \cup pa(V))$ the local preference $\kappa_V(\dot{v}|\mathbf{p}) < \kappa_V(\overline{v}|\mathbf{p})$ implies $\kappa(\dot{v}\mathbf{pr}) < \kappa(\overline{v}\mathbf{pr})$ given formula (7.7) holds.

So let $\kappa_V(\dot{v}|\mathbf{p}) < \kappa_V(\overline{v}|\mathbf{p})$ and let (7.7) hold, we show that this implies $\kappa(\dot{v}\mathbf{pr}) < \kappa(\overline{v}\mathbf{pr})$. We separate the outcome $\mathbf{c}$ of $ch(V)$ from $\mathbf{r}$ such that $\mathbf{r} = \mathbf{co}$ and inspect the left-hand side of the inequality under consideration, that is $\kappa(\dot{v}\mathbf{pco})$, first. Here, (7.2) gives us

$$\kappa(\dot{v}\mathbf{pco}) = \sum_{W \in \Sigma} \kappa_W(W(\dot{v}\mathbf{pco})|pa(W)(\dot{v}\mathbf{pco}))$$

We further split up the remaining sum into the sum over the children of V, the rest of the variables, and κ_V, which gives us

$$\kappa(\dot{v}\mathbf{pco}) = \kappa_V(V(\dot{v}\mathbf{pco})|pa(V)(\dot{v}\mathbf{pco}))$$
$$+ \sum_{W \in ch(V)} \kappa_W(W(\dot{v}\mathbf{pco})|pa(W)(\dot{v}\mathbf{pco}))$$
$$+ \sum_{W \in \Sigma \setminus (\{V\} \cup ch(V))} \kappa_W(W(\dot{v}\mathbf{pco})|pa(W)(\dot{v}\mathbf{pco})).$$

For variables in $\Sigma \setminus (\{V\} \cup ch(V))$, V does not appear in the local ranking tables, therefore we have

$$\kappa(\dot{v}\mathbf{pco}) = \kappa_V(V(\dot{v}\mathbf{pco})|pa(V)(\dot{v}\mathbf{pco}))$$

$$+ \sum_{W \in ch(V)} \kappa_W(W(\dot{v}\mathbf{pco})|pa(W)(\dot{v}\mathbf{pco}))$$

$$+ \underbrace{\sum_{W \in \Sigma \setminus (\{V\} \cup ch(V))} \kappa_W(W(\mathbf{pco})|pa(W)(\mathbf{pco}))}_{(A.6.15.a)}. \qquad (A.6.15)$$

We presupposed **pco** to be fixed and V does not appear in $(A.6.15.a)$, thus $(A.6.15.a)$ is a constant summand for $\kappa(\dot{v}\mathbf{pco})$. $\kappa_V(V(\dot{v}\mathbf{pco})|pa(V)(\dot{v}\mathbf{pco}))$ is evaluated to $\kappa_V(\dot{v}|\mathbf{p})$. So overall we obtain

$$\kappa(\dot{v}\mathbf{pco}) = \kappa_V(\dot{v}|\mathbf{p}) + \underbrace{\sum_{W \in ch(V)} \kappa_W(W(\dot{v}\mathbf{pco})|pa(W)(\dot{v}\mathbf{pco}))}_{(A.6.15.b)} + (A.6.15.a)$$

The same argumentation applies to the right hand side of the inequality under consideration, so for this we obtain

$$\kappa(\overline{\dot{v}}\mathbf{pco}) = \kappa_V(\overline{\dot{v}}|\mathbf{p}) + \underbrace{\sum_{W \in ch(V)} \kappa_W(W(\overline{\dot{v}}\mathbf{pco})|pa(W)(\overline{\dot{v}}\mathbf{pco}))}_{(A.6.15.c)} + (A.6.15.a)$$

We prosupposed $\kappa_V(\dot{v}|\mathbf{p}) < \kappa_V(\overline{\dot{v}}|\mathbf{p})$, this implies $\kappa_V(\dot{v}|\mathbf{p}) = 0$ with the normalisation condition of ranking functions, so the inequality $\kappa(\dot{v}\mathbf{pco}) < \kappa(\overline{\dot{v}}\mathbf{pco})$ is equivalent to

$$(A.6.15.a) + (A.6.15.b) < \kappa_V(\overline{\dot{v}}|\mathbf{p}) + (A.6.15.a) + (A.6.15.c)$$

and therefore we only have to prove $(A.6.15.b) < \kappa_V(\overline{\dot{v}}|\mathbf{p}) + (A.6.15.c)$. Together with (7.7), $\kappa_V(\dot{v}|\mathbf{p}) < \kappa_V(\overline{\dot{v}}|\mathbf{p})$ gives us

$$\kappa_V(\overline{\dot{v}}|\mathbf{p}) > \sum_{C \in ch(V)} \max_{\substack{\dot{c} \in \{c,\overline{c}\}, \\ \mathbf{p}_C \in \Omega_{pa(C)}}} \{\kappa_C(\dot{c}|\mathbf{p}_C)\}$$

which implies $\kappa_V(\overline{\dot{v}}|\mathbf{p}) > (A.6.15.b)$. By definition of OCF $(A.6.15.c)$ cannot be negative and therefore from $\kappa_V(\dot{v}|\mathbf{p}) < \kappa_V(\overline{\dot{v}}|\mathbf{p})$ we have $\kappa(\dot{v}\mathbf{pco}) < \kappa(\overline{\dot{v}}\mathbf{pco})$ under (7.7).

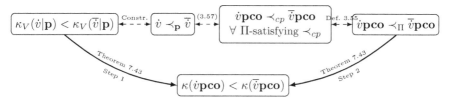

Figure A.1: Structure of the proof for Theorem 7.43 [EFKI16, Figure 5].

With this we now proceed to the next step: Since $\prec_\Pi$ is determined by comparing worlds ω, ω' of the form $\omega = \dot{v}\mathbf{pco}$ and $\omega' = \bar{v}\mathbf{pco}$, it suffices to prove the compatibility of κ to Π for such worlds. So let $\omega = \dot{v}\mathbf{pco} \prec_\Pi \bar{v}\mathbf{pco} = \omega'$. Then for all Π-satisfying relations $\prec_{cp}$, we have $\dot{v}\mathbf{pco} \prec_{cp} \bar{v}\mathbf{pco}$ which holds if and only if $\dot{v} \prec_\mathbf{p} \bar{v}$. By construction of Π, this means $\kappa_V(\dot{v}|\mathbf{p}) < \kappa_V(\bar{v}|\mathbf{p})$. From the first step of this proof, this implies $\kappa(\dot{v}\mathbf{pco}) < \kappa(\bar{v}\mathbf{pco})$, i.e., $\kappa(\omega) < \kappa(\omega')$, and so $\omega <_\kappa \omega'$. Figure A.1 illustrates this step of the proof. □

Proof of Proposition 7.45 [EFKI16]: Let $V \in \Sigma$ be a vertex with $\mathbf{p} \in \Omega_{pa(V)}$, $\mathbf{d} \in \Omega_{desc(V)}$ and $\mathbf{n} \in \Omega_{nd(V)}$ For Π we have $\dot{v} \prec_\mathbf{p} \bar{v}$ if and only if $\dot{v}\mathbf{pdn} \prec_\Pi \bar{v}\mathbf{pdn}$ by Definition 3.55. We also have that $\dot{v} \prec_\mathbf{p} \bar{v}$ is equivalent to $\kappa(\dot{v}|\mathbf{p}) < \kappa(\bar{v}|\mathbf{p})$ by construction. By the Markov Property (7.5) from the latter we obtain $\{V\} \perp\!\!\!\perp_\kappa nd(V) \mid pa(V)$, which which gives us $\kappa(\dot{v}|\mathbf{p}) = \kappa(\dot{v}|\mathbf{pn})$ by conditional κ-independence (Definition 3.18) for every $\mathbf{n}$. Therefore we have $\kappa(\dot{v}|\mathbf{pn}) < \kappa(\bar{v}|\mathbf{pn'})$ for any additional $\mathbf{n'} \in \Omega_{nd(V)}$. Since here a preference is preserved even if variables are configured differently, this does not hold for $\prec_\Pi$ in general. On the other hand, CP-independence gives us $\dot{v}\mathbf{pdn} \prec_\Pi \bar{v}\mathbf{pdn}$ for constant $\mathbf{d}$, but since $desc(V)$ is not κ-independent from V, preference does not hold for OCF in general. Therefore the concepts of independence in CP- and OCF-networks are different in general. □

Proof of Proposition 7.50 [EKI14, Proposition 1]: We show that the consistency condition (7.10) ensures the network to have a global OCF in accordance to (7.9) by reductio ad impossibilem. Assume there would be a pair of indices $1 \leq i, j \leq m$ such that $\kappa_i((\Sigma_i \cap \Sigma_j)(\omega)) \neq \kappa_j((\Sigma_i \cap \Sigma_j)(\omega))$. Definition 7.48 defines the local OCF of an OCF-LEG network to be marginals of the global OCF, so by (7.9), the assumption gave us

$$\kappa_i((\Sigma_i \cap \Sigma_j)(\omega)) = \kappa(\Sigma_i \cap \Sigma_j)(\omega) \neq \kappa(\Sigma_i \cap \Sigma_j)(\omega) = \kappa_j((\Sigma_i \cap \Sigma_j)(\omega))$$

which is a direct contradiction.   □

Proof of Theorem 7.52 [EKI14, Theorem 1]: The summation ensures that
the resulting function has the correct codomain, so to show that the global
OCF can be constructed according to (7.13) is an OCF, it suffices to show
that this function is normalised. We show this with the proof of [EKI14,
Theorem 1] which is a two-step approach: First, it shows that the local
OCF, which are normalised, are indeed marginals of the global function.
Second, it shows that the combination of these normalised OCF results in
a function which is normalised itself, as we can choose an outcome of the
variables such that there is possible worlds for which all local OCF are 0.

We show that the local ranking functions are marginals of the global one,
that is, $\kappa(\omega^h) = \kappa_h(\omega^h)$ for all $1 \leq h \leq m$ and all $\omega^h \in \Omega_h$. Let $\omega^h \in \Omega_h$ be
arbitrary, but fixed.

With $\omega \vDash \omega^h$ and $\omega^h = \mathbf{r}_h \mathbf{s}_h$, where $\mathbf{r}_h$ is a configuration of the variables of
$\mathbb{R}_h$ and $\mathbf{s}_h$ is a configuration of the variables in $\mathbb{S}_h$. By definition of the ranks
of formulas (3.10), this gives us $\kappa(\omega^h) = \min\{\omega | \omega \vDash \mathbf{r}_h \mathbf{s}_h\}$; the constraint of
the min-term fixes the configuration of $\mathbb{S}_h$ to $\mathbf{s}_h$. $\langle(\Sigma_i, \kappa_i)\rangle_{i=1}^m$ is a hypertree
on Σ, therefore the RIP guarantees that there are sets Σ_k, $k < h$ with $\mathbb{S}_h \subseteq$
Σ_k. We select such a set Σ_k. From the consistency condition (7.10) which
ensures that the local functions coincide on respective marginals we obtain
$\kappa_h(\mathbf{s}_h) = \kappa_k(\mathbf{s}_h)$. Additionally, if we remove a set from another and add it
again, we recover the original set, therefore $\Sigma_k = (\Sigma_k \backslash \mathbb{S}_h) \cup \mathbb{S}_h$ and hence for
the local ranking function we have $\kappa_k(\Sigma_k(\omega)) - \kappa_h(\mathbf{s}_h) = \kappa_k((\Sigma_k \backslash \mathbb{S}_h)(\omega) | \mathbf{s}_h)$.
Here, we set the propositional variables in $(\Sigma_k \backslash \mathbb{S}_h)^1$, to a configuration $\widehat{\mathbf{r}}_k$,
such that $\kappa_k(\widehat{\mathbf{r}}_k | \mathbf{s}_h) = 0$. This is equivalent to $\kappa_k(\widehat{\mathbf{r}}_k \mathbf{s}_h) - \kappa_h(\mathbf{s}_h) = 0$. This
step fixes $\omega^k = \widehat{\mathbf{r}}_k \mathbf{s}_h$ and therefore the propositional variables in $\mathbb{S}_k$ to a
configuration $\mathbf{s}_k$ such that $\omega^k \vDash \mathbf{s}_k$. We iterate this procedure over the
whole network, obtaining a sequence $(k_1, \ldots, k_p)$ of indices in $\{1, \ldots, m\}$
(with $k_1 = k$ and $k_p = 1$) such that $\mathbb{S}_h \subseteq \Sigma_{k_1}$, $\mathbb{S}_{k_1} \subseteq \Sigma_{k_2}, \ldots, \mathbb{S}_{k_{p-1}} \subseteq \Sigma_1$,
that is, $\Sigma_{k_1}, \ldots, \Sigma_{k_p}$ are the ancestors $(anc(\Sigma_h))$ of Σ_h. In the following we
refer to Σ_h as Σ_{k_0}. For each k_l, $l \geq 1$, we choose a configuration ω^{k_l} of the
variables in Σ_{k_l} such that $\omega^{k_l} = \widehat{\mathbf{r}}_{k_l} \mathbf{s}_{k_{l-1}}$ with $\widehat{\mathbf{r}}_{k_l}$ referring to the variables

---

1   Note that in general this is not $\mathbb{R}_k$, which is defined to be $\Sigma_k \backslash \mathbb{S}_k$.

in $\Sigma_{k_l} \setminus \mathbb{S}_{k_{l-1}}$ and $\kappa_{k_l}(\widehat{\mathbf{r}}_{k_l}|\mathbf{s}_{k_{l-1}}) = 0$, hence $\kappa_{k_l}(\omega^{k_l}) - \kappa_{k_l}(\mathbf{s}_{k_{l-1}}) = 0$. Since $\mathbb{S}_{k_{l-1}} \subseteq (\Sigma_{k_{l-1}} \cap \Sigma_{k_l})$ and due to (7.10), we have $\kappa_{k_{l-1}}(\mathbb{S}_{k_{l-1}}) = \kappa_{k_l}(\mathbb{S}_{k_{l-1}})$.

For the remaining hyperedges Σ_i, we move downwards, in ascending order of the indices, through the hypertree, starting at Σ_1, until we reach the first $\Sigma_j \notin anc(\Sigma_h)$. By the RIP, $\mathbb{S}_j$ is contained in one of the ancestors of Σ_h or Σ_h itself, and hence the outcomes of these variables have already been set to $\mathbf{s}_j$. We choose a configuration $\mathbf{r}_j$ of $\mathbb{R}_j$ such that $\kappa_j(\mathbf{r}_j|\mathbf{s}_j) = 0$, as above, and therefore $\kappa_j(\omega^j) - \kappa_j(\mathbf{s}_j) = 0$. We proceed downwards through the tree in this way, meeting all $\Sigma_j \notin anc(\Sigma_h) \cup \{\Sigma_h\}$, and choose configurations of $\omega^j = \mathbf{r}_j \mathbf{s}_j$ of the variables in all these Σ_j such that $\kappa_j(\mathbf{r}_j|\mathbf{s}_j) = 0$. In this way, we construct a (global) world ω_0 with $\omega_0 \models \omega^h = \mathbf{r}_h \mathbf{s}_h$ for the selected Σ_h, $\omega_0 \models \omega^{k_l} = \widehat{\mathbf{r}}_{k_l} \mathbf{s}_{k_{l-1}}$ for its ancestors, and $\omega_0 \models \omega^j = \mathbf{r}_j \mathbf{s}_j$ for the remaining Σ_j, such that $\kappa_{k_l}(\omega^{k_l}) = \kappa_{k_{l-1}}(\mathbf{s}_{k_{l-1}})$, $1 \leq l \leq p$, and $\kappa_j(\omega^j) = \kappa_j(\mathbf{s}_j)$ for the remaining Σ_j. We rearrange the sum for $\kappa(\omega^h)$:

$$
\begin{aligned}
\kappa(\omega^h) = \min_{\omega \models \omega^h} \Big\{ &\kappa_h(\omega^h) - \kappa_h(\mathbf{s}_h) \\
&+ \sum_{l=1}^{p} \big(\kappa_{k_l}(\Sigma_i(\omega^{k_l})) - \kappa_{k_l}(\mathbf{s}_{k_l}) \big) \\
&+ \sum_{\Sigma_i \notin (anc(\Sigma_h) \cup \{\Sigma_h\})}^{i} \big(\kappa_i(\omega^i) - \kappa_i(\mathbf{s}_i) \big) \Big\} \\
\leq \kappa_h(\omega^h) + \min_{\omega = \omega_0} \Big\{ &\sum_{l=0}^{p-1} \underbrace{\big(\kappa_{k_{l+1}}(\omega^{k_{l+1}}) - \kappa_{k_l}(\mathbf{s}_{k_l}) \big)}_{=0} - \kappa_1(\top) \\
&+ \sum_{\Sigma_i \notin (anc(\Sigma_h) \cup \{\Sigma_h\})}^{i} \underbrace{\big(\kappa_i(\omega^i) - \kappa_i(\mathbf{s}_i) \big)}_{=0} \Big\} = \kappa_h(\omega^h),
\end{aligned}
\tag{A.6.16}
$$

because $\kappa_1(\top) = 0$. Conversely, for each $\omega^h \in \Omega_h$ we have

$$
\begin{aligned}
\kappa(\omega^h) = \kappa_h(\omega^h) + \min_{\omega \models \omega^h} \Big\{ &\sum_{l=0}^{p} \underbrace{\big(\kappa_{k_{l+1}}(\Sigma_{k_{l+1}}(\omega)) \kappa_{k_l}(\mathbb{S}_{k_l}(\omega)) \big)}_{\geq 0} \\
&- \underbrace{\kappa_1(\top)}_{=0} + \sum_{\Sigma_i \notin (anc(\Sigma_h) \cup \{\Sigma_h\})}^{i} \underbrace{\big(\kappa_i(\Sigma_i(\omega)) - \kappa_i(\mathbb{S}_i(\omega)) \big)}_{\geq 0} \Big\}
\end{aligned}
\tag{A.6.17}
$$

It holds that $\kappa_{k_{l+1}}(\Sigma_{k_{l+1}}(\omega)) - \kappa_{k_l}(\mathbb{S}_{k_l}(\omega)) \geq 0$, since we have $\kappa_{k_l}(\mathbb{S}_{k_l}(\omega)) = \kappa_{k_{l+1}}(\mathbb{S}_{k_{l+1}}(\omega))$ and $\mathbb{S}_{k_l} \subseteq \Sigma_{k_{l+1}}$, hence $\kappa_{k_{l+1}}(\mathbb{S}_{k_l}(\omega)) \leq \kappa_{k_{l+1}}(\Sigma_{k_{l+1}}(\omega))$.

Therefore we obtain $\kappa(\omega^h) \geq \kappa_h(\omega^h)$ and altogether, $\kappa(\omega^h) = \kappa_h(\omega^h)$, as required. As each local κ_h is a ranking function, it follows immediately that $\{\omega | \kappa(\omega) = 0\} \neq \varnothing$, that is, κ is a ranking function. □

Proof of Proposition 7.55 [EKI14, Proposition 2]:

To show that $\Sigma_i \setminus \mathbb{S}_i \perp\!\!\!\perp_\kappa \Sigma_j \setminus \mathbb{S}_i \mid \mathbb{S}_i$ we have to show that $\kappa((\Sigma_i \setminus \mathbb{S}_i)|(\Sigma_j \setminus \mathbb{S}_i) \cup \mathbb{S}_i) = \kappa((\Sigma_i \setminus \mathbb{S}_i)|\mathbb{S}_i)$. This equation can be rewritten to

$$\kappa((\Sigma_i \setminus \mathbb{S}_i)|(\Sigma_j \setminus \mathbb{S}_i) \cup \mathbb{S}_i) = \kappa((\Sigma_i \setminus \mathbb{S}_i)|\mathbb{S}_i)$$

$$\Leftrightarrow \quad \kappa((\Sigma_i \setminus \mathbb{S}_i)|(\Sigma_j \cup \mathbb{S}_i)) = \kappa((\Sigma_i \setminus \mathbb{S}_i)|\mathbb{S}_i)$$

$$\Leftrightarrow \quad \kappa((\Sigma_i \setminus \mathbb{S}_i) \cup (\Sigma_j \cup \mathbb{S}_i)) - \kappa(\Sigma_j \cup \mathbb{S}_i) = \kappa((\Sigma_i \setminus \mathbb{S}_i) \cup \mathbb{S}_i) - \kappa(\mathbb{S}_i)$$

$$\Leftrightarrow \quad \kappa(\Sigma_i \cup \Sigma_j) - \kappa(\Sigma_j \cup \mathbb{S}_i) = \kappa(\Sigma_i) - \kappa(\mathbb{S}_i)$$

$$\Leftrightarrow \quad \kappa(\Sigma_i \cup \Sigma_j) - \kappa(\Sigma_i) = \kappa(\Sigma_j \cup \mathbb{S}_i) - \kappa(\mathbb{S}_i)$$

$$\Leftrightarrow \quad \kappa(\Sigma_j|\Sigma_i) = \kappa(\Sigma_j|\mathbb{S}_i)$$

$$\Leftrightarrow \quad \kappa(\Sigma_j|\mathbb{R}_i \cup \mathbb{S}_i) = \kappa(\Sigma_j|\mathbb{S}_i)$$

By prerequisite, Σ_i is a child of Σ_j, so applying the techniques used to prove Theorem 7.52, we can find a configuration such that in the summation (7.13) the values of the variables in $\mathbb{R}_i$ do not contribute to the rank of $\kappa(\Sigma_j|\mathbb{R}_i \cup \mathbb{S}_i)$ and thus $\kappa(\Sigma_j|\mathbb{R}_i \cup \mathbb{S}_i) = \kappa(\Sigma_j|\mathbb{S}_i)$, which completes the proof. □

Proof of Proposition 7.65: Let $\mathbb{C}_i, \mathbb{C}_j$ be to subsets over an alphabet Σ, $\mathbb{C}_i \subseteq \Sigma$ with c-representations κ_i according to Definition 3.33 and separators $\mathbb{S}_j = \mathbb{C}_i \cap \mathbb{C}_j$. Let $\kappa_i(\mathbf{s}) > 0$ if and only if $\kappa_j > 0$ for all configurations of $\mathbf{s}$.

If $\kappa_i(\mathbf{s}) = \kappa_j(\mathbf{s})$ for all $\mathbf{s}$, the proposition is trivially satisfied.

We inspect the case where there are i, j such that $\kappa_i(\mathbf{s}) \neq \kappa_j(\mathbf{s})$ for any outcome $\mathbf{s}$ of $\mathbb{S}_j = \mathbb{C}_i \cap \mathbb{C}_j$. The basic idea is that in these cases, we chose another c-representation for one of the OCF from the sets of Δ_i that satisfies the consistency condition.

We recall the function fal_Δ ((3.6), Page 42) which assigns to each world ω the set of conditionals in Δ that are falsified by ω. In parallel we define the function $fal_\Omega(\cdot) : \mathfrak{P}(\mathfrak{L}|\mathfrak{L}) \to \Omega$ that assigns to each set of conditionals the set of worlds that falsify these conditionals such that for a set of conditionals $\Delta = \{(\psi_1|\phi_1), \ldots, (\psi_n|\phi_n)\}$, $fal_\Omega(\Delta) = \{\omega | \omega \in \Omega, \omega \in fal_\Delta(\omega)\}$ as a kind a preimage of fal_Δ.

By definition of c-representations, the rank of a world greater than 0 if and only if the world falsifies conditionals in Δ. Let $\Omega^i_{\mathbf{s}}$ be the set of worlds $\omega^i \in \Omega^i$ that satisfy $\mathbf{s}$, that is, $\Omega^i_{\mathbf{s}} = \{\omega^i | \omega^i \vDash \mathbf{s}\}$.

We assumed $\kappa_i(\mathbf{s}) > 0$, $\kappa_j(\mathbf{s}) > 0$ hence $fal_{\Delta_i}(\omega^i) \neq \varnothing$ for all $\omega^i \in \Omega_{\mathbf{s}}^i$, as well as $fal_{\Delta_j}(\omega^j) \neq \varnothing$ for all $\omega^j \in \Omega_{\mathbf{s}}^j$. The sets $\{fal_{\Delta_i}(\omega^i)|\omega^i \in \Omega_{\mathbf{s}}^i\}$ and $\{fal_{\Delta_j}(\omega^j)|\omega^j \in \Omega_{\mathbf{s}}^j\}$ are $\subseteq$-ordered such that the first is a subset of the second. Since the ranking functions are c-representations the rank of a world is the sum of falsification impacts associated with conditionals and each of the above sets of conditionals thereby represents the rank of the worlds this set is assigned to. The inclusion-ordering on the sets implies a ranking ordering on the worlds, as well, for two sets of conditionals Δ, Δ', $\Delta \subseteq \Delta'$ implies $\kappa_i(\omega) \leq \kappa_i(\omega')$ for all $\omega \in fal_{\Omega_i}(\Delta)$, $\omega' \in fal_{\Omega_i}(\Delta')$. By definition of ranking functions it is $\kappa_i(\mathbf{s}) = \min\{\kappa_i(\omega^i)|\omega^i \vDash \mathbf{s}\}$, hence the rank of $\mathbf{s}$ is the rank a world associated with one of the $\subseteq$-minimal sets of conditionals. The actual rank of the worlds is defined by the falsification impacts of the conditionals in this sets, so we can raise the rank of $\mathbf{s}$ by raising the impacts associated with the conditionals in the $\subseteq$-minimal sets. Assume, without loss of generality, that $\kappa_i(\mathbf{s}) < \kappa_j(\mathbf{s})$, then we can achieve $\kappa_i(\mathbf{s}) < \kappa_j(\mathbf{s})$ be raising a falsification impact of each set by $\kappa_j(\mathbf{s}) - \kappa_i(\mathbf{s})$. Because (3.30) is a system of inequalities, this will lead to a different but correct solution of the system which then results in a different c-representation. We repeat this for all configurations $\mathbf{s}$ where $\kappa_i(\mathbf{s}) \neq 0$ and $\kappa_j(\mathbf{s}) \neq 0$, until the consistency condition is satisfied. □

A.7 Proofs for Chapter 8

Proof of Lemma 8.20 (confer [Tay17]): This is a result from a stoppered preferential relation being a preferential relation that does not contain infinite descending chains and the number of possible worlds being finite: Given a finite set of elements, the only possibility for a relation $\preccurlyeq$ to define an infinite descending chain is a circle in the relation, otherwise the finiteness of the elements lead to finite chains. $\qquad\square$

Bibliography

[Ada65]   Ernest Adams. The Logic of Conditionals. *Inquiry*, 8(1-4):166–197, 1965.

[Ada75]   Ernest W. Adams. *The Logic of Conditionals: An Application of Probability to Deductive Logic*. Synthese Library. Springer Science+Business Media, Dordrecht, NL, 1975.

[Ant97]   Grigoris Antoniou. *Nonmonotonic reasoning*. MIT Press, Cambridge, MA, USA, 1997.

[BBD+04]   Craig Boutilier, Ronen I. Brafman, Carmel Domshlak, Holger H. Hoos, and David Poole. CP-nets: A Tool for Representing and Reasoning with Conditional Ceteris Paribus Preference Statements. *Journal of Artificial Intelligence Research*, 21(1):135–191, February 2004.

[BCD+93]   Salem Benferhat, Claudette Cayrol, Didier Dubois, Jérôme Lang, and Henri Prade. Inconsistency Management and Prioritized Syntax-Based Entailment. In *Proceedings of the Thirteenth International Joint Conference on Artificial Intelligence (IJCAI'93)*, volume 1, pages 640–647, San Francisco, CA, USA, 1993. Morgan Kaufmann Publishers.

[BDDP06]   Jean-Francois Bonnefon, Rui Da Silva Neves, Didier Dubois, and Henri Prade. Background default knowledge and causality ascriptions. In Gerhard Brewka, Silvia Coradeschi, Anna Perini, and Paolo Traverso, editors, *Proceedings of the 17th European Conference on Artificial Intelligence (ECAI 2006)*, volume 141 of *Frontiers in Artificial Intelligence and Applications*, pages 11–15, Amsterdam, NL, 2006. IOS Press.

[BEK16]   Christoph Beierle, Christian Eichhorn, and Steven Kutsch. A practical comparison of qualitative inferences with preferred ranking models. *KI - Künstliche Intelligenz*, Volume 31, Issue 1:41–52, 2016.

[BEKI16]   Christoph Beierle, Christian Eichhorn, and Gabriele Kern-Isberner. Skeptical Inference Based on C-representations and its Characterization as a Constraint Satisfaction Problem. In

© Springer-Verlag GmbH Germany, part of Springer Nature 2018
C. Eichhorn, *Rational Reasoning with Finite Conditional Knowledge Bases*, https://doi.org/10.1007/978-3-476-04824-0

Guillermo Ricardo Simari and Marc Gyssens, editors, *Proceedings of the 9th International Symposium on Foundations of Information and Knowledge Systems (FoIKS 2016)*, volume 9616 of *Lecture Notes of Computer Science*, pages 65–82, Berlin, DE, 2016. Springer Science+Business Media.

[BEKI17a]   Christoph Beierle, Christian Eichhorn, and Gabriele Kern-Isberner. A Transformation System for Unique Minimal Normal Forms of Conditional Knowledge Bases. In Alessandro Antonucci, Laurence Cholvy, and Odile Papini, editors, *Symbolic and Quantitative Approaches to Reasoning with Uncertainty: 14th European Conference, ECSQARU 2017, Lugano, Switzerland, July 10–14, 2017, Proceedings*, pages 236–245. Springer International Publishing, Cham, DE, 2017.

[BEKI17b]   Christoph Beierle, Christian Eichhorn, and Gabriele Kern-Isberner. On transformations and normal forms of conditional knowledge bases. In Salem Benferhat, Karim Tabia, and Moonis Ali, editors, *Advances in Artificial Intelligence: From Theory to Practice: 30th International Conference on Industrial Engineering and Other Applications of Applied Intelligent Systems, IEA/AIE 2017, Arras, France, June 27–30, 2017, Proceedings, Part I*, pages 488–494, Cham, CH, 2017. Springer International Publishing.

[BEKIK16]   Christoph Beierle, Christian Eichhorn, Gabriele Kern-Isberner, and Steven Kutsch. Skeptical, Weakly Skeptical, and Credulous Inference Based on Preferred Ranking Functions. In Gal A. Kaminka, Maria Fox, Paolo Bouquet, Eyke Hüllermeier, Virginia Dignum, Frank Dignum, and Frank van Harmelen, editors, *Frontiers in Artificial Intelligence and Applications*, volume Volume 285: ECAI 2016, pages 1149–1157, Amsterdam, NL, 2016. IOS Press.

[BEKIK18]   Christoph Beierle, Christian Eichhorn, Gabriele Kern-Isberner, and Steven Kutsch. Properties of skeptical c-inference for conditional knowledge bases and its realization as a constraint satisfaction problem. *Annals of Mathematics and Artificial Intelligence*, 2018. Online first: February 2018.

[Ber16]   Elena Bernshteyn. Bayessche Propagationsmethoden für OCF-Netzwerke. Diploma thesis, Technische Universität Dortmund, Dortmund, DE, 2016. (in German).

[BKI14]   Christoph Beierle and Gabriele Kern-Isberner. *Methoden wissensbasierter Systeme*. Springer Vieweg, Wiesbaden, DE, 5. überarbeitete und erweiterte Auflage edition, 2014. (in German).

[BKO17]   Christoph Beierle, Steven Kutsch, and Andreas Obergrusberger. On the Interrelationships Among C-Inference Relations Based on Preferred Models for Sets of Default Rules. In Vasile Rus and Zdravko Markov, editors, *Proceedings of the Thirtieth International Florida Artificial Intelligence Research Society Conference, FLAIRS 2017, Marco Island, Florida, USA, May 22-24, 2017.*, pages 724–729. AAAI Press, 2017.

[BL04]   Ronald Brachman and Hector Levesque. *Knowledge Representation and Reasoning*. Morgan Kaufmann Publishers Inc., San Francisco, CA, USA, 2004.

[BMP97]   Hassan Bezzazi, David Makinson, and Ramón Pino Pérez. Beyond Rational Monotony: Some Strong Non-Horn Rules for Nonmonotonic Inference Relations. *Journal of Logic and Computation*, pages 605–631, 1997.

[BN98]   Franz Baader and Tobias Nipkow. *Term rewriting and all that*. Cambridge University Press, Cambridge, MA, USA, 1998.

[Boc01]   Alexander Bochman. *A Logical Theory of Nonmonotonic Inference and Belief Change*. Springer Science+Business Media, Berlin, DE, 2001.

[BOP13]   Jean Baratgin, David E. Over, and Guy Politzer. Uncertainty and the de Finetti tables. *Thinking & Reasoning*, 19(3–4):308–328, 2013.

[BP96]   Hassan Bezzazi and Ramón Pino Pérez. Rational Transitivity and its Models. In *Proceedings of the 26th International Symposium on Multiple-Valued Logic (ISMVL '96)*, pages 160–165, Washington, DC, USA, 1996. IEEE Computer Society.

[BT10]   Salem Benferhat and Karim Tabia. Belief Change in OCF-
            Based Networks in Presence of Sequences of Observations and
            Interventions: Application to Alert Correlation. In Byoung-
            Tak Zhang and Mehmet Orgun, editors, *Pacific Rim Inter-
            national Conference on Artificial Intelligence (PRICAI 2010):
            Trends in Artificial Intelligence*, volume 6230 of *Lecture Notes
            in Computer Science*, pages 14–26. Springer Science+Business
            Media, Berlin, DE, 2010.

[Byr89]   Ruth MJ Byrne. Suppressing valid inferences with condition-
            als. *Cognition*, 31:61–83, 1989.

[DBR02]   Rui Da Silva Neves, Jean-François Bonnefon, and Eric Ra-
            ufaste. An Empirical Test of Patterns for Nonmonotonic Infer-
            ence. *Annals of Mathematics and Artificial Intelligence*, 34(1-
            3):107–130, 2002.

[DHR13]   Emmanuelle-Anna Dietz, Steffen Hölldobler, and Marco
            Ragni. A Computational Logic Approach to the Abstract
            and the Social Case of the Selection Task. In *Proceedings of
            the 11th International Symposium on Logical Formalizations
            of Commonsense Reasoning (COMMONSENSE 2013)*, 2013.

[Die00]   Reinhard Diestel. *Graphentheorie*. Springer-Lehrbuch Master-
            class. Springer Berlin Heidelberg, Berlin, DE, 2000.

[DP96]   Didier Dubois and Henri Prade. Conditional Objects as Non-
            monotonic Consequence Relations. In *Principles of Know-
            ledge Representation and Reasoning: Proceedings of the Fourth
            International Conference (KR'94)*, pages 170–177, San Fran-
            cisco, CA, USA, 1996. Morgan Kaufmann Publishers.

[EFKI16]   Christian Eichhorn, Matthias Fey, and Gabriele Kern-Isberner.
            CP- and OCF-networks – a comparison. *Fuzzy Sets and Sys-
            tems*, 298:109–127, 2016. Special Issue on Graded Logical Ap-
            proaches and Their Applications.

[EKI14]   Christian Eichhorn and Gabriele Kern-Isberner. LEG Net-
            works for Ranking Functions. In Eduardo Fermé and João
            Leite, editors, *Logics in Artificial Intelligence (Proceedings of

the 14th European Conference on Logics in Artificial Intelligence (JELIA '14)), volume 8761 of Lecture Notes in Computer Science, pages 210–223, Cham, CH, 2014. Springer International Publishing.

[EKI15a] Christian Eichhorn and Gabriele Kern-Isberner. Qualitative and semi-quantitative inductive reasoning with conditionals. KI – Künstliche Intelligenz, 29(3):279–289, 2015.

[EKI15b] Christian Eichhorn and Gabriele Kern-Isberner. Using inductive reasoning for completing OCF-networks. Journal of Applied Logic, 13(4, Part 2):605 – 627, 2015. Special JAL Issue dedicated to Uncertain Reasoning at FLAIRS.

[EKIBB18] Christian Eichhorn, Gabriele Kern-Isberner, Katharina Behring, and Tanja Bock. Properties of (Nonmonotonic) Inference Relations with Reflections on System Z and c-Representations. Unpublished manuscript, 2018.

[ERKI18] Christian Eichhorn, Marco Ragni, and Gabriele Kern-Isberner. Rational inference patterns based on conditional logic. In Proceedings of the Thirty-Second AAAI Conference on Artificial Intelligence (AAAI-18), Palo Alto, CA, USA, 2018. AAAI Press.

[Fey12] Matthias Fey. Qualitative Semantiken für DAGs – ein Vergleich von OCF- und CP-Netzwerken. Bachelor thesis, Technische Universität Dortmund, Dortmund, Germany, 2012. (in German).

[Fin74] Bruno de Finetti. Theory of Probability, volume 1,2. John Wiley and Sons, New York, NY, USA, 1974.

[FL96] Michael Freund and Daniel Lehmann. On Negation Rationality. Journal of Logic and Computation, 6(2):263–269, 1996.

[Fol92] Richard Foley. The Epistemology of Belief and the Epistemology of Degrees of Belief. American Philosophical Quarterly, 29(2):111–124, 1992.

[Gab85] D. Gabbay. Theoretical Foundations for Non-Monotonic Reasoning in Expert Systems. In Krzysztof R. Apt, editor, Logics *and models of concurrent systems*, pages 439–457. Springer International Publishing, New York, NY, USA, 1985.

[GCK16]   Lupita Estefania Gazzo Castañeda and Markus Knauff. Defeasible reasoning with legal conditionals. *Memory & Cognition*, 44(3):499–517, 2016.

[Gil93]   Angelo Gilio. Probabilistic consistency of knowledge bases in inference Systems. In Michael Clarke, Rudolf Kruse, and Serafín Moral, editors, *Symbolic and Quantitative Approaches to Reasoning and Uncertainty*, volume 747 of *Lecture Notes in Computer Science*, pages 160–167. Springer Science+Business Media, Berlin, DE, 1993.

[GP91a]   Moisés Goldszmidt and Judea Pearl. On the consistency of defeasible databases. *Artificial Intelligence*, 52(2):121 – 149, 1991.

[GP91b]   Moisés Goldszmidt and Judea Pearl. System-Z+: A formalism for reasoning with variable-strength defaults. In Thomas L. Dean and Kathleen McKeown, editors, *Proceedings of the Ninth National Conference on Artificial Intelligence (AAAI'91)*, volume 1, pages 399–404, Menlo Park, CA, USA, 1991. AAAI Press.

[GP96]   Moisés Goldszmidt and Judea Pearl. Qualitative probabilities for default reasoning, belief revision, and causal modeling. *Artificial Intelligence*, 84(1-2):57–112, 1996.

[GS69]   Gerhard Gentzen and M. E. Szabo, editor. *The collected papers of Gerhard Gentzen*. Studies in logic and the foundations of mathematics. North-Holland, Amsterdam, NL, 1969.

[Hal05]   Joseph Y. Halpern. *Reasoning About Uncertainty*. MIT Press, Cambridge, MA, USA, 2005.

[Haw07]   James Hawthorne. Nonmonotonic Conditionals that Behave Like Conditional Probabilities Above a Threshold. *Journal of Applied Logic*, 5(4):625–637, 2007.

[HHM08]   John Harris, Jeffry L. Hirst, and Michael Mossinghoff. *Combinatorics and Graph Theory*. Springer US, New York, NY, USA, 2008.

[HKR09]   Steffen Hölldobler and Carroline Dewi Puspa Kencana Ramli. Logic Programs under Three-Valued Lukasiewicz Semantics. In Patricia M. Hill and David S. Warren, editors, *Logic Programming, 25th International Conference, ICLP 2009*, volume 5649 of *LNCS*, pages 464–478, Berlin, Heidelberg, DE, 2009. Springer.

[HM07]   James Hawthorne and David Makinson. The Quantitative/Qualitative Watershed for Rules of Uncertain Inference. *Studia Logica*, 86(2):247–297, 2007.

[HR09]   Steffen Hölldobler and Carroline Dewi Puspa Kencana Ramli. Logic programs under three-valued lukasiewicz semantics. In Patricia M. Hill and David Scott Warren, editors, *Logic Programming, 25th International Conference, ICLP 2009, Pasadena, CA, USA, July 14-17, 2009. Proceedings*, volume 5649 of *Lecture Notes in Computer Science*, pages 464–478. Springer, 2009.

[HS09]   Michel Habib and Juraj Stacho. Polynomial-time algorithm for the leafage of chordal graphs. In Amos Fiat and Peter Sanders, editors, *Algorithms - ESA 2009*, pages 290–300, Berlin, Heidelberg, 2009. Springer Berlin Heidelberg.

[KB83]   Donald Erwin Knuth and Peter B. Bendix. Simple word problems in universal algebras. In Jörg H. Siekmann and Graham Wrightson, editors, *Automation of Reasoning: 2: Classical Papers on Computational Logic 1967–1970*, pages 342–376. Springer Berlin Heidelberg, Berlin, Heidelberg, Germany, 1983.

[KI01]   Gabriele Kern-Isberner. *Conditionals in Nonmonotonic Reasoning and Belief Revision – Considering Conditionals as Agents*. Number 2087 in Lecture Notes in Computer Science. Springer Science+Business Media, Berlin, DE, 2001.

[KI02]   Gabriele Kern-Isberner. A Structural Approach to Default Reasoning. In Dieter Fensel, Fausto Guinchiglia, Deborah NcGuinness, and Mary-Anne Williams, editors, *Knowledge Representation 2002: Proceedings of the 8th International*

Conference (KR '02), pages 147–157, San Francisco, CA, USA, 2002. Morgan Kaufman Publishers.

[KI04]   Gabriele Kern-Isberner. A thorough axiomatization of a principle of conditional preservation in belief revision. *Annals of Mathematics and Artificial Intelligence*, 40:127–164, 2004.

[KI10]   Gabriele Kern-Isberner. Commonsense Reasoning. Unpublished lecture notes of the lecture Commonsense Reasoning 2010 at the computer science department in TU Dortmund University, 2010.

[KIE12]   Gabriele Kern-Isberner and Christian Eichhorn. A structural base for conditional reasoning. In Thomas Barkowski, Marco Ragni, and Frieder Stolzenburg, editors, *Human Reasoning and Automated Deduction – KI 2012 Workshop Proceedings*, pages 25–32, 2012.

[KIE13a]   Gabriele Kern-Isberner and Christian Eichhorn. Intensional combination of rankings for OCF-networks. In Chutima Boonthum-Denecke and Michael G. Youngblood, editors, *Proceedings of the Twenty-Sixth International Florida Artificial Intelligence Research Society Conference (FLAIRS 2013)*, pages 615–620, 2013.

[KIE13b]   Gabriele Kern-Isberner and Christian Eichhorn. Ocf-networks with missing values. In Christoph Beierle and Gabriele Kern-Isberner, editors, *Proceedings of the 4th Workshop on Dynamics of Knowledge and Belief (DKB-2013)*, Hagen, DE, 2013. FernUniversität in Hagen.

[KIE14]   G. Kern-Isberner and C. Eichhorn. Structural Inference from Conditional Knowledge Bases. In Matthias Unterhuber and Gerhard Schurz, editors, *Logic and Probability: Reasoning in Uncertain Environments*, number 102 (4) in Studia Logica, pages 751–769. Springer Science+Business Media, Dordrecht, NL, 2014.

[KIK11]   Gabriele Kern-Isberner and Patrick Krümpelmann. A Constructive Approach to Independent and Evidence Retaining Belief Revision by General Information Sets. In Toby Walsh, editor, *Proceedings of the Twenty-Second International Joint Conference on Artificial Intelligence (IJCAI'11)*, pages 937–942, Menlo Park, CA, USA, 2011. AAAI Press.

[KLM90]   Sarit Kraus, Daniel J. Lehmann, and Menachem Magidor. Nonmonotonic Reasoning, Preferential Models and Cumulative Logics. *Artificial Intelligence*, 44(1-2):167–207, 1990.

[KR14]   Gregory Kuhnmünch and Marco Ragni. Can Formal Nonmonotonic Systems Properly Describe Human Reasoning? In Paul Bello, Marcello Gaurini, Marjorie McShane, and Brian Scassellati, editors, *Proceedings of the 36th Annual Meeting of the Cognitive Science Society (COGSCI2014)*, pages 1806–1811, Austin, TX, USA, 2014. Cognitive Science Society, Inc.

[KTFF09]   Gabriele Kern-Isberner, Matthias Thimm, Marc Finthammer, and Jens Fisseler. Mining default rules from statistical data. In H. Chad Lane and Hans W. Guesgen, editors, *Proceedings of the Twenty-Second International Florida Artificial Intelligence Research Society Conference, May 19-21, 2009, Sanibel Island, Florida, USA*. AAAI Press, 2009.

[LB82]   John F. Lemmer and Stephen W. Barth. Efficient minimum information updating for Bayesian inferencing in expert systems. In Jay M. Tenenbaum, editor, *Proceedings of the Second National Conference on Artificial Intelligence, AAAI-82*, Palo Alto, CA, USA, 1982. AAAI Press.

[Lew73]   David Kellogg Lewis. *Counterfactuals*. Blackwell Publishers, Hoboken, NJ, USA, 1973.

[LM92]   Daniel J. Lehmann and Menachem Magidor. What does a conditional knowledge base entail? *Artificial Intelligence*, 55(1):1–60, 1992.

[LS88]   Steffen L. Lauritzen and David. J. Spiegelhalter. Local Computations with Probabilities on Graphical Structures and Their Application to Expert Systems. *Journal of the Royal Statistical Society. Series B (Methodological)*, 50(2), 1988.

[Łuk20]   Jan Łukasiewicz. O logice trójwartościowej. *Ruch Filozoficzny*, 5:169–171, 1920. English translation: On three-valued logic.

In: Lukasiewicz J. and Borkowski L. (ed.). (1990). *Selected Works*, Amsterdam: North Holland, pp. 87–88.

[Luk05] Thomas Lukasiewicz. Weak nonmonotonic probabilistic logics. *Artificial Intelligence*, 168(1-2):119–161, 2005.

[Mak88] David Makinson. General theory of cumulative inference. In Michael Reinfrank, Johan de Kleer, Matthew L. Ginsberg, and Erik Sandewall, editors, *Non-Monotonic Reasoning, 2nd International Workshop Grassau*, volume 346 of *Lecture Notes in Computer Science*, pages 1–18, Berlin, DE, 1988. Springer Science+Business Media.

[Mak94] David Makinson. General Patterns in Nonmonotonic Reasoning. In Dov M. Gabbay, C. J. Hogger, and J. A. Robinson, editors, *Handbook of Logic in Artificial Intelligence and Logic Programming*, volume 3, pages 35–110. Oxford University Press, New York, NY, USA, 1994.

[McC04] Pamela McCorduck. *Machines Who Think: A Personal Inquiry into the History and Prospects of Artificial Intelligence*. AK Peters Ltd, Wellesley, MA, USA, 2004.

[Mey98] Carl-Heinz Meyer. *Korrektes Schließen bei unvollständiger Information: Anwendung des Prinzips der maximalen Entropie in einem probabilistischen Expertensystem*. 41. Peter Lang Publishing, Inc., Pieterlen, CH, 1998. (in German).

[Par94] Jeff Bruce Paris. *The Uncertain Reasoner's Companion: A Mathematical Perspective*. Cambridge Tracts in Theoretical Computer Science. Cambridge University Press, Cambridge, UK, 1994.

[Par98] Jeff Paris. Common Sense and Maximum Entropy. *Synthese*, 117(1):75–93, 1998.

[Pea88] Judea Pearl. *Probabilistic Reasoning in Intelligent Systems*. Morgan Kaufmann Publishers Inc., San Francisco, CA, USA, 1988.

[Pea90] Judea Pearl. System Z: A natural ordering of defaults with tractable applications to nonmonotonic reasoning. In Rohit

Parikh, editor, *Proceedings of the 3rd conference on Theoretical aspects of reasoning about knowledge (TARK1990)*, pages 121–135, San Francisco, CA, USA, 1990. Morgan Kaufmann Publishers Inc.

[PK05]   Niki Pfeifer and Gernot D. Kleiter. Coherence and Nonmonotonicity in Human Reasoning. *Synthese*, 146(1–2):93–109, 2005.

[Poo88]   David Poole. A Logical Framework for Default Reasoning. *Artificial Intelligence*, 36(1):27–47, 1988.

[Ram29]   Frank P Ramsey. General propositions and causality. In David Hugh Mellor, editor, *Philosophical Papers*. Cambridge University Press, Cambridge, MA, USA, 1929.

[REB+17]   Marco Ragni, Christian Eichhorn, Tanja Bock, Gabriele Kern-Isberner, and Alice Ping Ping Tse. Formal nonmonotonic theories and properties of human defeasible reasoning. *Minds and Machines*, Volume 27, Number 1:79–117, 2017.

[Rei80]   Raymond Reiter. A logic for default reasoning. *Artificial Intelligence*, 13(1–2):81–132, 1980.

[REKI16]   Marco Ragni, Christian Eichhorn, and Gabriele Kern-Isberner. Simulating human inferences in the light of new information: A formal analysis. In Subbarao Kambhampati, editor, *Proceedings of the Twenty-Fifth International Joint Conference on Artificial Intelligence (IJCAI'16)*, pages 2604–2610, Palo Alto, CA, USA, 2016. AAAI Press.

[SPG14]   Giuseppe Sanfilippo, Niki Pfeifer, and Angelo Gilio. Probabilistic inference and syllogisms. In Angela Blanco-Fernandez, Gil Gonzalez-Rodriguez, and George Loizou, editors, *PROGRAMME AND ABSTRACTS, 7th International Conference of the ERCIM (European Research Consortium for Informatics and Mathematics) Working Group on Computational and Methodological Statistics (ERCIM 2014), December, 6-8, 2014*, page 120, 2014.

[Spo88]   Wolfgang Spohn. Ordinal Conditional Functions: A Dynamic Theory of Epistemic States. In William Harper and Brian

Skyrms, editors, *Causation in Decision, Belief Change and Statistics: Proceedings of the Irvine Conference on Probability and Causation*, volume 42 of *The Western Ontario Series in Philosophy of Science*, pages 105–134, Dordrecht, NL, 1988. Springer Science+Business Media.

[Spo12]   Wolfgang Spohn. *The Laws of Belief: Ranking Theory and Its Philosophical Applications*. Oxford University Press, Oxford, UK, 2012.

[ST12]   Gerhard Schurz and Paul D. Thorn. Reward versus Risk in Uncertain Inference: Theorems and Simulations. *The Review of Symbolic Logic*, 5:574–612, 2012.

[SvL08]   Keith Stenning and Michiel van Lambalgen. *Human reasoning and cognitive science*. Bradford Books. MIT Press, Cambridge, MA, USA, 2008.

[Tar30]   Alfred Tarski. Fundamentale Begriffe der Methodologie der deduktiven Wissenschaften I. *Monatshefte für Mathematik und Physik*, 37:361–404, 1930. (in German).

[Tay17]   Mariam Tayyem. Regelbasiertes Schlussfolgern: Modellierung psychologischer Studien mit Hilfe konditionaler Wissensbasen. Bachelor thesis, Technische Universität Dortmund, Dortmund, Germany, 2017. (in German).

[TB02]   Valerie A. Thompson and Ruth MJ Byrne. Reasoning counterfactually: Making inferences about things that didn't happen. *Journal of Experimental Psychology: Learning, Memory, and Cognition*, 28(6):1154–1170, 2002.

[TEKIS15a]   Paul D. Thorn, Christian Eichhorn, Gabriele Kern-Isberner, and Gerhard Schurz. Qualitative Probabilistic Inference with Default Inheritance for Exceptional Subclasses. In Jürgen Landes, editor, *progic 2015: The Seventh Workshop on Combining Probability and Logic*, Canterbury, UK, 2015.

[TEKIS15b]   Paul D. Thorn, Christian Eichhorn, Gabriele Kern-Isberner, and Gerhard Schurz. Qualitative Probabilistic Inference with Default Inheritance for Exceptional Subclasses. In Christoph Beierle, Gabriele Kern-Isberner, Marco Ragni, and

Frieder Stolzenburg, editors, *Proceedings of the 5th Workshop on Dynamics of Knowledge and Belief (DKB-2015) and the 4th Workshop KI & Kognition (KIK-2015) co-located with 38th German Conference on Artificial Intelligence (KI-2015)*, volume 1444 of *CEUR Workshop Proceedings*, 2015.

[Thi09]   Matthias Thimm.   Measuring inconsistency in probabilistic knowledge bases. In Jeff Bilmes and Andrew Ng, editors, *Proceedings of the Twenty-Fifth Conference on Uncertainty in Artificial Intelligence (uai 2009)*, pages 530–537, Corvallis, OR, USA, 2009. AUAI Press.

[TY84]   Robert E. Tarjan and Mihalis Yannakakis.   Simple Linear-Time Algorithms to Test Chordality of Graphs, Test Acyclicity of Hypergraphs, and Selectively Reduce Acyclic Hypergraphs. *SIAM Journal on Computing*, 13(3):566–579, 1984.

[Was68]   Peter Cathcart Wason. Reasoning about a rule. *Quarterly Journal of Experimental Psychology*, 20(3):273–281, 1968.

Index

© Springer-Verlag GmbH Germany, part of Springer Nature 2018
C. Eichhorn, *Rational Reasoning with Finite Conditional
Knowledge Bases*, https://doi.org/10.1007/978-3-476-04824-0

GPSR Compliance
The European Union's (EU) General Product Safety Regulation (GPSR) is a set
of rules that requires consumer products to be safe and our obligations to
ensure this.

If you have any concerns about our products, you can contact us on

ProductSafety@springernature.com

In case Publisher is established outside the EU, the EU authorized
representative is:

Springer Nature Customer Service Center GmbH
Europaplatz 3
69115 Heidelberg, Germany